Veiled EMPIRE

Veiled EMPIRE

GENDER *&* POWER IN STALINIST CENTRAL ASIA

DOUGLAS NORTHROP

CORNELL UNIVERSITY PRESS ◆ ITHACA AND LONDON

Frontispiece: An Uzbek bride and groom, 1927. (Courtesy RGAKFD.)

Copyright © 2004 by Cornell University

All rights reserved. Except for brief quotations in a review, this book, or parts thereof, must not be reproduced in any form without permission in writing from the publisher. For information, address Cornell University Press, Sage House, 512 East State Street, Ithaca, New York 14850.

First published 2004 by Cornell University Press
First printing, Cornell Paperbacks, 2004

Printed in the United States of America

Library of Congress Cataloging-in-Publication Data

Northrop, Douglas Taylor.
    Veiled empire : gender and power in Stalinist Central Asia /
Douglas Northrop.—1st ed.
        p. cm.
Includes bibliographical references and index.
    ISBN 0-8014-3944-2 (cloth : alk. paper)—ISBN 0-8014-8891-5
(pbk. : alk. paper)
    1. Women and communism—Uzbekistan—History—20th century.
2. Muslim women—Uzbekistan—Social conditions—20th century.
3. Veils—Social aspects—Uzbekistan—History—20th century.
4. Soviet Union—Relations—Uzbekistan.   5. Uzbekistan—
Relations—Soviet Union.   I. Title.
    HX546.N67 2003
    305.48'697'0958709043—dc22
                                                                2003020316

Cornell University Press strives to use environmentally responsible suppliers and materials to the fullest extent possible in the publishing of its books. Such materials include vegetable-based, low-VOC inks, and acid-free papers that are recycled, totally chlorine-free, or partly composed of nonwood fibers. For further information, visit our website at www.cornellpress.cornell.edu.

Cloth printing   10 9 8 7 6 5 4 3 2 1
Paperback printing   10 9 8 7 6 5 4 3 2 1

Sevimli rafiqam Mişelga
va jonajon ōğillarim Jeremi va Sayerga
bağişlayman

[Religion] is like a nail—the harder you hit it, the deeper it seems to go into the wood.

—Anatolii Lunacharskii, People's Commissar for Enlightenment, 1928

Dress, that splendid poesy of the feminine life . . . appeared to her eyes endowed with a magic hitherto unperceived. It suddenly became clear to her what it is to most women: the manifestation of an inward thought, a language, a symbol.

—Honoré de Balzac, *Une Fille d'Ève,* 1839

CONTENTS

MAPS

SOURCE ABBREVIATIONS

Archives

GARF: Gosudarstvennyi arkhiv Rossiisskoi Federatsii (State Archive of the Russian Federation, Moscow)

ÖzRKFFHMDA: Özbekiston respublikasi kinofotofonohujjatlar markaziy davlat arkhivi (Uzbek Central State Photo, Film, and Sound Archive, Tashkent)

ÖzRMDA: Özbekiston respublikasi markaziy davlat arkhivi (Uzbek Central State Archive, Tashkent)

PDA: Prezident devoni arkhivi (Presidential Archive, Tashkent; formerly Uzbek Central Party Archive)

RGAKFD: Rossiisskii gosudarstvennyi arkhiv kinofotodokumentov (Russian State Photo and Film Archive, Krasnogorsk)

RGASPI: Rossiisskii gosudarstvennyi arkhiv sotsial'no-politicheskoi istorii (Russian State Archive of Sociopolitical History, Moscow; formerly Soviet Communist Party Central Archive)

Published Sources

PSTZhMUz: *Pervyi s"ezd trudiashcheisia zhenskoi molodezhi Uzbekistana* (Tashkent, 1936), book chronicling the First Congress of the Laboring Female Youth of Uzbekistan

PV: *Pravda Vostoka,* Russian-language daily newspaper issued in Tashkent by the Communist Party's Central Asian Bureau

QÖ: *Qizil Özbekiston,* Uzbek-language Soviet daily newspaper issued by the Uzbek SSR's party and state organizations

ACKNOWLEDGMENTS

This book bears the imprint of many hands, and I am glad to acknowledge the generous assistance of many people around the world who helped make it possible. For help paving the road in Uzbekistan and Russia, I am grateful to Dilorom Alimova, Musallam Joraev, Renat Shigabdinov, and Liudmila Kolodnikova. The staffs of many libraries and archives did everything possible to help me at a time of great institutional and personal hardship; I deeply appreciate their trust and professionalism. Erkin Abdullaev, Raisa Li, and Shavkat Alimov, in Tashkent, and Liudmila Zapriageva, Vera Levanovich, and the entire staff of RGAKFD and RGASPI, in Moscow, went above and beyond the call of duty. At home I benefited immensely from the wisdom and advice of my teachers, in particular the late Alexander Dallin, my adviser at Stanford University, who provided space to develop my own voice and who is much missed. I also thank a series of other extraordinary mentors and friends: Norman Naimark, Daniel Segal, Jay Winter—and William Wagner, who first encouraged me by responding positively to the essay that eventually grew into this book.

My task was made easier by the wise advice of many perceptive colleagues. Among those who gave most generously of their time and insight by reading the entire manuscript were Lynne Viola, Adeeb Khalid, and Barbara Metcalf. At an earlier stage I benefited from the comments of many others, particularly Gail Lapidus, Roberta Manning, Christine Worobec, Peter Holquist, Francine Hirsch, Joel Beinin, Ronald Suny, Marianne Kamp, Terry Martin, Sandra Greene, Paula Michaels, Cassandra Cavanaugh, Amir Weiner, and my colleagues at the University of Georgia, especially Alexei Kojevnikov and Reinaldo Román. Thoughtful questions from audiences, commentators, and anonymous reviewers have left their imprint throughout. I am especially grateful to John Ackerman, who took a personal interest in this project and shepherded it through to publication at Cornell University Press, and to Barbara Salazar for her sharp, meticulous editing. Many others shared generously the fruits of their own work: Kate Fitz Gibbon and Andrew Hale for access to the remarkable photograph collection of the Anahita Gallery in Santa Fe, New Mexico; Dina Khojaeva for permission to use photographs by Max Penson; Elizabeth Constantine for a trove of newspaper and ethnographic materials; Shoshana Keller for archival notes from PDA; Cassandra Cavanaugh for a duplicate copy of Figure 10; Marianne Kamp for early photocopies from *Jangi jol;* Peter Blitstein, Terry Martin, Gábor Rittersporn, and Arch Getty for individual archival documents; and Joanne Young for an early play on women's liberation.

Earlier versions of parts of this book have been published and appear here by permission: "Subaltern Dialogues: Subversion and Resistance in Soviet Uzbek Family Law," *Slavic Review* 60, no. 1 (© American Association for the Advancement of Slavic Studies, 2001); "Languages of Loyalty: Gender, Politics, and Party Supervision in Uzbekistan, 1927–41," *Russian Review* 59, no. 2 (© 2000); and *"Hujum:* Unveiling Campaigns and Local Responses, Uzbekistan 1927," in *Provincial Landscapes: Local Dimensions of Soviet Power, 1917–53,* ed. Donald J. Raleigh (© University of Pittsburgh Press, 2001).

Financial support for book revisions was provided by the University of Georgia and its Center for Humanities and the Arts. The History Department and its chair, Ed Larson, generously defrayed the costs of map production, and Wendy Giminski of Campus Graphics did the cartography with consummate skill. Crucial funding during earlier stages of research and writing was provided by the Mellon Foundation; Stanford University; the Institute for the Study of World Politics; and the (initial) National Security Education Program. No less important has been the practical assistance and personal support received from colleagues and friends elsewhere. For helping me understand Central Asia, I am indebted to David Tyson, Kodyr Kholmatov, Ergash Umarov, and the Bakhadirov, Zakhidov, and Haqnazarov families, who made their homes my own. For friendship and generosity in Moscow, I thank Patricia Leigh, Alan Fahnestock, and Sergei Egorov.

Most of all, my family has supported me in ways that altogether surpass what I can acknowledge here. Michelle McClellan, in particular, has given as much to this book as I, and has given up as much for it. She has been a sounding board for my ideas, a demanding and perceptive reader at every stage, and someone whose passion for history reminds me every day why the subject matters. Yet beyond that, she has taught me about the other things in life that matter even more. It is to her and our ever-changing latest projects, Jeremy Padraic and Sawyer Tomlin, that I dedicate this book.

DOUGLAS NORTHROP

Athens, Georgia

NOTE ON TRANSLITERATION

This book is based on Uzbek- and Russian-language materials, a fact that raises complicated questions of transliteration. One must balance consistency with accuracy across several alphabet systems and decide whether and when to make exceptions for words familiar to English-language readers. Any approach is unavoidably idiosyncratic. My practice is to render Russian terms according to the Library of Congress orthography, excepting only such common terms as Soviet, Moscow, and Joseph Stalin. Uzbek has no generally acknowledged transliteration system, and the task is complicated by the use of six alphabets in the past century. No solution is perfect, but I have tried to be consistent within each alphabet and to cite sources in a way that scholars will recognize and that will enable them to locate the materials in question. In most cases I avoid Russian spellings of Uzbek words. The principal exceptions are Uzbek, Uzbekistan, and Tashkent, since these spellings have become common in English. I also use a hybrid spelling of *boi* (landlord) rather than the Uzbek transliteration, *boy,* to avoid confusing English-speaking readers. For certain other place names I provide Russian spellings in parentheses at first use (for example, Farghona [Fergana]). And I use *QÖ* as the abbreviation for *Qizil Özbekiston,* the main Uzbek-language Soviet newspaper, although the spelling varied as the alphabet changed: *Qzil Özbekiston, Qizil Ozbekstan, Kzil Özbekiston,* for example.

All of these matters are difficult and sometimes contentious. I do not pretend to put them to rest, but I hope that readers will forgive any inconsistencies and that they will focus on what is said rather than how it is spelled.

Veiled EMPIRE

Introduction

Banners waved, music played, and local newspapers reported an "unceasing hubbub of girls' voices, happy songs, [and] infectious dancing" among the crowds in early October 1935, when the First All-Uzbek Congress of Laboring Female Youth opened in Tashkent.[1] Amid triumphal Stalinist pageantry, several hundred young women arrived in the Uzbek capital city to discuss the issues and problems faced by indigenous women in Soviet Central Asia. The delegates came from throughout Uzbekistan and across the region, and a few hailed from farther away, from Moscow and other Muslim areas such as Azerbaijan. Most were young, married Uzbek peasant women who had joined the Young Communist League (Komsomol) after completing rudimentary schooling.[2] As such, they embodied the promise of Soviet liberation after nearly twenty years of Bolshevik power. Soviet press coverage related in glowing terms how far Uzbek women had come since 1917—and especially since 1927, when the Communist Party had with great fanfare launched a major ongoing campaign to improve the social status of women in Central Asia. The 650 young women at the congress—politically active, economically independent, and apparently eager to fight local manifestations of patriarchy—were taken as living evidence of this campaign's success. Soviet newspapers proudly noted that some delegates had even trained as parachutists (see Figure 1): a far cry from the strict practices of female seclusion and heavy

1. M. P., "Chudesnyi splav," *Pravda Vostoka* (hereafter *PV*), 3 Oct. 1935. For other accounts, see "Govoriat delegaty," *PV*, 4 Oct. 1935; Akmal Ikramov, "Bud'te smelymi i reshitel'nymi boitsami," *PV*, 10 Oct. 1935; Karimov, "Delo raskreposhcheniia zhenshchiny dovesti do kontsa," *PV*, 21 Oct. 1935; and several articles under the titles "S"ezd zhenskoi molodezhi Uzbekistana," *PV*, 5 Oct. 1935, and "Resheniia s"ezda—v massy devushek, molodykh zhenshchin," *PV*, 8 Oct. 1935.

2. According to statistics compiled at the congress, of the 650 women in attendance, 576 were younger than age 24; 495 were ethnically Uzbek; 424 had joined the Komsomol; 451 were married; 502 were peasants; and only 90 had more than an elementary education. See Özbekiston respublikasi markaziy davlat arkhivi (hereafter ÖzRMDA), f. 86, op. 10, d. 634, ll. 346–50, or the published records at *Pervyi s"ezd trudiashcheisia zhenskoi molodezhi Uzbekistana* (Tashkent, 1936), 123–25 (hereafter *PSTZhMUz*).

Figure 1. Basharat Mirbabaeva, Uzbekistan's first female
parachutist, Tashkent, 1935. (Courtesy ÖzRKFFHMDA.)

horsehair veils that were said to have shaped their everyday lives before the arrival of Soviet emancipation.[3]

Amid the pomp and circumstance, however, dissonant notes could be
heard. Even as they tried to leave listeners with an upbeat, inspirational message, many speakers pointed to continuing failures of the party's concerted effort to "liberate" the Muslim women of Uzbekistan. In one of the main
speeches at the congress, I. Artykov, a top leader of the Uzbek Komsomol,
tried to outline the profound yet contradictory meanings of Soviet power in
the ten-year-old Uzbek Soviet Socialist Republic. By 1935, Bolshevik efforts in
Central Asia had focused on women's liberation for almost a decade, and Soviet authorities and women's activists had mobilized the full force and considerable authority of the Stalinist state to make this vision a reality. What had

3. M. P., "Chudesnyi splav." See also "Boevaia zadacha komsomola Uzbekistana," *PV,* 12
Oct. 1935.

their efforts meant in practice? One of Artykov's examples, which recounted the life story of Ashur-Bibi Tashmatova, a young Uzbek girl orphaned early in life who now worked productively for the Soviet state, provides an unexpectedly revealing answer. Despite her notional status as a liberated Soviet woman, Tashmatova's biography actually served more to show the incompleteness of the party's efforts and to illustrate the severe constraints that existed on Soviet power in Muslim Central Asia during the 1930s.

Artykov started by describing her difficult childhood. After being orphaned at a young age, he said, Tashmatova had been raised by two older sisters. Unfortunately, one sister died when Tashmatova was just 9 years old and the other when she was 13. Her only brother was then working in a distant province, so she was left alone and soon found herself forced to marry her elder deceased sister's 45-year-old husband. This man already had seven wives, Artykov noted, not to mention business connections in Afghanistan (where he moved for several years) and personal links to prominent anti-Soviet figures. Tashmatova's life became still more difficult when her new husband returned from Afghanistan and started working as a Soviet official (of all things) in the town of Denau. Several times she ran away from him, but on each occasion he used his new government connections to have her caught and forcibly returned to him. Fortunately, Artykov said, at this point the Soviet police discovered his association with anti-Soviet "bandits," and he was condemned to death and shot.

To the assembled delegates, many Young Communists and all Stalinist heroes, this story of revolutionary justice must have struck an inspirational note. The Soviet courts had ferreted out a traitor and thus struck a blow simultaneously against the forces of political counterrevolution and cultural patriarchy. At last, they might have expected to hear, Soviet power had enabled Tashmatova to achieve economic independence, political liberation, and personal fulfillment. Artykov's story, though, took a different turn. "After her husband had been shot," he continued,

> other men courted and wooed her, and in the end she was again given forcibly into marriage, to one Jumamir Nasarov, the head of a local village soviet and before that a wealthy *boi* [landlord]. She was his second wife, and afterward he took a third. To prevent anyone holding him to account for his polygyny, he went to ZAGS [Zapis' aktov grazhdanskogo sostoianiia, the local Soviet civil registry office] and divorced both of his first two wives—but told them that according to the code of *shariat* [Islamic religious law] they [still] had to live [with him].

Fearing that Tashmatova's brother might return and see him mistreating his sister, and that he might then be denounced to Soviet authorities "as a former kulak and polygynist," Nasarov hired assassins to have him killed.

At this point Tashmatova surely could be forgiven some disillusionment with the Soviet cause. Yet she remained loyal, Artykov proudly declared, as she continued to plead for help from the authorities:

Ashur-Bibi went several times to the village soviet for help, asking for a divorce, but every time she was told that no divorce could be granted without her husband's permission.[4] Finally she turned to a local agronomist, who wrote to the district [capital], whence came a committee of inquiry that arrested Ashur-Bibi's husband. From there he managed to escape from custody, and—knowing that she had been the main reason for his arrest—he tried repeatedly, over several days, to kill her. Afterward he was again arrested and deported outside Uzbekistan.

At this point—at last—Ashur-Bibi Tashmatova seemed to be free. In 1931, Artykov said, she finally threw off her heavy black veil, joined the Young Communist League, and became a full-fledged Soviet worker, accepting a job as director of a crèche.

This was the moment of transfiguration required in any heroic Stalinist narrative. But what was her new, unveiled life like? How did it compare with the dark past? Artykov concluded his tale by describing Tashmatova's current home life, and made it clear that much still remained to be done:

> Now she has a third husband. He, Babahanov, is a Soviet worker, a Komsomol member, the assistant director and secretary of the village soviet. She also was married to him against her will. For five or six months they lived together well, but afterward he started to demand that she abandon her social work, started to beat her, and finally, making use of his position in the village soviet, wrote an attestation of divorce, put it in her coat pocket, gathered up all of his things, and left. When he was called before the district executive committee and asked on what basis he had written this attestation, he declared that it had been a joke.

By 1935, Artykov noted, she had lived with Babahanov for two years, but had experienced only insults and mockery, even occasional threats on her life. Shortly before the congress convened, moreover, she had come to Tashkent for training—and he mailed her a divorce. One more time she sought official help, turning to her local Komsomol and her district party leader for assistance—but, Artykov concluded ruefully, "they did nothing."[5]

The fluidity of social structures, the mobility of populations across supposedly inviolable international borders, and the stark weakness of government and party organizations—indeed, the active opposition to official policy on the part of local Soviet personnel—these are only some of the themes that emerge

---

4. She must have wished the village soviet to force her husband to grant her a religious (shariat) divorce, since he already had obtained a civil divorce at ZAGS.

5. She may have been seeking help to secure alimony, not necessarily trying to prevent the divorce. This story is taken from ÖzRMDA, f. 86, op. 10, d. 634, ll. 243–45. An edited version—omitting some of the most revealing information, such as the back-and-forth movement into Afghanistan—was published at *PSTZhMUz*, 63–64. Some stylistic editing in the published version is reflected in the story as quoted here.

through this story of an orphaned Uzbek girl shuttled from one abusive husband to another. Apparent, too, is the Soviet emphasis on measuring the political and cultural level of Central Asian Muslims through the character of their
intimate and family lives. Success in remaking Uzbeks as modern, civilized citizens was thought to flow from the party's success in transforming the social
position, legal rights, and cultural status of Muslim women. The tale of Ashur-
Bibi Tashmatova—and, no less important, the way Artykov chose to tell it—in
many ways serves as a microcosm of this book's larger narrative.

Central Asia as a Laboratory of Identity:
Women's Liberation and Soviet Revolution

This book seeks to offer a historicized interpretation of how contemporary
Central Asia's complex hybrid of social and cultural identities came into being.
It examines issues of cultural politics, gender relations, colonial power, and
everyday life in an effort to understand the changing face of Soviet Central
Asia and especially of Uzbekistan, the most populous Central Asian republic,
from before 1917 through the post-Soviet period. To do so it places Central
Asia in the wider context of the Islamic world's encounter with modern European colonialism and explores the peculiarities of its Soviet/Russian imperial
location, highlighting the mutually transformative nature of the colonial encounter that took place on the Soviet periphery. Soviet authorities no less than
their Central Asian subjects were reshaped through this protracted encounter,
and it was the ongoing interactions between these groups—unstable, perme-
able, and interpenetrated as they were—that in the end defined what it meant
to be both "Bolshevik" and "Uzbek."

Russian imperial leaders, officials, and elites had long staked a claim—tenuous and contested though it was—to Russia's "European" identity and its
rightful place among the world's "civilized" nations. From the late nineteenth
century on, this claim came increasingly to be linked to the practice of modern,
European-style colonial empire building, and to be justified through Russia's
self-proclaimed mission to transform, uplift, and modernize its imperial periphery, especially its most "backward" parts, such as Siberia, the Caucasus,
and, perhaps most visibly, Central Asia (see Figure 2).[6] And although tsarist
officials did not often intervene in local cultural matters, the colonial space of
Turkestan nonetheless served as a kind of civilizational laboratory, a place for
thousands of Russian men and women to work out who they were. In the imperial periphery they frequently referred to themselves as Europeans (rather
than Russians) to set themselves apart from indigenous Muslims. Central Asia

6. On this imperial mission, see Seymour Becker, "Russia between East and West: The Intelligentsia, Russian National Identity, and the Asian Borderlands," *Central Asian Survey* 10, no. 4
(1991): 47–64, or the Gorchakov circular, in *Major Problems in the History of Imperial Russia*,
ed. James Cracraft (Lexington, Mass., 1994), 410–11. On Siberia, see Yuri Slezkine, *Arctic Mirrors: Russia and the Small Peoples of the North* (Ithaca, 1994).

Figure 2. The colonial encounter: Russians and Muslims in tsarist Turkestan. (Courtesy Anahita Gallery, Santa Fe, N.M.)

became as crucial a space for the honing of self-definitions as for the colonial pursuit of military security, economic gain, and political power.

Before 1917 Central Asia thus helped make tsarist Russia European; after 1917, too, it continued to do so for Soviet Russia, even as it also helped define Bolshevism for the colonial world. Like their tsarist predecessors, the new Soviet authorities often acted in the name of Europe (however hazily it was defined) in their interactions with non-Russian populations. But Bolshevik activists and Soviet leaders were far more willing to intervene in local affairs, declaring it their business to remake, not just to administer, the Muslims of Turkestan. Seeing themselves as bearers of modern European cultural norms (such as gender equality) and as a transmission belt for European notions of social reform (which meant public health and hygiene as much as class revolution), groups of party activists arrived to recreate Central Asia in their image. Yet early Bolshevism itself was very much a work in progress; these activists' subsequent interactions with Central Asians gave them a chance to refine in their own minds this image of "civilization." They learned by doing, in short, what it meant to be European—and what it meant to be Bolshevik.

The present volume focuses on this process of intervention, transformation, and mutual self-definition during the first decades of Soviet power in Uzbekistan, from the establishment of national republics in Central Asia in the mid-1920s until the massive German attack of June 1941. These were the years of the Stalin Revolution: an era of massive state and party campaigns that sought nothing less than to build a new kind of civilization in the USSR. These all-encompassing campaigns aimed to restructure society, most obviously through rapid industrialization and the forced collectivization of peasant agriculture. They also aimed to create a new kind of Soviet citizen, through a "cultural revolution" that intended to produce a New Soviet Man (and, albeit usually less prominently, Woman). These were also the years of vast party purges and ultimately the nightmarish Great Terror of 1937–38. All of these campaigns had an impact on Soviet Central Asia: millions of Muslim nomads and peasants were settled on collective farms and put to work in new factories. In the later 1930s, top party officials were shot or sent to Siberia, while the landscape itself was reworked in huge projects such as the Farghona (Fergana) Canal, which aimed to boost cotton production by making the desert fertile. Indigenous populations were simultaneously recast, being taught the various components of "cultured" behavior: to read Marx and Lenin; to visit a doctor when ill; to appreciate modern science, engineering, and art; and to wash one's body with soap.

All of this is familiar to Soviet historians. But in southern Central Asia the turmoil of building a new world was also expressed in a qualitatively different key. In particular, during these years new identities—local, regional, and national—emerged from bitter struggles over gender roles and everyday family life. These struggles stemmed in part from attempts to answer the question: What is the proper social position for women in a modern society? This story obviously has parallels elsewhere and thus is part of a wider story of political power and cultural change under colonialism. Yet at first glance such a narrative may appear out of place in the Stalinist Soviet Union. The Stalin Revolution is often seen as marginalizing or ignoring women's issues: first overshadowed by the collectivization and industrialization campaigns, Soviet social and family policies became increasingly conservative during the 1930s, most visibly in the well-known 1936 decision to outlaw abortion. In Moscow the party's prominent Women's Department (Zhenotdel) was closed in 1930, and its successor, the lower-level Women's Section (Zhensektor), followed suit in 1934.

In Central Asia, though, local "special circumstances" kept the Zhenotdels alive for years.[7] In Uzbekistan, indeed, women's emancipation ultimately came in many ways to exemplify the entire Bolshevik Revolution. This unusual situation was largely the result of the Soviet state's peculiar position in Central

7. On the survival of Zhensektory in Uzbekistan, see Dilorom Agzamovna Alimova, *Zhenskii vopros v Srednei Azii: Istoriia izucheniia i sovremennye problemy* (Tashkent, 1991), 62–64, and Petr Matveevich Chirkov, *Reshenie zhenskogo voprosa v SSSR (1917–1937 gg.)* (Moscow, 1978), 71. A Zhensektor report from late 1936 or early 1937 is at Prezident devoni arkhivi (hereafter PDA), f. 58, op. 13, d. 1169, ll. 7–14. Unless otherwise noted, all subsequent PDA citations are also from f. 58, and thus specify only *opis'*, *delo*, and *list*. PDA unfortunately is closed to scholars. I am grateful to several colleagues for providing typescripts and notes from its holdings, all of which have been verified where possible. Some of these colleagues wish to remain anonymous. Of those I may acknowledge, I particularly thank Shoshana Keller for sharing her archival notes, recorded here as PDA(K).

Asia. Bolshevik revolutionaries had seized power in 1917 in the name of the oppressed—most obviously Russian workers, soldiers, and peasants, but also colonized peoples around the world. Yet Red Army soldiers and Communist officials soon found themselves assuming authority over most of the former tsarist empire, often over colonial populations that had not necessarily wanted Soviet power. This outcome produced enormous theoretical and practical problems for the Bolsheviks. Party leaders faced the difficulties of running a colonial empire under the banner of an anticolonial, liberationist ideology. In the end they were driven into a series of contingent choices that produced a Central Asian policy quite unlike that in Russia.

As committed Marxists, party activists—most of whom hailed from non-indigenous, non-Muslim European groups such as Russians, Jews, and Ukrainians—first sought allies among industrial workers. But Central Asia was an overwhelmingly rural place with few urban areas or factories, and Slavic immigrants, not native Muslims, dominated those that did exist.[8] The vast majority of these settlers resided in physically separate districts (and ethnically separate pockets) known as "New Cities" for their distinctive architectural styles and overwhelmingly European population. (See Figure 3.) Of the nearly five million people in the Uzbek SSR by 1930, only 8.5 percent were Russians or other "newly arrived" (*prishlye*) people—but as one would expect in a colonial setting, these groups were overrepresented and wielded disproportionate influence in both the major cities and the formal structures of political and economic power.[9]

At a loss to find an indigenous proletariat, local Bolsheviks sought other ways to translate the party's program for "building socialism" into the largely Muslim cultural world of Turkestan. At first they tried to transform Central Asia by simply repeating campaigns that had been employed in Russia. Antireligious campaigns, for example, criticized Muslim clerics as "class oppressors," and a large-scale land and water reform in 1925–26 aimed to redistribute these key resources to poor and landless peasants. By 1926, though, attacks on wealthy landlords and Islam had proved for the most part unsuccessful at creating either visible class identities or pro-Bolshevik sympathies among the vast majority of Uzbeks. The local Communist party was still tiny, isolated, and mostly alien to Muslim society. It numbered only a few tens of

8. The census of 1926 classified six out of seven Central Asians as "rural." Uzbekistan was relatively more "urban" (23.9 percent), but only by counting all towns with more than 20,000 inhabitants and some villages with as few as 500 (*Vsesouiznaia perepis' naseleniia 17 dekabria 1926 g. Kratkie svodki* [Moscow, 1927–29], 3:2–5, 27, and 47).

9. *Sredniaia Aziia v tsifrakh* (Tashkent, 1931), 9, lists 5.6 percent of the republic's total estimated population of 4,584,911 on 1 January 1930 as Russian and 2.9 percent as other, unspecified *prishlye* peoples. In 1926 this area had had a population classified as 74 percent Uzbek and 8 percent Tajik (ibid., 18–19). Most of the remainder was drawn from other indigenous Central Asian groups, such as Kazakhs and Kyrgyz. Indigenous (Bukhoran) Jews also represented a small percentage; they were distinct from the "European" Jews who were far more likely to hold positions in the Soviet apparatus.

Figure 3. Tashkent's New City. (Courtesy Anahita Gallery, Santa Fe, N.M.)

thousands of members, concentrated almost entirely in the cities and drawn disproportionately from the ranks of recent immigrants to Central Asia.[10]

In response, in late 1926 the party's top regional leaders in Tashkent, acting through the supervisory body of the Central Asian Bureau (Sredazbiuro), decided, partly at the urging of enthusiastic Zhenotdel activists, to try an approach that had no real counterpart or recent precedent in Russia proper.[11] This choice amounted to a belated admission that Muslim Central Asia was not, after all, always like Russia. Revolution in the colonial "East" henceforth was to be reshaped to address the area's specific needs and peculiar dynamics. Local society was patriarchal, and gender conflict coexisted in complicated ways with colonial conflict. Many Muslim women, the Zhenotdel reasoned, were forced to stay hidden in public and secluded at home, and hence saw themselves as victims of indigenous men, not just of the Russian colonial state. As an American political scientist, Gregory Massell, put it in 1974, party and Zhenotdel leaders thus developed an interpretation of Central Asian society in which all Muslim women were victims of patriarchal oppression and thus

10. In early 1926 the Uzbek SSR's Communist Party organization, the KP(b)Uz, reported a total of only 18,351 members and candidate members, or less than 0.5 percent of the republic's overall population. Within this group, Europeans outnumbered Uzbeks, 9,043 to 7,736; men outnumbered women 15 to 1; and almost a third were completely illiterate, with only 2.2 percent boasting a higher education (Z. Simanovich, "Itogi partiinoi perepisi v Uzbekistane," *Izvestiia TsK KP(b)Uz*, no. 1 [1926], 9–10).

11. It had been two centuries since Peter the Great ended the seclusion of elite Muscovite women.

functioned in Marxist terms as a "surrogate proletariat."[12] In this view, women represented a massive, latent group of potential allies that the party could mobilize by publicizing a message of gender equality and liberation. It seemed self-evident to many Soviet women's activists—many of whom hailed from Russia and other Slavic areas and had little experience in the Muslim world—that such a message would be welcomed at once by their Muslim sisters and adopted wholeheartedly by these assumed beneficiaries of emancipation. Therefore women's liberation was selected as the crucial strategy to find Bolshevik allies among the indigenous peoples of Central Asia; parallel efforts were launched in Azerbaijan and across the Soviet East.

Party activists in Tashkent launched this campaign in 1927, on the socialist holiday of International Women's Day (8 March), calling it a *hujum,* or assault, against the "moldy old ways" of female seclusion and inequality. This campaign took as its goal nothing less than the complete and immediate transformation of everyday life, or *byt* (in Uzbek, *turmush*), as measured especially in the realms of gender relations and family life. The hujum took various forms across Central Asia and elsewhere, but in Uzbekistan (as well as Tajikistan and Azerbaijan) it aimed above all at the eradication of the heavy head-to-toe veils of horsehair and cotton that many Muslim women (and girls over the age of 9 or 10) wore in the presence of unrelated men. In choosing to target these veils for destruction, Bolshevik activists followed and in important ways expanded the legacy of their tsarist imperial predecessors. They meant to show, as dramatically as possible, that Central Asia had been liberated and transformed according to Soviet ideals. Party optimists aimed at a swift campaign, despite the almost complete absence from party ranks of Uzbek women to help lead the effort.[13] Hopes thus fell to the mostly Russian activists of the Zhenotdel, who aimed to complete the heroic liberation of Central Asian women in less than six months—a schedule that would enable them to celebrate success by October 1927, the tenth anniversary of the Bolshevik Revolution.[14]

It is at this point that the present book begins. The campaign against the veil was complicated, contested, and contradictory; over the next fifteen years it transformed both sides. If it seems obvious that this campaign (quite liter-

---

12. Gregory J. Massell, *The Surrogate Proletariat: Moslem Women and Revolutionary Strategies in Soviet Central Asia, 1919–1929* (Princeton, 1974).

13. A reckoning in July 1927 found only 457 Uzbek women in the KP(b)Uz (ÖzRMDA, f. 86, op. 2, d. 27, l. 37). This figure represents less than 2 percent of the Uzbek Communist Party's membership rolls; it also indicates that an essentially invisible proportion (roughly 0.03 percent) of the overall Uzbek female population had been enrolled in the party.

14. PDA, op, 3, d. 1560, l. 57; ÖzRMDA, f. 86, op. 1, d. 5134, l. 25; Rossiisskii gosudarstvennyi arkhiv sotsial'no-politicheskoi istorii (hereafter RGASPI), f. 62, op. 2, d. 1205, l. 40b, and d. 1242, ll. 31 and 140ob. Except as noted, all RGASPI citations are from f. 62, op. 2 (the party's Central Asian Bureau), and thus specify only *delo* and *list.* Also see Serafima Liubimova, "Oktiabr' i truzhenitsa zarubezhnogo Vostoka," *Za partiiu,* no. 3 (1927), 77–80. On these activists, see *Khudzhum: Znachit nastuplenie* (Tashkent, 1987) and *Probuzhdennye velikim Oktiabrem: Sbornik ocherkov i vospominanii* (Tashkent, 1961).

ally) changed the face of Central Asia, it is equally important to see how it also changed Soviet activists themselves. This mutually reshaping intercultural encounter lies at the heart of the story, and I thus intend this book to be part of a wider narrative of European interactions with colonial subjects.[15] In particular, Uzbek women's behavior and status were taken to express the promise of Soviet power and validate its viability. Uzbek women thus occupied a central symbolic position in the protracted struggles between Soviet reformers and their Muslim opponents. All sides came to define their cultural practices and social values through the everyday customs of Muslim women. On the one hand, state action thus created unintended possibilities for women: a space where feminist concerns (under a different name) could survive and even thrive during the Stalinist period. Intensive efforts to transform and "liberate" Muslim women remained among the highest state and party priorities in Central Asia. On the other hand, this common ground of debate ultimately helped define a specific, local, and deeply gendered lexicon for both Central Asian Bolshevism and Uzbek national identity, and it left these women personally in a very difficult position, facing strong pressure from all sides.

The Uzbek woman's veil, in short, became far more than a simple piece of cloth. To Bolshevik activists it represented their "civilizing mission" and embodied all that was backward and primitive about Central Asia. Zhenotdel workers came to insist that Uzbek women publicly—and sometimes at gunpoint—throw off their veils. When unveiling came after 1927 to serve as an overarching symbol of the Soviet project in the colonial East, the curious metamorphosis was completed: a Marxist revolution promising class liberation had been transfigured into a project of gender emancipation. To many Uzbeks, both men and women, the veil was also likewise transformed. It was elevated in importance above many other customs and became symbolic of an entire way of life and a sense of self. Hence so-called traditional gender roles and behaviors persisted and even expanded, despite the best efforts of Bolshevik activists to stamp them out. Wearing a veil became more than a narrowly religious or moral matter; for many people it also became an act of political and national resistance to an outside colonial power.

Given the various and conflicting meanings with which the veil was invested, the tenacity with which it was both attacked and defended is understandable. In the longer term, the Soviet decision to focus on dramatic public unveilings proved counterproductive; by hardening Muslim hostility toward Bolshevik agitators perceived as foreign urban atheists, it made cultural change more rather than less difficult. And by deeming the veil a preeminent symbol of Muslim Uzbek culture, the Bolsheviks only gave it new strength.

15. See Peter van der Veer, *Imperial Encounters: Religion and Modernity in India and Britain* (Princeton, 2001), or Catherine Hall, *Civilising Subjects: Colony and Metropole in the English Imagination, 1830–1867* (Chicago, 2002), on this mutual transformation in the crucible of empire.

Conflict over the veil thus represents a story of resistance and power, but one far more complex than it first appears. Bolshevik leaders inadvertently reinforced the seclusion of Uzbek women in the short and medium term, effectively creating a powerful discourse of resistance to their own women's liberation policies. Despite stated goals to the contrary, that is, Soviet efforts played a large role in creating the veil as a national symbol and inscribing it as emblematic of a "tradition" that was in fact quite new.

By focusing on the frontier, then—the contact zone—between Slavic and Muslim worlds and on the shifting textures of everyday existence, one sees the Soviet imperial experience in a different light.[16] This approach highlights the complex processes of negotiation—not dictation—that shaped the social and cultural realm of family life. The meanings of Soviet power emerge here as provisional, unstable, always under debate, and continually changing. Soviet society was not always dominated and controlled, but frequently chaotic. In this view, the state was one actor among many—a powerful one, to be sure, but not always dominant in the struggles to shape the political, cultural, social, and economic worlds in which its citizens lived.

Colonial Power in an Anticolonial Empire:
An Orientation to Southern Central Asia

An appreciation of historical context is necessary to make sense of these events during the early Soviet period. By the mid-1920s much of Central Asia, once a hub of world trade, had been turned into a colony of the Russian empire, and the various peoples of Uzbekistan had weathered more than a half-century of Russian colonial rule.[17] The local societies and cultures of southern Central Asia were by no means static or isolated enclaves before the arrival of tsarist troops in the 1860s: the great Islamic cities of Bukhoro (Bukhara) and Samarqand (Samarkand) had been world centers of learning and major transit points on the Silk Road centuries earlier, and local wars for power, wealth, and territory were well under way in the early nineteenth century. (See Map 1A.) Nevertheless, the subsequent decades of tsarist occupation brought a bewildering array of changes in regional politics, economics, culture, and society. Russian colonists and soldiers expanded steadily southward after a series of successful military conquests in the 1860s and 1870s; after bitter resistance, the last

---

16. On the imperial "contact zone," comprising "social spaces where disparate cultures meet, clash, and grapple with each other, often in highly asymmetrical relations of domination and subordination," see Mary Louise Pratt, *Imperial Eyes: Travel Writing and Transculturation* (London, 1992), 4.

17. James Cracraft calls tsarist Central Asia "the very prototype of a classic colony" (*Major Problems*, 401). See also Nadira A. Abdurakhimova, "The Colonial System of Power in Turkistan," *International Journal of Middle East Studies* 34 (2002): 239–62. Adeeb Khalid notes that tsarist administrators saw Turkestan as Russia's European-style colonial realm (*The Politics of Muslim Cultural Reform: Jadidism in Central Asia* [Berkeley, 1998], 15).

Turkmen lands succumbed in the 1880s, and the final segment of the tsarist empire's southern border—with China and Afghanistan, in the high Pamir Mountains—was set in 1895. Local Muslim rulers and existing political structures were either officially pushed aside (as in the vast area incorporated by tsarist officials as "Turkestan") or subjugated (as in the khanate of Khiva [Khorazm, Khorezm] and the emirate of Bukhoro, both of which became protectorates).[18] (See Map 1B.)

These political shifts enabled—and provoked—social and economic changes. The nineteenth-century Russian threat, for example, helped create the *jadid* movement for social reform in Muslim areas of the tsarist empire. The jadids, as they were called (from the word for "new"), made the case for wide-ranging internal reform to create a new social order, one that would be modern yet still Islamic. (At the same time, analogous movements were appearing elsewhere in the Middle East and colonial world.) New tsarist railways, originally built to provide military security against possible threats from Muslim rebels as well as garrisons in British India, reoriented economic exchange patterns toward the Russian north. (See Map 1B.) A colonial economy developed: in the river basins of southern Central Asia, cotton production expanded at the expense of local food crops. Grain was imported by rail from the north, while cotton left by the same route. This arrangement later contributed to severe famine between 1917 and 1921, when the turmoil of revolution and civil war cut transportation networks and curtailed food imports. Grain prices soared, yet local production went down rather than up as the chaos and violence also disrupted irrigation networks. The planted acreage of food crops within Turkestan declined by almost two-thirds between 1917 and 1919, and thousands died.[19] Violent conflict erupted over access to food supplies, expressed in the appearance of bands of armed rebels, known in Soviet narratives as *bosmachi* (bandits). They were the sharp edge of a rural revolt against the cities, although they increasingly took on an anti-Soviet political and religious overlay and later, during the unveiling campaign, served to enforce adherence to non-Soviet ideals. These rebels—who called themselves *qörboshi*, from a title used by military and police officers in prerevolutionary Turkestan and Bukhoro—successfully attacked Soviet personnel and facilities, remaining active in places well into the 1930s.[20]

18. On the political history of the tsarist period, see Richard A. Pierce, *Russian Central Asia 1867–1917: A Study in Colonial Rule* (Berkeley, 1960), or Seymour Becker, *Russia's Protectorates in Central Asia: Bukhara and Khiva, 1865–1924* (Cambridge, Mass., 1968).

19. Total irrigated acreage declined from 7,395,238 to 2,822,111, a drop of 61.9 percent. Summer wheat suffered the steepest fall, of 79.0 percent. Alexander Park, *Bolshevism in Turkestan, 1917–1927* (New York, 1957), 37–38, also blames Soviet price controls and grain requisitioning.

20. For the Soviet interpretation, see S. Ginsburg, "Basmachestvo v Fergane," *Novyi Vostok*, no. 10–11 (1926), 173–202, and K[azimir] Vasilevskii, "Fazy basmacheskogo dvizhenii v Srednei

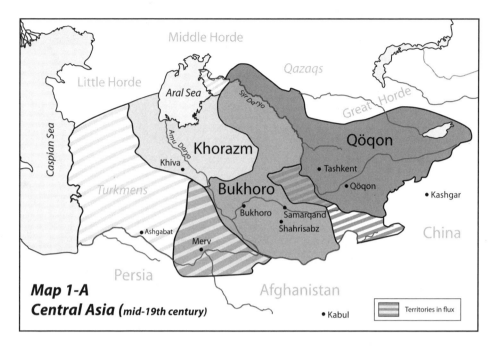

Middle Horde

Little Horde

Qazaqs

Aral Sea

Great Horde

Syr Daryo

Caspian Sea

Amu Daryo

Khorazm

Qöqon

Khiva

Turkmens

Bukhoro

Tashkent

Qöqon

Kashgar

Bukhoro

Samarqand

Shahrisabz

China

Ashgabat

Merv

Persia

Afghanistan

Map 1-A
Central Asia (mid-19th century)

Kabul

Territories in flux

Russian Empire
(Steppe Region)

Turkestan

Aral Sea

Semirech'e / Ettisuv

Syr Da'ryo

Vernyi
(Almaty)

Przheval'sk
(Qoraqöl)

Caspian Sea

Syr Daryo

Pishpek
(Bishkek)

Amu Daryo

Khiva

Shymkent

Transcaspia

Khiva

Samarqand

Tashkent

Namangan

Jalolobod

Krasnovodsk

Katta Qörghon

Qöqon

Andijon

Bukhoro

Jizzakh

Skobelev
(Farghona)

Farghona

Samarqand

China

Ashgabat

Merv

Shahrisabz

Bukhoro

Persia

Termiz

Afghanistan

India

Map 1-B
Tsarist Central Asia
(from 1895)

Kushka

Railway
(1881-1915)

Ironically, in many ways the stresses of colonial control on Central Asian society only increased after the (vocally anticolonialist) Bolshevik Party came to power in Russia in 1917 and the Red Army reclaimed tsarist possessions in southern Central Asia. The conceptual categories and formal structures of political life continued to shift at a dizzying pace, and by 1924 Bolshevik administrators had gone so far as to draw entirely new internal borders, creating the new national "republics" of Uzbekistan and Turkmenistan. Another republic appeared five years later, when Tajikistan was carved out of the Uzbek SSR; Kazakhstan and Kyrgyzstan, initially autonomous parts of the Russian Republic (RSFSR), received full republic status in 1936. (See Map 2.)

Indigenous identities were complex, multifaceted, and changeable, and they corresponded poorly to these new political borders. Such stark national distinctions, for example, meant little in places such as multilingual, multicultural Samarqand—the first capital city of the new Uzbek SSR—where most people wasted little time considering whether to call themselves Uzbek, Tajik, or something else. Most Central Asians did claim an identity as Muslim, but that common label masked a vast variety of local customs and religious practices.[21] Simple national and religious labels, in short, do not capture the multiple, layered, context-dependent nature of Central Asian identities. Personal self-conceptions here are better seen as a matrix, its components produced by an ongoing interplay of social institutions, religious practices, economic relationships, political structures, regional, clan, and local customs, generational and gender hierarchies, and occupational categories, as well as urban/rural differences and the deep historical divide between settled and nomadic groups. The matter of which identity was most salient in a particular situation (man? Muslim? Uzbek? Sart? farmer? father? from Tashkent? Surqosh?) depended on the precise issues under consideration and the individual in question, and frequently was impossible to pinpoint.

Despite the practical impossibility of drawing discrete boundaries in this complex cultural world, the state invested each Soviet Socialist Republic with a separate, officially sanctioned national identity, complete with its own political hierarchy, literary language, even alphabet. As post-Soviet scholarship has

---

Azii," *Novyi Vostok*, no. 29 (1930), 126–41. Archival discussions fill many *dela* at ÖzRMDA, f. 1714, op. 5. On the famine, see the work of Marco Buttino, especially "Ethnicité et politique dans la guerre civile: À propos du basmacestvo au Fergana," *Cahiers du monde russe* 38 (1997): 195–222; "Politics and Social Conflict during a Famine: Turkestan Immediately after the Revolution," in *In a Collapsing Empire: Underdevelopment, Ethnic Conflicts, and Nationalisms in the Soviet Union,* ed. Buttino (Milan, 1993); and "Study of the Economic Crisis and Depopulation in Turkestan, 1917–1920," *Central Asian Survey* 9, no. 4 (1990): 59–74.

21. According to the census of 1897, non-Muslim groups represented only 5.6 percent (of which Russians were 1.3 percent) of the population in the three southern provinces of Turkestan (Farghona, Samarqand, and Syr Daryo). The disparity was even greater in Bukhoro and Khiva, where by one estimate the population was 99.1 percent Muslim. See Michael Rywkin, *Moscow's Muslim Challenge: Soviet Central Asia* (Armonk, N.Y., 1990), 59, and Khalid, *Politics of Muslim Cultural Reform,* 16, 203.

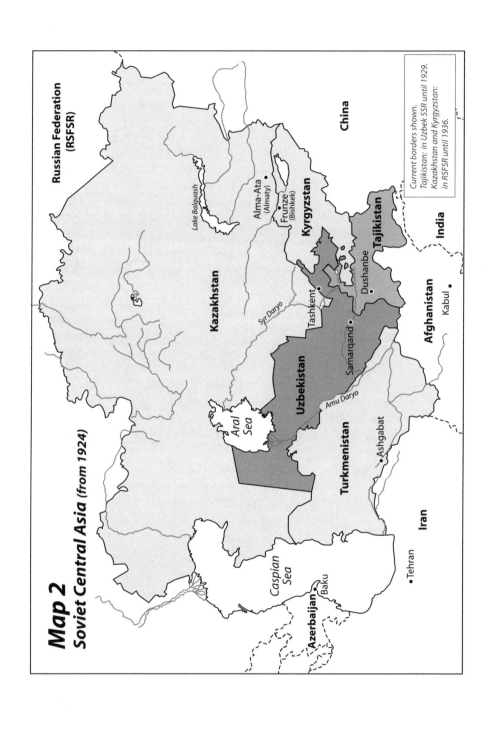

Map 2
Soviet Central Asia (from 1924)

Current borders shown.
Tajikistan: in Uzbek SSR until 1929.
Kazakhstan and Kyrgyzstan:
in RSFSR until 1936.

Russian Federation
(RSFSR)

China

India

Afghanistan

Kabul •

Iran

• Tehran

Kazakhstan

Kyrgyzstan

Tajikistan

Uzbekistan

Turkmenistan

Azerbaijan

Alma-Ata
(Almaty) •

Frunze
(Bishkek) •

Dushanbe •

Tashkent •

Samarqand •

• Ashgabat

Baku •

Lake Balquash

Syr Daryo

Amu Daryo

Aral
Sea

Caspian
Sea

shown, building such nations became one of the party's highest priorities all across the USSR.[22] In Central Asia, Soviet ethnographic teams collected folk tales and studied local customs to underscore the distinctiveness of each nation's supposedly ancient traditions—although many were, in truth, comparatively new. Uzbek women, for example, were said to wear one particular kind of veil, shown in the frontispiece to this volume. It consisted of two parts: a heavy cotton robe, or *paranji*, that covered the body and held in place a face screen of woven horsehair, called a *chachvon*. Turkmen women, by contrast, wore a *yashmak*, a lighter face covering that left the eyes, nose, and forehead visible, while Kazakh and Kyrgyz women veiled rarely, if at all. (See Figure 4.) Yet the ostensibly definitive Uzbek paranji and chachvon actually were quite new, having supplanted another veil (the lighter, less restrictive *mursak*) in the cities of southern Turkestan only starting in the 1870s. These heavier veils thus appeared only alongside or shortly after the establishment of Russian colonial power. Even by 1917 they were not universal, being worn primarily by urban women and those in reasonably affluent families.

Soviet power brought still more changes. Whereas tsarist administrators had for the most part been content to focus on issues of tax collection and military security rather than intervene in matters of local society or culture, Bolshevik activists and officials saw the world in very different terms. Central Asia, they thought, was a primitive region that had to be wrested out of its timeless past and thrown headlong into the modern (Soviet) era. (See Figure 5.) By doing so, the Bolsheviks hoped, they would enable Uzbeks, Kazakhs, and others to leapfrog over the capitalist period and move straight to socialism. Their success would showcase the promise of Soviet power for colonized peoples around the world, thus enabling the revolution to expand rapidly; this example would be (it *had* to be) more persuasive than competing, nonsocialist models of change, such as Kemal Atatürk's new nationalist state in Turkey. Complete transformation—political, social, cultural, economic—thus became the central goal of Bolshevik regional policy, as the party sought ways immediately to remake the men and women of southern Central Asia into true modern Soviet citizens.

Such efforts in some ways paralleled simultaneous campaigns to modernize the peasantry of Russia itself and other parts of the USSR. The historian Yuri Slezkine has argued this point most forcefully, contending that the Soviet project was fundamentally not that of a colonial empire but that of a modernizing state determined to transform its citizenry.[23] The point may sound reasonable;

22. Yuri Slezkine, "The USSR as a Communal Apartment, or How a Socialist State Promoted Ethnic Particularism," *Slavic Review* 53 (1994): 414–53; Ronald Suny, *The Revenge of the Past: Nationalism, Revolution, and the Collapse of the Soviet Union* (Stanford, 1993); and Terry Martin, *The Affirmative Action Empire: Nations and Nationalism in the Soviet Union, 1923–1939* (Ithaca, 2001).

23. Yuri Slezkine, "Imperialism as the Highest Stage of Socialism," *Russian Review* 59 (2000): 227–34. James C. Scott provides a wider framework for this view in *Seeing Like a State: How Cer-*

Figure 4. Gender and nation: Turkmen woman (left), 1931; Kazakh woman (right), 1930. (Courtesy RGAKFD and Anahita Gallery, Santa Fe, N.M.)

Soviet leaders, after all, insisted that their country was not an empire and that it was not at all colonial—that it was, in fact, anticolonial. From the party's perspective, Russian peasants also lacked basic literacy skills and rudimentary habits of personal hygiene (and Russian city dwellers were not much better). They too were seen as backward, primitive, patriarchal figures in need of transformation, and so were subjected to personal and political instruction at every turn: by traveling speakers, at organized demonstrations, through radio broadcasts, newspaper broadsheets, propaganda pamphlets, and study circles. All of these methods aimed to teach the categories, credos, and goals of the Revolution, to naturalize and internalize a Bolshevik way of seeing the world, partly by overcoming the so-called primitivism of everyday life. There were even rough analogues to the Central Asian unveiling campaign: during the initial radical phase of revolution after 1917, new family codes aimed to emancipate Russian women by expanding property rights, permitting abortion on demand, building child-care facilities, and changing divorce procedures and marriage law. The backward *baba* embodied much of what needed to be

---

tain Schemes to Improve the Human Condition Have Failed (New Haven, 1998). Among Central Asian specialists, Adeeb Khalid is one of the few to support Slezkine's view, although, as noted above, his work supports a contrary view of the pre-1917 period.

Figure 5. Uzbek village, Samarqand province, 1932. Note that no windows face the street. (Courtesy ÖzRKFFHMDA.)

changed in Soviet Russia, and local activists invested time and energy in associated cultural efforts, such as cutting the hair of Russian Old Believer women.[24]

Some elements of the Bolshevik approach to Central Asia, therefore, are not colonial per se. Yet it would be wrong to conclude from the surface similarities in representations of Slavic and Central Asian peasants that the USSR was no more than a modernizing state or that its policies did not differentiate meaningfully between regions. Even Slezkine has been willing to grant that Uzbek peasants differed crucially from their Russian counterparts precisely in having this colonial status.[25] Everyday private life mattered in Russia, but it became a central, all-pervading concern in Uzbekistan. Comparing the unveiling cam-

24. On views of Russian peasants as backward, see Lynne Viola, *Peasant Rebels under Stalin: Collectivization and the Culture of Peasant Resistance* (New York, 1996), 14–19, or Cathy A. Frierson, *Peasant Icons: Representations of Rural People in Late Nineteenth-Century Russia* (New York, 1993). On the other campaigns, see Daniel Peris, *Storming the Heavens: The Soviet League of the Militant Godless* (Ithaca, 1998); Elizabeth Wood, *The Baba and the Comrade: Gender and Politics in Revolutionary Russia* (Bloomington, 1997); and Irina Korovushkina Paert, "Popular Religion and Local Identity during the Stalin Revolution: Old Believers in the Urals, 1928–41," in *Provincial Landscapes: Local Dimensions of Soviet Power, 1917–1953,* ed. Donald Raleigh (Pittsburgh, 2001), especially 184–85.

25. In a published response to this author, Slezkine says that "good evidence and strong arguments" support the view that Soviet power in Uzbekistan was a colonial empire ("Imperialism as the Highest Form of Socialism," 231).

paign with the Soviet state's efforts to transform a recalcitrant Russian peasantry thus shows the common features of these encounters, but also makes clear the uniquely colonial and cross-cultural aspects of the Soviet attempt to build a particular kind of socialist modernity. Uzbek peasants were seen as qualitatively different from their Russian equivalents: speaking a different (and linguistically unrelated) tongue; professing an Islamic identity; in short, inhabiting a religio-cultural sphere perceived by both sides as distinct. On top of these distinctions came the experience of Russian rule and the formal structures (political, economic, and military) of modern colonialism. The apparently simple fact that the veil, as a principal marker of colonial difference, did not even exist in Russia but came to sit at the very heart of Soviet policy in Uzbekistan shows the centrality of ethnic and cultural difference in shaping Bolshevism for the non-Russian periphery.

One of my main premises, then, is that the USSR, like its tsarist predecessor, was a colonial empire. Power in the Soviet Union was expressed across lines of hierarchy and difference that created at least theoretically distinct centers (metropoles) and peripheries (colonies). Such lines of hierarchy and difference were simultaneously geographic, ethnic, political, economic, and cultural. Soviet policies, categories, and priorities had the effect of treating colonial people differently because of their special status along all of these axes. Hence, while it may not have been a classic overseas empire like that of the British or Dutch, the USSR did have a somewhat comparable political, economic, and military structure; a parallel cultural agenda; and similarly liminal colonial elites. It compares still more readily with the major overland empires: consider the Ottoman, Habsburg, or, especially, American cases.[26] The Soviet project's colonial component and the European-style civilizing mission it created for rank-and-file as well as prominent Bolsheviks served as important strands of party as well as Russian self-definition.[27]

The additional crucial layers of difference between Uzbeks and the metropolitan state made it harder for them to find common ground with Bolshevik activists who were struggling to bring the Revolution to Central Asia. To most of these (predominantly Slavic) activists, Uzbekistan was a more foreign place, and a different kind of foreign place, than a hypothetical village in rural Russia. Cross-cultural translation proved difficult, and many additional complications and new realms of misunderstanding soon emerged. Although Russian

26. I have benefited from discussions with Susan Solomon on these questions of definition. For attempts to apply such categories to the Soviet case, see Ronald Grigor Suny, "Ambiguous Categories: States, Empires, and Nations," *Post-Soviet Affairs* 11 (1995): 187–88; Karen Barkey and Mark von Hagen, eds., *After Empire: Multiethnic Societies and Nation-Building* (Boulder, 1997); and Dominic Lieven, *Empire: The Russian Empire and Its Rivals* (New Haven, 2000).

27. For a similar argument about the importance of work in the "periphery," see Jörg Baberowski, "Stalinismus an der Peripherie: Das Beispiel Azerbaijan, 1920–1941," in *Stalinismus vor dem zweiten Weltkrieg: Neue Wege der Forschung*, ed. Manfred Hildermeier with Elisabeth Müller-Luckner (Munich, 1998), 307–35.

peasants certainly had not welcomed party workers with open arms, a half-century of colonial rule left Central Asians even more suspicious of the Bolsheviks' self-proclaimed liberation.[28] Moreover, the party's decision to target specific indigenous social practices such as the veil for eradication ironically put Central Asians in a good position to resist state power. They did so by drawing on this perceived distinctiveness: by framing it in contradistinction and sometimes opposition to the state identified with (foreign, urban, colonial, Russian, Orthodox or atheist) Moscow.

Unlike its tsarist predecessor, however, the USSR was also a distinctively modern and modernizing state. In both center and periphery, that is, it sought simultaneously to build a polity with a common ideal of citizenship; and thus its insistent anticolonialism also needs to be taken seriously, as more than mere rhetoric. The unveiling campaign in some ways expressed this credo: it aimed to make Uzbeks into Soviet citizens rather than simply imperial subjects.[29] Thus even while it expressed colonial power and effectively applied cultural coercion to reinscribe colonial differences, it paradoxically tried to overcome this tsarist colonial lineage. By using the unveiling campaign to transform Uzbek society and culture, party leaders could claim their own status as civilized Europeans. At the same time, they also hoped this campaign would shoehorn indigenous Muslims into a lexicon of politics and cultural identity that Bolshevik rank-and-file workers could recognize. Success, after all, would leave Uzbek women and men approachable on the same terms as Russian peasants. To reach this goal, though, Uzbek women first had to take off their veils. They would still have a distinctive ethno-cultural identity, to be sure, but they would no longer be colonial, at least not in the sense of being differentially oppressed. The tsarist empire had to be recast, not abandoned: Soviet colonialism would be affirming and constructive, not oppressive or exploitative.[30]

Such an integral project was unusual for an imperial power: more often, colonial peripheries were kept, wherever possible, legally and conceptually separate from the metropole. In British India, for instance, colonial authority

---

28. Some scholars argue that Russian peasants were so distant from party activists that they too were colonized by the Soviet state. This is a potentially productive approach, but it risks blurring the distinction between modernizing states and colonial empires, the very issue raised by Slezkine. See Alvin Gouldner, "Stalinism: A Study in Internal Colonialism," *Telos* 34 (1977): 5–48; or more recently Stephen Kotkin, *Magnetic Mountain: Stalinism as a Civilization* (Berkeley, 1995), 33; and Tracy McDonald, "Peasant Rebellion in Stalin's Russia: The Pitelinskii Uprising, Riazan, 1930," in *Contending with Stalinism: Soviet Power and Popular Resistance in the 1930s*, ed. Lynne Viola (Ithaca, 2002), 100. Eugen Weber has made a similar argument in *Peasants into Frenchmen: The Modernization of Rural France, 1870–1914* (Stanford, 1976), 241, 485–96.

29. For a parallel colonial campaign in Russia itself, see Yuri Slezkine, "From Savages to Citizens: The Cultural Revolution in the Soviet Far North, 1928–1938," *Slavic Review* 51 (1992): 52–76.

30. Francine Hirsch eloquently makes a similar argument in "Toward an Empire of Nations: Border-Making and the Formation of Soviet National Identities," *Russian Review* 59 (2000): 201–26. See also her "Empire of Nations: Colonial Technologies and the Making of the Soviet Union, 1917–1939" (Ph.D. diss., Princeton University, 1998).

was justified in parental terms: supposedly mature British guardians were teaching allegedly less developed Indian children to grow up, become adults, and govern themselves. But this project was not meant to lead to assimilation or even equality, since it would not make the latter British, only more mature Indians. Thus some apparently interventionist British policies—such as the decision in 1829 to ban *sati* (the ritual burning of widows on their husbands' funeral pyres)—were justified in the name not of modernity and change but of defending tradition and purifying "true" Hindu practice—in essence, of making Indians better Indians.[31] The Soviet approach did not employ such arguments. It intended rather to create an altogether new, modern order, with enlightened citizens who shared a political status and common identity (one that coexisted with only a few permissible ethnic, cultural, and national differences). In this sense the USSR most resembled another atypical empire, one that likewise denied it *was* an empire: the United States. American visions of citizenship were similarly ideological and individual rather than ethnic or corporate. They, too, fitted awkwardly with some aspects of territorial expansion—especially given that this discourse on citizenship included a powerful strand arguing that anyone, at least in theory, could become an American. (Although, as in Soviet Central Asia, they might first need to drop certain linguistic, religious, or cultural markers coded as "foreign.")[32]

Frameworks and Debates: Gender, Power, and Empire

For decades scholars in the Soviet Union treated the history of the unveiling campaign, like the history of Central Asian women in general, straightforwardly as a case study in liberation, more or less unproblematically conceived.[33] From this point of view the hujum amounted to a heroic effort by the party to bring progress and civilization to a backward, oppressed, patriarchal region—and its success could be seen through a litany of statistics that demonstrated the vastly increased presence of Uzbek women in politics, industry, science, the arts, and academia. Western scholars for the most part ignored the

31. Lata Mani, *Contentious Traditions: The Debate on Sati in Colonial India* (Berkeley, 1998). This parental representation of British rule was modified after the uprising of 1857. See Bernard Cohn, "Representing Authority in Victorian India," in his *An Anthropologist among the Historians* (Delhi, 1987), 632–82.

32. See, for example, Sally Engle Merry, *Colonizing Hawai'i: The Cultural Power of Law* (Princeton, 2000). This picture is obviously complicated, especially by racial hierarchies in American culture and law, as during the Jim Crow era, and perhaps even more by the ambiguous position of Native Americans in U.S. discourses of citizenship. See Frederick E. Hoxie, *A Final Promise: The Campaign to Assimilate the Indians, 1880–1920* (Lincoln, Neb., 2001).

33. See the classic treatments by Khudzhuma Samatovna Shukurova, *Sotsializm i zhenshchina Uzbekistana* (Tashkent, 1970); Rakhima Khadievna Aminova, *Oktiabr' i reshenie zhenskogo voprosa v Uzbekistane* (Tashkent, 1975); and Bibi Pal'vanova Pal'vanova, *Emansipatsiia musul'manki: Opyt raskreposhcheniia zhenshchiny sovetskogo Vostoka* (Moscow, 1982). For a historiographical overview, see Alimova, *Zhenskii vopros.*

issue, Massell being the signal exception. Only a quarter-century after publication of *The Surrogate Proletariat* did a new generation of scholars start to reconsider the history of women in early Soviet Central Asia.[34]

My own interest is somewhat different, focusing on the mutually reshaping nature of the ongoing encounter between Soviet authorities and Uzbek society. This book seeks to probe how these power relations worked, how both sides used and were themselves transformed by the structures, goals, and techniques of Soviet power and colonial authority, and what this dialogue meant for identities on both sides. This story shows with particular clarity the ongoing, never-finished, iterative process through which identities are formed and reformed, and how power, in a multiplicity of realms, comes to be expressed, resisted, and reshaped. To explore these issues I draw upon three basic theoretical frameworks: gender, power, and empire.

This Central Asian struggle was waged over gender roles and relations as well as the symbols of fashion, national identity, and colonial power. In parts of southern Central Asia, Muslim women were envisioned as *by definition* always veiled, secluded, and submissive. For many Uzbeks the fight was expressed as opposition—sometimes violent—toward women who adopted "male" attributes and thereby questioned basic, socially accepted understandings of gender. It was a gender violation as well as a national and political threat, for example, for a woman to wear trousers or bobbed hair, to read books or work in public, or to show an unveiled face. More disconcerting still was the continued blurring and instability of gender lines as local Muslim women refused to be pigeonholed. Many unveiled, reveiled, and then unveiled again, depending on a kaleidoscope of shifting individual factors. They responded creatively to the challenges and patriarchies they encountered, both outside and inside the party, invoking various conceptions of female behavior and femininity as needed and appropriate.

Gender, in this sense, is a product of history, not biology: it is a social identity that structures human relationships, a pervasive interlocking set of attributes and qualities that are then naturalized as apparently fixed and embedded in the body. Gender attributes have served as a basic marker of social position, identity, and order in most human societies, even as they take widely

34. Marianne Kamp, a specialist in the Near East, has explored this area in greatest depth. She disavows a major interest in Soviet history, however, concentrating instead on feminist issues of subjectivity among the small group of indigenous female activists who supported the unveiling campaign ("Unveiling Uzbek Women: Liberation, Representation, and Discourse, 1906–1929" [Ph.D. diss., University of Chicago, 1998], 13). Others include Shoshana Keller, who studies Central Asian antireligious campaigns and sees the hujum principally as part of this wider attack on Islam ("Trapped between State and Society: Women's Liberation and Islam in Soviet Uzbekistan, 1926–1941," *Journal of Women's History* 10, no. 1 [1998]: 20–44), and Adrienne Edgar, who questions Massell's model elsewhere in Central Asia ("The Creation of Soviet Turkmenistan, 1924–1938" [Ph.D. diss., University of California, Berkeley, 1999], 145–201).

divergent forms historically and go beyond a simple, transhistorical dichotomy between "men" and "women."[35] The apparent fixity of gender categories, moreover, only obscures the cultural work that is always under way to
defend and retain them, and through them the overall social order. Identity is
most subversive when it is unintelligible, when regulatory norms are denied or
transgressed—when people, be they "women" or "men," weave back and
forth, mix and match, or refuse to stay in one place. Such norms therefore
need to be all the more carefully policed. The production of static, exaggerated images of feminine and masculine behavior serves this purpose, generating stereotypes in an attempt to fix identities and forestall or shortcut such
transformations.[36]

The contest over female veiling is a story as much about power as about
gender, and questions of power can be approached on several levels. Soviet
historians will note that I build on work on Stalinism that looks away from
Stalin the individual to the shifting textures and meanings of everyday life.
There are rapidly growing literatures on ethnicity, nationality, and the non-
Russian areas of the Soviet Union, on the one hand, and Soviet gender and
family life, on the other. This book ties these concerns together through a
focus on the imperial dimension of Soviet rule and the cultural and political
power of gender roles and family life—and their mutual, simultaneous construction. Moreover, the hujum, an organized assault on female seclusion in
the East, was launched immediately before the Stalin Revolution of collectivization, industrial development, and cultural change. It thus fits into well-
known narratives of Soviet history: the state's assertions of cultural hegemony
over the countryside, its efforts to crush organized religion, and its shift in the
1930s to a new mode of nationality policy, one less concerned with building
minority nations and more fearful of ethnicity as a potential locus for disunity.
Yet ironically, the continuing centrality of unveiling as a symbol of Soviet
power only underscored such abiding issues of ethno-national difference. The
outcomes and lessons of the unveiling campaign also raise serious questions
about the degree to which Stalinist control pervaded Uzbek society. If Bolshevik leaders found it so difficult to Sovietize Uzbekistan while at the height of
their powers, what does this say about the character and practice of Stalinism?
Power in the Soviet empire, as elsewhere, was negotiated and defined on the
ground, through the everyday interactions of the state with its citizens—an intricate process, but one that can be seen with particular clarity in the decades-
long effort to Bolshevize Central Asia.

35. To take one example, Thomas Laqueur, *Making Sex: Body and Gender from the Greeks to Freud* (Cambridge, Mass., 1990), shows this divide into two genders not to be universal. The *locus classicus* is Joan Wallach Scott, "Gender: A Useful Category of Historical Analysis," in her *Gender and the Politics of History* (New York, 1988), 28–50.
36. I am indebted to Mary Louise Roberts, who has shaped my thinking on these questions. These three sentences borrow from her lecture "The Fantastic Sarah Bernhardt: Gender and The-ater in Fin-de-Siècle France," delivered at the University of Georgia, 23 Oct. 2000.

This interpretation unavoidably raises the related and difficult issue of resistance to state power, a newly prominent topic in Soviet history. As archival materials have become available, the concept has been applied increasingly to non-Russian as well as both rural and urban areas of the USSR, but doing so is complicated and has proved controversial. Historical studies of resistance in the Stalin period in particular risk exaggerating the phenomenon, thereby minimizing the enormity and omnipresence of state power by implying that people could act more freely than was actually the case. They also run the moral danger of overlooking the ethical gray areas (or worse) among those who did try to oppose Soviet power, whether as members of the party hierarchy or as rebels. The rape and murder of unveiled women, for example, often had a political component, being constructed as an anti-Bolshevik and anticolonial act—but obviously such acts cannot be celebrated or valorized as heroic. Resistance came in multiple keys; such acts frequently had moral meanings that were simultaneously embedded in and supportive of local gender hierarchies and structures of patriarchal power.[37]

Yet resistance is a particularly effective lens in Uzbekistan, where previous historical experiences and a specific cultural context combined with the still-tenuous state of Soviet authority to produce a situation where many people perceived and were willing to fight for a real alternative to Soviet power. This perception added a crucial dimension to Uzbeks' resistance. Observing norms of female seclusion did not make them unthinking conservatives; the practices they defended were neither fixed nor unchanging, and in some cases developed only after 1927. But in the highly visible and politically charged context of the hujum, many men and women came to see new meanings in ostensibly simple acts of everyday life. Their resistance came to be embedded in such acts: it was contingent and relational, defined by local, historically produced social meanings. Such acts in Uzbekistan were invested with intent (being constructed as first political and then resistant) only in the context of and in constant dialogue with state policies and actions.

Resistance was such a potentially broad phenomenon in Stalin's USSR precisely because the party-state had such all-encompassing goals. Buying vegetables on the black market would not have been a political threat, for example, if the state had not chosen to ratchet such behavior into an at least potentially political act. Because the Bolsheviks aspired to control and shape all areas of Soviet citizens' lives, resistance could be produced almost anywhere. Hence the more the regime clamped down, the more it could feel threatened and could come to believe it was losing control. Resistance became something that could happen at home or among friends, in a whisper or even in silence, through a raised eyebrow or a mocking smile. It thus became far harder to police, as au-

37. See Sherry Ortner, "Resistance and the Problem of Ethnographic Refusal," *Comparative Studies in Society and History* 37 (1995): 173–93; and for an excellent overview, Viola, *Contending with Stalinism.*

thorities had to look for things much less visible than antistate demonstrations or the rare brave soul who stood up to denounce Stalin openly. In Soviet Central Asia, resistance came to include an almost endless variety of personal, practical coping mechanisms, individual adaptations and survival strategies, and instances of rule-breaking as well as decisions to pursue personal goals or enrichment rather than state priorities.

Resistance to state power is also a central concern of scholars in the field of subaltern studies, who as a group see the colonial state as a "dominance without hegemony," not a rule by consent.[38] These writers have shown how a society's "little people" can, through the unremarked and almost invisible behaviors of everyday life, wring concessions from, force compromises upon, even sometimes subvert state structures that appear overwhelmingly powerful. Subaltern studies first developed in the context of South Asian and Indian colonial history but have branched out to many other regions. James Scott, for example, has famously analyzed Malay peasant society to find such evasive forms of quotidian subaltern resistance as foot-dragging, pilfering, and verbal and nonverbal mockery.[39] Much of this group's sophisticated work underlies this book: it has, for example, shaped my view of resistance as a complex, widely dispersed, continually produced dialogic and discursive phenomenon.[40]

Yet while a few Soviet historians have noted its promise, the field of subaltern studies has for the most part ignored the USSR.[41] This neglect is particularly odd given the relevance of the Soviet state to many of its key concerns. As in the British Empire, for example, one finds multifarious resistance in Central Asia being directed against the colonial state. The Soviet government, however, differed in important ways from the Raj. It seized power in the name of the proletariat and declared itself to be a worker state—to be, in short, a kind of subaltern in power. How does Scott's dynamic change when the regime seeks consciously to champion the weak and give a voice to the downtrodden? When some previously subordinate indigenous groups come to be identified with the metropolitan state and indigenous elites face dispossession, harass-

38. Ranajit Guha, "Introduction," *Subaltern Studies* 1 (1982): xvii–xix. Hegemony is a concept elaborated by the Italian political theorist Antonio Gramsci. In simplest terms, Gramscian hegemony denotes a kind of social predominance, achieved more through consent than force. A group is hegemonic insofar as it persuades others to accept its political, cultural, and moral values. See *Selections from the Prison Notebooks of Antonio Gramsci,* trans. and ed. Quintin Hoare and Geoffrey Nowell Smith (New York, 1973), 57–58.

39. James C. Scott, *Weapons of the Weak: Everyday Forms of Peasant Resistance* (New Haven, 1985), and his *Domination and the Arts of Resistance: Hidden Transcripts* (New Haven, 1990).

40. Cultural anthropologists have effectively theorized these questions. See Martha Kaplan and John Kelly, "Rethinking Resistance: Dialogics of 'Disaffection' in Colonial Fiji," *American Ethnologist* 17, no. 1 (1983): 3–22. For the "dialogic" component, see Mikhail Bakhtin, *The Dialogic Imagination* (Austin, 1981).

41. For an invocation of Scott in Soviet history, see Viola, *Peasant Rebels,* 14, 38.

ment, disenfranchisement, and imprisonment, who is dominant? Who is subaltern? Polygamous husbands denouncing Soviet power or wives opposing domestic patriarchy? Men throwing rocks at unveiled women or Communist activists reporting their harassers to the secret police? The lines and hierarchies
can be difficult to draw, and the peculiar dynamics of the Soviet case, in which
a colonial state claimed an anticolonial and emancipatory legitimacy, created a
dizzyingly complex web of multiple context-dependent subalternities.[42]

If subaltern studies have largely ignored the Soviet case, it is even more
striking that postcolonial scholars have overlooked almost completely the pe-
culiarity of an avowedly anticapitalist and anticolonial yet undeniably imperial
Bolshevik state. But the Soviet empire was no less real and no less important
for being (in every sense) veiled. How did the crucible of empire differ in such
an ambiguous environment, where the ultimate aim—unlike that of the
British, German, Belgian, Dutch, or, for that matter, Japanese empire—was to
erase the marks of colonial difference? The uneasy Soviet symbiosis of modernizing state and colonial empire created endless contradictions. Similar issues had arisen elsewhere: in the United States, for example, in campaigns to
force Native Americans to acquire "enlightened" ideas of culture, civilization,
and citizenship, or the attempt to "Americanize" Mexicans in the Southwest
by "going after the women." (Mexican wives and mothers were targeted as
conduits to change their families' cultural habits, from diet and health to dress
and language.)[43] The closest parallel of all may have been the French campaign
in the late 1950s to gallicize Muslim women in colonial Algeria—strikingly, by
removing their veils. While French authorities were more ambivalent than
their Soviet counterparts about the ultimate goal of integration, let alone assimilation, their effort was directly inspired by the Bolshevik hujum of the
1920s.[44] Further, studies such as those of sati in India, *tianzu* (foot-binding) or
tianyou (the natural-breast movement) in China, clitoridectomy in East Africa,
cross-racial sex in Dutch Indonesia, or for that matter veiling and unveiling in

---

42. I am grateful to an anonymous reviewer for framing this issue so sharply. For another approach to power and overlapping identities in the Soviet context, see Caroline Humphrey, *Karl
Marx Collective: Economy, Society, and Religion in a Siberian Collective Farm* (Cambridge,
1983), especially chap. 7.

43. George J. Sanchez, " 'Go After the Women': Americanization and the Mexican Immigrant
Woman, 1915–1929," in *Unequal Sisters: A Multicultural Reader in U.S. Women's History*, ed.
Ellen Carol DuBois and Vicki L. Ruiz (New York, 1990), 250–63. On Native Americans, see
Hoxie, *Final Promise*.

44. On the Algerian campaign, see Meyda Yegenoglu, *Colonial Fantasies: Towards a Feminist
Reading of Orientalism* (Cambridge, 1998), 136–44; Winifred Woodhull, "Unveiling Algeria,"
Genders 10 (1991): 112–31; or David C. Gordon, *Women of Algeria: An Essay on Change* (Cambridge, Mass., 1968), 56–59 (on the Soviet inspiration, see p. 20). This effort to remove colonial
differences and hierarchies to create a single, undifferentiated "French" identity was never wholesale or unambiguous. In Algeria it was complicated by the triadic relationship of the state, indigenous populations, and colonial settlers (*colons*).

the wider Muslim world have shown the fundamental importance of gender in the functioning and legitimation of imperial systems, yet the Soviet empire has so far been virtually absent from such discussions.[45]

Finally, with rare exceptions Islamic historians too have largely overlooked the Muslim communities that lived under Russian authority during the nineteenth and twentieth centuries (and in some cases, such as that of the Volga Tatars, much longer).[46] Yet since the nineteenth century Tatars, Uzbeks, Azeris, and others have wrestled in distinctive ways with many of the same issues—Islamic modernism, school and family reform, the role of cultural and political nationalism—as Muslims in Turkey, Iran, Egypt, Syria, and Indonesia.[47] Thus this book is part of an emerging framework of Central Asian studies, and it is one of the first such archivally based studies. At a general level, Western scholars of Central Asia—few as they are—have disagreed bitterly over the degree to which decades of Russian and Soviet rule changed the region. Some argue that after 130 years of colonial control, modern Central Asians have been deeply Russified, and that only the most superficial aspects of local and Islamic identities survive. Others contend that Russian and Soviet leaders, their interventionist goals notwithstanding, had surprisingly little impact on the region or its people.[48]

I approach such questions through the realm of everyday life and cultural practices to see what the Soviet colonial experience actually meant in the day-to-day existence of ordinary people. The complexities of this process and the

45. On foot-binding, see Ping Wang, *Aching for Beauty: Footbinding in China* (Minneapolis, 2000), or Dorothy Ko, *Every Step a Lotus: Shoes for Bound Feet* (Berkeley, 2001). Tianyou has not been well studied: see Virgil Kit-yiu Ho, "The Limits of Hatred: Popular Attitudes towards the West in Republican Canton," *East Asian History* 2 (1991): 91–92. On clitoridectomy, see Susan Pedersen, "National Bodies, Unspeakable Acts: The Sexual Politics of Colonial Policy-Making," *Journal of Modern History* 63 (1991): 647–80, and Lynn M. Thomas, " 'Ngaitana (I will circumcise myself),' " in *Gendered Colonialisms in African History,* ed. Nancy Rose Hunt et al. (Oxford, 1997), 16–41. On the Dutch Empire, see Ann Laura Stoler, "Carnal Knowledge and Imperial Power: Gender, Race, and Morality in Colonial Asia," in *Gender at the Crossroads of Knowledge: Feminist Anthropology in the Postmodern Era,* ed. Micaela di Leonardo (Berkeley, 1991), 51–101, and her "Sexual Affronts and Racial Frontiers: European Identities and the Cultural Politics of Exclusion in Colonial Southeast Asia," *Comparative Studies in Society and History* 34 (1992): 514–51. On veiling, see Beth Baron, "Unveiling in Early Twentieth-Century Egypt: Practical and Symbolic Considerations," *Middle Eastern Studies* 25 (1989): 370–86. On sati, see Mani, *Contentious Traditions,* and Anand Yang, "Whose *Sati?* Widow Burning in Early Nineteenth-Century India," *Journal of Women's History* 1, no. 2 (1989): 8–33.

46. Two recent exceptions to this neglect among Islamic historians are Kamp, "Unveiling Uzbek Women," and Khalid, *Politics of Muslim Cultural Reform.*

47. For example, Joseph Massad, *Colonial Effects: The Making of National Identity in Jordan* (New York, 2001).

48. The political scientist William Fierman, for example, argues that Soviet policy amounted to a "failed transformation," in which Uzbek society remained at root non-Soviet, largely untouched by Soviet attempts to remake, "modernize," and control it (*Soviet Central Asia: The Failed Transformation* [Boulder, 1991]). The anthropologist M. Nazif Shahrani, by contrast, depicts a thoroughly Sovietized and fundamentally altered Uzbek society ("Central Asia and the Challenge of the Soviet Legacy," *Central Asian Survey* 12, no. 2 [1993]: 123–35).

shifting meanings attached to daily cultural practices emerge only through careful study. It is striking to see, for example, how the idea of an Uzbek identity (largely a Soviet creation) succeeded in structuring the worldview of Uzbeks; the unintended consequences of this early Bolshevik effort to bolster national pride are still felt. Yet at the same time this success does not mean that Uzbeks today are merely nationalist patriots or Muslim believers; they are neither simply Sovietized nor Russified nor Westernized. They are, in complicated, individual ways, all of these things and more. In the hybrid postcolonial world of contemporary Central Asia, such apparently distinct, even contradictory identity labels serve paradoxically to underpin and define one another.

In the end this book uses the bitter struggle in Uzbekistan over female veiling and seclusion during the 1920s, 1930s, and early 1940s to address fundamental questions about modern Central Asia. How did indigenous cultural and national identities emerge and evolve under Soviet colonial rule? How did these identities and definitions of political power and personal loyalty come to be expressed through the languages of gender and intimate behavior? How did the party's efforts to make Uzbek men and women into loyal allies initially backfire, creating resistance and a distinctly *non*-Soviet Uzbek identity? Is coercive modernization an appropriate or effective mode for social and cultural change? The underlying issues—of intercultural encounters and multiculturalism, gender relations, family trauma, and the unexpected consequences of state action—have wide relevance for scholars and students and for readers outside the academy.

Central Asia emerges here as fluid and at root historical, as a place both continually in creation and always offering multiple possibilities—not at all a society of timeless, unitary tradition. The paranji was attacked *and* defended in the name of ancient tradition, but actually became an Uzbek national emblem only through this struggle—and largely out of the party's efforts to eradicate it. Both tradition and its traditionalist defenders, then, were recent and historically specific creations, as was the supposedly eternal national struggle between Russians and Uzbeks. Such are the ironies, paradoxes, and complexities that start to emerge in the newly Soviet lands of Central Asia soon after the Bolshevik Revolution of October 1917.

CHAPTER 1

Embodying Uzbekistan

> In Bokhara the woman is described as conspicuous by her ab-
> sence. No man ever sets eyes upon a lady not his own, for in
> the street she is nothing but a perambulating sack with a black
> horse-hair screen where her face is likely to be. The women
> live in a strictly separate part of the house, often having its
> own courtyard and its own pond. Only now and again one
> meets them at dawn or nightfall, stealing out furtively to fetch
> water. They shrink at the sight of a stranger and veil them-
> selves in all haste. The children, of whom the usual quantity
> abounded, were suffering from sore eyes, a result of the all-
> pervading dirt amid which they live and the pestering flies that
> take advantage of defenceless babies.
>
> On the whole, women make the impression of children,
> and in the outlying districts, of savage children. They are inex-
> pressibly filthy in the villages and are everywhere on a far
> lower social grade than the men. One may say that the highest
> woman in the land is inferior to the lowest man.
>
> —American missionaries describing Central Asia, 1926

Pre-Soviet patterns of family life in southern Central Asia were neither universal nor unchanging—at least not until party action made them seem that way. Before 1927, and certainly before 1917, Central Asian Muslim men and women, adults and children, interacted in ways that varied greatly, both over time and from place to place. The cultural practices of everyday life, as expressed both within the family and between friends and neighbors, were undeniably and deeply gendered, yet at the same time remained multifaceted and fluid. Following the assertion of Russian colonial control in the mid–nineteenth century, though, and particularly under Bolshevik authority after 1917, certain patterns of gender relations—and in particular specific forms of female dress and seclusion—were deemed to be "customary" and timeless. They were then used, often quite effectively, as national markers in early Soviet Central Asia.

For its own reasons the party encouraged this development, seeing the creation of indigenous "nations" as a progressive step in Central Asia. At the same time, however, the Bolsheviks' remarkable success in creating distinct national identities quickly caught them on the horns of a dilemma. On the one hand, they had defined the new Uzbek nation in large part through its distinctive patterns of gender relations and customs of female seclusion, and especially through the heavy cotton-and-horsehair veils worn by Uzbek women. Yet by the mid-1920s they had also simultaneously declared these same practices to be primitive, dirty, and oppressive—a combination that had two serious consequences. First, the party had deemed the Uzbek nation in its current state to be by definition incapable of modernity or civilization, a judgment that led directly to the decision in 1927 to transform Uzbek society forcibly through its women. Second, this association of Uzbek national identity with social practices targeted for eradication was a gift to those who opposed Soviet-style reform, allowing them to portray themselves as defenders of the nation. The party thus inadvertently helped create a discourse of national-cultural resistance to its own women's liberation policies.

The East and Its Women

The equation of Central Asia with its women was not new in 1917. The image of an exotic, often veiled woman had long symbolized Central Asia—indeed, the entire Orientalized "East"—in Russian and European eyes. This ideal type, the "Eastern woman," was largely created by a series of Westerners who visited the region and, once returned safely home, wrote about what they had seen. Some of these visitors traveled to Turkestan, Khiva, Qŏqon (Kokand), and Bukhoro seeking adventure; others, pursuing scholarly ends; and still others, aiming to further diplomatic or military agendas. Whatever their purposes, the books they published were popular, attracting eager audiences from Britain to Russia.

These writers drew a picture that was in many ways grim, showing a despotic, primitive, almost timeless Central Asia—yet one that was also alluringly exotic. As one put it, "the East is, and ever was from time immemorial, the land of the most striking contradictions."[1] The Russian observer Nikolai Muravev, writing in 1822 about Khiva, described its "Uzbegs" as lazy, careless, and "extraordinarily dirty." Fathers ruled their children with an iron hand, he said, and life was governed by the dictates of religion. Unhappily, Muravev noted, the Uzbegs were "very low in the scale of enlightenment and education," being ignorant of nearly every Western science.[2] A generation later

1. Arminius Vámbéry, *Sketches of Central Asia* (London, 1868), 93.
2. Nikolay Muravyov, *Journey to Khiva through the Turkoman Country* (London, 1977), 159–61 and 163–66.

the Hungarian scholar Arminius Vámbéry, having disguised himself as a dervish to travel (he said) undetected, described the brutal tortures, ranging from starvation to eye-gouging, inflicted by the Khivan authorities in their zeal to defend religious law (see Figure 6). Apparently to underscore the shockingly barbarous character of the region, Vámbéry also included drawings of human heads being bought and sold.[3] The depth of Eastern savagery was not to be doubted, Vámbéry asserted, or the power of its rulers: "In a country where pillage and murder, anarchy and lawlessness, are the rule, and not the exception, a sovereign has to maintain his authority by inspiring his subjects with the utmost dread and almost superstitious terror for his person; never with affection. Even those nearest to him fear him for his unlimited power."[4]

Readers familiar with the work of Edward Said and other postcolonial theorists will immediately recognize the Orientalist tropes in these descriptions.[5] Such writings frequently accompanied and underpinned colonial expansion, justifying European rule while serving as a means of (European) self-definition. The Central Asian East was seen as unenlightened and primitive, thus practically begging for the introduction of civilization and progress by a more advanced West (or at least by the somewhat more advanced Russia, which had expanded into Central Asia during the nineteenth century). At the same time, the people of Turkestan are depicted as being different from and less than European. History had passed them by: Central Asia was perceived as timeless and unchanging. In 1887 the British cleric Henry Lansdell declared the Kazakh steppe to be an excellent exhibit of how people had lived at the time of the Old Testament, having what he called a "primeval character."[6] At the same time, Central Asian Muslims could not really act as autonomous individuals, since their lives were said to be governed by an unchanging religious fervor. As a result, the details of how particular people thought—their differences and disagreements, the nuances and changes in how they perceived the world and their place in it—became unimportant, and received generally short shrift.

Yet European and Russian readers' fascination with Muslim Central Asia ran deeper than knowing how Western travelers had, through clever disguises, subterfuge, and bravery, entered the domains of Oriental despots and lived to tell the tale. The very character of everyday life in the East seemed impossibly exotic and alluring, and these writers spent page after page chronicling the

3. Arminius Vámbéry, *Travels in Central Asia: Being the Account of a Journey from Teheran across the Turkoman Desert on the Eastern Shore of the Caspian to Khiva, Bokhara, and Samarcand Performed in the Year 1863* (New York, 1865), 169–72.

4. Vámbéry, *Sketches of Central Asia*, 90–91.

5. The *locus classicus* is Edward W. Said, *Orientalism* (New York, 1978). Some scholars dispute the applicability of an Orientalist framework in the Russian context: see the debate between Nathaniel Knight and Adeeb Khalid in *Kritika* 1, no. 4 (2000).

6. Henry Lansdell, *Through Central Asia* (Nendeln, Liechtenstein, 1978), 127–42. He described the "Kirghese," in modern parlance the Kazakhs.

Плѣнный персіянинъ въ Хивѣ.

Figure 6. A Russian view of Khiva: picture postcard of a Persian prisoner, nineteenth century. (Courtesy Anahita Gallery, Santa Fe, N.M.)

strange customs that shaped Muslim society. Of particular interest were the details of how women lived.[7] As George Curzon explained in 1889,

> I have frequently been asked since my return—it is the question which an Englishman always seems to ask first—what the women of Bokhara were like? I am utterly unable to say. I never saw the features of one between the ages of ten and fifty. The little girls ran about, unveiled, in loose silk frocks, and wore their hair in long plaits escaping from a tiny skull-cap. Similarly the old hags were allowed to exhibit their innocuous charms, on the ground, I suppose, that they could excite no dangerous emotions. But the bulk of the female population were veiled in a manner that defied and even repelled scrutiny. For not only were the features concealed behind a heavy black horsehair veil, falling from the top of the head to the bosom, but their figures were loosely wrapped up in big blue cotton dressing-gowns, the sleeves of which are not used but are pinned together over the shoulders at the back and hang down to the ground, where from

7. A good collection of documentary extracts is provided by Colette Harris, "Women of the Sedentary Population of Russian Turkistan through the Eyes of Western Travellers," *Central Asian Survey* 15, no. 1 (1996): 75–95.

under this shapeless mass of drapery appear a pair of feet encased in big leather boots.[8]

Female veiling and seclusion both illustrated and served as a metaphor for the generalized despotism that characterized the region. In the same vein as Curzon, Vámbéry provided an extended description of the secluded life led by the khan's wives in their harem.[9] Veils, harems, and polygyny served as powerful symbols, redolent of a supposed Eastern essence. Women—their dress, social customs, and particular restrictions—served as emblems of their society, both seductive and repellent; once one understood them, these writers implied, one would understand the East.

In the colonial context of tsarist Central Asia it is not surprising to find women being used as symbols of their people. Scholars have argued that cultural authenticity often inheres to the female sphere: gender and culture construct each other, and women are seen as markers of a society's identity.[10] But how much did these descriptions of an Eastern woman actually say about Central Asia? The authors who constructed this archetype were mostly non-Muslim outsiders—Russian, British, and Hungarian, among others. As such, their fixation with veiled women and harems as emblematic of an overarching, vague "East" reveals as much about themselves as it does about their supposed subject.[11] The creation of this primitive, despotic, and exotic East as an Other—as something utterly unlike Europe—served largely as a means of self-definition. For Russian writers, too, the ability to paint ethnographic pictures of primitive Central Asians may have helped bolster a sometimes shaky sense of Russia's proper place among the enlightened nations. Central Asia and its women provided Russia with a visible civilizing mission. As Dostoevsky put it in 1881, "In Europe we were Tatars, but in Asia we are also Europeans."[12]

Virtually all of these writers were male, and some lacked knowledge of local

8. George N. Curzon, *Russia in Central Asia in 1889 and the Anglo-Russian Question* (London, 1889), 174-75, quoted by Kathleen Hopkirk, *A Traveller's Companion to Central Asia* (London, 1993), 52.

9. Vámbéry, *Sketches of Central Asia*, 96. He also used women to show the power of religion, telling what happened when one man tried to see a veiled woman: both he and the unlucky woman were stoned to death (*Travels in Central Asia*, 170).

10. See Mani, *Contentious Traditions*, and Deniz Kandiyoti, "Women, Islam, and the State: A Comparative Approach," in *Comparing Muslim Societies: Knowledge and the State in a World Civilization*, ed. Juan R. I. Cole, 237–60 (Ann Arbor, 1992).

11. Exceptions do exist to this vague portrait of an undifferentiated "East" stretching halfway around the globe. Lansdell pointed out differences between Kirghese and Sart veiling practices, and Vámbéry sometimes depicts a surprising degree of male–female interaction. See Lansdell, *Through Central Asia*, 131, and Vámbéry, *Sketches of Central Asia*, 102–6. The general picture, however, stressed regional similarities, with female seclusion used as a metaphor for despotism.

12. Fedor Dostoevskii, *Polnoe sobranie sochenenii* (Leningrad, 1984), 27:36, quoted in Andreas Kappeler, *Rußland als Vielvölkerreich: Entstehung—Geschichte—Zerfall* (Munich, 1992), 176.

languages. Vámbéry may never have been permitted inside a harem, and Curzon admitted that he never saw the face of a woman of reproductive age. Despite such restrictions, these writers nevertheless claimed expertise on the most intimate customs of Muslim life. Vámbéry, for example, dwelled at length on the local rituals of birth, marriage, and death, focusing especially on the roles played by women. He explained that such ethnographic observations mattered, because "Central Asia in this respect is wrapt in considerable obscurity. To attempt to dispel this darkness may therefore not be deemed superfluous; and, the savage Polynesian and Central African having resisted vainly the spirit of inquiry, we will in like manner raise the veil from the rude and suspicious Œzbeg."[13] His choice of image here—the veil—is revealing. Most obviously, for Vámbéry and his fellow authors women represented a central site for the construction of knowledge about Central Asia, and thereby for the assertion of European scientific expertise and masculine power.

At the same time, as Sarah Graham-Brown has argued in her study of photographic representations of Middle Eastern women, it is striking to see the same tropes—especially the harem and veil—recurring throughout the accounts written by Western men decades and even centuries apart.[14] According to Curzon, an Englishman's first question about Central Asia was always to ask what its women were like; plainly there was (and still is) an element of the erotic in the fascination wielded by the Muslim East. The harem, to which nearly all access was banned, drew Western readers' attention thanks to the sexualized mystery attached to it. By describing harem life, authors therefore permitted their readers a vicarious thrill in entering the innermost sanctum of the exotic East. (They also fixated on parallel phenomena, such as foot-binding in China, when they visited other parts of the East.)[15] Similarly, the veil, both enticing and shocking to Western readers, remained a constant focus of attention. It served to demonstrate the power of patriarchal control over women and it raised a challenge to the imagination: these authors' detailed descriptions of Central Asian women's daily lives represented their attempt to

13. Vámbéry, *Sketches of Central Asia*, 98–99. In a sense, Central Asia as a whole is feminized in this discourse, being portrayed as an inert object simply awaiting its unveiling by Europeans.

14. Sarah Graham-Brown, *Images of Women: The Portrayal of Women in Photography of the Middle East, 1860–1950* (New York, 1988), 5–35. This observation does not mean that Western discourse on the East was always present, fully formed, and unchanging. This discourse too emerged gradually, with different men and women disagreeing about what features it comprised. While some tropes remained remarkably constant, others shifted over time, as is made clear below. See also Mohja Kahf, *Western Representations of the Muslim Woman: From Termagant to Odalisque* (Austin, 1992).

15. Dorothy Ko notes that foot-binding concealed Chinese women from view: "The benign European looked, but his gaze was not returned. Footbinding-as-concealment has rendered all objective—foreign—knowledge impossible. The footbound woman was thus fated to be the perpetual Other to the European man. In stubbornly refusing to be seen, she figured as a nagging reminder of China's alterity: mysterious, exotic, and resistant to foreign terms of understanding. It is no accident that she became the quintessential symbol of China itself in the nineteenth century" ("Bondage in Time: Footbinding and Fashion Theory," *Fashion Theory* 1, no. 1 [1997]: 13).

solve the "mystery" of what lay behind the veil.[16] Given that the point of female seclusion was to bar other men from knowing precisely that, such descriptions offered the reader an illicit thrill, promising vicarious access to the East's most protected and erotic domain.

As far as conceptions of Central Asia and its women were concerned, in many ways the Bolsheviks' assumption of power in 1917 brought few changes. At first, of course, other matters occupied party leaders' attention, most obviously the need to fight and win a civil war. Yet when they did devote time to thinking about Central Asia, one discerns a surprising degree of continuity across the supposed watershed of 1917. Many of the same tropes recurred, as Soviet writers—few of whom knew local languages and even fewer of whom were raised Muslim—drew upon prerevolutionary traditions of describing the East through such overarching, formulaic images. Many Bolshevik views sounded as much Orientalist as Marxist. Consider the description given in 1926 of Bukhoro ("The most typical Eastern city") by Serafima Liubimova, a prominent Russian women's activist who spent years working in Central Asia. After describing the city's charmingly "narrow, crooked little streets," the omnipresent mosques and minarets, and the bustling teahouses featuring exotic Eastern music and dancing, Liubimova declared that "all of this [strikes you] as soon as you take the first step away from the little Bukhoro train station—it makes the rest of the world fall away, and transports you to a fairy-tale world [skazochnaia obstanovka]."[17] (See Figure 7.)

From this perspective, Central Asia remained above all the Other, a land both attractive and repellent, seductive but at root primitive and despotic. As one foreign visitor sympathetic to the Soviet cause, Fannina Halle, later put it, "The Soviet East, like all Asia, like the whole East, whether Near or Far, is an alien, exotic land to our European feelings. And so any effort to grasp its alien quality emotionally is far better than all enumeration of names and figures, however systematic."[18] Painting with a very broad brush, Russian writers and ethnographers confirmed such judgments for a home audience with descriptions of Muslim areas, photo books, museum exhibitions, even picture postcards. Turkestan and the khanates of Bukhoro and Khiva were deemed backward places, with low literacy rates and few children (and virtually no girls) able to attend school; the poor health care and hygienic habits of the indige-

16. Graham-Brown, *Images of Women,* 70–91, 134–38. On the veil in the Western imagination, see also Ludmilla Jordanova, *Sexual Visions: Images of Gender in Science and Medicine between the Eighteenth and Twentieth Centuries* (Madison, 1989), 87–97. Yegenoglu, *Colonial Fantasies,* 12, argues that the colonial focus on unveiling Muslim women "was linked not only to the discourse of Enlightenment but also to the scopic regime of modernity which is characterized by a desire to master, control, and reshape the body of the subjects by making them visible. Since the veil prevents the colonial gaze from attaining such a visibility and hence mastery, its lifting becomes essential."

17. Serafima Timofeevna Liubimova, *Dnevnik zhenotdelki* (Tashkent, 1926), 21.

18. Fannina W. Halle, *Women in the Soviet East* (New York, 1938), 20.

Figure 7. Bukhoro's Old City, 1927. (Courtesy
ÖzRKFFHMDA.)

nous people sufficed to demonstrate the region's blighted, benighted nature.
Even the food, it was said, tasted bad.[19]

In the eyes of these early Bolshevik observers, much of the explanation for
these problems lay in the paramount importance of religion in Central Asian
life. Primitive, "barbaric" practices could thus be ascribed straightforwardly
to Islam, the opiate of the Muslim people. Although Qur'anic scriptures had
been written in Arabic (a language understood by few Central Asians) and despite their great antiquity, these texts alone sufficed to explain why specific
people acted in certain ways now, thirteen centuries later. Indeed, the supposedly primeval character of Central Asian Muslim society made it seem to these

19. For the allegations of backwardness, see ÖzRMDA, f. 86, op. 1, d. 8130, ll. 72–75; f. 94,
op. 1, d. 200, ll. 16–17; and RGASPI, d. 775, ll. 6–7. Uzbek food was disparaged at ÖzRMDA, f.
9, op. 1, d. 3399, ll. 5–6.

writers all the more reasonable to look far back in time for explanations, just as Lansdell compared Kazakh nomads to the Hebrew patriarchs of biblical times. Turkestan had not changed appreciably in centuries, and the Central Asian East, Bolsheviks said, possessed a "medieval way of life" (*srednevekovyi byt*).[20]

After 1917 just as before it, the Muslim woman served as a principal illustration for such views. Alluring and sensual, yet simultaneously a primitive and oppressed victim of patriarchal despotism, she embodied the contradictory essence of her culture. Depictions of the allegedly horrific lives lived by women in pre-Soviet Central Asia pepper the documents of the early 1920s, contrasting vividly with an accompanying picture of Leninist liberation. Bolshevik activists and writers always started by drawing a grim portrait of life under Islamic religious law (*shariat*) and the norms of Central Asian custom (*odat*). According to these accounts, before the Revolution females had been treated as property, more like cattle than humans. Veiled while still girls— sometimes at age 7 or 8—they were sold into marriage soon thereafter for a high bride-price (*qalin*). (Shariat norms permitted a girl to be married at 9 and a boy at 12 if their bodies were sufficiently developed; Bolshevik writers tended to overlook this latter stipulation in their expressions of disgust.) Soviet readers were told that often a young girl would be married to a man fifty years her senior, as one of his many wives. She would soon be infected with syphilis or worse, and her health would never recover. Thereafter the "harem life" kept her from education and productive labor, and thus from any hope of achieving economic independence and a measure of control over her life. Easily manipulated by her husband because of her ignorance, she most likely died young, wizened before her time.[21]

Once again images of veiling and seclusion were featured prominently to make this picture concrete. The power of Muslim patriarchy could, as before, be best appreciated by Western readers through the ideal type of an Eastern woman; the veil, more than anything else, conjured her to mind. Readers had come to expect such images. Accordingly, Soviet writers, like their bourgeois counterparts, stressed the extent of female seclusion throughout Central Asia, and drew their examples from regions (especially those later incorporated into the Uzbek SSR) with particularly strict customs in this regard. One prominent official in the Zhenotdel, Antonina Nukhrat, went so far as to say that the Uzbek woman "literally does not see the sun"; her colleague V. R. Kasparova

20. The phrase was common. See, for example, a report written in 1925 by the Uzbek SSR's Commissariat of Enlightenment (Narkompros) at ÖzRMDA, f. 94, op. 1, d. 33, l. 134.

21. Elements of this portrait appear frequently throughout the published and archival Soviet records of the period. The litany given here appears in the following sources, among others: RGASPI, d. 426, l. 56; d. 434, l. 25; d. 769, l. 44; d. 775, ll. 5–6 (from which the phrase "harem life" was taken); and d. 776, l. 90; "Zhizn' musul'manki (primechaniia k stikhotvoreniiu 'Sartianka')," *Krest'ianka*, no. 8 (1923), 40; L. I. Klimovich, *Islam i zhenshchina* (Moscow, 1958).

described Central Asian houses bereft of any windows facing the street, in order to keep women from public view.[22] Serafima Liubimova told of 50–year-old Uzbek women who had never left their quarter of Tashkent, and had never even heard of the European-style New City. The world known to these women, Liubimova asserted, rarely stretched beyond husband and kitchen. Barred even from the bazaar, they were required to wear heavy horsehair veils that stretched from head to toe at any time that a strange man might appear, lest he catch even the smallest glimpse of their body.[23] The Orientalist tone of such accounts sounds remarkably like that of contemporary missionaries—a similarity not as strange as it may first appear, given the party's shared interest in efforts at conversion, transformation, and redemption.

From Many, One: Patterns of Gender and Family in Pre-Soviet Central Asia

Of course, the severe limits of this—as any—ideal type should be made explicit. No single Eastern woman, however typical or emblematic, could possibly do justice to the multiplicity and variety of all the peoples she supposedly represented. Her always-unchanging visage—veiled and oppressed, apparently from time immemorial—obscured the fluidity of any human society. In particular, it missed the tensions and social ferment rocking Central Asia as it wrestled with the challenges of colonial control. Such a singular archetype at best represented only a narrow subsection of Central Asian society and ignored local social complexities and distinctions between regions, classes, and cultures.

The thinness of the documentary record before 1917 makes it difficult to draw firm conclusions about the position of women in pre-Soviet southern Central Asia. Yet surviving materials make it clear that Muslims in Turkestan and the khanates of Khiva and Bukhoro conceived of women's social roles in widely varying ways, and that the resulting variations in social practice were expressed in different cultures of everyday life. Particularly in the large cities of the southern river basins and among wealthier families, women observed rigid norms of female seclusion and many men maintained multiple wives. In other social locations, however—especially in more remote areas as well as in rural, nomadic, and lower-class families—women's lives were quite different. While underlying familial and social norms may have been no less patriarchal, these women did not necessarily veil at puberty, often had a strong public and social presence, and sometimes worked outside the home. Given the prevalence of poor rural villages throughout southern Central Asia, indeed, this pattern may have held for many and possibly most Muslim women much of the time.[24]

22. Antonina Ivanovna Nukhrat, *Oktiabr' i zhenshchina Vostoka* (Moscow and Leningrad, 1927), 19; and V. R. Kasparova, *Zhenshchina Vostoka* (Leningrad, 1925), 26.
23. Serafima Timofeevna Liubimova, *Sdvigi* (Tashkent, 1925), 6.
24. On regional differences, see H. Ismoilov, *An"anaviy özbek kiyimlari* (Tashkent, 1978), 35. On the class connotations of veiling see T. A. Abdullaev and S. A. Khasanova, *Odezhda*

In any case it is crucial to remember that Central Asian women themselves, their frequent portrayal in Russian accounts as helpless victims of patriarchal oppression notwithstanding, played an active role in creating the complex moral and ideological systems that underpinned Muslim society. Women no less than men were socialized into the various interlocking norms and patterns of daily life, believed in their propriety, and helped to replicate them in the next generation. Their actions in doing so, moreover, cannot be understood merely as a form of false consciousness or as complicity in their own oppression. Even women who observed the principles of strict seclusion, after all, could enjoy great influence within their households and communities. Women perceived as particularly devout gained moral authority among their relatives and neighbors. Some became *otins*, religious teachers with full oversight responsibility for other female believers. Otins enjoyed positions of very high status and honor, equivalent in some ways to that of mullahs and with a similar charge to uphold and spread the faith.[25]

Strict seclusion, then, was not universal in Central Asia, but rather was most prevalent in certain regions and among particular social circles. By 1917 the paranji and chachvon had become common among urban women of the southern river basins and could also be found in rural areas, mostly among wealthier families.[26] The heavy horsehair-and-cotton veil, however, existed scarcely at all on the nomadic steppe or in the mountainous regions of northern and eastern Turkestan, let alone among the many non-Muslim peoples of the wider Soviet East, ranging from Caucasian mountain dwellers to Buddhist Buriats to Koreans living in Siberia. As a singular emblem of that wide-ranging, exotic East, therefore, the paranji plainly had its limits.

If the practice of veiling was not universal, neither was it timeless. Not even among wealthy urban women in southern Central Asia had public veiling held

---

uzbekov (XIX–nachala XX v.) (Tashkent, 1978), 8; and M. A. Bikzhanova, "Odezhda uzbechek Tashkenta XIX–nachala XX v.," in *Kostium narodov Srednei Azii,* ed. O. A. Sukhareva (Moscow, 1979), 141. Similar class and urban linkages existed elsewhere in the Muslim world. The question of urban/rural differences in Central Asian female seclusion is vexed, but according to most reports rural women at this time were not secluded as frequently or as fully as their urban counterparts. See N. A. Smirnov, *Chadra (Proiskhozhdenie pokryvala musul'manskoi zhenshchiny i bor'ba s nim)* (Moscow, 1929), 11; N. P. Lobacheva, *Formirovanie novoi obriadnosti uzbekov* (Moscow, 1975), 17; Elizabeth E. Bacon, *Central Asians under Russian Rule* (Ithaca, 1966), 64 and 70–71; Harris, "Women of the Sedentary Population," 79; and O. A. Sukhareva, "Opyt analiza pokroev traditsionnoi 'tunikoobraznoi' sredneaziatskoi odezhdy v plane ikh istorii i evoliutsii," in *Kostium narodov,* ed. Sukhareva, 93. See also Kamp, "Unveiling Uzbek Women," 253–60.

25. See Habiba Fathi, "Otines: The Unknown Women Clerics of Central Asian Islam," *Central Asian Survey* 16, no. 1 (1997): 27–43. Women could gain status, even public status, in other ways: consider the accomplished female singers who issued a commercial recording in 1900 (Z. Nasriddinov, "Ikki taqdir: 'Hujum' harakatining 60 yiligiga," *Toshkent oqshomi,* 13 Apr. 1987). Contrary to Soviet assertions, too, girls' religious schools—although few—existed before 1917. See Edward A. Allworth, *The Modern Uzbeks* (Stanford, 1990), 132.

26. In addition to the sources noted above, see Liubimova, *Sdvigi,* 6, or RGASPI, d. 1199, l. 28.

sway since time immemorial. The idea of protecting women from the male gaze (or, more accurately, of protecting men from the sexual temptations thought to result from such a gaze) was itself the product of a particular place and time. While certain forms of obscuring female dress could be traced back to the pre-Islamic period, the details of veiling practices had shifted dramatically. Muslim women in Central Asia had worn a wide variety of veils over the centuries, some revealing more of their bodies and others less, in response to a variety of historical situations.[27]

In this long view, the paranji and chachvon were surprisingly recent innovations, appearing widely only after—and perhaps partly in response to—the Russian colonial conquest of the mid–nineteenth century. Until roughly the 1870s, upper-class Muslim women in Tashkent and other cities of southern Central Asia had demonstrated their good character by wearing a mursak, a veil that covered most of their bodies but left the face uncovered. The far heavier ensemble of paranji and chachvon, covering the entire body from head to toe, appeared only in the mid–nineteenth century and spread widely after the tsarist occupation of Central Asia in the 1860s and 1870s, first among younger women and then throughout Turkestani society. The reasons for this shift in fashion (and in related definitions of "character") are not entirely clear, but appear to be at least partially a response to the specifics of Russian colonization.[28] Even so, it took decades to displace the mursak altogether, and a few were still visible on the streets of Tashkent as late as 1910.[29] (See Figure 8.) The "tradition" of veiling with paranji and chachvon was far from a timeless, universal practice rooted deeply in the Central Asian past; nor was it self-evidently expressive of some vague Eastern cultural essence. Instead, this so-called tradition was both narrowly circumscribed in practice and modern in

27. For the more distant history of Central Asian female dress, see G. A. Pugachenkova, "K istorii 'parandzhi,'" *Sovetskaia etnografiia*, no. 3 (1952), 191–95; Abdullaev and Khasanova, *Odezhda*, 8; and Klimovich, *Islam i zhenshchina*, 3–14. Non-Muslim cultures, too, sometimes secluded women: the elite women of seventeenth-century Muscovy, for example, lived in terems.

28. The adoption of the paranji may represent a reaction to the arrival of unveiled (mostly Russian) women, and especially to the prostitutes who accompanied tsarist troops into Tashkent in 1865. The presence of these women—moral as well as religio-cultural aliens—could have added impetus to the shift already under way from the mursak to the paranji as a way of demarcating "proper" character. See K. Ian-Borisova, "Zhenshchina, uvidevshchaia svet," *Ekonomika i zhizn'*, no. 3 (1977), 29–30; and Allworth, *Modern Uzbeks*, 281. This argument is inconclusive, however, since there were indigenous prostitutes before the Russian invasion. See Jennifer M. Scarce, "Continuity and Modernity in the Costume of the Muslims of Central Asia," in *Cultural Change and Continuity in Central Asia*, ed. Shirin Akiner (London, 1991), 252–53; and Kamp, "Unveiling Uzbek Women," 41–45.

29. On the mursak and its gradual displacement, see M. A. Bikzhanova, "Mursak—Starinnaia verkhniaia odezhda uzbechek g. Tashkenta," *Trudy AN Tadzhikskoi SSR* 120 (1960): 47–53; Ismoilov, *An"anaviy özbek kiyimlari*, 31; Sukhareva, "Opyt analiza," 96; Bikzhanova, "Odezhda," 140–44; and Z. A. Shirokova, *Traditsionnaia i sovremennaia odezhda zhenshchin gornogo Tadzhikistana* (Dushanbe, 1976), 81.

Figure 8. Changing veils in Turkestan, late nineteenth century: three Sart women wear the mursak, two wear a paranji and chachvon. (Hordet, courtesy Anahita Gallery, Santa Fe, N.M.)

provenance, representing a specific response to the political and cultural challenges of modern colonial rule.

With these regional and historical variations in mind, it is not surprising to find a lack of unanimity among Central Asians about how women should act. The consensus among foreign observers was that Central Asian Muslim views of women's social roles flowed from a more or less widely accepted and unchanging interpretation of Islamic doctrine in which men stayed dominant and women subordinate. Islamic doctrine, however, was neither self-evident nor stable, and questions of family life and gender relations were contested and in continuous flux before the hujum of 1927. Some differences fell along rural/urban lines; others were regional, with important variations in, for example, the khanates of Khiva and Bukhoro as opposed to Turkestan. Educated Muslims, too, disagreed bitterly about the role women should play in society. One important group of reformers, the jadids, argued against their more conservative clerical colleagues for a multifaceted program of cultural reform and renewal. While much of their work focused on educational reform and other issues, one noteworthy plank of the jadids' reformist agenda focused on questions of women's rights. They argued that women should not wear the veil and that they should play a full and equal role in a modern—yet still Muslim—

society. The jadids thus represent an important indigenous voice arguing before 1917 for social reforms similar to those later adopted by the Soviet government; they were joined by other, generally small groups of indigenous leftists and socialists.[30]

Even this rapid sketch of the historical and cultural context of Central Asia shows both the multiplicity and the fluidity of Muslim cultural practices and ideals during the pre-Soviet period, especially with regard to women and their proper place in society. Despite the steady efforts of Soviet writers to create a monolithic, timeless "tradition" against which party policy could act, then, one finds complexity on both sides of the equation. This brief survey casts doubt on too-quick generalizations that use "Islam" as an all-encompassing shorthand for the panoply of intellectual dispositions and cultural practices that made up the highly complex world of southern Central Asia. Islam, in the unique form in which it was understood and practiced here, was not merely a collection of religious beliefs, ancient texts, and theological doctrines. Neither was it self-evident or unchanging. Instead, it was a worldview and cultural system continually in creation and with its content and emphases always in flux.[31] As a religion it rested ultimately on a foundation of both scripture and tradition, but scriptures need continually to be interpreted and reinterpreted, and traditions perceived, understood, and translated into new situations. Islamic "tradition," therefore—on this issue and others—was itself a modern, always-changing creation. Despite their pretense alone to speak for modernity, therefore, Soviet voices had to fight for that status in Central Asia. The encounter between Soviet power and Uzbek society is more properly seen as the meeting, in a colonial context, of two conflicting visions of modernity.

Inventing Uzbekistan: Defining an Uzbek Woman

Most Soviet writers ignored these complexities, drawing upon the prerevolutionary depictions of a Central Asian East to show it as primitive and despotic but enticing, as evidenced by its women. After 1917, however, colonial discourse did shift, as women came to signify a specific nation as well as a relatively undifferentiated East. Thus with the party's encouragement they played an important role in building separate national identities in Turkestan. A second major shift worked against such nation-building: Soviet writers increasingly treated indigenous women as emblematic of what was *wrong* with their nations, as symbols of what had to be changed to make Central Asia modern.

In most Russian discussions before 1917, the word "national" (*natsion-*

30. See Khalid, *Politics of Muslim Cultural Reform*; Edward J. Lazzerini, "Beyond Renewal: The Jadid Response to Pressure for Change in the Modern World," in *Muslims in Central Asia: Expressions of Identity and Change*, ed. Jo-Ann Gross (Durham, 1992), 151–66; and Allworth, *Modern Uzbeks*, 120–55.

31. For a similar analysis elsewhere in the Muslim world, see John R. Bowen's study of Indonesia, *Muslims through Discourse: Religion and Ritual in Gayo Society* (Princeton, 1993).

al'nyi), when applied to Central Asia, meant little more than "distinctive" or "non-Russian"—writers referred to "local national peculiarities," for instance. The region's various Muslim inhabitants were thought of as tribes or clans, perhaps proto-nations or "nationalities," but certainly not true nations on the level of Russians themselves. After 1917, however, such words increasingly took on a life of their own. While cases can be found of Soviet writers referring uncritically to one huge, expansive East, it also became a priority to parse this East into smaller bits. "National" no longer signified simply "native" or "distinct," but came to specify particular peoples within the multiethnic mosaic of Central Asia. Even the term used to discuss the indigenous peoples as a whole—the "principal local nationalities" (*mestnye osnovnye natsional'nosti*)—stressed multiplicity rather than unity.

This shift was not unique to Central Asia: new nations were being created, with elaborate effort, all across the young Soviet Union. The party welcomed this emphasis, counterintuitive though it may appear in the context of an internationalist socialist revolution, and however contested it remained in some Bolshevik circles.[32] The way party leaders integrated ethno-national identity into the structures of a new Soviet state had lasting consequences for all of its citizens, and for Uzbeks and other non-Russians in particular. Against the objections of Stalin and others, Lenin and his allies fought successfully to impart a federal configuration to the new USSR. In late December 1922 an ostensibly voluntary union was created of territorially defined and ethnically identified republics, instead of a single, unitary political entity of "Soviet Russia."[33] An ethno-territorial model of nationality was fundamental to this new state structure. Each republic received its own borders and an institutional umbrella—a capital city, bureaucracy, and physical infrastructure—that enabled an array of nation-building possibilities in the 1920s. National school systems, literary production, scientific, historical, and ethnographic work, economic development, and a range of political and institutional job opportunities all quickly emerged.

In Lenin's view, such changes were positive: nations, as products of capitalist economic relations, fitted into a classic Marxist stage theory of development. Even Stalin, who differed on the implications for Soviet policy, agreed that nations were an inescapable phase through which all human communities must pass.[34] Ultimately, they (like capitalism) would be superseded, but for precapitalist societies national development and nationalist movements were treated as progressive. Lenin drew a further distinction between great-power

32. Slezkine, "USSR as a Communal Apartment"; Suny, *Revenge of the Past*; and Martin, *Affirmative Action Empire*.

33. Moshe Lewin, *Lenin's Last Struggle* (New York, 1970). A different perspective is presented by Richard Pipes, *The Formation of the Soviet Union: Communism and Nationalism, 1917–1923* (Cambridge, Mass., 1964).

34. Iosif Stalin, "Marksizm i natsional'nyi vopros," in his *Sochineniia* (Moscow, 1946–53), 2:303.

nationalism, which oppressed others, and small-power nationalism, which formed in response to it. In places—such as Russia—that had been responsible for the national or colonial oppression of others, nationalism was to be combated without mercy and torn out by the roots. Among groups that had been victims of national or colonial oppression, by contrast—such as in the tsarist imperial periphery, where Russian power had created deep economic, political, and social resentment—the Leninist approach was to build socialism while encouraging indigenous development and national differentiation.

This analysis gave an important impetus to national development in non-Russian areas, especially once it took shape as the Bolshevik Party's official nationalities policy: a major effort in the 1920s to give Soviet power, across the USSR, a local face. Whether that local face would be Armenian, Ukrainian, Uzbek, or Yakut, non-Russian groups (at least those living in a republic, province, or autonomous district assigned to their ethnicity) found themselves the beneficiaries of an elaborate affirmative action program. This policy of "indigenization" (*korenizatsiia*) obligated party officials to enlist, instruct, and promote local cadres at every opportunity. The resultant crash training programs and mass social mobility aimed to create educated indigenous elites who—however imperfect their Marxist credentials—were schooled in, grateful to, and willing to defend these new national identities.

These elites started by defending their nations' new borders. Borders divide people, but in Central Asia they created people as well: when Soviet Turkestan was subdivided into several republics in the mid-1920s, these new boundaries helped produce a half-dozen or so nations, among them the Uzbeks. The irregular, twisting borders of Uzbekistan (shown in Map 3) were not invented at random—Soviet experts tried to divide economic resources fairly while following geographic features and perceived lines of ethnic settlement, not to mention administrative convenience—but no such territorial unit had ever before existed, and this one proved difficult to define.[35] Uzbeks and Turkmen had never before lived in separate, ethnically defined states. Kyrgyz and Kazakhs had not

---

35. On Soviet motivations and criteria, see the excellent discussion in Hirsch, "Toward an Empire of Nations." My Map 3 shows current political borders and names, reflecting many intermediate changes at the republican and provincial levels. Uzbekistan was at first a vaguely defined entity, continually in flux, so freezing it at any particular date is misleading. The most important changes after the initial national delimitation in 1924 were the separation of Tajikistan from the Uzbek SSR (in 1929) and the inclusion of Qoraqolpoghiston (in 1932). Individual provinces were variously created, renamed, redrawn, or abolished: Zerafshon disappeared, later to reappear as the southern part of Navoiy (the northern part came from Kazakhstan); Kenimekh was swallowed by Bukhoro; Namangan separated from Andijon in 1941, only to be erased in 1960 and then later reborn; Sirdaryo was fashioned from bits of Kazakh territory as well as from Samarqand and Tashkent; and Jizzakh was carved out of Samarqand and Surkhondaryo. For a political map of Uzbekistan on 1 Jan. 1927, before most of these changes took place, see *Vsesoiuznaia perepis' naseleniia 1926 g.*, vol. 15, following p. 200. Border shufflings continued throughout the Soviet period. See Lee Schwartz, "The Political Geography of Soviet Central Asia: Integrating the Central Asian Frontier," in *Geographic Perspectives on Soviet Central Asia*, ed. Robert A. Lewis (London, 1992), 58–64.

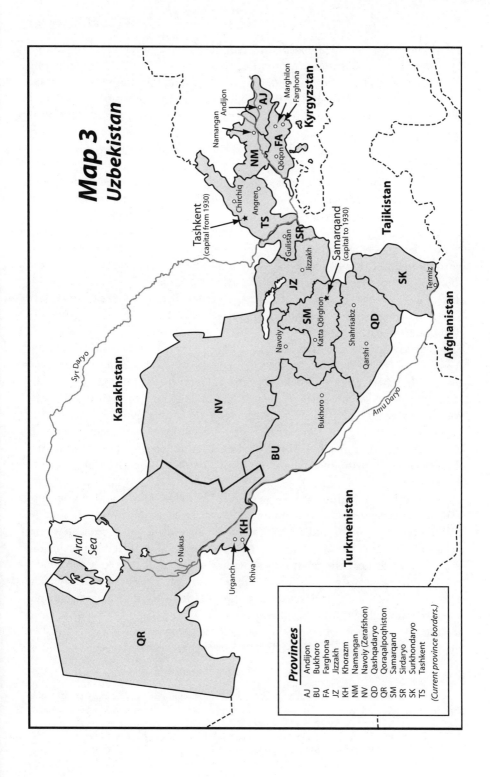

Map 3
Uzbekistan

Kazakhstan

Kyrgyzstan

Tajikistan

Afghanistan

Turkmenistan

Aral
Sea

Syr Daryo

Amu Daryo

Namangan
Andijon
Marghilon
Farghona
Qòqon

AJ
NM
FA

Chirchiq
Angren
Tashkent
(capital from 1930)

TS

SR
Gulistan
JZ
Jizzakh

Samarqand
(capital to 1930)

Navoiy
SM
Katta Qòrghon

Shahrisabz
Qarshi
QD

SK
Termiz

NV

Bukhoro

BU

KH
Urganch
Khiva
Nukus

QR

always been distinguished as separate nations, and had previously been known by different names: Kara-kyrgyz and Kyrgyz, respectively. The region's common literary language was Chaghatai; the multilingual inhabitants of many large towns were called Sarts, a name that fell into disuse after 1925. Although the term "Uzbek" had been used earlier, it was not altogether clear who was an Uzbek or what the label meant; the identity was provisional, fragile, still very much under construction.[36] Great differences of culture, language, and religion plainly divided the people of Uzbekistan. Once Bolshevik leaders had created geographical boundaries and called them national, then, much work remained to make these borders meaningful. This in turn meant defining through difference: devising ways to point out distinctions between the new nations.

What distinguished Uzbeks in Uzbekistan from other Muslims just across the border in, say, Kazakhstan? In providing an answer to this question, the party hoped to define—in essence, to create—an Uzbek national identity from the ground up. The search for definitions led in many directions. Linguistic differences, for instance, were deemed to separate Turkic Uzbeks from Persian Tajiks, although such supposedly straightforward distinctions were difficult to draw in areas with bilingual populations, as around the cities of Bukhoro and Samarqand. But even within Turkic culture, a range of careful distinctions were drawn within the broader sphere of Islamic practice to make clear the national differences among Uzbeks, Turkmen, Kazakhs, and others. One of the most promising avenues was to identify nations through their distinctive customs of daily life (byt), focusing particularly on locally gendered patterns of family behavior. Having long served as cultural emblems, women became the normative figures for each nationality: they stood for the inner domain of family, home, and spirituality, where the roots of cultural identity were taken to lie.[37]

Given the complexities of local settlement patterns, ethnic and clan groups spilled across the new borders, and a wide variety of gender practices could be discerned among them. But such local variety served the purposes of national demarcation, since codes of female behavior, especially of female seclusion, practiced on or near the territory of the new Uzbek SSR proved a convenient way of labeling a woman and her family as distinctly Uzbek, not merely Eastern. The veil was a particularly vivid marker of identity, and Soviet writers policed the boundaries that resulted, carefully distinguishing among various ("national") types of veils. Uzbeks living in Turkmen areas were distinguished by their "characteristic" veils—paranjis rather than yashmaks—and by differ-

36. The name was used during the medieval period, although not with a clearly ethnic meaning. See James Critchlow, *Nationalism in Uzbekistan: A Soviet Republic's Road to Sovereignty* (Boulder, 1991), 1; and Allworth, *Modern Uzbeks*.

37. I draw here upon Partha Chatterjee, *The Nation and Its Fragments: Colonial and Postcolonial Histories* (Princeton, 1993), 6, 121.

ent practices of female seclusion.[38] Uzbeks and Kyrgyz in the border area of Osh or Uzbeks and Kazakhs in southern Kazakhstan were identified along similar lines.[39] Sometimes it seemed that a woman and her family could be classified as Uzbek *because* she veiled in a certain way: in this sense, the paranji served as a creator of Uzbek identity. The leaders of the new Soviet republics— many of whom were beneficiaries of korenizatsiia—contributed to this sharp delineation of national customs. They used ethnographic distinctions to underpin competing land claims and to argue for redrawing and expanding their republics' borders.[40]

But such strict definitions did not fit the complex realities of Central Asian social practice, and the shortcomings were plain to see. As already noted, not all women who seemed Uzbek by other criteria in fact wore veils. Equally, however, not all veiled women were Uzbek. Indigenous Jewish women in Bukhoro, for example, wore the same paranjis and chachvons as their Muslim counterparts and shared other customs as well, yet no one—Jews, Uzbeks, or Bolsheviks of whatever ethnicity—argued that they were Uzbek.[41] Soviet writers mostly ignored the problem presented by these Jewish women as they nationalized the veil as a specifically Uzbek form of dress. Veiled women in local Roma (gypsy) communities were likewise ignored for similar reasons.[42] A handful of veiled European women—mostly Russian orphans born in Central Asia who married Muslim men—could also be found, but this image was so exceptional that it only underscored the Otherness of Uzbek veiling in general.[43]

Tajik women presented a similar but potentially more serious problem, since many Tajik veils, as shown in Figure 9, appeared virtually identical to the supposedly Uzbek paranji and chachvon. Until 1929 Tajikistan was part of the

38. RGASPI, d. 775, l. 6; and PDA, f. 60, op. 1, d. 4868, ll. 25–26. On the policing of national boundaries through women's dress, see V. Moskalev, *Uzbechka* (Moscow, 1928). A series of similar pamphlets was planned for 1930–31; see ÖzRMDA, f. 9, op. 1, d. 3425, l. 11.

39. For an example of secluded women in southern Kazakhstan being deemed Uzbek in 1929, see ÖzRMDA, f. 9, op. 1, d. 3404, ll. 37–38. Such distinctions could follow a circular logic: in Osh, for example, an unveiled Muslim woman must be Kyrgyz rather than Uzbek, because Kyrgyz women did not veil.

40. The republics fought over borders throughout the 1920s and beyond. Uzbek officials, for example, argued that the border in such places as Osh had stranded Uzbek communities that should be reunited with their co-nationals in the Uzbek SSR. See ÖzRMDA, f. 86, op. 1, d. 3423, ll. 47–59.

41. On Bukhoran Jewish women and their veils, see RGASPI, d. 787, l. 176, and d. 1157, ll. 24 and 38–40. (But the Danish geographer Ole Olufsen, who visited Bukhoro in the late 1890s, reported that they were unveiled: Hopkirk, *Traveller's Companion to Central Asia*, 53.) These women were "sold" into early marriages like Uzbek women, according to ÖzRMDA, f. 86, op. 1, d. 2597, l. 1020b.

42. RGASPI, d. 1239, l. 16.

43. Such cases horrified Russian readers. See "Russkaia devochka pod parandzhei," *PV*, 10 Apr. 1927; or RGASPI, d. 2072, l. 61, and d. 2073, ll. 26–29.

Uzbek SSR; until then, therefore, it served a political purpose to show that such cultural practices were held in common. And when after 1929 the two republics separated and it became more important to draw a stark distinction between Uzbeks and Tajiks, linguistic differences between Persians and Turks could be used. But party writers went further, portraying the paranji and chachvon as a specifically Uzbek form of dress. They portrayed the veils worn by Tajik women as culturally inauthentic, as either imposed or borrowed. Tajik women supposedly did not know how to make paranjis, and tended to buy them only when resident in the larger (Uzbek) cities. Only Tajik women in relatively "Uzbekified" areas, moreover, were said to do so. Such veils were reportedly rare in purely Tajik districts and even more infrequently found in Tajik villages. Hence they only mapped the extent of Uzbek influence on Tajik society.[44] In the end, then, both the paranji and the chachvon belonged to the Uzbek woman alone. Creating borders had helped to transform this veil from the symbol of a vaguely Eastern woman into a national emblem of the Uzbek people.

The new Soviet state employed other tactics to demarcate these new Central Asian nations: it created different alphabets and literary languages, for example. The deployment of science, however, was a particularly striking tactic in the dual construction of gender and nation. Working at the intersection of anthropology and biomedicine, Soviet scientific "experts" set out to define precisely what made a woman Uzbek.[45] They thus lent support to the view that national-cultural distinctions in Central Asia were objectively real and empirically measurable. Their authoritative manner and scholarly methods, too, gave this opinion a reassuring cast of impartiality.

Some of this work was highly technical, such as investigations of "scientific" phrenology—detailed studies of the different sizes and shapes of the heads found in various nations. One V. K. Iasevich, for example, a physician at Central Asian State University, in 1925–26 carried out a study of several hundred Uzbek women in Khorazm. His aim was to ascertain the unique biological characteristics of the Uzbek woman, and through her of the Uzbek nation. "It is necessary to stop [and study] the Uzbek woman," he argued, "because . . . [she] represents the most conservative element in the family, having long held on to and preserved tradition and the old style of life. . . ." Iasevich's study involved a detailed questionnaire concerning each woman's daily customs and life history, as well as complete physical and gynecological exams. Photographs were taken of supposedly typical subjects. Perhaps unsurpris-

44. See RGASPI, d. 2054, l. 118; and Shirokova, *Traditsionnaia i sovremennaia odezhda*, 81–85.

45. A few studied males along similar lines; for example, A. P. Shishov, "Mal'chiki uzbeki: Antropometricheskoe issledovanie," *Meditsinskaia mysl' Uzbekistana*, no. 1 (1928), 16–41. Women of other ethnic groups were the subjects of similar investigations: see the studies of Tajik women at RGASPI, d. 812, ll. 34–105.

Figure 9. Urban Tajik women, 1925. (Courtesy RGAKFD.)

ingly, the study encountered significant difficulties—many subjects had never seen European medical personnel, and often were seized with terror at the sight of medical instruments. A few women fainted in front of the cameras. Many questionnaires and exams were left incomplete, a fact noted in passing by Iasevich as he pressed onward with his scientific quest.[46]

In the end Iasevich defined the Uzbek woman through the dual languages of statistics and sexuality. His results, published in 1928 ("On the Question of the Constitutional and Anthropological Type of the Uzbek Woman of Khorazm"), included painstakingly detailed tables giving the statistical distributions of the measurements and descriptions of every conceivable body part—from spine curvature to skin tone to breast size—within the Uzbek female population of Khorazm. These distributions were compared with those of Russian, German, American, Jewish, and Norwegian women to demarcate the national differences more clearly. The voyeuristic quality of his project was then completed with photographs of six nude (and clearly uncomfortable) women (see Figure 10). Iasevich explained in dry, scientific language that they

46. V. K. Iasevich, "K voprosu o konstitutsional'nom i antropologicheskom tipe uzbechki Khorezma," *Meditsinskaia mysl' Uzbekistana,* no. 5 (1928), 35.

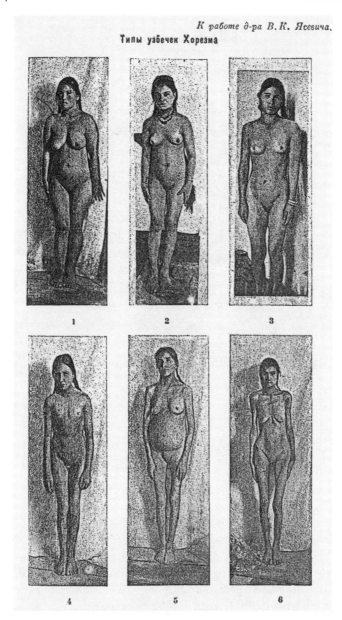

Figure 10. An anthropological view of the Uzbek woman, 1928.
(V. K. Iasevich, "K voprosu o konstitutsional'nom i
antropologicheskom tipe uzbechki Khorezma," *Meditsinskaia
mysl' Uzbekistana,* no. 5 [1928], 49.)

were meant as illustrations of the six principal body types he had found in Khorazm.[47]

If Iasevich's statistical tables were written for an audience of socio-medical specialists, other scientific work aimed at a wider audience. The well-known anthropologist L. V. Oshanin, for instance, was commissioned in 1926 to prepare a study of "the daily life and anthropological type of the Uzbek woman." Financed and closely supervised by the party's Zhenotdel and the government's Commissariat for Enlightenment (Narkompros), this study in many ways resembled Iasevich's. Once again several hundred Uzbek women, this time from Tashkent, were to be asked a series of questions about their daily lives and life histories and then subjected to detailed physical exams. The goal was to elucidate their biological essence, to isolate what was "typical" of the Uzbek people. Such a study was needed, Oshanin argued, because the topic was completely unexamined, and people did not know what features and behaviors should be considered characteristically or definitively Uzbek.[48] His party and state overseers agreed on the topic's importance, asking only that his study, in addition to its scientific merit, be made as accessible as possible to a popular readership. They encouraged him, for example, to include photographs of typical Uzbek women, and not to omit drawings of illustrative scenes of Uzbek daily life.[49]

One cannot help being struck by the intrusiveness of such studies. The anthropologists' questionnaires and exam records show an astounding attention to detail. Notwithstanding the deep cultural sensitivity of such questions in Central Asia, for Oshanin's study every conceivable body part (including the sex organs) was to be measured and categorized, and possibly photographed. Each woman then faced a series of probing questions about the intimate details of her family life: her age at sexual maturity, at first sexual act, at marriage, at childbirth, and so on.[50] Although couched in the language of science and discovery, these examinations represented a clear exercise of power: political (colonial), professional (scientific), and patriarchal (masculine). Scientists sought to gain an intimate knowledge of the most closely guarded areas of Uzbek family life, and used this knowledge to underpin their own claims to expertise and authority.

At the same time these studies served a more constructive purpose: they offered a sharp definition, in a very concrete and visible way, of what it meant to

---

47. Ibid., 49. It does not seem farfetched to see Iasevich's "scientific" investigation as overlaid with the erotic fantasies of earlier male visitors to the East. On such "scientific pornography," see Ann Laura Stoler, *Race and the Education of Desire: Foucault's History of Sexuality and the Colonial Order of Things* (Durham, 1995), 183–90.

48. Plans for this study, which does not seem to have been published, are at ÖzRMDA, f. 94, op. 1, d. 797, l. 89–89ob; and RGASPI, d. 776, ll. 146–47.

49. RGASPI, d. 1201, ll. 56–58; and ÖzRMDA, f. 94, op. 1, d. 797, l. 88.

50. See the physical examination forms at RGASPI, d. 776, ll. 143–144ob. A questionnaire on each woman's "social character" follows at l. 145.

be Uzbek. Such anthropological and biomedical studies concluded by pointing to physically distinguishing characteristics of this new nation, sometimes calling it a separate "race."[51] The scientific argument for a distinctive Uzbek identity was then made to as wide an audience as possible, as new museums and traveling exhibits illustrated through their displays of women's byt and biology the uniquely Uzbek features of the indigenous population.[52] Scientific policing of the boundaries between Central Asian peoples continued for decades, often including photographic "evidence" of Uzbek distinctiveness through its women.[53] Scientists continued to lend their voices and their authority to efforts to define who the Uzbeks were, helping to propagate a sense of national identity.

All of these Soviet efforts, taken together, started to bear fruit by the mid- to late 1920s—albeit not always in the way the party intended. They did so partly because they served Central Asian interests at least as much as those of the Soviet state. But for whatever reason, by 1930 an Uzbek national consciousness, however fitful and uneven, had started to take root, a remarkable development with momentous and lasting consequences. Anyone hearing Uzbeks today denigrate their Turkmen, Kazakh, or Kyrgyz neighbors as inferior would surely agree that a sense of national identity is a principal Soviet legacy to Central Asia, and to Uzbeks in particular. Uzbeks did not cease to see themselves as Muslims, to be sure, any more than they stopped being members of a certain family or clan or inhabitants of a particular region. But for many, this matrix of personal identity gained a new component—the Uzbek nation—that took on a real and growing importance.

Just as the party had hoped, moreover, this sense of Uzbek identity was based largely on customs of everyday life, and in substantial part on the supposedly distinctive veils and behaviors that defined an Uzbek woman.[54] The paranji and chachvon came increasingly to mark a woman as Uzbek in the eyes

51. On the tensions and ambiguities of Soviet discussions of "race," see the debate in *Slavic Review* 61, no. 1 (2002), especially among Eric Weitz, Amir Weiner, and Francine Hirsch.

52. See RGASPI, d. 774, l. 42; d. 793, l. 37; d. 801, l. 60. For a theoretical perspective, see Timothy Mitchell, *Colonising Egypt* (Cambridge, 1988), chap. 1.

53. V. Ia. Zezenkova, "Materialy po antropologii zhenshchin razlichnykh plemen i narodov Srednei Azii," in *Voprosy etnogeza narodov Srednei Azii v svete dannykh antropologii*, ed. L. V. Oshanin and V. Ia. Zezenkova (Tashkent, 1953), 57–60. Zezenkova, who carried out her work in 1944, included photographs of the different "types" of Uzbek women (pp. 89–111). Interestingly, like Iasevich and Oshanin, she sought to illustrate the ideal Uzbek woman—in the singular—but found it necessary to show a multiplicity of "types."

54. Scholars have found women being seen as repositories of nationhood in other Muslim parts of the former Soviet Union. See Gillian Tett, " 'Guardians of the Faith?': Gender and Religion in an (ex) Soviet Tajik Village," in *Muslim Women's Choices: Religious Belief and Social Reality*, ed. Camillia Fawzi El-Solh and Judy Mabro (Oxford, 1994), 128–51; and Nayereh Tohidi, "Soviet in Public, Azeri in Private: Gender, Islam, Nationalism in Soviet and Post-Soviet Azerbaijan," paper presented at the Middle East Studies Association of North America, 6–10 Dec. 1995, Washington, D.C.

of her co-nationals, just as they had done for Soviet ethnographers and scientists. A woman's dress became national, expressive of entire communities; it literally embodied an identity, both for her and for those around her, saying who they were and who they were not. A woman's decision to wear Russian-style shoes sometimes led even other women to denounce her as a prostitute who had abandoned her people; if she went further and unveiled, she had committed the ultimate transgression by renouncing her nationality to become Russian.[55] Women and families who moved into the European New Cities were lambasted as national traitors: not only had they learned to speak Russian, but they had abandoned Uzbek ways of life, most vividly by unveiling and wearing European clothes. All that remained of their former selves, according to one observer, was a propensity to sit on the ground during meals.[56] (See Figure 11.)

Such strict policing of the boundaries between national cultures went beyond what the party intended, sometimes leading to hostility between Uzbeks and Russians and also among some of the indigenous Central Asian nations.[57] The defense of each nation's cultural integrity was taken up by its own members, expressed largely in the same lexicon of byt—especially family life and practices of female seclusion—used by Soviet experts. One Uzbek man in Osh—a Communist Party member, no less—felt particularly strongly about policing these national boundaries after his marriage in 1927. To ensure that his family and any future children would remain Uzbek, he forced his new wife (listed as Kyrgyz, at least partly because she had not previously worn a veil) to don paranji and chachvon, a step that cost him his party membership card.[58] His willingness to risk this outcome speaks eloquently to the importance he attached to issues of national identity and to the degree to which he saw his own identity embodied in and expressed through his wife's paranji.

But if party and people were (for their own reasons) cooperating in this construction of nationhood, how did the equation of nation with gender come to backfire against Moscow? The answer lies in the unintended consequences of the methods chosen by the party to bring progress and modernity to Central Asia. As specific gendered behaviors became synonymous with a new Uzbek identity, they simultaneously encoded multiple and conflicting moral meanings—being deemed deviant and in need of change by Bolshevik women's activists and devout or patriotic and worthy of defense by Muslim conservatives (and now by Uzbek nationalists). It was only a short step for this new Uzbek identity itself to assume the same conflicting moral connotations. From the Soviet perspective, Uzbekness—defined through practices of veiling that seemed

55. See the records from 1925 and 1926 at RGASPI, d. 433, l. 36, and d. 776, l. 29.
56. RGASPI, d. 1202, l. 33.
57. Russian and Uzbek women could not work together in a factory at PDA, op. 2, d. 1371, ll. 23–25; an example of Uzbek-Jewish tension from 1924 is related at RGASPI, d. 162, l. 96ob.
58. RGASPI, d. 1684, l. 40ob.

Figure 11. Uzbek men and European fashion. (Courtesy Anahita Gallery, Santa Fe, N.M.)

primitive and oppressive—could readily be associated with notions of savagery, backwardness, and deviance. It practically cried out to be changed, rehabilitated, and transformed. This was an equation with ominous implications for later relations between Bolshevik leaders and Uzbek society, and it carried the seeds of an unwelcome if persistent association: between Uzbek national identity on the one hand and resistance to Soviet policies of women's liberation on the other.

Sovietizing Uzbekistan: Transforming the Uzbek Woman

If the first discontinuity of colonial discourse across 1917 was the creation of a specifically Uzbek rather than generally Eastern woman, the second was that Bolshevik activists were unable to emulate tsarist officials, who had—even while establishing a system of colonial rule—either ignored Central Asian culture or simply marveled at its exotic strangeness.[59] Bolshevik activists marveled too, even while denouncing their tsarist predecessors' exploitative policies. At the same time, these Bolsheviks found it impossible simply to leave Uzbekistan more or less alone. The point, after all, as Marx had said, was to

59. Tsarist administrators lived in a bubble almost completely isolated from their surroundings and were far more likely to ignore the inner workings of Central Asian society than to try to change them. One prerevolutionary guidebook to Tashkent, for example, focused for 520 pages on such attractions as the governor-general's home and the local Orthodox cathedral, mentioning only in passing the fact that Muslims also lived in Turkestan (A. I. Dobrosmyslov, *Tashkent v proshlom i nastoiashchem: Istoricheskii ocherk* [Tashkent, 1912]).

change the world, and it was simply unacceptable for Uzbek women in a Soviet state still to be wearing heavy black veils in public. The party's claim to rule in Central Asia was anchored in its emancipatory rhetoric, its promise to help the oppressed. This rhetoric seemed to apply particularly to Uzbek women, long the symbols of oppression in European eyes.[60] Party workers were thus impelled to attack the very veils that defined these women as Uzbek. This logic of emancipation drove the ostensibly anticolonial Soviet government to launch a project of cultural transformation in Central Asia that far surpassed in intrusiveness anything done by the tsarist state, or indeed by earlier colonial regimes in many other parts of the world.[61]

Most Russians living in Uzbekistan still made a point of calling themselves European, not Russian. In reports, statistics, and propaganda exhortations, they (together with other Slavic, Christian, and Jewish immigrants) drew the contrast starkly between European and local national ways.[62] Soviet evaluations of local customs—including the panoply of practices around female seclusion—found them lacking the requisite qualities of modern, civilized family life. Drawing such distinctions was a common practice in modern colonial empires, but again, the Soviet case differed from most in one crucial respect: party theory foresaw and official policy encouraged the ultimate erasure of such divisions. However long it might take, Uzbek men and women were to be remade into fully modern Soviet citizens. What did this mean? One important component was strict gender equality—a self-consciously secular and European vision of social and family life, a vision that was quite foreign to most Muslim Uzbeks (and, it should be said, hardly an accurate reflection of Russian family life either). But after 1917, Central Asia's perceived backwardness presented a golden opportunity for Bolshevik activists to assert membership in—and even leadership of—a European, enlightened movement for social justice. The new republic of Uzbekistan thus created Europeans as well as Uzbeks.

If anyone in Central Asia had to change, it was clear who it would be: European practices were the (modern) model to which (backward, primitive) Uzbeks had to adjust.[63] Uzbek customs were seen as unhygienic and unjust, as expressions of a social life that remained mired in the Middle Ages. The expertise of Soviet scientists and anthropologists was again deployed to support this depiction. Experts offered learned opinions that stressed the negative con-

---

60. See, for example, the effusive dedication page of *Za piat' let* (Moscow, 1925).

61. Native Americans may have faced something similar. See David Wallace Adams, *Education for Extinction: American Indians and the Boarding School Experience, 1875–1928* (Lawrence, Kans., 1995).

62. The label of "European" was claimed by nearly every non-Muslim group in the area. The main exception was the indigenous (Bukhoran) Jewish community.

63. In one factory, for example, Uzbek women reportedly were unable to work effectively or efficiently. The only exception was one *uzbechka* who improved dramatically after being put to work directly between two European co-workers. The latter's superior skill and diligence supposedly inspired her to raise her own level (PDA, op. 2, d. 1371, ll. 23–25).

sequences of Uzbek social customs, and portrayed them as emblematic of the despotic primitivism that characterized Uzbek culture. They carried out detailed studies of the "harmful survivals" (*vrednye perezhitki*) that structured Uzbek daily life, and carefully elucidated the associated risks to health and morality.[64] Hygiene was a particular concern, since that was a basic marker of modernity that Uzbeks supposedly lacked—despite the obvious concern with some kinds of cleanliness that ran through Central Asian daily life, from prescribed routines of hand washing to elaborate pollution taboos and religious requirements for ritual bathing. But Soviet activists had a different understanding of cleanliness and its purposes. For them the moral necessity of hygiene was driven by modern medical and scientific questions, not religious concerns about purity. It was linked to discourses of public health and tied into and justified by efforts to find and ameliorate the environmental causes of disease (tuberculosis, trachoma, worms and other parasites in the water supply). Yet despite the physical reality of microbes and their empirically verifiable effects on indigenous bodies, this public health campaign was not a disinterested, culturally neutral, altruistic enterprise. It was also deeply political, implicated in and contributing to the power relationships of colonial society. Ultimately it helped shape the wider cultural discourses that defined a modern, healthy, self-disciplined Soviet citizenry.

Women, once again, served as exemplars of their people: they showed readily the dirt, disease, and ignorance that gripped the Uzbek nation. This dual conflation of women with dirt and nation can be seen wherever issues of health and hygiene were discussed.[65] Soviet experts construed virtually every aspect of an Uzbek woman's life as dirty and unhealthful: one oft-cited statistic held that a demographic gap resulted, with only 889 Central Asian women to be found for every 1,000 men.[66] Early marriage, it was said, resulted in damage to the Uzbek woman's reproductive system, most likely compounded by several venereal diseases. Owing to her seclusion in the *ichkari* (women's quarter) of her home, her health suffered further from lack of exercise and exposure to sunshine and fresh air. She gave birth in horrendous conditions, and the rites surrounding childbirth only increased the danger to her and her newborn child. She then raised children in dirt and squalor, leading to astonishingly high rates of infant mortality. Any number of Uzbek child-care customs were

64. The language of "survivals" was explicit and unapologetic, defining these customs as vestiges of a developmental stage that European peoples had long left behind. The attention to health and dirt also bespeaks the Soviet state's efforts to claim the mantle of civilization and to create a self-disciplined citizenry. For lists of "harmful customs" crying out for study by Soviet scientists, see RGASPI, d. 1201, ll. 74–750b, and d. 1203, ll. 9–10.

65. Evidence for this paragraph is taken from ÖzRMDA, f. 737, op. 1, d. 185, l. 179; RGASPI, d. 769, l. 34; d. 775, ll. 6–8; d. 787, ll. 277–78; and d. 1211, l. 117; PDA, f. 60, op. 1, d. 4868, ll. 25–26; and Iasevich, "K voprosu."

66. The census of 1926 found a population imbalance in Uzbekistan, with 47 percent women and 53 percent men. The same proportion held for the overall Uzbek population in Central Asia (*Sredniaia Aziia v tsifrakh*, 18–19).

depicted as dangerously unhygienic: the *beshik,* or cradle, came under particular fire because it permitted a mother to leave her child unattended for long stretches (strategically placed holes and tubes were meant to obviate the need for diapers) and thus stunted proper development. With a pitying eye, Liubimova described the cumulative effect of such primitive customs. After reporting that one large medical study had found more than 45 percent of local women (9,772 of 21,626) to be seriously ill, she explained that the squalor of indigenous life was to blame:

> They are ill with syphilis, with rashes, with gynecological and skin diseases, with diseases of the eye. All of these sicknesses are connected by the fact that there is much filth in the *kibitki* and yurts; by the fact that both the sick and the healthy drink and eat from the same dishes, [and] sit on common cushions and blankets; [and by the fact that] for years at a time they do not wash their children, or wash themselves, or wash their clothes. According to one children's clinic in the Old City of Tashkent, 35 percent of the children in school never bathe at all.[67]

Dirt was everywhere; it seemed to characterize Central Asia and Central Asians. One feels here the horror of European activists, the sense that they wished to enlighten the savages, to transform local ways of life in Uzbekistan—and the belief that they were doing it for the Uzbeks' own good.

Having painted such a dire picture of Uzbek daily life, some party workers—especially those who came from the indigenous population—portrayed Soviet efforts to improve women's hygiene as a defense of the Uzbek nation. Uzbek women, they argued, had to be made into educated mothers able to raise strong, healthy children. In August 1925 the Uzbek party's top leader, First Secretary Akmal Ikramov, attacked the ignorance and stupidity of local folk healers (*tabibs*), some of whom reportedly advised syphilitic men to seek a cure by marrying a young girl. After denouncing such "barbaric, frankly idiotic methods [of treatment]," Ikramov said that they served as excellent illustrations of the prevailing conditions of everyday Uzbek life:

> If one pays strict attention to these facts, to the proper upbringing of the younger generation, then here one must start thinking about the fate of the Uzbek nation, about the proper cultivation of this nation. One must pay serious attention to [the need to] prepare, raise, and foster cultured mothers. A girl of 14 years, or one of 15–16 years, cannot become a mother and produce children, cannot raise them, and besides this, the

67. Serafima Timofeevna Liubimova, *Kommunist! Esli ty ne khochesh', chtoby narod vymiral, esli ty deistvitel'no zabotish'sia o razvitii narodnogo khoziaistva i kul'tury, esli ty ne bai, ne mulla i ne podderzhivaesh' mull i baev—ty dolzhen rabotat' po raskreposhcheniiu zhenshchin* (Tashkent, 1925), 3. Note that Liubimova is somewhat vague about her area: kibitki and yurts were nomadic tent dwellings of the steppe—not typical in Uzbekistan, and certainly not in Tashkent.

facts show that such a wife will be maimed and broken after her first births and will cease to satisfy her husband—from which [comes] polygamy, etc. The children of such a mother will be sick, and if all of this continues in the future, then nothing will come of it [but] the Uzbek nation will degenerate. It is necessary to consider this question seriously, to consider it from the point of view of the fate of the nation itself, of its culture and its material conditions.[68]

This call for change in a way extended earlier jadid arguments for internal reform; but Ikramov's negative views of Uzbek folk practices also set him apart from local society and identified him with Soviet power. Colonial theorists such as Albert Memmi portray such views as typical among colonized elites, who often develop mentalities of self-denigration and self-hatred.[69] Be that as it may, and leaving aside the difficult question of Ikramov's motives or psychological state, such calls for protecting the nation by protecting its mothers remained contradictory. For mothers to improve and safeguard the Uzbek nation's future, after all, they would have to abandon many of the practices that had made them both members and emblems of that nation.

More often, native women—in all their dirtiness and primitivism—served as shorthand symbols for their nation, and specifically for all that was wrong with it. Some indigenous Communists in Turkmenistan, for example, reportedly divorced their wives and married European women because the latter were less "illiterate and unclean."[70] Prominent party activists likewise called Uzbek women uncultured and illiterate. According to Yoldosh Akhunbabaev, chairman of the Uzbek Central Executive Committee, "It is impossible to compare European women with Uzbek women. The European woman understands something of cultural questions, and the Uzbek woman does not understand [them]."[71] Bolshevik activists thus focused on what they saw as basic efforts, such as teaching Uzbek women to use soap.[72] Such hygiene campaigns could be justified on public health grounds, to be sure, but in the eyes of European observers, they also underscored the primitivism of the unwashed

---

68. RGASPI, d. 445, ll. 43–44. In its very title, Liubimova's just-quoted booklet invokes a similar fear of the (Uzbek) nation's extinction. According to a different party report, also written in 1925, such perversions as those mentioned by Ikramov were "gnawing away at the health of the nation and leading to its degeneration." As this report put it, "An illiterate and enslaved mother cannot raise her children as healthy and cultured people. The facts of the degeneration . . . of women speak to the threat to the very existence of the Uzbek nation" (ÖzRMDA, f. 94, op. 1, d. 223, ll. 121–22).

69. Albert Memmi, *The Colonizer and the Colonized,* trans. Howard Greenfeld (Boston, 1965), especially 120–27.

70. RGASPI, d. 1202, l. 59.

71. RGASPI, d. 1688, l. 25. See also d. 1239, l. 27.

72. Examples of this soap-and-water campaign are at RGASPI, d. 769, l. 44; d. 774, l. 63; d. 1204, l. 35; and f. 507, op. 2, d. 118, l. 59; and Moskalev, *Uzbechka,* 23. Hygiene was applied as a judgment to other Central Asian nations—to Turkmen women at f. 62, op. 2, d. 799, l. 41, and Tajik women at d. 812, ll. 75–76 and 82.

Uzbek woman, and thereby her people's need to be led toward cleanliness and civilization.

The veil was so central to images of the Uzbek woman that it elicited a particularly heavy rhetorical attack.[73] Soviet writers denounced the paranji in every way possible: it was an economic hindrance, preventing women from working outside the home. It kept women physically enslaved and symbolized the oppression in which they lived. Zhenotdel activists denounced the veil (like the ichkari) in florid terms, as a "prison" from which Uzbek women had to be freed; and since no one else was defending women from oppression, they said, it fell to the party to do so. Their two most interesting lines of attack went further, portraying the veil as both dirty and deviant.

Criticisms of the veil's allegedly unhygienic character fitted nicely with the general portrait of illness and disease in Uzbek life. If Uzbek women's daily life was redolent of filth and if the paranji defined the Uzbek woman, then it followed that this veil must also be judged unhealthy and dangerous. Soviet doctors and propagandists argued that the paranji was to blame for many of the health problems that beset Uzbek women. According to one exemplary article written in 1925 by Liubimova ("The Paranji and Women's Health"), the veil kept Uzbek women from moving about and working outside, causing muscular weakness, flabby skin, and premature aging. This lack of exercise led to poor circulation and an accumulation of toxins, and often an early death.[74]

Liubimova became still more exercised as she traced a series of adverse health consequences to the paranji, many of which came to light only when the unfortunate woman became a mother. Her weak muscles meant that she would probably have difficulty giving birth, Liubimova said; either mother or child might die in childbirth, and birth deformities were common. Likewise, since only a mother who moved about briskly and exercised could hope to produce healthy breast milk, the restricted lifestyle dictated by the paranji meant that Uzbek children consumed milk in which the "poisons" of village life had accumulated. Once a young daughter herself donned the veil, she too was cut off from fresh air and sunshine and thus susceptible to various diseases: the chachvon also was to blame, because it did not permit fresh air to circulate, so that both poisonous carbon dioxide and harmful microbes were kept close to the face.[75]

Liubimova concluded by arguing that the paranji could fairly—if indirectly—be blamed for two other kinds of health problems. First, it produced ignorance, which in this context could be fatal. Veiled women were vulnerable to venereal diseases: ignorant of modern medicine, they understood neither the

73. This paragraph is based on RGASPI, d. 427, l. 16; PDA, f. 60, op. 1, d. 4981, l. 23; and Bibi Pal'vanova Pal'vanova, *Docheri Sovetskogo Vostoka* (Moscow, 1961), 28–29.
74. Liubimova's unpublished article is at RGASPI, d. 429, ll. 43–47; this part of her argument is from ll. 43–44. For a doctors' meeting to discuss such risks, see A. Nikolaeva, "Protiv parandzhi i chachvana," *PV,* 2 Mar. 1927.
75. RGASPI, d. 429, ll. 44–45.

means of transmission nor the symptoms nor the treatments for such serious conditions as syphilis and gonorrhea. Liubimova noted that these diseases could be spread either sexually or through close quarters and unhygienic practices, such as eating from common dishes. Yet their real cause, she argued, was the ignorance produced by the paranji. Uzbek women would contract a venereal disease from their husbands (who had picked it up "somewhere"), not recognize the initial signs of infection ("Often, particularly [in] a semicultured woman, the disease proceeds unnoticed"), and then bemoan the curses of fate, such as resulting stillbirths or permanent infertility. If any children lived, moreover, they were likely to be infected from birth.[76]

Second, the veil cut women off from the world physically, an indirect cause of other medical troubles. An Uzbek woman could not leave her husband or her family, even if she knew that staying would endanger her health. She could not venture outside to seek medical attention for a member of her family who fell ill or take that person to a hospital. She could not take her infant for regular preventive care, thus making it more likely that the child would die young—nor, Liubimova might have added, could she accept medical treatment from a male Soviet doctor. All of these tragedies Liubimova laid squarely at the foot of the paranji: "And so the paranji leaves the woman a flaccid, sickly body; weak lungs; difficult births; infertility and children sick from syphilis and gonorrhea; and an early, bitter old age."[77]

If attacks on the veil's health risks focused on dirt, criticism of its moral essence denounced it as deviant. By casting the issue of whether an Uzbek woman should veil in moral terms, Soviet activists—intriguingly—entered the argument against the paranji on its Uzbek Muslim defenders' own turf. Bolshevik denigrations of the veil therefore did not stop at the practical (its cumbersome weight, its propensity to spread germs). They went further, arguing that in its very essence the veil was spiritually harmful, morally unjust, and indeed fundamentally evil. As one local Communist put it as early as 1924,

> Communism is as incompatible with the *chadra* [veil] of native women as a dark night [is with] the full, bright sunshine of day. The chadra is the shameful mark of hoary centuries of despotism and slavery, darkness and ignorance; and besides this, [it is] an obstacle on the path toward the revolutionary advancement of the global working class.
>
> From this perspective every chadra that is torn away from a [woman's] face signals the victory of new life over the musty past, the victory of culture and light—communism.[78]

The veil thus served as antithesis to all the party stood for: it was darkness to the party's light, oppression to its liberation, ignorance to its wisdom. Whether

76. Ibid., l. 46.
77. Ibid., l. 47.
78. RGASPI, d. 427, l. 155.

one attributes such a view to the Enlightenment roots of the Bolsheviks' Marxist ethos or to the heritage of evangelical Europeanism shown by prerevolutionary Orientalists, it is unmistakable throughout the endless depictions of paranjis as prisons from which innocent women had to be freed.[79]

Sometimes this moral denigration took a slightly different line, imputing a range of character flaws to the act of donning a paranji. In an almost religious way, the veil could be blamed for causing wicked or sinful behavior. A fascinating, albeit extreme, example can be seen in the words of an Uzbek Communist who in 1927 addressed a local congress in Andijon (Andizhan):

> Together with the growth of socialist elements in the economy, there will be a decline in the debauchery [*razvrat*] of women. Really, does the paranji protect against depravity? Nothing of the sort; to the contrary, it leads to yet more of the same. Almost everyone knows that various forms of dissipation thrive among those who wear the paranji. For example, the love of one woman for another: this unhealthy phenomenon is very widespread among Uzbek women, [and] from this fact you [can] see that the paranji does not at all ward off debauchery.[80]

Casting moral aspersions on the veil and the women who wore it attacked the religious and moral defense of female seclusion at its heart. Rather than being a mark of devout piety, the paranji was said to drive women to immorality and deviance by turning them into lesbians.

Soviet writers thus constructed the veil as dirty and unhealthy, as well as evil, immoral, and unjust. It should therefore come as no surprise to find the hujum of 1927 targeting the paranji above all else. One party member had declared in 1925 that "Uzbek women are veiled, this has been their custom since ancient times; but as you can see, this is not normal. Thus it is necessary [for us] to take action so that they will remove their chadras."[81] The same paranji that defined the Uzbek people was thus held up against a European model and declared to be "not normal." In short, the nation itself—the same Uzbek nation that had been built up and encouraged by the party—was implied through its women's veils to be both dirty and deviant. Hence it became, in an important way, *wrong* to be Uzbek, at least insofar as Uzbekness was defined through these practices of daily life. Some Bolshevik workers were astonishingly frank, saying that their goal was to civilize the wild Uzbeks, to tame their fanaticism.[82] They seem not to have considered whether such an aim, so remi-

---

79. Jean Starobinski has argued that the Enlightenment sought transparency above all else, as expressed in its aim to unveil the secrets of nature—a perspective from which the paranji would appear unwelcome, morally threatening, and not a little ominous (*Jean-Jacques Rousseau: Transparency and Obstruction* [Chicago, 1988], especially 65–80 and 254–67).

80. ÖzRMDA, f. 837, op. 3, d. 150, ll. 138–39.

81. RGASPI, d. 436, l. 102.

82. ÖzRMDA, f. 86, op. 1, d. 2217, ll. 22–23.

niscent of prerevolutionary missionary rhetoric, could be seen as more colonialist than emancipatory.

Legacies

The negative construction of the Uzbek woman and her everyday life both underpinned and impelled the party's determination to remake Central Asia, a determination expressed most vigorously in the hujum of 1927. In launching this assault on female seclusion, party leaders aimed at nothing less than a thoroughgoing transformation of Uzbek culture and society. This transformation from primitivism to modernity would be measured in large part by the emancipation of Uzbek women from their paranjis. As one writer put it in 1925,

> A formal revolution in municipal life is taking place. The old Asian cities (Tashkent, Bukhoro), consisting of wretched little cottages, fashioned from clay and reeds, are earmarked for demolition. In their place will be built a new city of the European type, [which] although lacking in the picturesque "Eastern color," will on the other hand ensure the native population light, air, and cleanliness. . . . The struggle for women's liberation, for throwing off the age-old, nightmarish chadra of horsehair, completes the picture of enlightenment-propagandistic work now under way all across the territory of Soviet Central Asia.[83]

The sweeping ambition of this vision distinguished the Bolshevik brand of colonialism from its tsarist predecessor, and indeed the only real points of comparison—such as French efforts to remake Algeria—are equally modern phenomena.

Party leaders called upon Uzbek women to cast off their veils in the name of equality and freedom, trusting that the lure and promise of a European model of emancipation would attract the support and cooperation of millions of downtrodden women. The success of the campaign, they thought, was assured, because the interest of a veiled woman in her own emancipation would be self-evident. In a few cases this approach worked well; local Jewish women who wore the paranji, for example, could be encouraged to emulate their European Jewish sisters by unveiling.[84] The party, however, had not invested enormous time and effort to associate Jewish women with the veil. And for Uzbek women, matters were different because the paranji and chachvon had, in effect, been nationalized as Uzbek property. By definition, therefore, all Uzbek women wore the veil; it was what made them Uzbek.[85] Party activists

---

83. V. A. Gurko-Kriazhin, "Poezdka v Zakavkaz'e i Sredniuiu Aziiu," *Novyi Vostok*, no. 7 (1925), 370.

84. RGASPI, d. 787, l. 176.

85. The historian Marianne Kamp has argued the opposite: that the act of *un*veiling constituted an Uzbek nation ("Pilgrimage and Performance: Uzbek Women and the Imagining of Uzbekistan in the 1920s," *International Journal of Middle East Studies* 34 [2002]: 263–78). This could

thus had no group analogous to European Jewish women to which to point, no laudable models of women simultaneously Uzbek and unveiled. Hence these activists had to urge veiled Uzbek women to emulate foreign women by casting off their paranjis. In the context of a newly created national community and a half-century of European colonial rule, such advice was likely to be seen as tantamount to telling them to abandon their people.

Yet many Muslims in Uzbekistan had responded favorably to other aspects of Bolshevik nation-making, and had incorporated a sense of Uzbek identity in the intimate space of the family. The later Soviet attacks on the veil helped shape the particular features, definitions, outlook, and content of this new nationalism, but that is not to say that party policy, acting alone upon an inert Central Asian society, "created" Uzbek nationalism through the hujum. Neither did eloquent Muslim clerics (or millions of Uzbek peasants) bring this national community into existence by sheer force of will. The party's efforts to end female seclusion and remake everyday culture, after all, had not happened in isolation. Contemporaneous population migrations, new political borders, expanding education and literacy, linguistic differentiation, suppression of religious institutions, international struggles with the capitalist world, and battles with anti-Soviet bosmachi rebels, all shaped this process too and together produced recognizably modern national identities throughout Central Asia. Given the practical and symbolic centrality accorded to the women's liberation campaign after 1927, the hujum played an especially important role in catalyzing, shaping, and accelerating this process—but Uzbek nationality emerged through the struggle itself, not because a party master plan required it to do so.

Yet the conflicting associations of Uzbek women and their veils—nationally emblematic and thus good, disease-ridden and primitive and thus bad—created continuing problems for Soviet power in Uzbekistan. Once veils had been made into emblems of backwardness, the hujum represented the logical culmination of the party's efforts to remake and civilize Central Asia. The party, however, had also made veils into emblems of Uzbek nationality, and encouraged this national identity to develop and flourish—and therein lay the fateful contradiction. Party leaders showed a remarkable disregard for the resulting paradoxes. Mikhail Kalinin, chairman of the All-Union Central Executive Committee in Moscow, displayed an astonishing obliviousness—not to say vulgarity—when he described his vision of the future in a speech delivered in early 1928:

> There will be, of course, women of the East, but they will not have their specific peculiarities. They will not wear the paranji, they will not veil themselves, they will not live locked up in the walls of their huts. [Liubi-

---

be true only insofar as national identity was synonymous with the Soviet state and a personally pro-Soviet outlook.

mova calls out from the floor: "Remember qalin!"] They will not be sold for qalin. As soon as a woman emerges into the light, when others see that, unveiled, she is not so beautiful, then they will not buy her. (*Laughter from the audience.*)

    . . . I think that the time is not far off when we will no longer associate the Eastern woman with the idea that she is a woman who wears the veil. I think that the time is not far off when this connection between the veil and the woman of the East will disappear, and when we speak of the Eastern woman, this will signify only the territorial presence of this woman in the Eastern countries, and no more. There will be no other particular connotations [of the term]. So it seems to me that this time is not far off; [yet] I would like to make this not-too-distant day come still nearer. (*Applause from the audience.*)[86]

All Eastern women, therefore—and by extension the East itself—were to be stripped of any distinguishing features. The divide between colonizer and colonized would disappear: this was the ultimate goal of the Soviet empire. By returning to the former vocabulary of an undifferentiated East, moreover—and one with ugly women to boot—Kalinin obliterated such distinctions rhetorically. The idea that this outcome might not appeal to nations such as the Uzbeks, who had only just acquired a separate identity, did not appear to enter his thinking.

    The effects of such a miscalculation, along with the conflicting logic of constructing both nationality and backwardness through the same symbol, soon became plain. When the party's vision for modernizing Uzbekistan began with a hujum against the veil, Uzbek women and their paranjis served all too readily as a focus of cultural, religious, gender, and now national resistance to Soviet incursions into Uzbek society. Further conflict over the intimate space of Uzbek family life only stirred passions more deeply. From the Bolshevik perspective, the national thus became all the more deviant and worthy of attack. But for many Uzbeks, the fact that such gender roles and family practices had been made equivalent to one's sense of self and community gave a reason to fight all the harder to preserve them, since doing so now amounted to a struggle to preserve the Uzbeks as a people.

---

86. Gosudarstvennyi arkhiv Rossiisskoi Federatsii (hereafter GARF), f. 3316, op. 50, d. 14, ll. 4 and 2. (Reverse pagination in this *delo*.)

CHAPTER 2

Hujum, 1927

The "hujum"—the attack against old ways of life—began with the casting off of the paranji. Many of you saw a paranji at the Congress's exhibition hall.

This attire is not a simple dress like the ones we all wear, being changed into another; it is not a simple trading of one dress for another. It is a way of dressing that is connected to centuries-old religious statutes and institutions. . . . To throw off the paranji means to break [completely] with the old ways of life. It means quarrelling with mullahs, quarrelling with all kinds of old-style people in the family and neighborhood, it means standing in defiance of all that is old.

—Serafima Liubimova, Zhenotdel activist, speaking to a women's congress in Moscow, October 1927

Seclusion has a heritage of 1,345 years (that is, the length of the Mohammedan era). It cannot be eliminated in five or six years. The [Muslim] woman herself must want to throw off the paranji, but that is not yet the case.

—A Bolshevik analyst, December 1926

The new Soviet leaders of Central Asia did not act in a vacuum. They formulated policies and priorities in response to their perceived needs: political control and military security, food supply and economic production, and cultural work and the pursuit of an ideological mission. These needs in turn arose from the particular historical and political context of southern Central Asia. Party activists, in short, brought multiple goals to Central Asia, goals that intersected, overlapped, and sometimes conflicted. They sought to bring civilization and modernity to the primitive and backward parts of the Russian empire; to end tsarist oppression, thereby showing the promise of Soviet power to other colonized peoples; to feed the population, especially in urban areas, during a serious famine; to build a socialist economy that would become a contributing, productive part of the new Soviet state; and not least, to ensure the security of Soviet Russia.

Yet even after Red Army troops occupied the urban centers of tsarist Turkestan, local Bolsheviks felt more besieged than in control. The small Russian minority of a few hundred thousand, concentrated in the cities, was dwarfed by the nearly ten million inhabitants, mostly rural, of southern Central Asia.[1] Given its urban Russian associations, Bolshevik power remained tenuous well into the ostensibly Soviet period. The complexity of the social and political world of southern Central Asia, moreover—combined with party leaders' at best incomplete understanding of who the local players were and what their motives and goals might be—made the task of Soviet administrators all the more difficult.[2] For all of these reasons, they recognized the urgency of locating points of entry into Central Asian society and of finding local allies willing to support and defend the Soviet regime.

The international context also played a critical role in shaping Bolshevik actions. Before the idea of "socialism in one country" emerged as Soviet doctrine and gained acceptance in the late 1920s, party orthodoxy held that Bolshevism could not survive in Russia alone. Survival was thought to require revolutionary assistance from abroad, from the wider world proletariat. Many Bolshevik leaders believed that attention should be directed toward fomenting revolution in the industrialized countries of Western Europe and North America; others in the Communist International (Comintern) and party hierarchy argued that revolution would more easily start in the colonized world (the "East") and then quickly spread back to the industrialized metropoles. In either case, though, the international dimension of Bolshevik policy was crucial to the survival of the Soviet state. Especially from the second point of view, the Bolsheviks' actions in their own corner of the East—especially Central Asia, the Caucasus, and parts of Siberia—had to be considered carefully, with an eye to maximizing their public relations impact outside Soviet borders. Any policy in these regions had to have an international resonance and appeal, to display the promise of Soviet power for colonized people everywhere.[3]

1. In 1926 the official population of southern Central Asia (the Uzbek SSR with Tajik ASSR, the Turkmen SSR, the Kyrgyz ASSR, and the southern part of the Kazakh ASSR) was 9,616,365. Of this number, Russians accounted for approximately 5.8 percent (up from 2.2 percent in 1897). See Frank Lorimer, *Population of the Soviet Union: History and Prospects* (Geneva, 1946), 70; and Robert A. Lewis et al., *Nationality and Population Change in Russia and the USSR: An Evaluation of Census Data, 1897–1970* (New York, 1976), 149.

2. On the complicated ways in which Turkestani domestic politics intersected with Bolshevik interests and policies—ways that leaders in Moscow did not always understand—see Adeeb Khalid, "Tashkent 1917: Muslim Politics in Revolutionary Turkestan," *Slavic Review* 55 (1996): 270–96.

3. For the Comintern's retelling of the women's liberation campaign for its international public relations value, see RGASPI, f. 507, op. 2, dd. 24, 25, 89, 118, and 118a.

This grand vision of securing the allegiance of the colonial East was encumbered, however, by the presence of competing models for change and progress. Party leaders were only too well aware of international competitors, especially the reformist governments of Afghanistan and Turkey (and later, Iran). In Afghanistan, which shared a border with three Soviet Central Asian republics, a new leader, Amanullah Khan, launched a variety of internally controversial political, social, economic, and cultural reforms in the 1920s. By 1928 they included improvements in women's status (including unveiling the women of the royal family).[4] The new Turkish state loomed even larger as a potentially damaging competitor. Soon after taking power, Mustafa Kemal (later known as Atatürk) launched a wide-ranging program of social reforms intended to bring about national renewal. His reforms included a new Latin alphabet, an overhauled civil law code, educational secularization, and fashion reforms—to eradicate both the veil worn by Turkish women and the fez worn by Turkish men.[5] Given the cultural links between Anatolia and the largely Turkic world of Central Asia, Bolshevik leaders saw this program—which started in 1924 and was under way alongside Bolshevik efforts to remake Central Asia—as a particular threat. Uzbeks and other Soviet Muslims might draw inspiration from Atatürk; if that happened, the USSR risked losing the revolutionary initiative. The example (and potential threat) of Turkish unveiling thus helped drive the Soviet women's liberation campaign onward, farther and faster than might otherwise have been the case, lest the Bolsheviks' efforts appear, to both domestic and international audiences, to lag behind those of their bourgeois counterparts. International concerns consequently represented both an opportunity and a threat. Bolshevik analysts closely monitored developments abroad and measured their words carefully when they described such competing reform models in print.[6]

In working out what it meant to build a "Soviet" system in the foreign cultural and social world of Central Asia, party activists accordingly faced the dual constraints of the Bolsheviks' tenuous position (and thus the need to find

4. Leon B. Poullada, *Reform and Rebellion in Afghanistan, 1919–1929* (Ithaca, 1973), 66–91. (Women's issues, including the unveiling of Amanullah's wife, Soraya, are discussed on pp. 82–86.)

5. Jacob M. Landau, *Atatürk and the Modernization of Turkey* (Boulder, 1984); and A. L. Macfie, *Atatürk* (London, 1994), 136–48.

6. On the monitoring, see RGASPI, d. 776, l. 152–1520b, and d. 1685, l. 18. For discussions of Amanullah Khan and Afghanistan, see RGASPI, d. 1618, ll. 10–13; ÖzRMDA, f. 94, op. 1, d. 200, ll. 26–31; Evgenii Shuan, "Litso afganskoi zhenshchiny," *PV*, 17 Oct. 1928; and Smirnov, *Chadra*, 42–54. On Atatürk and Turkey, see RGASPI, d. 1212, l. 4; and ÖzRMDA, f. 837, op. 3, d. 150, l. 137; as well as "Novaia turtsiia," *PV*, 17 Oct. 1928; Iranduet, "Sushchnost' Kemalizma," *Za partiiu*, no. 2 (1927), 62–69; M. Krym-Ogly, "Shariat i novye zakony Turtsii o brake," *Antireligioznik*, no. 2 (1928), 27–32; and M. Kobetskii, "Novyi brachnyi zakon v Turetskoi respublike," *Kommunistka*, no. 5 (1927), 68–73. While Afghanistan and Turkey were uppermost in the minds of party leaders, unveiling efforts were also under way elsewhere in the Muslim world. See Baron, "Unveiling in Early Twentieth-Century Egypt."

allies) and Soviet policy's international implications (and thus the need to carry out dramatic reforms). Thus they needed both to enlist allies in the East (to ensure the Revolution's survival) yet simultaneously to remake and civilize those same allies (to prove their own credentials as Europeans and as modern, revolutionary socialists). It was a difficult situation. Central Asia had few large cities, virtually no indigenous industrial proletariat, and a wide religio-cultural and linguistic gulf that divided most Soviet officials from the local populace. Hence policies that made sense in classical Marxist terms—or at least in the terms Marxism had been filtered into and adapted to the peasant heartland of central Russia—did not easily apply. Neither theory nor experience offered much direct guidance, and the party's mission had to be reformulated and made appropriate for Central Asia (and thereby for the wider colonized world). It was not at all clear that the party should start with an attack on women's veiling and seclusion. The meanings of "Soviet power" in Muslim Central Asia were a work in progress, as party officials cast about and explored a variety of alternatives. It took almost ten years for them to decide to focus party policy on everyday life and culture, in particular on remaking the texture of Uzbek family life and gender relations. Many other possibilities were considered first and, for various reasons, abandoned and replaced.

Recasting Revolution for the East: The Emergence of Hujum as Party Policy

Party leaders in Tashkent devoted much of their attention immediately after 1917 to security issues (combating the Whites and thereafter the qörboshi). By 1923 or so, however, as part of the wider rebuilding process under way after the Civil War, they started to consider how to transform and Bolshevize Central Asia. Part of their answer was to build an infrastructure of administrative, military, educational, public health, and social welfare outposts to serve the local population. Given the enormous expense and logistical problems of doing so, though, this effort remained a long-term goal. Other apparently logical options were never seriously considered: reducing cotton production in favor of foodstuffs and grain crops, for instance, could have been portrayed as liberation from tsarist colonial policy, especially in light of the recent famines. Yet it also would have had serious consequences for the overall Soviet economy, hindering the emergence of an integrated, all-Union economic system based on a regional (and still colonial) division of labor. Such a step also carried political risks: by necessitating higher levels of cotton imports, it would create a potentially dangerous economic dependency on the hostile capitalist world.

Party leaders instead focused their efforts elsewhere. In part they derived their Central Asian policy from other national priorities, such as the broad effort to pursue a Leninist nationalities policy of indigenization, or korenizatsiia.

Since this policy required trained local cadres, many new educational programs were begun. Even alphabet reform helped: in late 1926 Arabic script
started to disappear from official usage and be slowly replaced by "modern,"
"international" Latin alphabets that were customized for the various Central
Asian nations. These alphabets, taught in Soviet basic literacy schools (*lik-
bezy*), helped bolster the new Soviet nations by producing distinct written languages (Uzbek, Kazakh, Turkmen) instead of the single, shared literary language of Chaghatai, which previously had united most of the region. This
script differentiation continued through later orthographic reforms (from
Latin to Cyrillic) in the late 1930s and 1940s. Equally important, these new
alphabets also cut off newly literate Soviet citizens in Central Asia from all preexisting literature—literature that was, not coincidentally, weighted heavily
toward religious writing and commentary—in favor of a blank slate, which
could be filled in by Soviet-trained authors.[7]

Another national priority for party officials, in the non-Russian periphery
no less than in the Russian heartland, was the hard-fought effort to combat
religion and religious "prejudice." Marx, after all, had famously denounced
religious belief as "the opium of the people." From a materialist, socialist
perspective, the institutional church—whether Orthodox or Lutheran, Muslim or Jewish, Buddhist or Zoroastrian—was a product of a society's economic base, and served principally to defend existing structures of social
domination and class exploitation. The religious faith of individuals, however sincere, was from this perspective a tragically misguided form of false
consciousness that served only to mask a baldly exploitative material reality.
Local activists and party leaders alike tried after 1917 to persuade suspicious
peasants, workers, and soldiers that God did not exist; that their church (or
synagogue or mosque) had misled them; and that priests, rabbis, and mullahs were hypocrites, seeking only their own wealth and class power. Only
the Soviet creed of progress and its vision of secular, socialist modernity,
they maintained, could speak with certainty; only it could offer a scientific,
objective view of human society and thus of the purpose, direction, and
meaning of human life.

This view of organized religion led the party to organize antireligious and
atheist campaigns across the Soviet Union. This story is familiar, at least in

7. On this reform, see GARF, especially f. 7543, and f. 1235, op. 124 and 125; RGASPI, dd.
1148 and 1607; and ÖzRMDA, f. 95, op. 5, dd. 591–602; also J. Axunbabajif, "Öktabir alifbesi
jolidaghi opportunizmgha bar ham berilsin," *Jangi jol*, no. 3–4 (1932), 6–7; and N. Tiuriakulov,
"K voprosu o latinizatsii tiurkskikh alfavitov," *Novyi Vostok*, no. 10–11 (1926), 219–22. Orthographic reforms modified the first Latin alphabet in 1935—dropping four vowels, removing the
principle of vowel harmony from written Uzbek and splitting it from other Turkic languages—and
then replaced it with Cyrillic in 1940. Counting the two prior Arabic scripts, the shift in post-
Soviet Uzbekistan to a (different) Latin alphabet thus represents the sixth alphabet system in
eighty years.

Russia proper: the details of the Bolshevik encounter with Orthodox Christianity have been well told by many scholars.[8] Local party activists and soldiers confiscated the church valuables they could carry (icons, serving platters, jewelry); the state followed, taking much of what was left (land, bank accounts, buildings). Members of the Orthodox Church hierarchy were alternately harassed and subjected to strict state oversight and control. Atheist organizations such as the League of the Militant Godless proselytized among peasants and workers alike. Civil law codes, which under the tsars had been religiously inflected (specific rules, for example, varied with the religious affiliation of a tsarist subject), were standardized and removed from church jurisdiction: the state asserted full control over the particulars of marriage, divorce, and inheritance.

Although the details are less well known, similar efforts were launched in other parts of the Soviet Union—such as, from the early 1920s, Central Asia and Uzbekistan.[9] Atheist societies here attacked the alleged hypocrisy and rigid dogma of Islam. Magazines and newspapers provided antireligious activists with primers on the fine points of Qur'anic doctrine and sought to highlight what they saw as superstitious, oppressive aspects of local custom. Sometimes they used evangelical techniques, relying on circuit riders, movie screens, radio broadcasts, and scientific demonstrations. Such work was intentionally confrontational, often setting out to ridicule those who held a strong religious faith. Atheist activists challenged local clerics to produce rain on command, for example, or to show clear, immediate evidence of God's displeasure in the face of blasphemous shouts. As in Russia, the Central Asian campaign included a hardheaded assault on the human resources, institutional frameworks, and financial foundations of organized religion. This effort included asserting control over the Muslim clerical hierarchy, closing most religious schools, restricting opportunities for pilgrimage to Mecca, and confiscating the sizable assets held by religious endowments (*waqf*). Many mosques were shut down; some were turned into Soviet clubs, offices, even—in a step particularly galling to believers—antireligious centers.[10]

But in Uzbekistan as in Russia, such campaigns elicited responses that for the most part disappointed party leaders and antireligious activists.[11] Most

8. William B. Husband, "*Godless Communists*": *Atheism and Society in Soviet Russia, 1917–1932* (De Kalb, Ill., 2000); Peris, *Storming the Heavens;* and Glennys Young, *Power and the Sacred in Revolutionary Russia: Religious Activists in the Village* (University Park, Pa., 1997).

9. Shoshana Keller, *To Moscow, Not Mecca: The Soviet Campaign against Islam in Central Asia, 1917–1941* (Westport, Conn., 2001); and on the later period Yaacov Ro'i, *Islam in the Soviet Union: From the Second World War to Gorbachev* (New York, 2000).

10. For an example, see Z. A. Astapovich et al., eds., *Velikii Oktiabr' i raskreposhchenie zhenshchin Srednei Azii i Kazakhstana (1917–1936 gg.)* (Moscow, 1971), 383.

11. Husband, "*Godless Communists,*" 130–58, and his "Soviet Atheism and Russian Orthodox Strategies of Resistance, 1917–1932," *Journal of Modern History* 70 (1998): 74–107; also Young, *Power and the Sacred*, 147–91.

Uzbeks refused to participate. Many simply ignored the party's efforts. If pressed to respond, they tended to disagree with or even attack those who criticized or denigrated Islam. For Soviet workers, such efforts did pay one kind of dividend: they produced a heroic narrative of Bolshevik struggle, and thereby helped define party self-identity. They also produced a dramatic martyrdom for a few unfortunate activists, such as the writer and social reformer Hamza Hakimzoda Niyoziy—the "singer of the Revolution"—who was killed by a mob in 1929.[12] In the end, though, this frontal assault did not cause Islam to crumble, partly because of its relatively decentralized structure. Islam took many and complex forms in Central Asia, and there was no single institution or hierarchy (like that headed by the Orthodox patriarch or Holy Synod) that alone commanded obedience. The various Sufi orders acted independently, with only an indirect relation to such institutional figures as the mufti. Hence policies that focused on formal institutions had a limited effect, and party leaders had to seek other options.

They invested high hopes in a major campaign in 1925–26 that aimed to redistribute land and water rights from allegedly wealthy bois (and clerics) to poor peasants and hired farmhands. This campaign—arguably the most Marxist attempt that was made to translate Soviet power into Central Asia— proceeded with great fanfare. It was modeled on the land reforms carried out in Russia during and after 1917 (which amounted, in practical terms, to formalizing the already accomplished peasant seizures of Russian landed estates). A similar redistribution in Central Asia, it was hoped, would create a loyal indigenous constituency of new landowners willing to support Soviet power. This outcome, in turn, would aid the party's other efforts, such as indigenization and the assault on Islam. The land and water reform did bring changes to the Uzbek countryside, but the task was made easier by the immense acreage abandoned by hundreds of thousands of people who fled across the Afghan border.[13] Perhaps because actual expropriation and physical transfer were not always involved, this reform thus yielded fewer dramatic shake-ups of the local social order than originally envisioned—and fewer beneficiaries who emerged with new land and therefore an undying gratitude to Soviet power.

Redistribution, further, did not always proceed according to plan. Soviet personnel were so few that they often could not supervise land transfers; local administrators were not reliably under Bolshevik control; and land registers, where they existed, could not be trusted to show the actual owners once Uzbek

12. Keller, To Moscow, Not Mecca, 247–55. On Hamza's death, see p. 186.

13. According to Nazif Shahrani, roughly a million people left Turkestan and Bukhoro in the early 1920s, mostly for Afghanistan ("Pining for Bukhara in Afghanistan: Poetics and Politics of Exilic Identity and Emotions," in Türkistan'da Yenilik Hareketleri ve Ihtilaller: 1900–1924, ed. Timur Kocaoglu [Haarlem, Netherlands, 2001], 371). Michael Rywkin calculates that fully one-quarter of the arable land in Uzbekistan and two-thirds in Tajikistan were abandoned (Moscow's Muslim Challenge, 42).

villagers heard of Soviet plans. Most crucially, rural Central Asians did not adopt the key categories of class identity and concepts of class warfare ("poor" peasants struggling against rich "exploiters") as readily as Bolshevik workers had hoped and expected. Uzbeks of nearly all degrees of affluence tended to share a common distrust of reforms propounded by foreign, urban, atheist Bolsheviks. This rural alienation paralleled the party's experience in post-1917 Russia, but if anything, it was stronger in Central Asia, where religious, cultural, and linguistic factors only deepened suspicion of the party's motives and goals.[14]

Only after each of these policies had been launched but fallen short of expectations did party leaders in Tashkent start to consider women's liberation seriously. Of course, the turn to gender as an idiom for liberation did not arise out of thin air, nor was it simply a random choice among various policy alternatives. Issues of women's status had long served as a powerful metaphor for the state of Central Asian society. Women's daily life was thought to express a deeper essence, to embody a local culture and spirit. Hence by challenging local ideas of femininity (and thus, at least by implication, masculinity), one could effectively alter the bases of social order. The emphasis on women's emancipation further fitted the party well on ideological grounds: among the first Soviet decrees in 1917 had been one granting full civil equality to women. No less an authority than Friedrich Engels could be mobilized to justify the stress on sexual oppression as an analogue to class oppression, especially in preindustrial societies.[15] Finally, given the religious aspects of local patriarchy, women's liberation could be seen as a way to jump-start the faltering antireligious campaign.

But still, this decision was neither inevitable nor self-evident. Contrary to Soviet writers' argument that women's liberation had always been at the core of regional policy, this supposedly fundamental approach had waited in the wings for nearly a decade. The decision to make it a centerpiece of the Bolsheviks' civilizing mission emerged piecemeal, through a step-by-step process of experimentation, feedback, and analysis. This process culminated in 1926 when a sufficient number of party leaders came to agree on two propositions: that in Central Asia all other options had failed, and that gender relations were crucial to the area's wider social order. At this point a surrogate proletariat could be identified and the hujum could begin. But many people both inside and outside the party saw the women's liberation campaign as no more than

14. On this land and water reform, see RGASPI, dd. 773, 802, and 1222; the films *Bakht Kuyashi* (1926) and *Kiyatva* (1937); or S. Liubimova, "Po Srednei Azii," *Kommunistka*, no. 4 (1926): 56–59; A. Kh., "Po kishlakam Zerafshana," *PV*, 7 Jan. 1927; and Joshua Kunitz, *Dawn over Samarkand: The Rebirth of Central Asia* (New York, 1935), 169–214.

15. From Frederick Engels, *Origin of the Family, Private Property, and the State* (New York, 1972), 129, originally written in 1884: "The first class opposition that appears in history coincides with the development of the antagonism between man and woman in monogamous marriage, and the first class oppression coincides with that of the female sex by the male."

the successor to the land and water reform, as the latest in a so far unsuccessful series of attempts to remake Central Asian society and culture.[16]

The decision to substitute gender for class at the heart of Central Asia's revolution rested on a specific analysis of the social position of Muslim women. Despite obvious differences among them (of age and wealth, for instance), Muslim women were, in this view, fundamentally united by a common experience: they were all victims of the oppressive structures of patriarchal Islamic society. Hence Bolshevik analysts contended that they represented an enormous latent revolutionary ally, one merely awaiting the requisite Leninist injection of political consciousness. Shifts in women's status would then have a ripple effect, creating social change from the ground up and leading ultimately to a thoroughgoing transformation of local culture and politics. Since female subordination was a basic part of the Muslim social order, for instance, and since this subordination was justified by Islamic doctrine, ending it would also reduce or eliminate the power of religious clerics—something the antireligious campaigns had never managed to do. It would also make millions of Muslim women into passionately loyal Soviet boosters, some of whom could then be trained to fill government and party posts and thereby provide an indigenous face for Soviet power, as required by the policy of korenizatsiia. It would thus at a stroke solve some of the party's most pressing problems in Central Asia. Hence the Zhenotdel was joined in its efforts by the full range of Soviet and party organizations: the Young Pioneers, Komsomol, trade unions, local governments, atheist clubs, peasant unions, and the Red Army, among others.

Once the focus of Soviet work had been shifted to women's liberation, it still remained to define precisely what that liberation meant. Ultimately, by late 1926, regional party leaders decided (at least in Uzbekistan and a few other places) to equate the idea with eliminating the veil. But like the decision to focus on women's issues in general, that equation was not inevitable: it too resulted from debate and from experience—from trial and error among the forms of "women's work" already under way in southern Central Asia. The women's campaign elsewhere—in Turkmenistan, Kazakhstan, and Kyrgyzstan, not to mention the wider Soviet East—concentrated on other issues altogether. These issues ranged from foot-binding among Chinese communities in Siberia to the prevention of blood feuds and bride abductions, as well as the provision of heavy winter coats for mountain women in the Caucasus (where Soviet power thus focused on covering rather than uncovering local women).[17] Clearly the party was willing to consider a range of particular methods to reach the ostensibly universal goal of women's liberation.

In Uzbekistan specifically, Zhenotdel and party workers had tried a wide range of approaches to improve the position of Muslim women before 1926,

16. PDA, op. 2, d. 1410, l. 118; and RGASPI, d. 769, l. 8.
17. On these other campaigns see Halle, *Women in the Soviet East*, 177–78; ÖzRMDA, f. 86, op. 1, d. 6570, l. 19; and GARF, f. 6983, op. 1, d. 18, l. 5, and d. 80, l. 10.

but initially the idea of a massive, forcible attack on the paranji hardly entered their thinking. After the establishment of a Central Asian Zhenotdel in 1919, most early forms of women's work had little to do with the veil. They included the construction of women's clubs, ABC schools to fight illiteracy, Red Corners, Red Boats, Red Yurts, Red Teahouses, and mountaineer women's Red Huts. Party and state publishers issued books, magazines, and brochures—complemented by a stream of documentary and feature films—purporting to show the meaning and power of Soviet-style liberation. Women's artels or cooperatives appeared, along with special stores (*lavki*) and markets open only to women. New laws banned polygyny, underage marriage, and the practice of bride-price. Meetings of Eastern and Muslim women were convened, and groups of these women occasionally traveled to Moscow. In June 1921 one such delegation of seventy-eight women met Lenin in person.[18]

Together all of these forms of women's work created within Zhenotdel and party circles the framework for a narrative of liberation, a story in which heroic party activists struggled against immense odds to raise the consciousness of oppressed, primitive Muslim women.[19] An article in 1922 implored the Russian-speaking readership of *Turkestanskaia Pravda*, "European women, come to the assistance of your dark sisters!"[20] Despite the many problems that hindered the Zhenotdel's early efforts—ranging from budget and staff constraints to communications problems and language gaps to violence—these efforts were portrayed as the thin edge of a wedge that ultimately would lead to the inevitable emancipation and transformation of the East. "The ice is breaking," one Zhenotdel report concluded in 1924:

> [Our] work among women in Turkestan is starting to show its influence [both here] and in the neighboring republics of Bukhoro and Khorazm, where the conditions of women's slavery are particularly difficult, [where] the influence of the Muslim clergy knows no bounds. Work is starting there, where until recently they did not want to hear the speeches of women at all-party meetings, where Zhenotdel workers were arrested on the street for a single conversation with a man, where European women working for the Zhenotdel were exposed to the danger of being poisoned or killed, where they themselves had to wear the chadra in order to penetrate the Muslim family.[21]

This kind of heroic narrative ultimately helped both to justify the analysis of Muslim women as subject to unparalleled oppression by patriarchal Central

---

18. A. Rozanova, "Priezd zhenschin narodov Vostoka v Moskvu," *Kommunistka*, no. 14–15 (1921), 36–37.

19. For examples, see RGASPI, dd. 427–431; T. Mubashira, *Sovet Sharqi khotin-qizlarini ozod qilish tarikhidan* (Tashkent, 1978); and A. Chernysheva, *Chto dala zhenshchine Vostoka Oktiabr'skaia revoliutsiia* (Tashkent, 1926).

20. Quoted in Astapovich, *Velikii Oktiabr'*, 332.

21. PDA, f. 60, op. 1, d. 4868, ll. 25–26.

Asian society and to support the turn to gender, through the hujum, as an appropriate idiom for Soviet liberation.

Yet note that in this story of heroic emancipation, unveiling per se remained, at best, a minor, supporting theme. Veils were not the principal focus of Zhenotdel activists—indeed, in the report just quoted, Soviet women's activists sometimes donned the veil to go about their work.[22] Such curious images raised the specter of activists going native, and thus, from the perspective of Moscow, risking the loss of their mantle of civilization and modernity. But even more, they show the kinds of complicated cultural mixing that took place in many imperial settings around the world.[23] In Soviet Turkestan, both sides changed and adapted: Uzbeks acquired a national identity, but Russian women's activists found themselves paradoxically bringing liberation while wearing a prime marker of female subjugation. In later accounts, such patterns of dress were usually portrayed as a clever ruse, a tactical step designed to fool Muslim men and gain access to Muslim women; but before 1926 it was less clear that this approach was either tactical or temporary.

Before 1926, too, very few indigenous women cast off their paranji and chachvon as a way to show personal liberation. Although some cases were reported in party annals, they usually involved only a few women acting individually—not in large groups—and almost always at demonstrations or gatherings convened at great distances from their homes. Most commonly, public unveiling during this period was a gesture by handfuls of Central Asian Muslim women brought hundreds of miles to Moscow to attend party congresses, or gatherings of the Communist International. These women, cut off from friends and family, in the midst of a world they may not have understood (many spoke little or no Russian), sometimes could be induced to toss off their veils as a dramatic statement to the assembled, mostly Slavic delegates, who would applaud loudly and then go back to other business. These women usually reveiled for the trip home, and there are few signs that they were criticized for doing so.[24]

---

22. An image of Russian women activists in indigenous (Kyrgyz) dress is at Astapovich, *Velikii Oktiabr'*, 165. The Anahita Gallery, Santa Fe, N.M., has a similar photograph of Russian men in Bukhoran dress.

23. For example, John L. and Jean Comaroff, *Of Revelation and Revolution: The Dialectics of Modernity on a South African Frontier* (Chicago, 1997), 218–73.

24. Such unveilings—of Azeri as well as Central Asian women—are at N. Sardjeva, "Buyuk jasoratning munosib vorislari bõlaylik," *Partiya turmush,* no. 6 (1987), 81. Among the first reported were in 1919, described by Laziz Aziz-Zoda, "Oyposhsha," *Gulistan,* no. 4 (1967), 6, and in 1921 at Özbekiston respublikasi kinofotofonohujjatlar markaziy davlat arkhivi (hereafter ÖzRKFFHMDA), 2410; Pal'vanova, *Docheri sovetskogo Vostoka,* 10; and Carol Eubanks Hayden, "Feminism and Bolshevism: The *Zhenotdel* and the Politics of Women's Emancipation in Russia, 1917–1930" (Ph.D. diss., University of California, Berkeley, 1979), 204–8. After 1923 these scattered reports become more frequent. An American visitor, Anna Louise Strong, alleged that only ten Uzbek women had unveiled by 1924 (*Red Star in Samarkand* [New York, 1929], 261).

So the act of unveiling remained uncommon, even marginal, before 1926. It was constructed as a symbolic act mostly for external consumption, as a signifier to foreign audiences, especially in Russia, that the Eastern woman—and thereby the East—was being transformed. Within Central Asia itself, by contrast, one finds only scattered positive references to unveilings, usually in Moscow or other distant cities.[25] Occasionally local Bolsheviks denounced the Central Asian paranji or the Azeri chadra as a prison, one that represented a health hazard and kept women economically enslaved and dependent, but such references generally were made only in passing. The slogan "Down with the paranji!" was proposed in Tashkent as early as 1924, for example, but does not appear to have elicited much enthusiasm at the grassroots level, and outbursts against the veil were rare even within the Zhenotdel.[26] In sum, the veil's supposed social dangers and harmful effects were at best a secondary matter before 1926.

Indeed, party policy before 1926 was fairly clear that while unveiling could serve a symbolic purpose in particular cases, it should not be a central focus of Zhenotdel attention. In fact, the reverse was more the case—many Bolsheviks in positions of authority argued vocally *against* unveiling, contending that it was premature, or worse, a distraction that would only harm party interests.[27] At the First Congress of the Peoples of the East, held at Baku in 1920, for example, the delegate Khaver Shabanova-Karaeva declared,

> The women of the East are not fighting merely for the right to walk in the street without wearing the chador, as many people suppose. For the women of the East, with their high moral ideals, the question of the chador, it can be said, comes last in priority. If the women, who form half of every community, are set up against the men and do not enjoy the same rights, obviously it is impossible for society to progress; the backwardness of Eastern societies is irrefutable proof of this.[28]

In the same vein, the Red Army leader Mikhail Frunze in May 1920 told the 118 delegates at the First Congress of Turkestani Women—including many Uzbek and Tajik women, all of whom attended while wearing their veils—that in the eyes of Soviet authorities their paranjis did not imply anything negative about them or their political outlook. In fact, during the Civil War these veils even served a military purpose. The delegates could help liberate Turkestan, he declared, adding that "under the paranji beats an honorable heart, that under

25. RGASPI, d. 421, l. 6; d. 427, ll. 68–69; d. 435, l. 165; d. 442, ll. 63 and 67; and d. 779, ll. 1 and 10.

26. On the slogan in 1924, see Halle, *Women in the Soviet East,* 171. For early arguments against the veil, see RGASPI, d. 427, l. 9; d. 428, l. 64; and d. 429, ll. 43–47.

27. In addition to the specific cases cited below, see RGASPI, d. 427, ll. 72–73, and d. 443, l. 140.

28. John Riddell, ed., *To See the Dawn: Baku, 1920—First Congress of the Peoples of the East* (New York, 1993), 204–5.

the paranji [one] may faithfully serve the Revolution, and the paranji sometimes hides a courageous scout for the Red Army."[29] Soon thereafter, one of
the seventy-eight Muslim women who met Lenin in Moscow in 1921 declared
that "even though we still wear the veil, we are nonetheless free."[30] In 1923
party leaders in Central Asia had cracked down on those who called for unveiling Uzbek women as guilty of a "Left deviation," and notably, as late as
August 1925—only slightly more than a year before the hujum started—the
main speaker at an all-Uzbek Zhenotdel meeting portrayed unveiling as positively un-Bolshevik, arguing that ensuring the "economic and material security
of women is the fundamental path for the solution of the 'woman question,'
really [this matter] should for the most part be settled through economic measures." A Bolshevik, moreover, had to "oppose the jadids' understanding of
women's liberation (liberation by throwing off the paranji and appearing in
public places) and [instead] promote the complete political and economic independence of women."[31] In the light of what followed, this argument is nothing short of remarkable. Before 1926 the very idea of unveiling Uzbek women
appeared to many Bolsheviks a jadidist preoccupation, a leftist deviation, and
a notion contrary to the party's true interests in economic liberation. Attention
devoted to the veil only distracted Bolsheviks from their true calling.

Multiple voices therefore existed within the party with regard both to the
importance of the veil and to what should be done about it. Yet just as it was
not an accident that women's liberation became a party priority when other
policies proved disappointing, it was not a random outcome for the Zhenotdel
to focus on the veil when other forms of women's work made little headway.
The veil had long served in European eyes as a fundamental trope of the East,
one that explained the region and embodied its people. This view, which Bolsheviks shared with their tsarist predecessors and West European travelers,
helped shape the policy alternatives on which the party could draw as it considered how best to liberate Muslim women. The veil was such a dramatic
symbol of the primitive East that any attempt to overturn it would have great
international resonance: it certainly established a stark visual contrast between
dark, gloomy seclusion and the bright light and progress of a Soviet future. Finally, the fact that Atatürk in Turkey and Amanullah Khan in Afghanistan had
launched unveiling campaigns also pushed Bolshevik activists onward, lest
such a dramatic statement of liberation first be made by a bourgeois rather
than communist state. Party discussions in 1926 include specific references to
the Turkish and Afghan examples, and Soviet press discussions of Atatürk and
Amanullah became steadily more critical as their implied competition became

29. His words were paraphrased by Pal'vanova, *Docheri sovetskogo Vostoka*, 46. Frantz
Fanon likewise observed that Algerian women could conceal weapons under their veils to fight
French colonial authorities (*Studies in a Dying Colonialism* [New York, 1965], 61–62).
30. Rozanova, "Priezd," 36.
31. RGASPI, d. 445, l. 37. For the 1923 crackdown, see d. 1212, l. 122.

greater.[32] When other efforts to remake Central Asia through its women faltered, then, the paranji and chachvon remained as logical alternatives on which to focus party work.

The hujum's origins were thus multipolar, with inputs from local Communists and jadids; from Zhenotdel workers at the grassroots and regional level; from high-ranking party leaders and women's activists in Moscow, Tashkent, and Baku; and even from the pressures of international politics and the Comintern. The actual mechanics of the decision to launch a hujum against female veiling and seclusion have been discussed by Massell and Soviet scholars, so I will address them only briefly here.[33] The forceful slogan "TO THE ATTACK!" ("*K NASTUPLENIIU!*") emerged by June 1926, at a meeting of Central Asian women's workers, and by autumn had come to be defined in Uzbekistan as an attack against female veiling and seclusion. The proximate impetus for this campaign did not come from below—from local Zhenotdel or party workers— but from high in the Bolshevik hierarchy, namely the leaders of the Sredazbiuro and Kavkazbiuro, the party's chief regional supervisory bodies for Central Asia and the Caucasus. From its headquarters in Tashkent, and with the support of superiors in Moscow, the Sredazbiuro, in a series of circular letters and speeches to closed party gatherings between September and December 1926, proposed that the party devote itself completely to an assault against the "byt oppression" of Central Asian women. Special commissions were created, staffed by some of the most prominent Bolsheviks in Central Asia; they were given several months to lay the groundwork for a major women's liberation campaign. All Soviet and party organizations were directed to help. The public component of this campaign was to begin on the upcoming holiday of International Women's Day, 8 March 1927.[34] Party optimists dared to hope that they

32. On the perceived pressure from Turkey and Afghanistan, see RGASPI, d. 776, l. 152–1520b, and d. 808, l. 4–40b; or Serafima Liubimova, "Bor'ba na ideologicheskom fronte," *Kommunistka*, no. 4 (1926), 74–75. To show the more critical treatment of Atatürk, in particular, compare the tone of these works with Kasparova, *Zhenshchina Vostoka*, 83.

33. Massell, *Surrogate Proletariat*, 226–28, 233–34, and 239–44. For more or less canonical expressions of the Soviet view, see Shukurova, *Sotsializm i zhenshchina Uzbekistana*, 175–200; Aminova, *Oktiabr' i reshenie zhenskogo voprosa*; Pal'vanova, *Emansipatsiia musul'manki*, 163–201; and Alimova, *Zhenskii vopros v Srednei Azii*, 19–32.

34. On these commissions, Sredazbiuro directives, and the appearance of the veil in priority lists, see PDA, op. 2, d. 1374, ll. 9–10; d. 1398, ll. 201–2; and op. 3, d. 1598, ll. 21–22; and RGASPI, d. 771, ll. 75 and 77, and d. 773, l. 62. On prominent participants, see PDA, op. 2, d. 1374, ll. 9–10. The public starting point of the hujum was a speech in September 1926 by the Sredazbiuro's director, Isaak Abramovich Zelenskii, that announced the campaign to a provincial meeting of women's workers. It was immediately published under his name as *Za raskreposhche-nie zhenshchiny* (Tashkent, 1926). Similar steps were under way in Baku, where the Kavkazbiuro organized a parallel unveiling campaign among Azeri women: see Jörg Baberowski, "Stalinismus als imperiales Phänomen: Die islamischen Regionen der Sowjetunion, 1920–1941," in *Stalinismus: Neue Forschungen und Konzepte*, ed. Stefan Plaggenborg, 113–50 (Berlin, 1998). Both regions kept in contact about the campaign, sending progress reports and discussion transcripts back and forth; see, for example, a collection of Azeri materials at RGASPI, d. 1696.

would complete the liberation of Central Asian women very quickly, in no more than six months—a schedule that would permit them to celebrate success by October 1927, on the tenth anniversary of the Bolshevik Revolution.[35]

To be sure, these initial announcements were on one level cautious, since the specific contents of the attack varied by republic, social position, and local setting. Each republic received its own national form of the hujum. In Turkmenistan and Kyrgyzstan the campaign focused on eradicating qalin, polygyny, underage marriage, and illiteracy. In Uzbekistan and Azerbaijan, by contrast—the two republics most prominent in the eyes of party leaders, and which also came to define the hujum for international audiences—the focus fell squarely on the abolition of female seclusion and veiling.[36] Initially, too, only Communists and their immediate families were required to participate. Only after this political vanguard had demonstrated by personal example the transformation of their own family lives would the campaign be broadened, in concentric circles, to others thought most likely to participate: trade union members, factory workers, and schoolteachers.[37] Finally, the hujum did not at first apply everywhere. The Sredazbiuro announced that only three areas in Uzbekistan (Tashkent, Farghona, and Samarqand) were ready to take part initially—and even there, only in the cities and in those villages and small towns that had a viable party presence. Other provinces, such as Zerafshon, were said to be nearly ready to join the campaign, but local land and water reforms had to be finished first. And in still other provinces, such as Surkhondaryo, Qashqadaryo, and Khorazm, party leaders in Tashkent suggested no more than merely asking the sparse local party organizations whether the time would soon be right for such a campaign.[38]

Despite these qualifications, important themes had emerged by late 1926. The use of personal example by a supposed vanguard; the tensions and contradictions between class identities and one's outlook on questions of gender relations and family life; and the decision to use the criminal courts to combat perceived opposition—all continued into the 1930s and beyond.[39] The choice of assault as the preferred mode of women's work in Central Asia, too, required that new methods be adopted, stressing coercion over persuasion and emphasizing sudden, dramatic transformation over slow, steady change. Zhenotdel workers did not discontinue earlier forms of women's work: they continued to build women's clubs, to stock women's shops, and to draw Muslim women into basic literacy schools. But starting in late 1926, the issue of the veil, which only a year earlier had been denounced as a "jadidist distrac-

35. PDA, op, 3, d. 1560, l. 57; ÖzRMDA, f. 86, op. 1, d. 5134, l. 25; RGASPI, d. 1205, l. 40b, and d. 1242, ll. 31 and 1400b; and Serafima Liubimova, "Oktiabr' i truzhenitsa zarubezhnogo Vostoka," *Za partiiu*, no. 3 (1927), 77–80.
36. PDA, op. 3, d. 1598, ll. 21–22.
37. RGASPI, d. 769, ll. 5 and 7.
38. RGASPI, d. 773, l. 125; and PDA, op. 2, d. 1374, ll. 9–10.
39. RGASPI, d. 771, ll. 75, 77, and 97–106.

tion," started to be discussed as an urgent problem, one with important economic, public health, and demographic, not to mention political, implications. The veil appeared with increasing frequency on party and Zhenotdel priority lists, and by March 1927 this horsehair-and-cotton ensemble had come to sit squarely at the center of Soviet policy in Uzbekistan.[40]

Zhenotdel workers found their time and energy directed increasingly to the organization of public demonstrations, preferably on a grand scale. These gatherings of hundreds or thousands of Muslim women (and men, as observers) heard fiery speeches and inspirational reports about the meanings of Communist liberation. If all went well, the women in attendance then dramatically cast off their paranjis and chachvons en masse, sometimes into a central heap to be set on fire. By dint of repetition and prominence of place, such public unveilings became a currency of Bolshevik political discourse in Central Asia during and after 1927; large-scale party congresses, conferences, and meetings frequently included at least one such dramatic act of unveiling to open or close the proceedings.[41] (See Figures 12 and 13.) The Soviet narrative of liberation—telegraphed whenever possible to a wider, especially international, audience—came to depend crucially on this public, even theatrical act of individual emancipation. The act of unveiling was expected to correspond with (and perhaps also to bring about) a great leap upward in each woman's political level and a total transformation of her cultural outlook. Women's clothing, in short, served as a kind of "symbolic subversion" that was meant to overturn the old ways completely. (Similar struggles over other kinds of radical female dress and hair styles were under way around the world at this time, far outside the USSR.)[42]

The party's decision, contingent as it was, to focus on the veil in Central Asia had an array of fateful and largely unanticipated consequences. The leaders of the Sredazbiuro did not know in advance whether a mission of class liberation could function through a lexicon of gender transformation (although they certainly hoped that it could). The contradictions and tensions that re-

40. For priority lists, see RGASPI, d. 807, l. 5; and PDA, op. 2, d. 1397, ll. 1–15. For arguments against the veil in late 1926, see RGASPI, d. 427, l. 16; d. 429, ll. 43–47; and d. 774, ll. 62–66.

41. Two examples are RGASPI, d. 1238, l. 58, and d. 1248, l. 82. Two films dramatize unveilings at Rossiiskii gosudarstvennyi arkhiv kinofotodokumentov (hereafter RGAKFD), 3965-II and 13196.

42. The most sustained analysis of fashion—especially female fashion—as "symbolic communication" is by Diana Crane, *Fashion and Its Social Agendas: Class, Gender, and Identity in Clothing* (Chicago, 2000), especially 99–131 (the quoted phrases are from pp. 99 and 126). Crane discusses subversive fashion discourses in Western Europe and the United States. Also see Mary Louise Roberts, *Civilization without Sexes: Reconstructing Gender in Postwar France, 1917–1927* (Chicago, 1994), especially 63–87. In China women who bobbed their hair were killed in 1927 on the pretext that their short hair marked them as Communist radicals. See Karl Gerth, "Nationalizing Consumption, Consuming Nationalism: The National Products Movement in China, 1905–1937" (Ph.D. diss., Harvard University, 2000), 359.

Figure 12. Burning veils at a Soviet meeting, 1927. (Courtesy ÖzRKFFHMDA.)

sulted from this choice to launch a hujum against female seclusion in Uzbek-istan—and ultimately to make this hujum virtually synonymous with Soviet policy in Central Asia—are complex. In the end, this choice shaped the en-counter between Soviet power and Uzbek society in long-lasting ways, and its influence is still felt today.

Flames for the Future: Uzbek Society and the Hujum

What followed the large-scale demonstrations on International Women's Day (8 March) in 1927, with the spectacle of thousands of women casting off and burning their veils? How did Uzbek society respond? Given the political im-portance attached to the hujum, confidential Soviet government and party re-ports sought from the very beginning to answer that question in detail. These sources have their own agendas, biases, and omissions. They certainly offer an unparalleled view of how Soviet officials perceived Uzbek society, but it can be harder to discern individual Uzbeks' motivations. If a particular person op-

Figure 13. Uzbek woman unveiling, 1927. (Courtesy RGAKFD.)

posed the hujum, for example, was that opposition the result of neighborhood or family pressure, or of sincere anger at the Soviet state (because it had attacked Islam, seized local lands, or for some other reason)? If a Muslim woman did not *say* that her husband or father oppressed her, what does this silence show? Obviously it does not prove that she was able to speak her mind or act of her own free will: perhaps she had been frightened into silence by that very man; or perhaps the documents are incomplete. On the other hand, if she *is* recorded as saying that she was a victim of patriarchy and therefore supported the hujum, can that assertion be accepted at face value? Local Communists could have forced her to say so, or she could have been trying to gain alimony or other benefits from the state—or a too-eager Soviet author may simply have put words in her mouth.

Such questions frequently have no satisfying answers. One is often left to impute individual motives, partly by observing how groups of people acted and partly by considering how widely disparate sources record the same or similar events. Many opinions were expressed and actions carried out in ways that correlated with a particular setting—a man might permit (or compel) his wife to unveil at a Soviet meeting, for instance, but reverse course once they returned home, denouncing the hujum and allowing (or forcing) her to reveil. Other declarations fit a particular source location: passionate avowals of support, for example, are rife in local reports sent upward to party superiors. One strategy is to look for cracks, for dissonances: to find places where people asserted opinions that were situationally unpopular, even dangerous, or to locate sources that record events or utterances that were contrary to the institutional interests and political perspectives of their authors. These records are more likely to be candid and accurate; they are also more likely to reflect strongly held views—if one comes across a man far from any Soviet outpost, for instance, who faces down his neighbors and insists that women should unveil, or likewise finds a woman who stands up at a party congress and denounces the hujum.

While reading any of these sources on Uzbek women, outside observers must be doubly sensitive. Central Asian society *was* generally patriarchal, and it can be dangerous (if not morally suspect) to valorize the mistreatment of women as simple resistance to a colonial or Stalinist state—by reading an unproblematically heroic content into forcing a woman to stay veiled, for example, or preventing her from seeing a doctor or learning to read, or attacking, raping, or murdering her if she transgressed local norms.[43] Fashion theorists have held that subversive dress (such as, in this case, an unveiled face) can be a kind of "nonverbal resistance"—here directed against local patriarchy, not the state.[44] Yet it is equally dangerous simply to impose foreign notions of liberation, ignoring their associations in the Central Asian context with the structures, ideals, and personnel of a historically colonial political order. There is, first, an obvious risk of ethnocentricity: of assuming that European ideas of gender equality are (or should be) a universal goal or a standard measure of social and cultural progress. Far better to admit that such concepts as freedom have meanings that depend at least partly on perspective and context, and to be cautious about cultural imposition. Some Uzbek women acted in ways that implied that gender was not always their most salient identity—still less that they agreed with a Soviet/feminist/jadid analysis that saw them primarily as the victims of patriarchy. Some, such as otins and older women, already held positions of influence and authority. Many may have concluded, quite rationally, that they preferred indigenous patriarchy to an external, possibly imperialist kind of liberation. Others concluded some-

43. On the complexities of internal hierarchies and subordination and the problem of patriarchy, see Viola, *Contending with Stalinism,* 5: "Engagements with resistance should not obscure but illustrate the complexities of societies, their internal and sometimes unappealing divisions, their own dominants and subordinates, and the fact that resistance could be coerced from within just as compliance with the regime could be."

44. Crane, *Fashion and Its Social Agendas,* 100.

thing altogether different and enthusiastically supported the Soviet campaign, but it would be patronizing and incomplete to say that theirs is the only legitimate female response.

So Uzbek women were not a single entity, and neither were Uzbek men. Even through the obscuring filters and categories of party language, and with the methodological caveats in mind, these confidential Soviet documents permit a glimpse of the wider Uzbek society beyond party circles, and of its responses to the hujum. In particular, they show this variety, pointing to the emergence of multiple understandings of Uzbek national "tradition." Reactions in Uzbek society covered a wide spectrum, from those of enthusiasts sincerely affiliated with Soviet power to those passionately opposed to it. The largest group lies between these extremes: it included those who changed their minds and those whose position depended on the forum and the specific issue under discussion. Such multiplicity should come as no surprise: Uzbekistan was not yet three years old, and it was far from a monolith. Obvious differences of political heritage (between Turkestan, Bukhoro, and Khiva, for instance) were only one division within this new Uzbek identity. Regional, ethnic, generational, professional, and rural/urban identities, among others, influenced how people reacted to the idea and practice of unveiling.[45] Even Uzbeks who joined the Communist Party came in many stripes; it was not always clear what they understood Bolshevism to be. Likewise, those who opposed the hujum did so for a variety of reasons. Finally, views changed over time. The initial successes in March, when thousands of veils were reportedly burned, dwindled in subsequent months. By summer it seemed to many observers that few faces remained unveiled.[46]

As might be expected in any complex society, therefore, Uzbeks reacted to the hujum in a vast number of individual ways. Some were vocally supportive of the unveiling effort, even wishing that it could be accelerated. This group is easy to find: their voices were zealously sought out and highlighted in Soviet records, and their story has been chronicled by generations of Soviet scholars and more recently by Western feminist historians.[47] Some, notably, were Uzbek men who for a variety of political and personal reasons had internalized Bolshevik values sufficiently to believe in and act in support of Soviet programs. One low-ranking Uzbek Communist man was rebuked in 1927 for overeagerness: when a peasant had asked him for permission to wait a day be-

45. For an example of regional differences, contrast the upbeat portrayal of Marghilon at PDA, op. 3, d. 1533, ll. 9–11, with the pessimism of Zerafshon at RGASPI, d. 1242, l. 214. On generational conflicts, see RGASPI, d. 1226, l. 63. For villages "lagging" behind cities, see RGASPI, d. 1214, l. 16, or d. 1247, l. 226. Also see Allworth, *Modern Uzbeks,* 176–88.

46. On the early successes, see PDA, op. 2, d. 1410, ll. 20–24, or nearly any issue of *Pravda Vostoka* from March 1927. The later slowdown, especially during the summer, is discussed below and at RGASPI, d. 1246, ll. 91–95.

47. See, for example, Shukurova, *Sotsializm i zhenshchina Uzbekistana,* or Kamp, "Unveiling Uzbek Women."

fore unveiling his wife, he had refused, saying that it was simply impossible to wait, that the peasant's wife must be unveiled that very day.[48] While it was in Soviet interests to exaggerate (or fabricate) such accounts, they do appear to represent a small but real strand of Uzbek society. Most obviously, this group of supporters included such high-ranking Communists as Akmal Ikramov, Faizulla Khojaev, and Yoldosh Akhunbabaev, men who worked as top leaders in the Uzbek state hierarchy and in the party's Central Asian Bureau, and thus helped design and implement the unveiling effort. Many of these leaders had strong personal ties to the jadids and other indigenous leftist or socialist groups: until 1920, for instance, Khojaev had been a leader of the Young Bukhoran Party.[49] By most accounts these men worked hard and sincerely for the hujum after 1927. They did so for many reasons, not least because it fitted into their local as well as Muscovite vision of cultural change. The jadids, after all, had argued for unveiling well before 1917: the idea had an indigenous constituency long before Soviet reformers arrived in Central Asia.

From this perspective, neither national identity nor religious obligation required Uzbek women to retain their paranjis and chachvons, and one did not have to be a strict Marxist materialist to think so. The jadids had made this argument from a religious perspective, and some Muslim clerics (called "progressives" by Soviet observers) continued to propound such ideas after 1927, arguing that the paranji and chachvon lacked Qur'anic roots. In their view, veils originally had emerged out of the social tensions of warfare and class exploitation that existed under the khans. Since the conditions that led to fears for women's honor no longer existed, they concluded, unveiling now was no sin.[50] Other progressive clerics conceded that the veil had existed during the Prophet's time, but argued that it also predated Islam among upper-class women. In general, they asserted, veils were linked to specific local conditions; they were not a universal obligation for all believers. Why, they asked, did Muslim Tatar women veil rarely and Kyrgyz women not at all?[51] These mullahs and *eshons* (Sufi masters) even went so far as to invite believers to public unveilings, and to unveil their own wives there.[52] Their attitude toward Soviet power per se is not always clear, but at least some saw themselves as Soviet allies. One reportedly ended his preaching with a cry of "Long live Soviet power, long live the Communist Party!"[53] Unfortunately, as he soon discovered, party leaders did not return his ardor.

For many local women, gender concerns were at least as important as these

48. RGASPI, d. 1214, ll. 73 and 130.
49. Khalid, *Politics of Muslim Cultural Reform*, 295, and also his "Society and Politics in Bukhara, 1868–1920," *Central Asian Survey* 19, no. 3–4 (2000): 367–96.
50. RGASPI, d. 1205, l. 90b.
51. RGASPI, d. 1214, ll. 7–9.
52. RGASPI, d. 1211, ll. 94 and 204; d. 1213, l. 1050b; d. 1214, l. 55; d. 1240, l. 160b; d. 1246, l. 75; and d. 1247, l. 206.
53. RGASPI, d. 1213, l. 1050b.

general political issues of social reform. From their perspective, the hujum was a herald of change, a welcome portent of greater equality in male–female relations. One old woman in a generally sympathetic crowd, for example, was quoted by the OGPU (Ob"edinennoe gosudarstvennoe politicheskoe upravlenie, the Soviet secret police) in 1927 as saying, "Our time is past, but the young ones, of course, must unveil." Such quotations sound like precisely what the state hoped to hear, and indeed they may have been shaped, massaged, or fabricated by overeager secret police officers. Yet some Muslim women clearly did see in the hujum opportunities to reshuffle existing social hierarchies and overcome perceived inequities. Hundreds, even thousands of women threw off their veils and kept them off. A handful went so far as to join the Zhenotdel, working assiduously to unveil others and to eliminate indigenous patriarchy wherever they saw it. A few, such as the prominent women's activist Tojikhon Shadieva, became visible personal icons of liberation, with their life stories recounted in popular books, newspapers, museum exhibits, and inspirational films.[54]

Who were these women that responded to the Soviet call? Some were the wives and relatives of Communist Party members, especially high-ranking ones, who faced strong pressure to liberate their families at the outset of the unveiling campaign. Desperately poor female beggars and especially prostitutes—few of whom had worn veils in any case—also sought Zhenotdel aid and support. Other Uzbek women unveiled for just the reasons party activists expected: they resented the restrictions placed on local women. In this sense, and for these women, the Soviet campaign brought new possibilities, even a real kind of liberation. Leaving aside for a moment the problem of coerced unveilings, the positive appeal of the Bolshevik vision is arguably evident in the social locations of women who flocked to the cause. Local women who unveiled in the hujum's early days hailed disproportionately from marginal social positions: orphans, widows, and runaway girls, for example, sought refuge in Soviet institutions and women's clubs far out of proportion to their overall numbers.[55] In part this may have been due to their socialization in (and financial, physical, even emotional dependence on) state institutions. Equally plausible, however, is the possibility that they were enabled to unveil by their structural position outside local kin networks. They were thus less constrained by male relatives or social pressure, and perhaps more able to act as they wished.

But despite these pockets of support for the Soviet project of unveiling Uzbek women, such welcoming voices were conspicuous mostly for their rar-

---

54. On Shadieva, see R-l', "Osvobozhdennye velikim Oktiabrem," *Rabotnitsa*, no. 30 (1934), 29–30, or S. Normatov, *Tadzhikhon* (Tashkent, 1966). Her life was the subject of an uplifting film in 1934 (RGAKFD 3965), and later of museum exhibits (V. Tatarinov, "Zavidnaia sud'ba," *Sel'skaia pravda*, 8 Oct. 1974).

55. Such socially marginal women are discussed at *PSTZhMUz*, 63–66; "Uzbechka-prokuror," *PV*, 18 Nov. 1929; and R. Bozhko, "O chem rasskazala staraia fotografiia," *Partiinaia zhizn'* (Tashkent), no. 3 (1969), 73–75.

ity.[56] The vast majority of contemporary sources, especially those not meant for public dissemination, relate varying types and degrees of opposition to the hujum. They demonstrate what appears to be the emergence and rapid solidification of a newly defined "traditional" Uzbek culture in the face of Soviet transformative efforts. "It is a secret to no one," stated one highly classified OGPU report, "that in Uzbekistan 95 percent of the population is against the unveiling of women. If this is so," the report continued with remarkable understatement, "then too-sudden approaches to the issue may provoke some misunderstandings."[57] Indigenous opposition came in a bewildering variety of forms, made use of all possible outlets, and bedeviled party activists at every turn. The strength of popular resistance shows that in this initial onslaught, Soviet efforts made little headway in dislodging the cultural hegemony of so-called traditional ideals of women's role and status in Uzbekistan, particularly as these understandings had come to be expressed through customs of female veiling and seclusion. Indeed, the party arguably created much of this passionate resistance after 1927 by deciding to attack the veil. This strategic decision inadvertently created strong discourses of resistance, framed in terms of morality as well as national-cultural authenticity, and in the end left the paranji and chachvon more stable and universally worn than before.

Uzbek women and men drew upon the experience and lessons of a half-century of Russian rule, extending existing techniques of anticolonial resistance into new realms when Bolshevik tactics proved more interventionist and intrusive than those of their tsarist predecessors. Formal resistance, first of all, could be—and was—expressed within the institutional structures established by Soviet authorities. Opponents of the hujum sought to subvert the Soviet campaign from within, for example by packing local *mahalla* commissions with people sympathetic to their views. (The mahalla was the virtually all-Muslim neighborhood in which most urban Uzbeks lived.) Signed letters and petitions arrived at Soviet offices, complaining openly about the use of high-pressure tactics to persuade Uzbek women to unveil. Some protests were delivered in person by group delegations, which occasionally went so far as to threaten Soviet personnel and facilities physically. Groups of women also brought petitions requesting permission to don the veil again.[58]

Outside official channels, too, southern Central Asian society could draw on many resources. As tsarist authorities had discovered during major rebellions in 1898 and 1916, preexisting cultural languages of legitimacy and political power in Central Asia could readily be used to express disagreement with state

56. RGASPI, d. 1250, l. 42.
57. RGASPI, d. 1214, l. 2.
58. Protest delegations (allegedly inspired by class enemies) are at RGASPI, d. 1226, l. 73, and d. 1238, l. 10. Women demonstrate in protest and ask permission to reveil at d. 1224, l. 74. An example of a protest letter, with threat included, is at d. 1214, l. 95. Some petitions supported the Soviet cause, for instance requesting that action be taken against "anti-Soviet agitators"; their credibility may be questionable. See ÖzRMDA, f. 1714, op. 5, d. 663, ll. 5 and 18.

authorities perceived as unlawful or corrupt. Such deep structures of political culture and religious community were now mobilized against the Soviet project of liberation. Most of the *ulamo* (the wider group of Islamic theologians and scholars), for example, objected to unveiling on religious grounds, and many mullahs used their positions of prominence and respect to preach against unveiling as a sin advocated by foreign, urban, atheist Bolsheviks. These so-called traditionalist (*qadimist*) clerics believed that jadids erred when they said that a devout Muslim woman could unveil. To the contrary, they argued, the Qur'an specifically mandated that honorable women be shielded from the view of men outside their immediate families.[59] Soviet sources are obviously a deeply flawed lens through which to explore the fine points of such theological reasoning, but diligent police investigators saw the desperate need for Soviet activists to know and understand the types of rhetoric they would face, and hence preserved wherever they could the details of such arguments. These clerics cited specific passages from the Qur'an to contend that Muhammad's revelation on female seclusion and veiling, in addition to being well suited to the conditions of his society (namely, the need to protect nonslave women from sexual overtures and attempts at seduction), also had a general applicability:

> The prophet Muhammad commanded [us] to veil women; it follows that the unveiling of women violates the principles of religion.
>
> Woman is a debauched creature. God, of all lusts, gave nine-tenths to the woman, and only one part in ten to the man. The veil of woman's lust is the paranji. The unveiling of women entails the debauchery of the entire world. Cursed be the days of our life! Cursed be those who are the first to proceed with the unveiling of women, and who show an evil example.[60]

Many mullahs preached in this vein publicly at mosques and privately to small meetings at home, concentrating on the apocalyptic implications of unveiling. The hujum, which would leave not a single woman honorable, was a harbinger of the end of the world; faithful Muslims were enjoined to pray for God's deliverance from Soviet power.[61] Mullahs, eshons, and *murids* (Sufi adepts, or disciples of a Sufi shaykh) directed men not to unveil (or permit the unveiling of) wives, daughters, sisters, and mothers. If these men saw an unveiled woman, they had committed a sin, the cleansing of which required mandatory ablutions.[62]

Clerical efforts also targeted women directly. Uzbek women and girls were organized into special religious schools and activities (few of which had ex-

---

59. RGASPI, d. 1214, ll. 6–7, 33, 37–38, 125. On preexisting languages of political change through violence in the Qöqon khanate, see Beatrice Forbes Manz, "Central Asian Uprisings in the Nineteenth Century: Ferghana Under the Russians," *Russian Review* 46 (1987): 267–81.

60. RGASPI, d. 1214, l. 15.

61. Ibid., ll. 20, 125, and 157.

62. Ibid., l. 119.

isted before), where they heard Zhenotdel activists denounced as "prostitutes striving to nationalize women" and were exhorted not to unveil lest the world come to an end.[63] In a self-consciously Muslim culture, and with committed Bolsheviks on the ground few and far between, such clerical efforts had an impact. Patriarchal oppression alone cannot explain why so many veiled women made the choice to remain covered and why others decided now to veil for the first time. Women in the village of Marhamat, near Andijon, were reportedly so affected by one mullah's "enthusiastic" reading of the Qur'an that they burst into tears and fell to the ground, overcome by emotion.[64] In a nearby village, twenty-five women reveiled after a similar meeting.[65]

Opposition expressed informally represented an even larger problem for Bolshevik activists. Springing from the view of a large and growing number of Uzbeks that certain codes of gender behavior, such as female veiling, were proper and should not be changed, these subterranean expressions of discontent were hard to pin down and thus hard to stop. Rumors spread like wildfire in 1927, and efforts to stamp them out, much less to identify the parties responsible, appeared hopeless. Mixing religious precepts with tales (sometimes true, often exaggerated) of Soviet excesses in the unveiling campaign, such rumors became the currency of Uzbek discourse and were perhaps the most effective means of communication available on either side, serving rapidly to bolster Uzbek Muslim solidarity against perceived Bolshevik interlopers. For political reasons, therefore, secret police and party reports chronicled these rumors carefully.

Some popular tales drew on the apocalyptic views of Muslim clerics, perceiving the end of the world to be nigh. When a severe earthquake in August 1927 badly damaged the Namangan area, for example, it was taken to show God's displeasure that Uzbek women had removed their veils. Other rumors focused on Soviet tactics and motives. Bolshevik personnel sometimes used armed force or financial coercion to compel women to expose their faces, tactics that were taken to show that they hoped to make all women into prostitutes, and thereby to destroy the Islamic religion and Uzbek culture. Still other stories held out hope for rescue from unlikely quarters. Britain would soon declare war on the USSR to stop the dishonoring of Central Asian women, ran one tale, capitalizing on the well-known hostility between the British and Soviet governments. The qörboshi would reappear, said another. Finally, speculation ran rampant about the party's practical intentions and the views of its top leadership. One rumor had high officials in Moscow on the verge of shooting Uzbek party leaders for carrying out the unveiling campaign against orders. Another asserted that the Uzbek leadership was about to thumb its nose

63. The quotation is from RGASPI, d. 1242, l. 208. See also d. 939, l. 18; d. 1214, l. 124; d. 1234, ll. 3–4; and PDA, op. 3, d. 1598, l. 39.
   64. RGASPI, d. 1214, l. 88.
   65. Ibid., l. 124.

at Moscow by issuing a decree banning the hujum.[66] The fabric of these rumors is rich, and they served important social functions even as they reveal a good deal about how Uzbeks understood the world. However obsessed Soviet authorities were with the accurate, even encyclopedic recording of these tales, however, even the substantial coercive resources of the OGPU proved powerless to stop them.

Other resistance was passive, or at least hard to see in the surviving sources. Women could simply stay home rather than face Soviet activists, and men could send their wives far away to avoid the unveiling campaign.[67] But many Uzbeks were not reluctant to challenge Soviet authority openly, and active, visible resistance was also widespread. Most obviously, pressure could be brought to bear against anyone who appeared to support the goals and tactics of the hujum. The crucial factor was the growing cultural hegemony of these patterns of intimate and family life, patterns now reified through state and party action as characteristic of both Uzbek and Muslim tradition. Given the dominance of such views in determining proper social practices, the life of a Soviet sympathizer could quickly be made miserable. In the face of unrelenting opprobrium, insults, even threats of violence everywhere—at home, on the street, at the bazaar, with family or friends—many Uzbek men as well as women who might have supported the hujum opted out, deciding it was easier and safer to keep a low profile.

Men, holding positions of familial authority in a patriarchal society, felt some of this pressure. It was their responsibility to see that "their" women (wives, daughters, sisters, mothers, even neighbors) stayed veiled and observed the requirements of seclusion. Those who unveiled their wives or who allowed their wives to unveil faced ostracism or worse. A few such men were attacked and even killed for their failure to defend traditional mores, but more often the silent treatment proved sufficient. One Mukhamedjan Akhmetjanov, a peasant from the village of Yavva, learned this lesson the hard way, enduring severe criticism after his wife unveiled. The Soviet secret police report that tells his story carefully notes that Akhmetjanov's village accusers were "former bureaucrats of the emir," and thus, from the Soviet perspective, persons of dubious character. This fact, however, likely held little comfort for Akmetjanov when all of his neighbors were told that "he unveiled his wife, and thereby violated the Muslim law; therefore it is forbidden to have anything to do with him, or even to visit his home."[68]

<hr>

66. For views of the apocalypse, see RGASPI, d. 1205, l. 10, or d. 1214, ll. 23 and 114. On prostitution and alleged Bolshevik coercion and hypocrisy, see d. 1058, ll. 25–26; and PDA, op. 3, d. 1549, ll. 1–140b. Rumors about the international situation are at RGASPI, d. 1061, ll. 13–14, and about bosmachi at d. 1201, l. 124. For the party's intentions and the allegedly imminent demise of Yoldosh Akhunbabaev, the Uzbek president, see d. 1242, l. 214, and d. 1248, l. 93.

67. RGASPI, d. 1214, ll. 104–5 and 148.

68. Ibid., ll. 12 and 145. Other examples of such ostracism, felt by indigenous Communists, are at ll. 17, 20, and 105.

But Uzbek women were caught most squarely in the middle of this struggle, and it was they who bore the brunt of social pressure. Zhenotdel activists tried many arguments to induce them to unveil, and some local Communists resorted to coercion. The various sanctions of family, friends, and neighbors, however, were far more immediately daunting, and they wielded more influence on most women's behavior. Within the home, husbands could and did prevent their wives from attending Soviet meetings or parades, and threatened divorce if they unveiled.[69] Outside the home, the "social opinion of the mahalla" was firm: any unveiled woman was assumed to be the equivalent of a prostitute, and could be treated as such.[70] Fights broke out when schoolchildren taunted classmates about their newly unveiled mothers—who had, they shouted, taken up prostitution.[71]

Unveiled women bolstered themselves for harsh criticism every time they stepped outside, onto the kind of street shown in Figure 14. Raised in a culture that stressed honor as a paramount female virtue, they faced mockery and ridicule at every turn. According to Soviet sources, many decided against unveiling, "fearing social opinion—mainly that of their mahalla and especially that of the street gossips, the guardians of 'shariat order.' "[72] The continual mutterings of "prostitute" from passersby had an effect, sometimes reducing the demoralized women to tears; they pleaded for help from Soviet authorities, saying that soon they would be driven to reveil.[73] Yet Uzbek women, too, played multiple roles in this conflict—some (veiled) women as well as men were behind the harassment and insults. One young woman, upon hearing a veiled woman call her a prostitute, snapped; she "made a scandal, tearing off [the other woman's] paranji and then beginning to beat her, only afterward wanting to take [the harasser] to the police."[74]

However unpleasant the street abuse, Uzbek women faced a more extreme form of pressure: violence, either real or threatened. Women who unveiled or even considered doing so ran a real personal risk, especially if they lived outside the Russified New Cities of major urban areas, and the risks escalated considerably if they tried to persuade other women to follow their example. Many reports of violent opposition to the hujum appeared in the periodical press and have been chronicled by Massell and by Russian and Central Asian scholars. Suffice it to say that the classified materials only reinforce the view

69. Ibid., ll. 28, 38, 115, 146–47, and 154.

70. The phrase is from RGASPI, d. 1203, l. 15. On the equivalence of unveiling and prostitution, see d. 1214, l. 105, and d. 1242, ll. 163 and 167.

71. RGASPI, d. 1214, l. 56.

72. Ibid., l. 14. On the "hysterics" that greeted the sight of an unveiled woman, see PDA, op. 3, d. 1598, l. 33.

73. RGASPI, d. 1214, ll. 148 and 153, and d. 1248, l. 91. These authorities were not always sympathetic: some Uzbek Communists were threatened with expulsion for mocking unveiled women; see d. 1250, l. 55.

74. RGASPI, d. 1214, l. 38. Other examples of women as harassers are at PDA, op. 3, d. 1598, l. 37, and RGASPI, d. 1205, l. 12.

Figure 14. Street in the Old City. (Courtesy Anahita Gallery, Santa Fe, N.M.)

that Uzbekistan in 1927 was a dangerous place for an unveiled woman—or for a women's activist, whether she was European or Uzbek. Thousands of women survived attacks intended to intimidate them and rapes meant to illustrate their "dishonored" status. Hundreds more did not survive; Soviet hagiographers memorialized these victims as martyrs, a small consolation. Some murders were accompanied by gruesome mutilations, many by rape. Often relatives of the victims—husbands, fathers, brothers—carried out the killings to expiate a perceived smirch on the family honor.[75] The continued domination of non-Soviet understandings of the social meanings of such acts, however, supported the belief that such murderers had done nothing wrong. Even when Soviet courts managed to catch and punish them, the killers often became martyrs to the cause of Muslim justice.[76]

Taking Stock: Initial Outcomes and Soviet Authority

This multifarious resistance had the effect of essentially—and very quickly—stopping the hujum in its tracks. The problems besetting the Bolshevik campaign became clear by the autumn of 1927, when the first serious effort was made to pause and take stock. What had been accomplished during the first six months of all-out effort against the veil? Not much, it seemed, when it came to

75. Among the many reported cases of attacks, rapes, and murders, see an example at RGASPI, d. 1206, ll. 87–88. Mutilations are at d. 1214, l. 93. An example of violent threats is at ÖzRMDA, f. 737, op. 1, d. 185, l. 216. Note that some men died as a result of these attacks as well: see RGASPI, d. 1214, l. 38. Martyrs are memorialized at d. 1242, l. 1400b.

76. RGASPI, d. 1214, l. 75.

the benchmark criterion of how many women had thrown off the paranji and chachvon and kept them off. After some early successes—the standard claim was that 100,000 Uzbek women (about 6 percent of the total in Uzbekistan) had unveiled shortly after 8 March—the vast majority had reversed themselves and reveiled, a fact admitted in dozens of internal party reports. As a worker in Farghona province wrote, "The campaign is at the stage where . . . for every eight that unveil, nine reveil."[77] Another explained in late 1927 that the tide had turned during the summer, saying that now "the picture is completely different, characterized by the *phenomenon of a mass reveiling* of those who had unveiled at the start of the hujum." Perhaps only a tenth of the initial 100,000 women were still unveiled in December, this report noted, and many specific examples supported the general depiction of gloom: "In Marghilon, out of 3,000 unveiled, 2,600 have veiled again. In the large village of Pskent (the former district center), out of 1,500 unveiled, 1,470 have veiled again."[78]

If reveiling was a slap in the face to Bolshevik activists, they at least thought they knew where they stood in its aftermath. Either a woman was unveiled or she was not; at a minimum, this clear dichotomy would be easy to measure. Or would it? By late 1927 many ostensible success stories retained a decided air of ambiguity. Some women, it transpired, had removed a paranji and chachvon, only to cover their faces with scarves or heavy overclothes, or to turn away out of "shyness" whenever a man looked at them. Others agreed to unveil when far away, but refused to return home without donning traditional garb. Still others unveiled at Soviet demonstrations or meetings, but reveiled before walking onto the street. "Go ahead and kill me," one woman reportedly told party activists, "but I will not walk unveiled into my mahalla."[79] Even women who sympathized with the Soviet agenda had been socialized into the norms and values of local society, so that a clean break was difficult. Just as salient, they worried about the practicalities of living a permanent, publicly unveiled life. Threats of violence sometimes made it impossible to hold women's meetings, and many women and men thought it simply too dangerous to consider unveiling. As one man, a jadidist cleric, put it when challenged, "I am not against unveiling, on the contrary, I personally have fulfilled it 100 percent in my family. At home, my wife does not veil when men come to visit, or at meetings. If she veils when she goes out onto the street, that is only because 35 percent of the inhabitants in the mahalla are fanatics, and I fear that they would count me as [their] fervent enemy."[80] His self-defense shows both how a

77. RGASPI, d. 1202, l. 88.
78. RGASPI, d. 1242, l. 116; emphasis in original.
79. RGASPI, d. 1214, l. 14. For alternative veils, see PDA, op. 3, d. 1549, ll. 12–140b; or RGASPI, d. 1240, l. 36. Women's "shyness" is at RGASPI, d. 1058, l. 27. Unveiling away from home is at d. 1214, l. 123, and d. 1217, ll. 77–78; only during Soviet meetings at d. 1247, ll. 49 and 1370b.
80. RGASPI, d. 1214, l. 2. Threats preventing meetings are discussed at d. 1225, l. 74. Another expression of the perceived danger of unveiling is at d. 1214, l. 107.

woman's actions were seen to reflect on her husband and how the threats of severe consequences made even sympathetic Uzbeks reluctant to run the risks of
unveiling.

The evidence shows overwhelmingly that by late 1927 these traditional
views of family relations and gender roles pervaded virtually all strata of
Uzbek society. Increasingly, such views encompassed female veiling and seclusion. Even within party ranks, where one might expect to find the most energetic proponents of the Soviet cause, few Uzbeks appeared willing to dissociate
themselves from local society and culture. Uzbek Communists as a group had
been raised under the same system of symbols and beliefs as their neighbors,
and many held similar attitudes toward Russian colonial authorities as well as
views of how society should be organized. Few knew much Marxist theory or
understood the intricacies of Bolshevik policy. Even high leaders were not im-
mune to common assumptions: Akmal Ikramov, first secretary of the Uzbek
party, admitted that he thought poorly of a woman who smiled upon meeting
him in the street. Revealing her teeth, according to prevailing cultural codes,
had marked her as dissolute.[81]

Ikramov's fealty to traditional views pales by comparison with the recalcitrance of his colleagues. Many Uzbek Communists treated unveiled women
badly, insulting, ridiculing, and even attacking and trying to rape them.[82] The
unveiled wives of party members joined in the harassment, mocking the
shabby, inexpensive clothes of their unveiled working-class sisters.[83] By doing
so they plainly demonstrated the limits of class and politics on female cama-
raderie and sympathy, even within the small, ostensibly united group of unveiled women. And the primary loyalty of most Uzbek Communists (the vast
majority of whom, after all, were men) lay not with the party but with local
cultural and social networks; if it came to a choice, their decision was clear.
Burhan Babaev, a village Communist since 1918, threatened to kill his wife if
she had any contact with his newly unveiled sister-in-law. When other party
members asked whether he would unveil his wife and take her to the demonstration on 8 March, Babaev declared, "Let them kick me out of the party, but
I will not unveil my wife, and I will not take her to the demonstration. I have
lots of money now, and I give a percentage of it [as alms] to the peasants. Besides this I have a large garden, a house, and forty head of cattle, so I have no
need for the party and can make do without it. Let them kick me out of the
party, but I will not unveil my wife."[84] Many Uzbek Communists held such
views on women's proper role in 1927.

But indigenous Communists had at least in theory been selected for their po-

81. PDA, op. 4, d. 1208, ll. 34–40.
82. RGASPI, d. 1242, l. 39; d. 1246, l. 11; and d. 1247, l. 179.
83. RGASPI, d. 1217, l. 132, and d. 1240, l. 37.
84. RGASPI, d. 1214, l. 23. Ergash Umarov, a Communist from Urgut, declared in a similar
spirit that he would sooner die than permit his wife to unveil (l. 31).

litical views, and so some of them should have sympathized with the hujum, or at least not have opposed it. These potential allies of the Soviet cause, however, felt the same pressures and fears as other Muslims, and few were willing to risk social disapproval—much less their personal safety—to support the unveiling campaign. The mahalla could be unmerciful, and most local Communists lived their day-to-day lives there, among thousands of noncommunists. A few left, opting out by moving to the Russian-populated New Cities.[85] Such a drastic step sometimes appeared to be what the party wanted: certainly being willing to renounce Uzbek Muslim ways in favor of a European appearance marked them as loyal allies. At one women's demonstration in 1927, for instance, police permitted only men "wearing European clothes or walking with a brief-case" to attend; those dressed in "national" garb (such as the heavy robes known as *chopons*) were held back until the demonstration had concluded.[86]

There were other, intermittent efforts to retool indigenous ideas about masculinity and male prerogative by changing male attitudes and attire, but they usually remained subordinate to what was seen as the core gender transformation, the one taking place among women.[87] Further, most male Muslim party members were not prepared to abandon their old lives altogether, and those who stayed faced ostracism, insults, and physical threats if they contemplated unveiling their wives.[88] Although directed repeatedly to provide a personal example of women's liberation, some Uzbek Communists admitted that they feared their neighbors' poor opinion. They argued that their wives did not know how to act without a veil, even how to walk and talk. Further, they contended, having an unveiled wife would lose them whatever authority they had in the eyes of the masses.[89] In the end, many native Communists followed their neighbors' example, failing to bring their wives to demonstrations, refusing to unveil them once there, or, if all else failed, later forcing them to reveil.[90] In the Uzbek capital city of Samarqand in late 1927, according to confidential party materials, fewer than 10 percent of Uzbek Communists could boast of having an unveiled wife, and fewer than 5 percent had actually spoken in favor of unveiling.[91]

The evidence thus suggests that in its first months the unveiling campaign left Soviet control over southern Central Asia no less tenuous than it had been

85. ÖzRMDA, f. 837, op. 3, d. 150, l. 178.
86. RGASPI, d. 1214, l. 37. Attendance policies at this meeting were curious, since Russian men and working-class males were also excluded.
87. Acknowledgment of the need for work among men could be found as early as 1924; it was said to be necessary "for the elimination of byt superstitions that bring about women's oppression" at RGASPI, d. 163, l. 47. For a later example, in which the activist Vinnikov argued in 1931 that men were just as important as women in any effort to eliminate the paranji, see PDA, op. 7, d. 866, ll. 84–85.
88. RGASPI, d. 1214, ll. 17, 20, and 105.
89. Ibid., ll. 15, 23, and 144.
90. PDA, op. 3, d. 1598, l. 16; and RGASPI, d. 1207, l. 11; d. 1225, l. 107; and d. 1242, l. 38.
91. RGASPI, d. 1214, ll. 25 and 31.

before. By sparking bitter resistance, indeed, and contributing to the renewed strength of anti-Soviet qörboshi rebels, the hujum appears to have left Bolshevik leaders rather weaker—the exact opposite of what had been intended—and made local party work more difficult. In the face of a continuing wave of violent unrest (mentioned in Soviet materials as "incidents" or "excesses") it was far from clear that the local balance of power lay with party-sanctioned authorities. One local official declared his willingness to kill President Akhunbabaev if he mandated unveiling.[92] A peasant who killed an Uzbek woman for convening a liberation meeting in his village marched straight to the local Soviet government office to declare proudly what he had done.[93] Both were typical of the new Uzbek "traditionalists," men and women who took up the banner of cultural defense as a means of resistance. In many cases they incited anti-Soviet violence, whether by breaking up meetings or hunting down and killing Communists.[94]

A colorful but not atypical example is related in a top-secret OGPU report of April 1927, which describes an attack on a women's liberation meeting in the Farghona Valley, near the town of Pop. The meeting of 2,000 people had been held (more than a little provocatively) at the village mosque. Shortly after it opened, shouts were reportedly heard coming from the audience: "Thrash 'em, beat 'em!" The crowd, actually more of a mob, was thrown into turmoil, and all the women present tried to flee. The crowd then advanced on the members of the Commission for Women's Liberation, boxing them into a corner with such force that they were pushed through the walls of the mosque. More shouts rang out: "Beat all the Soviet workers and their wives for their disgraces!" The commission fled in panic. Angry Uzbeks then went from door to door looking for Soviet workers and commission members, breaking windows and doors as they went.[95] This episode—one among many—vividly illustrates the strength, energy, and extent of popular reaction to the unveiling campaign. It also shows the profound weakness of Soviet workers, forced to flee the very citizens they purported to lead.

The hujum failed in these early months to live up to party leaders' hopes: certainly it did not succeed in recasting Uzbek society along modern, Bolshevik lines in time for the Revolution's tenth anniversary in October 1927. In many ways it did the opposite, strengthening anti-Soviet resistance and providing it a new, powerful foundation in the language of gendered "tradition." By making dramatic public unveilings central to and emblematic of the Soviet vision for Uzbekistan and the entire Soviet East, moreover, it raised the ultimate stakes for women's liberation. Yet the head-on, public confrontation over female seclusion made little immediate headway. Passions in 1927 ran high on all

92. Ibid., l. 35.
93. Ibid., l. 111.
94. Attacks on the party and OGPU are ibid., ll. 31 and 100.
95. RGASPI, d. 1214, l. 52. Another disastrous meeting is related at l. 92–920b.

sides, from Bolshevik activists busily working in the Zhenotdel to conservative clerics preaching in local mosques. Publications, demonstrations, even violent altercations reveal plainly the depths of feeling, showing the centrality of paranji and chachvon to each group. Party activists and their opponents alike produced, disseminated, and consumed antagonistic discourses of gender and family relations, and veiled Uzbek women did not turn out to be the unquestioned allies Bolsheviks expected them to be. The veil itself, ostensibly a simple piece of cloth, encapsulated multiple contradictory layers of meaning and identity. It encoded religion, politics, and ethno-nationality as well as ideas about gender relations and family life. These layers grew only more complex and interwoven through this confrontation in the hujum. Conflicts over the discourse of the veil, over what it meant to be veiled, came to be fought with increasing bitterness in this part of the new Soviet empire.

CHAPTER 3

Bolshevik Blinders

The party and Soviet power have put a great task before us:
the liberation of women. Some comrades, speaking here on
this question, have expressed the opinion that there is [too
much] influence by clergy, bois, etc., that it is not yet the time
to move toward women's liberation, that it is not yet the sea-
son. I would say these comrades err when they say "the mass"
is not ready, that under the masses one can see bois and merchants and clergy. There is, of course, some displeasure with
the liberation [campaign], but if we are to speak of the working class, then the picture is entirely different. And that is ex-
actly what we must do, speak of the class opinion. Our [guid-
ing] principle must be that of class.

—A Bolshevik activist, Hashimov, speaking to a local party
congress, 1927

I wore the paranji until 1928, and was sick all the time;
toward the end I was losing my eyesight. But when I threw off
the paranji, I became healthier and more cultured than before.

—An Uzbek housewife, Najmi Rasulova, in the late 1930s

By late 1927 Bolshevik activists at the Zhenotdel and elsewhere knew that
unveiling was not going according to plan. The fact that it had encountered difficulties came as no surprise to grassroots party and Soviet workers, many of
whom bore personally the brunt of violent reactions. But while Uzbek Communists as a group did not welcome the hujum, the women of the Zhenotdel, mostly
non-Muslim and largely European, generally did support the cause of unveiling
as emancipation. They were deeply concerned about its lack of progress, and
along with powerful allies in the upper party apparatus, they tried to understand
what was happening, to turn the tide, and to make the hujum a success. Doing so

required these true believers—and it is they I mean by "Bolsheviks" here, not the Uzbek rank-and-file members—to react appropriately to the patterns of mostly negative social response that had greeted the unveiling campaign.

The responses of these Soviet observers were confused at best and chaotic at worst. If a silver lining existed, it was in the real discussion made possible by confusion and chaos: initiatives often emerged from lower levels of the party. This was not, in practice, a tightly controlled, centralized, authoritarian party. Yet while disagreement and debate could have permitted local flexibility and thus been turned into a strength, such potential remained for the most part unrealized. The very categories of analysis that Bolsheviks brought to Central Asia prevented them from understanding, let alone coping with, Uzbek responses and resistance to the hujum. Ideologies—by which I mean something wider, deeper, and more pervasive yet more diffuse than a simple set of formal doctrines or consciously voiced political beliefs—played a key role.[1] Bolshevik habits of mind, or ideological filters, helped harden party resolve to continue harsh attacks on the veil even after it was clear that such tactics were not working well.

Information Gathering and Analysis

How did party leaders respond to the hujum's troubles? Their first impulse was to seek accurate information on what they called the "popular mood." They hoped such data would enable them to understand Uzbek social responses and perhaps ultimately to direct them. Given Central Asia's divergence from any ideal of information control, however, this was easier said than done. With poor communications, long distances, few staff or material resources, and little contact between rural or provincial areas and the central government, Uzbekistan presented stark challenges to the data collector. The Central Asian Zhenotdel first requested, then ordered, and finally begged unions and local party organizations to send complete reports on the progress of the hujum, convinced that if only they could discover what was happening on the ground, they would be able to understand and respond properly.[2] The

---

1. I draw on William H. Sewell Jr., who calls ideology something that is "at once constraining and enabling," that is "anonymous, collective, and constitutive of social order" ("Ideologies and Social Revolutions: Reflections on the French Case," *Journal of Modern History* 57 [1985]: 60 and 85). In Sewell's words, "Ideology must be seen neither as the mere reflex of material class relations nor as mere 'ideas' which 'intellectuals' hold about society. Rather, ideologies inform the structure of institutions, the nature of social cooperation and conflict, and the attitudes and predispositions of the population. All social relations are at the same time ideological relations, and all explicit ideological discourse is a form of social action" (p. 61).

2. Government officials complain about the quality of information at RGASPI, d. 1247, ll. 44–45. Requests included questionnaires, reports, statistical forms, and detailed lists of unveiled women, complete with spaces for name, age, social class, hometown, party and marital status, workplace, date of unveiling, literacy, and husband's workplace and party status. See ÖzRMDA, f. 737, op. 1, d. 185, l. 121; or RGASPI, d. 1247, ll. 80–81, and d. 1250, ll. 70–83.

resulting files show plainly the chaotic state of this information-gathering effort and reveal the deep confusion that beset the campaign.

Difficulties came in many varieties. Some information was lost in the mail, misplaced by staff workers, omitted by lower-level employees, or, in the many areas with no Communists or Soviet-affiliated workers, never recorded in the first place.[3] The fluidity of the situation on the ground, with reveilings rapidly reclaiming women from the ranks of the unveiled and the difficulty of measuring "tactical" unveilings (those reveiling in their own mahalla, for instance, or those covering their faces with a scarf rather than a chachvon) made aggregate statistics, so beloved by party leaders as a proxy language through which to express progress, at best dubious. More insidious from a Soviet perspective, some local reports intentionally misrepresented the facts or put an inaccurate spin on events, errors that could be caught only through the time-consuming, expensive technique of sending out investigative brigades to verify local claims.[4] One village electoral commission leader submitted a false report that twenty-five women had participated in an electoral meeting; upon verification, it turned out that only four women had been present, and that they were elderly women who had merely sat outside the door drinking tea.[5]

Grassroots materials tend to yield the most damning glimpses of popular antihujum sentiment, yet reports prepared by local organizations for higher authorities frequently accentuated the positive, stressing success stories and minimizing problems, perhaps in the hope of avoiding interference from the central party and government.[6] Locally reported statistics often included any woman who had ever been unveiled, whether or not she remained so; sometimes a woman might unveil at more than one meeting and be counted separately on each occasion. It also seems possible, to say the least, that some local authorities simply pulled their (often eerily precise) numbers from thin air.[7]

---

3. ÖzRMDA, f. 86, op. 1, d. 4231, l. 147. See RGASPI, d. 1250, l. 5, for workers losing lists of unveiled women. For partial data, see ÖzRMDA, f. 737, op. 1, d. 185. Many local staffers were illiterate, a serious problem that hindered not only the gathering of data from the localities but also the transmission of policy directives down the party chain of command. See f. 245, op. 1, d. 168, ll. 128–29.

4. An investigative brigade discovered that a local women's commission existed only on paper at RGASPI, d. 1250, l. 107. Unions put a positive spin on their unveiling successes in a report to the party at ÖzRMDA, f. 737, op. 1, d. 185, ll. 256–60.

5. ÖzRMDA, f. 86, op. 1, d. 5719, l. 15. This "meeting" took place in 1929.

6. See the alleged triumphs in unveiling village women reported by the Tashkent party at RGASPI, d. 1250, l. 49, or the generally upbeat report from Farghona at d. 1242, ll. 174–77.

7. In early May 1927, for example, the Farghona provincial party organization reported 3,389 unveiled women in the New City of Marghilon (Margilan); 2,648 in Besh-ariq; and 1,086 in Aravan (Astapovich, *Velikii Oktiabr'*, 190–91). Meanwhile the Andijon regional party committee admitted, "An exact accounting of unveiled women is completely lacking. The district committees report approximate numbers, which often are far from the corresponding reality. The Naryn district committee reports that there are 2,000 unveiled women in the district, but local reports attest that there never were more than 368, and that 50 percent of these have reveiled. The Qorghon Tepe district committee tells of 1,495 unveiled women, [but] in personal discussions workers of

For all these reasons locally generated statistical reports came under scrutiny at the republican and Central Asian levels, especially when they went too far and lost all connection to reality. Some doubt was expressed by eyewitnesses: one Communist told a meeting in May 1927 that he attended a plenum in Urgut "where they said, 'Here we have so-and-so-many unveiled women,' but when I walked on the street, I did not meet a single unveiled woman, [and] if I met [a woman] without a paranji, that did not matter, since her face was covered with something else."[8] First Secretary Akmal Ikramov expressed his doubts in a major speech of October 1927, blaming the troubles on interregional competitiveness:

> I remember when, at the plenum of the Commission for Liberation, we gave a good evaluation to one district or region, and the other districts were offended; their secretaries, in particular, were offended. When we gave Qöqon a good evaluation, saying that Karimov was working magnificently, that he had unveiled 67,000 women, and so on, then Tashkent said that they had not [merely] 67,000, but still more women unveiled, and so forth. And the Samarqand comrades once said—although in the city there was, in total, [only] 40,000 women—according to their word they had 70,000 unveiled (*laughter from the audience*).[9]

No matter why inaccurate data reached the central authorities, the obvious shortcomings of local reports alarmed top decision makers. Zhenotdel activists and high party leaders responded in several ways. First, they tried to reduce the stress on raw statistics as the only way to demonstrate or evaluate achievement. Instead, they encouraged local workers to explain the social behavior, both positive and negative, that lay behind the numbers. Their success in this effort remained less than complete, as local authorities continued to shower the Central Asian Bureau and Zhenotdel with statistical tables, but the intent was clear. Zinaida Prishchepchik, director of the Uzbek party's Zhenotdel, declared in May 1927 that the party should not become bogged down in empty disputes over numbers:

> How many women have unveiled in Samarqand province? Comrades, I think that Allah himself does not know this. I think that making an accurate inventory is an utterly impossible thing. There was an attempt in Zerafshon to make a list of all women. If you make a list of all 70,000 or 80,000 unveiled women, then you may find some comrades who declare their opinion that this figure is incorrect. Today's unveiled [woman] may wear the paranji again tomorrow, and thus [any] counts are inaccurate.

that district declare that the distant villages have only groups of 10 to 15 people [unveiled]" (RGASPI, d. 939, l. 17). Other cases of exaggeration and puffery are related at d. 1240, ll. 36–53.

8. RGASPI, d. 1240, l. 47.

9. RGASPI, d. 1238, l. 7. Local officials often did not have an opportunity to respond to such charges; an exception is at d. 1239, l. 6.

If we consider the strict measure, in which the unveiled woman does not reveil and begins to walk freely about the village, well, then, that would be another discussion, but unfortunately, that is not the situation today.

Together with [lists of] 70–80,000, probably, there are [other lists showing only] 30,000. It is difficult to speak about this now. Recently a verification was carried out that showed the figure of 30,000 was probably more accurate. Comrades, people attack and argue, saying that if this figure were to be checked again, then perhaps yet another result would be obtained. Nobody can decide this debate, and that is not the issue we set before you. We give a rough figure, one that gives the overall picture of what we face. It seems to me that we will not have a scholastic argument here, but the mere fact that so many women have unveiled shows that we undoubtedly have taken great strides in our work. Now we need to shift [our attention] to the matter of strengthening these accomplishments and preparing [our] forces toward this goal.[10]

Central decision makers also responded to the information deficit by declaring candor to be a cardinal virtue. Calls for self-criticism (*samokritika*) were sincere, at least as voiced by the central apparat, which undoubtedly hoped to elicit criticism of lower-level officials along with a better sense of what was happening in the localities.[11] This candor extended to the press: investigative reporters were dispatched to the provinces to chronicle setbacks, find mistaken party tactics, and report on violent resistance to the hujum.[12] Most public discussions did avoid the deep pessimism of classified reports—violence against unveiled women was portrayed in print as a nuisance, as merely a counterpoint to the inexorable, heroic onward march of liberation—but the articles stand in stark contrast to the largely sanitized press of the early 1930s.[13] Official approval of frank reporting may have meant to promote full disclosure by local authorities, but asking those authorities to evaluate their own records remained a recipe for disaster, so the publicity also aimed to induce local whistle-blowers to report difficulties. In all these ways party leaders hoped to subvert lower-level officials' control over information and its dissemination to the outside world.[14]

10. RGASPI, d. 1240, l. 620b.

11. Some high-level Uzbek Communists did call for intensive "verifications" of the upper reaches of the party. See PDA, op. 4, d. 1208, ll. 36–38; or RGASPI, d. 1238, ll. 83–84.

12. One early example is A. Nikolaeva, "Pervye itogi (Tashkentskii okrug)," *Kommunistka*, no. 8 (1927), 52–54. A later compilation was Adalis, "Voprosy khudzhuma," *Revoliutsiia i kul'-tura*, no. 12 (1929), 29–40.

13. For example, see Khairova, "K voprosy o zhenskom obrazovanii na Vostoke," *Kommunistka*, no. 6 (1928), 86–87.

14. This reasoning parallels that of J. Arch Getty, who argues that central leaders in Moscow used samokritika to attack local satraps and fiefs. The intent was to create an alliance of top leaders with the rank and file to squeeze mid-level "chieftains" (Getty, *Origins of the Great Purges: The Soviet Communist Party Reconsidered, 1933–1938* [Cambridge, 1985], 24–25).

Local candor, in other words, was far more likely if central leaders had access to independent sources of information. Newspaper reporters and party investigative brigades served this purpose, but they were expensive ways of gaining scattershot glimpses of local conditions. Party leaders also enlisted urban students as an intelligence-gathering force, urging them to spend vacations in the villages teaching peasants basic literacy skills while also carrying out political enlightenment and propaganda work. While in the countryside, the students were asked to keep detailed diaries, and to report immediately any urgent problems with the hujum, both to the local Zhenotdel and to the Central Asian party hierarchy in Tashkent. When they returned, students were expected to report on the number of unveiled women and who they were; the "mood" of various social groups; cases of forced unveiling by local authorities; the degree to which local Communists had liberated their own families; the state of literacy and educational work; and crimes directed against the women's liberation campaign.[15] Soviet authorities hoped these data would provide a better glimpse of rural society than the figures provided by local officials; it was no surprise, therefore, that these students frequently faced a hostile reception and difficult working conditions in the villages.

The true information breakthrough came when the Soviet secret police (OGPU) agreed to prepare a series of detailed, highly classified field reports about the hujum and its progress. As S. G. Shimko, the assistant director of the Central Asian Zhenotdel, noted confidentially in late 1926, party leaders in Tashkent had had little opportunity to see unvarnished popular sentiment. They were limited to observing Uzbek men and women at congresses and other meetings, "where there is always feigned enthusiasm."[16] To be sure, the OGPU had its own limitations and biases; like other Soviet bodies, it had a largely European staff, and thus was far from omniscient in the culturally foreign milieu of Central Asia. It also had a vested interest in finding anti-Soviet opposition and thereby justifying its own existence. Yet among Soviet institutions, the secret police had a strong claim on available resources. And with a comparatively extensive network of staff and informants and less of a vested interest in the women's campaign, the OGPU was better positioned to deliver high-quality, forthright intelligence about the hujum. Its institutional credibility rested on a reputation for candor, an ability to present leaders with uncomfortable facts, and during the late 1920s a stream of such reports arrived on the desks of central policy makers. Today these reports represent the best source available on the immediate Uzbek social responses to unveiling.[17] The decision to devote precious OGPU resources to such an investigation, more-

15. RGASPI, d. 1204, ll. 35–360b.
16. Shimko's letter requesting OGPU assistance is at RGASPI, d. 776, l. 140–1400b.
17. A raw sample is provided in the Appendix. I have found fourteen full reports: ten from 1928 and four from 1929. They are cited individually below, but in the aggregate are at PDA, op. 4, d. 1235; and RGASPI, dd. 1692, 1694, and 2064.

over, shows the high priority top party leaders accorded to the women's liberation campaign.

The reports by police investigators, party activists, reporters, and vacationing students were meant to show the strength and variety of Uzbek responses to the hujum; they actually do at least as much to illuminate their creators. They show how central policy makers perceived and understood Uzbek society, and how they evaluated tactics in terms of past performance and future promise. But even the secret police could not overcome the inherent contradictions between what it saw and the ideological expectations it faced in framing reports. This tension between the dual, dueling imperatives of surveillance and interpretation is ever present in the classified sources. How did Soviet eyes see Uzbekistan? In addition to the Orientalist visions already discussed, they drew some regional distinctions: the Uzbek SSR could be seen as a collection of discrete areas with their own peculiarities and idiosyncrasies, and not necessarily having much in common.[18] These differences, occasionally described with subtlety and discernment, implied the need for sensitivity to each area's particular features. Each was seen as being at a certain level or stage of sociocultural as well as economic development. Such differences made it possible to deem unveiling premature in some districts, or to explain why it proceeded more quickly in, say, Bukhoro than in Khiva.[19]

However important the regional factors, though, Bolsheviks could not concede that they drove Uzbek social dynamics. Why, after all, were different regions not at the same level of development—and so what lay behind the differential reception accorded the hujum? One basic answer fitted a Marxist perspective: conflict between social classes drove all aspects of human history, and so it too must determine the outcome of the hujum. In the classic view (held by or at least known to party true believers, although admittedly not by many unschooled rural Communists), changes over time in a society's relations of production shifted the power balance between existing and emerging, dominant and subordinate social classes. These shifts, in turn, drove human societies through a more or less inevitable succession of socioeconomic stages: from feudalism to capitalism, for example, and thence to socialism. This stage theory of history applied universally. Hence Central Asia's future could be known with certainty: currently judged to be at the precapitalist, feudal stage, it would inevitably follow Russia, Europe, and other more "advanced" areas. Moreover, since all social conflict amounted to the expression of antagonistic class interests (sometimes well hidden by a cultural "superstructure," sometimes not), class identities and struggles were the main explanatory vehicle that would shed light on Uzbek society.

18. See RGASPI, d. 1214, ll. 14–25 and 143–52, and d. 1240, l. 10.

19. These arguments were not necessarily consistent: the "backwardness" of Bukhoro's emir allegedly created a backlash, manifested in vigorous unveiling in 1927; yet a similarly retrograde regime in Khiva explained why the hujum ran into trouble there. See RGASPI, d. 1214, l. 76; Halle, *Women in the Soviet East,* 171–75; and Strong, *Red Star in Samarkand,* 261–73.

Almost all Soviet reports, whether classified or not, carefully identified the class origins of anyone accused of antihujum sentiments. The Muslim clergy, in particular, was treated as a unitary class and a particular enemy of Soviet power. This view, which amounted to an unspoken party mantra—"class to explain, clergy to blame"—rested on a chain of logical propositions. Uzbek society was said to consist of discrete socioeconomic classes (rather than clans or local, regional, or religio-cultural/ethno-national communities). Poor men and nearly all women were oppressed by these class relations, and thus were at least latently sympathetic to a Soviet message of class liberation. Opposition to Soviet power and the hujum hence emanated from a narrow class stratum at the top of Uzbek society, made up largely of Muslim clerics and wealthy bois, not from a broad religio-cultural consensus that crossed class lines. From the party's perspective, a dominant stratum might influence the masses, but its structural position was weak because it relied ultimately on force, and its members were few against the exploited masses. As a result, effective party work to unmask the class character of this dominant group's ostensibly religious position would change the way most Uzbeks saw them. This chain of reasoning led to the conclusion that cooperation and conciliation with class enemies was impossible: only the resolute pursuit of policies—such as the hujum—that defended the most oppressed groups within Uzbek society would lead to the triumph of Soviet power in the hearts and minds of working Uzbeks.

These ideas, while internally consistent, were poorly suited to Uzbek society, and together they led to startlingly flatfooted analyses. Soviet writers described the opposition to unveiling as coming from "nonproletarian elements"; that is, from mullahs, merchants, and "other nonlaboring elements." Loyal support for the party line on women's liberation, on the other hand, came from poor peasants, hired farm workers, and schoolteachers.[20] Reveiling, when it occurred, showed only successful "agitation" by the wives of Muslim clerics and bois. By contrast, in those areas "where bois and mullahs were isolated and opposed by the poor [classes] from the beginning, there was hardly any reveiling, and the bois' wives had no success."[21] From the Bolshevik point of view, the true contest was for the loyalty and allegiance of the "middle" peasantry (seredniaki), who had not yet allied themselves with poor laborers to achieve class liberation. The time for such a grand class alliance, they concluded, was now.[22]

Not all party activists were so dogmatic. Occasionally—particularly in confidential reports—they offered more subtle suggestions, focusing less on class purity than on the need to overcome the cultural hegemony of traditional gen-

20. RGASPI, d. 1211, l. 198; d. 1226, l. 61; and d. 1242, l. 199; and ÖzRMDA, f. 737, op. 1, d. 185, l. 257.
21. RGASPI, d. 1242, l. 30.
22. RGASPI, d. 1247, l. 115.

der values.[23] Even in secret Soviet discussions, however, most work plans followed a focus on class as the principal (and often only) defining feature of social identity. "Can the hujum be continued?" asked one top-secret report in early 1927. It was a remarkable question to pose, but the answer was calculated to reassure worried party members:

> It is completely true that the campaign for real liberation is being carried out against a background that is sufficiently gloomy that one may raise the question, is it necessary to go further with these sacrifices, would it not be more sensible and prudent to curtail the work that is under way, and to shift to a period of persuasion [rather than attack].
>
> It might be proper to insist, completely categorically, on such a course, if in fact among the allies of this campaign there were no workers, if there were no poor peasants. But the party directive has elicited a response from the workers and peasants, it has found support among the youth and the best part of the party membership. This speaks to the rightness of this directive, to its timeliness. In the ranks of those who hamper [us], who disrupt and ruin the work under way, we find reactionary forces, both in the form of open enemies—bois, clerics, and merchants—[and] hidden enemies, in the form of a certain high-ranking element in the party, which one way or another—in the past, and in most cases now as well—has had close links (of blood, politics, etc.) with the enemy groups, or those who still to this day have not yet broken away from [their] religious beliefs.[24]

From this perspective, there was no room for tactical compromise with class enemies and no space for dalliances with supposedly progressive clerics. However sympathetic such figures might appear to the goal of unveiling, they remained class enemies and could not be trusted.[25]

Nearly every Soviet report purporting to offer an overview of Uzbek social dynamics, whether on the hujum, land reform, or other policies, began by pigeonholing social responses into specific neat, predetermined boxes. The most salient feature of any Uzbek was her or his social class, not any religious, cultural, regional, or ethno-national identity.[26] Even reports on the hujum, where gender might be expected to play a paramount role, could not easily disentangle gender from class identity. These classes, delimited with careful precision, divided Uzbek society into two opposed camps of allies and enemies. Central Asia may have borne little resemblance to the classic European societies of nineteenth-century industrial capitalism analyzed by Marx, but party thinkers nonetheless worked out ways to categorize Uzbek society through the lens of

23. For one such exception, see RGASPI, d. 1242, ll. 124–26.
24. PDA, op. 3, d. 1598, l. 38.
25. RGASPI, d. 1213, l. 100.
26. For an example, see the report at PDA, op. 3, d. 1598, ll. 21–40.

Figure 15. Class enemies or allies? Uzbek men in conversation. (Courtesy Anahita Gallery, Santa Fe, N.M.)

class and class conflict. (See Figure 15.) Given that party and OGPU investigators were often told to find and report on the "mood" of each social class, moreover, such interpretations became self-fulfilling, and these analytic categories shaped Bolshevik data even before they had been gathered.[27] Everyone fitted into a distinct box, with little room left for doubt or ambiguity.

Through a Glass, Darkly: Uzbek Society through the Lens of Class

Bolshevik analysts began with their presumed class allies. Native Communists and Komsomol members came first, despite the problems with their sympathies and actions.[28] Presumed class allies also included several groups without direct, formal links to the party or Soviet power: industrial workers; peasants, especially poor and middle peasants; educated groups, especially schoolteachers; and women themselves. Marxist analysts deemed these groups exploited by their class positions in Uzbek society, and thus saw them as natural sup-

27. See the questionnaires at RGASPI, d. 1201, ll. 105–60b.
28. Reportedly only 5 percent of Samarqand's Communists supported the hujum, and many declared themselves to be religious believers. Others ridiculed unveiled women, or permitted their own wives to unveil only in the New Cities (PDA, op. 3, d. 1598, ll. 23–26; and RGASPI, d. 1211, l. 93; d. 1214, l. 31; and d. 1242, l. 208). Problems in the Komsomol seemed almost beyond hope; see PDA, op. 4, d. 1208, ll. 36–37.

porters of a class-based message of liberation. Once Soviet policies such as the hujum and land and water reform became better known, these groups were expected to respond more or less straightforwardly in support.

Problems in the party and Komsomol were not ignored, but detailed internal discussions rarely considered how thoroughly these Uzbek men (and the few women involved) had been socialized into the values, behaviors, and worldview of Muslim society. How far were their motivations class-driven? How much did they know of, let alone support, Bolshevik political doctrine? One might think the answers manifest from the evidence already adduced. From the party's perspective, however, Uzbek Communists were by definition the class vanguard of Uzbek society, and thus ipso facto the leading edge of Soviet power in Central Asia. If their behavior in the hujum showed problems, only two explanations could be proffered. Either they had not understood the campaign, in which case accurate explanation and good political counsel would change their hearts, minds, and deeds; or they were hidden class enemies who had inveigled a party card to subvert the Soviet mission from within. In this case, they had to be punished and expelled from the party, but their presence would not show any deeper problem: after all, they did not really belong to the party, they were only using their membership cards for cover.[29]

For such a proletarian organization as the Bolshevik Party, industrial workers ranked at the top of any list of allies. In Central Asia, the indigenous working class was tiny, and so could offer political support only in the long term. Nonetheless, Bolshevik writers expected a combination of factors—higher education and literacy levels, greater economic independence for women, exposure to urban culture, the benefits of trade union membership, and the experience of industrial labor itself—to produce a proletarian consciousness, with a concomitant Bolshevik sensibility, among those workers that did exist. Party activists thus anticipated strong support for unveiling among urban workers, and trumpeted its early manifestations:

> The majority of workers removed the paranji from their wives even before 8 March (Qōqon, Andijon, Tashkent). Before 1 May there was a new wave of unveilings among the wives of trade union members (1,520 women in Qōqon). . . . In the mahallas of Qōqon where workers live, almost no paranjis remain. . . . In Andijon all the workers at the creamery removed the paranji from their wives, and there is not a single case of reveiling. The wives of workers (at a meeting in Andijon) despairingly cut into the party members for not liquidating seclusion among their own wives with sufficient strictness. Some workers' wives declared that their husbands had long been ready to raise the issue of unveiling, but

29. PDA, op. 3, d. 1598, ll. 37–38. The belief that explanation will persuade true Communists to do the right thing is expressed at d. 1533, ll. 59–60.

that it had been awkward [*neudobno*] to do so before the beginning of the hujum.[30]

Factory workers were depicted as strong allies, sometimes impatient with the party's slow pace in unveiling women, and willing to overcome violent resistance in the pursuit of liberation. In this narrative they sometimes served as better personal examples than Uzbek Communists: several lists of trade union members asserted that most had unveiled and perhaps even stayed uncovered.[31]

In the overwhelmingly rural environment of Central Asia, however, party activists knew that peasant attitudes would be critical. Secret police and other reports show that rural Uzbekistan did not welcome the hujum. The writers of these reports, though, framed their story differently, relying on the notion of deep class divisions in Uzbek peasant society. Peasants may have appeared to resist the hujum, that is, but such resistance did not accord with the class interests of poor and middle peasants, who should sympathize with Soviet aims. (They were expected, for instance, to welcome the labor of newly unveiled women.)[32] Opposition could thus be assumed a priori to originate from other sources, most likely the wealthy, "exploiter" peasants known as bois (Russianized as *bais* or *beks,* later referred to as the Central Asian analogue of kulaks) or other class enemies, such as Muslim clerics.[33] Occasionally a vague "hostile stratum" of middle peasants bore some blame.[34] By contrast, poor peasants and hired farmhands were described, generally without much supporting evidence, as sympathetic allies.[35] When mobs of undeniably poor peasants stormed Soviet buildings, killed unveiled women, or otherwise expressed displeasure with Bolshevik policies, explanations followed from first principles: either these poor peasants had fallen under the influence of class enemies or the party itself was to blame for not making clear the political character of women's liberation and its connection to the class interests of poor peasants.[36]

If Bolshevik analysts were whistling in the dark by assuming the latent sympathy of Uzbek peasants, they similarly believed that most Uzbek women sup-

---

30. RGASPI, d. 1240, l. 120b.

31. PDA, op. 3, d. 1598, ll. 28–29; RGASPI, d. 1211, ll. 93, 135, and 191; and ÖzRMDA, f. 737, op. 1, d. 185, ll. 187–90, 257, and 265.

32. RGASPI, d. 1247, l. 221.

33. An Uzbek government report of 1931 blamed antihujum violence and terrorism on such class enemies, who sometimes acted by "using the politically unknowing [*nesoznatel'nye*] forces of the poor peasants and hired farmhands" (ÖzRMDA, f. 6, op. 2, d. 462, l. 27).

34. RGASPI, d. 1205, l. 8; and PDA, op. 3, d. 1598, l. 29.

35. RGASPI, d. 1199, l. 15, and d. 1211, ll. 93 and 193. A rare exception, admitting that poor peasants could oppose the hujum because of the difficulties of the "personal moment" of unveiling, is at d. 1203, l. 16.

36. The party blamed itself at RGASPI, d. 1199, l. 17, and d. 1240, ll. 140b-15.

ported the goals and techniques of the hujum. Women, deemed universally oppressed by patriarchal Muslim society, seemed from the Bolshevik point of
view self-evidently core allies in the unveiling campaign. Soviet sources bravely
declared—again without much evidence—that the "mass" of women were
sympathetic, and that their *aktivnost'* (activism; energy and devotion to the
cause) was growing inexorably as Soviet efforts became more widely known.[37]
They retained this belief in the face of all evidence to the contrary—evidence
that the same investigators reported faithfully. They testified that some women
resisted unveiling but had been forced to comply by husbands or party workers; that others flatly refused to consider it without new clothes or better protection against street harassment; and that still others actively demonstrated
against the entire policy.[38] Given their exploited position in Uzbek society,
though, women—particularly lower-class women—could not actually oppose
their own emancipation. The apparent paradox thus explained itself. Either
these women had been intimidated or brainwashed by class enemies, or they
did not understand Soviet aims, or party tactics had been to blame. Actual opposition could be no more than scattered "incidents," and so was of no great
concern. This reasoning enabled a classified report of May 1927 to describe
decidedly ambivalent female attitudes toward unveiling, and then to blithely
ignore them:

> In Khojent province mass work began when mahalla commission
> members gathered and were told that the unveiling campaign required
> meetings to be held in each mahalla. Mass meetings began, to which . . .
> all women were required to come without their paranjis. Women came,
> leaving their paranjis at home, hanging muslin in front of their faces,
> with lamentations and wailing (they wept that in this guise they would
> not rise to heaven, that after death they would not be buried in a grave,
> etc.). . . .
> [But] in general, the question of women's liberation has penetrated the
> broad mass of laborers in the city, both organized and unorganized. In
> general, a mood of support for the annihilation of [female] seclusion has
> been created, although long, sustained work is still needed to strengthen
> the already attained results, to deepen and broaden them.[39]

A final group in the camp of class allies, dubbed the "progressive intelligentsia" by Soviet writers, occupied a problematic, ambiguous position. This
group, consisting mostly of teachers, did not have a clear class interest linking

37. Women's aktivnost' was reported to have grown "colossally" at RGASPI, d. 1240, l. 17.
38. PDA, op. 3, d. 1598, ll. 27–28; RGASPI, d. 1225, l. 74; and ÖzRMDA, f. 837, op. 3, d.
150, l. 136.
39. RGASPI, d. 1240, l. 14.

it to the Bolshevik cause, yet Soviet analysts noted native intellectuals' general support of the hujum. They explained these people's support by reference not to such plausible local factors as their jadid heritage but to their relatively high educational level.[40] In some cases "intellectuals of a Soviet mood" (*sovetski-nastroennaia intelligentsia*), often drawn from a younger generation, were more stalwart allies than native Communists; in others they were too "passive" in their work for women's emancipation and not willing to fight for the Soviet cause.[41] As a group, teachers received a positive evaluation for their sympathy with the Soviet project and for unveiling their wives, but the ambivalence of their class position limited their usefulness and produced politically "immature" views among them. This equivocal standing caused their advice—they often urged party leaders to wait, or to slow down or moderate their confrontational methods—to be tarred with the brush of "immaturity," and frequently ignored as a result.

Soviet analysts also parsed Uzbek society into discrete bits when they described a camp of enemies. Not surprisingly, all its members—clergy, bois, merchants, and former bureaucrats of the emir—were found to have class interests deeply antagonistic to an emancipatory proletarian revolution. Their shared domination of capital and labor made them social exploiters; this position was now fundamentally threatened by the Soviet project. Thus they formed the core of opposition to the hujum, sweeping other social groups along by any means available. Just as they supposedly instigated resistance to other Soviet policies—land reform, tax policy, new electoral rights—they allegedly spread malicious rumors about the hujum and misled peasants, workers, and women about Soviet intentions, browbeating them into submission and whipping up an anti-Soviet frenzy.[42]

Wealthy landowners and merchants fitted logically onto this Bolshevik enemies list, and so (in a slightly different way) did the emir's former bureaucrats. Each had analogues in revolutionary Russia, where the Bolshevik Party had reaped a political windfall in 1917 by denouncing the propertied classes (*tsenzovoe obshchestvo*), broadly defined. These Central Asian groups were similarly blamed for the problems now facing Soviet Uzbekistan. Top-secret OGPU reports on the "popular mood," for instance, found antihujum sentiments rife among the bourgeoisie. Merchants and bois allegedly harassed unveiled women, calling them prostitutes and offering to take payment in sexual favors; sent their wives to protest forced unveiling as well as Soviet tax hikes; and,

40. RGASPI, d. 1211, ll. 137 and 192–93; and d. 1240, ll. 13 and 41.
41. The phrase is from RGASPI, d. 1238, l. 68. For a more negative judgment, see d. 1242, ll. 208–9, where female teachers were accused of abandoning their veiled sisters by fleeing to marriage in the New Cities.
42. PDA, op. 3, d. 1598, ll. 31–32; and RGASPI, d. 1214, ll. 145–46. As one writer put it, bois and mullahs were "trying to use their weakening authority" by playing on the "dark instincts of the less conscious elements" ("Staryi gorod i ego prestupniki," *PV*, 24 June 1927). For the fear these formerly dominant groups were said to feel, see ÖzRMDA, f. 9, op. 1, d. 3397, l. 6.

most troubling of all, "held the masses under their influence."[43] Similar anti-hujum views, of course, had been reported among peasants and workers. The key difference was their class position: for peasants, resistance to unveiling was ("objectively") aberrant, showing a lack of education or manipulation by class enemies. For the bourgeoisie, by contrast, anti-Soviet feelings were not only expected but required, since they expressed an elemental class antagonism. Identical behavior thus showed their deeply anti-Soviet character and justified harsh reprisals.

Yet however badly bourgeois groups fared in the Soviet estimation, definitions of class could not be quite the same in Uzbekistan as in Russia. Party leaders always maintained that the Muslim clergy were the main enemies of women's liberation; indeed, they were the principal oppressors of the Uzbek lower classes and the main hindrance to a modern Central Asia. This oppression might be masked by spiritual or cultural arguments, but a keen Marxist intellect saw through that charade. The mullahs' class position could be traced back to the Islamic conversion, when an educated group of newly arrived Arab-Iranian "holy men" became preachers and established dominance over local trade routes.[44] Although the scholars, teachers, and mullahs of the contemporary ulamo—much less the mystics of the various Sufi orders—did not constitute a formal clergy in the same sense as the Russian Orthodox hierarchy, this fact did not slow Bolshevik analysts appreciably. In their view, the clerical "aristocracy" had kept their economic grip for centuries, even into the Soviet period, as evidenced by their continued wealth and power, wielded through and by mosques, religious endowments, and individual mullahs. The clergy maintained this hammerlock through an elaborate system of religious, cultural, and economic rituals, in which female seclusion played an integral role. Uzbek women's paranjis therefore flowed less from the dictates of morality than from the need to preserve a particular class structure. Soviet power threatened this cozy state of affairs, party analysts concluded, and thus the Muslim clergy vigorously opposed every Bolshevik move.

As we have seen, Soviet writers frequently distinguished two groups among the clergy. "Conservative" clerics—meaning roughly the qadimist scholars and teachers of the ulamo, although the label was sometimes used more widely—were those who stood against the hujum and made no secret of their views.[45] Preaching against unveiling, spreading rumors about Soviet intentions and mistakes, and frightening Uzbek women into reveiling by misrepresenting the international situation: none of it, in Soviet eyes, was beneath or beyond

43. PDA, op. 3, d. 1549, ll. 10–12, and d. 1598, l. 34; RGASPI, d. 1199, l. 20, and d. 1214, l. 16.
44. RGASPI, d. 1242, l. 208.
45. PDA, op. 3, d. 1598, ll. 32–33.

these conservative clerics, and hypocrisy and cowardice were the least of their sins.[46] When an unveiled Uzbek woman fell victim to attack or murder, conservative clerics were portrayed as lurking behind the scenes, whether as instigating, directing, or indirectly inspiring the act.[47]

"Progressive" clerics, by contrast, drew on the jadidist heritage to support the ultimate goal of unveiling. Although critical of some Soviet methods, they might thus on the surface seem to be allies: some preached in praise of Soviet power, and a few Tatar jadids celebrated International Women's Day.[48] Ikramov cited one such cleric in a major speech of October 1927, declaring that "in the words of one of the prominent jadids, Munavvar Qori, it is obvious that 'if there were no Soviet power, then we would not have been able to liberate our women from the paranji, and would not have been able to take up those issues with which Soviet power is now dealing.' "[49]

But Ikramov quickly went on to call Munavvar Qori "our active opponent." From the party's perspective, the notion of a progressive clergy was tricky, and despite their support for Soviet goals, such clerics could not be welcomed with open arms. However progressive their politics might seem, they made strange bedfellows for an atheistic party. In the end their class position made such a choice intolerable, and the jadids, who could have been valuable allies, had to be denounced as enemies. In this case, the goal of unveiling was subordinated to the wider interest in class purity. The jadids' interest in unveiling, moreover, made this group in some ways more dangerous than open oppositionists. Party leaders feared losing the initiative in women's liberation: in several cases Uzbek women had confused jadids with Communists, thus missing the fact that true liberation came only in October 1917.[50] Jadidist clerics had to be stopped from making use of such confusion to challenge Soviet claims to leadership and power.[51]

On one level, this shared focus on women among Communists and jadids shows the centrality of gender roles in defining visions of social order. At the same time, the confusion demonstrates the limits the party faced in using Uzbek women as revolutionary symbols. In the Central Asian context, programs equating unveiling with liberation were neither only nor strictly Bolshevik; and once unveiling became a top priority, popular confusion between jadid and Zhenotdel programs became politically dangerous. This danger in turn pushed the party to redouble its efforts while questioning the sincerity of

46. Ibid., d. 1549, ll. 10–12; RGASPI, d. 1061, ll. 13–14, and d. 1214, ll. 21–22.

47. The baleful influence of such clerics could be discerned where antihujum sentiment ran highest, according to ÖzRMDA, f. 737, op. 1, d. 185, ll. 143–44.

48. RGASPI, d. 1203, l. 18. Criticism of Soviet methods is at PDA, op. 4, d. 1208, ll. 36–38.

49. RGASPI, d. 1238, l. 2. On Munavvar Qori, see Khalid, *Politics of Muslim Cultural Reform*, 95–96.

50. RGASPI, d. 1206, l. 46.

51. PDA, op. 3, d. 1549, ll. 10–12; and RGASPI, d. 1242, ll. 500b-51.

jadids' commitment to women's liberation.[52] By this point no retreat on women's unveiling could be considered, not even if such efforts were having a counterproductive effect on Uzbek attitudes toward Bolshevik power.

Confrontation or Persuasion: Ideology and the Debate over Tactics

The ideological lens also influenced the evaluation of an initially wide variety of unveiling tactics. When local Soviet workers received in 1927 a sweeping mandate to attack harmful customs that oppressed women, such as the paranji, they responded in dissimilar ways. Broadly speaking, they advocated techniques that fell along a continuum from hard to soft, and a lively debate ensued as to the relative merits of the two approaches. In practical terms, neither extreme enjoyed much immediate success: no tactics on offer seemed able to create an unveiled, literate, employed, and socially active Uzbek womanhood. Hence neither camp, hard or soft, won the unqualified approval of party higher-ups. As their shortcomings became plain, too, each strategy—the details of which usually were devised by activists operating under their own authority—faced severe criticism by party and police investigators and by high Soviet officials. The original vagueness of high-level directives generally escaped blame, but in the end the ideological predispositions of top Bolsheviks played a decisive role in the differential evaluation of arguably similar practical outcomes. While both hard and soft approaches encountered difficulties, then, their different ideological implications and perceived political associations proved crucial in the intraparty struggle to define Soviet Central Asian policy.

Advocates of hard and soft lines based their conflicting policy prescriptions on fundamentally different analyses of the hujum's troubles. Hard-liners saw the problem as an insufficiently resolute approach to class enemies; they called for strict tactics of uncompromising confrontation. In their view, the campaign's initially limited scope—focusing on wives of party, government, and union members, and in only a few major urban areas—was partly to blame. Unveiling, they argued, should be a kind of permanent revolution in gender relations, being broadened as far and as quickly as possible: to outlying regions and districts, rural villages, and the nonparty masses.[53] Antihujum resistance,

---

52. At a district congress in February 1927, one speaker argued that even progressive clerics did not wholeheartedly support female unveiling. He cited a mullah who had declared that unveiling was lawful according to shariat, but fled when challenged to unveil his wife. In the speaker's view, this showed the slyness and treachery of his ilk. "Enemies are starting to attach themselves [to our program]," he concluded, "in order to draw the masses toward them" (RGASPI, d. 1196, ll. 10–11).

53. Trotsky is associated with the concept of "permanent revolution," but (not surprising in 1927) I have found no citations of him in this context. On expanding beyond the party, see RGASPI, d. 1241, l. 20. On moving into outlying areas and villages, see d. 1239, l. 34, and d. 1249, l. 94.

they declared, came from class enemies, to whom no quarter could be granted. Muslim clerics in particular were the wellspring of antihujum opposition, but their exploitative class position by definition prevented them from enjoying wide popular support.[54] Hence they should be "isolated and neutralized": criminal charges should be brought against anyone who spoke against unveiling.[55] Soviet courts and laws should protect unveiled Uzbek women from harassment and should make an example of those who did not observe Bolshevik norms of women's rights.[56] Even widespread opposition to unveiling within party and Komsomol ranks did not call for reexamination of the hujum; hardliners took it as evidence of the presence of hidden class enemies, who by stealth had worked their way into the Soviet apparatus. Since by definition antihujum attitudes amounted to a display of (anti-Soviet) class colors, these opponents had to be rooted out without hesitation or mercy. Thus purges were needed to weed out Communists who resisted unveiling their own wives or showed insufficient zeal in prosecuting the unveiling campaign.[57] Indeed, violent attacks on unveiled women only showed the need to stay the course, since they revealed the desperation of anti-Soviet class enemies whose backs were now against a wall.[58]

By contrast, adherents of a softer approach felt that the hujum's difficulties could be traced to too much rather than not enough confrontation. This group argued that pressuring women to unveil while not simultaneously guaranteeing their physical and economic security could only backfire, since it would alienate the very people whose support the campaign hoped to gain. It might even force women into prostitution.[59] True change would come to Central Asia only slowly, through persuasion, not coercion; the party had first to subvert the cultural hegemony of traditional values and gender roles by changing the way Uzbek men and women saw the world and their place in it. This group thus proposed a more differentiated vision of unveiling, arguing that Uzbek women would remove their paranjis voluntarily only when activists turned away from dramatic veil-burnings toward the more humdrum, day-to-day business of pro-

54. RGASPI, d. 1247, l. 222. Other groups that shared control of socioeconomic resources, such as parents and the older generation in general, allegedly shared the clergy's attitude. See d. 1242, l. 208.

55. The quotation is from RGASPI, d. 1212, l. 122. On criminal charges, see PDA(K), op. 3, d. 152, l. 7.

56. General calls for show trials to protect women are at PDA, op. 3, d. 1533, ll. 59–60, and op. 4, d. 1208, ll. 36–38.

57. See PDA, op. 4, d. 1208, ll. 36–38; RGASPI, d. 1238, ll. 83–84, and d. 1242, ll. 119–22.

58. ÖzRMDA, f. 737, op. 1, d. 49, ll. 39–40.

59. They pointed to cases in which indiscriminate use of "administrative pressure" had unfortunate consequences, providing anti-Soviet groups with rhetorical ammunition. See PDA, op. 3, d. 1533, ll. 10–13 and 23–25; d. 1598, ll. 16–18; op. 4, d. 1208, ll. 36–38; and RGASPI, d. 1238, ll. 920b-93; d. 1242, ll. 23, 38–39, and 122; d. 1245, ll. 23, 32–33, and 36. For allegations that too rapid unveiling could lead to prostitution, see RGASPI, d. 1205, ll. 806–9; d. 1214, ll. 2–3 and 32–33; or PDA, op. 3, d. 1549, ll. 3–4, and d. 1598, ll. 29–31.

viding women with economic and institutional support in the form of education and training programs.[60] Cities and villages, too, had to be treated differently; stringent insistence on immediate unveiling everywhere was premature and counterproductive, as it provoked violent resistance. Instead of universal, unwavering confrontation, this group maintained, it was preferable to calibrate the work to each locality, even if work in some particularly difficult regions had to be slowed: to paraphrase Lenin, better to work slower but better.[61] Finally, supporters of a soft approach saw the strict class purity of the means as less important than the ultimate end of women's liberation. They urged activists to make use of all resources at hand; in particular, they urged cooperation with progressive clerics, who after all sympathized with the goal of unveiling. It might even help to seek a *fatwa* (religious edict) to permit unveiling, they mused, since it would legitimate the campaign in the public eye.[62]

Taken as a whole, this nuanced vision of a differentiated approach held promise for overcoming some of the problems encountered in 1927. It represented a clear alternative to the hard-line vision of continuing, ever-sharper conflict, and in many ways fitted the conciliatory, go-slow attitude of Soviet policy during the 1920s, under the aegis of Lenin's New Economic Policy (NEP). But by 1927 Lenin had been dead for three years; NEP was falling out of favor, along with its main corollary in nationality policy—korenizatsiia, the effort to indigenize local party and state apparatuses. In Central Asia, moreover, such soft-line, conciliatory policies curried suspicion through their jadidist associations. Some party officials labeled such views "nationalist," pointing out their lack of class consciousness. By rejecting overly cautious, tepid approaches to women's liberation, these officials wanted to prove that Soviet power, not jadid reformism, was the true revolutionary force in Central Asia. On a practical level, too, the vast financial and other resources required to build an effective women's infrastructure could not be guaranteed, so the promise of a less expensive kind of liberation, attained through dramatic demonstrations and heroic pronouncements rather than massive budget outlays, also held substantial appeal.

In practice, of course, hard and soft approaches were not always easily dis-

---

60. On voluntary unveiling, see RGASPI, d. 1225, ll. 74 and 106. On economic independence, see ÖzRMDA, f. 837, op. 3, d. 150, l. 174. Intellectuals argued that economic and cultural support would lead women, bit by bit, to unveiling: see RGASPI, d. 1214, l. 33.

61. For such invocations, see the reports from Samarqand and Oltiariq at RGASPI, d. 1240, l. 330b, and d. 1245, l. 31. For recommendations that work be slowed where necessary, see d. 1240, ll. 10 and 48. Some activists called for slower unveiling lest the women involved stray into prostitution or a dissolute life, or otherwise prove bad examples: see PDA, op. 3, d. 1533, ll. 24–25. Some party committees were criticized for beginning too soon; see the top-secret reprimand received by the Surkhondaryo Zhenotdel for violating orders to delay the hujum at RGASPI, d. 1214, l. 110. On the need to treat city and village differently, see d. 1212, l. 122.

62. See RGASPI, d. 1238, ll. 2 and 920b; d. 1240, l. 34; and d. 1242, ll. 210–12; and PDA, op. 4, d. 1208, ll. 34–35.

tinguishable. Various officials took different positions on a variety of issues, and changed their views over time; for that matter, individual resolutions and pronouncements were not always internally consistent. Insofar as two camps existed, moreover, neither dominated early policy discussions. Both had important supporters, and the written record shows a vigorous exchange of views within the party over these basic questions of strategy and tactics. Both groups had early successes in implementing proposals to help unveiled women: the establishment of support groups, for instance, sat side by side with the passage of strict laws against insulting or attacking unveiled women.[63] By late 1927, however, activists with hard-line views had started to enjoy comparatively greater success in the policy arena. Since proponents of a softer line tended to be those men and women best able to see and understand social responses on the ground—local activists and schoolteachers, for instance, including many ethnic Uzbeks and the few Russians who knew local languages—this outcome had unhappy consequences for the campaign's later success. With hindsight, the seeds of these consequences are evident in the debates that took place in late 1927 over the hujum.

In these debates, the hard line was criticized for excesses, for riding roughshod over local sensibilities and thus providing fodder for anti-Soviet enemies to whip up popular antagonism to Soviet rule. "Crude, clumsy approaches to the issue [of unveiling] have led to discontent among the population, and even partial unrest," said one report, in something of an understatement; lengthy discussions of the dangers of using coercion, "pressure" (*nazhim*), or "administrative rule" (*administrirovanie*) featured prominently in nearly every confidential field report on the hujum.[64] The campaign's rhetoric seemed to lend itself to such methods—the word "hujum," after all, was translated from the Russian *nastuplenie* (attack or onslaught)—but it soon became apparent that such tactics could easily backfire. OGPU observers reported case after case of coercion, few of which had the desired long-term effects. Local activists threatened men with fines, arrest, long imprisonment, even death if they did not permit their wives to attend Soviet meetings or to unveil, and sometimes carried out these threats.[65] In an eerie echo of tsarist practice, Soviet police rounded up prominent men (especially mullahs) for brief jail stays around Soviet holidays, such as May Day.[66] In Namangan, remarkably, peasants even appealed to the OGPU for protection against lower-level Communists, complaining that these officials bran-

63. On support groups, see RGASPI, d. 1250, ll. 28–29; one such law was published as "O predostvalenii osobykh l'got zhenshchinam po okhrane ikh cherez sudebnye uchrezhdeniia ot nasilii i oskorblenii po povodu sniatiia parandzhi," *Sobranie uzakonenii i rasporiazhenii rabochego i dekhkanskogo pravitel'stva UzSSR*, 1927, sec. 1, no. 1, art. 56, pp. 234–35.

64. The quotation is from RGASPI, d. 939, l. 17.

65. PDA, op. 4, d. 1208, l. 34; and RGASPI, d. 939, l. 17, and d. 1214, ll. 75 and 98.

66. RGASPI, d. 1211, l. 208, and d. 1240, l. 150b.

dished pistols and sometimes opened fire on the peasantry to force local women to unveil.[67]

Veiled Uzbek women faced the same sanctions, and cases of sobbing women being dragged bodily to meetings by Soviet police pepper the documents.[68] But women also encountered special hurdles. Some Soviet factories refused to keep women employees who failed to unveil, and some officials refused to hear petitions and grievances from veiled women.[69] Some zealous local officials threatened to prosecute unveiled women if they reveiled; others empowered the general citizenry forcibly to unveil any women they encountered. In Osh, a heavily Uzbek region of southwestern Kyrgyzstan, informal troikas roamed the streets and unveiled any covered woman they saw.[70] Most women did not welcome such tactics. When one party member ripped off his wife's veil at a public meeting, for instance, she reportedly shrieked and fell into the nearest irrigation ditch (*ariq*). In the ensuing tumult, all the other women ran away.[71] When four women at a similar meeting in the village of Kum were unveiled by force, all other women present fled the scene, vowing never again to attend a Soviet event.[72]

From the Soviet point of view, the outcomes of these coercive tactics were less than ideal. The difficulties brought about by intemperate approaches are well illustrated by a mahalla meeting held in Old Tashkent on 23 July 1927. According to a classified party report on the incident, this meeting—held in a former mosque—showed both the torpor of Soviet efforts and the popular antagonism bubbling just beneath the surface. "From conversations with women before the meeting," the report began, "it became clear that the favorite methods [of preparation] . . . had been intimidation by so-called guards (mahalla plenipotentiaries); while giving notification of meetings, these guards had threatened no-shows with a fine (from 60 to 300 rubles), the husband's arrest, or, more mildly, the husband's expulsion from his trade union." Such techniques yielded a list of twenty-five women reportedly willing to unveil, and in the end about fifty women and thirty men, mostly Young Communists, turned up at the meeting. But attendance was no guarantee of success, it transpired, because once at the meeting,

> naturally, no kind of enthusiasm or élan could be felt. It was not aroused by the report by a member of the mahalla commission, either, [one that

---

67. RGASPI, d. 1211, l. 209. This source describes a meeting in Shur-Qorghon at which a peasant asked the district committee leader whether veiling was to be voluntary. The official whipped out a revolver and demanded to know, "What business is it of yours?" The peasants did not respond well to this approach; they surrounded the official and drove him onto a roof, from which he opened fire. Partly because of such altercations, peasants' hunting weapons were soon confiscated—a further restriction that must have added to the regime's unpopularity.

68. RGASPI, d. 1202, l. 84; d. 1211, l. 208; d. 1214, l. 123; d. 1225, l. 106; d. 1240, l. 85.

69. RGASPI, d. 1242, l. 172, and d. 1250, l. 28.

70. RGASPI, d. 939, l. 17; d. 1211, l. 211; and d. 1214, ll. 111 and 130.

71. RGASPI, d. 1211, l. 206.

72. RGASPI, d. 1214, l. 126.

was] popular and thorough enough but that dragged on for an hour and a half. It was obvious that no kind of preparation had preceded the meeting, as after the report confusion and embarrassment settled in: the women did not manifest any readiness to remove [their] paranjis, and [so] the organizers started mass-meeting agitation [among them].

This informal, individual lobbying, however, had an effect opposite from that intended:

As discussion proceeded, a member of the Communist Party since 1919, Gazi Khojaev, a worker on the local city committee and president of a mahalla commission, took the floor to give a fiery speech *against* unveiling, indicating the incorrectness of the party line in its work among women [and] protesting against the coercion used by local party workers in their work on unveiling. His speech provoked a stormy protest from one part of the audience and passionate support from the other. For ten minutes the meeting remained utterly disorganized. The flickering light of torches, shouts, the crush of the throng, the disorderly music—all of this would have produced on a passing viewer the impression that it was some kind of barbaric festival.

This vivid depiction was far from the image party leaders had intended for Soviet liberation. By this point, though, the carefully orchestrated script of emancipation had been left far behind; only with "great effort" was "a relative degree of order" restored.

Finally, they got around to the gala unveiling of women. Even as the din and hubbub continued, a portion of the women began to throw off their veils. A list of unveiled women's names was recorded by a police officer.

At this moment the husband of one of the unveiled women was detected in the back rows, having appeared with a knife and intending to kill his wife. He was arrested.

Then a scandal broke out by the meeting's exit: a few women wanted to leave to breast-feed their infants. Some youths by the door—clearly members of the mahalla commissions—refused to allow them to leave. Somebody intervened on the women's behalf. The result was a stormy squabble.

During the course of the entire meeting, mullahs rushed up and down the walls of the mosque, arriving just in time for the hottest moments, just as if somebody had notified them beforehand.[73]

Plainly, such meetings showed little promise of creating sympathy for the Bolsheviks, let alone of yielding many permanently unveiled women. The

---

73. This report is at RGASPI, d. 1206, ll. 25–26 (emphasis in original).

hujum was meant to help the Soviet cause, not hurt it, but these coercive tactics often backfired. Class enemies were only too willing to pounce on Soviet mistakes: large demonstrations broke out in Namangan, for example, protesting the hujum and Soviet power itself. With crowds numbering upwards of 500, these were an ominous development.[74] Given the tenuous nature of Soviet control, real dangers loomed, and party activists were enjoined not to use more force to unveil Uzbek women.

The hard line was thus culpable for going too far too fast and for ignoring the importance of free will in unveiling. But as Lenin had said in his famous pamphlet *"Left-Wing" Communism, an Infantile Disorder,* such errors in judgment could be seen as the product of insufficient political maturity, not of incorrect principle.[75] They could therefore be corrected incrementally, by moderating the overeagerness that made activists rush ahead too quickly. Proponents of a soft line faced a much harsher political verdict. According to their critics, they erred in their basic premises and allegedly violated the most axiomatic Soviet principles. Their strategies, tactics, and advice were thus fundamentally misguided, and in the end could serve only to indicate where Soviet policy ought not to go.

Perhaps most fundamentally, the soft-liners appealed to Uzbeks for the wrong reasons: they used gentle, "cultural" approaches rather than an uncompromising attitude of confrontation toward class enemies. Bolsheviks should seek to transform Uzbek society completely, hard-line critics sniped, a goal they could not accomplish by permitting a Muslim framework to dictate the terms of discussion. They denounced, for example, a rash of cases in which local party officials had enlisted Muslim clerics as allies. In some instances they sought religious dispensation to authorize unveiling; in others they asked mullahs to preach about the harmful effects of the paranji, sometimes even asking them to lead the family circles (*kruzhki*) that lay at the heart of the Soviet agitation effort.[76] The motivations of these officials are often obscure but sometimes they defended their views openly, urging the party at large to make use of progressive clerics.[77] Such appeals fell increasingly on deaf ears, as top-level decision makers saw no excuse for reliance on class enemies in the clergy.[78] This approach, they felt, would only muddy the waters by diluting

74. RGASPI, d. 1242, l. 172. See also "Provokatsiia mull," *PV,* 6 Sept. 1927.

75. An English version is in *The Lenin Anthology,* ed. Robert C. Tucker, 550–618 (New York, 1975).

76. RGASPI, d. 1203, l. 49, and d. 1238, l. 920b. One local party official mixed this approach with coercion, arresting imams who refused to order women to unveil (d. 1214, l. 98).

77. RGASPI, d. 1240, l. 34, and d. 1242, l. 212. Several factors seem to have been at work. Some officials no doubt hoped to improve the unveiling campaign's dismal success rate, or at least to reduce the frequency of violent attacks and threats by enlisting religious support. Others seem to have approached the clergy for the same reasons as their neighbors: they sought religious counsel as to whether the hujum should be supported, tolerated, or opposed. Still others appeared genuinely confused, unable to snap the deep links between religion and politics.

78. PDA, op. 4, d. 1208, ll. 34–35.

Bolshevik claims to a distinctive message of class liberation. The veil could not be treated as a matter of character or religious obligation; once that concession was made, hard-liners contended, the argument had already been lost.

When they tried to persuade women to unveil, moreover, the soft camp sometimes employed tactics fully as counterproductive as the arm-twisting of hard-line activists. On many occasions local officials took persuasion too far, sweetening the deal for women by offering rewards for unveiling. These rewards, amounting in practice to bribes, became a major problem when—as happened all too frequently—the promises could not be kept. As one confidential report put it:

> There are also cases when female workers tried to force Uzbek women to unveil with the aid of various material inducements, such as [promises] that in the city they can have gold teeth put in, they will be given a pretty dress, paid work will be found for them, places will be found for them in school, etc. When these Uzbek women arrived in the city, of course, they received nothing that was promised, and as a result they returned to the village, where some of the deceived women reveiled themselves, and some of them started to agitate against the later unveiling of other women.[79]

Similar unhappy outcomes led to sharp criticism from party superiors.[80] Women, after all, were meant to see the merits of emancipation and to choose to unveil for the proper political, even spiritual reasons, not because the party had acted as the highest bidder. Given the financially strapped condition of overextended local agencies, too, promises of material benefits often could not be kept. Lower-level officials were directed not to promise gold teeth, pretty dresses, or anything else as inducements to unveil.

Another startling departure from party policy by the soft camp, discussed only in whispers at closed meetings in 1927, shows both how Bolshevik policy could be misunderstood as it trickled down to the party rank and file and how financial pressures shaped practical outcomes on the ground. The problem arose when lower-level party and Zhenotdel organizations showed an unexpectedly entrepreneurial spirit by, of all things, taking up the business of buying and selling paranjis. The reasons for veil brokering varied, but in each case it appears to have made sense to the activists involved. On the one hand, these workers said, empowering women by giving them financial independence was a high Soviet priority. Uzbek women had limited economic resources, but many could sew; and inasmuch as paranji production represented a form of "women's work," it seemed logical that new Soviet women's artels could profitably specialize in their manufacture.[81] On the other hand, many women who had unveiled demanded financial compensation: in casting off their veils they

79. RGASPI, d. 1247, l. 224. Other cases of bribery are at d. 1214, l. 18, and d. 1238, l. 74.
80. RGASPI, d. 1239, l. 33.
81. RGASPI, d. 1249, l. 15.

had, in practical terms, discarded a very valuable item of clothing, and it was not unknown for local party or Zhenotdel bodies to pay a sum as recompense.[82] Yet money was tight at the local level, so sometimes these local bodies decided to resell the paranjis on the open market. Done properly, such sales could garner hundreds of rubles, enough to recover the party's money and even possibly make a profit.[83]

The impetus for reselling veils, in nearly all cases, is recorded as coming "from the unveiled women themselves," and local activists insisted vehemently that it caused no anti-Soviet gossip. On at least one occasion paranjis were sold as a fund-raiser at a Farghona factory, with proceeds used to purchase equipment for Soviet women's clubs and Red Corners.[84] Nonetheless, such revelations shocked the women and men responsible for supervising the central party and Zhenotdel. No matter what local activists said, these higher-level officials feared that class enemies would use such stories to create anti-Soviet propaganda, and they insisted that such practices could not be tolerated. An accurate accounting of all discarded paranjis must be kept, and under no circumstances were any to be sold.[85]

Where, then, had the soft line gone wrong? Its basic error was pursuing slow, steady, incremental change rather than crushing the resistance of class enemies in one fell swoop. The go-slow approach implied at least a temporary accommodation with powerful elements within native society, not a total and immediate transformation of Uzbek gender roles. Such an accommodation, according to its boosters, held out the possibility of greater long-term success by unveiling as many women as possible and keeping them unveiled. Yet the stress on accommodation and compromise, not to mention the similarity of such suggestions with jadidist views, made them politically suspect. Especially as the overarching framework of NEP waned in strength, the proponents of such soft cultural approaches found it increasingly difficult to use persuasion as a template for party policy. Such views continued to appear in the sources after late 1927, but with diminishing frequency—and increasingly only as illustrations of mistakes made along the road to liberation.

With both hard and soft tactics bearing little fruit by late 1927, where could party policy go? As long as women's liberation remained a priority, the problem was acute, and lower-level activists begged for strategic as well as tactical guidance amid the chaos.[86] In this atmosphere, real debate continued to swirl within party ranks over how, if at all, to continue the hujum. As the dispute over tactics shows, the party encouraged such freewheeling discussion. Both

---

82. Such cases were discussed by party control commissions at PDA, op. 3, d. 1549, ll. 4–7.

83. RGASPI, d. 1245, l. 23. See also PDA, op. 3, d. 1533, ll. 14–16. To these women, it was a question of priorities: was the hujum about the veil per se, or was it aimed at a more fundamental liberation, of which the paranji was only the most visible symbol?

84. PDA, op. 3, d. 1533, ll. 23–26.

85. RGASPI, d. 1245, l. 31, or PDA, op. 3, d. 1533, ll. 16–18.

86. See one delegate's pleas to a local congress at ÖzRMDA, f. 837, op. 3, d. 150, l. 140.

hard and soft camps—albeit not always so neatly delineated in practice or necessarily so labeled by their adherents—fought for the ears of top party leaders
in Samarqand (the Uzbek capital until 1930), Tashkent (the headquarters of
the Sredazbiuro), and Moscow. High-ranking leaders encouraged this debate,
both for its own sake and by default through their indecision. Befuddled by the
hujum's failure to attract popular support, these top leaders found it by far the
easiest to criticize all sides, but much more difficult to suggest plausible alternatives. In the end, this sharp internal debate led to remarkably little flexibility
in devising fresh policy prescriptions. Constrained by their cultural preconceptions and ideological categories, party leaders continued badly to misread
Uzbek society and culture. In the end they could do little better than to direct
Bolshevik grassroots workers to try the same tactics, the ones that had already
failed, only this time to do it better.

In the face of hundreds of deaths and rampant violence, the party opted, in
essence, for more of the same: party and Zhenotdel activists were told to stay the
course. The key, according to top party leaders in the Soviet Uzbek government,
and the only way to overcome the difficulties that had beset the hujum, was to
improve what these leaders rather amorphously called the "quality" of Soviet
work. In other words, Bolshevik policy was not at fault—it simply had not been
carried out properly. This conclusion created a mostly unremarked tension in
the written record: between simple optimism, on the one hand, that Bolshevik
efforts would inevitably triumph if only the quality of work could be improved,
and, on the other hand, grim pessimism in classified OGPU and other reports
about the near-total lack of popular support for Soviet-led unveiling.

While party and Zhenotdel workers thus were directed to gather better information about Uzbek society and to study the antihujum opposition, their
primary focus was inward.[87] They were to concentrate on bettering themselves
and their work, and unveiling would follow naturally. Party and trade union
members, Soviet workers, and Zhenotdel activists were told repeatedly to provide visible examples of women's liberation in their own lives, by unveiling
themselves—or, for men, by unveiling their wives, daughters, sisters, and
mothers.[88] But beyond the power of personal example, the party's self-criticism focused on technical problems that hindered the organization and implementation of the women's liberation campaign rather than basic issues of principle or strategy. According to these reports, work on the hujum was
characterized by "bungling" (golovtiapstvo) at every turn; it was weak, careless, disorganized, and lacking in effective leadership. Far too often women's
work was a priority on paper only, a topic that was rarely discussed, much less
pursued, by all levels of the party organization.[89]

87. PDA, op. 3, d. 1533, ll. 19–26, and d. 1549, ll. 13–140b; and RGASPI, d. 1245, ll. 32–36.
88. For one example of many, see PDA, op. 3, d. 1533, ll. 20–23.
89. See RGASPI, d. 1247, l. 223; and PDA, op. 3, d. 1533, ll. 23–25, and op. 4, d. 1208, ll.
38–39.

All of this was true. But however real such "technical" problems were—and they did, emphatically, exist—naming them as the root cause of the hujum's difficulties meant that remedies also were deemed to be technical. Women's liberation, as measured by the core criterion of public unveiling, stayed the top priority, and the special hujum commissions continued their work. All parts of the party organization were directed to continue assisting in the effort; the Zhenotdel alone could not carry the entire load. Lower-level party committees had to follow directives on women's liberation more closely and actively, announced the Central Asian Bureau, and the courts and Soviet administration at all levels had to pay more attention to the unveiling campaign.[90] Additionally, attention to the quality of work lay at the heart of these prescriptions: it had to be improved by all concerned. Instead of being a scattershot, hit-or-miss priority on International Women's Day, women's liberation needed to be "deepened," improved, and made a systematic and permanent part of Soviet policy.[91] Staff vacations or temporary absences could no longer be permitted to interrupt the campaign's momentum, and the qualifications of staff workers in women's clubs and local Zhenotdels had to be improved from their generally dismal level. These women would at a minimum be taught to read, and perhaps even given a bit of training in "political literacy" too.[92]

The first order of business for a renewed hujum thus was not to rethink fundamentals but rather to strengthen and deepen the "already attained accomplishments" of women's liberation. Party leaders saw their task principally as recovering momentum that had, they thought, been lost during the summer of 1927, when many Zhenotdel workers had gone on vacation. As a result, even repeated violent attacks against unveiled women did not change the central focus on dramatic public unveilings: despite plentiful evidence to the contrary, the women's liberation campaign was judged to be moving in the proper direction. The violence only showed that class enemies were willing to take advantage of a brief period in which Soviet efforts had flagged.[93] Important work had been done, party leaders maintained, although to date it only amounted to "a drop in the sea," since hundreds of thousands of veiled women remained. The main forms of work—public demonstrations, education and training courses, lectures and "family evenings," strict legal protection for unveiled women—should remain unchanged, but had to be redoubled in vigor.[94] The

90. ÖzRMDA, f. 837, op. 3, d. 150, l. 134; and PDA, op. 3, d. 1533, ll. 22–24, and op. 4, d. 1208, ll. 37–40.

91. RGASPI, d. 1211, ll. 44 and 186; and PDA, op. 3, d. 1533, ll. 22–25, and op. 4, d. 1208, ll. 34–38.

92. PDA, op. 3, d. 1533, ll. 21–26; and RGASPI, d. 1242, ll. 590b and 65.

93. ÖzRMDA, f. 737, op. 1, d. 419, ll. 39–40. On vacations, see f. 837, op. 3, d. 150, ll. 195–97.

94. ÖzRMDA, f. 837, op. 3, d. 150, ll. 132–33 and 167; and RGASPI, d. 163, l. 54.

all too common phenomena of reveiling and rumor-mongering, finally, would be combated by more effective education and explanatory work.[95]

The various difficulties encountered by local women's activists throughout 1927, so richly documented in the classified party and OGPU reports, could not be totally ignored. Yet party leaders in Samarqand, Tashkent, and Moscow consistently treated antihujum sentiment as "incidents," as isolated events explained by the "excesses" of particular local party and Zhenotdel officials, not as manifestations of systemic problems or opposition. Such "events," one report of July 1927 declared, did not reflect the masses' true sentiments toward Soviet power. Its author, S. G. Shimko, argued optimistically that "the process of liberation is continuing among the nonparty mass of peasants," despite the presence of an "insignificant quantity" of reveiled women. Such "excesses," she concluded, while unfortunate, "are having little influence on the masses."[96]

Since party policy was focused inward, on improving the quality of work rather than looking outward to see why Soviet unveiling had provoked such bitter resistance, the archival record inevitably says more about Bolshevik activists and the Bolshevik worldview than it does about Uzbek society. Few nonindigenous party members had much firsthand knowledge of or empathy for the Uzbek language, religion, or culture, and many party leaders continued to rely on class relations as the assumed principal motor of social conflict. They did so even when fissures appeared that suggested that class per se was not the best or even necessarily a particularly useful concept to explain social responses to the hujum. The underlying ideological filter of class categorization, though, underpinned the fateful decision to continue a forceful strategy of confrontation—a hujum—to bring about female unveiling.

Unveiling as Marxist Liberation? Class vs. Gender in the Hujum

For these Bolshevik true believers, just how important was women's liberation? The hujum, its success measured in piles of discarded or burned veils, was in some ways an odd choice as a centerpiece for Marxist social, political, economic, and cultural policy in the region. Was the campaign, at root, aimed at a revolution of class relations or of gender roles? Could it be both simultaneously? Zhenotdel and party workers had been directed to rely on class allies to liberate Uzbek women from the veil; the two objectives were held to be mutually reinforcing.[97] It soon became clear, however, that this dual imperative did not always work cleanly in practice. Choosing a gender-based campaign to

95. RGASPI, d. 1247, ll. 168 and 179. Rumor-mongers were legally accountable; see d. 1248, l. 93, and Aleksandr Rogov, "Po kishlakam i aulam Srednei Azii: Pod znakom 'khudzhuma,'" *Za partiiu*, no. 1 (1928), 93.

96. RGASPI, d. 1202, l. 82.

97. PDA, op. 3, d. 1533, l. 24.

define a class-directed policy raised constant tensions. Which mattered most, class or gender? Different Bolsheviks had different answers: on this as on other matters, the party had no shortage of conflicting views. Even in the increasingly hard-line realm of official policy, however, the tension between class concerns and women's liberation contributed to confused outcomes. The Bolsheviks' class-sensitive theoretical approach to Uzbek society, on the one hand, and their practical attention to the end result of unveiling Uzbek women, on the other, gave rise to policy contradictions and conundrums. These are most easily seen in the treatment of Uzbek women at opposite ends of the socioeconomic spectrum.

First, what was to be done with the wives of Muslim clerics and bois? As women, they were, according to the terms of Soviet doctrine, necessarily oppressed by the patriarchal structures of Uzbek society, just like their poorer sisters. In some ways, indeed, they might be seen as *more* oppressed, forced to live with the men most directly responsible for enforcing norms of female seclusion. Yet these women also benefited personally from their husbands' economic resources and positions of social respect, and Soviet documents record such wives leading antihujum demonstrations, disrupting Soviet women's meetings, and persuading other Uzbek women to reveil.[98] In most cases, class appeared to trump gender for these women: party activists concluded that because the wives of Muslim clerics and bois generally shared their husbands' class position, they could simply be excluded from the liberation campaign.[99] Exceptions were made, but only in special circumstances, such as for very young women who were the second, third, or fourth wives of rich, elderly bois—especially if they had grown up poor and now wanted to leave their husbands. (The prominent Zhenotdel activist Tojikhon Shadieva had just such a story.)[100] But most wives of Muslim clerics and bois were deemed to be class enemies. As such they could not vote in Soviet elections; their petitions to authorities or their wailing appearances outside government offices were deemed class provocations to be ignored.[101] Once this view came to be known, Muslim clerics reportedly sent their wives on many such missions, perhaps hoping to point out the inconsistencies in the party's ostensibly universal message of women's liberation.

Consider too the class tensions at work within the comparatively small group of unveiled women. These tensions arose even over such deceptively

98. The wives of bois were said to occupy positions of social respect, so their personal example mattered (RGASPI, d. 1214, l. 36; and PDA, op. 3, d. 1598, l. 28).

99. PDA, op. 3, d. 1560, l. 347. Such exclusions were justified because poor peasant women were said to resent wealthy women's class privileges (it was unclear how this resentment coexisted with their social respect). See I. Depovskoi, "Shtab zhenarmii (v zhenotdele zerafshanskogo obkoma)," *PV,* 20 Dec. 1926.

100. Normatov, *Tadzhikhon.*

101. On the franchise, see ÖzRMDA, f. 86, op. 1, d. 4432, ll. 17–21. The restrictions had an impact: one group of student investigators reported that of 24,957 women in Old Andijon in September 1927, only 14,954 had voting rights. Further, only 1,557 had actually voted in the most recent election—and only 182 of these women had been unveiled (RGASPI, d. 1202, l. 48).

simple matters as what unveiled women were to wear. What would replace the
paranji and chachvon? Having urged (and sometimes forced) women to discard their veils, should the party be responsible for providing them new
clothes? If so (or even if not), what should their new wardrobe look like? As
early reports trickled in from the localities, unforeseen debates sprang up
around these questions. Uzbek women clearly had many reasons to be reluctant to throw aside their paranjis, but prominent among their expressed motives was a lack of presentable clothes to wear in public. This objection could
simply have served as an excuse to avoid unveiling, yet it does seem to have
been an important consideration for at least a subset of Uzbek women who
were willing in principle to consider unveiling. Certainly this issue highlighted
the class divisions among Uzbek women as a whole.

Simply tossing off her veil would leave an Uzbek woman in no more than a
robe (*khalat*) and underdresses (*ichkilar*), the latter being garments never worn
in plain view outside the home. They were the psychological and sociocultural
equivalents of a Russian woman's brassiere, panties, and slip. The prospect of
appearing in public in such clothes horrified these women (not to mention
their husbands, fathers, and brothers).[102] If they were to unveil, these women
argued, they needed to break free entirely from Uzbek fashions and appear in
a completely different kind of dress. Thanks partly to the preexisting cultural
discourses of liberation, many of these women evinced a desire to wear European fashions. Party records show many such women asking their husbands—
or better yet, the party—to provide them with new European-style clothes.

From one point of view, such requests fitted well the culturally transformative aim of Soviet liberation. Certainly Soviet publications, especially the
party's own Uzbek-language women's journals, made every effort to inculcate
European ideals of fashion that would define a sophisticated, cultured woman.
(See Figure 16.) Promises of fashionable dresses therefore could be seen to fit
into the broader aims of Bolshevik policy. They also could be a way to miti-
gate poor Uzbek women's resentment of affluent and well-connected Communists. Providing comparatively expensive, high-quality European clothing—
ideally free of charge—to all Muslim women who expressed interest could
serve not only as a way to persuade more women to unveil but also to make it
harder for affluent women to ridicule the shabbiness of a poor woman's garb.

What, then, was the problem? Some of the difficulty stemmed from the fact
that party leaders saw poor Uzbek women as the Soviet state's core class allies,
and thus as the most likely to unveil, with or without material inducements.
But as the least affluent members of society, these women by definition had
little or no money to spare. Not only were they reluctant to discard—let alone
burn—their expensive paranjis and chachvons, they also lacked means to buy
new clothes to replace them.[103] Some poor women reportedly unveiled but

102. PDA, op. 3, d. 1598, l. 27.
103. RGASPI, d. 1242, l. 162, and d. 1246, l. 91.

QANDAJ KIJINIŞ KERAK?

Figure 16. "How should one dress?" European fashions for the Uzbek woman, 1937. (Marjamxan, "Qandaj kijinish kerak?" *Jangi turmush,* no. 1 [1937], 29.)

then, lacking a wardrobe and ashamed to wear underclothes in public, never left home, an outcome that was disappointing to Soviet hopes of a free, unveiled, socially active womanhood.[104] By contrast, the unveiled wives of Soviet workers and party members could easily afford European clothes, boasting "Paris shoes [and] silk stockings, and straightaway [taking] on a European appearance."[105] Thus it was not surprising that poor women threatened not to unveil unless the party outfitted them similarly.[106]

104. On staying home, see RGASPI, d. 1214, l. 153; on shame, see PDA, op. 3, d. 1598, l. 27.
105. RGASPI, d. 1203, ll. 50–51. Such dress is called "Russian" at d. 1242, l. 162.
106. RGASPI, d. 1058, l. 26. One woman marched into a local Zhenotdel office demanding money to buy clothes; her request was refused (d. 1240, l. 61).

In the end, financial pressures doomed the idea of providing unveiled women with new dresses; the funds to outfit many thousands (or millions, if the campaign went well) of Uzbek women lay far beyond the Zhenotdel's limited budgetary means. Party leaders complained that calls for new clothes ignored the enormous expense that would be involved.[107] Women may want new clothes, a variety of speakers declared bravely at conferences and congresses across Uzbekistan, but liberation is not simply about fashion and European styles.[108] As one Sonam Mirzaeva announced to a meeting of unveiled women in March 1927, "Many women say that without good clothes it is impossible to unveil. This is an incorrect view: we unveil not to show off [our] fashion, but to become free women."[109]

The party hierarchy welcomed such heroic declarations, arguing that despite the demand for European clothes and the revulsion against wearing undergarments as outerwear, women should nonetheless wear their own national garb.[110] Some speakers argued for distinctly Uzbek fashions as a means of national-cultural preservation, saying that women should "preserve [our] national dress, not change it and not become European."[111] Many other activists, especially among the men, showed a remarkable lack of concern about the practical and psychological problems faced by unveiled Uzbek women. At one local congress in Andijon, for example, one Ashurov pointed out that not all husbands would be able to afford European clothes for their wives. But he went on to argue, in essence, that Uzbek underclothes might become all the rage, saying that "many maintain that if an Uzbek woman who has unveiled does not go about in European dress, then she may face various [forms of] mockery [nasmeshki] and pesterings [pristavaniia] from men. Thus the insufficiency of money for European clothes is partly [to blame] for hindering a mass unveiling of women. But perhaps when the unveiling of women becomes typical, then [maybe the] dress now worn by Uzbek women will become a favorite of Russians!"[112] Such flippancy—or studied obliviousness—likely offered little consolation to newly unveiled Uzbek women, who knew full well that their Russian counterparts were not about to don khalats and ichkis. In no case, though, party leaders declared, should local party bodies reward women for unveiling by giving them money.[113] Perceived fiscal limits here constrained both class ideology and gender solidarity; poor women enjoyed little assistance

107. RGASPI, d. 1240, l. 280b.
108. RGASPI, d. 1203, ll. 50–51; and PDA, op. 3, d. 1549, ll. 110b-120b.
109. RGASPI, d. 1250, l. 28.
110. ÖzRMDA, f. 837, op. 3, d. 150, l. 174; and RGASPI, d. 1211, l. 110; d. 1239, l. 33; and d. 1250, l. 530b.
111. RGASPI, d. 1240, l. 280b. Such statements suggested the potential for a Central Asian woman to be "modern" yet simultaneously Uzbek, not European. Although the details remained undefined, this unspoken shift from the trope of cultural transformation created a tension that persisted in later discussions of fashion.
112. ÖzRMDA, f. 837, op. 3, d. 150, l. 139.
113. RGASPI, d. 1239, l. 33.

from their party comrades, who continued to wear (or to have their wives wear) silk stockings and shoes from Paris.

At the other end of the socioeconomic spectrum from both bois and Communists, some of Uzbekistan's most desperate women—prostitutes—also presented a dilemma for party activists. From the Bolshevik perspective, these women represented the most clearly exploited subset of Uzbek womanhood—if there was a female Uzbek surrogate proletariat, surely prostitutes stood at its head—and thus the most likely to welcome Soviet-sponsored liberation. At the same time, they were not, for the most part, veiled to begin with; and therein lay the dilemma. Uzbek culture placed a high priority on familial honor, and a woman's sexual abstinence before marriage and fidelity within it played a paramount role in defining that honor. Prostitutes thus represented the antithesis of a "good" Uzbek woman; many proper, upstanding Uzbek women reacted with disdain or disgust upon meeting a prostitute in the street. Devout women would, at the least, shun their society, lest their character be besmirched by association. Since most prostitutes did not wear veils, moreover, an association between "unveiled" and "prostitute" already existed before the hujum began.[114]

Zhenotdel activists faced the difficult task of overcoming this association, of persuading Uzbek women and men that a woman could be both moral and unveiled—a task further complicated by the party's simultaneous desire to redefine in a nonreligious way what it meant to be moral. Yet if these activists included actual prostitutes in the women's liberation campaign—trying to reform them by teaching job skills or inviting them to women's clubs—they risked the entire effort, since the presence of such women would compromise women's liberation and the unveiling campaign in the popular eye. In the end, prostitutes' class interests proved less salient than their morally dubious status, and the risk of tainting the hujum with even a whiff of prostitution was judged too great. As Olimpiada Ermakova, a high-ranking Zhenotdel worker, told her comrades in September 1927, "As soon as you fuss over two or three prostitutes, hundreds of the people we need will run away from us."[115] Prostitutes' desperate plight was thus subordinated to the greater good of liberating all Uzbek women, and party activists, ostensibly the defenders of the downtrodden, effectively disavowed the only sizable group of urban Uzbek women who

---

114. Prostitutes thus represented a cautionary tale for Bolshevik activists. Forced to sell their bodies and bearing the brunt of degradation and disease, which to Zhenotdel activists was the logical outcome of patriarchal society, prostitutes also embodied what could happen to independent women without job skills. Since many unveiled ("liberated") women were disavowed and turned onto the streets by male relatives, unless the Zhenotdel could offer them education and job training, they too might be driven into prostitution—an outcome that would only strengthen the popular association of unveiling with prostitution. The Zhenotdel's disavowal of prostitutes also held the implicit message that unveiled Uzbek women would be on their own—a further disincentive to unveiling.

115. PDA, op. 3, d. 1533, l. 21. Ermakova was director of the Farghona provincial Zhenotdel.

were already unveiled. Rather than trying to change the way Uzbek men and women saw prostitutes—as economically disadvantaged women in need of compassion and aid, not the targets of moral scorn—party and Zhenotdel leaders directed grassroots workers to take popular attitudes into account. Practicality overcame principle, and all contact with prostitutes was kept separate from the "regular" track of women's liberation.[116]

In one sense the exclusion of prostitutes from the universal promises of Soviet women's liberation represented a nod to the culturally sensitive approaches of the soft line, and resolutions of late 1927 do include other examples of culturally sensitive methods, although most are conceptually undeveloped amid the general language of class confrontation. Unveiling would not succeed until Uzbek women themselves joined the struggle, one report declared; better institutional support was needed to persuade them to participate.[117] Other reports declared that efforts directed at men—changing their ideas of masculinity and especially teaching them not to insult unveiled women—were essential.[118] Such scattered references show that at least some party members recognized the crucial importance of what they called "social opinion." Most of the documentary record, though, shows little understanding within the party, especially at the middle and upper levels, of how to appeal to the masses, how to create the required "mood" of popular support for mass unveiling.[119] The Andijon Communist cited earlier, Ashurov, for example, argued that attacks on unveiled women resulted simply from "curiosity." The way to overcome the violence, he said, was to unveil more women:

> It is necessary to raise the question of how to defend unveiled women from hooliganism. Such actions toward unveiled Uzbek women occur because [they] have always [before] walked about while veiled, which is to say, [the attacks] result from curiosity. When such [unveiled] women were rare, then it was even harder for them; but now, when there are already many unveiled, people do not pay them so much attention. When unveiling is a mass phenomenon, there will be no such [violent] actions from men at all.[120]

116. Ibid., ll. 24–26; and RGASPI, d. 1245, l. 36. Immediately after her words quoted above, indeed, Ermakova called for a "series of show trials" to identify and weed out prostitutes from women's clubs and corners (*ugolki*). The Zhenotdel, she said, washed its hands of these women. "Lists of verified prostitutes" were to be prepared and handed over to local party organizations, which would be "pressured" to deal with the problem. "It is their affair," Ermakova concluded, "not the Zhenotdels'."

117. ÖzRMDA, f. 837, op. 3, d. 150, l. 139; and RGASPI, d. 1249, ll. 28–29, and d. 1250, l. 28.

118. See RGASPI, d. 1225, l. 74, and d. 1250, l. 28.

119. For undeveloped mentions of "mood," "social opinion," and "mass appeal," see PDA, op. 3, d. 1598, ll. 39–40; and ÖzRMDA, f. 837, op. 3, d. 150, ll. 138 and 181.

120. ÖzRMDA, f. 837, op. 3, d. 150, l. 137.

Ashurov's analysis lacked much depth of insight into the social and cultural factors at work in the violence against unveiled women. His simple prescription to increase the numbers of unveiled women until they were no longer a curiosity lacked many crucial intermediate steps, and on its own was unlikely to persuade many Uzbek women to cast off their paranji and chachvon.

This sort of straightforward optimism can be found throughout Soviet discussions of late 1927 and beyond, showing plainly the limits of any internal rethinking of the hujum. Party leaders were either oblivious of reports of anti-hujum sentiment or willing to pretend, to themselves and their superiors, that deep-seated resistance did not exist. Most resulting directives ignored the problems, just as they ignored the contradictions in the party's ostensibly class-driven policy. The assumptions and ideological filters many Bolsheviks had brought to Central Asia pushed them into untenable positions. All it took to unveil Uzbek women was effort, they declared heroically; the power of Soviet ideas and personal example would inspire, more or less mechanically, all Uzbek women and girls to cast off their veils.[121] But when antihujum resistance was too obvious to be denied, the tactics they suggested demonstrated a yawning gap between their worldview and the problems facing Uzbek women. Consider a resolution passed in August 1927 by the party and Komsomol cells of Buka, a small town south of Tashkent:

> *Resolved:* That recently cases have been noted of women reveiling, [a situation] that has been promoted by certain inhabitants of Buka village: Umar Umangaliev, and the mullah Jalil and his relatives. . . . [Therefore,]
> 1. In order that unveiled women will not fall under the influence of the above-named persons and their stooges, it is essential to convene next Friday a women's meeting, with a report on the international situation and about the lives and conditions of women in the European states. For this purpose we ask the district party committee and the district hujum commission to spare a speaker [to address] this topic.[122]

To the party members who devised this plan, a lecture on European conditions may have seemed an excellent way to appeal to Uzbek women; it is unlikely, however, that many of the women in question saw it as particularly relevant to their situation in weighing whether or not to reveil.[123]

---

121. One district party secretary outside Tashkent reported in September 1927 that "in one village of 65 households not a single woman has yet unveiled, that is to say, in this village the population is more prosperous and the women are very difficult to unveil. Notwithstanding all this, a hujum commission has been established in the village, and we hope in short order, with the help of this commission, to unveil 100 percent of its women" (RGASPI, d. 1247, l. 183).

122. Ibid., l. 167.

123. Other efforts were made to galvanize women to unveil by organizing demonstrations about the international situation, such as to protest British interference in Afghanistan (RGASPI, d. 1211, l. 201, and d. 1214, l. 17). Since many Bolsheviks were concerned about such issues, they may have assumed that they mattered to Uzbek women and men too (ÖzRMDA, f. 837, op. 3, d. 150, ll. 130–32).

Momentum, Revolutionary Rhetoric, and the Problem of Initiative

By late 1927 Bolshevik policy had come to be based firmly on a profound mis-reading of Uzbek society and culture as structured fundamentally by class cleavages and conflicts. While some Bolsheviks and pro-Soviet Uzbeks, particularly those working at the grassroots level and those with jadidist sympathies, were aware of the problems and contradictions in party policy, they could do nothing about them. The hujum continued to stress attack and confrontation, and put a premium on rapid, complete, public unveiling as the chief measure of emancipation. An unveiling campaign that aimed at an immediate, dramatic, thorough transformation of primitive Central Asia reflected fundamental Bolshevik predilections and predispositions. Marxist theory assured party activists that triumph was inevitable, that history was on their side. Such reassuring certainties helped drain even violent resistance of lasting significance, or of the potential to force a real rethinking. The hujum drove itself onward; the rhetorical momentum of the campaign and its perceived importance made it impossible to turn back.[124]

Party leaders saw the unveiling campaign as a crucial exhibit of what Soviet power could do, of how Bolshevism was bringing modernity and liberation to the colonized East. As such, it had international implications far beyond the immediate goal of liberating Uzbek women. The Zhenotdel could not permit itself to be outflanked. In order to keep the revolutionary initiative, the hujum had to be more resolute than Atatürk's "bourgeois" efforts to unveil Turkish women or the efforts of Amanullah Khan in Afghanistan.[125] Party investigators thus saw a greater threat from the indigenous left—from "progressive" clerics, for example—than from the hujum's self-declared enemies on the conservative right. One top-secret internal report warned of "that enormous danger" which faced the party, arguing that "if we weaken [our] leadership in the struggle for [women's] liberation, then the clergy will carry the mass of women away [from us], on a road of religious influence."[126] Initiative was the key, and the need to keep it in Bolshevik hands kept hard-line, uncompromising policies ascendant. Appeals for caution, for a less confrontational approach, could be—and were—depicted as a danger to the entire process of women's liberation, and indeed to the Soviet revolution itself.[127]

This expansive view of the hujum's significance also hindered any reconsideration of its course. The efforts in autumn 1927 to take stock of the campaign wound up more concerned with specific tactics than with overall strategy, since the general direction of policy had been settled. The unveiling effort,

124. PDA, op. 3, d. 1598, l. 39.
125. On the need to oppose "bourgeois" policies within Soviet borders, see RGASPI, d. 1203, l. 18.
126. PDA, op. 3, d. 1598, l. 40.
127. ÖzRMDA, f. 837, op. 3, d. 150, l. 178.

originally devised as a straightforward, quick campaign, had become much more complicated. These additional layers of meaning made the hujum's promise of a dramatic cultural transformation central to Soviet regional policy and staked the party's credibility on the outcome. Once the stakes had been pushed so high, no retreat was possible. Despite widespread resistance, confrontation—indeed, attack—had to remain the order of the day.

CHAPTER 4

The Chust Affair

> Those who make claims about Chust are incorrect when they
> say that it is a lesson for all the provinces. No, it is only family
> fisticuffs [*semeinoe mordobit'e*], having no [general] social
> character . . . and cannot be a lesson for the other provinces.
>
> —A Zhenotdel activist, Aleksandrova, May 1927

> We began questioning the people . . . and, as usual, failed to
> get any definite information. That is invariably the case in the
> East; a story always sounds clear enough at a distance, but the
> nearer you get to the scene of events the vaguer it becomes.
>
> —George Orwell, "Shooting an Elephant"

How did the Soviet–Uzbek encounter over the hujum play out in
practice? An episode in Chust, a medium-sized town just west of Namangan
in the Farghona Valley (see Map 4), in the spring of 1927 tells the tale.
Sparked by the women's liberation campaign and precipitated by local officials' abusive tactics and coercive policies, the "Chust affair" was the product
of a specific cultural and political context, although it seemed to party officials to flare out of nowhere. It was not unique; similar minirevolts broke out
around this time in other parts of Uzbekistan and Central Asia.[1] As the most
visible and threatening flash point of resistance, however, it was paid close attention by the party. "Chust" became shorthand for the wider phenomenon,
and this rebellion was discussed extensively, both at closed party meetings

---

1. See the descriptions of a mass march on Andijon to demand the release of several detained
imams and the arrest of a local party secretary at ÖzRMDA, f. 86, op. 2, d. 92, ll. 28–30. Other
serious "incidents," meriting the "most severe repression," are listed at RGASPI, d. 1198, ll.
41–42; and ÖzRMDA, f. 86, op. 2, d. 92, ll. 32–42 and 49–51. Chust was deemed more or less
"characteristic" of such uprisings at PDA, op. 3, d. 1598, l. 17.

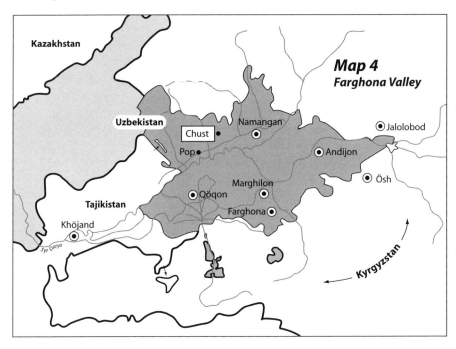

and in the periodical press. The episode shows both the depth of religio-cultural consensus that emerged to oppose Soviet policies and the tenuousness of Soviet rule in the Uzbek countryside. It further illuminates the deep disconnect between most Uzbek citizens and state and party authorities. This disconnect went beyond a simple ethnic difference—many of the local Bolsheviks involved in this story were Uzbek—and was as much about urban/rural differences, social class, personal power, political ideologies, and the complexities of how to carry out a new kind of colonial rule that acted in the name of liberation.

Precursors and Contributing Causes

Soviet sources are vague on the background to the uprising. Officials had little interest in describing Chust, its neighboring town of Pop, or indeed much of rural Farghona until hindsight brought about an abrupt change after the revolt in April 1927. Later Soviet reports tended to stress preexisting local factors that are difficult to verify, such as an allegedly large number of clerics living in the mahalla of Qorghonchi, the neighborhood where trouble erupted. But Bolshevik activists did often choose confrontational locations for their public unveilings and women's liberation meetings, and internal party reports point to an ancient saint's tomb in this mahalla, which could have made it a religious center.[2] In addition to such purely local characteristics, the inhabitants of Chust shared with other Central Asians the general experiences of Soviet rule: the Red Army's suppression of the qörboshi, Soviet implementation of a redistributive land and water reform, and finally, in March 1927, the start of a massive campaign to unveil Muslim women. With Soviet authorities showing relatively little interest in popular wishes, and with regional traditions of rebellion against authorities perceived as corrupt or illegitimate, any spark had the potential to ignite pent-up frustration into open rebellion.

The few extant early materials make it clear that the party hierarchy had little or no sense of popular sentiment in Chust before April. After a visit in January 1927, for example, one activist had written a positive report praising the town's progress in and support for women's liberation.[3] This report drew a picture of thousands of women in Chust already unveiled—without a prostitute among them—and described the allegedly high esteem in which their fellow townspeople of both sexes held these women. Other particulars, however, make the reader wonder. The population figures were dubious: of the town's 14,000 inhabitants, 9,000 were said to be women. This was noted as "strange," but even odder was the claim that 10,000 women in Chust had unveiled. Arithmetic aside, one wonders about such pervasive unveiling, especially so early—before 8 March—and also about the unspoken implications of the offhand observation that none of the (few) European women in the area could speak Uzbek, and that none of the Uzbek women knew any Russian. (In 1880 Chust had had only 96 Russians in a town population of almost 20,000, and the figures were scarcely different at the next reckoning, in 1912.)[4] Communication under such conditions must have been limited at best, resulting in only the shallowest knowledge of the area and its people among party activists. The "high esteem" for unveiled women, in particular, was likely the product of wishful thinking by an overly optimistic visiting Russian activist.

With only such reports to rely on, it is no surprise that when social unrest did appear, it seemed (from the Soviet point of view) to flare out of nowhere, and local Bolsheviks were caught flatfooted and dumbfounded. Ranajit Guha has noted that colonial governments often perceive peasant revolts as "wildfires" or "thunderstorms," "earthquakes" or "epidemics," using metaphors

2. On the 380-year-old tomb of a local saint and the large number of clerics alleged to live nearby, see RGASPI, d. 1211, l. 208, and d. 1240, l. 15. According to a local ethnographer writing in the 1990s, in the late nineteenth century Chust had 84 mosques, or one for approximately every 220 inhabitants (Kh. Sanaqulov, *Chust: Ommabop tarikhiy-etnografik ocherk* [Tashkent, 1991], 12).

3. The report is at RGASPI, d. 1213, ll. 4–50b. Its author is unnamed and the signature is illegible. A similarly upbeat report from before April 1927 is at d. 1217, l. 57.

4. The vast majority (18,545 of 18,690, or 99.2 percent) were categorized as Sarts, plus a handful of Tatars, Jews, Indians, and an odd group of 55 Germans (Sanaqulov, *Chust*, 12 and 48).

drawn from nature to express the allegedly elemental, unpredictable nature of peasant behavior.[5] After a decade of Soviet rule and more than a half-century of direct Russian/Central Asian interaction, however, the social unrest provoked in 1927 was nothing if not explicable. While Soviet officials remained oblivious, the Farghona countryside had by then been made into a tinderbox. The party's decision in March to launch an assault against the veil worsened the situation appreciably, and matters came to a head barely a month later. The final catalyst came in mid-April, when local authorities bungled a women's liberation meeting in Chust. It spiraled out of control, triggering an unforeseen chain of events and pushing this discontent into the open.

The Affair: Perceptions, Agendas, and Retellings

The facts of the case are difficult to know with certainty. Told differently by various informants with their own perspectives and agendas, the story also changed in accordance with the audience and the purpose. I begin with the internal party reports generated during and immediately after the crisis, when the accuracy of information was at a premium and before the "facts" had been overly analyzed, filtered, and processed. According to these reports, mostly written by local (Chust-Pop) and provincial (Farghona) officials for their party superiors in Samarqand and Tashkent, the basic story went something like this.[6] Party workers had convened a women's liberation meeting in Chust on 15 April 1927, but Muslim clerics showed up too, making a nuisance of themselves and obstructing the meeting by denouncing the hujum. Local Bolsheviks, annoyed, decided to make these clerics promise in writing never again to speak against the unveiling of Uzbek women, and asked the police for help in securing such statements. When word spread the next day that clerics had been arrested, a crowd of 400 gathered in front of the building occupied by the local soviet and *ispolkom* (executive committee). The crowd's demands quickly led to the release of the arrested mullahs, but when one newly freed cleric admitted signing a statement promising not to criticize the hujum, the crowd attacked him. A policeman then intervened to defend the mullah; the crowd turned on this officer and killed him. These early reports concluded with the subsequent arrest of eight men accused of responsibility for the murder.

Reading these reports, one cannot help being struck by their dry, schematic flavor. They are telegraphic with facts, not even naming the mullah who was attacked (Abbos Maksum) or the policeman who died defending him (Uzoqboi Tashmatov). Their basic message, however, was plain: the unpleasantness

5. Ranajit Guha, "The Prose of Counter-Insurgency," in *Selected Subaltern Studies,* ed. Ranajit Guha and Gayatri Chakravorty Spivak (New York, 1988), 46–47.

6. The best example, on which this paragraph is based, is a report of the Farghona party provincial committee (*okruzhkom*) at RGASPI, d. 1208, l. 67. Similar reports are at d. 1242, l. 175; and PDA, op. 3, d. 1598, ll. 17–18.

in Chust had resulted from the manipulation of local passions by unscrupulous Muslim clerics. One report written in early May by a Pop district official implied that unseen sinister forces had hijacked this women's liberation meeting. It alleged that the crowd was gathered a full four hours early, and that by the time the meeting was called to order, some "thirty elements in turbans" (that is, Muslim clerics) had appeared to hinder its work.[7] Yet despite such machinations and the violent outburst that ensued, these local officials maintained stoically in their reports to superiors that overall, the women's unveiling campaign in Farghona was going well.[8] By putting the best possible spin on bad news, they may have hoped to escape increased oversight and supervision in the future.

These lower-level party and state officials had the advantages of being close to the events and having immediate access to eyewitnesses. But they also had a strong interest in telling the story in a certain way, in highlighting certain facts and omitting others. Many other details thus emerge only in the classified contemporary materials prepared by the Soviet secret police. In this episode, at least, the OGPU had fewer axes to grind; certainly it had no interest in hiding local mistakes, and arguably had less invested in any particular spin on the Chust events. While their language and presentation make it clear that secret police investigators were far from the objective observers they pretended to be (they had a strong institutional interest in highlighting local security problems, for instance), their reports are the best available and are, by comparison with other party studies, quite subtle and discerning. No less important, they also show the base of raw material (the "facts") available to later party analysts. Although some of the fine points of what had happened in Chust remained vague, these reports added a wealth of detail.[9] In particular, they illuminated the contributory and causative role of local party workers' mistakes and highhandedness. They also provided a clear view of popular sentiment, spotlighting the depths of pent-up frustration in Chust and the passionate anti-Bolshevik sentiments that had been produced by mid-April by such Soviet policies as the hujum.

The single best contemporary source on the events in Chust is a secret police

7. PDA, op. 3, d. 1549, ll. 4–5.
8. See, for example, RGASPI, d. 1242, l. 77.
9. The initial top-secret OGPU report on the unrest, written on 19 April, was confused. It asserted that a crowd of 50 had forced a rapid release of the imprisoned mullahs on 16 April, but a crowd of 400 returned the next day for no apparent reason, attacked the Raiispolkom building, seized a policeman, and killed him with his own rifle. It thus separated the imams' release from the attack and omitted Abbos Maksum entirely (RGASPI, d. 1214, l. 53). Other discrepancies are minor. Was the crowd first promised that the mullahs would be released the next morning, causing them to spend the night outside the town soviet building, or were they first turned away empty-handed and the mullahs only released the next day when a more numerous assemblage appeared? Did Tashmatov try first to shout the crowd away from Abbos Maksum, or did he simply shoot into the air? Contradictory information is at d. 1213, l. 78, and d. 1240, l. 15–150b.

report of 2 May 1927 sent to S. G. Shimko, the director of the Central Asian Bureau's Zhenotdel, in Tashkent.[10] The story told in this report (and a handful of others) contrasts starkly with that told by local party officials. According to the OGPU, women's liberation before mid-April had proceeded slowly but steadily, with roughly 250 women in Chust choosing to unveil. Although Ashurkulov, the chief secretary of the local party cell, had wanted to cancel the fateful meeting on 15 April when he saw Muslim clerics (neskol'ko ulemistov) among the gathered crowd of 200, in the end he called it to order and gave a report about the meaning of women's liberation. After his report, the audience was invited to ask questions. Some asked whether they could speak freely, without fear of repercussions. They were assured that they would face no reprisals. With that, some of the clerics in attendance—reportedly joined by merchants and even a few peasants—went on the offensive, taking issue with the main points of Ashurkulov's presentation and citing the tenets of shariat to argue forcefully against the unveiling campaign. According to another report, they asked Ashurkulov "tricky" (kaverznye) questions; that is, questions he could not answer.[11] At a loss to respond, bested by the superior reasoning of supposedly backward and primitive mullahs, Ashurkulov apparently judged discretion the better part of valor and simply declared the meeting over. The crowd dispersed peacefully, perhaps feeling that the local party had been taught a lesson and put in its place.

No doubt humiliated by this debacle, Ashurkulov and his party colleagues could not have wanted Muslim clerics to have the last word. They only compounded their problems, however, when they opted to arrest the mullahs who had spoken out. It was this mistake and its unfortunate consequences (along with Ashurkulov's ineptitude and unpreparedness at the initial question-and-answer session) that were too embarrassing for the local party to include in the reports it sent up the chain of command.[12] But they were not too embarrassing for the OGPU, which noted in its classified reports that while returning from the meeting Ashurkulov had met Saifutdinov, the secretary of the party district

10. Except as noted, the rest of this section is based on this report by Berman and D"iakov of the Central Asian OGPU office in Tashkent: RGASPI, d. 1213, ll. 77–79; this paragraph is based on l. 77. This report is also a principal source for the summary prepared by Zinaida Prishchepchik, Zhenotdel director for Uzbekistan, at d. 1240, l. 15–150b.

11. RGASPI, d. 1211, l. 208. Another OGPU document cites examples of the questions that stymied Ashurkulov: "Soviet power gives freedom of conscience, it has divided church from state; how then can you try to abolish the shariat, [thereby] mixing yourself up in religious affairs?"; "The paranji is a religious institution—are you really right to abolish it?"; "You say that unveiling is to proceed voluntarily, but why [then] were we called [to this meeting] by the police?" (d. 1240, l. 15).

12. The Farghona party did admit mistakes in letters sent downward to the localities, urging them not to make promises (such as not to arrest clerics) that would not be kept. (See the directive at RGASPI, d. 1249, ll. 95–96.) Such admissions were rare in reports sent upward. In one partial exception, a Pop official noted that part of the blame must be borne by local activists who did not simply expel the clerics when they spoke out on 15 April. For this reason, he said, it was "our mistake," and the party had gone on to make matters worse (PDA, op. 3, d. 1549, ll. 4–5).

committee (raikom); they had agreed that the clerics who expressed opposition to the unveiling campaign would have to promise not to do so again. Reneging, therefore, on his promise of no reprisals, Ashurkulov on 16 April dispatched police officers to arrest the mullahs. This action provoked an immediate response: a crowd of fifty soon gathered to request that the clerics be freed. Local authorities' refusal only fueled the flames; a larger crowd of 200 appeared the next morning (17 April) to repeat the same demand, its numbers quickly swelling to as many as 400 when these entreaties were rebuffed. In the face of what the OGPU euphemistically called the "insistence" of the crowd, the leaders of the town soviet finally capitulated and released the arrested mullahs on bail.[13]

The secret police materials thus stress the role of the local party's mistakes and its use of high-handed tactics that flouted local opinion and provoked open rebellion. The rest of the police narrative casts yet more doubt on the veracity and completeness of the story as told by local officials. According to the OGPU, one of the freed clerics, the imam Mullah Abbos Maksum, soon met the crowd not far from the town soviet building and told them that he had signed a promise not to agitate further against the unveiling campaign. This news reportedly enraged the crowd, now more of a mob. Indignant bystanders pelted Abbos Maksum with questions, demanding to know why he had signed such a promise "without having the agreement of the population for doing so." Shouting "Ur, ur!" ("Thrash him, hit him!"), the throng then threw themselves upon Abbos Maksum and started beating him unmercifully. The policeman Uzoqboi Tashmatov happened to be nearby; he was reportedly on the way to return his gun to the police station before leaving on vacation. Seeing what was happening, Tashmatov tried to intervene and save the imam, but the mob quickly turned on him. His attempt to disperse the throng by shooting into the air only inflamed the crowd further, and they killed him.[14]

Most frightening to the local party, however, must have been what followed Tashmatov's murder. Although the story as related by local officials stopped abruptly at this point, skipping ahead to the arrest of eight men alleged to have participated in the attack, OGPU documents show that the rampaging crowd did not immediately subside:

> After [Tashmatov's death] shouts could be heard from the crowd of "Beat the Europeans and drive them out of here!" The effect of [such] excesses not far from the city soviet produced panic among the Soviet and party workers, who fled and scattered. The mass [of people], wanting to track down these [workers], in its turn flung themselves onto the trail of those who had run away, but not [succeeding in] overtaking any

13. RGASPI, d. 1213, l. 78.
14. Ibid. The mullah was not killed; as discussed below, he reappeared in a different guise in later tellings of this story. The fact that Tashmatov was armed and had inflamed the crowd by discharging his weapon was another ambiguous detail omitted in the story told by local officials.

of the office workers, knocked out the windows of the city soviet building and broke down the doors and walls of [its] employees. After this a rumor rushed through the crowd that everything that had happened was known to Namangan and Qöqon, and that supposedly army troops were now on the way from there. These latter tidings compelled [everyone] to disperse to their houses.[15]

This OGPU narrative, of course, is neither perfect nor complete. But in stark contrast to the local reports, it offers a convincing explanation for what had happened in Chust. It provides a relatively unvarnished view of how the party's own ill-advised actions helped create the crowd that grew steadily in size and hostility, and ultimately provoked violent attacks on Soviet personnel and property. Most striking of all, it captures something of the charged atmosphere of mid-April 1927, laying bare the frightening depth of anti-Soviet feeling among the populace and the tenuous character of the party's control in the countryside around Chust.

One might expect these events to have had a sobering effect on party leaders in Tashkent and elsewhere: such a grave rupture in the fabric of public order required a firm response and perhaps even a rethinking of the policies that helped bring it about. How, then, did the party respond to the Chust affair? Local accounts minimized the significance of the unrest, stressing the rapidity with which it was contained. Eight arrests quickly followed Tashmatov's murder: that seemed to local leaders a fitting end to the story, and they mostly failed to mention the later measures that were taken to chastise the Communists of Chust.[16]

Again, however, the highly classified police documents yield a different view. Disseminated on a need-to-know basis, these documents reveal the deep concern felt by top party leaders about the events in Chust. These leaders immediately sent a special commission from Qöqon to investigate; it soon issued reprimands and disciplinary sanctions against errant local Communists.[17] Commission members met with local party cells and visited local mahallas, even calling a meeting of peasants in Qorghonchi, the mahalla where the trouble had started. This meeting was induced to name the "ringleaders" (*zachinshchiki*) of the unrest. In the end, investigators prepared a list of 127 names, ranging from Komsomol members to the wives of mullahs, all of whom allegedly had participated in the violence.[18] Further, a detachment of Red Army soldiers and mounted police soon arrived from Namangan to en-

15. Ibid.

16. For example, see RGASPI, d. 1208, l. 67, and d. 1213, l. 79.

17. According to the OGPU, by early May the Farghona okruzhkom had removed Ashurkulov from his post, issued a reprimand to the local party cell, and referred the entire raikom, "especially Saifutdinov," to the party's control commission for further disciplinary action (RGASPI, d. 1213, l. 79).

18. The selection of names likely served many purposes. Forced to name someone—anyone—the peasants in attendance may have chosen personal enemies or rivals for land, trade, or power.

force public order, a deployment that reportedly caused "great alarm and commotion [*perepolokh*] among the mass of the population." Fearing arrest, many peasants took to spending the night anywhere but their own homes.[19] Unlike local leaders, the OGPU did not shrink from the grim details, and it told how close the party felt it had come to the precipice of outright rebellion in Chust. Only the deployment of troops and the imposition of martial law had brought the situation under control. Soviet power seemed certain to face continuing difficulties if it kept interacting with Uzbeks through policies such as the hujum.

Narrativizing Resistance: Anti-Soviet Opposition Contained and Explained

These OGPU documents show the depth of anti-Soviet feelings in rural Farghona, feelings pushed into the open by the unveiling campaign. In the aftermath of rebellion, the yawning gulf between self-consciously European Soviet and party workers—even those of Uzbek ethnicity, such as Ashurkulov and Saifutdinov, who often came to places like Chust from nearby cities—and the bulk of Uzbek society grew even wider. The hujum had meant to increase the number of Bolshevik sympathizers in Uzbek society, after all, not drive them away. Although in hindsight the Chust affair seems tailor-made to serve as a red flag to alert party leaders to popular alienation, no such warning penetrated the mental categories of Bolshevik analysts and decision makers. While on one level the violence might have led to a reorientation of women's liberation policy (and perhaps a reduction in confrontation), many party members in positions of authority were unable to think what was for them the unthinkable, to see the depth and cross-class pervasiveness of anti-Soviet feeling manifest in these responses to the hujum. This reluctance is clear in the way these Bolsheviks coped: they changed the story of Chust as they told and retold it, both to others and to themselves.

Later accounts of the Chust rebellion, written for internal as well as public audiences, are very revealing of Bolshevik worldviews and cultural preconceptions. By stages the episode was narrativized; it became "the Chust affair." The events of April 1927 proved remarkably flexible in serving a variety of purposes and audiences. This narrative plasticity may not be a surprise in the many newspaper accounts that obviously were meant for didactic ends. Yet even highly classified internal party reports show the same or similar narrative changes. Such shifts thus show more than simple manipulation by propagandists. Rather, they show party writers coping with a potentially terrifying incident, one with unhappy implications for their professional success and even

---

But such concerns do not seem to have troubled investigators; in any case, they would have found it difficult to untangle such agendas.

19. Except as noted, the information on party responses in this paragraph is taken from the OGPU report at RGASPI, d. 1240, l. 150b.

personal safety, by making it steadily less threatening in the retelling. They contained and explained the events of April 1927 in terms they could understand, terms shaped by their cultural preconceptions and ideological blinders. Unfortunately, each stage of narrative reinterpretation pushed the party's collective analytical head further into the sand, making it less likely that high-level policy makers would understand what was actually happening in Uzbek society or have the information to respond appropriately.

In creating a narrative out of the disparate facts at their disposal, these analysts had first to explain what had happened in Chust and then to arrive at an understanding of why. Of course, no documents, not even the contemporary classified OGPU reports, offer a transparent view of what happened in Chust in mid-April 1927. Even these sources have a specific limited perspective on the events in question; they too pass human experiences through a multilayered process of perception, selection, interpretation, and representation as they come to be fixed in textual form. Nevertheless, with increasing distances of time and space from the original events, these narratives became increasingly revelatory of their interpreters rather than their subjects. It is illuminating to see how, once the immediate crisis had passed and the initial emergency reports had been filed, party thinkers began to make sense of Chust.

In explaining the rebellion—to themselves, initially—these analysts first chose in a variety of ways to minimize its importance. While this choice may be counterintuitive (why devote analytic energy to studying a phenomenon of no great import?), it served a deeper purpose. It contained the unrest and opposition; it made it manageable. By treating this episode as an isolated event rather than one with systemic implications, by seeing Chust as an occurrence without deep causes, analysts could avoid unpleasant questions about the overall strength of Soviet power in Central Asia, an edifice whose health was closely tied to their own interests and even their survival. Party writers spoke of the "Chust events" or of the "incidents" that had occurred, telling the story as a neatly packaged narrative. Indeed, the very act of naming it "the Chust affair" (*Chustskoe delo*) recognized but simultaneously circumscribed its importance, localizing and containing the phenomenon as having something less than general relevance. One analyst made the point explicitly, arguing that Chust's difficulties showed only a local problem, that nothing similar was happening elsewhere.[20]

Second, Bolshevik analysts explained what had happened in Chust through the prism of class conflict. Such an approach appealed to party thinkers both for ideological reasons and because few had the kind of in-depth personal knowledge of Uzbek culture that might have suggested alternative understandings of Central Asian social dynamics. The party's internal discussions of Chust thus took eyewitness descriptions of events and assimilated them to the categories expected in Soviet analysis. The resulting portrait seemed both more

20. Ibid., l. 320b. See also Aleksandrova's argument in the chapter epigraph.

explicable and reassuring. When the Chust affair was shoehorned into a class-based analytical scheme, it no longer signified broad-based popular resistance to the hujum or against Soviet power. When the opposition was portrayed as class-specific, it became less overwhelming.

According to this interpretation, unrest had broken out in Chust because of the area's high concentration of class enemies, particularly bois and the clergy; these class enemies had carried out antihujum agitation among local peasants; they further planned an "attack" (*napadenie*) on state, party, and Soviet workers, which led directly to the death of Tashmatov.[21] In contradiction to eyewitness and initial OGPU reports, these analyses portrayed the bulk of local society ("the general mass of the peasantry") as sympathetic to Soviet authorities.[22] Any reservations of the masses about Soviet-style women's liberation merely showed the shortcomings and negligence of party workers in permitting Muslim clerics to manipulate the populace rather than innate peasant conservatism or historically produced anticolonial sentiment.[23] Expressing a mixture of optimism and wishful thinking, these reports asserted that one commonly found reactions of shame and disgust among the peasantry at what the class enemies had done, and revulsion at the disgrace they brought upon the poor, laboring population of Chust. People in the local mahallas, in fact, allegedly had begun (voluntarily, it was implied) the task of unmasking these "great exploiters and their stooges" (*krupnye ekspluatatory i ikh prispeshnikov*).[24]

Going Public: Narrative Refiguring into a "Revolt of the Mullahs"

News of what had happened in Chust could not be hidden—rumors, at least, were bound to circulate—so the affair could not simply be swept under the rug. It became necessary in the weeks and months after April 1927 to retell the story, to re-present and explain it to a wider public. Newspapers at all levels published extensively on the rebellion, helping disseminate the party's interpretation: I focus here on a series of articles printed in *Pravda Vostoka*, the Communist Party's principal newspaper of record in Central Asia.[25] While in some ways these articles offer a skewed version of the story, they do reveal how Bolshevik activists thought about themselves, about Central Asian society, and about their place in it.

21. ÖzRMDA, f. 86, op. 1, d. 5602, l. 7. For similar reasoning, see RGASPI, d. 1249, ll. 95–96, where Chust is described as "a center of trade and a nest of the reactionary clergy, whose influence on the population is still strong."

22. PDA, op. 3, d. 1598, l. 17.

23. Ibid., d. 1549, l. 14–140b; and RGASPI, d. 1211, l. 207.

24. PDA, op. 3, d. 1549, ll. 4–5.

25. Other newspapers, including the Uzbek-language press (such as *Qizil Özbekiston*, hereafter *QÖ*), also discussed the Chust affair; but as the organ of the Sredazbiuro as well as the Uzbek party and government, *Pravda Vostoka* was the mouthpiece of and for Soviet power across all of Central Asia, and thus shows the party's public self-representations most readily and authoritatively.

Strikingly, the differences between most newspaper accounts and all but the most candid internal party materials are relatively minor, differences more of degree than of kind. Many of the analytical devices that shaped internal reports also characterized newspaper articles. The only real difference was a further loss of subtlety in the periodical press, not surprising given its propagandistic and instructional tone. The press had after all already come under fire for adding to the problems of the women's liberation campaign—for "sowing panic" by focusing on such negative outcomes as the attacks on unveiled women and the multitude of women who reveiled, while they were accused of mostly ignoring the campaign's accomplishments. Editors and reporters were told to moderate their candor, to black out bad news and put more effort into inspiring the masses.[26] In the pages of *Pravda Vostoka,* therefore, the story of Chust had fewer shades of gray and more of black and white. It offered less ambiguity in its protagonists and more caricatured class explanations. The story was repackaged as a narrative set piece, with a preordained happy ending.

The first mention of problems in Chust appeared in print astonishingly rapidly, on 23 April 1927, while the Farghona party was still trying desperately to reestablish order in the countryside and Red Army troops had marched in to occupy Chust. The initial public announcement, however, struck a very different tone. Buried in a long article touting the success of women's liberation in Farghona (the subtitle read "More than 10,000 Uzbek Women Unveiled in Pop District"), it meant to reassure rather than alarm readers.[27] Its author, Igel', an activist in the neighboring village of Pop, minimized the importance of unrest in Chust, mentioning it as an aside affecting only a minor backwater. Trouble had broken out, he remarked, "in the large village—although it is called a 'city'—of Chust." He went on to argue that a small number of "reactionary elements," specifically "bois, mullahs, and eshons" who opposed women's liberation, had instigated the violence; that the people of Chust, by contrast, supported Soviet power; and that the incident had not derailed the party's progress toward its goal of unveiling Uzbek women.

Igel''s story of the rebellion shows a creative reworking of the narrative, a reworking that redounded to the party's benefit and was not encumbered by the "facts" as they had been reported by the OGPU. His telegraphic account of

26. "Sowing panic" was denounced at PDA, op. 4, d. 1208, l. 38. Shimko explicitly directed the press not to be candid, mandating "complete silence" on matters showing setbacks to Soviet aims [*polnoe zamalchivanie iavlenii obratnogo poriadka*], such as reveilings and murders (RGASPI, d. 1210, l. 22).

27. This and the following paragraphs are based on Igel', "Chachvan ne derzhitsia: Krupnye rezul'taty 'nastupleniia' v Ferganskom okruge," *PV,* 23 April 1927. This claim of massive unveiling in Pop district strains credulity. The rural population around Chust and Pop represented a tiny fraction of Uzbekistan's roughly 5 million people. Given the party's oft-repeated (albeit itself questionable) claim that 100,000 women had unveiled between March and May across all of Uzbekistan, a figure of 10,000 in Pop district seems wildly disproportionate.

the unrest omitted elements that cast party or Soviet authorities in a bad light, exaggerated or fabricated items critical of Muslim clerics and other class enemies, and imagined a response, polarized along class lines, that had little in common with reality. After introducing Chust as a place with a "motley" (*raznosherstnoe*) population that included a "notable number of influential clerics, bois, and merchants," he asserted that these class enemies had shown up at a women's liberation meeting and asked "sly questions . . . [that] had a poor influence on the mood of the meeting." Igel' omitted any mention of how Ashurkulov's promise of free speech had elicited these questions, skipped altogether the arrests of mullahs that had abrogated that promise, and ignored the party's repeated refusal to compromise even as a hostile crowd gathered outside the town soviet building. Instead, Igel' simply said that the next morning a "small group" (*kuchka*) of hostile people, made up largely of mullahs, had marched to the Ispolkom—apparently out of the blue—and started shouting denunciations of Soviet power. When a policeman, Uzoqboi Tashmatov, spoke up in defense of Soviet authorities, the group had seized and beat him to death. A mullah had also been beaten for promising not to oppose women's liberation, Igel' noted, but the connection between the two men was not spelled out, nor did he note that the mullah's statement had been signed at the behest of local authorities, and so might have been less than completely voluntary.[28]

Igel''s imaginative powers were most apparent, though, in his account of what followed. The rampaging crowds that went on to destroy the Ispolkom building and hunt down the local soviet workers figured nowhere in his story. Instead, he invented a profound, if deeply implausible, pro-Soviet sympathy among peasants in and near Chust. The "vile crime" of Tashmatov's murder, Igel' said, had inflamed the peasantry; they attended his funeral in strength, and his tomb became a site of pilgrimage. They demanded that the killers be apprehended and face the strictest punishment, and expressed shame that the murder had happened in their area. Igel' wrote: "At one meeting an old, poor peasant expressed his indignation with impassioned, short phrases, and with tears in his eyes: 'I am from the mahalla of Qorghonchi, which the peasants are calling rotten [*parshivaia*]. It is not we who are rotten, but there are some rotten ones among us. They must be found and judged by a strict public court. They have left a shameful, indelible stain on all of us.'"

Many of *Pravda Vostoka*'s readers—by definition the Russian-speaking population of Central Asia—had no way of knowing whether such statements had been fabricated, but they must have been reassured to read such sentiments expressed by their ostensible class allies among the poor peasantry. Igel' had succeeded in recasting the narrative along class lines, with a bottom line calculated to calm party loyalists who might have heard disquieting rumors

28. There were other differences in Igel''s narrative, such as his failure to note that Tashmatov had been armed, and his hard-to-believe assertion that Ashurkulov's initial report on 15 April had not even mentioned the paranji, but limited itself to general comments on women's rights.

about their colleagues being hunted down and beaten, or worse. He summarized bluntly the lessons taught by the unrest: "The incident in Chust shows graphically that the bois, the clergy—all the enemies of the party are taking steps to hamper the liberation of enslaved Uzbek women. But with every day [these enemies] endure ever greater defeats; with every new criminal step they provoke still greater indignation from the laboring peasantry." He concluded in upbeat terms, returning to the successes of women's liberation embodied by the 10,000 women allegedly unveiled in Pop district. A terrifying episode was refashioned and drained of fear in this retelling: the unpleasantness in Chust had no real significance, Igel' implied, but was only a signpost of progress on the road to the inevitable triumph of Soviet women's liberation.

After Igel''s piece, nothing further about the unrest in Chust appeared in *Pravda Vostoka* for several months. This long silence, which in its own way speaks eloquently to the difficulties faced by Soviet authorities trying to impose order in the countryside and identify guilty parties in Chust, was broken only in late August, four and a half months after the rebellion. At last, officials announced, they were prepared to try the murderers and looters of Chust. The number of accused had by this time increased from eight to eighteen, and *Pravda Vostoka* sent a special correspondent, V. Frenkin, to Chust to write about the case. Framed by the judicial proceedings, Frenkin's series of articles further simplified the story, transforming it into a melodrama with ultimate justice on the side of the Bolsheviks, a tale of triumph through adversity, of heroic victory over vicious class enemies. Most important, the narrative showed the party as firmly in control, with exemplary punishments being meted out to class enemies.

The first of these articles, a backgrounder, appeared on 29 August. Although most court proceedings had already taken place (testimony was heard from 22 to 27 August), Frenkin's first piece only set the stage, providing a framework to help readers understand the courtroom drama to come. Questions of fact, though, were not left for the trial. Instead, Frenkin again—preemptively—told the story of Chust, a now-Manichean tale that began with a description of the entire district of Qorghonchi as virtually synonymous with class enemies. By constructing a fresh category of enemies, *Kurganchintsy* (that is, residents of Qorghonchi mahalla), Frenkin pushed the Soviet narrative a step further:

Kurganchintsy

With what inexpressible loathing up to now have the peasants of Chust pronounced this word!

Chust is divided into four parts. In three live peasants; the fourth, called Qorghonchi, is populated primarily by clergy and the local "aristocracy."

Users of force, petty tyrants, aggressors [who dominate] water supplies, "landlords" in the time of the khanate, bosmachi during the years
of revolution: the Kurganchintsy even now remain enemies of all that
draws the peasantry toward freedom.[29]

Frenkin thus highlighted the enemy for his readers, simultaneously circumscribing it in both class and spatial terms. He made the Chust violence less
threatening by depicting it as a limited danger, one created by specific conditions in one particular district of a certain town in rural Farghona and, by implication, nowhere else.

After so specifying the enemy, Frenkin told his version of the story of those
crucial days in mid-April 1927. After recounting how the initial meeting of 15
April was marred by Muslim clerics who opposed the hujum (although ne-
glecting to mention Ashurkulov's promise that they could speak freely),
Frenkin admitted that the local party had erred in making arrests. After this
point, though, the blame fell completely on noncommunist shoulders. "This
mistake was just what the Kurganchintsy were waiting for," Frenkin wrote,
imputing a high degree of organization and planning to anti-Soviet forces. At
the instigation of a Muslim cleric, he continued, a crowd had gathered to demand the mullahs' release. Here Frenkin changed the tale again, leaving out
the repeated official refusals of these demands and asserting that the crowd
was told immediately that the mullahs would be freed the next morning at
eleven o'clock. The throng, however, refused to wait and immediately attacked the local soviet building. Shouting "Save our shariat!" the mob freed
the imprisoned clerics by force and then started to destroy the ispolkom's offices. When a nearby policeman, Tashmatov, merely tried to talk to some of
the people involved (Frenkin omitted entirely his defense of Abbos Maksum),
his temerity drove the mob's leaders "frantic with rage" (*raz"iarilis'*) and they
chased him. Finally catching the exhausted officer when he fell into an irrigation ditch, they ignored his pleas and entreaties for mercy and commenced
beating him. One Sufi adept, Tuichiboi Baibabaev, seized Tashmatov's rifle
and started beating him on the head with its butt; another, Pulatbek Begmatov, finished off the victim by hurling rocks at him. Other Kurganchintsy then
set upon the corpse, and "Tashmatov was literally ripped to pieces."[30]

Frenkin's version of the Chust affair thus simultaneously named the worst
offenders individually (removing the mob's frightening faceless quality) and
stressed their brutality by using language that described them like a pack of
wolves. Even better, from the perspective of class justice, his narrative alleged

29. F-n [V. Frenkin], "Chustskoe delo," *PV,* 29 Aug. 1927.
30. Ibid.

that the actual acts of violence were committed by Muslim religious figures, specifically these two murids (Sufi adepts or disciples). Frenkin then went further than Igel' in describing what came next. Hoping to show a deep popular sympathy for Soviet authorities, sympathy that would both isolate the revolt and its leaders and reassure the Russian-speaking readers of *Pravda Vostoka,* he fabricated a further episode more or less out of thin air:

> *For Soviet power*
>
> Among the labyrinth of streets, across the fields, rumors about the revolt of a small group of mullahs, detested by the peasantry, was embellished in one of the three peasant parts of Chust. A terrible indignation seized everyone. With shouts of "When will they give us peace!" and "We are going to save our [Soviet] power!" peasants armed themselves with what was at hand—*ketmens* [hoes], *teshas* [adzes], and sticks—and, numbering about 500, moved threateningly against the Kurganchintsy. The crowd kept growing, increasing as peasants abandoned their field work [to join]. When the Kurganchintsy, preparing to continue their excesses, heard about the approaching peasants, they scattered in an instant. Order was restored. The peasants thoughtfully tidied up the Ispolkom [building], calming its workers [as they did so].
>
> The "revolt of the mullahs" was liquidated.[31]

The wishful thinking that party writers projected onto Uzbek society is nowhere better expressed than in this vision of poor Uzbek peasants leaping to the defense of their white-collar brothers and sisters and then "thoughtfully tidying up" their ravaged offices.

And Justice for All: The Courtroom as Instructional Theater

Successive retellings had transmuted this popular rebellion from a broad-based insurrection, one triggered by party high-handedness and coercion in the unveiling campaign, into a "revolt of the mullahs." At this point a coda was added to the story to show the enactment of Soviet class-based justice. Igel' and Frenkin, among others, had shifted the public narrative of what happened in April, thereby bringing the past under control. Their view, in which the peasantry ultimately saved the day despite unfortunate mistakes by the party, had drained the violence in Chust of most of its fear. All that remained was to claim the present and future. To do so the party seized the opportunities presented by a public trial of the accused Chust criminals in August 1927.

This trial promised authorities a chance to control the story's final retelling,

31. Ibid.

one that would codify the Soviet narrative as accurate by using the ostensibly objective forum of a court of law to display the "facts" of the case and certify them as true and beyond question. This story could then be used endlessly for the instruction of the masses; Frenkin, after all, had been sent to Chust for just such a purpose.[32] The trial was not concerned primarily with questions of individual truth, of determining the factual accuracy of particular accusations. Rather, it aimed at a higher truth: justice measured in class terms. Such bottom-line justice had to be disseminated widely for maximum effect, so courtroom proceedings were staged consciously for public consumption and instruction. The Chust trial thus developed earlier precedents—and foreshadowed later, more famous Soviet show trials—in seeing justice as a performance, one that used the courtroom as its theater.[33]

When seen as theater, the trial makes sense. The plot was neatly packaged, with protagonists clearly marked as good or bad and a virtually preordained ending; there was never much doubt that the class enemies in the dock were criminals or that they would be convicted. The instructional nature of the proceedings easily explained and excused a certain flexibility on questions of fact; artistic license required that a story line be massaged to allow effective retelling. Regular newspaper reports kept public interest engaged, doling out each act of the drama like a serialized novel, with enough suspense, violence, and sex to keep the audience reading. Only a few months earlier *Pravda Vostoka* had acquired the equipment to print photographs; this technological innovation now made it possible for readers across Central Asia to *see* what was happening in the distant town of Chust and to visualize the drama for themselves. *Pravda Vostoka* spared no expense: Frenkin's articles were illustrated with pictures of almost all the main players, conveniently labeled for easy identification: "the accused" (for a group shot of the eighteen men on trial); "the direct murderers of policeman Tashmatov" (for the two Sufi adepts Baibabaev and Begmatov, presumed guilty before trial); "members of the court" (for the three judges, one of whom was female); and "the procurator and *obshchestvennyi obvinitel'* " (for the prosecution team). Not coincidentally, all the faces pictured belonged to ethnic Uzbeks, a necessary conceit to

32. A class-conscious party proposal to use the trial and sentencing for public instruction, to "use the mood of the poor" in aiding women's liberation work, is at PDA, op. 3, d. 1533, ll. 21–22.

33. The Chust proceedings predated by almost a year the Shakhty trial of "wreckers," which opened in May 1928 and is often seen as the first use of sensational public justice in the Stalinist USSR. Such theaters of justice were pioneered earlier by Soviet authorities in Central Asia, however, particularly over women's liberation. Chust was not unique in this regard: for roughly contemporary murders in Achi and Dyumen that also were used for public instruction, see *PV*, 13–27 Apr., 26 May–29 June, and 23–31 Aug. 1927. Scholars have also found other precursors in Russia well before 1928. See Elizabeth A. Wood, *Performing Justice: Agitation Trials in Revolutionary Russia, 1920–1933* (Ithaca, forthcoming); or Julie Cassiday, *The Enemy On Trial: Early Soviet Courts on Stage and Screen* (De Kalb, Ill., 2000).

give the impression that justice was being determined by Uzbeks themselves, not by Russian Bolsheviks in Tashkent or their superiors in Moscow. Only the defense advocate, who occupied a tricky, anomalous role in this performance, was neither named nor pictured.

Frenkin started by noting the strong popular interest in the drama. His first article explained that the peasantry, horrified at Tashmatov's murder, had demanded such a trial. Once it had been convened, Frenkin described the scene at the eye of the storm, the Red Teahouse (*choihona*) that had been converted into a makeshift courtroom. Already crammed with people, this court could not accommodate the more than 3,000 people who wanted to attend. The people crowding the streets outside were too packed to move as more and more peasants arrived, reportedly abandoning their fields to see the spectacle. Although it is impossible to evaluate the accuracy of such descriptions (as unlikely as parts of them sound), Frenkin thought it important to assert that at least half of the crowd was female, and to say that the talk in the streets was of nothing but the trial.[34]

In his next article, published on 31 August, Frenkin offered a detailed report of the court proceedings, showing how the judges had succeeded in "unmasking" the truth of what had happened in Chust. The story, as retold to and by the court, continued to change. The accused were depicted unsparingly, as spineless and shifty, as lacking the masculinity that would have made them real men: they could not even bring themselves to admit what they had done. Frenkin expended much ink in elaborating the ways in which these "pathetic and shameless" men had tried to escape Soviet justice. They all had denied involvement in the violence. Several, including the two murids accused of murder, protested that they had not even been present: Baibabaev maintained that he had been working in the fields, and Begmatov insisted that he was buying meat at the market at the time of the killing. Others, such as the clerics Akmedjan Abidov and Mirsagdulla Akhunbabaev, stated that they had tried to avoid trouble by staying at home. At least two of the accused looters, Mirza Rakhimov and Ibrohim Khoja Mulladjanov, took a different tack, arguing that they stalwartly supported Soviet power; while they admitted rushing into the Ispolkom building, they insisted they had done so not to attack but to warn the workers there of the danger they faced.

Frenkin scornfully dismissed these stories as cowardly attempts to hide the truth. Under the sarcastic headings "Ia ne ia, i loshad' ne moia" (I am not me, and the horse isn't mine) and "My za sovetskuiu vlast'" (We are for Soviet power), he painstakingly refuted each account. Long quotations from several peasants' testimony punched holes in the alibis of those who said they had been elsewhere. Then Khaltam Kalandarov, an ispolkom worker, forcefully contradicted those who said they had raced into the building to warn its occupants. Kalandarov (who also helpfully gave an Uzbek face to the outpost of

34. F-n [V. Frenkin], "Chustskoe delo," *PV*, 29 Aug. 1927.

Soviet power under attack) rebutted Rakhimov's testimony by declaring that when the latter burst into his office, not only had he not warned Kalandarov, but he had started to destroy property and beat him severely. In the end, Frenkin concluded, the accused in the dock were shown to be cowards and liars. Three witnesses who had helped them concoct alibis were added to the trial, charged with perjury.

Frenkin's second shift of the narrative bolstered the Soviet view that the Chust violence had been instigated and directed by a highly organized, dedicated group of anti-Soviet class enemies. Under the heading "Podpol'naia rabota kipela . . ." (Clandestine work was boiling), he alleged that the head of the Qorghonchi mahalla's "clerical commission," one Sultan Said Akhmedov, had convened a secret gathering of clergy well before the fateful women's liberation meeting of 15 April. Akhmedov's conclave (which Frenkin may have fabricated or at least greatly embellished) supposedly declared that unveiled women were no longer to be considered legally married, that husbands who permitted their wives to unveil were no longer to be counted as believing Muslims, and that the time had come to speak out against the hujum. The arrests on 16 April had provided the perfect pretext for this cabal to put its dastardly plan into action. Frenkin thus again localized the root cause of the violence in the manipulations of a small group of class enemies.

Frenkin's final modification further altered the tale in a way that contradicted the classified OGPU account and, for the sake of ideological clarity, made the Chust narrative much less ambiguous. Several narrative elements shifted; one of the most visible was the anomalous role of the imam Mullah Abbos Maksum. He had played a central role in the secret police account: he was the cleric attacked for promising not to oppose the hujum, the cleric to whose defense Tashmatov had come and thus indirectly the cause of Tashmatov's death. Yet most subsequent Soviet narrations had omitted Abbos Maksum entirely. His narrative position was more than a little awkward: as a clergyman, he should have been an enemy, not someone willing to do what the party asked by agreeing not to oppose the hujum. Clerics, moreover, were supposed to lead (or manipulate) the population in religious fervor—not be accused of having an insufficiently strong religious commitment, bludgeoned, and then almost lynched by a crowd of peasants. Abbos Maksum's specific role in the unrest was even harder to explain, since it raised the specter of Tashmatov's having been killed for defending a class enemy—and a class enemy, no less, who had come under attack only because of mistakes made by local Communists.

So it is not surprising that most party narrations omitted Abbos Maksum. But Frenkin went much further, recasting him in a more ideologically appropriate role. Calling it "a pity" that the trial had not permitted the audience to feel the real danger represented by the clerics and merchants in the dock—the trial apparently succeeded too well at containing and belittling these class enemies—Frenkin lamented that the judges had never even seen Abbos Maksum.

Why did that matter? Because, Frenkin declared, Abbos Maksum was the "main inspirer" of the assault on the Ispolkom, allegedly having given the signal for the attack with a nod of his head. "This signal," Frenkin continued, "was understood by the crowd of mullahs in an instant, and they threw themselves against the Ispolkom and then started after the policeman, with impassioned shouts of 'They beat Abbos Maksum! A holy war! Save our shariat!' " *Pravda Vostoka* thus solved the dilemma of Abbos Maksum by assimilating him, by inventing a new role more appropriate for a clergyman. Transformed from victim into ringleader, he now fitted the expected categories of Soviet ideology.

The didactic tone and purpose of Soviet public justice became completely clear in Frenkin's last three articles on Chust, which appeared in *Pravda Vostoka* on 4 September. Through summaries of the closing arguments by prosecution and defense and a full quotation of the court's final decision, the Soviet narrative was certified publicly with the badge of judicial authority. In all three segments readers imbibed the same interpretive line: Frenkin left no doubt about the conclusions one should reach. He began with the prosecution's closing argument, delivered by the (ethnically Uzbek) procurator, Ishmatov. Ishmatov's summation described the accused as a sly and crafty group of mullahs, bois, and merchants who had a hidden, irreconcilable hatred for peasants. He then headed off any defense strategy that might try to portray this group of "bandits" as anything less than a highly organized, conspiratorial anti-Soviet band of class enemies, declaring that "with irrefutable clarity, this trial has exposed the real political essence of what these former 'landlords' have said, planned and organized in advance against peasant power. The faces sitting in the dock are the faces of organized and deliberate counterrevolutionaries and murderers."

Faced with such an argument and surrounded by an audience stoked up to express unrelenting hostility, the defense put up little fight. Frenkin did maintain a pretense of objectivity (as was required by the format of court proceedings) by including a brief description of the defense's closing argument, but he simultaneously guided readers on how to evaluate it. The still unnamed defense advocate certainly played the strangest role of all in this judicial performance, since as an officer of the court he had the anomalous obligation to defend class enemies. If the trial had been scripted for public enlightenment, though, it required a conviction. Therefore the defense could neither do too well nor be too convincing, either to the judges or to the public audience. The defense advocate based his brief summation on the notion that the accused men were peasants manipulated by others, that they were "unknowing lambs" (*nesoznatel'nye iagniata*). Even while appearing to attempt to exculpate the defendants, then, the public defender bolstered the party's overall position that clerics and class enemies lay behind the violence, contending only that the men in the dock were the victims of mistaken identity. Frenkin reported this argument with a rhetorically raised eyebrow, ensuring that readers saw how skeptically the audience—people who, after all, supposedly knew these men—reacted to this idea. He began by quoting the defense advocate, who asserted:

> "The head of the clergy, Abbos Maksum, is guilty of everything. He got the masses worked up. He forced [these] unknowing, benighted, ignorant peasants to speak out [against unveiling]. . . ."
>
> An involuntary smile ran across the faces of the many thousands of people watching.
>
> . . . "Peasants?"
>
> "These Kurganchintsy are a band of mullahs, eshons, and merchants—and now they are peasants?"

In the face of this incredulous reaction from the audience, Frenkin reported, the defense advocate rested his case and took his seat. All that remained was a last word from the accused, delivered in a way that, according to *Pravda Vostoka,* only underscored their shiftiness and spinelessness: "And all of them—who had tried to destroy the Ispolkom, who were directly or indirectly the murderers of Tashmatov—with one voice repeated insolently, over and over again, 'We have always stood—and we still stand—for "our" Soviet power.' "

Frenkin's final, sarcastic quotation marks completed his task. Questions of guilt and innocence had taken on an entirely new appearance once the Chust uprising was refigured into a revolt of the mullahs. If the revolt was synonymous with a specific social class, after all, all that the court had to do to prove guilt was to demonstrate membership in that class. Hence, since the accused were alleged to be lying about their peasant status—since they were actually mullahs and merchants—they must ipso facto also be guilty of Tashmatov's murder and the destruction of the Ispolkom building. Their class identity was their badge of criminality, and no further proof of specific wrongdoing was necessary.

Frenkin made clear that the accused were meant to leave an unfavorable impression. Lest there be any misunderstanding, though, *Pravda Vostoka* also published the court's official verdicts and sentences. This final statement on the case was reprinted in full, verbatim, the better to instruct a wide readership. The court's decisions did contain a few surprises. Three of the eighteen men accused were acquitted for lack of evidence, and the three accused of perjury during the trial were also released. Such actions lent an aura of fairness and objectivity to the proceedings and bolstered the authority of the guilty verdicts rendered against the other men. The Sufi students accused of direct responsibility for Tashmatov's murder, Baibabaev and Begmatov, were sentenced to death by shooting, with confiscation of all property. Ten others were sentenced to five years in prison and a further loss of rights for three years after their release. Further, a special court was called to hear the remaining cases, particularly of two men who had fled Chust before they could be arrested, and notably also to try the alleged clerical masterminds of the plot, Abbos Maksum and Sultanboi.[35]

It may not be surprising to find such narrative permutations in the retellings of the Chust story in *Pravda Vostoka*. The newspaper, after all, was a public Soviet forum. Of course its writers and editors would portray the party in a positive light (and its purported enemies in a negative one) whenever the facts allowed—and they might invent a few facts along the way. Yet these narrative changes are not just window dressing created by calculating propagandists. The shifts in the story as told by *Pravda Vostoka* strikingly resemble those in the internal, confidential party materials. They were merely a more extreme version of the views these writers expounded to themselves and to each other; they show the same coping mechanisms as Bolsheviks tried (mostly unsuccessfully) to make sense of the violence in Chust. Both public and private sources apprehended these events through the same analytic and cognitive categories, and the story changed accordingly until it portrayed the unrest and violence as caused and manipulated by a small group of clerical class enemies. This depiction in turn helped make it impossible for the party to consider cooperation with sympathetic clerics, or to consider reducing the confrontation inherent in the hujum.

Consequences and Legacies

The many public and private tellings of the Chust story show a great deal about the Bolshevik storytellers, if perhaps less about the story itself. Yet in at least one respect an important difference does exist between the newspaper accounts and internal reports. Public forums such as *Pravda Vostoka*, virtually without exception, had to belittle the ultimate significance of the Chust affair. Anxiety about its implications could not be shown in public, so the real fear in Bolshevik ranks can be glimpsed only in internal reports. Although many analysts did succeed in denying and explaining away the Chust rebellion, and although this success did influence subsequent policy decisions, at least a few Communists, particularly at the local level, saw Chust as more than mere sound and fury, signifying nothing. Despite the brave public statements in *Pravda Vostoka* and elsewhere, Chust lingered in the minds of party activists

35. "Prigovor," *PV*, 4 Sept. 1927. It is unclear whether these later trials took place. There were good reasons that Soviet authorities would not wish them to be public: two of the accused were not in custody, so the swift and sure arm of Soviet justice might seem neither; the evidence against Sultanboi (probably the same Sultan Said Akhmedov who had been accused of organizing clerical opposition in Qorghonchi) seems at best weak; and the evidence against Abbos Maksum must have been fabricated completely, since he was a victim of the violence, not an instigator. Moreover, no mention was made of legal action against the party secretary and other officials who had provoked the riots, even though Frenkin's article of 29 August had promised that they, too, would be tried.

(and their opponents) all across Uzbekistan. It colored their subsequent actions with respect to the hujum and perhaps to other issues as well.

One visible legacy of the Chust affair noted by Soviet observers was a deeply troubled unveiling effort, both in the Chust-Pop area of rural Farghona and elsewhere. Such difficulties showed that the party's explanation for what had happened in Chust failed to win universal acceptance and also demonstrated the thoroughness and speed with which informal information networks spread the news of rebellion across Uzbekistan and beyond.[36] Such whisperings were particularly dangerous while the qörboshi still were a potential threat; some of these anti-Soviet rebels reportedly had encamped just across the Afghan border.[37] One internal party report complained that the Chust events were "used by hostile forces" to reveil women, and that in some completely unveiled villages all the women had again donned paranji and chachvon.[38] In Farghona, where the uprising had occurred and news presumably spread most quickly, the picture was especially bleak. The raikom secretary Saifutdinov said that party heavy-handedness in Chust had led to the reveiling of all but a handful of the 16,000 unveiled women in his district. Ignoring his own role in that heavy-handedness, he lamented that he would be pleased to find a mere 100 women still unveiled.[39] The bottom line, to those Bolsheviks able to see it, was unhappy. Uzbeks could and did conclude that although the ultimate balance of force in southern Central Asia might lie with the Red Army, short-term, local, or carefully calibrated resistance was still quite possible. The balance of power at any given point in the thinly staffed reaches of the Uzbek provinces did not necessarily favor the Soviet state.

Despite the party's success in controlling newspaper coverage and in generating rhetorical accounts that contained and belittled the class enemies who allegedly lay behind this outburst of violence, the name of Chust remained in the minds of party leaders and analysts long after April 1927. It represented in party discourse an always-present danger. When an uprising several months later in the village of Oq-er threatened to explode into violence, another article in *Pravda Vostoka* stated explicitly that a Chust-like tragedy had been avoided only by the timely actions of local officials.[40] And local party organizations across Uzbekistan, however optimistic they sounded in reports sent up the chain of command, remained deeply shaken. One high-level provincial official arrived in Rishtan in late April 1927 and immediately directed local Commu-

36. The party was aware of the dangers of gossip about the uprising. Activists were told to carry out an extensive campaign of "explanatory work" to disseminate the Soviet view of what had happened (PDA, op. 3, d. 1533, l. 15).

37. PDA, op. 4, d. 1208, ll. 38–39.

38. RGASPI, d. 1249, l. 92.

39. RGASPI, d. 939, l. 17. As noted above, Saifutdinov's claimed high-water mark of 16,000 unveiled women in the district was likely an exaggeration.

40. A. P., "Provokatsiia mull," *PV,* 6 Sept. 1927.

nists to arrest the area's mullahs in advance of May Day, as the tsars had done with political enemies before state holidays.[41] Superiors quickly counter-manded his order, but the episode shows the anxiety that gripped many party members in the immediate aftermath of the rebellion, as danger seemed to be everywhere.

Chust was a flash point, showing the tensions within Uzbek society and il-luminating social responses to the hujum (and to other Soviet policies, such as the land and water reform). Its proximate cause, the women's liberation meet-ing held in the "holy mahalla" of Qorghonchi, was only that, the immediate impetus. The party's arresting of local clerics after promising not to do so and its attempt to force mullahs not to speak out on matters of deep moral and cul-tural concern were but the last straw for many Uzbeks in Chust, and they cat-alyzed a dramatic public display of anger. Yet while Uzbekistan's Bolsheviks could not avoid seeing this flash—and many were very frightened—the party as a whole could not come to grips with its daunting implications. On one level, Communists in Tashkent and Samarqand saw the revolt as inexplicable, all the more so given their frequently reiterated expectation that the popular masses—especially the enormous mass of poor peasants—would stand with them. At the same time, given the limited insight of a largely European party hierarchy into the inner workings of Uzbek society, the thunderclap of vio-lence had to be explained within the cultural and ideological vocabulary that was available.

Within an analytical approach deeply structured by external considerations, then, Bolshevik analysts arrived at an explanation for the Chust affair: first, local party leaders had made mistakes in executing a generally correct policy, and second, class enemies had seized upon these mistakes to whip up anti-Soviet feelings. Through successive retellings, the story of Chust proved mal-leable; it was a plastic narrative that increasingly came to resemble this Soviet view. Narrative elements were omitted, embellished, slanted, and invented as needed to make the story fit. The all too visible anti-Soviet actions of poor peasants and others did not show this deeper truth, so they had to be ignored. Perhaps Soviet writers believed the episodes of spontaneous peasant support they invented: it is impossible to know. But they wanted so badly for them to be true—they *needed* them to be true—that they may have made them so, by dint of belief, within their own heads and in private party discussions.

Party leaders thus confronted an episode of violent popular resistance that by rights should have terrified them about the direction and effects of Soviet policy. But through repeated retellings they remade what had happened, coped with it, and arrived ultimately at a version that solidified their resolve not only to continue the hujum but to accelerate it. Soviet authorities in essence con-structed their own vision of an Uzbek society—one riven by class conflict, with tearful peasants proclaiming loyalty to the party and demanding harsh show

41. The episode was related by Prishchepchik at RGASPI, d. 1240, l. 150b.

trials—by projecting their wishes for that society onto the raw material at hand. By minimizing the long-term implications of the violence, moreover—by calling it an "affair," an "incident"—they also contained its power. In the end, the cultural work that went into creating a malleable, tightly circumscribed Chust affair succeeded: it was made into an object lesson for the masses—instead of being, as it could and should have been, an object lesson for the party.

CHAPTER 5

Subaltern Voices

> It was the colonialist's frenzy to unveil the Algerian woman, it
> was his gamble on winning the battle of the veil at whatever
> cost, that were to provoke the native's bristling resistance. . . .
> We here recognize one of the laws of the psychology of colo-
> nization. In an initial phase, it is the action, the plans of the
> occupier that determine the centers of resistance around which
> a people's will to survive becomes organized.
>
> —Frantz Fanon

> I will not bare my wife; for Soviet power is exposing women
> and corrupting them, but they will uncover my wife only when
> they shoot me.
>
> —Imetdin Nizamutdinov, a resident of Bukhoro, March 1928

Conflict over female seclusion and veiling in Central Asia only intensified
after 1927. How did Central Asian Muslims respond to Soviet readings of their
society and culture? How did Uzbek eyes see Soviet power, expressed in the
hujum? What were the cognitive categories and discursive constructions used
by Muslim society to respond to these Soviet campaigns? In the sources preserved in Soviet archives it can be difficult to find the kinds of indigenous voices
that answer such questions. Where they exist, these voices have been filtered
through Bolshevik lenses of selection and interpretation. To address such questions, therefore, one must read Soviet reports against the grain of their intended
purpose—ideally in combination with other forms of evidence. The difficulties
are real, but careful readings can detect such hidden voices. They show that in
the face of a continuing attack against female seclusion in conjunction with
other Soviet assaults, such as forced collectivization, most Uzbek men and
women came by the 1930s to resist these party efforts with increasing vigor and
coherence. In the end, just as the party's analyses of Uzbek society say more

about the party than about Uzbeks, so Uzbek discourse on the hujum—its exaggerations, inaccuracies, points omitted or altered in retellings—reveals more about Central Asian ideological and cognitive categories than about the Soviet campaign.

For many Uzbeks the hujum was a blank slate, an empty canvas on which to inscribe their hopes, fears, and dreams. Yet this canvas was not created in a vacuum; many of its background colors had been filled in. Like party analysts (albeit from a very different perspective), individual Uzbeks understood and reacted to the world around them in ways that were structured by their historical experiences, material resources and opportunities, and cultural, religious, and ideological predispositions.[1] Such considerations did not determine what any particular actor would do—far from it—but they circumscribed a finite world of possible responses and shaped the lexicons in which such responses were elaborated, explained, and defended. Uzbek Muslims were not primitive or ignorant, as party writers thought: decades of tsarist rule in Central Asia had shaped quite rational opinions about who Russians were and what they wanted, and ten years of Bolshevik rule had added further notions about Communists, who mostly were seen as alien atheists and city folk. This mix of stereotype and hard-won experience was refracted by Uzbek Muslims through a particular religio-cultural and ideological lens, shaped in significant part by an always evolving, uniquely Central Asian brand of Islam. (See Figure 17.)

From party activists' perspective, the ideas about Bolshevism and Soviet power that resulted were misguided and inaccurate: misunderstandings and misconceptions characterized both sides of the Uzbek-Soviet encounter. Spotty education and limited knowledge of the Russian language kept most Uzbeks from talking with foreign Bolsheviks, let alone understanding why the party had decided to pursue policies such as the hujum. Most Uzbek men and women thus assimilated Soviet actions into their preexisting conceptions of the world. They interpreted the hujum, above all, in apocalyptic terms—less as an emancipatory campaign by a modernizing government than as a storm or plague sent by Allah to test or punish Muslim believers. In virtually all segments of Uzbek society, unveiling was seen as a sign of God's displeasure with Central Asian society. Its moral connotations served as a harbinger of the end times. Such views had real consequences: once the struggle over female seclusion had been cast in apocalyptic terms as a battle between good and evil, no retreat or compromise was possible. Just as had happened within the party, the hujum was recast as an epic battle between two faiths. And again, competing voices—in this case the jadids, who had lent a voice of indigenous support for unveiling—were marginalized, discredited, and written out of the story. By

1. This approach draws on Pierre Bourdieu's concept of the *habitus*, in which an ever-changing calculus of material and cultural-symbolic factors influences every historical actor's outlook and actions. See his *Logic of Practice*, trans. Richard Nice (Stanford, 1992), 53–60.

Figure 17. Ritual blessing as a bride departs for her new
husband's home, 1929. (Courtesy RGAKFD.)

1930 the dialogue on both sides had narrowed appreciably; and as we shall
see, this confrontation only begat more of the same.

Hegemony, Power, and the Dilemmas of Control: Soviet Unveiling and Uzbek Responses

Just as there was no single, monolithic hujum, there was no universal response
to it. Regional differences were implicit in the hujum's piecemeal approach: serious attempts to unveil local women did not begin in Qashqadaryo until
1928, for example, and a similar delay occurred in Tajikistan (part of the
Uzbek SSR until 1929), where central authorities often knew virtually nothing
about the most basic conditions on the ground.[2] The success of local unveiling
efforts also varied dramatically. Party analysts in Tashkent and Samarqand ex-

2. RGASPI, d. 2056, l. 139, and d. 2066, l. 1.

plained trouble in distant villages by arguing that anti-Soviet clerics and others sought out and moved into areas where the hujum had been slow to start, but it was harder to say why in 1928 unveiling seemed to be more stable, albeit at a lower level, in areas where no hujum had yet been launched officially than in those where it had.[3] While remote areas near the Afghan border were slow to unveil, it was more surprising—and much more embarrassing—to see similar difficulties close to the heart of Soviet regional power.[4] Of Uzbekistan's three major cities, only Bukhoro was seen as an unambiguous success; its allegedly complete unveiling was held up as an inspiration.[5] Samarqand, by contrast, the first Soviet capital of Uzbekistan, was less of a model: when unveiled rural women from nearby villages came to the city, they complained of being mocked and laughed at by veiled urban women.[6] Most troubling was Tashkent, long the center of Russian presence in Central Asia (and after 1930, the Uzbek capital city). It was one of the worst laggards: activists from Bukhoro complained openly about the baleful influence of Tashkent's failure on other districts.[7]

Soviet and party workers insisted many times that female unveiling was proceeding well.[8] The credibility of such assertions is not self-evident, as it was in the interest of these writers to exaggerate or invent popular enthusiasm in reports sent up the chain of command. Likewise speeches or reports meant for public consumption tended to strike an upbeat tone. Yet in at least a few places—particularly in the Russified New Cities of major urban areas, where Soviet control was comparatively secure—significant numbers of Uzbek women could and did remove their paranjis and chachvons in relative, sometimes temporary safety.[9] These women expressed one kind of subaltern voice—they were buffeted by social pressure and sometimes faced great danger for walking about unveiled, yet nonetheless acted bravely to stake out posi-

---

3. PDA, op. 4, d. 1235, ll. 18–20, and Otdel RiD TsK KP(b)Uz, *Rezoliutsii Uzbekskogo Soveshchaniia rabotnikov sredi rabotnits i dekhkanok* (Tashkent, 1929), 8.

4. On the Afghan border, see PDA, op. 5, d. 815, ll. 176–77. On regional distinctiveness, see PDA, op. 7, d. 866, ll. 80–82, and op. 10, d. 662, ll. 157–62; and RGASPI, d. 2052, ll. 45–48.

5. PDA, op. 10, d. 662, ll. 99–100; RGASPI, d. 1713, ll. 26–27, and d. 2055, ll. 1–6; and *Vsesoiuznoe soveshchanie otvetstvennykh sekretarei komissii po uluchsheniiu truda i byta zhenshchin* (Moscow, 1930), 54–55. Problems with this portrait of Bukhoro are discussed below.

6. RGASPI, d. 2059, l. 11.

7. RGASPI, d. 2051, ll. 257–58. As Mariia Muratova, director of the Sredazbiuro Zhenotdel, put it to a Central Asian Congress of Women's Workers in late 1929, "In the backward areas of Bukhoro and Qashqadaryo we have mass unveiling, and we have no reveiling. But the leading province of Tashkent, the Farghona Valley, plus Samarqand: [they] are very much the leading provinces on the other side. What is going on? What is really happening is that Bukhoro has unveiled and has pulled Surkhondaryo, Qashqadaryo, and Zerafshon after itself, and we have mass unveilings. But esteemed Tashkent sits tight, pulling after itself all of the Farghona Valley and Samarqand; they look at each other, they moan and groan, they just go on like this [*po okhaiut, po akhaiut i tak i zhivut*]" (ibid., l. 239).

8. One example among many is PDA, op. 3, d. 1560, l. 344.

9. See, for example, the OGPU report from 1929 at RGASPI, d. 2064, ll. 18–19.

tions in support of greater gender equity. Their subaltern status is even more apparent given their frequently marginal social positions. But subalternity in Stalinist Uzbekistan came in multiple, overlapping, and contradictory shades: given Soviet military supremacy, the character of Stalinist rule, and the Russian colonial legacy, from another point of view Uzbeks—*all* Uzbeks—were subaltern, subject to the changing whims of authority. From this perspective unveiled women—who after all were connected with, socialized in, and fiercely protected by Soviet state and judicial institutions—had strong links to power, even as they fought personal battles against indigenous poverty, patriarchy, and social disapproval. In Soviet Central Asia, dominance and submission were highly complex, layered, context-dependent matters.

So in some social circles and certain geographical spaces the unveiling campaign made headway. But the party also gained a different and in some ways more profound success by about 1930. The high priority accorded the hujum, with its attendant publicity and large investment of political capital, succeeded fundamentally in marking the act of unveiling with Soviet colors and thus in shifting its cultural connotations within Uzbek society. One of the party's deepest fears in 1927 had been that, having chosen a hujum for women's emancipation as the centerpiece of its Central Asian policy, it might lose the initiative and be outflanked on the left. Other competing models of liberation, international (Turkey, Afghanistan) and domestic (the jadids), had also included unveiling as an integral part of needed social reform. This fact threatened to muddle in the popular eye the association of "Soviet" with "unveiling," and pushed party activists to accelerate the hujum all the more resolutely.

By 1930 the party seems to have won this battle. "Reform," meaning unveiling, now meant the hujum, and it was associated unquestionably with the Bolsheviks. The handful of apparent exceptions only proves the point.[10] After much discussion in 1927, both public and classified materials fell almost completely silent on the Turkish and Afghan unveiling efforts. And given the indigenous reform tradition among jadidist clerics, it is noteworthy that they too featured only rarely after 1927 in discussions of women's liberation.[11] The historian Adeeb Khalid has shown that many individual jadids joined the party or Soviet government during and after the Russian Civil War of 1917–21, and for many Uzbeks, this fact probably added to the hujum's most lasting legacy: the

10. One cleric described the party's campaign of 8 March 1928 as being carried out by "our jadids," by which he meant the Bolsheviks (RGASPI, d. 1688, l. 124). The jadid label was thus discredited as it became synonymous with—not an alternative to—Soviet power. Similarly, when another cleric in 1929 denounced Amanullah Khan's reforms in Afghanistan, he did so by calling them "Bolshevik" (d. 2064, l. 25).

11. Scattered references to "progressive clergy" unveiling their wives and preaching a Qur'anic basis for female unveiling are at RGASPI, d. 1419, l. 3; d. 1688, ll. 120–21; and d. 1694, ll. 31–32. A rare later mention of Turkish unveiling is in a news brief, "5 dekabria—vseturetskii zhenskii den'," *PV*, 12 Dec. 1934.

deep association of unveiling and liberation with Soviet power, rather than as something with indigenous Muslim roots.[12] This was an important victory: the party had fought hard for this discursive association, and from its point of view it triumphed when it squeezed out its international competitors as well as the jadids.

Yet this success did not have unambiguously positive consequences. By 1930 unveiling had also become, in the eyes of many Uzbeks, a far less positive thing than when it was associated with the jadids. By wresting conceptual ownership of the hujum away from reformist Muslim clerics, the party helped doom its chances of success in the short to medium term by removing its main source of indigenous support. Unveiling became alien, recast as a Russian, Bolshevik, foreign, atheist, urban effort to remake Central Asia. Hence it was only a short step for nearly any Uzbek—even one with jadidist sympathies—to join in resisting the hujum. Residual voices in favor of unveiling, too, could easily be tainted by or accused of complicity with Soviet power.

OGPU documents as well as other party and government materials from the late 1920s make clear the two basic, interrelated problems the Soviet state faced in trying to administer, much less transform, Central Asia. The first was evident in the Chust debacle: a failure to overcome the cultural hegemony of non-Soviet ways of seeing the world. These codes of cognition, belief, and practice drew on a distinctively Central Asian Muslim heritage, and on the parts of that heritage now nationally specific to Uzbeks. Women could obtain a Soviet divorce, for example, if their husbands refused to allow them to unveil or to attend school. But without an Islamic divorce according to shariat, which required a husband's assent, Soviet officials admitted that it was impossible for a woman to live in Uzbek society.[13] If the party wanted women to unveil, some Uzbeks retorted, party members and Soviet workers were welcome to unveil their own wives. They should, however, leave the rest of us alone.[14]

Despite the best efforts of activists to inculcate a socialist sensibility, most Uzbek women and men spent their days in an altogether different cultural framework, one that in some ways grew stronger after being called "traditional" and placed under attack. The Bolshevik approach backfired by seeking to impose "enlightened" (foreign) ways of thinking. The party's self-appointed transformative purpose in Central Asia often took the form of what to Uzbek eyes seemed cultural insensitivity. Urging women to unveil was only the most obvious example. Soviet social welfare institutions also alienated their Central Asian clientele by, for example, serving inappropriate food. One crèche was reported in November 1928 to have served pork sausage (*kolbasa*) to the chil-

12. Squeezed thereafter by the Soviet government's anticlerical campaigns and discredited when parts of their program were hijacked by party activists, many suffered an unhappy end (Khalid, *Politics of Muslim Cultural Reform*, 281–301).

13. ÖzRMDA, f. 86, op.1, d. 5885, l. 7750b.

14. This sentiment was common. See PDA, op. 4, d. 1235, ll. 84–85; and RGASPI, d. 1694, ll. 106–7.

dren in its care, and thereby to have driven local Muslim parents to withdraw all their children.[15] Unfortunately for the party, most Uzbeks faced with such attitudes could simply withdraw from everyday contact with Soviet institutions.

Even carefully planned attempts to use major socialist holidays (such as 8 March) to challenge customs of female seclusion did not always turn out as planned. Such holidays aimed to strike an upbeat tone: thousands of women unveiling, smiling as sunlight hit their faces for the first time, ignoring threats of violence; a range of support institutions being dedicated, and scores of women promoted to positions of authority; even a few fringe class enemies being caught up in the wave of enthusiasm for women's liberation.[16] Yet public spaces were contested, and these texts of liberation could easily be subverted and remade into demonstrations of Bolshevik weakness and isolation. Consider the description given by the Bukhoro OGPU of a "flying demonstration" through the city held on the eve of International Women's Day, 1928, which chose a particularly confrontational time and place for its agitation:

> On 7 March many women drove about in an automobile with posters and carried out flying meetings. At this time a crowd of spiritual leaders, prominent bois, and [former] bureaucrats of the emir [had gathered] at the Liabi-Hauz mosque and were preparing for prayer. At this time up drove the automobile with the women, and they started to hold a mass meeting [*mitingovat'*]. Seeing the women, the crowd of those praying, about sixty people, ran up on all sides around them, saying, "Look at the devils who have driven here. God save us Muslims from this shame and give us back our old life. Now we have neither Uraza nor prayer, and our wives are debauching themselves, but thanks be to God that God has not punished us with an earthquake as he did in Namangan."[17]

Even discounting the class language used to describe the men involved, it is plain that this situation could not have been comfortable for the carload of women. Instead of a tightly scripted demonstration showing the promise of Soviet women's liberation, they suddenly found themselves surrounded by a crowd of unruly, hostile men. It not only was impossible to carry out effective agitation but quite likely left them fearing for their personal safety. As one Qodyr Salomov, from a village outside the city, declared roundly about the same time: "We will not allow our wives to go to a meeting and we will not permit [them] to unveil. And if the government sends some male delegate [to

15. ÖzRMDA, f. 9, op. 1, d. 3373, l. 70. A separate case in 1930 involved a *stolovaia* (canteen) that served only Russian foods such as borscht and *kotlety* rather than *palov* or local specialties (d. 3427, l. 183). While serving pork or alcohol might have been an intentional strategy to attack Islamic strictures, in most cases simple obliviousness seems more to blame.

16. RGASPI, d. 1688, ll. 120–23, and d. 1694, ll. 31, 35–37, 52–56, and 65–68.

17. RGASPI, d. 1694, l. 33. Uraza is a holiday marking the end of the Islamic holy month of Ramadan.

persuade us otherwise], then we'll gather together a few people and we will kill him; if it is a woman [who is sent to us], then we will rape [her]."[18] Such situations in and around Bukhoro—the city that was the party's principal success story of women's liberation—illustrates vividly the uncertainty of day-to-day control of public spaces, and shows that they had not been ceded altogether to the Bolsheviks.

Perhaps most disturbing to Soviet authorities were signs by 1929 that resistance to the hujum was being valorized, that opposition to unveiling was becoming a marker of Uzbek religious virtue and national-cultural identity. Party activists complained that despite their efforts to locate, ostracize, and punish offenders, men who murdered unveiled women often were not seen as criminals, but rather were admired by their neighbors.[19] When a cobbler in Bukhoro killed himself rather than live with the shame of his wife's unveiling, his piety and his courage in choosing suicide over capitulation were greatly esteemed.[20] In 1929 the Stalinist period had begun, at least in the sense that Stalin had consolidated political power in Moscow, but in Central Asia one still finds oppositionist Uzbek Muslims declaring themselves openly. When one woman in Bukhoro province decided to remove her paranji, her husband told her that she was no longer his wife but a prostitute, and he banished her from their home. When her father arrived to plead her case, the husband denounced him as an infidel. He then declared, "Do with me what you will, but I am not afraid of the authorities. If their leaders come to me, I will knock their heads off."[21]

Short of saying that all such statements were invented, how can they be explained? They make sense given the continuing acceptance of certain views of what defined a good Uzbek and Muslim. Partly thanks to the hujum, the cultural hegemony of such views became only more firmly entrenched. Consider the case of Mukhetdin Imedjanov, a rural official and party member in a village outside Tashkent. He came to the OGPU's attention when in May 1929 he declared publicly that he did not mind being denounced for opposition to the hujum, stating that "I am afraid of nobody, and I declare to everyone that I am a true Muslim." "Even a thousand notes" in the newspaper, he announced, "will not cow or intimidate me, or make me change my mind."[22] Imedjanov's views were at odds with party policy, and by stating them openly he risked losing his party membership card. But his attitude, expressed after more than two full years of effort on the hujum, shows the depth of opposition

18. Ibid., l. 39. Other subversions of Soviet spaces—funerals, electoral meetings, and so on—are at PDA, op. 4, d. 1235, l. 8; and RGASPI, d. 2057, ll. 60–64, and d. 2064, ll. 290b and 480b.

19. Strong, *Red Star in Samarkand*, 255 and 291.

20. RGASPI, d. 1688, l. 124, and d. 1694, ll. 34 and 65. His case was unusual, and I have found no men who followed his example. Violence was more commonly directed against wives, sisters, mothers, and daughters.

21. PDA, op. 4, d. 1235, l. 17.

22. RGASPI, d. 2064, l. 49.

to the unveiling campaign within party ranks and the vast distance that remained for the hujum to succeed.

The second basic (but related) problem faced by Soviet authorities was the issue of control. On any given day in most places in Uzbekistan, Soviet dominance was not nearly as firm as it first appeared. Uzbek men and women resisted Bolshevik authority on a host of issues—collectivization, agricultural taxes, the forced planting of cotton, and grain collections; urban unemployment and taxes on merchant trade; and voting rights and the closure of mosques.[23] Small groups of armed anti-Soviet qörboshi stayed active well into the 1930s, and their intermittent incursions from Afghanistan still posed a security problem.[24] Soviet control over many (especially rural) areas remained tenuous. To be sure, by the late 1920s Soviet power in Central Asia was not ("objectively") vulnerable to being toppled from within. As in Chust, the party could always shuttle troops to hot spots to enforce its version of law and order, and the Red Army served as an ultimate guarantor of power.

Yet many episodes also show the everyday limits faced by Soviet officials. In October 1928, for example, an unruly crowd of 500 peasants marched to Qöqon to protest the women's liberation campaign. Startled local Communists reacted quickly, immediately arresting the march's leaders, but the message that rural Uzbeks did not want a wholesale transformation of gender roles was unmistakable.[25] Five months later, in another small town near Namangan, a Soviet women's meeting held shortly after International Women's Day was surrounded by a crowd of local men. Reportedly using sticks, knives, and their teeth as weapons, they attacked the gathering and killed a village activist, the male teacher Ahmad Ali Ziyaev.[26] On another occasion, a supposed Soviet sympathizer, one Omon Islamov, ensured that the hujum made no headway in his area. After giving a (presumably critical) report on the paranji at a women's meeting in Tashkent, Islamov ceded the floor to a colleague, Badal'-Khoja. The latter proceeded to invite the women in attendance to cast off their paranjis and chachvons. This, however, was too much for Islamov, who according to the OGPU flattened Badal'-Khoja with a vicious punch and then proceeded, in full view of the meeting, to kick and punch him into unconsciousness:

23. RGASPI, d. 1692, ll. 125–29; d. 2004, l. 260b; d. 2062, l. 12; and d. 2064, ll. 26–330b. On the agricultural tax, for instance, one Soviet inspector was told, "Do what you will with me, but I won't pay" (d. 1692, l. 31).

24. One such band was alleged in April–May 1929 to have killed thirty-nine Soviet citizens in Tajikistan, including three unveiled women (Kazimir Vasilevskii, *Islam na sluzhbe kontr-revoliutsii* [Moscow, 1930], 52). Bekhtiarova, a woman's club worker in Andijon province, told a Moscow congress in March 1930 that another band had doused a woman in kerosene and burned her alive for having unveiled. They then surrounded a Soviet school and lit it aflame, killing the female teacher and several pupils (GARF, f. 6983, op. 1, d. 157a, l. 293).

25. ÖzRMDA, f. 1714, op. 5, d. 663, ll. 86–89.

26. RGASPI, d. 2064, l. 23.

A panic arose, and [people started] running from the meeting. There was a crush at the doors, and a few women threw themselves out the window. No one tried to defend Badal'-Khoja, because in that area Omon Islamov is considered a dictator.

Having satiated himself with the beating, Islamov left quietly.

At the present time [three weeks later] Badal'-Khoja is confined to his apartment, ill, and he [continues to] spit up blood.[27]

Merely having sufficient armed force to guarantee military control, then, does not tell the full story of daily life in Soviet Uzbekistan. Given that Red Army troops could not simultaneously be garrisoned everywhere, the everyday texture of Soviet rule did not involve military power except as a background assurance of authority, something that could be invoked in extremis (if an armed rebellion broke out, for instance). More commonly, at any given moment in a particular village or town, the local calculus of forces—even in strictly military terms—was unlikely to favor the handful of party and Soviet workers. Death threats were common, as in the following anonymous letter of April 1928 to village administrators in Farghona province:

To the authorities in Auchi, Kalacha, and Shaykhan:

You have greatly offended the local population [by saying] that men and women should be together [in everyday social life]. There is [therefore] nothing extraordinary if we come to you before Hayit Ramazon [to say that] you, the women, and the teachers await punishment. . . .

As punishment we will bury alive in the earth, cut off the hands, cut out the tongues and throw into the river all the [Soviet] officials of the three villages, the teachers and those studying in their schools. We are eighty people [strong]. God gives [us the authority to do this] and we will come. What we say to everyone, from small to great, is: You must be upright. If these words are not heeded, then you [must] prepare yourself for death.[28]

This letter and others like it provoked consternation; they certainly drew the OGPU's attention, and they show the difficult context in which local staffers acted. Bursts of violent opposition were clearly possible, especially when provoked.[29] Since Red Army intervention, if needed, could take a considerable time to arrive, the promise of Soviet support and protection may have seemed

27. RGASPI, d. 1693, ll. 11–12.

28. A copy, translated into Russian, is at RGASPI, d. 1694, l. 50. For a less anonymous threat, see the Communist confronted with death threats from his neighbors for working on the unveiling campaign (ll. 64 and 75). Hayit Ramazon is the feast that marks the end of Ramadan.

29. In March 1929, party coercion in the unveiling campaign provoked the population near Naryn to convene an extralegal trial of Soviet workers, which ended when one was severely beaten, whereupon a rampaging crowd of 350 scoured the area looking for more government officials (RGASPI, d. 2064, ll. 22–23).

a distant prospect and a hollow comfort, even in some urban areas. A crowd in Samarqand, shouting about the need "to rip such people out by the roots," attacked a member of the local mahalla commission in 1928. The official, Fathullaev, reportedly was fortunate to escape with his life.[30] Russians and other Europeans remained foreign, many rarely venturing outside the Russified New Cities. For the relative handful of Muslim and native Central Asian activists, the isolation could be intense. Surrounded by neighbors, friends, and relatives without a Bolshevik outlook, affiliation, or identity, these staffers tended to revert to their social and cultural upbringings, and mostly made use of their connections to state power for other ends.

Post-Soviet historical scholarship has stressed how the Soviet system constructed itself from the bottom up, especially through the structuring power of language and linguistic categories. Writers such as Stephen Kotkin, Jochen Hellbeck, and Amir Weiner have argued compellingly for a more sophisticated understanding of power in the Stalinist system, a view in which power is multivalent and dispersed throughout society in language and ways of thinking, not just crude physical force wielded from the top. Drawing evidence particularly from the 1930s and 1940s, these historians have shown how Soviet citizens adopted Bolshevik language and how this language then shaped the way these citizens saw the world. From this perspective, Stalinist categories succeeded in defining the worldview, discursive universe, and personal identities of Soviet men and women.[31] But these writers focus principally on the East Slavic cultural world of Russia and Ukraine, from which most Bolsheviks came, and so do not address the complications created by a different set of social, cultural, religious, and linguistic categories in the non-Slavic areas of the colonial periphery. In Muslim Central Asia, the linguistic creation of a Stalinist Soviet subject was a far slower and more painful process.

Despite Moscow's undeniable power by 1930, Uzbek men and women were still quite capable of stepping back and seeing Soviet power from outside. They could readily imagine an alternative to Bolshevik rule, and that alternative, based on a partly preexisting and partly redefined cultural and religious framework, was more appealing to many of them than the Soviet one on offer. Further, the new concept of an Uzbek nation—ironically developed and encouraged by the party—provided another proximate locus around which individual and group identities could coalesce. Such identities were rooted, too, in the context of sixty years of Russian colonial rule. Finally, these non-Soviet alternatives were simultaneously spurred and shaped in their specific content, symbolic language, and political goals by the ongoing experience of

---

30. RGASPI, d. 1694, l. 59.
31. Kotkin, *Magnetic Mountain;* Jochen Hellbeck, "Fashioning the Stalinist Soul: The Diary of Stepan Podlubnyi (1931–1939)," *Jahrbücher für Geschichte Osteuropas* 44 (1996): 344–73; and Amir Weiner, *Making Sense of War: The Second World War and the Fate of the Bolshevik Revolution* (Princeton, 2001).

Soviet power, and particularly by the hujum and other Bolshevik efforts to modernize Central Asia.

But the fact that Uzbeks were reacting against the hujum to frame and express their views does not mean that they were simply "speaking Bolshevik," as Kotkin would have it, much less "thinking Bolshevik," in Hellbeck's provocative view.[32] Rather, they were in constant dialogue with Bolshevism and with themselves. Many Uzbeks ignored or dismissed Marxist pretensions that the tide of history was with the Soviet state and did not agree that total Bolshevik victory was only a matter of time. They believed, rather, that Soviet power was a plague sent by Allah. They thought and hoped it was a temporary scourge and would pass away like a bad dream or a storm in the night. After large-scale resistance by the qörboshi had been suppressed, few Uzbeks believed that they alone could defeat the Red Army militarily. But they still hoped for deliverance from external factors: by divine intervention, or by an attack from the USSR's enemies (or possibly both, if God willed Britain, say, to declare war on the Soviet Union). Their underlying ability to see a meaningful alternative, to visualize a way—however fraught with difficulty it might be— in which Soviet power could come to an end, adds a crucial dimension to their resistance.[33] Their belief in a viable non-Soviet future made it easier to fight back against the hujum and the wider Bolshevik project.

The lack of everyday control by Soviet authorities and the power of non-Soviet ideals help explain the existence of widespread, even growing opposition to the hujum after 1928. This opposition was expressed in a broad spectrum of resistance, both in word and in deed. Violence against Soviet-style women's liberation remained the most serious problem. In some instances it involved direct attacks on the state or party, as in Chust, but it took many other forms as well. When Zhenotdel activists visited Uzbek homes to agitate among local women, for example, they were expelled forcibly by husbands, brothers, and fathers.[34] Uzbek men dragged their wives away from Soviet meetings, either preemptively, lest they dishonor themselves by unveiling, or afterward, in fury if they had unveiled.[35] In some villages dogs were set loose in the streets to

32. On "speaking Bolshevik," see Kotkin, *Magnetic Mountain*, 198–237. Hellbeck goes further, portraying Soviet citizens as a group as trying to internalize Soviet values before and apart from the state; in his view, even apparent dissenters must be seen as subjects in crisis, riven with a "longing to overcome their painful separation from the collective body of the Soviet people" (Hellbeck, "Speaking Out: Languages of Affirmation and Dissent in Stalinist Russia," *Kritika* 1 [2000]: 92, 96).

33. Stephen Kotkin makes the good point that resistance is qualitatively different if those resisting cannot imagine a meaningful alternative to the existing system (personal communication). We disagree, however, on whether it was possible at that time for Soviet citizens to do so. His work on Magnitogorsk stresses the negative: despite the complex negotiations and unofficial survival strategies on display at Magnitka, Kotkin sees them ultimately as attempts to accommodate the system, not overturn it.

34. RGASPI, d. 2057, l. 60.

35. RGASPI, d. 1689, l. 55, and d. 2057, l. 60.

prevent Soviet women's meetings from convening.[36] These and other uses of force had one common aim: to prevent individual Uzbek women from unveiling, and failing that, to dissuade others from following their example. Sometimes intimidation could suffice. Women who had unveiled and refused to reveil were threatened with death.[37] Occasionally threats were made, too, against men who permitted "their" women to remove paranji and chachvon. One top-secret report of May 1929 quoted Ghafurjon Muminjanov, a resident of Old Tashkent, as saying:

> Eleven years have passed since Soviet power was established. If it lasts another ten years, there will not be a single honorable woman [left]. All of them will become prostitutes. [A few days ago] my son-in-law came to me requesting permission to unveil his wife, my daughter. I declared categorically to him that in the event of his wife's unveiling I will kill either him or her. This is not an empty threat. What I say must be carried out.[38]

Whether Muminjanov was sincere or not, many Uzbek men did follow through on such threats, and acts of physical violence dotted the landscape of the late 1920s.

Yet overt action is not the only road to resistance. The historian James Scott and others have described other "weapons of the weak," tactics used particularly by peasants and colonized peoples who face radically unequal power balances. These tactics include rumors, gossip, folktales, songs, gestures, and jokes, all of which may be used by subaltern groups as a "theatre of the powerless" that "insinuate[s] a critique of power while hiding behind anonymity or behind innocuous understandings of their conduct."[39] While this view may impute a higher than warranted level of intentionality and unity to an anti-regime critique embedded in rumor, jokes, and gossip, it nonetheless makes an important point. Many forms of passive and half-hidden resistance, in which opposition could be expressed through mockery or even through acts of apparent acquiescence and submission, existed in Central Asia. Women traveling by horse-drawn cart near the Afghan border, for instance, were overheard singing a sarcastic song about the failings of Soviet power: "In the co-op there are no wares [to buy], and Soviet power has no might, [so] I won't take off my paranji."[40]

Party workers in the localities reported a widespread mood of "passive opposition" to the hujum ("If my wife wants to go to the meeting, let her go, I'm not stopping her").[41] Women who wished to support the unveiling campaign faced insult and harassment in their homes and on the streets of their mahal-

36. RGASPI, d. 1699, l. 91.
37. RGASPI, d. 2064, ll. 20 and 280b.
38. Ibid., l. 50.
39. Scott, *Domination,* xii–xiii. Also see his *Weapons of the Weak.*
40. RGASPI, d. 1681, l. 108.
41. RGASPI, d. 1698, l. 70.

las—not necessarily violent, but a powerful disincentive nevertheless. Even apart from the danger of violent reprisals, an unveiled woman faced ordeals against which Soviet courts and laws offered little protection. She could be spat upon and called a prostitute by neighbors; she faced mockery and insults whenever she ventured out into the street.[42] As Scott points out, for a system of everyday cultural policing to work, it must have a "shared worldview. Neither gossip nor character assassination, for example, makes much sense unless there are shared standards of what is deviant, unworthy, impolite. In one sense, the ferociousness of the argument *depends* on the fact that it appeals to shared values that have been, it is claimed, betrayed."[43] In this light, consider what happened one day in 1928 to Kozmey Nasretdinova, a member of the local hujum commission in the town of Katta Qorghon (near Samarqand), when she walked past a neighbor in her mahalla. The neighbor, Naqil Sufiev, reportedly swore at her "with uncensored words" and then exposed himself to her as she walked by.[44] Everyday life in the mahalla was not easy for an unveiled woman.[45]

The spectrum of resistance in Uzbekistan included many creative solutions to the problem of how to oppose a state that in extremis could always rely on an army to enforce its version of law and order. Uzbek men and women learned after Chust how to push the party and Soviet government to the brink without provoking martial law. Crowds still gathered and demanded (not always successfully) the release of men arrested for speaking out against women's liberation.[46] Gossip, rumors, and mutterings on the street criticized Soviet policies; they were very hard to answer, much less stamp out.[47]

Perhaps most interesting are the ways Uzbek women and men subverted the party's own logic and language. In 1929, for instance, one husband arrived at a women's liberation meeting shouting that its leaders were not legitimate rulers, they were bosmachi for having invited his wife without his permission. "Bosmachi" was the party's preferred term of opprobrium for anti-Soviet groups. When the chair of the local mahalla commission tried to calm the vis-

42. See RGASPI, d. 1694, l. 79, and d. 1699, l. 91.

43. Scott, *Weapons of the Weak,* xvii.

44. RGASPI, d. 1694, l. 124.

45. It was not necessarily easier for men who supported the hujum. According to a top-secret OGPU dispatch from Namangan, in February 1929 one such man, named Damulladjanov, accompanied his wife to a Soviet school to enroll her and enable her to unveil. En route to the school they were confronted by a Khoja Qasymboi, who "started to curse Damulladjanov in all possible ways, calling him a soul for sale [*prodazhnoi dushoi*], reproaching him for having fallen under the influence of unbelievers, and finally threatening to 'make short work' of him if Damulladjanov unveiled his wife. In view of this threat, Damulladjanov backed away both from the schooling and from the removal of [his wife's] paranji" (RGASPI, d. 2064, l. 8). Note that the wishes of his unnamed wife are never mentioned.

46. RGASPI, d. 1694, l. 26, and d. 2064, ll. 22–23; ÖzRMDA, f. 1714, op. 5, d. 663, ll. 86–87.

47. For an example, see RGASPI, d. 1694, l. 64.

itor, moreover, he was attacked with a knife. In other cases the Soviet narrative of liberation was used against itself. Zhenotdel activists saw it as a necessary first step, for example, to persuade veiled women to attend a Soviet meeting or to visit a women's club. That visit was conceived as the thin edge of a wedge that would lead inexorably to unveiling, education, and complete Sovietization. The hujum's opponents used the same reasoning to argue that Uzbek women should not take even a small step that could be interpreted as support for the regime. They stretched the negative associations of public unveiling to the less immediately dangerous acts of speaking with Zhenotdel workers or attending a meeting. As one Tashkul Rahimov said when he was asked to bring his wife to a meeting, "If any [women] go, then it may be said that their paranjis have already been removed."[48] By equating the first step away from devout behavior (talking with an infidel about liberation) to the horrors of the last (public prostitution), such arguments aimed to prevent Uzbek women from having anything at all to do with the hujum, and thus to cut the Soviet campaign off at the knees.

Crafting Practices of Resistance: Enacting Female Seclusion in Everyday Life

In one sense it is possible to measure resistance to the hujum straightforwardly, by looking at the prevalence of veiling and seclusion. The evidence suggests that such lived social practices persisted and even spread by 1930. They cut across Uzbek society, being dominant in almost every social group and in nearly every geographic area. Equally noteworthy are their changing associations, as they became nationalized as authentic expressions of a new Uzbek collective identity.

The extant evidence, both archival and published, demonstrates clearly the prevalence of female seclusion and veiling in Uzbekistan in the first years after 1927. This was not merely a picture created by imaginative OGPU officers who sought to justify their positions by finding nests of opposition. While scattered cases or quotations may have been edited, exaggerated, or invented, and while the OGPU's agenda and language must be considered, the basic picture of widespread and growing antihujum sentiment is clear. Many other observers with different personal and institutional interests found similar problems. Although by 1930 party and Zhenotdel activists had had almost three years to implement the hujum, Uzbek women had not swarmed to welcome Soviet-style liberation. Even the OGPU struggled to explain the bitter opposition it found among groups of supposed class allies as well as class enemies. One of the Soviet Union's top women's activists, Antonina Nukhrat, reported glumly in late March 1929 that "almost 90 percent" of Uzbek women still

48. PDA, op. 4, d. 1235, l. 7.

wore the paranji.[49] Although some party reports claimed that progress was being made, many others disagreed, suggesting that veils were becoming more common rather than less, especially in rural areas, even among the wives of indigenous Communists.[50] After one unveiled woman fended off a rape attempt outside Bukhoro in 1929, other village women reportedly donned veils even while working in the fields. Rural women stayed home as rumors spread that bosmachi would attack any unveiled women they found doing agricultural work.[51]

A similar picture characterized most urban areas. Confidential party investigations found few veiled women in Bukhoro by 1929, but other cities offered a different panorama. Virtually all the women of Shymkent, a heavily Uzbek region of southern Kazakhstan, were reported to be wearing "traditional" veils, whether or not they had done so in the past.[52] In almost every Uzbek town, girls showed up at Soviet schools—when they came at all—wearing paranjis and chachvons.[53] Women donned their veils to participate in Soviet elections and meetings.[54] (See Figure 18.) Urban women, particularly in the Old Cities, reportedly laughed at unveiled women. The wives of Communists and factory workers sometimes led this mockery, and indeed allegedly observed codes of female seclusion more strictly than other women.[55] One confidential party report of mid-1928 stated that "administrative pressure" had induced between 750 and 800 women to unveil in one Tashkent mahalla, but they had thrown off only their oldest and most worn paranjis and then quickly reveiled, leaving only 147 actually liberated.[56] "We have more than 300 Uzbek men working in Uzbektorg," declared the delegate Nazarova to a trade union congress in December 1929, "but not a single wife [of theirs] is unveiled. On 8 March we unveil women, and the next day they once again wear the paranji."[57]

Veiling and seclusion were common during the late 1920s among nearly all social strata. However discomfiting to OGPU and party investigators, in this regard little seemed to distinguish class enemies from allies. The Muslim clergy, of course, supposedly led the charge, preaching in support of female seclusion and veiling and denouncing the broad sweep of Soviet policy. Clerics, the secret police concluded, took advantage of the slowdown in Soviet

49. GARF, f. 6983, op. 1, d. 5, l. 125.
50. For positive reports, see PDA, op. 5, d. 866, l. 115; ÖzRMDA, f. 86, op. 1, d. 6585, l. 195; and RGASPI, d. 1492, l. 30.
51. RGASPI, d. 2057, l. 63, and d. 2066, l. 22.
52. RGASPI, d. 2055, ll. 1–6, and d. 2072, l. 22.
53. RGASPI, d. 1700, ll. 37–38.
54. For an image of veiled Uzbek women being lined up to vote, see ÖzRKFFHMDA, 1-46448.
55. RGASPI, d. 1699, l. 9; and PDA, op. 5, d. 815, ll. 175–76, and d. 866, l. 30.
56. RGASPI, d. 1714, l. 67.
57. ÖzRMDA, f. 736, op. 1, d. 1161, l. 27. For a similar case in Farghona, in which a factory's 500 Uzbek workers all had veiled wives in 1929, see RGASPI, d. 2051, l. 203.

Figure 18. Soviet demonstration, mid-1920s. (Courtesy ÖzRKFFHMDA.)

work during the summer of 1927 to spread their invidious message of inequality and murder.[58] But according to the OGPU, clerics were not alone in instigating anti-Soviet hysteria. Bois, merchants, and former bosmachi and emirate bureaucrats also made the blacklist as anti-Soviet elements who stood at the root of all opposition.[59] These groups allegedly saw their position of economic advantage being threatened and hence, with rare exceptions, lashed out to protect their class interests.[60] Supposedly troubled that women would no longer be treated as property, these men saw the hujum as another kind of expropriation, much like the land and water redistribution. One was quoted as saying that unveiling was merely an extension of Soviet land reform, since it aimed to seize the second, third, and fourth wives of bois and transfer them to the poor

58. RGASPI, d. 1690, l. 15, and d. 1694, l. 43. The clergy were allegedly behind a wave of murders of unveiled women at d. 2063, l. 185.

59. RGASPI, d. 1694, l. 44. Folk healers [*tabibs*], who reportedly worked to keep the population away from Soviet doctors and sometimes told pregnant women that for the sake of their unborn child's health they should be sure to wear paranji and chachvon, were also sometimes on this list (d. 1681, l. 114, and d. 1710, l. 38).

60. A forceful statement of this position is at ÖzRMDA, f. 9, op. 1, d. 3397, l. 6. Exceptions are at RGASPI, d. 1419, l. 3; d. 1688, l. 121; d. 1694, ll. 31 and 36; and d. 2064, l. 290b.

landless peasants who had to hire themselves out as field hands.[61] (This was a common view, as many Uzbeks also saw the hujum as transferring women from male control to that of the state.) The OGPU said that groups of "wealthy exploiters" had called clandestine meetings to plan anti-Soviet activities, plotted violence and made death threats against unveiled women, used economic pressure against poor peasants to encourage them not to unveil their wives, and helped bring about a near-total reveiling in many regions.[62]

In describing attitudes toward the hujum among supposedly sympathetic social groups, by contrast, the OGPU tried doggedly to put a brave spin on what it found, even as the detailed data continued to contradict such upbeat views.[63] In all five official social categories of allies (the Soviet/party elite; industrial and service workers; the native intelligentsia, principally teachers; peasants, especially poor peasants; and women themselves) the popular "mood" fell well short of what party leaders had hoped. The group of local Communists, Komsomol'tsy, and Soviet officials, first, was small, and as we have seen, its members remained reluctant to participate in the hujum. Some spoke out publicly against it and others even tried to rape unveiled women. One Soviet worker (although not a party member) in Rishtan declared in mid-1928 that he would fight to the death against the hujum, and that if he were killed in this struggle, his death would be holy.[64] Industrial and service workers also failed to support the hujum as expected. One trade union member reportedly threatened to kill his wife and mother if they attended a Soviet meeting, and the OGPU found significant ill will toward the hujum among cottage industry (*kustar*) workers too. One, Israil Kasymov, was quoted in March 1929 as saying, "Let the Soviet authorities shoot me, but I cannot tolerate the shame that my wife had an unveiled face and wandered around at meetings. I will be against the hujum always and everywhere, and I must in every possible way defend the interests of religion."[65]

Since education—particularly in the nonreligious "new method" schools run under Soviet auspices—was thought to correlate with support for enlightened notions of women's rights, the relatively small group of educated Uzbek

---

61. RGASPI, d. 1694, ll. 2 and 121.

62. PDA, op. 4, d. 1235, ll. 7–10; and RGASPI, d. 1419, l. 20b; d. 1694, ll. 3, 18, and 57–59; and d. 2064, l. 20. In Zerafshon province, one boi, Qalandar Dusamov, was quoted as declaring that unveiled women would "boil in hell" unless they reveiled, and if they did not, he said, any man who so desired could use them sexually as he wished (PDA, op. 4, d. 1235, l. 7).

63. A good example is a top-secret OGPU summary of May 1928, in which stoic claims of "general support" for unveiling bracket a report in which little support of any kind can be seen. After a brief opening paragraph hailing local unveilings on 8 March, the authors, Astrov and Popov, spent more than eight pages relating a litany of resistance, obstruction, failure, and opposition. They then conclude with one jarring sentence: "All of the above-mentioned abnormalities, it goes without saying, in no way aid in the development and deepening of work for liberation" (PDA, op. 4, d. 1235, ll. 16–24).

64. PDA, op. 4, d. 1235, ll. 11, 19–23, and 89–90.

65. RGASPI, d. 2064, l. 28. The trade union threat is at d. 1694, l. 6.

men and women, many of whom served as schoolteachers, were expected to support the hujum. While some did, others grumbled that the unveiling campaign was premature. Some refused to help at all. One male teacher sent to work in a village outside Bukhoro beat his wife severely when she unveiled, and drove the few local women who had been unveiled to cover themselves again.[66] And teachers could be intimidated like anyone else: one female teacher at a girls' school in Marghilon received an anonymous note threatening death if she did not reveil and stop teaching. She shuttered her small school and again donned paranji and chachvon.[67]

Of course the OGPU expected to find allies among the poor peasants (*bedniaki*) and landless agricultural laborers (*batraki*) and possibly among a segment of so-called middle peasants (*seredniaki*) as well. Rural opposition was thought to emanate from wealthy bois, either directly or through manipulation and exploitation. Yet dozens of local reports show widespread, not class-specific, rural antipathy to the hujum. Peasants complained about the party's refusal to hold sex-segregated meetings, declared that unveiled women should be killed, and advised women to leave a meeting if they did not wish to be treated as prostitutes.[68] "The government intends to convert us Muslims into infidels [*kofirs*]," said one poor peasant recorded by the Andijon provincial OGPU in mid-1928. "If God does not deliver us from this government, then our situation will become worse—it does not give even the poorest [of us] the chance to live."[69] One poor peasant in Zerafshon declared in 1928, "I believe in God; so let the government shoot me, but I will not unveil my wife for anything."[70] Such opposition to the unveiling campaign was overlaid on the long-standing urban/rural tensions that characterized Central Asian society. Most Zhenotdel activists were based in cities or the larger towns and visited villages only when they had to, looking down on what they saw as the primitive conditions of rural life. Peasants in rural villages (*qishloqs*) sensed this disdain, and resented party activists who came from the city and demanded that local women unveil, particularly when urban women and the wives of Soviet workers had yet to do so.[71]

Even peasants who benefited from other Soviet policies shared this rural antipathy to the hujum. Rural Uzbeks specifically perceived Bolshevik demands that women unveil as a quid pro quo for the land redistribution of 1925–26. Whether or not the party intended such a link, this connection was drawn by

66. The teacher outside Bukhoro is reported in an OGPU dispatch at RGASPI, d. 2064, l. 9. Grumbles about premature attacks on the veil and at reveiling by teachers' wives are at PDA, op. 4, d. 1235, l. 22.

67. RGASPI, d. 2064, l. 20.

68. PDA, op. 4, d. 1235, ll. 10–11; and RGASPI, d. 1688, l. 126, and d. 1694, l. 19. These reports were dismissed as isolated incidents.

69. PDA, op. 4, d. 1235, l. 16.

70. RGASPI, d. 1694, l. 84.

71. PDA, op. 4, d. 1235, l. 10.

peasants across Uzbekistan. In a conclusion deeply revealing of rural priorities, moreover, many poor peasants declared, in essence, that if unveiling was the price of Soviet land, then the Bolsheviks could have it back. One peasant, Irka Pulatov, declared: "The government gave us the land, and for this [now] wants to unveil our women. The land stands right here, out in the field; if the government needs it, then let them take it back. But you can't throw off the paranji and stay a Muslim."[72] The hujum thus reduced rather than built support for Soviet power in the countryside. It unified Uzbek peasants against Soviet power—a trend that only accelerated once the broader all-Union campaign of forced collectivization began in 1929.

The comparative handful of party activists scattered across Uzbekistan faced the difficult task of building momentum for the unveiling campaign in an increasingly hostile environment. The momentum, rather, seemed to be in the other direction, as a massive wave of reveilings swept across Central Asia. While a few Bolsheviks bravely asserted that the number of women involved was exaggerated, the near-unanimity of these mostly classified reports and the fact that it was not something that Soviet analysts wanted to proclaim make it likely that the phenomenon was rather *more* common than reported.[73] Reveilings could be (and were) blamed on Muslim clerics, rumors, earthquakes, or the fear created by violent attacks on unveiled women.[74] Whatever the cause, though, most Uzbek women who removed their veils in 1927 thought better of it as time went by. One report from Buvaida said that only 50 of the 1,800 women who had unveiled there remained uncovered in 1928.[75] Table 1 illustrates the problem with official Soviet statistics from urban and rural locales in Farghona province. It is easy to feel the frustration of Zhenotdel staffers who confronted this phenomenon. Semagina, the secretary of the Farghona provincial Zhenotdel, prepared for her superiors in 1928 a long list of women, listed by name and subdivided by mahalla, who still wore the paranji. Her list was full of names of party members and Soviet officials whose wives were still veiled, and it filled four full pages. The gaze of the state and secret police, however, proved insufficient to discipline such officially transgressive behavior. The individual names in Semagina's report are not terribly meaningful, but her summary descriptions suggest the scope of the problem:

> The Qizil Trnok mahalla . . . had 160 unveiled women, of whom 7 remain unveiled, but 153 have covered themselves [again]. . . .
> Chankallik, Kakhayat mahalla: 35 women had unveiled, but all have [now] reveiled, beginning with the wife of the mahalla commission president, Madal'baev Datkhojanov. . . .

72. RGASPI, d. 2057, l. 61. For other cases, see d. 1419, l. 20b, and d. 1694, ll. 37 and 65.
73. See PDA, op. 4, d. 1235, ll. 12 and 84; RGASPI, d. 1712, l. 53, and d. 2051, l. 174. For an assertion that the phenomenon was exaggerated, see d. 2055, l. 16.
74. Such explanations are offered at RGASPI, d. 1690, l. 13.
75. ÖzRMDA, f. 1714, op. 5, d. 663, l. 88.

Table 1. Number of unveiled women in Farghona province, selected locations, 1928–1929

Location	March–June	July	August	January
Isfara-Guzar mahalla, Old Qöqon	90	65	30	25
Navoiy mahalla, Qöqon	50	35	20	15
Yarmazar village, near Marghilon	10	10	—	—

SOURCE: RGASPI, d. 1694, l. 41.

> Tashkalik Guzar Commission: A total of 25 women unveiled, among them Soviet delegates [*delegatki*], but at present all of them have reveiled. . . .
>
> Salkashen mahalla: 43 women unveiled, of whom four remain unveiled. All the others have veiled [again], including the wife and daughter-in-law of the president of the mahalla commission. . . .
>
> Bakhmal'bob mahalla: Virtually all the wives of staff workers and party members are veiled. . . .
>
> Kal'voi mahalla: Of 15 unveiled women, all have veiled again, not excepting the wife of the mahalla commission president. . . .
>
> Tandir-Saz mahalla: Of 20 unveiled women, all 20 have reveiled, among them the wife of the mahalla commission president. . . .
>
> Qizil Yulduz mahalla: All the unveiled women of this mahalla have reveiled.[76]

Semagina's list continued in this vein, naming dozens of neighborhoods and villages that either had reverted to or had for the first time adopted near-universal female seclusion.

Even the party's successes were less impressive when probed in depth. Comparatively few women stayed unveiled, as shown by data from Tashkent in Table 2. Other measures of success seemed equally flimsy. One women's meeting of 1928 in rural Khojent drew 600 attendees, but only 100 were unveiled; the remainder wore paranjis or covered themselves in other ways.[77] The large-scale public unveilings on 8 March and the massive bonfires of paranjis and chachvons often amounted to less than met the eye, being "formal" unveilings, often coerced.[78] As the Tashkent Zhenotdel reported about its Women's Day celebration in 1928,

> It is necessary to note that the discarded paranjis were, as a rule, very old, torn, and dirty. The women explained that they were making themselves dresses out of the newer paranjis, and [thought it therefore] a shame to discard them. Typically, after throwing off the paranji, women were ashamed to show their faces—even to other women—and [so] cov-

76. RGASPI, d. 1688, ll. 197–980b.
77. RGASPI, d. 1694, l. 68.
78. RGASPI, d. 1690, l. 12.

Table 2. Number of women unveiling, Tashkent City, 1927–1929

Mahalla	1927	1928	1929	Permanently unveiled
Shur-Tepe	4	15	21	13
Olmazar	7	18	42	29
Kar-Yagdy	7	57	74	19
Türk-Yangi-Shahar	28	49	81	10
Shatek	10	41	52	8
Navoiy	6	16	29	13

SOURCE: RGASPI, d. 2064, l. 48.

ered up with shawls or their sleeves. It was very difficult to assume that a woman would decide tomorrow to walk unveiled about the city. Therefore, the statistic of 4,947 people [unveiled], although it has been verified formally, is not an [accurate] index of the number of those actually unveiled.[79]

A year later, in 1929, the Muslim celebration of Hayit Ramazon fell less than a week after 8 March. The Tashkent OGPU noted that huge crowds gathered for religious observances on 12–13 March, and only a handful of unveiled women could be seen. Where were the thousands of proud supporters of the hujum, visible only four days earlier? They had not disappeared. Noting that many veiled women wore European stockings and shoes (that is, Russian-style *chulki* and *tufly*), the secret police deduced that the wives of Soviet workers and other "unveiled" women were now numbered among the vast crowds wearing paranji and chachvon.[80] Across Uzbekistan and throughout local society, female seclusion had persisted and even increased by 1930.

How did these practices become nationalized? The link between nationality and gender has many parallels in other colonial situations. Frantz Fanon suggested that the veil became a locus of resistance in Algeria not only because it was important in indigenous culture but also because French colonial authorities deemed it worth fighting over.[81] And in an influential study of India, Partha Chatterjee has argued that anticolonial resistance frequently starts with a defense of the inner domain of spiritual culture, a domain often associated with women and emblematic of the nation.[82] But the closest parallel comes from the work of Leila Ahmed, a historian of modern Egypt:

The veil came to symbolize in the resistance narrative, not the inferiority of the culture and the need to cast aside its customs in favor of those of

79. PDA, op. 3, d. 1560, ll. 339–40.
80. RGASPI, d. 2064, l. 29.
81. Fanon, *Studies in a Dying Colonialism,* 63. See chapter epigraph.
82. Chatterjee, *Nation and Its Fragments,* 6, 9, 26, and 116–57.

the West, but, on the contrary, the dignity and validity of all native customs, and in particular those customs coming under fiercest colonial attack—the customs relating to women—and the need to tenaciously affirm them as a means of resistance to Western domination. . . . [T]he resistance narrative thus reversed—but also accepted—the terms set in the first place by the colonizers. And therefore, ironically, it is Western discourse that in the first place determined the new meanings of the veil and gave rise to its emergence as a symbol of resistance.[83]

This situation was much like the one in Uzbekistan in 1930. Once each side had invested the paranji with its respective core values, the veil came to symbolize both resistance and transformation, and it literally embodied the struggle over Central Asia. In the eyes of many Uzbeks, conflict over the hujum became an arena of national struggle, especially but not exclusively between Russians and Uzbeks.[84] The unveiling campaign was portrayed as an attempt "to destroy the Uzbek nationality": one man in Andijon province was quoted as declaring that "unveiled women lose their nationality along with their paranjis, and stop being Uzbek."[85]

This new Uzbek national identity had a strong religious component; in many ways it grafted a particular thread of Central Asian Islamic practice onto a growing sense of national community. Many Uzbeks framed the national and colonial struggle against Russian Bolsheviks simultaneously as a defense of Islam against the kofirs. "Russification" meant many things—unveiling, wearing European clothes, eating pork, drinking vodka, converting to Orthodoxy—but all connoted to varying degrees a decision to abandon Uzbek Muslim culture and so to "denationalize."[86] A woman in Farghona province reportedly agitated among other women against the hujum in 1928 by arguing,

83. Leila Ahmed, *Women and Gender in Islam: Historical Roots of a Modern Debate* (New Haven, 1992), 164.

84. "Russians have seized our homeland," bemoaned one group of Uzbeks (RGASPI, d. 1694, l. 18). Uzbek Communists were denounced for doing the bidding of their Russian masters in the unveiling campaign (PDA, op. 4, d. 1235, l. 2). In 1929 Akhmedova, the president of a factory committee, reported bitter national tensions among female workers in Bukhoro: "There is such a muddle [*katavasiia*] at the moment that if the matter is not investigated, the working masses will disintegrate once and for all. There is at present a move of the Uzbeks against the Tajiks, the Tajiks against the Uzbeks, both together against the Jews, and so on. Right now the national question is very sharp. There is no educational work, and no other work is being carried out now. Everything revolves around these squabbles. The entire factory is raging" (RGASPI, d. 2055, l. 12).

85. PDA, op. 4, d. 1235, l. 86. In a similar case, a Muslim cleric argued that the unveiling campaign was meant to humiliate the nation before Russians, and it was better to die than submit (RGASPI, d. 1688, l. 122).

86. One rural man denounced Uzbeks who ate in Russian canteens (*stolovye*) as giving in to the government's alleged aim of turning all Muslims into kofirs. Few Uzbeks prayed any more, he lamented. "What kind of Muslims are these?" he asked. "It would be better to cross oneself in front of an icon" (RGASPI, d. 2064, l. 250b). Another Muslim cleric charged the Komsomol with wishing all Uzbek youth to "leave the Muslim faith" in order to turn them into Russians and "long-haired kofirs" (d. 1692, l. 137).

"The Russians want to convert us to the Orthodox faith, to take us into the army and turn us into prostitutes. Don't take off your paranji, lest you become idolaters and after your death descend to hell."[87] The hujum made such a neo-traditionalist interpretation of Muslim culture, if anything, more strongly rooted as a fundamental aspect of Uzbek identity; religious activity soon opened one to charges of nationalism, and vice versa.[88]

Women of the World, Unite?
Class, Agency, and the Predicaments of Liberation

The central contradiction of the party's ostensibly Marxist approach to Central Asia was its decision to focus on a campaign that aimed at liberation along lines of gender rather than class. This decision had immense consequences for the party's ideological coherence, and it also had the effect of putting Uzbek women in a very difficult position. By making women's social behavior emblematic of society itself, both proponents and opponents of the hujum put these women squarely in the middle of a bitter struggle. These women's choices about how to live their lives were thus fraught with complexity and not infrequently with danger. Both sides tended to respect the choices of only those women who conformed to their vision and treated contrary female voices as illegitimate or inadmissible.

How did Uzbek women respond? The view held by Soviet as well as some Western feminist scholars stresses their positive reaction, heroically burning their veils and signing up for literacy classes and job-training programs in the face of vicious attacks by local men.[89] Much evidence, however, suggests that Uzbek women often responded much like Uzbek men. For obvious reasons this evidence can be difficult to tease out of Soviet sources; issues of class and agency also cloud the picture. It is impossible, too, to render definitive judgments about "the" Uzbek woman, or to speak too sweepingly about all Uzbek women. Yet some Uzbek women did play a role in undercutting the Soviet narrative of liberation, and many others resisted—or at a minimum did not support—the wholesale recasting of gender norms by a foreign, urban, infidel Bolshevik regime.

The classified OGPU reports of 1928 and 1929 consistently listed women as among the party's chief allies, and party activists usually assumed that opposition must be coming from local men. All Central Asian women had to be, by definition, at least latently sympathetic to the hujum, and secret police writers tried to depict them as such. Painting with a broad brush, they asserted that

87. PDA, op. 4, d. 1235, ll. 22–23.
88. For a later example (from 1937), see PDA, op. 13, d. 3, ll. 220–22.
89. The classic Soviet accounts already cited include this interpretation. Among Western writers, Kamp laudably strives to restore agency to Uzbek women rather than their Russian "elder sisters," but by minimizing or discounting evidence of female sentiment against the hujum, ultimately does so only for some.

women's aktivnost' was growing rapidly, that Uzbek women were becoming ever more "enthusiastic" about unveiling—in short, that all was falling into place as required by the party's ideological expectations.[90] The details, however, largely contradicted such broad assertions, and the picture of male recalcitrance as a hindrance to the hujum is incomplete. While the spectrum of women's reactions was complex, it is striking that most Uzbek women, the ostensible beneficiaries of Soviet liberation, did little to welcome it, and a few fought actively against it. Many Uzbek women expressed reluctance to unveil before local Communists had unveiled their own wives, or in the absence of more effective legal protection. The small group of unveiled women denounced local officials for not punishing men who harassed or attacked liberated women.[91] Most common was a simple but stalwart unwillingness to participate: most Uzbek women flatly refused to have anything to do with the hujum. Some sent excuses and regrets when summoned to Soviet meetings.[92] A huge number of Muslim women, in most places by far the majority, refused to participate in Women's Day festivities, while others attended only reluctantly. Some unveiled briefly under pressure, but quickly donned paranji and chachvon afterward.

Some women reveiled because of threats from husbands, fathers, brothers, and neighbors, but not all female reluctance can be ascribed to threats and violence. At least equally important was these women's shared socialization into gendered norms of public deportment, and specifically into concepts of female seclusion that had become increasingly definitive of national as well as religio-cultural identity. Many Uzbek women were anxious about transgressing the behavioral norms of shariat that showed them to be "good" women.[93] Some women even took the lead in organizing opposition to the hujum.[94]

Soviet and OGPU analysts had imagined women as a unitary class that would respond predictably to the promise and practice of emancipation, but the complications posed by class cleavages among Uzbek women continued to be an issue. Occasionally women not otherwise seen as Soviet allies (such as the wives of bois and mullahs) unveiled and joined the hujum.[95] More commonly, though, OGPU and party writers explained female reluctance to unveil as the product of male coercion or the result of a dubious class position or both. As a group, the wives of bois and mullahs were said to share their hus-

90. RGASPI, d. 1419, ll. 30b-4, and d. 1713, l. 125.

91. RGASPI, d. 1694, ll. 6–7, 38, 65–66, and 76. On l. 84, women in Old Tashkent are quoted as saying, "They are killing us, our husbands do not permit us to go to meetings, Soviet and party workers are not unveiling their wives, and on top of this they jeer at the unveiled. Therefore it is essential for the authorities to take tough measures against the opponents of women's liberation in order to deliver us from insults and mockery."

92. RGASPI, d. 1694, l. 85.

93. RGASPI, d. 2057, l. 65.

94. See RGASPI, d. 1684, l. 68, and d. 2064, l. 480b.

95. RGASPI, d. 1688, l. 187, d. 2062, l. 12, and d. 2064, l. 42.

bands' views: they more than other women were blamed for opposing the hujum by word and deed, and for spreading anti-Soviet rumors.[96] In the party's eyes their only redemption was that they were probably manipulated by their husbands. Bois and clerics were judged devious enough to send their wives to unveil at Soviet demonstrations, either to subvert the party's leadership of the women's liberation campaign or to petition Soviet authorities for the right to vote.[97] If, as unveiled women, they succeeded in gaining the franchise, their husbands would be able, the OGPU feared, to influence Soviet elections. Despite the protections enacted to restrict voting to "sympathetic" classes, at least one boi's wife reportedly won election to a local soviet, raising the specter of behind-the-scenes sabotage by class enemies.[98] From the party's perspective, then, any and all female opposition was explained and its significance diminished by being ascribed to class-alien elements.

If women's behavior and dress were seen by all sides as emblematic of the overall social order, women had to play a crucial role in social and cultural development. They were historical actors, after all, not putty waiting to be shaped by Zhenotdel activists or their opponents. Uzbek women's bodies were the terrain for a struggle over the shape of Central Asian society. Hence these women were caught in the middle, and they had to consider the practical outcomes of their actions. Many no doubt stayed veiled to avoid street harassment and violent attacks. Yet these women made individual decisions about how to live their lives, decisions shaped by a host of competing factors that were specific to each woman and her particular situation.

Neither party activists nor Muslim traditionalists could pretend to have won the unswerving allegiance of all Central Asian women by the early 1930s. Since both groups saw themselves as locked in an epic struggle and each saw its own views as self-evidently correct, a serious problem arose: how to explain why some women did not wish to follow the correct path. Both groups solved this problem by circumscribing female free will. They dealt with inconvenient women's voices by deciding that only women with the correct view were truly autonomous actors, able to express their desires. Other women had been manipulated or oppressed into acting the way they did—but if they could be properly enlightened and freed to express themselves, they obviously would choose to live according to the correct code of social practice.

Party analysts conceded that a few female fortune-tellers and folk healers (tabibs) might stand against the unveiling campaign, but it was far more common, they contended, for opposition to come from women who "look upon liberation from the point of view of their husbands. In this is expressed the centuries-old socioeconomic and religious structure of village life: the wife is a

96. PDA, op. 4, d. 1235, ll. 22–23.
97. RGASPI, d. 1684, l. 68; d. 2059, l. 90; and d. 2071, l. 13; and ÖzRMDA, f. 86, op. 1, d. 5085, l. 700.
98. RGASPI, d. 2059, l. 11.

thing, the possession of [her] husband. Consequently, it is inappropriate to speak about a truly independent, definite opinion on questions of liberation from this group."[99] Such women, then, could not think for themselves. Soviet analysts nevertheless insisted that most Uzbek women, especially among the poorer social strata, remained supportive of unveiling. Female opposition to the hujum represented a form of false consciousness, and it could be dealt with accordingly. When a group of bois' wives and elderly women in Osh, for example, petitioned the OGPU in March 1928 for permission to reveil, officials decided that their husbands were manipulating them. Perhaps contradictorily, several of the women were arrested as provocateurs.[100]

A similar argument was expressed by Uzbek opponents of the hujum. It was a first principle for most mullahs and eshons that all honorable Muslim women wished to remain veiled.[101] Lest there be any doubt, though, they preached that women should not unveil even at their husbands' request, since doing so would send them to hell.[102] They also praised positive examples of female behavior, such as the Uzbek woman in Old Tashkent who, reputedly unveiled by force, was too pious to bear such shame and indignity. She begged Allah to let her die, and he granted her wish. According to the story as told by a local cobbler to OGPU informants, she quickly fell ill and died on the second day, then "of course rising to heaven."[103]

A second line of argument rose out of the Soviet government's decision not to outlaw the paranji. Uzbeks who opposed the hujum could thus argue that since party activists could not force women to unveil, the choice was up to them. Identifying the final "them" in this sentence, however, was not always easy. Sometimes Uzbek men exhorted women not to unveil, saying that they were free to stay covered because Bolshevik authorities could not force them to do otherwise.[104] At other times these men declared that since unveiling was a matter of free will, no one could force "us" to unveil "our" women. In this view the choice belonged to husbands, who feared that their wives' "weak wills" would not permit them to refuse Soviet exhortations to unveil.[105]

This limited view of female choice, in which only certain actions were recognized as legitimate, served on both sides as a male constraint on female action. High-level male Bolsheviks trumpeted women's right to choose their way of life when that choice meant unveiling, but showed great reluctance to accord the same weight to a contrary female opinion. Male Muslims praised publicly the piety of women who chose to remain veiled, seeing their actions as a true expression of Uzbek Muslim identity, but did not accord unveiled

99. PDA, op. 4, d. 1235, l. 91.
100. RGASPI, d. 1689, l. 55.
101. RGASPI, d. 1688, l. 122.
102. RGASPI, d. 1694, l. 40.
103. RGASPI, d. 2064, l. 490b.
104. RGASPI, d. 1694, l. 18.
105. Ibid., l. 65, and d. 2082, l. 1140b.

women the same respect. This contest over female roles, status, and behavior focused the attention of both sides on women's bodies, but less out of concern for women per se than out of the utility of those bodies as a mutually agreed (if unspoken) ground of conflict over the social order.

Yet this story is still too simple; any discussion of agency must extend beyond the ways Uzbek women were controlled and constrained by men. Women, too—again on both sides—shared the same tendency to privilege only certain women's voices as legitimate. Most Zhenotdel activists were women, but they mirrored the reluctance of their male party colleagues to admit that an Uzbek woman might freely choose not to unveil. And of course a number of Uzbek women also spoke out in support of female seclusion and veiling. Refusing to admit that any good Muslim woman would voluntarily unveil, they invoked the same arguments as Uzbek men, blaming unveiling on Soviet coercion.

But despite all the obstacles, millions of Uzbek women did act, deciding from day to day how to live their lives. Their actions do not necessarily speak for themselves. The vast majority of Uzbek women were illiterate, and few were interviewed by dispassionate outsiders interested in asking about their opinions or motivations. Most of the surviving documentary record was compiled and written by Soviet, party, and secret-police officials. Yet careful readings can find ordinary Uzbek women's voices even here; they bubble up through the cracks and fissures of official sources. What do they say?

These women varied widely in their responses to the invitation to unveil. Some welcomed the hujum; party writers gave them prominence of place whenever possible. Stories of Uzbek women who faced down threats to attend school or a demonstration or to unveil pepper the documents.[106] Such cases showed the essential rightness of the party's approach, and so, to paraphrase Voltaire, had they not existed, they would have had to be invented. Some, indeed, may have been invented: vehement Marxist quotations from the mouths of Uzbek peasants do make the skeptical reader wonder. Yet other voices also emerge from these reports, particularly from the highly classified internal documents, showing Uzbek women as less universally receptive to the hujum than the party had hoped.

Leaving aside for the moment those comparatively rare women who openly supported the hujum, how did the broad majority of Uzbek women act? The largest single group numbered in the millions: women who appear in the documents only through their absence. These women avoided Soviet workers, tried to ignore the hujum, and probably went about their daily lives much as before. Their views and beliefs can only be guessed at. Yet many reports make plain the creativity demonstrated by the ostensibly silent Uzbek woman in adapting the conflicting demands of the hujum to her world. She might remove paranji and chachvon, for instance, but cover herself just as completely with a

106. RGASPI, d. 1694, ll. 37 and 66–67, and d. 2057, l. 62.

shawl or cloak. Or she could unveil at a demonstration, only to reveil before reaching home.[107] Measuring any particular woman's support for the hujum—or even whether she should be counted as unveiled—was a tricky issue. When forced by party or Soviet officials to unveil or participate in a demonstration—particularly in large urban areas and the New Cities—many women showed themselves masters of *seeming* to cooperate. Often they did so only when and insofar as they had to, acting provisionally and temporarily. Their decisions correlated with spatial considerations, wearing the veil (or not) depending on expectations in a given locale. As the Andijon Zhenotdel put it in an unusually perceptive and discerning report written in early 1928:

> In the beginning [we] tried to prepare an accounting of the veiled and the reveiled, but afterward became convinced that it was impossible to take such an inventory. After 8 March, the paranjis that had been cast off and burned stuck tenaciously [*trudno pristaet*] to the women's faces. Under the various influences of byt traditions, the stagnation and ignorance of the local men, and the agitation of socially alien elements, women reveiled themselves again with paranjis, with the sleeves of their cloaks [*khalats*], or with shawls. This category of "temporarily unveiled" is difficult to count as either "unveiled" or "veiled." Many women go unveiled at meetings, in family circles, and also in the New City, but in their own mahalla walk about veiled. It is the same in the villages.[108]

This report went on to describe conditions in the city of Namangan, where only 200 of the 600 nominally unveiled women actually went through daily life without a veil. "An exact reckoning," it noted, "is not possible, given the state of our apparatus and [local] conditions of everyday life." The tactical uses of the veil then became clearer as the author described local women's day-to-day lives. When jobs were available at the local cotton processing and dairy factories, for example, enterprise managers announced that only unveiled women would be considered, so many women left their veils at home when they went to apply. "The Uzbek woman is very cautious," the report concluded: "She boldly and confidently walks to women's meetings—unveiled. And to [Soviet] family circles; she goes [unveiled] wherever she knows that she will not run into insults, ridicule, and mockery. [But] it is hard to find unveiled women at the bazaars, or on the lively streets of the Old Cities. Here [the Uzbek woman] tries to cover herself, that is, [she veils] in those places where insults can most often be heard directed at the unveiled."[109] Uzbek women re-

---

107. See RGASPI, d. 2056, l. 56; and ÖzRMDA, f. 86, op. 1, d. 5719, l. 16, and f. 736, op. 1, d. 933, l. 640b.

108. RGASPI, d. 1690, l. 11.

109. Ibid., l. 13.

fused to adopt the whole package of a transformed way of life as it was offered by the party, despite many Bolsheviks' assumption that such a transformation would follow more or less automatically. Instead, women made tactical and strategic choices: to unveil, to reveil, or to do neither or both, depending on individual situations and personal predispositions.

If most women crafted their actions carefully and avoided politically charged situations whenever possible, others expressed their views quite directly. Some, unable to avoid confrontations with party activists, flatly refused to go along with Soviet liberation. They left little doubt about their views of how a woman should act. One woman, the wife of a trade union member and party worker, declared that she would not unveil even if her decision meant that her husband would be dismissed. Another, the wife of a Communist, threatened to abandon him and their children if he forced her to unveil; the vigor of her insistence left the local party at a loss on how to proceed.[110]

Other forms of resistance were collective. Several cases were recorded in 1928 and 1929 of Uzbek women undercutting the hujum through means that to party and OGPU writers were subversive. These women went to Zhenotdel demonstrations and meetings in order to speak out against the unveiling campaign. They ridiculed unveiled women: cases continued to crop up of party members' wives leading the mockery.[111] A similarly corrosive effect was traced to the many antihujum songs and subversive rhymes that spread among Uzbek women, which seemed impossible to stamp out.[112]

Most startling of all was the willingness of at least some Uzbek women to engage in active and occasionally violent resistance to Soviet efforts to emancipate them. A few women were accused of organizing anti-Soviet and antihujum groups.[113] Such cases were rare, but because of their explosive implications they were discussed only privately, in highly classified OGPU reports. Most violence directed against the hujum, to be sure, came from Central Asian men, but these scattered cases of female violence are more important than their numbers suggest. They show women acting as historical agents (albeit not in a way the party welcomed), and they demonstrate strong support among at least a subgroup of Muslim women for non-Soviet patterns of female seclusion and veiling. Such women quickly latched on to various Bolshevik "mistakes," such as the brokering of veils, to make their case to other Uzbek women.

Consider a classified report sent to Moscow by the Central Asian OGPU in mid-May 1929. It described a meeting of 200 women, held two weeks earlier in the village of Sultan-Obod, in rural Andijon, called by Qoriyahon Bibi Otun

110. ÖzRMDA, f. 736, op. 1, d. 1161, l. 27; and RGASPI, d. 1690, l. 12. See also RGASPI, d. 1694, l. 65, for a group of thirty women in Tashkent flatly refusing to unveil.

111. RGASPI, d. 1694, l. 23, and d. 2057, l. 139.

112. See RGASPI, d. 1681, l. 108. Another antiregime and antihujum song from the Old City of Farghona was quoted by the local Zhenotdel chief, Olimpiada Ermakova, at d. 1688, l. 218.

113. RGASPI, d. 1684, l. 68, and d. 2064, l. 480b.

Abbas Khojaev, a female *bakhshi*.[114] One woman in attendance declared that Soviet authorities "deceived us on 8 March: they took away our paranjis, [saying] that they would be returned the next day. The paranjis were not returned to us. The local workers divided [them] among themselves and made some of them into blankets." She specifically named a police officer, a Russian woman named Pal'vanova, and also accused a Zhenotdel worker named Kurbanhon, who "took away the best paranjis and is selling them at the bazaar." "We must go to the authorities on May Day," she concluded, "and demand that they return our paranjis to us."

But on May Day events quickly spun out of control. The OGPU recounted the story as follows: After some of the official festivities drew to a close, the wife of a former district administrator, Ugul Bi Rajababaeva, had addressed a group of women with a resounding battle cry: "Whoever is for Soviet power— let them stand aside. But those who are for a revolution—follow me!" All twenty women present declared their agreement with this anti-Soviet revolution and marched behind Rajababaeva to see a senior police officer, Pirnazarov. They asked him to return the paranjis that his wife, Hamidova—the secretary of the local party cell—had taken on 8 March. Rajababaeva then "threatened [him] with a knife that she had concealed on herself"—she had hidden it under her paranji—and Pirnazarov "took fright and ran away." From this point matters spiraled from bad to worse. Another informal women's gathering allegedly took place two days later at the home of a poor peasant, Mirza Karim Churak. The ten women in attendance again "decided to demand the return of the paranjis that had been taken on 8 March." They went straight to Hamidova and Pirnazarov's apartment, three of them armed with knives "and the rest with stones." One, Marhamathon Mulla Sultanova, declared on the way, "We will tear Hamidova to bits and make ourselves paranjis from her hide."

Hamidova, fortunately for her, was not home. But as the frustrated female battalion returned, it confronted unveiled women on the street, "savagely beating" one of them, Khojihon Bibi. In light of this episode, it would be an understatement to say that not all Uzbek women responded positively to the hujum. Yet the need to treat women as revolutionary allies shaped the party's subsequent responses. After intensive investigations by the local police and the Andijon provincial OGPU, three people were arrested and two were accused of playing a "passive role" in the violence. Yet only one of the accused was a woman (Rajababaeva, who was arrested). Even though the violence had been carried out by a roving gang of angry armed women, the truly responsible parties were judged to be the men who *must have* been lurking behind the scenes,

114. This report, on which the three subsequent paragraphs are based, is at RGASPI, d. 2064, l. 51–510b. A bakhshi is now a folk singer or bard; during this period the term also meant folk doctor, sorcerer, or magician.

such as the peasant (Mirza Chulak) at whose house the final meeting was held, or the passively complicit mahalla president, Usman Dulak Hudaiberdiev.

While most Uzbek women, then, simply refused to take part in the hujum, a few went much further. These women, no less than their male compatriots, were raised to see themselves as good Muslims, and now they were also patriotic Uzbeks. And for most the Bolsheviks' invitation to liberate themselves was not very appealing. Their reluctance followed partly from the dangers faced by unveiled women, but also from the way these women saw the world. The strongly negative associations of unveiling—its links with prostitution, immorality, decadence, and unbelief—only grew stronger when Zhenotdel activists tried to force the issue.

The resulting alienation from Soviet authorities—who proved strikingly unable to overcome these beliefs—led even women who sympathized with the party's aims to feel betrayed. Twenty unveiled schoolteachers in Samarqand, for example, expressed this view in a forceful petition submitted to city hall in 1928. They demanded that the Samarqand City Soviet resolve the question of unveiling "once and for all, before 8 March."[115] In their view, Soviet officials did not understand what the world looked like to an unveiled woman. The petition began by asking how they were supposed to have benefited from Soviet liberation:

> In the past, when we languished [at home, surrounded by our] four walls, we endured the outrages of our husbands; now we liberated women appear as prostitutes in the imaginations of women who still wear the paranji.
> Is this the reward of a proletarian government to us?

With that rhetorical question hanging, the schoolteachers launched a harsh critique of the party's unveiling policy. "Having started [to pursue] the issue," they alleged, "you did not drive it to a conclusion and then [you] started to say that unveiling is a matter of the free will of women themselves. Based on this declaration, nearly all of the women who still wear the paranji are denouncing us for having sold out our faith, calling us shameless and dogs of the street." Veiled women, not Uzbek men, were singled out here as responsible for the harassment: the complexities are plain, as is the frustration of the few women who had done as the party asked and thrown off the veil. "At the time of our liberation," they pointed out, "you told us that with regard to people who responded badly to liberation and liberated women, you would take the very strictest measures. In this we still are not satisfied. On the streets, at weddings, in other gatherings, everywhere and all around, we see and hear [nothing but] scornful attitudes and bad opinions, both from men and from women who are

---

115. This petition, from which the subsequent summary and quotations are taken, is in Russian translation at RGASPI, d. 1692, ll. 51–52.

not unveiled." Reporting such episodes to the Zhenotdel, the city soviet, or the raikom, they admitted, did sometimes get results: arrests and some convictions followed. "But," they noted, "this has not at all given us any guarantee against cases of murder during our trips out of town or likewise the ferment caused on secluded, out-of-the-way streets by the appearance of [our unveiled] faces. Against whom, then, can our lifeless body be avenged?"

If even we, they continued, the loyal followers of Lenin, are treated this way—facing insults and humiliation with every step—then "nothing will be left for us but to shout '*Voidod!*' [Help!] and to shout it not once but thousands of times."[116] As the petition drew to a close, these women made it clear that they had reached the limits of their endurance. "We will not be able to do it any more," they said, unless the state did what they asked. "If you really intend decisively to attack the paranji," they declared, new and much more decisive action was needed. They then presented their list of demands:

> 1. If a woman in a paranji brings wares to the market, let no one buy from her.
> 2. Cooperatives are not to sell goods to women in paranjis.
> 3. The judicial organs are not to hear the requests of women in paranjis.
> 4. Women in paranjis are not to be given medicines by clinics and drugstores.
> 5. Members of the party and Komsomol, if their wives wear the paranji, are to be removed from their positions.
> 6. The daughters and sons of merchants are not to be accepted in Soviet schools.

"If you do not implement these requests of ours before 8 March," the petition concluded, "then do not blame your Red teachers if they once again begin to wear the paranji."

Such demands for a more coercive approach make perfect sense coming from the small, embattled group of unveiled women. The sense of impatience verging on betrayal felt by the party's ostensible allies is palpable in the willingness of these unveiled women to make nonnegotiable demands of the Soviet government. Their temerity makes visible the growing distance by 1930 between Soviet authorities and even their closest friends in Uzbek society.

Voices of Resistance: Preaching, Prophets, and Rumors

These acts of resistance speak clearly about Uzbek sentiment toward the unveiling campaign. But what else can be learned from the words of Uzbeks? How did they explain their views of the women's liberation campaign? The

---

116. "*Voidod!*" literally means "Help!" but is uttered only at moments of extreme distress, sorrow, and despair, as at a death in the family.

documentary sources, again, do not yield easy or transparent answers: most were filtered, selected, and often translated by party workers, and the portrait of Muslim religious doctrines or Uzbek nationalist beliefs that results must of necessity remain incomplete. Yet historians are fortunate that Soviet authorities and the OGPU were so interested in these questions. Even when they did not understand what they heard and even when they kept it secret, these authorities meticulously recorded many Uzbek voices, including, perhaps especially, those of resistance.

It is possible to discern important aspects of how many Uzbeks saw Soviet power in these party and state sources. These Uzbek men and women frequently expressed themselves in a religious/moral lexicon, in which the hujum was understood in apocalyptic terms, as a sign of the end times. In essence, the unveiling campaign was a punishment from Allah, sent for reasons only he could know, most likely to test Muslim believers. Rather than being seen through the lens of liberation, as the party wished, the hujum was assimilated into and explained in terms of Muslim theology and Uzbek culture. Its meanings thus bore little resemblance to those intended by Zhenotdel and party workers. Signifying not progress but the danger and depths of the political, cultural, and moral crisis faced by Central Asian society, it was a blank canvas onto which Uzbek Muslims projected their hopes, dreams, fears, and anxieties. Reactions to the hujum—both the narrowly religious, especially as expressed by the clergy, and the wider, more amorphous popular discourse—reveal some of the contours of Uzbek Muslim identity. They also show the shape of an increasingly coherent non-Soviet vision of social order. These utterances suggest much about how Uzbeks saw the world and how they understood their place in it.

Religious discourse, first, served as a visible language of moral values and cultural authenticity. As the Soviet assault against the veil entered its third year, few Muslim clerics—even former jadids—were willing to express support for the hujum, even had the party wanted them to. Cases of open clerical opposition, by contrast, were rife. Nearly all the recorded words of mullahs and imams from 1928 and 1929 express categorical opposition to the hujum; some reportedly moved to remote areas or sent their wives away to escape being asked to unveil.[117] These clerics saw themselves as the moral guardians of society, as the cultural bulwarks of propriety and faith—and justifiably so, given the high esteem in which they usually were held. Hence they used their bully pulpit to bolster the cultural hegemony of specific Muslim beliefs and behaviors. After 1927 in Uzbekistan, thanks largely to the hujum, this meant above all female seclusion.[118]

---

117. PDA, op. 3, d. 1560, l. 347, and op. 4, d. 1235, l. 19. An exceptional eshon who supported the hujum is at RGASPI, d. 1694, l. 36.

118. Some examples, in addition to those cited below, are RGASPI, d. 1692, l. 138, and d. 2064, l. 19.

The flavor of these clerical views emerges from the extant speeches and writings preserved by the Soviet secret police. While one needs occasionally to read between the lines and certainly to compensate for the OGPU's class imputations, it is plain—and consistent with the other evidence already adduced—that mullahs made a concerted effort to link unveiling with a variety of social ills. On one level unveiling meant Russian Orthodoxy and a loss of Uzbek nationality, and therefore was an act that could be practiced only by traitors. Another line of attack linked unveiling with various social dysfunctions and pathologies. The hujum aimed to make women abandon their husbands, according to one mullah; another argued that it was intended to mobilize women for the army. Still other associations were based on moral concerns, such as attempts to link uncovered female faces with dishonor. Women should not go to Soviet meetings, according to one imam, because "there they can become Russified and lose their conscience and honor."[119] A woman without her paranji was the functional equivalent of a prostitute, and some clerics agreed that she could (and, for deterrent purposes, perhaps even should) be treated as such. Unveiling was fundamentally shameful, and it betrayed a deep moral failing.[120]

As a sin, too, unveiling held deeper implications for the body national than other social ills. Citing specific passages from the Qur'an, these clerics argued that Allah's truth, as revealed by Muhammad, required women to veil in the presence of men outside their immediate family. God punished anyone who violated this law, they declared. Women would go to hell if they unveiled, even if they did so at their husbands' behest. Men sinned by permitting their wives to unveil, and they risked being excluded from the mahalla's social life and permanently ostracized as an infidel, or kofir.[121] In these clerics' judgment, the hujum was an unmitigated disaster that had brought bloodshed to the allegedly peaceful land of old.[122]

The supposed tranquility that had existed before the hujum framed a complementary clerical argument, one that posed a positive alternative to Soviet unveiling. These mullahs and imams did not merely attack the hujum; they also propounded a different vision of what society should look like. This vi-

119. PDA, op. 4, d. 1235, ll. 35–36.

120. On prostitutes, see RGASPI, d. 1688, l. 123; d. 1694, ll. 33 and 38; and d. 2064, l. 19. The associations with moral corruption and dissipation are at d. 1694, l. 18; and PDA, op. 4, d. 1235, l. 17.

121. RGASPI, d. 1688, l. 123, and d. 1694, ll. 34, 40, 56–57, 72, and 79–80. A mullah denounced men whose wives attended Soviet meetings (not to mention those who were unveiled) as "*souteneurs*" (ponces, pimps) and said that such men would no longer be permitted at ritual prayer (*namoz*) (Em. Iaroslavskii, "Antireligioznaia propaganda i kul'turnaia revoliutsiia," *Revoliutsiia i kul'tura*, no. 5 [1928], 33).

122. "To throw off the paranji is forbidden, [see] how this led to a whole series of murders, which we have observed in different regions of our Uzbekistan. We now [again] live calmly; we will live quietly and peacefully [if we are left to live] according to the old ways. Why do you want bloodshed?" (RGASPI, d. 2064, l. 290b).

sion was based on Muslim piety and devout observance of religious and cultural norms. Yet in response to the hujum, these religious and cultural views were reimagined to give women new prominence. In the past women usually had not been welcome in mosques, but now Muslim clerics preached to them and even trained them to proselytize for continued adherence to codes of veiling.[123] While religious scholars and clerics tarred unveiling with negative associations, they praised women who practiced seclusion as virtuous and honorable. When a Soviet activist tried to convince one Mirza Ota Sharafov that the veil oppressed women, for instance, he rejoined, "Of course for debauched women, for those not content with their husbands, the paranji was a prison; but for honorable women, on the contrary, they would sooner agree to die than to give it up."[124]

These clerics generally interpreted the hujum not as an unwanted intervention by a powerful non-Muslim colonial government but as a part of God's plan. However unpleasant, the hujum was a manifestation of divine will, a plague sent to punish or to test Muslim believers. It arose from the internal failings of Muslim society, not the superior military might and political power of Bolshevik Russia. Allah had sent the hujum to Central Asia, ran one common line of thought, because Uzbek Muslims, through their shortcomings, had brought it upon themselves. The OGPU transcribed one village discussion outside Tashkent in March 1929, at a rural *iftor* (meal to break the Islamic fast) attended by seventeen rural clerics and middle peasants:

> ... Imam Nugman-Makhjum, having read an extract from the Qur'an, explained: "These are the words of God. [This is what] they mean: 'My offspring will do many things: they will not acknowledge God, they will insult shariat [and] religion, they will take away the property of others. Unclean scoundrels will be running things, Muslims will become unbelievers, women will lose their conscience and uncover their faces, children will not respect their elders, and they will stop going to the religious school [*madrasa*].' "
>
> Dost-Domullaev [the host, son of a prominent imam] answered, "This is indeed that time, and that government. Women have lost their conscience and youth their respect for adults. They have seized the property of others. [But] in all of this we are the guilty ones. We have not paid the *ushury* [religious tax], we have engaged in money-lending, we have had five wives [shariat permitted only four], we have drunk heavily, we have led depraved and debauched lives. For all of this God has sent us the Bolsheviks!"
>
> Mukum-Khojaev (an imam, son of a Sufi shaykh) [said], "Brothers, this has been done not by the Russians but by Muslims themselves. They

123. RGASPI, d. 1694, ll. 5 and 65.
124. RGASPI, d. 1688, l. 122.

have forgotten God, they have unveiled [their] women. What kind of a true-believing government is this! It has set us one against another. This government wants to destroy religion, to convert everyone into an unbeliever, to subordinate [everything] to itself."[125]

Uzbek Muslims had not lived according to God's commandments, and the unveiling campaign either was a wake-up call or, more ominously, showed God's sweeping displeasure with Muslim society and his intention to destroy all of humanity. By contrast, when Amanullah Khan's regime in Afghanistan collapsed in 1929 after it had tried to implement similar reforms of women's status, the news was taken to show that Afghans had been spared because Afghan society was more devout and religious.[126] Soviet policy in the hujum was thus reconceived and recast as punishment visited by an angry God upon his disobedient children.

This understanding of the hujum led to a corresponding view of how Central Asians should respond. If we Muslims caused this plague, clerics reasoned, then by our actions and repentance we may hope to end it. Hence they advised Uzbeks to focus on bettering themselves by piety, devoutness, and faith, and enjoined them not to cooperate with Soviet authorities, who promulgated a message of sin and godlessness. Some mullahs urged the party to slow its campaign. They used logic and the party's own words to argue that unveiling was obligatory only for Communists and members of the Komsomol and trade unions.[127] Others called meetings to denounce the hujum, not coincidentally scheduling them at the exact times of the party's "family circle" meetings.[128]

Other techniques were more direct and forceful. Uzbeks who sympathized with the party or who unveiled were ostracized, excluded from religious services and barred from obtaining religious burials for dead relatives.[129] In March 1928 one inhabitant of Vabkent, a small town outside Bukhoro, explained how open demonstrations could stop the unveiling campaign:

> In Tashkent, too, the authorities ordered the people to unveil women, but there [the inhabitants] were cleverer. They gathered [a crowd of] as many as a thousand people and declared to the authorities, "For sixty-two years, ever since the Russians took Turkestan, we have paid them taxes and given [them] soldiers, but nobody in all this time has disturbed our religion. We are your citizens, [but] if you want to unveil our wives,

125. This discussion is transcribed in a top-secret OGPU report at RGASPI, d. 2064, l. 25.
126. Ibid., ll. 25 and 26ob.
127. PDA, op. 4, d. 1235, ll. 18–19; and RGASPI, d. 1688, l. 122, and d. 1694, ll. 33 and 36.
128. RGASPI, d. 1688, l. 187.
129. Burials were withheld to retaliate for disenfranchisement of eshons in Soviet elections (ÖzRMDA, f. 86, op. 1, d. 5719, l. 16, and d. 5885, l. 691). All religious services were withheld in 1930 from kolkhoz peasants on the grounds that by joining a Soviet enterprise that was based on expropriated land, they were no more honorable Muslims than unveiled women (PDA, op. 5, d. 866, l. 115).

then [you will have to] begin by shooting us." It turns out that the government is afraid when lots of people come out against it, and in Tashkent, when these thousand people spoke out, the authorities had a good talk with the people and canceled the unveiling of women. Our people have a weak faith, but if only they held to their beliefs more strongly and gathered a crowd of five hundred against the government, then everything would be in its place and as many women as have now unveiled would not have done so.[130]

The problem, then, lay not in the superior power wielded by Bolshevik authorities but in the insufficient resolve and weak faith of Uzbeks. But all was not lost; popular pressure could still yield results, and religious, spiritual, and national reform might yet save the day. These mullahs believed that a display of unity and piety, manifested in large crowds agitating for moral and national ends, could successfully challenge Soviet power and put the world right.

These arguments were not unique to clerics. Many Uzbek women supported such positions, invoking a moral and religious discourse that denounced the hujum as synonymous with sin and hell. The Uzbek OGPU cited one such case in June 1928:

An inhabitant of Kara-Palvan village (Yangi-Qorghon district, Andijon province), Muriya-Bibi Akhunbaeva, was invited to read holy books for deceased women from that village. Making use of [the fact that] more than a hundred women gathered at funerals, Muriya-Bibi started to agitate among them against the removal of the faranji. Hearing of this, the president of the village soviet wrote her a letter directing her to cease this agitation. Reading this note, Muriya-Bibi threw off her chachvon and began to shriek hysterically, with the aim of exciting the religious-minded and attracting them all the more to her side.[131]

Such women, dismissed as "savage" by party activists, joined their male co-nationals in denouncing their unveiled sisters as no longer Muslim.[132] In 1929 party activists spotted two veiled women in Gijduvan making the rounds with a Qur'an, an unusual sight given the low literacy level among women. Upon investigation the activists discovered that these women had come all the way from Tashkent to agitate among women for the need to stay veiled.[133]

The overall thrust of this religious discourse is clear: it aimed to rehabilitate Central Asian Muslim society by reforming it from within and unifying it

130. RGASPI, d. 1694, l. 36. Another unfavorable comparison of Bolsheviks with tsarist authorities is at l. 5.

131. Ibid., l. 113. "Faranji" is an alternate spelling—Uzbek words sometimes interchange *f* and *p*. For another association with sin and hellfire, see d. 1419, l. 40b.

132. PDA, op. 4, d. 1235, l. 22. For the "savage" description, see op. 8, d. 886, l. 24.

133. RGASPI, d. 2082, l. 1140b. Other cases of women speaking out against the hujum are at PDA, op. 4, d. 1235, l. 11, and RGASPI, d. 1694, l. 7.

against Soviet power. The ultimate aim of ending Soviet control was hardly a secret, but the Bolsheviks per se were almost incidental to the drama. Like the various enemies defeated (with God's help) by the Israelites of the Old Testament, they were really only foils, spurring Uzbek Muslims to look inside and regenerate their faith. Decadence and corruption were the true enemy, which had to be overcome for propriety and justice to be restored. Muslim clerics thus prayed publicly for Soviet power to be crushed and called for a "second revolution, as a result of which power will pass into the hands of the Muslims."[134] Mullahs in Namangan province threw down the gauntlet in 1929, addressing a crowd with calls for a jihad against female unveiling. This language of combat included promises of heaven for those who died as martyrs in the struggle and for those who slew the enemies of morality and justice.[135]

Calls for massive demonstrations to force the Soviet regime to rescind the unveiling campaign—not to mention calls to jihad—relied on this underlying optimism, the belief that Uzbek Muslims, through their own efforts, could still turn the tide. But some more pessimistic religious figures interpreted the stress and upheaval of the late 1920s in a different light. The presence of unveiled women on public streets could be seen as a test for Uzbek believers, to make them behave better; but it could also be read as a sign that all hope had been lost, for this world at least—that Allah had willed the hujum onto Central Asia as a sign of the end times. Without the prospect of ultimate victory over the evil and corruption represented by the Bolsheviks, indeed, only apocalypse remained. For some Uzbeks, then, unveiling signaled that the end of the world was nigh.[136]

Such views are common in times of severe social strain; scholars of millenarianism have found similar phenomena around the world. Often prophets of apocalypse arise under such conditions to lead revitalization movements, movements that seek (with supernatural help) to protect indigenous culture from an alien, often colonial power.[137] They make it possible for indigenous society to retain its conceptual independence—in this case, to preserve the ability of Uzbeks to conceive of a world outside the political structures, linguistic categories, and cultural frameworks of the Soviet state. While Uzbek sources mention only a few such prophets or charismatic leaders, the wider doomsday reading of the hujum that was common in southern Central Asia fits well into this broader literature.

Uzbeks with such an outlook took the hujum's main features and projected

134. PDA, op. 4, d. 1235, ll. 18–19.

135. RGASPI, d. 2082, l. 1100b.

136. For examples of this linkage, see RGASPI, d. 1694, ll. 4, 18, and 39–40, and d. 2064, l. 29.

137. Michael Adas, *Prophets of Rebellion: Millenarian Protest Movements against the European Colonial Order* (Chapel Hill, 1979), especially xxi–xxii and 186–87. See also Silvia L. Thrupp, ed., *Millennial Dreams in Action: Studies in Revolutionary Religious Movements* (New York, 1970); and Michael Barkun, *Disaster and the Millennium* (New Haven, 1974).

them into the future, concluding that the total collapse of society and morality was inevitable. In this dystopian vision, social order would disintegrate, faith would disappear, and life as it currently existed would end. As one Safar Gharibov explained in 1928, current trends raised horrifying prospects: "Among unveiled women no shame remains. Today they are throwing off their paranjis, tomorrow their dresses, and bit by bit they will be laid bare. Now we are in the hands of infidels, God help us. Either take this government away or let our land collapse. Where is our emir? The shariat no longer exists among us, and the time of kofirs has begun."[138] Gharibov's vision expressed the deep fears engendered by the hujum: nakedness would inevitably spread after civilization's retaining walls were breached. Party activists invested enormous energy in a public relations effort to say that this was not the outcome they wanted. But the nightmares conjured by the unveiling campaign reveal how its opponents—both self-styled devout Muslims and patriotic Uzbeks—saw the world, and what they thought mattered most.

The story of one Uzbek millennial prophet shows how the act of unveiling could be associated with eternal damnation and hellfire, and how Muslim Uzbeks could be urged to keep the day of final judgment firmly in mind whenever they had to interact with Bolsheviks. Ironically, this prophet, named Rising Moon, was a woman. Her story was preserved and told in 1929 by Anna Louise Strong, a pro-Soviet American visitor to Central Asia. According to Strong, Rising Moon presided over a series of women's meetings in southern Uzbekistan. With the blessing of local religious authorities, she reminded her listeners of their duties as wives, and painted a grim picture of the hujum's consequences:

> The emotion of a wife's soul must strictly correspond to that of her husband. If he is merry, she also must be merry; if her lord is sad, let her with looks and sentiments share his woes. . . .
>
> Oh, my sisters! great is the power of the husband over his obedient wife. Wherefore, when a wife is seriously ill, let her husband strike her on the back and say: "Ye evil ones, who lead mankind into trouble, begone at once from this beautiful body!" Then the devil, which dwells between skin and flesh especially to torment her, will leave immediately. . . . But only if she is a true wife, submissive to her husband.
>
> A man must not be soft nor come under his wife's influence. From time to time let him make her feel that he is the head of the household, by appropriate chastisement or even blows but not in such manner as to injure permanently.
>
> When the sun shall burn out, when the stars shall fail, when the hills shall move, when the seas shall boil, when souls ascend in steam, when

138. RGASPI, d. 1694, l. 36. Similar fears of total nakedness—meaning the abandonment of all social moorings and moral standards—have been voiced by people opposed to new fashions in other parts of the world. See Roberts, *Civilization without Sexes*, 72–74.

the lists of men are read, when the heavens are open and the fires of hell await—then shall every soul give an account of itself on the Terrible Judgment Day. . . . Fear that hour, O my sisters! Do not unveil your faces before men, as counsel the wicked Bolsheviks. Do not draw down on yourselves the wrath of God.[139]

This kind of voice was not at all what Zhenotdel and party workers expected to hear from Uzbek women.

Yet even this bleak vision held out some hope for Uzbek Muslims. Society would end, but a new, utopian order would arise from its ashes. Thus the disasters of Soviet rule could be assimilated into a broader theological scheme in which they served as harbingers, however painful, of God's final kingdom on earth. As another mullah declared,

> They [Bolsheviks] want all the people to become kofirs, and this is a sign of doomsday. I have read in the [holy] books that at the end of the world, Muslims will cast aside their faith and go over to another, and others will be cast into caves until the appearance of the imam Mahdi and Jesus. After this appearance the kofirs will be annihilated and [only] Muslims will remain. We are now, therefore, living through signs of the end times and we must pray even more diligently.[140]

Even if the hujum connoted apocalyptic doom, then, it was a necessary step toward a final era of justice and piety.

Many of these hopes and fears can be discerned in the words of ordinary Uzbeks, often recorded by the party and OGPU under the general rubric of "rumors." Psychologists find rumors and informal storytelling to be instructive: as such tales travel through society, they are said to be brought into line with the beliefs and worldview of those doing the telling and retelling. The stories thus change over time, being "leveled and sharpened" and made "more concise, and more easily grasped and told." Thus rumors and gossip serve complex emotional as well as social and intellectual purposes. In the words of Gordon Allport and Leo Postman, a rumor "rationalizes while it relieves": "Most rumors, and most gossip too, are far from idle. They are profoundly purposive, serving important emotional ends. Just what these ends may be both teller and listener are usually unable to say. They know only that the tale seems important to them. In some mysterious way it seems to alleviate their in-

---

139. Quoted in Strong, *Red Star in Samarkand*, 245–47.

140. RGASPI, d. 1694, l. 33. Another imam argued that "Soviet power has turned the entire world inside out: it does not recognize faith, and is destroying it. Now the end of the world has begun, the people have stopped praying and do not go to the mosque. Now they are unveiling all the women, and if the women unveil themselves, then everyone will be kofirs; the Muslim inhabitants do not need to suffer this. God has opened up the land and all of these people are seizing it for themselves. Now the government feels its strength, but this will not be for long, since in our [holy] books God promised us that this [regime] will end" (l. 39).

tellectual uncertainty and personal anxiety."[141] Even as they ascribe and extract meaning from a social environment, too, rumors and gossip permit the reteller to slap out at a collectively reviled target. The terms in which a rumor is framed serve simultaneously to normalize and justify such revulsion. Gossip and rumor thus knit a community together, continually redeclaring its shared values and serving as a kind of social glue.

The fabric of rumors circulating through Uzbek society in the late 1920s and early 1930s—notwithstanding their perhaps skewed presentation by concerned OGPU officers—expose some of these earthly hopes and heavenly dreams, the hidden beliefs and deepest fears of the women and men involved in their transmission.[142] Uzbek stories fused these deep passions and hatreds with a complicating dose of sex and anxiety. Some of the rumors imputed scurrilous motives for the unveiling campaign, or alleged that the party wanted to destroy Central Asian society. Others generated hope for their listeners and retellers, either immediately or in the life hereafter. In either case, their content and presentation show Uzbeks making sense of the hujum and using it to create a vision of a non-Soviet future. Unveiling, in short, served as a narrative gateway to a different social order. Either the removal of paranjis and chachvons would bring down the Soviet regime—perhaps by provoking international war—or it signified the end of the world and thus the coming of a heavenly kingdom on earth.

The first of three main kinds of rumors disparaged the aims behind the unveiling campaign. The party wanted women to cast off their paranjis in order to enlist them in the Red Army, one story alleged; another asserted that Soviet workers would kidnap any young woman who attended women's meetings.[143] Most such tales started with a kernel of truth and then recast, amplified, and exaggerated it to show the supposedly evil motives of Zhenotdel activists. For example, it was whispered (not inaccurately) that Uzbek women could be forced to unveil if they showed up at Soviet meetings. Another rumor—perhaps based on episodes of veil brokering—posited that the paranjis seized by the party were being used by the wives of Soviet workers.[144] From this perspective, unveiling appeared as yet another state expropriation, like the land

---

141. Gordon W. Allport and Leo Postman, *The Psychology of Rumor* (New York, 1965), 75, 37, vii. See also Raymond Firth, "Rumor in a Primitive Society," *Journal of Abnormal and Social Psychology* 53 (1956): 122–32; Adas, *Prophets of Rebellion*, 145; and Scott, *Domination*, 145–48.

142. On the methodological issues, see David Arnold, "Touching the Body: Perspectives on the Indian Plague, 1896–1900," in *Selected Subaltern Studies*, ed. Ranajit Guha and Gayatri Chakravorty Spivak, 404–13 (New York, 1988); or Luise White, *Speaking with Vampires: Rumor and History in Colonial Africa* (Berkeley, 2000). For the specifically Soviet issues, see Viola, *Peasant Rebels*, 45–66; and Sheila Fitzpatrick, *Stalin's Peasants: Resistance and Survival in the Russian Village after Collectivization* (New York, 1994), 286–96.

143. PDA, op. 4, d. 1235, l. 17; and ÖzRMDA, f. 86, op. 1, d. 5719, l. 16.

144. RGASPI, d. 2057, l. 139. On the rumored coercion, to mention but one instance, see I. Rigin, "Pod znakom bor'by s parandzhoi," *Kommunistka*, no. 5–6 (1929), 58–59.

and water reforms or high Soviet taxes on private trade. Perhaps most interesting were the rumors that the party did not intend to stop at unveiling. One
tale alleged that the Zhenotdel wished to efface all gender differences, making
men and women indistinguishable. Muslim women besieged local activists
with questions, seeking assurances that the party would not make them wear
men's trousers in place of their customary bloomers.[145]

The second general variety of rumor promised hope for the here and now,
holding that party activists' failure to unveil Uzbek women was inevitable, and
that as a result the Soviet state would disintegrate. The reestablishment of
proper Muslim authority was only a matter of time, and a plain alternative to
Soviet power was, if not imminent, at least easy to see. Such stories noted that
the hujum was limited in scope—it did not apply to foreign nationals, for instance—and anyway was proving to be a flop.[146] These rumors often painted a
picture of party authority collapsing in other, usually distant parts of Uzbekistan. "In other cities" women were said to be reveiling, or even to be banned
from appearing in public without a paranji.[147] Akhunbabaev, the Uzbek president, supposedly was speaking out (elsewhere) against the unveiling campaign,
and his own wife and mother still wore the paranji and chachvon.[148] The
hujum, in short, was said not to be working.

Soviet power also was believed to be doomed in the face of an international
array of powerful forces aligned against it. An attack by the great powers was
allegedly imminent, an attack that would come to the aid of devout, besieged
Central Asians and would overwhelm Moscow's paltry forces. Rumors about
the international situation and the impending collapse of the Soviet Union recurred frequently. The secret police may have been especially sensitive to such
stories in view of Soviet officials' deep fears in this regard, but some Uzbeks
did look outside the USSR for deliverance. Perhaps on the theory that the
enemy of one's enemy is a friend, many hoped for and predicted an attack by
England, by Poland, even by the Afghans, Americans, and Japanese in league
against the Red Army.[149] The British allegedly were so offended by the spectacle of Russian infidels forcing Muslim women into prostitution by unveiling
that they would cause Bolshevik kofirs to be defeated on the battlefield, as had
happened in 1929 to Amanullah Khan in Afghanistan.[150] In other stories, the

145. The delegate Maksudova reported such questions to a conference at RGASPI, d. 1699, l. 97.
146. PDA, op. 4, d. 1235, ll. 7 and 17; and RGASPI, d. 1694, l. 34.
147. RGASPI, d. 1694, l. 18; and ÖzRMDA, f. 86, op. 1, d. 5885, l. 689.
148. RGASPI, d. 1682, l. 100b, and d. 2064, l. 480b.
149. For these permutations, see RGASPI, d. 1694, ll. 3 and 64, and d. 2064, ll. 260b, 29, and 490b. On the international situation and the impending collapse, see PDA, op. 4, d. 1235, ll. 17–19; RGASPI, d. 1419, l. 3; d. 1688, l. 122; d. 1692, l. 125; d. 2064, l. 25; and ÖzRMDA, f. 86, op. 1, d. 4434, ll. 270–71.
150. Amanullah was said to have been defeated because he wanted to unveil Afghan women. The shame of bare faces supposedly led England to back his ouster and to support the killing of men with unveiled wives (RGASPI, d. 2055, l. 18).

former emir was poised to return from Afghanistan to kill in vengeance all the unveiled women he found. Such a war would rescue Central Asia from the unveiling campaign, and the USSR would cease to exist.[151]

The final type of rumor also offered hope, but looked more to heaven than to England for deliverance. Those who saw the unveiling campaign as contravening the laws of shariat and morality felt confident that they could anticipate God's negative reaction to it. Allah would surely respond by destroying the enemies of Islam, and he did not need the British army. Whispered rumors in 1928–29 said that the initial stages of this heavenly retribution were already visible. God was wreaking personal vengeance on those who opposed his wishes. He sometimes struck at individuals: a bus that struck and killed a female schoolteacher and four students on their way home from a Soviet meeting, for instance, served as a sort of technological finger of God.[152] He sometimes operated on a larger scale: natural disasters, particularly earthquakes, signified deep divine displeasure with female unveiling. Rumors circulated wildly that tremors were increasing, and that they would peak around International Women's Day.[153] Like the apocalyptic visions of preachers and prophets, such rumors foresaw in the end a heavenly kingdom, a utopia made possible by divine intervention against the Bolsheviks. In Farghona province, for instance, a mullah in the village of Begovat announced that the end of the world was coming, that it would bring freedom to all Muslims, and that all unveiled women would be buried alive as punishment for what they had done.[154] Devout believers were reassured that they needed only to persevere, to hold on, and they and their way of life would prevail. Such a view reestablished and normalized a vision of social order contrary to the party's official "scientific" worldview of Marxist dialectical materialism. It thus enabled Uzbeks to continue to believe in a non-Soviet future, an outcome that facilitated further resistance in the 1930s.

The rumors that provoked such dismay among party officials thus crystallized into clearly discernible patterns. They appeared to have a life of their own, and nothing Bolshevik activists did could convince Uzbeks that such stories were false. The stories seemed so real to their listeners that in some sense they *became* true as local common sense or received wisdom, and thus helped stitch together the new nation of Uzbeks. The men and women involved did not see themselves as liars, as telling tales that were intentionally false. They were simply sharing information and passing along stories that corresponded

151. RGASPI, d. 1688, l. 124, and d. 1694, l. 125; and PDA, op. 4, d. 1235, l. 85. On the emir's alleged plans, see RGASPI, d. 2057, l. 176.

152. RGASPI, d. 1688, l. 138.

153. For examples, see RGASPI, d. 1419, l. 3; d. 1689, l. 55; d. 1694, l. 18; d. 1699, l. 119; and d. 2063, l. 185. Christians in Central Asia—mostly Russian Orthodox—also saw earthquakes as God's revenge, in this case for church closings (d. 2067, l. 71). See Adas, *Prophets of Rebellion*, 140–41; and Barkun, *Disaster and the Millennium*.

154. RGASPI, d. 1694, l. 125.

with the way they expected the world to be. Thus these rumors about the hujum illustrate the "constructive character" of memory.[155] Habit, emotion, cultural conventions, attitudes, and expectations all came together to shape such collective perceptions and to influence how such stories were remembered and retold. These stories in turn then formed the basis for a new collective memory that was fleshed out in the years that followed.

Mutual Misreading and the Creation of Conflict

By the early 1930s the picture was, from a Bolshevik perspective, dishearten-ing. Disdain toward the hujum had long since turned into antipathy. Party ac-tivists confronted veils almost anywhere they looked, and the practices of fe-male seclusion seemed only to be more common in many areas, particularly in the countryside. Party analysts were flummoxed by the near-universal resis-tance provoked by the Bolshevik campaign to unveil and liberate Uzbek women. When the Soviet state had suddenly declared a variety of everyday be-haviors to be political, it essentially created vast new spheres of potential op-position and resistance. And as traditional gender practices grew more rather than less widespread, and with veiled women at least officially exempted from coercion, such resistance became increasingly hard to confront, police, or eradicate. Customary behavior was thus made into a conscious act, a national Uzbek act, and even (in a double irony, given that Soviet power had helped create the Uzbek nation) an anti-Soviet act. While not every woman who wore a paranji did so to make a political statement, the party's unrelenting focus on the veil had invested women's dress with additional layers of significance. For many Uzbeks, Bolshevik action effectively revitalized the veil and made it worth defending, investing it with rich new meanings as both a symbol of resistance and a sign of national-cultural authenticity.

155. Allport and Postman, *Psychology of Rumor*, 49–60.

CHAPTER 6

With Friends Like These

But before leading this struggle [for women's liberation], we ourselves must be pure, like crystal, and not like the former procurator of the Beshkent raion, Shurkurov, and others. How can such people lead the struggle?

—Comrade Polianskii, speaking at a meeting of procurators and judicial workers, Bukhoro, 1941

The main reason our laboring women are kept in ignorance [*chahalatda*] is the paranji. This means that our Communists and Komsomol members must be first in line against the paranji: this struggle must be carried out by explaining it to the broad masses, and also by our own example.

Truly, most Communists, Komsomol members, and responsible workers we meet [do] so. But along with this we also see a number of Communists, Komsomol members, and responsible workers who to this day are preserving religion and its remnants [*salqitlari*], strictly observing the requirements of shariat, [not] living in the new ways within their families, and not doing any work at all against the paranji.

—An article in the Uzbek party's women's journal, *Jangi jol*, 1934

Soviet military and political control was established in Central Asia by the early 1920s, but Bolshevik activists on the ground occupied a very weak position for years thereafter. Few as they were, lacking financial resources, largely ignorant (and frequently disdainful) of local cultures, and possessing a Marxist program designed for an industrial society, these activists in many ways seemed fish out of water. Their decision in 1927 to focus party policy on an attack against the veil only accentuated many of these problems. How could Soviet authorities in Uzbekistan go about finding—or creating—sympathetic cohorts of indigenous men and women? The critical need for such cohorts, after all, had initially motivated the hujum and had helped make korenizatsiia, or "nativization," the major expression of Soviet nationality policy during the 1920s. Efforts to build local cadres, in particular, promised to create a new kind of Soviet administration, one that would be both culturally fluent and politically aware, and thus far better able to pursue to completion such policies as the hujum.

By the early 1930s these efforts appeared to bear fruit. The Communist Party of Uzbekistan (KP[b]Uz) managed to raise its proportion of members classified as ethnic Uzbeks from barely a third in 1927 to almost 60 percent in early 1932—and if one counts candidate members and Young Communists, to nearly three-quarters by July of that year.[1] But what sorts of people were these new Uzbek Communists? What motivated them to join the party? What did Bolshevism mean to them? Gregory Massell has argued that these indigenous cadres, even such top leaders as Akmal Ikramov and Faizulla Khojaev, were essentially a faceless, interchangeable mass that adjusted their words carefully, adapted to the party line quickly, and accepted Moscow's orders without audible complaint. "To all intents and purposes," Massell writes, "they were largely anonymous agents of power and change, filling temporarily some slots on the assembly line of a great social upheaval."[2]

When approached from the perspective of colonial studies, though, this group looks quite different. Scholars of empire have focused intensely on just such groups in settings around the world: indigenous elites who occupy a curious intermediate position in the structures of colonial power.[3] They were often liminal, being fully accepted by neither imperial authorities nor local populations. Yet they played a crucial mediating role between these worlds, and indeed were instrumental in bringing about their mutual transformation. Uzbek Bolsheviks personally embodied many of the complexities and contradictions of this Soviet colonial project. Appearing to have been co-opted by the metropolitan state and linked to its power, they were denounced as national traitors; yet since they were simultaneously well positioned and frequently all too eager to subvert that state and its interests in practice, these men and women give unique insight into the paradoxical functioning of the Soviet colonial system. Indeed, the later prominence of orphans and others without strong kin ties suggests continuing Soviet ambivalence about indigenous cadres that were both locally integrated and politically powerful.[4]

1. RGASPI, d. 2938, l. 23, and Gerhard Simon, *Nationalism and Policy toward the Nationalities in the Soviet Union*, trans. Karen Forster and Oswald Forster (Boulder, 1991), 32.

2. Massell, *Surrogate Proletariat*, xxxii–xxxiv.

3. Classics include Frantz Fanon, *Black Skin, White Masks* (New York, 1967); and Homi K. Bhabha, *The Location of Culture* (London, 1994). More recently, see Comaroff, *Of Revelation and Revolution*, 2:63–118; and Hall, *Civilising Subjects*, 140–73.

4. Two obvious examples are the first post-Soviet leaders of Uzbekistan and Turkmenistan: both Islam Karimov and Saparmurad Niyazov are orphans who rose through Soviet ranks.

The party and Soviet apparatus was overwhelmingly male (85–90 percent or more), but the small group of female Communists and Soviet workers occupied a unique and symbolically critical position.[5] Together these groups show the importance of looking at the Soviet system from a vantage point outside Moscow. Initiative in party policy and self-governance—even in defining something as apparently basic as what made someone a good Bolshevik—emanated not just from the Kremlin but from an ongoing interplay of Soviet authorities in Moscow and Tashkent on the one hand and local Uzbek cadres in rank-and-file and mid-level positions on the other. These cadres, in short, were not faceless ciphers. They expressed themselves in many ways, often in open contravention of party directives, and left a lasting imprint on the character of Bolshevik rule in Central Asia.

These men and women ultimately helped to define the idiosyncratic character of Stalinist politics in this part of the Soviet empire. The Central Asian location mattered, because the hujum had provided a language for Soviet identity in Uzbekistan. It enabled particular patterns of gender and family relations to serve as a shorthand synonym for political loyalty (or disloyalty) to the Soviet cause. It thus provided Bolsheviks with a more or less coherent language of authority in Central Asia and shaped the way the party related to its own members. Certain gendered practices—especially female seclusion and veiling, but also such supposed misdeeds as polygyny, underage marriage, and the payment of bride-price, or qalin—were deemed incompatible with party or Soviet membership and taken to reveal a disloyal, "anti-Soviet" character. This equivalence effectively broadened the sphere of the political in Central Asia and impelled the party to adopt ever more thorough and intrusive means of surveying and disciplining its own ranks.

Throughout the 1930s an almost continuous series of investigations and purges vetted party members on these and other questions. From the perspective of party leaders, the need for such surveillance was clear in the startling numbers of Communists found still veiling their wives and practicing polygyny. The purges of the 1930s in Central Asia, in fact, were partly justified—and to a degree impelled—by the perception that class enemies, as revealed by their veils, lurked within the Soviet apparatus. This perception was itself a product of the decision to make unveiling synonymous with Bolshevism in Central Asia. It also shows another unspoken contradiction at the heart of Soviet regional policy. Korenizatsiia stressed the need to expand indigenous cadres as quickly as possible, at almost any cost; but the hujum simultaneously created new criteria by which to assess those same cadres in Central Asia, and was used to exclude many from their newfound positions of authority. Paradoxically, then, when Soviet authorities needed every supportive body they

5. The proportion of women in the Uzbek party grew between 1926 and 1932 from less than 7 percent to almost 13 percent, but these figures include Russian as well as indigenous women. See Table 3.

could find, Uzbek Communists functioned less as a progressive vanguard than as the most carefully monitored, disciplined, and in some ways non-Soviet group in the region.

The Personal as Political: Communists and the Power of Example

When the Central Asian party organization designed the hujum in late 1926, it opted not to appeal immediately to all Uzbeks to unveil. Instead the hujum started only in a few carefully chosen regions and among members of the party and Soviet apparatus. These regions and organizations were deemed most ready and best suited, both ideologically and practically, to be the vanguard of change. Every Muslim member of the party, the Komsomol, or a Soviet organization was called upon to be a "personal example" of new, Soviet norms of family life in the struggle against "moldy old ways."[6] The hope was that the self-evident superiority and greater justice of these new forms of intimate life would be apparent to all, and the rest of Uzbek society would emulate the example of their more politically advanced brethren.

This decision to focus first on the relatively small group of Uzbeks in the party and Soviet apparatus came partly from the fact that these men (and the handful of women involved) were the most accessible to Soviet and Zhenotdel activists, and were somewhat more likely to speak or understand Russian, the language of most such activists, than was the Uzbek population at large. Party leaders assumed that these men and women were by definition the most sympathetic to Bolshevik campaigns such as the hujum. They had, after all, voluntarily affiliated with the party, so how could they not be politically sympathetic? With hindsight, other reasons could explain a decision to join the party—most obviously, the pragmatic advantages of control over state resources and institutions. But in the mid-1920s such possibilities were not the immediate top concern of party leaders. Once the Bolshevik mission in Central Asia had been reinterpreted as being fundamentally concerned with gender roles, these leaders assumed that this reorientation of party policy would be supported by rank-and-file Communists, or at least by those with the requisite levels of seniority and political consciousness.[7]

The decision to focus on Soviet and party personnel led to a stream of resolutions, directives, and exhortations in 1927 and afterward aimed at Uzbek Communists. Front-page editorials trumpeted, "Communist, be an example!"[8] Party members were ordered to be moral exemplars in every possible way: no drinking, bribe-taking, or visiting of prostitutes could be counte-

---

6. S. Liubimova, "Uroki 'nastupleniia,'" *Antireligioznik*, no. 2 (1928), 23.

7. Some analysts argued that party members who did not observe Soviet norms of women's liberation tended to be candidate rather than full members (PDA, op. 3, d. 1548, l. 30).

8. "Kommunist, bud' primerom!" *Sem' dnei*, 7 Jan. 1927, 1.

nanced, for example.[9] Their role in remaking Uzbek everyday culture was particularly important: by unveiling their wives and observing new Bolshevik rather than old Muslim rituals of family life (*oktiabriny* and Red weddings, for example, not religious ceremonies to mark circumcisions, weddings, or funerals), they would inspire relatives, friends, and neighbors to follow their example.[10] It was crucial, explained a Sredazbiuro circular of January 1927, that individual Communists and Komsomol members lead the way:

> Until Communists themselves, in their own bands, beginning with their own families, become pioneers and fighters for the real liberation of women, we will not overcome the byt survivals of the masses. . . .
>
> The overcoming of superstitions in everyday life, the liquidation of women's seclusion and inequality in the party ranks will be a huge victory in overcoming the ignorance and backwardness of the broad mass of the population.
>
> The example of 25,000 members and candidate members of the party will inspire hundreds of thousands of followers from the nonparty masses.[11]

Communists were not to wait for others to act, but had to play "the decisive role in this struggle" through "personal example." Uzbek Bolsheviks in Farghona heard in 1927 that they faced "shame" if the nonparty masses unveiled first.[12] In other regions, such as Surkhondaryo, the hujum was aimed *only* at Communists, explicitly leaving all other social groups alone, at least for the time being.[13]

This approach put the small group of indigenous Soviet and party personnel in a tricky and in some ways impossible position. In 1926 the average party cell was responsible for twenty-five villages, an enormous number; even by mid-1932, the Uzbek party had barely 80,000 members, concentrated mostly in the cities and representing roughly 1.5 percent of the five million people who lived in the Uzbek SSR.[14] Vastly outnumbered by their noncommunist neighbors,

---

9. Drinking was criticized at PDA, op. 4, d. 1235, ll. 89–92; RGASPI, d. 1214, ll. 99, 117, and 149. On bribery and corruption, see PDA, op. 4, d. 1235, ll. 84–87; and ÖzRMDA, f. 9, op. 1, d. 3397, l. 113, and f. 86, op. 1, d. 5719, l. 16. Visits to prostitutes came under fire at RGASPI, d. 1242, l. 208, and d. 1245, l. 560b.

10. See PDA, op. 3, d. 1598, ll. 14–17; RGASPI, d. 1212, l. 141; and Astapovich, *Velikii Oktiabr'*, 378–79. These Soviet ceremonies did occur but they were not common, and their main distinguishing feature was the lack of religious ritual. A Red wedding could be simply a wedding without bride-price or a religious ceremony (RGASPI, d. 2071, l. 26).

11. RGASPI, d. 1210, l. 33.

12. RGASPI, d. 1033, l. 11.

13. ÖzRMDA, f. 737, op. 1, d. 185, l. 209. In later years the scope was broadened beyond the party.

14. RGASPI, d. 775, l. 9, and d. 2938, l. 23. The Uzbek party had 80,206 members on 1 July 1932. This figure included European as well as indigenous Communists. Fewer than half were full members; most were candidate members and Komsomol'tsy.

these party workers were caught, as one put it, "between two fires."[15] On the one hand, the party demanded they unveil their wives, sisters, mothers, and daughters—a step that, as some pointed out, had not been mentioned when they signed up for a party card.[16] But if they did as the party asked, they faced a negative reaction from most of their friends and neighbors—the very people whom their example was supposed to inspire. Internal party documents list such fears expressed by rank-and-file Bolsheviks, ranging from anxiety about ostracism to worry about death threats.[17] They offered anguished protests that an unveiling campaign would not inspire the wider populace, but would only inflame it further against Soviet power. These local reports depict a society divided into two hostile camps—Communists and Komsomol members on one side, everyone else on the other—with no links between them. One early reaction to the hujum reported among nonparty Uzbeks, indeed, was the exclamation, "Thanks be to Allah that we are not Communists!"[18]

Such appeals by the rank and file, however, did little to move party leaders in Tashkent, who continued to say that the power of example would carry the day, and to those who complained they retorted that the path to women's liberation might be bloody, but it was nonetheless essential.[19] If lower-level Communists were reluctant to participate, party leaders in the Sredazbiuro and the upper reaches of the Uzbek republican hierarchy said, they were willing to use "the strictest measures" to force them to do so.[20] Recalcitrant Soviet and party officials faced ultimatums and immediate deadlines: the president of one district executive committee was given twenty-four hours to unveil his wife.[21] Party leaders declared themselves untroubled by such pressure within party ranks, explaining that the wider population would never unveil unless "responsible workers" did so first, and contending that the continuing presence of superstitious elements in the party ran the risk of discrediting its overall program.[22]

At a deeper level, the insistence on immediate, complete unveiling among party and Soviet cadres rested on the judgment—central to the hujum—that the political level and affiliation of an Uzbek man or woman emerged from and was expressed most clearly in the texture of his or her daily life. It was thus simply "not loyal" for a Communist not to unveil his wife.[23] As early as

15. PDA(K), op. 3, d. 1168, ll. 34–35.
16. RGASPI, d. 1247, l. 219.
17. See RGASPI, d. 1214, ll. 27, 31–32, 69, 96, 100, and 144.
18. RGASPI, d. 1211, l. 9. On two hostile camps, see ÖzRMDA, f. 86, op. 2, d. 92, ll. 28–30. Another report from 1929, in which "all peasants" are reported to "detest Communists," is at RGASPI, d. 2072, l. 22.
19. RGASPI, d. 1685, ll. 97–99.
20. RGASPI, d. 1715, l. 27.
21. RGASPI, d. 1211, l. 210.
22. A. Kostygin, "Zadachi antireligioznoi raboty sredi zhenshchin," *Antireligioznik*, no. 4 (1929), 57; *Sredneaziatskoe 6-e kraevogo soveshchanie rabotnikov sredi zhenshchin* (Tashkent, 1928), ii; and RGASPI, d. 1196, l. 15.
23. RGASPI, d. 1694, l. 45.

January 1927, a party circular had declared that "there is no place in the party for wavering Communists" while the party was on the verge of complete victory in women's liberation.[24] From here it was only a short step to say, as the Third Uzbek Party Congress did that November, that female seclusion was "incompatible" with party membership.[25] Such declarations opened the possibility of expelling from the party those who refused to carry out a hujum within their families—of using the ostensibly private sphere of family life as a benchmark by which to purify Bolshevik ranks. Veils were extremely useful in this regard: they unmasked those "overtly hostile" to Soviet power, especially those who stood in opposition "from beneath the cover of a party card." (Note the metaphorical interplay between various kinds of covering and uncovering.) As an internal report put it in the spring of 1927, the time had come for new tactics, for a move away from persuasion and toward "isolating the party from those who are ideologically alien to [it], those who, after almost ten years of Soviet power, have not been able to reeducate themselves."[26]

Of course, this focus on forcing Uzbek Communists to unveil their wives again gave rise to troubling questions of women's agency. By treating the way a woman dressed as transparently revelatory of her husband's (or brother's, son's, or father's) social and political views, this approach effectively erased women as actors in the party's internal narrative of liberation. In a campaign purporting to be about personal emancipation this erasure may appear curious, but few Communists or even Zhenotdel workers objected on such grounds, since virtually all Muslim women were presumed to welcome Soviet liberation.[27] Party members were thus pressured to use any means necessary to unveil their wives. Some husbands threatened divorce (which could leave a woman penniless, living in the street), others used beatings, and others ripped paranjis off by force, provoking shrieks, tears, and sometimes injuries.[28] But, as one report asked, if a Communist is unable to induce his own wife to unveil, how can he possibly lead the masses toward socialism?[29]

Bolshevizing the Party: Class, Gender, and Political Loyalty

Veils and their absence thus emerged out of the hujum as a currency of loyalty in Central Asia. The language of gender and family relations became a lasting shorthand for political outlook. The question whether someone was a good

24. RGASPI, d. 1210, l. 33.

25. This decision, which was widely cited and helped lead to the "verification" (proverka) of party rolls discussed below, is quoted at ÖzRMDA, f. 737, op. 1, d. 419, l. 38.

26. These two sentences are from PDA, op. 3, d. 1598, ll. 37–38.

27. Such objections were raised at RGASPI, d. 1197, l. 45; d. 1211, l. 10; and d. 2056, l. 190; ÖzRMDA, f. 837, op. 3, d. 150, l. 177; PDA, op. 2, d. 1410, ll. 23–24; and S. Smidovich, "Iz byta sem'i kommunista," Kommunistka, no. 6 (1928), 28–29.

28. See PDA, op. 3, d. 1545, l. 16; and RGASPI, d. 1199, ll. 83 and 200; d. 1203, l. 52; d. 1214, ll. 17 and 40; d. 1240, l. 11; and d. 1692, l. 100.

29. ÖzRMDA, f. 837, op. 3, d. 150, l. 177.

Communist could be answered by looking at his or her behavior at home, in the intimate space of the family, and on the street, in the everyday social space of the mahalla. It was not the only measure, as Communists were also evaluated according to more standard Soviet criteria: their class position, level of religious observance, knowledge of Marxist-Leninist theory, even their level of literacy. But the distinctive features of Central Asian society—only a minuscule number of indigenous proletarians, few with any knowledge of Marx, living in a cultural framework seen as deeply influenced by religious concerns, and even high officials with only rudimentary reading and writing skills—militated against using such factors alone.[30] Several years of effort, for example, succeeded in reducing the overall illiteracy rate within the Uzbek party only from 25.8 percent in 1926 to 24.9 percent in 1932.[31] The Central Asian party needed a way to locate other proofs of an individual's attitude toward Soviet power. This was a task for which questions of everyday culture and family life proved eminently suited.

The quotidian practices of the Uzbek family thus came to be read as a text that revealed its authors' attitude toward Soviet power. This text had many facets: participating in neighborhood and religious feasts (töy); observing Muslim holidays (Ramadan, Navröz); showing an affinity for local groups or clans; arranging or attending ritual circumcisions—any such acts had negative implications for a Communist's standing in the party. But veils in particular were used as an external, visible signifier of a woman's (and her family's) otherwise internal and hidden sympathies. A refusal to observe Soviet norms of unveiling, monogamy, and equality marked a family as anti-Soviet, as standing in league with class enemies, or even as themselves being class enemies in disguise.[32] Conversely, unveiled women were almost by definition loyal. They could and did cite the date on which they cast off their paranji as a totem of entry into the Soviet camp; it served as an emblem that warded off nearly any criticism.[33]

30. For an example of purging along other criteria, see the OGPU discussion of Uzbek "national chauvinism" at RGASPI, f. 81, op. 3, d. 127, ll. 205–33. (Thanks to Terry Martin for this document.) In 1926, 13 percent of party members were listed as "officially [religious] believers" at f. 62, op. 2, d. 775, l. 19. Although the sources merit caution, Akhunbabaev was reported illiterate in 1923 and to have only shaky Russian skills in 1929. See Ella K. Maillart, *Turkestan Solo: One Woman's Expedition from the Tien Shan to the Kizil Kum* (London, 1938), 191–92; and Strong, *Red Star in Samarkand*, 108–9, who makes her view clear when she discusses the "difficult" task of "mak[ing] intelligent Marxians out of Central Asians" (226).

31. RGASPI, d. 775, l.9, and d. 2938, l. 23. These figures include the entire Uzbek party, both European and Muslim Communists. Admittedly, they stretch over a period in which total membership was expanding quickly, and the proportion of indigenous Communists was growing even more rapidly.

32. See RGASPI, d. 2051, ll. 136–37; ÖzRMDA, f. 6, op. 2, d. 462, l. 34; and D. I. Manzhara, "Chto pokazala chistka partii," *PV*, 7 Mar. 1930.

33. The dates provided were fluid and served clear political purposes. In later decades, many women insisted they had unveiled before 1927 (in 1925, 1924, even 1919) to stake their claim to status as a heroic pioneer. One woman said she was moved to unveil upon hearing the news of Lenin's death in 1924 (O. Usmanov, "Zhenshchiny-aktivistki," *PV*, 22 Nov. 1940).

Regional politics thus became simultaneously broader and more intimate as party writers sought to link the languages of Uzbek gender practices and Soviet class politics. One resolution of late 1928 declared, "Our attack on the old ways of daily life, on the slavery of women, is one of the elements of our general attack on the bois and kulaks, on all of the capitalist and feudal elements of the city and village."[34] The veil also came to be caught up in local expressions of Kremlin power struggles. As Stalin overcame his rivals for supreme party authority in the late 1920s, for example, several resolutions depicted the continuing presence of the paranji within party ranks as a threat from the Right, a petty bourgeois deviation more dangerous than open opposition.[35] One writer argued that the Uzbek party was afflicted with a "secret sickness": many Communists showed signs of "feudal-bourgeois ideology" by refusing to participate in women's liberation work.[36]

Just as the hujum was conceived as an expression of the class struggle in Central Asia carried out through gender roles, the party now aimed to unmask the class enemies lurking within its ranks by seeking out gender malfeasance. One man who declared himself against the hujum was—apparently on that basis alone—deemed a boi and thus a class enemy of Soviet power.[37] In Uzbekistan, where class identities (in Soviet terms) were often vague or contradictory, party investigators argued that social groups were demarcated by both class and gender in ways that underpinned and mutually reinforced one another. Specific gendered behaviors were thus a form of class in practice, and the simplest way to find class enemies was to look for opposition to the hujum. When a group of party and Soviet workers in Kassan, a village near Andijon, in mid-1927 declared their opposition to the unveiling campaign, a classified GPU report focused on identifying and categorizing the group's members. Although all served as "responsible workers" (otvetrabotniki) in the party or Soviet apparatus, one was now identified as a "fervent nationalist," another as "the son of a famous boi who earlier had served as an imam," another as a boi who lost land in the Soviet land reform, and yet another as the brother of a man exiled from Uzbekistan "as a socially dangerous element." It went on: "All of this group declared categorically that they would not unveil their wives. This group is supported by the bois, clergy, and the well-to-do element of Kassan."[38] Through such reports Soviet writers created a new political language in which class identities flowed partly from one's view of gender relations.

The discovery of antihujum sentiment within the party, combined with this equation of veils with political disloyalty, gave rise after 1927 to increasing

34. RGASPI, d. 1685, l. 88.
35. I. Zelenskii, "V bor'be za raskreposhchenie zhenshchin," Za partiiu, no. 4 (1927), 42; and RGASPI, d. 2055, l. 36, and d. 2063, l. 11.
36. RGASPI, d. 1247, ll. 21–22.
37. RGASPI, d. 1240, l. 100b.
38. RGASPI, d. 1214, l. 127.

calls for a "Bolshevization of the party."[39] However odd this sounded—was the party not, by definition, Bolshevik?—it rested on the belief that many, even most Central Asian Bolsheviks did not deserve such a label. One investigator alleged in 1927 that 99 percent of the party organization in Vabkent (near Bukhoro) was made up of "alien elements"; others contended that ethnically Uzbek party members hoped to create an "Islamized communism."[40] Proof lay largely in Uzbek Communists' gender practices: mistreatment of women revealed those who had only "by chance" found their way into the party.[41]

Bolshevism was seen as a deep, essential identity, not something captured by mere possession of a party card. True Bolsheviks expressed themselves not only by public political declarations but also in the ongoing fabric of daily life, and from this perspective Uzbek Communists fell short. Anxious officials in Tashkent worried throughout the 1930s that the continuing presence of veils and seclusion within party ranks not only diluted the Bolshevik message of liberation but polluted those most responsible for carrying it out. They declared the need to purify the party through its family life and gender relations, an effort in which a party or Komsomol card would offer no protection.[42] This step was meant to weed out the alien elements that had latched onto the party, and involved both a strict evaluation of new applicants and a careful examination of existing members.[43] As the Zhenotdel leader Mariia Muratova declared again in 1930, the veil was simply incompatible with party membership, and any Communist who disagreed faced expulsion:

> . . . it is incompatible [*nesovmestimo*] for a party member to be in the party and Komsomol if his wife, sister, or mother is veiled. Every Communist must be required to fulfill this directive. And to that Communist who resists, who does not want to carry out this party directive, who wants [to preserve] the remnants of feudal relations and seclusion, to that Communist and Komsomol member [we say]: there is no place [for you] in the party and Komsomol.[44]

Out of the campaign to end female seclusion, then, gender practices emerged as a principal language of Bolshevism in Uzbekistan.

The adoption of everyday cultural practices as a shorthand for political

---

39. See, for example, RGASPI, d. 1239, l. 27, and *Rezoliutsii III partiinogo kurultaia* (Samarqand, 1927), 20.

40. The report from Vabkent is at RGASPI, d. 1202, l. 5. On "Islamized communism," see Ramzi, "Metody antireligioznoi raboty sredi musul'manskogo naseleniia," *PV,* 5 Dec. 1927; or Critchlow, *Nationalism in Uzbekistan,* 172.

41. ÖzRMDA, f. 86, op. 10, d. 634, l. 246.

42. See such a declaration from 1935 at *PSTZhMUz,* 40.

43. RGASPI, d. 2057, l. 37, and d. 2064, l. 26.

44. ÖzRMDA, f. 9, op. 1, d. 3427, l. 459. Other declarations of this point were made earlier, and appeared in large numbers starting in 1928. See RGASPI, d. 1695, l. 98.

loyalty had important consequences. Most obviously, it vastly expanded the sphere of potential disloyalty and made the party's task much more difficult. Since customary practices within the home could now be read as political opposition, party and secret police investigators had to be far more intrusive to vet Uzbek men and women as "loyal." The Uzbek party, like others in Central Asia, was impelled to carry out a series of investigations and house-cleanings throughout the late 1920s and 1930s, exercises that ultimately spiraled almost out of control. They began with the *proverka,* or "verification," of 1928–29.

This proverka, the first sustained practical effort to apply gender relations and family life as a principal criterion for cleansing the Uzbek party, required a major outlay of time and resources and represented a high priority for party leaders.[45] In some ways it set the stage and provided a language for the purges that followed in the 1930s. Communists were told in February and March 1928 that each of them faced an individual verification by party investigators, so now more than ever they must be examples to their friends, relatives, and neighbors in matters of women's liberation.[46] Failure to do so would reveal them as class-alien elements, criminal, corrupt, and immoral; as supporters of class enemies now locked into a hidden struggle against Soviet power, and thus deserving of expulsion from party ranks.[47] Top Bolshevik leaders helped frame the campaign, showing Moscow's interest in these questions: Emel'ian Iaroslavskii, head of the all-Soviet executive bureau of the Union of Atheists and a member of the party's Central Control Commission presidium, noted in a speech of 1929 that the campaign applied to rank-and-file members as well as their superiors. He explained its aims:

> In the future we will be checking up on the ranks of our party. . . . [They] must be cleansed of all alien elements; of the corrupted, the bureaucratized, [those who have] attached themselves [to us], the ideologically alien. Is it possible to consider a person ideologically suited to be a Communist [if he] locks up his wife, holds her under the paranji, forbids her to go to meetings; [if he] teaches his children in the Islamic school [madrasa]; [if he] relies in his work on some mullah or other—really, can

45. See RGASPI, d. 1691, ll. 18–23 and 27–28; "O rezul'tatakh proverki rukovodiashchikh kadrov i o khode chistki partii v Srednei Azii," *PV,* 3 Oct. 1929; and "Ferganskie bai," *PV,* 6 Oct. 1929. Similar campaigns were carried out elsewhere in Central Asia: see the Turkmen effort described at ÖzRMDA, f. 6, op. 2, d. 462, ll. 133–34; the Kyrgyz campaign at RGASPI, dd. 1707–8; or S. Zalesov, "Zhenshchina v bytu otvetstvennykh rabotnikov Kirgizii," *Za partiiu,* no. 5 (9) (1928), 88–90.

46. "Proverim direktivy partii o raskreposhchenii zhenshchin: Za usilennuiu proverku," *PV,* 1 Mar. 1928. The official text launching the campaign, over Zelenskii's signature, was published at "O proverke vypolneniia direktiv po raskreposhcheniiu zhenshchin partaktivom osnovnykh natsional'nostei," *PV,* 1 Mar. 1928.

47. See RGASPI, d. 1522, ll. 35–44, and d. 2051, ll. 136–37; and "8 marta i proverka partiinogo aktiva," *PV,* 9 Feb. 1928.

we consider such a person our own [*rodnyi*], a Leninist Bolshevik? It would be better for us to have fewer people in the party, but to have party members who accept the whole of our program, and not just parts [of it]. . . . We will need to check up on our party's ranks in this way, particularly in the national organizations of the East. A party member may pay his membership dues very well, he may attend meetings punctually, but we need to ask him, to verify, how he relates to his wife, how he relates to his sister, to his children. Does he support any of the forms of social-byt oppression that hinder us from carrying out our socialist measures? We need to check up on him like this, and not only from the point of view of whether he pays his membership dues.[48]

The proverka, then, was to be the leading edge of a general purge in which a crucial factor was the veiled or unveiled status of the females in a Communist man's family and the character of the family life they lived.[49] (A contemporaneous verification of female Communists also was under way, but it raised a different set of issues, as we shall see.)[50]

The party worked to cleanse and purify its ranks through both surveillance and discipline. Central party organizations first dispatched teams of investigators to conduct a member-by-member evaluation to single out Communists who transgressed Soviet norms of gender relations and family life.[51] A brigade sent to investigate the rural district of Chash-Tepe, for example, concluded:

> The party *aktiv* in all of the villages have a good attitude toward issues of women's liberation, and are the first to unveil their wives. Two rank-and-file party members, [however,] have not unveiled and do not wish to unveil their wives: Nizametdinhoja Turakhojaev, party card #827319, and Raskhulla Mukhammadjonov, party card #827320. They have not unveiled their wives, and to the cell's questions about why they have not unveiled, they answer, "We ourselves will know when to unveil [our wives]."[52]

Once the hujum had politicized the most intimate details of their home lives, Uzbek members of the party and Soviet apparatus found few spaces that,

48. Emel'ian Iaroslavskii, "Reshitel'nee udarim po bytovym perezhitkam," *Kommunistka*, no. 1 (1929), 30–31.

49. RGASPI, d. 2057, l. 36.

50. K. Mezhol', "Predvaritel'nye itogi proverki kommunistok," *Kommunistka*, no. 20 (1929), 3–7.

51. For general plans for these investigations, see RGASPI, d. 1204, ll. 2–30b; and ÖzRMDA, f. 9, op. 1, d. 3371, l. 105. For examples in practice, see RGASPI, d. 1242, ll. 107–13; d. 1250, ll. 41–42 and 105–8; d. 2071, ll. 34–37; and d. 2082, l. 114–140b; ÖzRMDA, f. 9, op. 1, d. 3392, l. 248–480b; and f. 245, op. 1, d. 222, ll. 119–200b; and especially PDA, op. 4, d. 1235, ll. 85–90; and op. 5, d. 852, ll. 38–44.

52. PDA, op. 3, d. 1545, ll. 16–17. The aktiv included sympathizers—those who cooperated with and worked alongside local Communists.

Figure 19. Kolkhoz family, Samarqand province, 1932. Note the Russian samovar and chairs. (Courtesy ÖzRKFFHMDA.)

in theory at least, were not subject to the state's gaze of information gathering, analysis, and enforcement. The proverka empowered—and indeed encouraged—investigators from the OGPU and control commissions to ask for personal details of each Communist's family and social life. Some party members were grilled about their drinking habits.[53] Others were photographed in mixed company, eating meals or relaxing at home, as shown in Figure 19: such images were meant to display model behavior for other Uzbeks in new, "European" domestic spaces. But investigators focused especially on how Uzbek men interacted with their wives and female relatives. Were these women veiled, secluded, and illiterate, or did they lead a productive, constructive, Soviet-style social life? It was difficult to avoid these investigations: some Uzbeks left the party voluntarily to protest the hujum, but even so were interrogated afterward by control commissions.[54]

The confidential reports of these investigations show the sorts of information considered most valuable in deciding whom to purge. They illustrate in particular the party's steady focus on the political meanings of family life. To take just one example, a confidential protocol from Osh, written in March

53. See the interrogation at RGASPI, d. 1248, l. 50–500b.
54. RGASPI, d. 1242, l. 155, and d. 1691, l. 20.

1928 at the start of the proverka, listed party members by name, nationality, position, and party standing ("Hamidjon Eshankhanov, Uzbek, president of local peasant union party committee in Osh. Party member since 1918, poor peasant, no party reprimands"). It then carefully noted the character of each member's home life ("Married since 1922, married in the old [religious] way, wife illiterate, has a child, [wife is] a member of peasant union [but] does no work for them at all"). The investigating commission's decision was then recorded ("Because of the religious customs in his family life, Comrade Esh-ankhanov is issued a warning. [He is] directed to strengthen the Communist influence on his family life and to liquidate his wife's illiteracy").[55]

By combining the results of many such investigations, party officials hoped to gain an accurate portrait of the Uzbek party, and through it, perhaps, of Uzbek society at large. They compiled statistics on women's liberation among Communists and Komsomol members.[56] They prepared long lists of unveiled women, including nearly a dozen "identifying characteristics" both to specify the woman in question and to aid analysts who wanted to understand why some unveiled and others did not.[57] More ominously, party and police investi-gators also prepared lists of *veiled* women. These lists likewise provided de-tailed information about specific women, but here served to provide activists with leverage over veiled (or reveiled) Communist women and wives. One re-port, for instance, noted that a veiled woman received a Soviet pension; in other words, pressure could be brought to bear by threatening to withhold financial support.[58]

The party's control commissions did not shy away from bad news.[59] In fact, they were directed to seek out scurrilous details about the everyday behavior of Uzbek men in the party. (Female Communists usually were exempted from this mud slinging.) The commissions themselves sometimes came under fire, mostly for insufficient zeal: a lack of prosecutions was assumed to show a commission's failure, not good news about local Communists' byt practices.[60] Hence the commissions tried to elicit as many accusations as possible. Individ-ual Bolsheviks were obligated to report byt misconduct—an obligation that was often ignored but occasionally enforced. In one case, two Communists faced party discipline for not reporting a friend who had carried out a ritual circumcision of his newborn son and kept his wife veiled.[61] No doubt the deci-

55. RGASPI, d. 1691, ll. 27–28. Similar reports are throughout dd. 1690, 1691, and 1694.
56. RGASPI, d. 1247, l. 113; d. 1520, l. 182; and PDA, op. 3, d. 1548, l. 80.
57. The form used to compile such data is at RGASPI, d. 1247, l. 46. For examples of lists, see d. 1247, ll. 35–37; d. 1250, ll. 21–26, 31, 46, 61, 70–83, and 87–90; and d. 1688, l. 165.
58. RGASPI, d. 1688, l. 197; d. 1690, l. 75; d. 1692, l. 120; and d. 1704, ll. 80–83.
59. On these commissions, see PDA, op. 3, d. 1560, ll. 60–61 and 342–44, and op. 9, d. 975, ll. 42–44.
60. RGASPI, d. 1197, l. 65, and d. 1242, l. 127.
61. RGASPI, d. 1211, l. 199. On the obligation to report violations, see *Rezoliutsii Uzbek-skogo Soveshchaniia rabotnikov sredi rabotnits i dekhkanok* (Tashkent, 1929), 3, and RGASPI, d. 1204, l. 20b.

sion to publish appeals for any and all "compromising materials" (*kompro-metiruiushchie materially*) on Communists proved more successful in generating leads, but the complaints that resulted must have served many agendas (discrediting or removing rivals, to name only one).[62]

Obviously these problems influenced the picture that emerged from the control commissions' reports, so caution is in order when one interprets the results. Other factors, however, worked in the opposite direction to minimize the number of accusations. And while taken alone these reports are not conclusive about the actual state of everyday conduct in the party, they do illuminate the party's perception of that state. It was this perception that partly impelled the further purges during the 1930s: the sense that the Uzbek party was deeply hostile to the hujum and Soviet women's liberation. There were exceptions, but many Communists declared open opposition to the unveiling campaign; others were "unmasked" as organizers of behind-the-scenes resistance to it. A potpourri of noncommunist attitudes was turned up, revealing party members who threatened or beat women who wished to unveil; harassed Zhenotdel activists; practiced polygyny, bride-price, and underage marriage; and took sexual advantage of—even raped and murdered—unveiled schoolgirls, women, and activists. Control commission investigators announced that they had defined a new category of crime: insults suffered by unveiled women at the hands of Soviet and party workers.[63] Further, the vast majority of Uzbek Bolsheviks stood accused of hindering party efforts by inaction. Even those Communists who had unveiled their wives, investigators wrote, "stand to the side" when called upon to work for women's liberation, and this passivity represented a major threat to the hujum's continued success.[64]

The fundamental problem from the perspective of party and Zhenotdel leaders was that, as a group, Uzbek Communists had not internalized Soviet norms of family life, and in fact seemed little different from their compatriots outside the party. Soviet colonialism, after all, was distinctive in wanting to *overcome* colonial difference and subordination, to erase it and build a new, modern, anti-imperial kind of empire. The indigenous Soviet elite (along with the group of unveiled women) was supposed to be the crucial starting point in this effort, to be the thin edge of a wedge of sociocultural transformation. Thus it was all the more disconcerting when this group appeared not to be changing, but rather to be masking their sympathy for the old ways and simply using state resources for their own ends. It was particularly damning that Uzbek Communists seemed mostly uninterested in the requisite inner transformation (of political outlook, personal consciousness, and civilizational level) that lay at the heart of this Soviet project. Such reluctance suggested that non-

---

62. One such advertisement is in *PV*, 19 Dec. 1929.

63. RGASPI, d. 1694, l. 15. The first section of this paragraph is drawn from reports already cited.

64. On this passivity, see RGASPI, d. 1211, l. 198, and d. 1691, l. 23.

Soviet affiliations, loyalties, identities, and outlooks ran far deeper than the strategists of the hujum had assumed.

Most frustrating and alarming of all was the frequency with which Communist wives and even some female Communists continued to wear the paranji and chachvon.[65] When waves of reveiling swept through Uzbekistan each year after celebratory veil-burnings on International Women's Day, Communists led the way. In 1929 women's activists complained that only 8 women out of 1,000 remained unveiled in Sharikhan, a rural district outside Andijon, once local party members reveiled their wives.[66] *This* power of example, of course, was not what party leaders had intended, although it did allow them (reassuringly) to blame scapegoats at the local level. Top party leaders concluded that many rank-and-file Uzbek Bolsheviks had shown themselves to be more Uzbek than Bolshevik: their primary loyalty belonged to Uzbek Muslim culture rather than to party directives to lead a hujum against it. The unsettling pattern of antihujum sentiment turned up by this proverka marked these Communists as disloyal and thus not worthy of party membership. At this point party surveillance ended and discipline began.

Soviet investigators perceived veiling, polygyny, and the other forms of "feudal-boi" relations with women to be a mass problem within the Uzbek party, and hundreds of Communists were punished accordingly.[67] Members of the control commissions, secret police officers, and judges and prosecutors brought to bear a range of sanctions: from a confidential suggestion that a comrade improve his ways to public humiliation, expulsion from the party, even criminal prosecution. For some forms of misconduct—as in the case of the man who invited only attractive women to Soviet meetings—the exact punishment is unspecified in the archival record.[68] Other sanctions reached outside the party proper: one directive of 1928 barred Communists with veiled wives from standing for election to Soviet posts.[69] Such wide latitude gave the commissions flexibility in responding to individual investigations. Depending on the seriousness of a violation—or the political connections of the accused—certain acts could be deemed a true political threat, while others (albeit not many) might warrant only a slap on the wrist.

Party discipline thus took many shapes, the two most significant of which were expulsion and shame. The proverka identified people whose very presence discredited the Soviet cause and unceremoniously expelled them, offering

65. See RGASPI, d. 1690, ll. 13–14, and d. 1693, l. 25.
66. RGASPI, d. 2051, l. 137.
67. One estimate is that the proverka of 1928–29 considered 34,801 Central Asian party members, of whom 5,667 faced disciplinary sanctions. Of these, 761, or 13.4 percent, were disciplined for reasons related to the women's liberation campaign (ÖzRMDA, f. 6, op. 2, d. 462, l. 34; and Manzhara, "Chto pokazala chistka partii," 2). This proportion appears low in comparison with other figures related below.
68. RGASPI, d. 1214, l. 1150b.
69. ÖzRMDA, f. 9, op. 1, d. 3427, l. 460.

a moral lesson to other Communists on the need to observe party directives and unveil their wives.[70] Similar steps were taken in the Uzbek Soviet and trade union organizations. Sometimes these individuals were referred to the criminal courts for prosecution: one Nizamutdin Khojaev, for instance, was expelled from the party and then put on trial for speaking out against the hujum.[71] In the end roughly one in ten Uzbek Communists overall lost his party card in this way during the proverka of 1928–29; in some places the figure was much higher.[72]

Public shame also was used against Communists who refused to unveil their wives, or who forbade them to attend schools or public meetings. Party cells and local committees harangued those who had not lived up to their Bolshevik obligations. The judgment of comrades and the glare of publicity were meant both to embarrass offenders and to inspire others to do what was necessary to avoid such humiliation. To reach a larger audience, these local episodes were then recounted in newspaper articles, editorials, even newsreels that discussed the progress and findings of the proverka. Although the underlying concept was in some ways misguided—during this period shame could be brought to bear more effectively within the mahalla to force a woman *to* veil—it certainly had a political impact. It may also have had a personal effect, especially among higher-ranking party officials. First Secretary Akmal Ikramov argued that investigators should focus on making examples of high-ranking Communists who kept their wives secluded. If a people's commissar or the head of the All-Uzbek Ispolkom were to be publicly humiliated and expelled, Ikramov reasoned, the public would take notice and the hujum would proceed more rapidly. He did not, however, suggest any specific individuals who deserved to be singled out.[73]

On a Pedestal or in a Glass House? Female Communists in the Spotlight

Most of the party's efforts to survey and discipline its members' family lives rested on the unstated assumption that Uzbek Communists were men. The

70. RGASPI, d. 2057, l. 36. On accusations of discrediting the party, see PDA, op. 3, d. 1560, l. 347.

71. RGASPI, d. 1211, ll. 198–99; d. 1240, l. 110b; and d. 1250, l. 55. On the unions, see d. 1238, l. 69; d. 1681, l. 1030b; and d. 1682, l. 104.

72. Approximately 10 percent of the Communists in Farghona, Samarqand, and Qöqon were expelled for these reasons, but at least one district lost as much as 70 percent of its membership in this proverka (albeit not only for reasons related to women's liberation). While such statistics are always open to doubt, one account estimated that 7 percent of the Uzbek party were expelled for violating Soviet norms of women's liberation, and that another 6 percent were expelled for their religious customs, some of which may have related to gender issues (ÖzRMDA, f. 86, op. 2, d. 27, l. 320b; RGASPI, d. 1691, l. 22, and d. 1713, l. 124; and A. Mitrofanov, "K itogam partchistki v natsrespublikakh i oblastiakh," *Revoliutsiia i natsional'nosti*, no. 1 [1930], 32, and no. 2 [1930], 36–37).

73. PDA, op. 4, d. 1208, ll. 37–38. For a sample newsreel, see the Osh aktiv undergoing a proverka on questions of women's liberation in 1929 (RGAKFD 2059 [Khronika No. 36/215]).

proverka essentially asked whether a Communist was trustworthy by looking at how he treated his female relatives. Had he unveiled his wife? Did he permit her to attend school, work outside the home, and take part in Soviet activities? Quite apart from the issues of female agency—if he acted to unveil his wife, did her wishes matter?—this approach ignored the real possibility that a Communist or a Soviet worker could be female.[74]

The vast majority of Central Asian Communists were indeed men, and the proportion grew even larger if Russian and other non-Muslim party members were excluded.[75] Yet as Table 3 shows, a few Uzbek women—around 3,500 by the mid-1930s, or perhaps 0.2 percent of the indigenous female population—did join the party. For political reasons, they wielded a symbolic importance completely out of proportion to these tiny numbers; their stories were told in a wide variety of Soviet accounts, usually in a heroic or hagiographical vein.[76] Some of these women became Communists as the result of diligent Soviet efforts, such as the discussion circles that met at women's clubs and the many educational, literacy, and job-training programs that sought to prepare new Soviet cadres.[77] Others were the wives, sisters, or daughters of male party members. Still others, as already noted, came from socially marginal positions: widows, orphans, and runaways who found shelter and protection in Soviet institutions, and thus stood outside powerful local kin networks.

However they came to the Soviet camp, this small group of Uzbek female activists and Communists occupied a fascinating, anomalous, and in some ways contradictory position. On the one hand, their gender marked them as privileged within the Soviet order, and their unveiled faces provided an almost unassailable degree of political protection. (See Figure 20.) They enjoyed a special status because of their symbolic importance as personal exemplars of Soviet liberation and also because they represented a unique solution to the party's problems in Central Asia. Uzbek men could provide an indigenous face for Soviet rule (as required by korenizatsiia), but as a group they consistently violated the norms of women's liberation (as required by the hujum). Uzbek women appeared to avoid this contradiction: they both personally embodied the promise of the hujum and served the goals of korenizatsiia. In the world of the hujum, then, Uzbek women benefited doubly from the affirmative action

74. Consider the views of Muratova and Iaroslavskii, quoted above.

75. In January 1932, after several years of korenizatsiia, the Uzbek party had enrolled 47,749 indigenous members, candidate members, and Komsomol'tsy (69.8 percent of its total membership), and this fraction reached 73.8 percent six months later (RGASPI, d. 2938, l. 23). As shown in Table 3, however, these proportions are well ahead of the ratio of indigenous to nonindigenous women in the KP(b)Uz.

76. *Khudzhum: Znachit nastuplenie;* Pal'vanova, *Emansipatsiia musul'manki,* 163–201; or *Probuzhdennye velikim Oktiabrem,* in addition to the annual portraits on 8 March in local newspapers. Kamp, "Unveiling Uzbek Women," also focuses on this group.

77. PDA, op. 3, d. 1545, ll. 20–22.

Table 3. Communist Party membership, Uzbekistan and Central Asia, 1926–1933, by gender and ethnicity

	1926	1927	1928	1929	1930	1931	1932	1933
Uzbekistan*								
All Communists	18,351	26,610	34,028				68,495	
Women								
Number	1,236	2,049	3,029	3,229	4,406	6,830	8,856	8,006
Percent	6.7%	7.7%	8.9%				12.9%	
Indigenous women†								
Number		457	1,021	1,303	2,222	3,934		3,522
Percent		22.3%	33.7%	40.4%	50.4%	57.6%		44.0%
Central Asia								
All Communists	34,925		46,410	53,404	61,510	87,709	106,708	
Women								
Number			3,578	4,687	6,440	10,327	14,282	
Percent			7.8%	8.7%	10.5%	11.8%	12.3%	

Note: Includes candidate and full members.

* Excludes Tajik and Qoraqolpogh areas.

† Includes principal local nationalities.

Source: RGASPI, d. 775, l. 8; d. 2676, l. 8; and d. 2938, ll. 1 and 23; PDA, op. 9, d. 976, ll. 28–29; ÖzRMDA, f. 86, op. 2, d. 27, ll. 34 and 37; and Z. Simanovich, "Itogi partiinoi perepisi v Uzbekistane," *Izvestiia TsK KP(b)Uz,* no. 1 (1926), 9–10.

policies of the Soviet state.[78] Building their numbers became a very high priority, and intense effort went into the identification and training of hundreds of young women to fill party and state positions.[79]

The substantive criteria for evaluating promising female recruits were very loose. As females they were ipso facto politically sympathetic and thus almost automatically qualified to join the Soviet camp. At a demonstration outside Bukhoro in 1930, for example, all women who threw off their paranjis were given party membership cards (as candidate members), whether they wanted them or not. The fact that many had no idea what the word "Communist" meant and few participated in any subsequent party activities throws doubt over even the tiny membership numbers claimed by the party.[80] Such indiscriminate recruiting created problems: many of these women had few bureaucratic skills and no administrative training. Most were illiterate, or at best had only a rudimentary ability to read and write. Some attended special Soviet

78. Such policies provoked resentment among those who did not benefit from similar preferences, such as non-Uzbeks who sought to find paid work in Soviet institutions: ÖzRMDA, f. 736, op. 1, d. 932, l. 118. Terry Martin characterizes the USSR as an "affirmative-action empire."

79. These efforts fill scores of files in the state and party archives. For example, see PDA, op. 5, d. 818, ll. 19–30 and 58–61.

80. Mitrofanov, "K itogam," no. 2, 38.

Figure 20. The new Uzbek woman: reading *Qizil Özbekiston* (*Red Uzbekistan*), 1930s.
(Max Penson, courtesy Dina Khojaeva, collection Anahita Gallery, Santa Fe, N.M.)

training courses, which lasted anywhere from a few weeks to two years, depending on specialty, but a brief reading of their academic records finds few
who distinguished themselves in the classroom. Even after graduating, many
were unable to meet the technical requirements of their new jobs.[81] When a
new judicial regulation stipulated that court cases relating to women's issues
be heard by a panel that included at least one female judge, some of the
women who were quickly empaneled to meet this requirement turned out to be
illiterate and thus unable to read the Soviet laws they were charged to enforce.
Other female judges arrived at court wearing paranji and chachvon, removed
them to hear the day's cases, and then donned them to walk home again.[82]

Such personnel problems hindered the efficiency of Soviet administration
and created problems the already chaotic and understaffed bureaucracy could
scarcely afford. Yet the fault here lies with party practices, not with the
women. The eagerness, even impatience to put Muslim women in visible positions of authority led to placements without sufficient concern as to whether
the women in question were prepared, or even interested. This approach left

81. See ÖzRMDA, f. 86, op. 1, d. 7096, ll. 23–23a; f. 86, op. 10, d. 773, ll. 54–55; and PDA,
op. 2, d. 1375, ll. 30–32. A sample of academic records is at ÖzRMDA, f. 904, op. 12, d. 109, l.
115.
82. Strong, *Red Star in Samarkand,* 284.

untrained women in an untenable position: those suddenly serving as judges, procurators, and government administrators soon realized that they had been hired as showpieces, and complained bitterly about this tokenism to anyone who would listen. At a meeting in 1929 of workers who had been promoted to administrative posts (*vydvizhentsy*), one delegate complained that her co-workers looked at her "as if at an exhibit" and refused to help her learn what her administrative job entailed. Others told of being promoted into positions that required extensive paperwork and long meetings in Russian, even though they were completely illiterate and some of them could not understand the Russian language. They passed their days unable to understand what happened at the office, and were frustrated when their pleas for additional education and special help went unheard.[83]

Despite their lack of technical skills, however, these women in the party and Soviet apparatus enjoyed a remarkable degree of job security and protection during the massive political upheavals and turmoil of the Stalinist 1930s. Their gender did not save them all, to be sure—especially in the massive all-Union purges of 1937–38, a paroxysm to which even such prominent women as Tojikhon Shadieva succumbed—but it did give them a dramatic advantage.[84] When the class position of Communists came under investigation in 1929, for instance, female Bolsheviks could be exempted from the inquiry. They were shielded explicitly during the proverka, and according to the party press, they also were not to be expelled for the otherwise cardinal sin of "passivity" or for certain moral failings, such as having a child out of wedlock.[85] When in 1933 a new rule required that all full members of the party be literate, it reportedly threatened a "considerable" number of indigenous female Bolsheviks with expulsion or with demotion to candidate membership or "sympathizer" status.[86] The party thus organized intensive literacy courses on an emergency basis for Communist women, a step it took again in 1936, during the "exchange of documents" (*obmen dokumentov*), which also aimed to weed out other, principally male, party members.[87]

Virtually no effort was spared to keep local women in the party. A. A. Tsekher, secretary of the Uzbek party, wrote a confidential letter to district and provincial-level party officials in late 1936 or early 1937 calling on them to ensure the proper treatment of local women's activists and to forgive their

---

83. PDA, op. 5, d. 851, ll. 1–20.

84. On the victims of 1937–38, see *Özbekistonning yangi tarikhi* (Tashkent, 2000), 2:385.

85. Mezhol', "Predvaritel'nye itogi proverki kommunistok," 4–5.

86. PDA, op. 9, d. 960, ll. 78 and 81–85, and d. 976, ll. 28–29. The proportion of illiterate women members of the Uzbek party rose as recruitment proceeded, climbing from 19.7 percent in 1929 to 31.7 percent in 1931, but these aggregate figures include Russians and other non-Uzbeks. The percentage was reportedly higher among indigenous women (RGASPI, d. 2676, l. 8, and d. 2938, l. 23).

87. Anan'eva, "Rastut riady aktivistok," *PV*, 8 Mar. 1937; ÖzRMDA, f. 86, op. 10, d. 772, l. 59.

inevitable mistakes. The training, development, and promotion of such activists, Tsekher said, was "a large-scale political matter for the entire party,"
and each party leader needed to protect and nurture every single one of them.
Only by painstakingly creating such female cadres, he continued, would it be
possible to inculcate a wider "socialist spirit, to raise the cultural level of the
female masses, and to liquidate survivals of the past in their consciousness and
daily life."[88] The unveiled faces of these activist women served as a totem, one
that marked them indelibly as personally loyal, politically valuable, and thus
worthy of retention in party ranks. Their gender, combined with their willingness to affiliate publicly with the Soviet cause, created a presumption of loyalty, which usually protected them from the kinds of intrusive inquiry into
their family and home lives that plagued many of their male colleagues.

Yet even as they benefited from special training courses, preferential hiring
policies, and uniquely protected positions during party purges, these women
faced particular scrutiny and were held to an especially high moral standard.
They may have been placed on a pedestal, that is, but their exalted status put
them always in public view. Now they lived in glass houses. This intense
scrutiny makes sense given the party's running battle to persuade Uzbek men
and women that unveiled women were not lacking in moral fiber, let alone
that they were tantamount to prostitutes. The political capital of female Bolsheviks thus was caught up in their moral standing—and while their private
home lives often escaped detailed investigation, their public behavior attracted
the attention of party and secret police monitors lest they discredit the Soviet
cause. Alongside the virtually universal assumption that all indigenous women
were revolutionary allies lay the fear, expressed in whispers, that a few ill-
chosen women might do more to damage the cause of women's liberation than
thousands could do to advance it. The ambivalence, confusion, and uncertainty about how to proceed when that seemed to be the case is visible in the
exceptionally strict (and secretive) policing and punishment of women's activists accused of prostitution and moral degradation.

These cases were uncommon and almost always were treated as top-secret
matters. The party could not admit publicly that a Soviet Uzbek Communist
woman—who had by definition been brought to consciousness by the
hujum—could show signs of moral turpitude or political inconstancy.[89] Soviet
courts faced further difficulties in considering these cases because the accusations of moral failings and prostitution appeared regularly as a language of
protest against the hujum. Yet in at least some instances party and Soviet investigators took the accusations seriously, an atypical response that suggests—

---

88. PDA, op. 12, d. 172, l. 136.
89. One rare and fascinating exception was a show trial held in Kurgan-Tyube to combat
"hooliganism" among unveiled women. The defendants were accused of "drunkenness and de-
bauchery" with local men. It was hoped that their expulsion would improve the female cadres that
remained (ÖzRMDA, f. 86, op. 1, d. 5594, l. 2300b).

although obviously it does not prove—that the charges may have had some merit. On these occasions the party and police moved quickly to limit possible damage. In several top-secret cases, individual Zhenotdel staff workers were convicted of a range of corrupt practices, moral failings, even open opposition to party policy. Some women's workers had accepted bribes—of cash or "gifts" like silk dresses—from Uzbek men to overlook violations of Soviet byt laws.[90] One activist "sold" her twelve-year-old daughter into marriage, thus violating at least three new laws, and was sentenced to three years in prison.[91] Other local Zhenotdel activists worked against rather than for Soviet efforts, telling women that the hujum was misguided, that they should not unveil, and that Soviet power would soon collapse and be replaced by the emir, who would seize unveiled women upon his return.[92] One woman, elected to lead the village soviet in Besh-Ariq, turned up in 1929 at the center of a sordid web of nepotism, bribe-taking, and matchmaking that ended in murder.[93]

The need for disciplinary action to combat corruption and open opposition seemed clear—at least once investigators were sure that misconduct had occurred, and that it was not merely a story planted by class enemies to discredit loyal workers. When party, police, and judicial authorities heard accusations of moral rather than political failings among female Communists, though, questions of verification and punishment became more vexed. How, after all, should a "good" woman act in Soviet Uzbekistan? Not according to preexisting Muslim moral codes—the hujum's central goal had been to pull Uzbek women out of religiously justified seclusion. But alternative notions of "Communist morality" were at best a work in progress. Births out of wedlock, for example, no longer counted as evidence of poor character, at least not officially, but ambiguities remained. Take the case of a woman who was fired from her factory job in 1930 for a moral transgression: she had smoked in public. The act of smoking, though, was simultaneously being held up in other party circles as a token of female liberation. Ultimately the woman's dismissal was overturned and the factory's director disciplined, but definitions of Soviet morality remained vague, as shown in several other ambiguous cases.[94] What of the women in 1936 who turned up drunk, boisterous, and singing at the top of their lungs late at night in mixed company? What of the female students being trained for responsible Soviet positions who crept out of their dormitories after dark to consort with men? Such activity was fairly common among young male students and usually merited only a slap on the wrist. Officially,

90. RGASPI, d. 775, l. 19; d. 786, ll. 8 and 11; d. 1214, l. 150; and d. 1224, l. 39.

91. Strong, *Red Star in Samarkand*, 293–94. The laws involved would (at a minimum) have covered underage marriage, bride-price, and forced marriage.

92. RGASPI, d. 1214, ll. 135 and 158, and d. 1690, l. 73.

93. ÖzRMDA, f. 86, op. 1, d. 6573, l. 114. See also "Tak bylo v Besh-Aryke," *PV,* 25 Sept. 1929; and "Kalianovshchina—baiskoe kontrnastuplenie," *PV,* 12 Jan. 1930.

94. For these contrasting views, see ÖzRMDA, f. 9, op. 1, d. 3427, l. 305, and f. 86, op. 1, d. 3680, ll. 28–30.

women faced the same rules—but these cases were hushed up. The young women involved were frequently expelled from school, the Komsomol, or the party, lest such behavior tarnish the Soviet cause by association.[95]

It is especially interesting to see how the party dealt with accusations of prostitution and pandering among Zhenotdel workers and female Communists. Such accusations arose frequently, and indeed served as the stock in trade of Uzbeks who opposed the hujum. Sometimes allegations of pandering appeared to mean the organization of arranged marriages, a service long provided by Uzbek *sovchilar* (matchmakers).[96] Accusations of prostitution usually meant that a woman had appeared in public with an unveiled face, not that she had accepted money for sex. Verification of such charges thus presented a major problem. Ultimately it fell to doctors to provide a judgment—rooted in medical rather than political or moral authority—as to whether a woman was a prostitute. Accused Zhenotdel workers could thus find themselves forced to undergo gynecological examinations, a degree of physical intrusiveness far surpassing in intimacy the investigations of home and family life faced by their male colleagues.[97]

But investigative records and some horrified party discussions indicate that in at least a few rare cases these accusations struck the mark. Some prostitutes had originally joined the party or Soviet organizations, it is true, a fact that created problems for the Zhenotdel.[98] These women were already unveiled, and they certainly fitted the profile of socially marginal groups who were disproportionately represented in the hujum. Special difficulties arose, however, when a handful apparently continued working as prostitutes, at least occasionally, while serving in party positions—and in very rare instances, even allegedly to have used their access to vulnerable Uzbek women to organize prostitution rings among the newly unveiled.[99] The provincial control commission and OGPU quickly intervened in mid-1927 when such accusations were leveled against a local Zhenotdel director, Babajanova, in the small town of Sharikhan, outside Andijon. She was removed from her job for pandering and abuse of power (she allegedly fired an assistant who refused to cooperate). The case became the focus of a top-secret investigation and a cause célèbre in party circles. Babajanova's name was never mentioned in public, but it appeared thereafter in highly classified party reports to show the need for caution in working with Uzbek women.[100]

95. ÖzRMDA, f. 86, op. 1, d. 7998, l. 77, and op. 10, d. 1273, ll. 46–51 and 59.
96. RGASPI, d. 1694, l. 8. For examples of such accusations, see d. 1213, ll. 111 and 132; and Liubimova, *Dnevnik zhenotdelki,* 13–15.
97. RGASPI, d. 1214, l. 128.
98. Ibid., ll. 50, 121, and 131; d. 1245, l. 36.
99. RGASPI, d. 939, l. 7, and d. 1214, ll. 2–3.
100. Records from and later references to the case are at RGASPI, d. 1211, l. 229; d. 1213, l. 111; d. 1214, l. 84; and d. 1690, l. 73; and ÖzRMDA, f. 86, op. 2, d. 92, ll. 37–38. Babajanova's guilt is contested by a report of the provincial control commission at RGASPI, d. 1213, l. 132.

Finally, the decision to treat Uzbek women as the personal embodiments of Soviet policy had real implications for questions of women's agency. These issues were particularly confused in party thinking on such issues as whether female Bolsheviks had the ability to choose their own dress and lifestyle. Some Communist and Komsomol women ignored party directives while retaining their membership cards. One Communist woman—a party member since 1920—chose in 1933 to marry a man who already had a wife.[101] Other female Communists and Komsomol members chose to stay veiled and secluded during the 1930s, or to reveil more or less quickly after their initial decision to throw off the paranji and chachvon.[102] One Zhenotdel worker even presented herself to a proverka commission while wearing a paranji. When asked about her dress, she retorted, "I want [to stay veiled], what business is it of yours?"[103]

Such decisions appeared bizarre to party leaders, who thought female reluctance to unveil could only be evidence of male intimidation or an insufficiently raised consciousness. But as Uzbek female Communists, these women were by definition the vanguard's vanguard, and thus should have political consciousness sufficient to make "correct" decisions.[104] Their failure to do so showed that unveiling, emancipation, Bolshevik sympathies, and party membership were not necessarily so equivalent as had been assumed. To the small group of female Communists and Komsomol members, a party card could mean many things: employment, influence, access to resources, legal protection, or alimony enforcement, for example. The opportunity to inspire the masses in "socialist construction" appealed to some but apparently not to others. Yet because of the uniquely protected political position held by these women and the party's desperate need to demonstrate that it could attract, train, and retain Uzbek women, the question could not be forced, as it was with Uzbek men. One thus finds a curious paradox: at least a few veiled Uzbek women continued to be card-carrying members of the Bolshevik party in Stalinist Uzbekistan years after the hujum, even during the purges of the 1930s.

Cultivating a Colonial Elite: State Power and Its Limits

As the treatment of Uzbek Communist women as well as men shows, while the use of gender relations as a language of political authority drove internal party investigations to expand their scope and intrusiveness, the all-seeing gaze and vengeful arm of Soviet power were less than perfect in practice. In point of fact, and to return for the most part to the male rank-and-file Communist ma-

---

101. PDA, op. 9, d. 968, ll. 196–97.

102. For a Communist woman veiled in 1934, see PDA, op. 9, d. 971, ll. 81–83. Girls in the Komsomol are veiled in 1939 at op. 15, d. 81, ll. 10–11.

103. Mitrofanov, "K itogam," no. 2, 38.

104. PDA, op. 3, d. 1598, l. 26; and ÖzRMDA, f. 9, op. 1, d. 3427, l. 458, and f. 837, op. 3, d. 150, l. 170.

jority, both the surveying and disciplining functions of the proverka were sub-verted in many ways—intentionally and unintentionally—by the very party members who were under examination. Complaints from Zhenotdel activists and party leaders about the ineffectiveness and inconsistency of party discipli-nary measures recur throughout the archival records. Although the Third Uzbek Party Congress had declared in late 1927 that party members faced ex-pulsion if they did not unveil their wives, many Uzbek Communists with veiled wives passed muster in the later proverka, some receiving only a mild repri-mand.[105] Even more troubling, several men expelled from the party and Kom-somol as "alien elements" soon gained readmission.[106]

The party's attempt to survey and thereby control its membership encoun-tered many problems. Some difficulties resulted from the general chaos of party administration, which still plagued Soviet authorities during their second decade in power. According to one source, up to half of the Uzbek Commu-nists investigated by the proverka showed up for interviews without any docu-mentation, saying that their party cards had either been lost or never been is-sued.[107] Information gathering was hindered further by the many comrades who tried to hide evidence of their own (and their friends', relatives', and neighbors') non-Soviet family lives.[108] They answered questionnaires in ways intended to mislead superiors, and some local party cells simply ignored viola-tions committed by their members.[109] Even the control commissions faced se-rious problems: some members turned out to have several wives, were hostile to the idea of including women, and proved quite prone to delegate investiga-tive responsibility to the localities; that is, to the very people who were the tar-gets of inquiry.[110] Lower-level "investigations" could thus yield dubious re-sults: one report of 1928 stated proudly that of the 299 Communists investigated to date, only two or three had wives who still wore the paranji.[111]

Such evasions and misrepresentations did not come as a surprise to party supervisors; indeed, they only proved the need for a proverka. The most damn-ing indictment of its implementation, however, was published while the cam-paign was still under way, in late 1928, in the Central Asian Bureau's journal, Za partiiu.[112] The article argued that the groundwork for the proverka had been laid "hastily"; those whom it would affect were not told about the cam-paign's motives, only "rudely [informed that it would be] some kind of

105. PDA, op. 3, d. 1533, ll. 58–60; op. 4, d. 1235, ll. 10–12; and op. 5, d. 815, ll. 173–74.
106. RGASPI, d. 1692, l. 122; d. 1694, l. 118; and d. 2052, l. 29.
107. Mitrofanov, "K itogam," no. 2, 41.
108. RGASPI, d. 1713, l. 124.
109. PDA, op. 5, d. 852, l. 38; and ÖzRMDA, f. 86, op. 1, d. 7998, l. 85.
110. ÖzRMDA, f. 9, op. 1, d. 3397, l. 113; RGASPI, d. 1690, l. 23–23ob; Zalesov, "Zhen-shchina v bytu," 89; and Iaroslavskii, "Reshitel'nee udarim," 29.
111. RGASPI, d. 1690, l. 79.
112. I. Ustalyi, "Protiv chachvana i zatvornichestva (Itogi proverki partaktiva uzbekskoi orga-nizatsii)," Za partiiu, no. 9 (13) (1928), 95–97. The draft is at ÖzRMDA, f. 86, op. 2, d. 27, ll. 32–33ob.

'purge.' " Personnel problems continually dogged the work; many commission members, especially in the Old Cities, were illiterate. Very few (only 14 percent) were women, and these were mostly non-Muslim; only 5 percent of commission members were Uzbek women. "To our shame," the article continued, some party cells did not create verification commissions (*proverkomy*) at all, and hindered the efforts of external investigators, declaring that it was none of their business. One party secretary flatly refused to let a visiting proverkom see his cell's records. In other places, local meetings had a "mechanical character," with an "automatic raising of hands" that avoided dealing with issues: they simply passed resolutions declaring that they were in compliance with all directives and concluding that no further investigation was necessary. Ostensibly to save time, party cells in Samarqand "refused to translate the verification commission's report into Uzbek, notwithstanding the presence at meetings of a large number of Uzbek women who do not understand Russian."[113]

Such difficulties plainly hindered an efficient cleansing of the Bolshevik body politic and show the Soviet system in Central Asia as less than the perfectly oiled machine its leaders wanted to build. Yet these problems also contributed, in a curious way, to the overall logic of political purification through the investigation of gender relations. Party leaders were only too well aware of the hindrances facing the proverka, and of opposition from rank-and-file Bolsheviks over the hujum and unveiling. This fact, however, only convinced them of the need for further vetting and purges of party ranks in the 1930s. They had to continue until the Uzbek party, as measured by the now sanctified criterion of family life and gender relations, matched the long-sought (but always apparently receding) ideal of a loyal, politically advanced cadre in Central Asian society.

Throughout the 1930s and beyond the party paid close attention to the home lives of its members, interpreting "byt character" as an expression of one's political level and leanings. A good Communist had to live as a Communist should—with a family based on trust and equality rather than force and patriarchy, and in which wives and daughters did not veil, but rather attended school and worked outside the home. Yet despite the party's continuing efforts to survey, discipline, and mold their behavior, Uzbek Communists as a group did not adopt the new Soviet ways as quickly or completely as their superiors in Tashkent and Moscow hoped. Polygyny, qalin, and underage marriage continued to be observed within party ranks; one kolkhoz's Komsomol secretary was caught in 1939 selling his sister for a bride-price of 7,000 rubles.[114] The problem was particularly vivid in the persistence of veiling and seclusion, which remained the criterion par excellence of liberation. In one Tashkent ma-

113. Ustalyi, "Protiv chachvana," 97, added a sarcastic aside: "See how deeply the Samarqandtsy have mastered the procedures of economics!"

114. PDA, op. 15, d. 1383, ll. 39–41. See also op. 10, d. 141, l. 32; op. 15, d. 1383, ll. 45–47, and d. 1388, ll. 18–21.

halla only five of nineteen Communists had unveiled their wives by 1934, and long lists of veiled women in party and Soviet organizations appeared throughout the 1930s and into the 1940s.[115] Even some female Communists and Komsomol members continued to wear the paranji and chachvon, and many cases were reported of women casting off their veils and either reveiling immediately or refusing thereafter to leave their homes.[116]

These problems were obvious to party investigators. To many, especially the European Communists who had been posted to Central Asia, they appeared very serious. One political brigade leader, M. Piatkova, reported in May 1931 after a two-month investigation of villages in Marghilon province that party directives about women's liberation *"have not even been read* by the local organizations." She had diligently addressed the local aktiv and gone to meetings of the local party and Komsomol, she said, to stress the need for improvement, but "they listened to me and . . . the party members only sat there, keeping perfectly silent—not a single one of them made a sound (to say that they needed to unveil their wives, all of whom are veiled). And when they were not forced to speak about this question, all of them, as one, stayed silent."[117]

The situation at the district level was no better. Not knowing any Uzbek, Piatkova had sought staff help to aid her work with unveiled women, to prepare them to serve as the next generation of activists. But she found no interest and received no assistance from officials in the district party, Soviet, or Komsomol organizations. In such a situation, she noted, "it is difficult to expect positive results. Among these organizations there is a devilish stagnation and sluggishness. In general I consider the situation catastrophic." In Piatkova's view, local Communists' failure to understand and support women's liberation and the unveiling campaign meant grave danger for all other party programs: "Women here not only are not prepared for collectivization, but [will] stay aloof from it for an entire half-century. The misgivings of the [local] party are completely [responsible for the fact that] in Central Asia the disruption of collectivization may come from women." Given such unqualified judgments ("I

115. For the Tashkent report, see "Azadliq dushmanlarigha qarshi!" *Jangi jol,* no. 3 (1934), 4. For lists, see those from 1934 at "Plenum Sredneaziatskogo Biuro TsK VKP(b)," *PV,* 15 Sept. 1934; from 1935 at PDA, op. 12, d. 880, l. 15; and ÖzRMDA, f. 86, op. 10, d. 634, l. 246; V. Bashalov, "Rabota sreda zhenskoi molodezhi—zabytyi uchastok (Uzbekistan, Chechnia, Dagestan)," *Izvestiia TsK VLKSM,* no. 19 (1935), 7–8; from 1936 at ÖzRMDA, f. 86, op. 10, d. 772, l. 92; and from 1940 at PDA, op. 15, d. 1383, ll. 44–53, and Mastura Avezova, "Okonchatel'no unichtozhit' parandzhu!" *Pravda,* 15 Jan. 1940.

116. For more examples of veiled female Communists and Komsomolki in the 1930s, see PDA, op. 9, d. 971, l. 83; ÖzRMDA, f. 86, op. 10, d. 632, l. 88; and Mitrofanov, "K itogam," no. 2, 38. On temporary unveilings and refusals to leave home, see PDA, op. 5, d. 852, ll. 43–44; and Kostygin, "Zadachi," 57.

117. RGASPI, d. 2695, l. 40; emphasis in original. All quotations in the next paragraph are from this source.

consider the situation catastrophic") as well as these key political linkages to wider state priorities, it is clear why party leaders would want to redouble efforts to ensure proper gender attitudes among Uzbek Communists.

Simply put, the persistence of gender misconduct and female seclusion represented an ongoing problem for the party because these issues continued to define political loyalty. To be sure, other questions of everyday culture also attracted the attention of Soviet Central Asian authorities. By 1938, for example, male Komsomol members and party officials in Uzbekistan came under fire for a range of personal habits—not shaving, not washing, not brushing their teeth, as well as wearing forms of masculine "national dress" (such as khalats) that were deemed inappropriate for "cultured socialist people" in the wider world.[118] When agents of the Turkmen secret police came up short in arrests of counterrevolutionaries in 1937–38, they filled their quota by going to the Ashgabat marketplace and rounding up all men who wore beards, on the theory that they were likely to be mullahs.[119] But such nationalized forms of masculinity and men's fashion remained a subordinate theme in the prewar period; it was veils that were prima facie indicators of political outlook. Some lists of male party members in the 1930s specified for each individual only the most important information: name, age, social position, date of party membership, and wife's status as veiled or unveiled.[120] One speaker at a major Uzbek women's congress in 1935 said that enlightened husbands did the proper thing when they forced their wives to unveil.[121] This continuing focus on gender distinguished the politics of the Soviet empire in Central Asia. Even well after the formal dissolution of the all-Union Zhenotdel in 1930, local party cells in Uzbekistan faced regular audits of their women's liberation work, audits that often concentrated on the personal lives of party members. One Tashkent mahalla investigation in 1937 immediately focused on the fact that the local Communists' wives were still illiterate and veiled.[122] Two years later, a Tashkent Komsomol examiner prepared a list of local teachers and Young Communists who insisted that their wives stay veiled and who kept them from studying, working, or participating in any other form of Soviet-sanctioned social life.[123] Another investigative brigade, visiting a rural kolkhoz in 1940, chronicled various problems in the women's campaign and then listed by name the party and Komsomol members whose wives were veiled.[124]

118. RGASPI, f. M-1, op. 2, d. 134, ll. 47–49. Thanks to Peter Blitstein for this document.
119. GARF, f. 8131, op. 37, d. 145, ll. 46 and 56–57. I am grateful to Gábor Rittersporn and Arch Getty for this reference.
120. See such a list from 1931 at ÖzRMDA, f. 6, op. 2, d. 462, ll. 137–41.
121. ÖzRMDA, f. 86, op. 10, d. 634, l. 252.
122. ÖzRMDA, f. 837, op. 32, d. 346, l. 33. A similar report from 1931 is at f. 86, op. 1, d. 7287, ll. 21–22.
123. PDA, op. 14, d. 1092, ll. 1–2.
124. PDA, op. 15, d. 1383, ll. 50–53.

Languages of Loyalty: Gender Relations and the Cycle of Party Purification

When a series of purges rocked the Uzbek party during the 1930s, then, this gendered language of loyalty was available to guide those who wished to purify the party.[125] And while the exact dynamics of these purges are still poorly understood, in Central Asia no less than the USSR at large, it is clear that those responsible for implementing them in Uzbekistan did draw on this language, linking issues of gender propriety with concerns about political soundness. In 1930 *Pravda Vostoka* announced that the recent party purge had unmasked those "Communists" (carefully surrounded by quotation marks) who had spoken out against women's liberation as the bearers of class-alien influence within the party.[126] In 1932 readers of the Moscow journal *Revoliutsiia i natsional'nosti* similarly learned that the principal form of anti-Soviet activity in the Turkmen SSR was opposition to the women's liberation campaign.[127]

But it was in the wider and better-known party purges of 1936 and after that the links between gender liberation and internal party politics appeared most explicitly. A series of articles in *Pravda Vostoka* in March 1936 showed how deeply the two had become intertwined.[128] Communists were criticized for keeping their wives veiled, and the violence experienced by women's activists was bemoaned; such problems were said to require greater political vigilance. Perhaps most striking was the way gender concerns permeated the language of denunciation, as reported at local mahalla party meetings in Tashkent: "Many of our comrades have learned to speak beautifully about women's liberation, but do nothing for it," announced one employee of a local women's club. "Here, today, from this very tribunal, Ayupov, the secretary of the city soviet's party committee, read us an entire lecture about women, while in his own mahalla he has in fact done nothing for them." *Pravda Vostoka* went on to note that "not all Communists have engaged in active work for women's liberation," and urged all party committees to examine how individual Communists "fight for women's liberation" as a way to gauge their aktivnost' and to decide whether to expel them from party ranks.[129]

As Party Secretary Tsekher explained at the Samarqand City Party Conference, held at the same time, such issues mattered because of their place in the broader class struggle being waged by the party:

125. Michael Rywkin has identified seven purges in Central Asia between 1930 and 1938 (*Moscow's Muslim Challenge*, 108).

126. Note the title of Manzhara's article, "Chto pokazala chistka partii: 'Kommunisty,' vystupaiushchie protiv raskreposhcheniia, byli provodnikami baiskogo vliianiia," *PV,* 7 Mar. 1930.

127. G. Aronshtam, "K chistke natsional'nykh partorganizatsii," *Revoliutsiia i natsional'nosti,* no. 5–6 (1933), 14.

128. In addition to those quoted below, see M. Dzhurabaev, "Navedem obraztsovyi poriadok (K itogam partkonferentsii Oktiabr'skogo raiona)" and "Vragi raskreposhcheniia: Po materialam upolnomochennogo Komissii partiinogo kontrolia," both in *PV,* 23 Mar. 1936.

129. "Na raionnykh konferentsiiakh: Oktiabr'skaia," *PV,* 17 Mar. 1936.

Work among women is [now] acquiring an especially acute meaning. In his criminal activity, the class enemy we [now confront] in Uzbekistan is concentrating more attention on the struggle against women's liberation.

The facts of the discrediting of female activists, of the best women workers, of the leading kolkhoz women; the methods of terror against women; the marriage of underage [girls]—[these are] far from isolated occurrences. All of this shows that many party organizations have not taken this sphere of work under their attention, under their leadership; the enemy realizes this quickly and makes use of our weak spots.[130]

Women in veils within party ranks thus represented a "weak spot" that could threaten the entire Bolshevik program. Only ridding the party of such alien elements would ensure its political purity and enable its members to be "pure, like crystal," as they had to be.[131]

The hujum therefore provided a language for denunciations within the party. Yet this language was not merely a smoke screen to hide "real" issues in the purges. Gender transgressions, as defined by the party, did continue among party and Komsomol members; and since regional politics by the 1930s had become in important ways synonymous with gender practices and the remaking of everyday culture, this reality itself also drove the purges onward. Soviet leaders in Moscow and Tashkent confronted a party as well as a society that was in their terms polluted in gender relations and hence in political outlook, a party that was at root un-Soviet. Thus the party had to look again (and again) at its membership rolls to weed out those who did not belong.

Exhaustive investigations of the party aktiv and rank-and-file members continued throughout the 1930s as the scope of possible punishment expanded greatly.[132] Obviously many other factors—not least political input and direction from Moscow—also contributed to the qualitatively different and far more violent Great Purges of the later 1930s, which affected all levels of the Uzbek party organization. Between 1936 and 1938 the vast majority of Uzbek Communists lost their membership cards and many their lives. Akmal Ikramov and Faizulla Khojaev, two leading architects of the hujum, were arrested in 1937 and sentenced to death in the last major show trial. They were the most famous victims, but the wider statistics at the middle and lower levels of the Uzbek party are truly staggering. According to the historian Michael Rywkin, the massive purge in 1937 alone removed 70.8 percent of members of district

---

130. A. A. Tsekher, "S chest'iu nosit' vysokoe zvanie chlena partii," *PV*, 29 Mar. 1936.

131. ÖzRMDA, f. 904, op. 10, d. 91, l. 40, quoted above as an epigraph.

132. For two such cases, see ibid., ll. 4–5, and f. 837, op. 32, d. 346, l. 33. Shame continued to be used by both the Uzbek- and Russian-language press. See "Xatin-qizlar arasida ishlash unutilgan," *QÖ*, 4 Feb. 1936; "O rabote sredi zhenshchin v Oktiabr'skom raione goroda Tashkenta," *PV*, 26 Aug. 1935; and Z. Ipatova, "Bol'she vnimaniia rabote sredi zhenshchin (Partkonferentsiia Iangi-Iul'skogo raiona), *PV*, 5 Mar. 1940.

party committees and 55.7 percent of lower-level cadres. The Uzbek party's central committee changed completely: barely half of its members won reelection in 1937 and just 6 percent in 1938.[133] By 1939, too, the Uzbek party's membership rolls had once again shrunk dramatically, to just 35,087. Ethnic Uzbeks were particularly hard hit: from a high-water mark of almost three-quarters of the party membership in mid-1932, in the heyday of korenizatsiia, they now accounted for just 47 percent of those left on party rolls.[134]

Neither the proverka of 1928–29 nor the "document exchange" of 1933 matched the later purges in scope, method, or goals. Nor did the proverka and its logic, ultimately traceable to the hujum, *cause* the uniquely violent catharsis of 1936–38. The Great Purges, after all, were not limited to Uzbekistan. Within the context of the Soviet East, however, these prior events and this pre-existing logic did lend a particular flavor to the denunciations that followed. The indigenous Soviet elite—that very small group that bridged metropole and colony—found its first generation of leaders targeted specifically by these criteria. Rarely in other parts of the USSR were enemies of the people identified principally through their antipathy to women's liberation, as they were in this Uzbek party resolution of 1939:

> The placidly opportunistic attitude of some local party, Soviet, Komsomol, and judicial-investigative organizations in the struggle to liquidate manifestations of feudal-serf relations toward women has resulted in hostile elements stirring up counterrevolutionary activities in this area. Organizing a struggle for the liquidation of feudal-serf survivals in relations toward women is a part of the sharpening class struggle.
>
> Enemies of the people, national fascists, spies, wreckers, and saboteurs, now holding leadership positions in the [Uzbek] republic, have long counted on ruining the party's and government's measures to liberate women, and [have] in every possible way hampered the growth of [women's] social-political and productive aktivnost'.[135]

Gender talk and the jargon of Stalinist paranoia combined here to form a dual justification for internal purification, making the peculiar flavor of the Uzbek purges emerge with particular clarity.

Questions of gender relations were fundamental to the language of Soviet politics and authority in post-hujum Uzbekistan. Thus accusations of gender or family misdeeds possessed more local resonance than charges of, say, Trotskyism (although that charge was also used). And as the articles published in *Pravda Vostoka* in 1936 show, concerns of family life and accusations of

---

133. Rywkin, *Moscow's Muslim Challenge,* 107–8; and Donald S. Carlisle, "Modernization, Generations, and the Uzbek Soviet Intelligentsia," in *The Dynamics of Soviet Politics,* ed. Paul Cocks et al. (Cambridge, Mass., 1976), 247.

134. Allworth, *Modern Uzbeks,* 264; and RGASPI, d. 2938, l. 23.

135. PDA, op. 15, d. 81, ll. 10–11.

transgressions within the intimate space of the home figured more prominently as a justification for purges, especially at the middle and lower levels of the party hierarchy, in Uzbekistan than elsewhere. But again, from Moscow's perspective this justification was not a sham. This unrelenting, insistent attention to the fabric of everyday culture shaped the way the party evaluated and related to its members for many years. The repeated investigations of gender infractions led every time to the discovery of further disloyalty and thus to calls for even greater vigilance. This paranoia, combined with the inability of even experienced Bolshevik activists to transform Central Asian cultural practices, made Uzbek Communists as a group seem unreliable and even, in a basic way, non-Bolshevik. Their underlying foreignness—as measured by such alien and, after 1927, politically charged customs as veiling—practically impelled further house-cleanings by the control commissions.

The continuing presence of veils within the party also fitted neatly with Stalinist views of "enemies within." In the 1930s this ideological resonance may even have encouraged the purges to proceed further and faster than would otherwise have been the case. Ultimately, too, it channeled decisions about whom to purge, pushing authorities to look at specific members of this indigenous elite—with grave consequences, it goes without saying, for those Uzbeks who found themselves targeted.

CHAPTER 7

Crimes of Daily Life

The great October Revolution for the first time in the history of civilization obliterated all inequalities of women with men. It broke, it smashed to the end all of the bourgeois-capitalist laws that kept women in slavery. . . .

Only Soviet power has brought women liberation and given them rights equal to men.

—A report by judicial authorities in Namangan on the continuing efforts to fight criminal violations of women's rights, 1941

We must address this question very seriously. We can no longer be patient with violations of women's rights. Our country is growing [and] moving ahead, the collective farms are growing, culture is expanding, we are moving forward on all sides with regard to women. We must take care to help them. Among us Uzbeks it is said that only a crazy person gets mixed up in family matters between a husband and wife. This is not so: what about the cases in which signals arose of [bad] relations between husband and wife, [but] based on this sentiment no attention was paid and bad results [followed]. This [advice to leave family affairs alone] is the invention of bois and the religious clergy and only serves their hostile ends.

—Comrade Abdurakhmanov, addressing a conference of Stakhanovite kolkhoz women, 1940

Many European colonial regimes of the late nineteenth through mid–twentieth century attempted to govern vast numbers of subjects with a comparative handful of officials, soldiers, and settlers. Since direct physical force and coercion alone could not guarantee imperial power, these regimes needed other means to control indigenous populations. Laws and legal norms often served this purpose, creating codes of behavior against which colonized individuals could be measured. If all went well—from the standpoint of colonial authorities—these norms would be so fully internalized by colonial subjects that no massive police force would be needed. The defense of indigenous women against oppression was one common justification for using the law in this way, as when British authorities decided in 1829 to ban the practice of sati, or widow burning, in India. The postcolonial theorist Gayatri Spivak has argued that in this case, the protection of Indian women from Indian men helped justify colonial British rule. Such a law became, she says, "a signifier for a *good* society which must, at such inaugurative moments, transgress mere legality, or equity of legal policy. In this particular case, the process also allowed the redefinition as a crime of what had been tolerated, known, or adulated as ritual."[1]

By the late 1920s Soviet Central Asian authorities had passed a series of laws to address the problems posed by such Uzbek "rituals."[2] These laws established an important new category of criminal offenses: crimes of daily life, or *byt* crimes. They involved the definition of new norms for personal behavior and new legal templates to govern and shape patterns of everyday family life. Many of these new rules took effect piecemeal after 1917, and a large number were introduced between 1924 and 1926, immediately after the creation of the Soviet Central Asian republics. Marriage codes underwent radical changes at this time, for example, as women received a legal guarantee of equality in personal rights.[3] Polygyny, forced marriage, and bride-price (qalin) were banned. The legal age for marriage was raised from 9, as (nominally) permitted by the Islamic code of shariat, to 16. The explicit consent of both parties became essential: forcing a woman to marry against her will carried a potential sentence of five years in prison. Reforms in divorce procedure and property law safeguarded women's rights and at least in theory ensured women a degree of economic independence.[4] New laws also addressed women's personal safety: it became illegal to mistreat or insult a woman, and in particular to use force or

1. Gayatri Chakravorty Spivak, "Can the Subaltern Speak?" in *Marxism and the Interpretation of Culture,* ed. Cary Nelson and Lawrence Grossberg (Urbana, 1988), 298. Also see Spivak, "The Rani of Sirmur," in *Europe and Its Others,* ed. Francis Barker et al. (Colchester, 1985), 1:144. On the wider use of law by colonial powers, see Comaroff, *Of Revelation and Revolution,* 365–404; Lauren Benton, *Law and Colonial Cultures: Legal Regimes in World History, 1400–1900* (Cambridge, 2002); Upendra Baxi, " 'The State's Emissary': The Place of Law in Subaltern Studies," *Subaltern Studies* 7 (1992): 247–64; and Michael R. Anderson, "Islamic Law and the Colonial Encounter in British India," in *Institutions and Ideologies,* ed. David Arnold and Peter Robb (Richmond upon Thames, 1993), 165–85.

2. Each nationality received a distinctive set of "crimes"—specific to Kazakhs, Turkmen, Uzbeks, and so on. See ÖzRMDA, f. 86, op. 1, d. 4434, l. 206.

3. See PDA, f. 60, op. 1, d. 4868, ll. 103–4; and ÖzRMDA, f. 86, op. 1, d. 2772, l. 148.

4. Divorce was easier to obtain, and child support and alimony became obligatory on the part of the spouse with a greater degree of financial independence, usually the husband. See RGASPI, d. 1224, l. 55; and ÖzRMDA, f. 86, op. 1, d. 2217, ll. 22–23, and d. 4434, ll. 208–9.

coercion to induce her to wear a veil or remain in seclusion.[5] When violence greeted the hujum during and after 1927, special laws were passed and confirmed by the Soviet Supreme Court deeming politically motivated attacks on women "counterrevolutionary" state crimes, "terrorist acts" meriting the death penalty.[6] The Soviet state thus expressed wide-ranging, intrusive goals in designing a panoply of laws. Party activists sought no less than to overturn the fundamental character of what they saw as the most intimate and closely guarded spheres of Uzbek social life.

By 1940, when Soviet authorities claimed success in liberating Uzbek women from these crimes of everyday life, the very existence of such laws served an important propaganda function. As Uzbekistan's president, Yoldosh Akhunbabaev, put it,

> The Soviet woman is the happiest woman in the world.
>
> The party of Lenin and Stalin has given women rights identical with men and [women] have now become active participants in the socialist construction of the USSR. Women's centuries-long lack of rights and chains of oppression have been obliterated once and for all. Women in the Soviet [Union] possess all political and personal rights guaranteed by the Stalin Constitution.[7]

Legal reform, then, was a principal strategy used to realize the Soviet vision of an unveiled, fully equal, socially active Uzbek woman, and thus to create a truly Soviet Uzbekistan. But there was also another side to this effort. In 1940 party leaders announced that in Uzbek society, as in the Uzbek party, one could infer the continuing presence of anti-Soviet class enemies from the high rate of crimes committed against women.[8] Class enemies and byt crimes went hand in hand: in a circular logic, each was taken to reveal the other.

The campaign to liberate Muslim women through law cannot be judged a mere success or failure; it played out in a manner that was neither simple nor straightforward. Party leaders and women's activists made concerted efforts to emancipate Uzbek women through legal, judicial, and police action—and Uzbek individuals reacted to, often subverted, and sometimes reshaped these efforts. As Nicholas Dirks has argued with reference to British law in India, the imposition of legal norms by a colonizing power can create a discursive sphere in which the contradictions of colonial rule both flourish and are laid open for

5. "O predostavlenii osobykh l'got zhenshchinam po okhrane ikh cherez sudebnye uchrezhdeniia ot nasiliia i oskorblenii po povodu sniatiia parandzhi," in *Kompartiia Uzbekistana v bor'be za reshenie zhenskogo voprosa v period stroitel'stva sotsializma (1917–1937 gg.),* ed. R. Kh. Aminova et al. (Tashkent, 1977), 74–75.

6. See ÖzRMDA, f. 6, op. 2, d. 462, ll. 28–29; f. 9, op. 1, d. 3417, l. 135; and f. 86, op. 1, d. 5602, ll. 1–3; d. 5885, ll. 382–83; and d. 6574, l. 42.

7. ÖzRMDA, f. 2454, op. 1, d. 412, l. 140.

8. Ibid., l. 137.

all to see, a situation that certainly existed in Soviet Central Asia.[9] The legal encounter between Soviet power and Uzbek society resulted in complex processes of interplay and negotiation.

By using law to define and enforce "proper" behavior, party activists hoped to change the terms of debate within Uzbek society, to accumulate what Pierre Bourdieu calls "symbolic capital" by creating a new "official version of the social world."[10] These activists made a series of choices to define the new laws, deeming certain customs—and simultaneously not others—subject to legal action and judicial penalties. The contingent aspects of their choices can be seen in the extensive debates on which "crimes" to include, how to define them, and how harshly they should be punished. Zhenotdel activists, in particular, fought to persuade their colleagues and the regional party leadership to carry out a wide-ranging effort to protect indigenous Muslim women through law. Once Soviet legislators arrived at a canonical list of byt crimes, though, such signs of ambivalence were erased wherever possible and muted wherever not. Soviet police officers, prosecutors, and judges, many of them Europeans from outside Central Asia, then took up the cause, setting out to survey the population, enforce the new rules, and reshape Central Asian daily life. Uzbek men and women in turn responded to these new laws in a variety of inventive ways, making their voices heard both inside and outside the Soviet system and producing ultimately a negotiated outcome on the ground. The path to Soviet-style women's liberation turned out to be anything but smooth.

Custom Criminalized: Defining a Canon of Byt Crimes

Each of the new laws was announced with great fanfare and publicized widely. Soviet officials justified new legal norms in humanitarian terms, as required by the party's self-proclaimed duty to defend the most defenseless members of Central Asian society. This rhetoric ran deeper than mere tactical political propaganda: many Bolsheviks felt the duties of their civilizing mission quite sincerely. They painted a horrific picture of Uzbek social life, portraying each new law as self-evidently progressive and humane—as nothing more than the moral expression of modern common sense. Before 1917, Zhenotdel workers declared, Uzbek women had lacked even the most rudimentary rights and protections, being treated like property, equivalent to cattle. Soviet officials saw qalin as a form of "speculation in women," denounced polygyny as "kulak exploitation of female labor," and said that the harm caused to young girls' sexual health by underage marriage was contributing to the "degeneration of the

9. Nicholas B. Dirks, "From Little King to Landlord: Colonial Discourse and Colonial Rule," in *Colonialism and Culture*, ed. Dirks (Ann Arbor, 1992), 175–208.

10. The phrase is from Richard Harker et al., eds., *An Introduction to the Work of Pierre Bourdieu: The Practice of Theory* (New York, 1990), 13. On "symbolic capital," see Pierre Bourdieu, *Language and Symbolic Power*, ed. John B. Thompson (Cambridge, Mass., 1991), 166–67.

[Uzbek] nation."[11] In Bolshevik eyes, too, the alleged prevalence of pederasty among Uzbek men showed prerevolutionary Uzbek society to be little more than a den of iniquity and perversion.[12] New Soviet rules, in short, were needed to protect Uzbek women and children from the patriarchal oppression that dominated their everyday lives.

By 1927, calls could be heard for standardization of such norms across the Soviet state. One party report argued that the current patchwork of "decrees, resolutions, directives, [and] orders" did not constitute a coherent legal framework, and that one was badly needed.[13] The result, it was hoped, would be a single seamless web of family law to govern everyday life, one both consistent internally and easy to explain and enforce. Yet the party's debates over the new category of byt crimes reveal internal divisions as well as the contingent aspects of Soviet policy in Central Asia. Even while newspapers and pamphlets trumpeted the inexorable and inescapable logic of Soviet legal liberation, archival records show vividly the constructed nature of this supposedly seamless web. In the end an accepted canon of byt crimes did emerge, but neither its shape nor its exact contents were obvious at the outset. Party activists came to focus on certain Uzbek customs as "oppressive," for instance, while ignoring others that might equally have been included (such as the practice of keeping newborn infants in a cradleboard, or *beshik*, for hours at a time).[14] These choices, while not altogether arbitrary—they certainly drew on Orientalist preconceptions—reveal more about these party members and their views of the world than about the problems facing Uzbek women.

Throughout 1927 wide-ranging discussions within the party and in discussion circles at Soviet clubs debated the question of byt crime and found few predetermined answers. The mostly European members of the Zhenotdel argued forcefully for attention to what they saw as the patriarchal oppression of Central Asian women. The Zhenotdel had institutional and ideological interests in promoting such discussions, but other party bodies—also staffed disproportionately by non-Muslims—agreed with its bleak portrait of Uzbek family life. Not all agreed, however, that women's work should be the party's

11. RGASPI, d. 2081, l. 16. For more on this theme, see Cassandra Cavanaugh, "Backwardness and Biology: Medicine and Power in Russian and Soviet Central Asia, 1868–1934" (Ph.D. diss., Columbia University, 2001), 262–323. On early marriage, see RGASPI, d. 1224, l. 55. The polygyny quotation is from PDA, op. 10, d. 141, l. 32, and qalin from A. I. Nukhrat, "Usilit' massovuiu rabotu Sovetov sredi natsionalok," *Vlast' Sovetov*, no. 6 (1933), 8–9.

12. Pederasty was called a common sex crime in a report of 1928 at ÖzRMDA, f. 86, op. 1, d. 5602, l. 22–220b.

13. RGASPI, d. 1199, l. 21. For early efforts, see Suleimanova, "Zarozhdenie Sovetskogo ugolovnogo prava v Uzbekistane," *Sovetskoe gosudarstvo i pravo*, no. 10 (1948), 65–69. For the text of byt laws before the standardization of 1926–27, see I. A., "Bytovye prestupleniia," *Vestnik iustitsii Uzbekistana*, no. 4–5 (1925), 27–30. An exhaustive list of changes considered thereafter is at ÖzRMDA, f. 86, op. 1, d. 5885, ll. 321–62.

14. An unsuccessful attempt to include such practices was made by Rafail Samoilovich Gershenovich, *Perezhitki starogo byta i ikh vred dlia zdorov'ia* (Tashkent, 1940).

top legal priority while other issues—such as land and water reform—remained so urgent. The comparatively few indigenous Muslim Communists, nearly all male, also lobbied for the party to direct its efforts elsewhere, contending that attacks on the Uzbek family would only backfire. Even the few Muslim Soviet women were not of one mind: some wanted immediate legal reform to protect and improve the status of all Uzbek women, while others preferred to focus on job training, literacy courses, or social welfare work.

These tensions—between Zhenotdel and party leaders, newly arrived Europeans and indigenous Muslims, and women and men—were expressed in the debates over how (and even whether) to proceed with family law reform. Overlaid on these structural and personal divisions were differences of ideology, temperament, and method. Although the situation was obviously complicated, the legal arguments again clustered around two broadly distinct approaches. Some Bolsheviks argued that new family and marriage codes should arise organically from local conditions, not party dictates. As long as such laws underpinned the party's economic aims, they should be drawn as flexibly as possible, and no laws should be passed without the support of local populations.[15] This group stressed the merits of persuasion, publicity, and the strict observance of legal norms and due process. Other activists, especially within the Zhenotdel, rebuffed this approach, contending that the widespread existence of patriarchal injustice showed indigenous Central Asian populations to be the least qualified to influence Soviet policy. This group was willing to employ coercion, duress, even, if necessary, violence in pursuit of the overarching goal of women's liberation, without being unduly slowed by attention to legal niceties.

Many Soviet police officers and judicial workers felt strong pressure to produce results. The general Soviet ethos and practice of "socialist competition" (sotsialisticheskie sorevnovaniia), carried out here between Central Asian republics and cities on women's liberation and other matters, likely contributed to the pressure.[16] Such campaigns put careers on the line, creating powerful incentives to cut corners to "increase the tempo," to speed up Soviet judicial proceedings related to women.[17] This approach encouraged coercive tactics and an increasingly indiscriminate use of "administrative pressure" (administrativnyi nazhim). Lower-level officials stretched police powers and used the judicial apparatus in an extralegal way. Intimidation played a role: clerics were arrested, as in Chust, merely for speaking out against the unveiling campaign.[18] Many local Soviet bosses ordered male neighbors and subordinates—some-

---

15. ÖzRMDA, f. 245, op. 1, d. 222, l. 118. See also RGASPI, d. 1240, l. 180b.

16. On a women's liberation competition between the people's commissariats of justice in Uzbekistan and Turkmenistan in 1929–30, see G. L., "V zashchitu zhenshchin," *PV,* 1 Nov. 1929; "Sorevnovanie po raskreposhcheniiu zhenshchin," *PV,* 11 Dec. 1929; and ÖzRMDA, f. 837, op. 6, d. 105, ll. 210–11. Also see the contest of 1930–31 between Bukhoro and Tashkent at A. S., "Istoriia odnogo dogovora," *PV,* 24 Feb. 1931.

17. ÖzRMDA, f. 837, l. 6, d. 105, ll. 210–11.

18. RGASPI, d. 2071, l. 24.

times at gunpoint—to unveil their wives. Uzbek women faced fines, jail time, or loss of employment if they refused to unveil.[19] Roving bands, or troikas, patrolled the streets of major cities to remove paranjis and chachvons by force. In one fairly typical case, a local Zhenotdel leader, Maisurdjanova, walked up to a veiled woman standing in line at a store in 1929 and "without a word" ripped off her paranji.[20] Another tricked women into giving up their paranjis and then refused to return them, ordering that those who resisted be arrested. Sometimes doors to Soviet meetings were locked and no one was permitted to leave until the women removed their veils. After coercing women to attend meetings, local officials frequently prepared lists of those who refused to unveil, threatening dire consequences such as land confiscation. One local party secretary declared that such veiled women, along with their husbands, were counterrevolutionaries and would be exiled "far, far away."[21]

Ignoring legal technicalities in all of these ways made sense to many frustrated Soviet officials. The growth of "terrorist acts" against unveiled women, they argued, showed that Bolshevik repressive tactics had been too "weak."[22] While "administrative methods" might backfire, they admitted, activist women had to be protected by any means necessary. As the Sredazbiuro's top leader, Isaak Zelenskii, put it in 1928 in a top-secret letter to Akmal Ikramov, head of the Uzbek party,

> We cannot tie our [hands] with the procedural norms of the [criminal] code. Without a doubt we have here the makings of a civil war, and [our] means of struggle must be appropriate to the situation that is developing. In cases where there is insufficient basis to prosecute [those who] aid and abet [crimes against women], we must use administrative means of repression. With regard to certain groups of complicitous elements—bois, eshons, counterrevolutionary elements—I consider it perfectly possible to use exile, confiscation of property, and arrest.[23]

Mere procedural norms, then, could not be permitted to hinder the greater good of women's liberation.

But this attitude was not universal among party leaders, nor was it widely evident among rank-and-file workers. Many forcefully rebuffed this line of thinking, arguing instead for strict adherence to legal norms and proper procedures to eradicate byt crime. Perhaps fearing to be criticized as weak-willed

---

19. Among many examples, see RGASPI, d. 1211, ll. 205–11, and all of d. 1214; ÖzRMDA, f. 86, op. 2, d. 92, ll. 28–36; and PDA, op. 3, d. 1598, ll. 16–19.

20. A. Red., "Blagodeiateli baev i mull," *PV*, 26 Dec. 1929. See also RGASPI, d. 1211, l. 211, and d. 1214, l. 130.

21. RGASPI, d. 1214, l. 116. On these other tactics, see d. 1206, ll. 25–26; d. 1214, ll. 21 and 60; d. 2057, l. 177; and d. 2064, l. 21.

22. ÖzRMDA, f. 9, op. 1, d. 3397, l. 109.

23. RGASPI, d. 1692, l. 840b.

bourgeois sentimentalists, they offered mostly practical rather than theoretical arguments to make their case: heavy-handed tactics drove Uzbek women away from the party, they contended, persuading them to stay home and avoid Zhenotdel and Soviet meetings altogether. Defining so many indigenous customs as crimes and punishing them harshly, further, was counterproductive, and the use of pressure tactics and "administrative methods" (*administrirovanie*) only reduced the party's public authority, discredited local Communists, and persuaded Uzbek men and women to listen once again to their mullahs.[24]

Starting in 1927 and continuing throughout the 1930s, then, repeated party declarations "categorically" abjured the use of force or coercion to support Soviet laws. By 1934 the prominent Bolshevik Semen Dimanshtein stated publicly that administrative measures in women's liberation had hurt the party and brought about a "recidivism" of female seclusion.[25] From this perspective persuasion and education, not harsh penalties and state coercion, were the most effective way to make new Soviet byt codes a reality.[26] As one delegate, Smirnov, put it in 1930 at a local party congress, twenty-three activist women had been murdered so far that year, but fully thirty-four people had already been put to death in response: certainly proportionate, if not excessive, he implied. Moreover, jailing an otherwise honest worker who merely "marries and takes a wife who is not 16 or 17, but 14 or 15," was in his view, in a broader sense, harmful to Soviet interests. In such cases, the young wife would be thrown on the street and forced to fend for herself; her husband would emerge five years later a resentful "semibandit," no longer honorable, with a hardened anti-Soviet attitude. "Such is our punitive policy," Smirnov concluded, "and I think that in such cases we go too far."[27]

Such disagreements highlighted the difficulties of creating a single, uniform set of laws to govern Soviet family and marital relations. Simply adopting the laws used in Russia was not an option. In Russia and elsewhere, de facto mar-

24. These arguments are at RGASPI, d. 1690, l. 74; V. Kasparova, "Itogi 3-go Vsesoiuznogo soveshchaniia sredi zhenshchin Sovetskogo Vostoka," *Izvestiia TsK RKP(b)*, no. 25–26 (100–101) (1925), 2–3; and A. P., "Provokatsiia mull," *PV*, 6 Apr. 1927.

25. S. Dimanshtein, "Bor'ba na ideologicheskom fronte v Srednei Azii," *Revoliutsiia i natsional'nosti*, no. 12 (58) (1934), 26.

26. ÖzRMDA, f. 9, op. 1, d. 3370, ll. 60–61; f. 86, op. 1, d. 5881, l. 126, and d. 5885, l. 252. As Khalbibi Yoldasheva, a kolkhoz farmer from Nurat district and survivor of a byt attack, told the First All-Uzbek Congress of Female Youth in 1935, it was tempting to think that the immediate destruction of all religious institutions would solve all Soviet problems in Uzbekistan, but "life itself shows otherwise." Such difficulties were cultural and complex, she said, and "therefore we need to raise here as a very pressing matter the question not only of punitive measures but also of educational measures. Because a person who does something illegal [out of] political backwardness may [yet] by means of educational work submit to our influence" (f. 86, op. 10, d. 634, l. 252).

27. ÖzRMDA, f. 86, op. 1, d. 6096, ll. 244–45.

riages had legal standing—an approach that was meant to undercut the sanctity of religious weddings. Aleksandra Kollontai and other prominent Bolshevik women's activists proclaimed personal freedom in intimate affairs to be a guiding principle; in one Central Asian discussion of byt laws, a similarly minded delegate declared sexual freedom to be a primary goal of Soviet power and therefore Communists "must not forbid or punish [any] sexual union."[28] In Central Asia, however, authorities faced different problems: in the name of personal freedom, an Uzbek man might ignore Soviet views on underage marriage and live with a teenage girl—or with several preteen girls. Such goings-on could not be welcomed by any good Bolshevik, so in Central Asia, cohabitation without official sanction was a political threat. As an Uzbek government report sent to Moscow in 1928 explained, "local conditions" drove Soviet Central Asian authorities to contradict the Russian Republic's legal codes by recognizing only legally registered marriage as a permissible basis for cohabitation.[29]

Difficulties and disagreements created by such local conditions cropped up every step of the way, and efforts to define a canon of byt crimes proceeded fitfully. Which crimes should be included? Circumcision ceremonies? Drunkenness? Bad parenting? Prostitution? All of these and more were mooted as possible crimes.[30] Even the veil itself was considered: should it be a crime to wear the paranji? Even when most party and Zhenotdel activists could agree that a particular Uzbek practice oppressed women and therefore had to be changed, they often were tripped up by the details. How should the crime in question be defined? Who was responsible for it? How harsh should penalties be, and how strictly should they be applied? Drawing on long-standing Orientalist images of the East as well as Marxist ideas of exploitation, most Zhenotdel workers could in the end agree that certain Central Asian marital practices should be ended. Yet in each case these well-intentioned general beliefs proved difficult to translate into specific laws.

By 1926 the Uzbek criminal code had banned qalin in any form, for example, defining it in Article 222 as payment of money, cattle, or any other property to obtain a wife. While punishments varied according to social position, the person paying bride-price and the person accepting it faced identical penalties: up to a year in jail or at forced labor along with confiscation of all property involved in the transaction.[31] Soviet women's rights commissions

---

28. This delegate, Nazarov, expressed his views at ÖzRMDA, f. 904, op. 1, d. 200, l. 90b.

29. ÖzRMDA, f. 86, op. 1, d. 4434, l. 208.

30. Uzbek feasts (*töylar*) with circumcision ceremonies were criticized in 1940 at ÖzRMDA, f. 837, op. 32, d. 2066, ll. 60–61 and 103. The case of a woman convicted in 1936 of being a criminally bad mother—largely because of her drunkenness—is at f. 86, op. 10, d. 772, ll. 49–51. In 1929 the head of the Bukhoro Zhenotdel argued that prostitution was a byt crime, and that prostitutes should be punished accordingly (f. 9, op. 1, d. 3397, l. 110).

31. ÖzRMDA, f. 86, op. 1, d. 2772, l. 148.

claimed credit for the application of this law to both payer and payee, and Uzbek courts were ordered, given the "class character" of qalin, to apply these punishments strictly.[32] By contrast, Soviet legislators agreed that the girls who were—in Bolshevik terms—being bought and sold were not guilty and should not be punished.

This apparently even-handed approach, however, gave rise to unexpected problems. Most visibly, it undercut Soviet efforts to enlist allies among the poorer groups in Uzbek society. In many cases poor peasant men and agricultural wage laborers were being penalized for violating the statute: unable to afford bride-price as a lump payment, they had "banked" qalin in the form of personal labor. But the law did not distinguish between such "exploited" men (forced to work for wealthy landowners to have a chance to marry) and their "exploiters." Hence in 1930 Soviet legislators amended the law to exclude personal labor as a form of qalin. Legal and logical contortions remained, however: wealthy bois who accepted personal labor as qalin remained criminally liable even as the men who paid it escaped penalty.[33]

Few byt issues inspired more unanimity among party leaders and Zhenotdel staffers than polygyny. Nearly all Soviet legislators agreed that the practice was harmful to women and should not be permitted anywhere in the Soviet Union. Such agreement, however, was not by itself enough to create effective laws, since loopholes, flaws, and shortcomings quickly appeared in every effort the party made to end the practice. The Uzbek criminal code in 1926 promised a jail term of up to one year for men who took a second (or third or fourth) spouse, and declared that all weddings must henceforth be registered at local civil registry offices (ZAGS) to be recognized as legal.[34] Apart from the issue of compliance, however, the complexities of Uzbek social life soon seeped through this ostensibly unambiguous prescription. How could the party require all marriages to be registered at ZAGS? What about existing (religious) marriages? What about the many regions in which it was impossible to find a ZAGS office? After a sharp debate within party ranks, such factors helped bring about a decision in 1928 to recognize as legally binding all pre-existing religious marriages, and to require ZAGS registration only for new weddings.[35]

This apparently reasonable decision, however, solved only the uppermost layer of problems. Many logical flaws remained, as one party member, Kurbanov, noted at a closed-door gathering. If all religious marriages now had legal force, he asked, then what about existing polygynous marriages? Was the

32. ÖzRMDA, f. 86, op. 1, d. 3933, ll. 88–89, and d. 6570, l. 55.

33. ÖzRMDA, f. 86, op. 1, d. 5885, ll. 387–88; d. 6571, l. 71; and d. 6574, l. 41.

34. ÖzRMDA, f. 86, op. 1, d. 2772, l. 148, and d. 3618, ll. 4–11. The penalties also applied (theoretically) to a woman who married more than one husband.

35. See the sharp debate at ÖzRMDA, f. 904, op. 1, d. 200, ll. 8–12; and "Novyi zakon o brake, sem'e i opeke," *PV*, 25 Sept. 1927.

Soviet state sanctioning polygyny? Surely not; that would be inconceivable.[36] But if not, how could a monogamous family structure be determined? Only a few possibilities logically existed. Would it be in order of seniority—would a first wife automatically be considered legal, with later spouses shorn of all rights? Would the decision be left to each family (meaning, in practice, the husband) to choose one wife to keep, with the others thrown out onto the street, publicly shamed, and perhaps driven into prostitution? Kurbanov's blunt question left the party with three equally unpalatable choices: to permit such injustices to cast-off wives; to legalize polygyny; or to permit a married man to live with many women while legally being married to only one of them.

Such problems boggled the mind, and indeed the party never directly addressed the issue of existing polygynous marriages. Once banned, to be sure, polygyny was never legalized in Soviet Uzbekistan, but it did achieve a kind of de facto recognition. Zhenotdel workers and local women's clubs encouraged women in polygynous marriages to seek a divorce and to pursue the alimony and child-care support to which they were legally entitled. Yet they were never required to do so, nor were their marriages declared illegal or defunct. The Uzbek criminal code technically only forbade an already married person from entering into another marriage, not from continuing an existing multiple marriage. "Life itself," Kurbanov declared ruefully, "forces [us] into this compromise" (Sama zhizn' zastavliaet idti na etu ustupku).[37] His words could serve as a motto for the overall Soviet effort to transform Uzbekistan through law.

The contingent and flexible nature of byt crime emerges with particular clarity in the creation and definition of underage marriage as a culturally specific category of criminal act. Once again party activists tried to make the law as orderly and straightforward as possible. The possibility under shariat rules for girls to marry at age 9 (and boys at age 12) plainly horrified Zhenotdel workers. Even though Islamic codes stipulated that such marriages could occur only with sexual maturity, party writers tended to overlook this qualification in their push to protect children—particularly young girls—from the dangers of underage marriage.[38] As early as International Women's Day in 1924, for example, the party announced its intent to raise the minimum marriage age for girls from 9 to 16 and for boys from 12 to 18, marshaling and later developing a wide range of arguments in explanation.[39] Underage marriage allegedly led to infertility and was blamed for reducing Uzbek women's life expectancy to between 40 and 50 years. Shortened life spans created a dramatic demographic imbalance, leaving, in the aggregate, only 889 women for

36. Kurbanov's speech is at ÖzRMDA, f. 904, op. 1, d. 200, ll. 80b-90b.
37. Ibid., l. 9.
38. One report alleged in 1925 that only in the "more cultured parts" of Uzbekistan did families wait until their daughters reached age 14 before giving them in marriage; in others (such as Qashqadaryo, Surkhondaryo, and Khorazm) marriage as early as age 9 was said to be common (ÖzRMDA, f. 86, op. 1, d. 2217, l. 22).
39. PDA, f. 60, op. 1, d. 4868, ll. 103-4.

every 1,000 Uzbek men. This shortfall in turn fueled a vicious circle, creating perverse incentives for unmarried men to marry young girls.[40]

Responding to such arguments, the Uzbek SSR's Central Executive Committee in October 1925 approved the idea of raising the marriage age to 16 for girls and 18 for boys. Penalties went into effect for parents who permitted or caused their children to marry sooner; prosecutions quickly widened to include clerics who performed such weddings as well as the matchmakers (sovchilar) who arranged them.[41] By 1928 women's activists called for this age restriction to be standardized across the USSR; one Uzbek report to Moscow noted with pride that the age stipulations in Uzbekistan applied equally to both local and European boys and girls.[42] Tensions persisted under the surface, however, and in closed, confidential debates Soviet legislators discussed the complicated intersecting questions of race, nation, health, and the law.

Some difficulties were practical. How could a legal minimum age—*any* legal minimum—be established, skeptics asked, given the lack of accurate birth records to fix the age of a bride- or groom-to-be?[43] Simple, proponents replied: carry out medical examinations of all prospective marriage partners. The ZAGS office in Old Tashkent was typical: its director set aside a private room in which Soviet personnel asked Uzbek brides to remove their paranji and chachvon for a visual inspection. Despite the violation of Uzbek gender propriety, this procedure was compulsory and could not be refused on grounds of modesty or morality. If ZAGS workers judged the bride younger than 16, she was sent to a medical doctor for a full evaluation. The doctor's word would be final: without a medical certificate the prospective bride could not marry, at least not in the eyes of the state.[44]

Although practical issues remained—in many areas Soviet-trained doctors were rare—such scientific authority offered unassailable prestige to a party that believed it was implementing a Marxist-Leninist science of society. Indeed, medical authority justified the very creation of a category of underage marriage, as scientific objectivity was used to show in gruesome detail the health consequences of the practice.[45] The reluctance of Uzbek women to submit to medical examinations—especially by male doctors—was either ignored

---

40. A. Smirnova, "Pochin po bor'be s religiei na Vostoke," *Kommunistka*, no. 8 (1929), 27; *Trud i byt zhenshchiny Vostoka: Materialy Vsesoiuznogo soveshchaniia komissii po uluchsheniiu byta zhenshchin Vostoka* (Moscow, 1928), 115; and Emine Mukhitdinova, *Revoliutsionnaia zakonnost' i bytovye prestupleniia na Vostoke* (Moscow and Leningrad, 1929), 27–28.

41. The new rule is at ÖzRMDA, f. 86, op. 1, d. 2342, l. 331. Clerics were prosecuted in 1929 at d. 5885, l. 388. The statute was amended in February 1930 to make matchmakers criminally liable: d. 6571, l. 71, and d. 6574, l. 41.

42. ÖzRMDA, f. 86, op. 1, d. 4434, l. 208, and d. 4902, l. 4.

43. "Novyi zakon o brake, sem'e i opeke."

44. ÖzRMDA, f. 86, op. 1, d. 3620, l. 398–980b.

45. See the painfully detailed doctor's report of genital damage to a 10-year-old girl, Fatima-Bibi Nabirova, who was beaten senseless by her 48-year-old husband shortly after being forced to have sexual relations with him (report by Nikiforov, quoted by Liubimova, *Sdvigi*, 7–8).

or dismissed as superstition and ignorance. Transgressing conservative gender norms was, after all, the central point of the hujum; until popular outcry forced important procedural changes in the early 1930s, violations of religious ideas of feminine privacy were a small price to pay to prevent future harm, and in any case helped to overcome local superstitions.[46] Doctors, not politicians, were thus empowered to answer the core question in this debate: How young was too young? What made a marriage count as "underage"?

This question obviously lay at the heart of the issue. Virtually all Zhenotdel workers could agree that 9-year-old girls were too young to marry. But what about girls of 13? Could they be mature enough, physically and emotionally, to live as wives and mothers? Would they become so at 14? At 15? At 16? Where, how, and why should a legal line be drawn? Did the physical changes of puberty, such as first menstruation, connote the crucial degree of maturity, or should less tangible psychological and emotional questions also be considered? Should legislators develop a common, standardized approach across the USSR, or should the existence of hundreds of locally distinct ethnic groups, living in widely varying environmental and socioeconomic conditions, permit variation? The extensive discussions of such questions showed the boundaries of criminal behavior to be far less clear than party activists wanted to admit. Flexibility was the order of the day. For their part, top party and government leaders had no preconceived notions of what the law should be and refused to offer any guidance to local officials. Rather than set all-Soviet standards, in fact, in June 1926 the Presidium of the All-Union Soviet of Nationalities in Moscow declared explicitly that this was a local matter: each republic and autonomous republic should set its own legal age for marriage, "in consultation with the broad masses of the laboring population."[47]

Questions of difference within and between ethnic groups—based on racial as well as national factors—thus entered public policy, as local authorities enjoyed virtually free rein to decide regionally and racially appropriate marriage ages. The resulting laws varied widely across the USSR: in some parts of the Caucasus girls were permitted to marry as early as age 13. Yet everywhere science underpinned these decisions and could be used to explain the disparities. A Doctors' Commission met in Samarqand in October 1925, for example, and justified 16 as the specific minimum permissible age for Uzbek girls to marry. The doctors explained their conclusion as a scientific rather than political matter. "Unlike women of the Caucasus," they said, "who may be considered mature at 13 years of age," Uzbek girls

---

46. Exams by male doctors in medical offices were replaced in 1930 by a more culturally sensitive procedure. ZAGS workers henceforth verified a bride's age with a certificate from the local village soviet or mahalla commission, if necessary supplementing this document with affidavits and other evidence. If doubts remained, a medical team was sent to the bride's home to carry out a physical examination. But these doctors were only to be women, and they bore criminal responsibility for the accuracy of their conclusions. See ÖzRMDA, f. 86, op. 1, d. 6556, l. 162.

47. ÖzRMDA, f. 86, op. 1, d. 2342, l. 337.

at this point are only starting to menstruate. That is, their ovaries are still preparing for reproductive functions, and the appearance of first menstruation does not mean that a woman can become a mother.

While one finds exceptional cases of menstruation at 8 or 9 years of age, such cases exist not only in southern but also in central Asia and even in northern Europe, and by no means show a girl's maturity and ability to carry out healthy reproduction.

Difficult conditions of everyday life and universal malaria delay the sexual development of Uzbek girls behind those of the Caucasus. Members of the Doctors' Commission, in the course of their many years of work in Uzbekistan, have almost never seen an Uzbek girl who is fully developed at 15 years of age. Typically only at 16 years do the tubercles of the mammary glands start to appear, the muscles start to thicken and the skeletal system forms itself into compact masses. The Doctors' Commission considers early marriage to be harmful, as the cause of a large percentage of gynecological illnesses, as a reason for the frequent infertility and high mortality of the female population of Uzbekistan (889 women for every 1,000 men) and also [the high mortality] of children.[48]

Skeptics might wonder how nearly all Uzbek girls, of all regions, conditions, and social classes, matured virtually simultaneously on their sixteenth birthday. The special government commission charged to set a new marriage age, however, accepted this recommendation without objection, declaring that Uzbek girls should not be permitted to marry until they reached age 16. Rare exceptions could be made for 15-year-old girls, but only with a doctor's permission to certify physical maturity.[49]

The power of medical authority here is remarkable. Yet the force with which these public health arguments were expressed reveals their very instability and lack of popular acceptance. While within Soviet circles it was virtually impossible to argue that there should be no such thing as underage marriage—images of 9-year-old child brides resonated too strongly in European eyes for that—fierce arguments continued over nearly all of the details. Some women's activists argued strongly for raising the age of marriage higher than 16: one proposed in 1928 that girls be allowed to marry only at 17 and boys at 20—or better still, that the age be 18 for both boys and girls.[50] Similar calls for a universal marriage age of 18 reverberated for years in party circles, ultimately taking official form in a party resolution of 1938.[51] Other party members, however—including many indigenous male Communists—took advantage of top-level uncertainty to fight in the opposite direction, seeking to whittle the marriage age downward. Local Communists spoke their minds, en-

48. Ibid., l. 327.
49. Ibid., l. 331.
50. ÖzRMDA, f. 904, op. 1, d. 203, ll. 41–42.
51. PDA, op. 14, d. 114, ll. 17–18.

couraged by the flexibility (or indecision) of top party and government bodies. In February 1929, in fact, the Uzbek Supreme Court declared that marriages in violation of the law could nonetheless be recognized in "all cases where the recognition of such marriages does not harm the situation of the women [involved]."[52] The rules, the court appeared to be suggesting, were not necessarily so strict after all.

Discipline and Punish: Enforcing the Soviet Ideal

Although the precise meanings of "byt crime" thus remained unstable and open to debate, once the category had been created and its canonical content more or less defined, party leaders and Zhenotdel activists sought to put it into practice. The first requirement was publicity: much effort was devoted to spreading the word, especially among indigenous women, about the details of the new Soviet laws. Authorities issued a range of publications, including hundreds of articles in the periodical press along with brochures, leaflets, and proclamations printed in native languages. Radio broadcasts, public speeches, and face-to-face meetings at local teahouses and legal-aid clinics (konsultatsii) supplemented this effort.[53] Party leaders also saw a pressing need for new legal institutions, especially for courts strong enough to enforce the new laws and to supplant the religious judges (known as qozi) who enforced shariat norms.[54]

A consensus within the party called for strict enforcement of the new byt rules. Sympathy had its place, but only for the victims of byt crime: an intricate system of pensions and payments compensated those who were martyred or attacked in the liberation campaign.[55] Elaborate procedures ensured that Soviet laws were observed and unwanted outcomes prevented. In 1928, for instance, one Uzbek man submitted an official complaint when five ZAGS officials insisted on interviewing his daughter individually at her wedding to ensure that her consent was voluntary.[56] An internal government report portrayed peasants in 1930 waiting at ZAGS offices for several days while bu-

---

52. ÖzRMDA, f. 9, op. 1, d. 3417, l. 135.

53. These efforts aimed to explain the differences between Soviet laws and those of shariat and odat, on the one hand, and of the tsarist empire, on the other. See ÖzRMDA, f. 9, op. 1, d. 3368, l. 570b; f. 86, op. 1, d. 4444, ll. 4 and 14; f. 95, op. 1, d. 1927, ll. 72 and 1400b-41; f. 736, op. 1, d. 1161, l. 35; and f. 904, op. 1, d. 296, l. 267.

54. These judges were officially recognized well into the 1920s. For some crimes defendants could choose between Soviet and qozi jurisdiction, and in some areas qozi authority was accepted by local soviets. In Zerafshon qozi were the only judges available until 1926 (PDA, op. 2, d. 1368, ll. 82–83, and op. 3, d. 1598, ll. 44–45). See N. N. Fioletov, "Sudy kaziev v Sredne-Aziatskikh respublikakh," Sovetskoe pravo, no. 1 (25) (1927), 132–46, and his "Sudoproizvodstvo v musul'manskikh sudakh (sudy kaziev) Srednei Azii," Novyi Vostok, no. 23–24 (1928), 204–17. Soviet officials also used ad hoc bodies to fight byt crime; alimony brigades, for instance. See ÖzRMDA, f. 95, op. 1, d. 1927, ll. 1400b-41.

55. For martyrs, payments went to surviving relatives. See ÖzRMDA, f. 86, op. 1, d. 4337, ll. 63, 72, 79–800b, 85, 142, 146–47, and 374, and f. 904, op. 1, d. 313, l. 36.

56. RGASPI, d. 1694, l. 121.

reaucrats completed the necessary paperwork to register their marriage.[57] Such caution was no accident. Another confidential report of 1928 said that this stringency was producing a deterrent effect: people in Farghona were said to be whispering that Soviet courts were punishing byt crimes and attacks harshly and so such acts were best avoided.[58]

Efforts to eradicate byt crime played an important role in the Soviet colonial and cultural mission to Central Asia. If women were a surrogate proletariat, legislation to protect them served as "an instrument of the dictatorship of the proletariat in the Uzbek SSR."[59] Anti-Soviet forces in Central Asia could be identified through their byt practices and their attempts to persuade others not to observe Soviet codes, so only the "fire of criminal repression" against byt offenders would annihilate the class enemies that confronted Soviet power.[60] As a draft resolution of the Third All-Uzbek Congress of Soviets put it in mid-1929, there were strong links between terrorism, byt crime, and class conflict. "The struggle around questions of [women's] liberation is one of the most important spheres of the class struggle," it said. In the context of a sharpening fight against "reactionary elements," "every terrorist act committed against liberated women and active workers for liberation must be considered a counterrevolutionary act directed against the measures of Soviet power."[61]

The Uzbek Supreme Court agreed, having already declared in August 1928 that any "murder or serious attack against a woman in connection with her liberation from all types of oppression, and in particular against a woman who has unveiled," henceforth qualified as a terrorist act, a counterrevolutionary crime, under Article 64 of the Uzbek criminal code. Such acts were capital crimes, subject to the death penalty.[62] The Court restated this decision in 1929 and again in 1930 and 1931. In January 1930 the decision was broadened to include threats of murder or violent attack. In February 1930 the Presidium of the All-Union Central Executive Committee in Moscow ratified this broader definition, thus demonstrating the Center's continuing interest in the political implications of Eastern women's liberation.[63] The Presidium's timing was re-

57. ÖzRMDA, f. 86, op. 1, d. 6574, l. 44. ZAGS procedures included medical examinations as well as red tape: for the groom, a marriage required a doctor's certificate of good health, a personal statement regarding his family situation, and an attestation from the mahalla commission that he was old enough to marry and had no other wives; for the bride, a signed profession of consent to the marriage was necessary, along with a statement from a Zhenotdel worker giving an opinion about the bride's age and whether the marriage appeared voluntary, and a confirming statement from the mahalla commission to certify age and consent once again (d. 3620, l. 3980b).

58. ÖzRMDA, f. 86, op. 1, d. 4450, l. 12.

59. ÖzRMDA, f. 95, op. 1, d. 1927, l. 118.

60. ÖzRMDA, f. 9, op. 1, d. 3397, l. 216.

61. ÖzRMDA, f. 95, op. 1, d. 1927, l. 2270b.

62. ÖzRMDA, f. 6, op. 2, d. 462, l. 28; f. 86, op. 1, d. 5883, l. 92, and d. 5885, ll. 382–83. Soviet law previously treated the murder of unveiled women as a "simple" (rather than political) crime (f. 9, op. 1, d. 3397, l. 1090b).

63. The Moscow decision, over the signature of Avel' Enukidze, is at ÖzRMDA, f. 904, op. 1, d. 313, l. 30. It was published at S. Akopov, "Bor'ba s bytovymi prestupleniiami," *Revoliutsiia i*

markable, since this decision came just as the central Zhenotdel in Moscow was facing abolition. Even here, though, the problems of constructing clear legal categories were plain. The most extreme penalty—capital punishment— was declared to apply first and foremost to those of dubious class backgrounds (who were believed to have "instigated" and "inspired" the attacks), not to the "semiconscious," ignorant, misled poor peasants who often actually committed the murders.[64] Yet it was hard to identify the shadowy figures lurking behind the scenes, and women's activists resented pardoning or reducing the sentences of actual murderers, even if they were from a supposedly sympathetic social class.[65]

The existence of "terrorist" and antistate crimes against the hujum and its workers called for a zero-tolerance policy: all Soviet byt laws must be enforced. The courts went to work, trying to impose discipline, swift and severe, on an all too unruly Uzbek society. Rapid investigations, speedy trials, and strict punishments lay at the heart of this campaign to make the new codes of everyday life a reality. Speed, deliberate or not, was applauded; by late 1928 the Uzbek lower courts were ordered to consider and conclude cases of byt violations in no more than a week.[66] For years, expeditious justice remained a high priority: in 1941 courts in Namangan decided 86 percent of their byt cases in less than three weeks.[67]

Punishments were stern, even at the possible risk of individual miscarriages of justice. One father, convicted in 1929 of facilitating an underage marriage, was sentenced to a year in jail before the Uzbek Supreme Court threw out his conviction when he proved his daughter had been of legal age to marry.[68] However regrettable such cases, party activists saw the danger of insufficient vigilance as far greater. By 1929 President Akhunbabaev argued for increased use of the death penalty to deter byt crime; such cases were trumpeted pub-

natsional'nosti, no. 4–5 (1930), 65. The All-Union Supreme Court reached a similar decision in 1929; see Chirkov, *Reshenie zhenskogo voprosa*, 186. On the inclusion of threats, see ÖzRMDA, f. 9, op. 1, d. 3417, l. 135. Later restatements are at f. 6, op. 2, d. 462, l. 29; f. 86, op. 1, d. 5885, l. 585; d. 5602, ll. 1–3; and d. 6570, l. 55; and f. 95, op. 1, d. 1927, l. 139–390b.

64. In mid-1927 an illiterate farmhand was accused of stabbing his wife sixteen times. Normally he would have faced the death penalty, although she survived. Upon his conviction, however, the farmhand's social position and illiteracy earned him a dramatically reduced sentence— only five years in prison (RGASPI, d. 1060, l. 11).

65. On attempts to apply a differential class analysis to identify categories of capital crime and the perpetrators of such crimes, see ÖzRMDA, f. 9, op. 1, d. 3397, ll. 6, 11, and 214–15, and f. 86, op. 1, d. 5885, ll. 380–81 and 765. A particularly eloquent argument from 1939 that crimes against women revealed the "dirty hands" of the "counterrevolutionary clergy" is at PDA, op. 15, d. 81, ll. 10–11.

66. This directive in November 1928, which noted that such cases could take from five to eight months to wend their way through the courts, is at ÖzRMDA, f. 86, op. 1, d. 5885, l. 389.

67. ÖzRMDA, f. 904, op. 10, d. 91, l. 49.

68. T. T. Inoiatov, "Sudy sovetskogo Uzbekistana v bor'be s feodal'no-baiskimi perezhitkami," *Trudy SAGU*, n.s., Juridical Science 4, no. 124 (1958): 29.

licly, to show the power of Soviet justice in action.[69] Delays, suspended sentences, and muddled thinking on whether particular acts qualified as capital crimes were all blamed for reducing the deterrent effect of Soviet law.[70]

To show the seriousness of Soviet efforts, judicial workers spent much time compiling statistics on byt crime and its enforcement. In reports to higher-level courts and to officials in the women's liberation commissions and the Zhenotdel, these workers carefully recorded the details of each crime in long tables that listed the identity and social origin of each defendant. They chronicled individual acts of byt crime, hoping to track and analyze broader trends and to improve police and prosecution efforts to stamp out such phenomena. Such tables usually listed the disposition of each case and specified the punishment; the number of criminals fined, imprisoned, or shot showed that progress was being made.[71] The flip side, however, was less encouraging: statistics from the Uzbek Commissariat of Justice (Narkomiust) showed nearly all kinds of byt crime, even the most serious, apparently rising, not falling, in the late 1920s. (See Table 4.) These figures are neither transparent nor conclusive. Some of the sharp increase reflects more careful reporting procedures, especially after the Uzbek Supreme Court certified crimes against women to be counterrevolutionary acts. Many more incidents never showed up in Soviet chronicles. But the increase is likely not entirely an artifact of improved reporting. Narkomiust said that the situation was worsening with every passing year, that the "general population" was involved in these crimes (in addition to the expected "anti-Soviet elements"), and that "doubtless" the trend would continue.[72] Thousands of women and a smaller number of men were beaten to ensure their continued adherence to non-Soviet codes of female seclusion.[73] Hundreds of unveiled and activist women had been killed in Uzbekistan by 1929, as retribution and to warn others contemplating the same path.[74] Juma Juraev, a peasant living outside Bukhoro, reportedly mused, "Unveiled women are leading all the others astray. We have two unveiled women in our village, and [by] looking at them, others are being corrupted. I think these two women need to be killed."[75] Incrementally better prosecution rates provided cold comfort to Zhenotdel workers and party activists who confronted such attitudes.

By 1929 terrorist acts against women were being reported in every province

69. For Akhunbabaev's sentiments, see RGASPI, d. 2080, l. 15. Two examples of publicity are M. Grek., "K rasstrelu!" PV, 10 Feb. 1929, and "K vysshei mere," PV, 29 May 1929.

70. Such difficulties reportedly increased after 1928, when fully 73 percent of death sentences pronounced had actually been carried out (ÖzRMDA, f. 86, op. 1, d. 5885, l. 384).

71. For examples of such tables, see RGASPI, d. 2057, ll. 211–200b; and ÖzRMDA, f. 86, op. 1, d. 4450, l. 14.

72. ÖzRMDA, f. 95, op. 1, d. 1714, l. 7.

73. RGASPI, d. 1694, ll. 37–38, 68–69, and 89–92.

74. PDA, op. 6, d. 743, ll. 36–37.

75. RGASPI, d. 1694, l. 19.

Table 4. Crimes of daily life, Uzbekistan, 1927–1929

Crime	1927	1928	1929*
Speaking out against women's liberation	15	41	86
Qalin (bride-price)	105	†	192
Forced marriage	101	179	124

* First half only.
† Illegible.
SOURCE: ÖzRMDA, f. 95, op. 1, d. 1714, l. 7.

of Uzbekistan, and local activists begged for help and protection. They tracked hundreds of incidents month by month on color-coded graphs showing the numbers of Uzbek women raped, assaulted, and killed.[76] Rape-murder combinations were common, serving as a particularly chilling disincentive to any woman thinking about joining the Soviet cause.[77] The most extreme cases were truly horrific—some involved mutilation and dismemberment—and seemed to confirm the party's worst preconceptions about the bestiality of its opponents. One female activist in Qashqadaryo reportedly was killed in 1929 by a group of seventeen men; another unveiled woman was killed by her husband when she was eight months pregnant.[78] In one of the most disturbing tales, three Uzbek Communists were accused of raping and maiming an unveiled woman and then doing the same to her two-year-old daughter.[79] While such tales could have been embellished by the party or police to show the depravity of anti-Soviet forces, at least some seem credible; and for the most part these reports were kept highly classified, not disseminated as propaganda (not surprisingly, given the negative impact such news had on women who were considering unveiling). Table 5 shows a substantial increase in prosecutions for byt terrorism: by 1929 nearly two-thirds of death sentences meted out for counterrevolutionary crime under Article 64 were related to the hujum. The battle against byt violence had come to lie at the heart of Soviet criminal justice in Uzbekistan.

This stress on byt misconduct did not end in 1929. Published sources and archival documents show a steady stream of calls in party and government circles throughout the 1930s and into the 1940s to redouble efforts to enforce byt laws. Bekhtiarova, a women's club worker, told a gathering of her col-

76. Examples of such graphs are at RGASPI, d. 1694, ll. 16 and 101. Similar reports are at ll. 9–10, 12–14, and 86–92; and PDA, op. 4, d. 1235, ll. 83–92. A report from 1929 citing hundreds of cases emanating from every province of the UzSSR is at RGASPI, d. 2056, ll. 203–4, and the disquiet over sharp increases is at ÖzRMDA, f. 95, op. 1, d. 1927, ll. 70–71.
77. On rape, see RGASPI, d. 1694, ll. 123–24, and d. 1699, l. 91.
78. Qashqadaryo is at PDA, op. 5, d. 821, l. 3; the tragic pregnant woman is at RGASPI, d. 1692, l. 53.
79. RGASPI, d. 1520, l. 222.

Table 5. Prosecution and sentencing of byt terrorists, Uzbek SSR, 1927–1929

	1927	1928	1929*
Prosecutions for byt terrorism†			
Number of cases	5	25	44
Byt terrorism as percent of all prosecutions under Article 64	0.5%	1.2%	8.8%
Sentences for byt terrorism			
Number of criminals convicted	12	45	170
Number sentenced to death	5	27	124
Percent sentenced to death	42%	60%	73%
Byt terrorists as percent of all death sentences under Article 64	2.9%	25%	63%

* First eight months only.

† "Terrorism" includes all crimes certified as terrorist and counterrevolutionary acts under Article 64 of the Uzbek criminal code.

SOURCE: ÖzRMDA, f. 9, op. 1, d. 3397, l. 213; f. 95, op. 1, d. 1927, l. 92.

leagues in Moscow in 1930 that forty activist women had been murdered in Andijon province over the past year, noting that it was very difficult to work in such conditions.[80] Andijon provincial courts came under fire again in 1932, when they produced only two death sentences in response to 284 byt crimes.[81] The First All-Uzbek Congress of Female Youth in 1935 focused a great deal of attention on byt crime; speakers declared the need to "judge [offenders] with all the severity of revolutionary law."[82] Shortly thereafter leaders in Moscow underscored the crucial importance of the issue: on 16 May 1935 the Presidium of the All-Union Soviet of Nationalities noted the "especially important political meaning of protecting the rights of national-minority women" and called on local procuracies to pay special attention to byt crime. Punitive measures with regard to forced marriage, underage marriage, and qalin required "decisive strengthening," the resolution continued, and the full Soviet of Nationalities would take up the issue of counterrevolutionary crimes such as the murder of liberated (unveiled) women. The All-Union procurator, the infamous Andrei Vyshinskii, was directed to report regularly on the quantity and nature of such cases.[83]

In the later 1930s one finds articles in both the central and Central Asian press criticizing poor efforts to eradicate byt crime, along with laments that

80. GARF, f. 6983, op. 1, d. 157a, l. 293.

81. ÖzRMDA, f. 86, op. 1, d. 7996, l. 259.

82. *PSTZhMUz*, 87 and 93. The congress sparked an upsurge in the prosecution of cases, according to V. Tadevosian, "Usilit' bor'bu s prestupleniiami protiv raskreposhcheniia zhenshchin-natsionalok," *Sotsialisticheskaia zakonnost'*, no. 11 (1938), 36–37.

83. ÖzRMDA, f. 837, op. 13, d. 21, ll. 14–15.

the murder of unveiled and activist women, the marriage of underage girls, and the driving of young women to suicide by self-immolation were increasing rather than declining.[84] In 1936 the Uzbek government increased byt crime penalties, with higher maximum sentences for some violations and new minimums without any stated maximum for others.[85] In late 1938 the Uzbek SSR procurator, V. T. Kukharenko, called for redoubled attention to women's cases and the continuing problem of byt crime, and judicial organs came under renewed scrutiny in 1939 and 1940.[86] As Akhunbabaev put it in 1940, "It is obvious that this excessive tolerance [liberal'nichanie] toward criminal violations of Soviet laws cannot lead to a decrease in the number of crimes committed against women's liberation. In certain districts the [increasing] number of terrorist acts directly reflects the activization of enemy elements."[87] Finally, on the eve of war in late May 1941, *Pravda Vostoka* published another clarion call for renewed assault on the continuing problem of byt crime.[88]

The very fact that such resolutions continued to be necessary—the declaration in 1939 vowed that the murder of "not a single activist woman" could be permitted in 1940—suggests that Soviet success was less than total.[89] Party activists continued to publicize Soviet laws and tried to create a moral discourse to undercut customary byt practices, portraying unveiled women as virtuous, upstanding citizens, for instance, and polygynous marriages based on qalin as squalid, oppressive, and evil. But bringing about such moral revaluations was difficult, no matter what scripts were tried. "Spontaneous" public demonstrations were one common tactic. Crowds gathered to protest murders of unveiled women and Soviet personnel; frequently they shouted for the death penalty against those responsible.[90] In one case in the 1930s, a murder in Katta Qorghon reportedly elicited a crowd of seventy angry women marching "with red flags to the District Committee [to demand] that the murderer be surrendered to them." Only when a local official explained that lynching was not permitted under Soviet law, but that the murderer would receive punishment at the hands of Soviet courts, was the crowd said to be mollified.[91]

Show trials—or "demonstration trials," in which the judicial process was

---

84. Iv. Babintsev and V. Turetskii, "O raskreposhchenii zhenshchin v Azerbaidzhane," *Revoliutsiia i natsional'nosti*, no. 3 (73) (1936), 54–55; and "Ot VII k VIII s"ezdu Sovetov Soiuza SSR," *Revoliutsiia i natsional'nosti*, no. 11 (81) (1936), 76.

85. ÖzRMDA, f. 86, op. 10, d. 1092, ll. 58a-60.

86. "Reshitel'no borot'sia s maleishimi narusheniiami prav zhenshchin," *PV*, 28 June 1938; Khursan Makhmudova, "Feodal'no-baiskie perezhitki v Uzbekistane," *Pravda*, 28 Dec. 1940; PDA, op. 15, d. 16, l. 13; and ÖzRMDA, f. 837, op. 32, d. 2066, ll. 47–48.

87. ÖzRMDA, f. 2454, op. 1, d. 412, l. 131.

88. Nafisa Khairova, "Usilit' bor'bu protiv feodal'no-baiskikh perezhitkov," *PV*, 29 May 1941.

89. The phrase is from ÖzRMDA, f. 837, op. 32, d. 2066, l. 34. On terrorism against women in 1941, see f. 904, op. 10, d. 91, ll. 2–97.

90. For example, PDA, op. 3, d. 1560, ll. 340–43.

91. Halle, *Women in the Soviet East*, 191.

employed for a publicly didactic purpose—also played a central role in the attempt to create moral change through the dispensation of justice.[92] (See Figure 21.) These trials functioned as educational theater—to teach Soviet justice, popular obedience, and ideas of class identity and revolutionary punishment. They were expected to curtail acts of violence against women, and other byt violations as well.[93] As even foreign visitors could readily discern, such propaganda trials were intended for public education, not individual justice. Guilt in the customary sense was not the issue; often the accused did not deny his actions. The goal was to convince the audience and the public that what he had done was wrong: "In the 'show-trials,' not only does the judge descend to take part in the battle, but all local political and social organizations are incited to dramatize the proceedings. Civilian bodies pass resolutions demanding the highest penalty. The trial itself is held in a large hall, or even in the open air, and by the size of the attendance is reckoned the measure of its success."[94] One such trial convicted one Nur Ali of killing his newly unveiled wife. He was sentenced to death and his accomplices to various prison terms, but the trial was deemed a success mostly because the audience of 5,000 peasants applauded the outcome, even renaming their village after the ill-fated victim, Aloliatbibi.[95]

Show trials and publicity continued throughout the 1930s and beyond. At a party congress in 1940, for example, one speaker recited case after case of brutal murders of Soviet women activists in 1939. While such a litany might have been depressing, in each case the speaker noted carefully that the culprits had been found, tried, and usually sentenced to death—news that drew a steady stream of applause.[96] One party report asked what would be the point of holding trials out of the public eye, in out-of-the-way rooms, without mass involvement: the masses would lose the opportunity to educate themselves by witnessing a trial and seeing the strict Soviet punishment meted out. Private trials, it concluded, "are of little use."[97] Top Central Asian Bolsheviks complained in late 1938 or early 1939 about the paucity of public trials—reportedly only 10 percent of court cases dealing with byt crime were open to the public, a fact that Usman Yusupov, the new first secretary of the Uzbek party, and others saw as clearly insufficient.[98] Public humiliation for those convicted,

---

92. Their ritualistic and scripted nature has already been seen in Chapter 4, so I will not offer a close analysis of another byt trial—the Kakharov affair, the Kapa trial, or any of the many others. See ÖzRMDA, f. 1714, op. 5, d. 663, ll. 1–89; and RGASPI, d. 2056, ll. 109–24; d. 2064, ll. 12–120b and 22–23.

93. RGASPI, d. 1239, l. 32.

94. Strong, Red Star in Samarkand, 291 and 298–99.

95. Ibid., 292. For other foreign visitors' accounts of such trials, see Maillart, Turkestan Solo, 243–53; or Halle, Women in the Soviet East, 126–39.

96. ÖzRMDA, f. 837, op. 32, d. 2066, ll. 46–47. A trial was quickly organized when Yoldasheva told the First All-Uzbek Congress of Female Youth in 1935 about a violent attack she suffered (f. 86, op. 10, d. 634, l. 251).

97. ÖzRMDA, f. 95, op. 1, d. 1927, l. 71.

98. PDA, op. 15, d. 16, l. 13.

Figure 21. Uzbek criminals under arrest. (Courtesy Anahita Gallery, Santa Fe, N.M.)

after all, did not end at the courtroom door. Throughout the prewar period newspapers splashed coverage of these trials prominently across their pages, and newsreels and documentary films provided footage for all to see.[99]

Subaltern Dialogues: Soviet Law as a Starting Point

Bolshevik activists and party leaders were not alone in having ideas about how Uzbek social life should be lived, and despite occasional appearances to the contrary, their debates did not proceed in isolation from Central Asian society. Many party members, even some of those new to Uzbekistan, believed that Soviet law could advance only with the support of local populations. Perceived or expected social responses often colored Soviet views about how to proceed or about whether a particular law would work. Despite the undeniable and sometimes overwhelming power of the Stalinist state during the late 1930s and early 1940s, the expressed or anticipated views of Uzbek men and women not

99. For example, "Ubiitsy Khasiiat prigovoreny k rasstrelu," *PV,* 4 Dec. 1928; Vl. Kin., "Vragi raskreposhcheniia zhenshchin," *PV,* 23 July 1935; and Iu. Bekarevich, "Ubiistvo Tokhta Abdul-laevoi," *PV,* 26 June 1939. For films about activists' murders in 1930, with coverage of the trials and convictions and later memorial services for the victims, see RGAKFD 10521 or 10526.

directly connected to Soviet power produced modifications, extensions, and even occasional withdrawals of official legal norms. Such social responses are fundamental to the complicated processes of cultural negotiation that shaped the changing meanings of Soviet law in Central Asia.

Many Uzbeks outside the party simply ignored the new laws, while others appropriated and subverted Soviet rules and the new judicial system in a wide variety of fascinating and creative ways. In the words of the historian William Wagner, who has studied legal reforms and family life in the late tsarist Russian empire, "although the law affects behavior, it is far easier to change the law than to use it effectively to inculcate specific values, control behavior, or shape social relations in conformity with ideals."[100] This observation is borne out in Stalinist Central Asia. Despite the dramatic show trials that meted out exemplary punishment for qalin and polygyny, for example, these practices continued largely unabated, albeit sometimes in altered forms to avoid the gaze of Soviet police, ZAGS officials, and Zhenotdel activists. Soviet women's workers privately admitted that many byt laws had what they called a "declarative" rather than substantive character, given the resolutely non-Soviet sensibility of most Central Asians.[101] The spectrum of social responses to Soviet attempts to enforce this new legal category of byt crime was broad, fascinating, and complex, ranging once again from vocal support and open hostility at the two extremes to apathy and subtle forms of mutual accommodation in the middle. But many thousands of Uzbek men and women used the "weapons of the weak" against these Soviet incursions. From positions both inside and outside the Soviet system they emulated peasants and colonized peoples around the world by generating "hidden transcripts" that spoke back to governmental and judicial structures of power.[102]

Some Uzbek men and women chose openly to resist Soviet efforts to define and eradicate these crimes of daily life. They made speeches opposing the creation of crimes out of customary practices; they organized large-scale public meetings to show their opposition; they submitted petitions asking for a reconsideration of the new Soviet laws. They appeared to believe their voices mattered: in 1928, for example, one workers' meeting in Farghona's New City voted publicly, 50–16, against the idea of raising the marriage age for girls to 17.[103] Archival records from the hujum's early days in 1927 show Zhenotdel workers unhappily contemplating organized crowds of several hundred people marching in protest, and the arrest of ringleaders failed to dissuade others. By 1929, party reports complained that antihujum "agitation" had taken on a

100. Wagner, *Marriage, Property and Law in Late Imperial Russia* (Oxford, 1994), 383.

101. RGASPI, d. 1685, l. 85.

102. Scott, *Weapons of the Weak* and his *Domination*. As noted above, subalternity in Soviet Uzbekistan was multilayered and context-dependent. In many situations outside state control, Uzbek opponents of the Soviet state dominated social interactions.

103. ÖzRMDA, f. 904, op. 1, d. 203, ll. 109–12.

"systematic, organized character" (allegedly led by Muslim clerics), and that verbal assaults against Zhenotdel activists were occurring all across the Uzbek SSR. Instances of open protest against the unveiling campaign and Soviet byt legislation continued throughout the 1930s.[104]

Perhaps the most common form of resistance to the new laws was simple refusal to observe them in practice. In some cases and in some regions violations of Soviet byt norms only became more flagrant once they were written into law. While it is difficult to evaluate the extent to which the commission of byt crime represented a form of protest or civil disobedience, clearly the widespread—in some cases virtually universal—infraction of these new laws could not be ignored. Violent byt crime remained an especially problematic phenomenon from the perspective of party leaders. It was all the more serious given the ongoing weakness of Soviet control in Central Asia, and as violent resistance was also visible elsewhere in the Soviet countryside (in Russia, Ukraine, and Kazakhstan, for instance) after the start of Stalin's collectivization campaign.[105] In Uzbekistan, local newspapers had initially shown the hujum's difficulties with remarkable candor. "YET ANOTHER VICTIM," screamed one headline in November 1927: "Having recently thrown off the paranji, Achil'deeva is savagely strangled by her husband."[106] Only when Zhenotdel and party officials complained that such reports made people reluctant to cooperate did the tone of newspaper coverage shift in the 1930s.

Rampant violations of Soviet byt laws remained a cause of concern within the party leadership as well as the Zhenotdel. The codification of such behaviors as crimes, after all—and their placement in a linked pyramid of criminality, with "counterrevolutionary" attacks at its pinnacle—marked all byt transgressions, whether violent or not, as intolerable political acts. The persistence of such acts may not be surprising in the late 1920s, during the initial turmoil around the hujum. Rape, murder, and the occasional mutilation of unveiled women and Zhenotdel activists occurred with regularity—by one estimate as many as 2,500 women in Uzbekistan had been killed by 1930—along with an apparently endless stream of cases involving polygyny, qalin, and forced veiling and seclusion.[107] Even when the large number of rapes and "insults" to women and terrorist acts that qualified as counterrevolutionary crimes under

104. ÖzRMDA, f. 86, op. 1, d. 5885, ll. 381–82, and f. 1714, op. 5, d. 663, entire; and RGASPI, d. 1688, l. 187.

105. On other parts of the USSR, see the five-volume documentary collection *Tragediia Sovetskoi derevni: Kollektivizatsiia i raskulachivanie. Dokumenty i materialy, 1927–1939*, ed. V. P. Danilov, R. T. Manning, and L. Viola (Moscow, 1998–2004).

106. "Eshche odna zhertva," *PV*, 14 Sept. 1927.

107. RGASPI, all of d. 1214; ÖzRMDA, f. 86, op. 1, d. 5885, ll. 380–91; and PDA, op. 5, d. 815, ll. 175–78. The figure of 2,500 murders is from N. Ibragimova and F. Salimova, "Opyt raskreposhcheniia zhenshchin respublik Srednei Azii i Kazakhstana i ego burzhuaznykh falsifikatory," *Kommunist Uzbekistana*, no. 8 (1985), 83–89.

Article 64 are excluded, the remaining categories of byt crime produced almost one out of every ten cases heard in the Uzbek criminal justice system in 1929.[108]

Lamentations that the party was losing the war against byt crime continued throughout the 1930s and beyond. Polygyny, the buying and selling of women, and underage marriage were all reportedly common on collective farms throughout the 1930s.[109] Urban areas fared little better: in 1935 one district of Tashkent alone prosecuted nearly 200 byt crimes: 53 beatings, 56 rapes, 36 cases of "opposition to liberation," 6 underage marriages, 17 nonpayers of alimony, 8 "hooligans," 3 instances of polygyny, and several cases of murder and threats to commit murder.[110] Prosecutions for qalin and underage marriage increased dramatically in 1938 and 1939, and the rate of byt murder, sex crimes, and beatings appeared to some observers also to be growing.[111] An official list of byt cases from Khorazm in 1940–41 included murder, attempted murder, rape, underage marriage, and beatings to prevent wives from attending school or training courses.[112] Women were still married against their will; in several cases in 1939, 1940, and 1941, husbands forced their wives to wear paranji and chachvon, even though they faced hard labor or up to three years' incarceration for doing so.[113] Dozens of "terrorist acts" in the Uzbek SSR were reported in 1939, with fully three times as many female as male victims; the ill-starred town of Chust alone saw at least eighteen murders of unveiled women in 1939–40.[114] No wonder that at a conference of procurators held in late 1941—after the war against Hitler had started—each of these Uzbek officials reported dozens of byt cases and discussed the unfortunate "shortcomings" (kamciliklar) that continued to mar the realization of women's legal rights and hindered the war effort.[115]

Resistance through noncompliance was not the only Uzbek response to Soviet byt laws. In many cases Uzbek men and women did not withdraw completely from interactions with Soviet structures, but instead creatively negoti-

108. *Materialy k otchetu Tsentral'nogo Komiteta KP (bol.) Uzbekistana V-mu Partiinomu kurultaiu* (Samarqand, 1930), 58.

109. For reports from 1933 and 1940 see PDA, op. 9, d. 968, ll. 194–98; and ÖzRMDA, f. 2454, op. 1, d. 412, ll. 130 and 146.

110. ÖzRMDA, f. 86, op. 10, d. 772, l. 62.

111. The rate of qalin and underage marriage prosecutions in the Uzbek SSR more than doubled, growing from 152 in the first half of 1938 to 213 in the first four months of 1939 (PDA, op. 15, d. 1383, ll. 39–41).

112. ÖzRMDA, f. 904, op. 10, d. 91, ll. 2–9.

113. PDA, op. 15, d. 81, ll. 10–11, and d. 1388, ll. 18–19; ÖzRMDA, f. 86, op. 10, d. 634, l. 27; f. 904, op. 10, d. 91, ll. 50–53 and 91; and f. 2454, op. 1, d. 412, l. 130; and RGASPI, d. 1213, ll. 48–49.

114. ÖzRMDA, f. 837, op. 32, d. 2066, ll. 35–42, 46–48, and 101, and f. 2454, op. 1, d. 412, ll. 131, 135–36, and 144.

115. ÖzRMDA, f. 904, op. 10, d. 91, ll. 42–46.

ated this relationship to produce benefits for themselves, even if doing so conferred an implicit legitimacy on Soviet authorities. Soviet cash, for instance, was used to pay bride-price obligations, although it also wove participants into the Soviet economy and confirmed the state's basic power to define and circulate socially agreed units of value.[116] Despite a common reluctance to observe the precise stipulations of the new laws, moreover, it is striking that large numbers of Uzbek men and women still traveled to local ZAGS offices to register their marriages legally. (See Figure 22.) Yet simultaneously, indigenous populations took steps both overtly and covertly to make the new system work to their advantage and did their best to modify that system's exact provisions.

Reforms in divorce procedures, for example, had aimed to improve the situation of Muslim wives, who according to shariat could be divorced without alimony, child custody, or cause. All a husband needed to do was repeat three times the word "leave" (*taloq*), a simple option not available to wives. Initial reports suggested that Soviet reforms had given women greater latitude to act. One survey found that women initiated fully 91 percent of 450 divorce applications filed in Tashkent in 1927. Soviet procedures thus gave these women a measure of legal agency as well as state protection, both from angry husbands seeking revenge and from the possibility of being left penniless in the street.[117]

Yet in addition to the obvious problems, such as ensuring that alimony and child-support awards were actually paid, Soviet divorce reforms ran into—and sometimes caused—unexpected difficulties. Critics noted that even with a Soviet divorce an Uzbek woman would not be accepted socially unless her husband also gave her a shariat divorce—a step Soviet courts were powerless to coerce and without which she remained a social pariah.[118] Even when indigenous women took advantage of Soviet divorce, the outcome was not necessarily what the party wanted. In some areas women reportedly decided en masse to divorce their husbands, a step that on the surface looked consistent with Soviet women's liberation but that overwhelmed the government's paltry support structures and opened the party to rhetorical attack from those who argued that the Bolsheviks wanted to destroy Central Asian society. By 1928 the party was forced to organize a campaign against Uzbek mass divorces, notwithstanding the contradiction to its promises of female autonomy and independence.[119]

In other cases men rather than women took advantage of Soviet divorce procedures. Some husbands divorced their unveiled wives and invented reasons to satisfy ZAGS officials: "poor housekeeping," for example. If such a petition were granted, the ex-wife could often be driven by social opprobrium to reveil and return to him.[120] Fictitious divorces also permitted multiple wives.

116. Thanks to Peter Holquist for urging me to clarify this point.

117. The Tashkent survey is at RGASPI, d. 1224, ll. 50–52. The need for protection emerged when men attacked their ex-wives; see d. 1690, l. 2.

118. ÖzRMDA, f. 86, op. 1, d. 5885, l. 7750b; and RGASPI, d. 2057, l. 255.

119. RGASPI, d. 1713, l. 148.

120. RGASPI, d. 1247, l. 228.

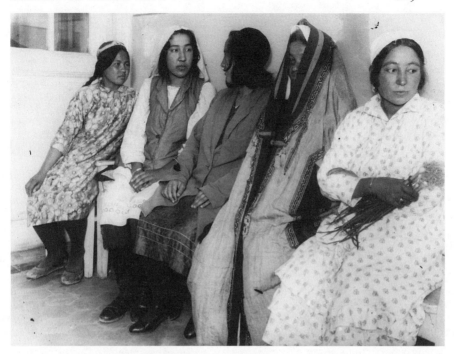

Figure 22. Uzbek girls awaiting examination to obtain permission to marry, ZAGS office, Tashkent, 1925–26. (Courtesy RGAKFD.)

Even village Communists used this technique to keep two or three wives. All were married according to shariat, but only one wife was legal in the eyes of the state.[121] Strange "third parties" were sometimes spotted lurking near ZAGS divorce proceedings; Soviet officials did not know who they were or what their business might be, speculating only that they were engaged in "pandering" (*svodnichestvo*).[122] Calls for rapid and easy divorce might sound revolutionary, ZAGS workers concluded, but given imperfect information and Soviet ignorance of local culture, they often only ensured that young Central Asian women would continue to be bought and sold like cattle.[123]

Soviet attempts to ban qalin, too, quickly ran into trouble as the new laws were bent, broken, and subverted at every turn. According to one report from 1928, qalin was "almost legal" in Khorazm province, since it happened in plain sight and was rarely prosecuted. Party investigations turned up continuing evidence of the practice on a massive scale throughout the 1930s and into the 1940s, with bride-price ranging as high as several thousand rubles, forty-

121. ÖzRMDA, f. 6, op. 2, d. 462, l. 6.
122. ÖzRMDA, f. 9, op. 1, d. 3397, l. 95ob.
123. This argument was also made about Turkmenistan; see ÖzRMDA, f. 9, op. 1, d. 3427, l. 38.

five head of cattle, and large quantities of grain.[124] The only real changes resulting from the Soviet effort to ban qalin was a shift away from cattle in favor of more easily concealed cash payments and the frequent portrayal of bride-price transfers as wedding gifts.[125] Such payments were easily concealed from the gaze of Soviet police and prosecutors; in some cases, local authorities assisted in the deception. Local police officers were known to drive away party investigative brigades, offering their big-city visitors assurances that they had been mistaken, that byt crimes like qalin did not exist in *this* region.[126] Tactics on the ground were creative. In 1928, for instance, one man accused of rape and forced marriage tried to turn the tables on his accuser. He argued that she had accompanied him willingly, that they had sexual relations voluntarily, and that only afterward did she demand qalin as a form of blackmail. Although his story failed to sway the Soviet court, it is remarkable in its attempt to recast him as the victim of qalin rather than the criminal.[127]

The very weakness of Soviet efforts to enforce the new rules against qalin can be discerned in the records of successful prosecutions. With thousands of instances of bride-price spread all across Central Asia, criminal accusations generally came to light only when some aspect of the contractual arrangement went awry. Perhaps a man who paid qalin in the form of labor decided to seize his bride before working the full agreed term; possibly the young woman refused to participate in an arranged marriage; in some cases, the bride's father reneged on the deal and refused to accept the agreed-upon amount in payment.[128] The wronged party could then threaten to turn to Soviet courts, but this was a step taken only in extremis, after negotiations had failed, since no Soviet court was likely to enforce such a marriage contract. In fact, such an appeal could well lead to jail time and fines for all the men involved, including those who lodged the complaint. For this reason, barring the unlucky few who happened to be visible to Zhenotdel investigators—either because they occupied positions of Soviet or party authority or because they had the ill fortune to be present during a spot check or intensive local audit—marriages in which qalin arrangements proceeded smoothly to all parties' satisfaction rarely surfaced in the Soviet courts.

The reported cases thus tend to be exceptional. Each story, of course, no matter what its particulars, served to underscore the self-consciously European horror of many Slavic party activists at what they saw as the buying and selling of young girls. But few indigenous Muslims saw it that way. For them,

124. The report from Khorazm is at RGASPI, d. 1690, l. 2. One partial audit in 1936 found hundreds of cases during the previous year (PDA[K], op. 12, d. 638, ll. 96 and 105). Also see RGASPI, d. 1214, l. 4; d. 1694, ll. 8 and 114; d. 2057, l. 255; ÖzRMDA, f. 86, op. 1, d. 5885, l. 392; PDA, op. 4, d. 1235, ll. 12–13, and op. 9, d. 968, ll. 196–97; and Akopov, "Bor'ba," 62.
125. ÖzRMDA, f. 9, op, 1, d. 3397, l. 88, and f. 86, op. 1, d. 4902, l. 20.
126. RGASPI, d. 1224, l. 48.
127. ÖzRMDA, f. 1714, op. 5, d. 322, ll. 83 and 98.
128. ÖzRMDA, f. 86, op, 1, d. 5885, ll. 387–88.

qalin was a far more complicated transaction, involving moral statements and the establishment of familial alliances as much as a simple economic transfer. Thus only in a truly extraordinary circumstance would a party to a qalin transaction actually complain to Soviet authorities. These cases therefore show the boundaries of customary behavior by revealing what acts violated local norms flagrantly enough to trigger such a drastic step. Complaints were lodged when one woman was "sold" many times but never actually given in marriage, or when a father or brother tried to squeeze extra money out of a prospective bridegroom. In 1927 one local official sold his ("very pretty") sister three times for qalin, but he faced trial only when his neighbors complained that he kept the money and refused to give his sister in marriage to any of the suitors. Another rural Uzbek man was reported in 1936 to have sold his adult daughter to five men over two years; and in 1940 a father was accused of selling his 15-year-old daughter for 4,400 rubles and other material goods, but after the wedding, it was charged, he seized his daughter, sent her into hiding in Kazakhstan, and threatened to resell her unless her new husband paid an additional 10,000 rubles.[129] Such actions violated accepted codes of behavior among neighbors and clearly incited anger among prospective husbands. These cases therefore show Uzbek men using and manipulating the Soviet legal apparatus to fight a battle antithetical to the one party activists thought they were fighting. Soviet courts were being used to *enforce* rather than overturn the boundaries governing the practice of qalin in Uzbekistan.

Similar patterns characterized Soviet efforts to stamp out polygyny. Although intensive local investigations continued to turn up hundreds of violations in the 1930s, Soviet activists found it very difficult to make headway in enforcing legislation barring multiple spouses. One delegate to the First All-Uzbek Congress of Female Youth in 1935 complained that men in her region who married second and third wives received paltry sentences of only a month or two in jail, after which they returned home and laughed at local women's workers, taunting them with the question, "What are you going to do [about it]?"[130] Deception, too, played a role: many men obtained false certificates from local mahalla commissions stating that they were unmarried, which permitted them to register a new bride at ZAGS. Others never registered their religious weddings at the local ZAGS office.[131] One unhappy party activist, E. Mostovaia, called such practices "hidden bigamy," explaining that if an Uzbek wife did not produce a son, she could be taken to ZAGS and divorced in the eyes of the state. Her husband would then marry another wife but refuse to grant the first wife a shariat divorce. Given the difficulties in making legal

129. These cases are from RGASPI, d. 1250, l. 54; PDA(K), op. 12, d. 638, ll. 96 and 105; and ÖzRMDA, f. 2454, op. 1, d. 413, l. 72.

130. ÖzRMDA, f. 86, op. 10, d. 632, l. 209; and PDA, op. 10, d. 141, l. 32.

131. Mukhitdinova, *Revoliutsionnaia zakonnost'*, 29–34. For a case from 1937, see ÖzR-MDA, f. 837, op. 32, d. 346, ll. 29 and 32.

cases stick (not to mention associated claims for child support and alimony), she could not remarry and had to remain with him.[132] Finally, some men with several wives—including some local Communists—went so far as to argue that they were serving the Soviet cause by staying married to all of their spouses. They were *protecting* these women, they contended, in view of the dangers that faced an uneducated cast-off wife and the impossibility of her earning an independent yet honorable living. If the party had not insisted that he stay married for the sake of social justice, said one such local official, Kadyrov, in 1929, he would of course have divorced all but one of his wives.[133]

Kadyrov's chutzpah may have been unusual, but his playfulness with Bolshevik categories and legal limits was not unique. Similar patterns of flexibility and creativity were also visible in the rules on underage marriage. Local audits consistently turned up evidence of massive violations of the Soviet laws that set minimum marriage ages for girls and boys. Again, these cases were likely only the tip of the iceberg, since for the most part only couples who sought to register their marriages with Soviet authorities turned up in such audits. The number of completely unregistered marriages—such as that of a 16-year-old girl discovered living with her husband in 1939—can only be guessed at.[134]

Even among marriages registered at ZAGS, however, underage brides were common. Local audits of civil registry records turned up hundreds of cases in the late 1920s, and such violations showed no sign of decreasing during the 1930s and early 1940s. They likely increased when the minimum marriage age for girls was raised to 18. One audit in 1935–36 found many marriages of 12- and 13-year-old girls and located hundreds of underage marriages spread across fifty-four of the sixty-one districts under investigation. The girls involved were mostly between the ages of 11 and 15, although some were as young as 8 or 9. Another report from 1940 listed a series of cases in which 13- to 16-year-old girls were withdrawn from school, veiled, and married to older men.[135]

Uzbek parents—both fathers and mothers, it is important to note—employed various strategies to marry off their daughters before they attained the requisite age. Subterfuge was a principal tactic. Once ZAGS offices required an official certificate (*spravka*) to prove a girl's age, for example, the production of false spravki became a cottage industry. Occasionally a bribe was required—one woman was prosecuted in 1939 for offering 200 rubles to a mahalla commission worker to obtain a false spravka for her 17-year-old daughter—but many local Soviet workers and mahalla commission members were

132. E. Mostovaia, "Pervoe vsesoiuznoe soveshchanie Komissii po uluchsheniiu truda i byta zhenshchin-vostochnits," *Vlast' Sovetov*, no. 9 (1928), 8.
133. ÖzRMDA, f. 9, op. 1, d. 3397, l. 114.
134. PDA, op. 14, d. 1092, ll. 1–2.
135. ÖzRMDA, f. 86, op. 1, d. 5718, l. 208, and f. 2454, op. 1, d. 412, ll. 130 and 139; and PDA(K), op. 12, d. 638, ll. 95 and 105.

only too happy to oblige.[136] Even doctors, whose scientific expertise served as the court of last resort for girls seeking permission to marry, could be induced to cooperate. Substantial numbers of inflated age certificates were discovered as late as 1941, despite the existence of criminal sanctions against medical fraud.[137] If a ZAGS official appeared reluctant to register a marriage, the applicant's family could assure him or her not to worry, that the family would be responsible for dealing with any troublesome Soviet investigators—and given the sympathy of local police and Soviet officials, such investigators were unlikely to look very hard.[138]

Substitution was another simple but effective way to deceive ZAGS officials. One 8-year-old girl in Jizzakh was able to marry a 28-year-old man in 1929 thanks to her older sister's willingness to appear at ZAGS in her name to pass the medical examination, and similar cases appeared throughout the 1930s.[139] In some circumstances, men tried substitution too: in 1929 an Uzbek man who wished to marry but was denied a health certificate when he was diagnosed as syphilitic sent a healthy man to the doctor in his place. Unfortunately for him, the plan was discovered, apparently by chance, and he was arrested.[140] Many similar cases, however, probably went undetected.

These patterns of deception—and the culpability and dubious loyalty of many in the Soviet judicial, police, and civil registry apparatus—emerge with particular clarity in a case recounted by one Sarymsakova, a ZAGS employee from Andijon, to an Uzbek party congress in 1929. According to her, local authorities were often complicit in dodging the requirements of Soviet byt law, and mahalla commissions frequently committed "criminal mistakes" in cases of underage marriage. The corrosive influence of such behavior on Soviet authority could be seen in the story of an unnamed 12-year-old girl who was to be married in Andijon in 1929. As Sarymsakova told it, the local mahalla commission had provided the girl with a spravka falsely attesting that she was of legal age to marry. The commission then sent her to the ZAGS office, first dressing her in a heavy khalat to make her appear more solidly built and placing cotton wadding on her chest to give a misleading impression of her physical development. Sarymsakova became suspicious and, surmising that the girl was younger and slighter than she appeared, sent her to a doctor for examination. When the doctor fixed the girl's age at not more than 11, her marriage application was denied. But the story did not end there. Sarymsakova herself

136. PDA, op. 14, d. 1092, ll. 1–2. Other cases of girls as young as 12 being given spravki attesting to their legal age for marriage—often with the connivance or support of local officials—are at ÖzRMDA, f. 86, op. 1, d. 3031, l. 11, and d. 3626, l. 103; and RGASPI, d. 1690, l. 14.

137. ÖzRMDA, f. 904, op. 10, d. 91, ll. 5–6.

138. ÖzRMDA, f. 86, op. 1, d. 5594, ll. 2340b-35.

139. RGASPI, d. 2080, l. 1. For a similar case from 1935, see ÖzRMDA, f. 86, d. 10, l. 634, l. 225.

140. ÖzRMDA, f. 86, op. 1, d. 5594, l. 236.

endured repeated harassment from a local police officer, Sabirjon, who insisted that she had been wrong to request the doctor's exam.[141]

Reworking Bolshevism from Within: The Uzbek Soviet Apparatus

Sarymsakova's tale of woe shows the potential for another subversive response by Uzbek men and women to Soviet byt law, namely, working within Soviet institutions to transform them. Many Uzbeks who gained Soviet or party positions used their newfound authority to block the hujum. This strategy amounted to nativization of the Soviet apparatus—a principal goal of the party's korenizatsiia policy—but in a way that party leaders neither expected nor wanted. Obviously not all Uzbeks responded identically, and some served in Bolshevik posts with distinction and loyalty. Sarymsakova, for one, presented herself to the congress in this light, and no evidence exists to contradict this depiction. Yet many professions of support appear strategic: either situational or designed to further personal and ideological agendas. And not all Uzbeks reacted with support. More often, Uzbek personnel in the Soviet and party apparatus either actively or passively hindered the effort to stamp out byt crime.

It is not always possible to determine whether such obstruction was a product of conscious action (or inaction) or whether it resulted from bureaucratic inertia, disorganization, a lack of training, or some other cause. (This uncertainty was useful, and it helps to explain why such weapons of the weak can be so effective.) Clearly, some of the difficulties that marred the unveiling and legal reform campaigns were not the products of intentional, conscious resistance. The massive efforts to recruit Uzbek cadres during the early decades of Soviet power—seen with such high hopes by Bolshevik leaders in Moscow and Tashkent as the crucial step in providing the Central Asian populace with indigenous models of socialist behavior—required government agencies and party organizations to rely on ill-trained, semiskilled, and sometimes completely illiterate local personnel.

This situation had unhappy consequences for the effectiveness of Soviet justice no less than for the efficiency of Soviet administration. Some Central Asian staff workers were unable to understand the "formal juridical language" used in laws, and were at a particular disadvantage when these laws had not yet been translated from Russian into indigenous languages.[142] Others refashioned Soviet institutions and authority to work in a way consonant with their own expectations and experiences: one customs officer arrested a woman in

---

141. Ibid., l. 232.
142. See the discussions of Turkmen staff members and campaign delays in the early 1930s at ÖzRMDA, f. 6, op. 2, d. 462, ll. 10–11 and 94–134; and f. 9, op. 1, d. 3397, ll. 96–107. A similar report on the Uzbek campaign is at f. 736, op. 3, d. 77, ll. 5–110b; also see RGASPI, d. 1224, ll. 46–59. Sometimes the ethnically Russian staff could not address indigenous populations: see a speech to Tajik women delivered in Uzbek at RGASPI, d. 1694, l. 20.

1929, for example, when she appeared before him without a veil. *Pravda Vostoka* complained that Soviet courts in Uzbekistan had, under the direction of some indigenous judges, taken on a tinge of shariat norms. Men had been convicted of entering a house with unveiled women inside, and found guilty of drinking alcohol, although neither action was an offense under the Soviet criminal code.[143]

Bureaucratic snafus and lack of preparedness also give the lie to portraits of an all-knowing, all-powerful Soviet state. Reports on the ZAGS apparatus, for example, depicted an organization chronically short of supplies, funding, and personnel. An investigation of the Tashkent office in 1926 found workers taking personal "fees" of 10 to 15 rubles to register marriages to supplement their low salaries; similar problems turned up in the 1930s.[144] Such ZAGS offices discredited rather than enforced Soviet efforts: many staff workers simply accepted marriage-age attestations at face value, making no effort to verify the identity of the women who appeared in front of them. In some places registrations proceeded by rote, with applications rubber-stamped in two or three minutes. In other cases Uzbek male staffers were reprimanded for abruptly unveiling prospective brides to "evaluate" their ages, a phenomenon that must have provoked strongly negative reactions from many brides (and grooms). Attempts at reform, such as disbanding some of the most egregious age-certification commissions, seemed to make little difference.[145]

Similar problems cropped up in the courts, where judges and procurators faced manifest difficulties in trying to punish Central Asian crimes of daily life. Many such cases collapsed from neglect, incompetence, or sabotage before reaching trial. According to one internal report, the proportion of failed cases in Uzbekistan reached nearly 50 percent by 1930. But even when problems resulted from ineptitude as much as conscious obstruction, higher party leaders and investigators, conditioned by the hujum, frequently saw them as evidence of political deviance and opposition. The same report argued that the high rate of byt cases failing to reach trial showed the prevalence of "Right-opportunist practices" in the Central Asian judicial system. "This shows," it concluded, "how in many places the courts do not serve us, or the proletarian state, or the proletariat, or the party, or the laboring masses, but rather the kulak, either openly or in a roundabout manner."[146]

Although such accusations appear overblown—and the use of such politically loaded tags as "kulak" reveals more about party priorities than it does

143. M. Grek., "Shariat v sovetskom sude," *PV,* 13 Dec. 1928; and Iu. Larin, *Evrei i antisemitizm v SSSR* (Moscow and Leningrad, 1929), 13.

144. The 1926 investigation led to calls, apparently not implemented, for the centralization of marriage registration at *raion* and *volost'* centers, leaving only birth and death registries with local offices (ÖzRMDA, f. 86, op. 1, d. 3620, l. 398).

145. See several reports written in the early 1930s: ÖzRMDA, f. 9, op. 1, d. 3417, l. 138; f. 86, op. 1, d. 6297, l. 43, and d. 6556, l. 162.

146. RGASPI, d. 2691, ll. 30–31.

about the Uzbeks in question—the evidence does suggest that many Uzbek staff workers during the 1920s and 1930s consciously used their positions to hinder the Soviet legal and juridical campaign. From the perspective of party leaders, such subversion from within the Soviet apparatus could be maddeningly hard to trace and eradicate. Foot-dragging and purposeful obfuscation, after all, easily resembled genuine confusion, all the more when high illiteracy rates and poor communications made chaos a more or less normal state of affairs. Police and court paperwork could be lost accidentally or intentionally. Some local officials hid the murder of women activists from their superiors in Tashkent.[147] All of these problems flowed from the perceived need to involve Uzbek men and women in the campaign to stamp out byt crime, both as part of the korenizatsiia effort and to give credibility to the ostensibly universal norms of personal behavior enshrined in the hujum and the new byt codes. Reliance on Uzbek personnel, however, opened up other unintended possibilities.

Soviet documents portray the failure of local police officers, prosecutors, and judges to recognize the political nature of byt crimes as a major cause of the problems. As a result, women's activists contended, local officials were reluctant to punish byt criminals with the requisite severity. Men arrested for "insulting" unveiled women could sometimes gain release in as little as two hours.[148] The need for a different kind of rapidity—for Soviet justice to be swift as well as sure—remained a continuing theme, suggesting that delaying tactics were common. Many indigenous officials were not particularly concerned about eradicating underage marriage, polygyny, and qalin; unannounced local audits and confidential investigations found a persistent pattern of failure among local courts and police districts to press for the rapid resolution of such cases. In Khorazm province, for example, byt cases could take several years to reach a conclusion in the late 1920s.[149] Similar lamentations about judicial foot-dragging were heard throughout the 1930s and 1940s.[150]

Only a small percentage of cases, moreover, ever worked their way through the system to conviction and punishment. An audit in 1928 found 120 cases of underage marriage at one local ZAGS office in Old Bukhoro, but noted that only 10 cases were prosecuted that year in the entire province. During the same year, courts in Andijon province heard only five such cases.[151] Even violent crimes fell between the cracks of prosecutors' workloads. Officials in Khorazm reported 20 prosecutions for the murder of activist women in 1928, a figure included in the official total of 203 such murders for the year in Uzbekistan. Yet an independent investigation discovered that at least 68 such murders had occurred in Khorazm province during 1928, mostly unreported and

147. Strong, *Red Star in Samarkand*, 257.
148. PDA, op. 3, d. 1598, l. 35.
149. *Rezoliutsii Uzbekskogo soveshchaniia*, 16.
150. ÖzRMDA, f. 904, op. 10, d. 91, ll. 7–10; and Iuldash Saidov, "V Surkhan-Dar'e oslablena rabota sredi zhenshchin," *PV*, 5 Sept. 1939.
151. ÖzRMDA, f. 86, op. 1, d. 5885, l. 386.

unpunished.[152] Indeed, some local officials appeared eager to reclassify the most serious crimes downward (although doing so was deemed a "Right deviation")[153] by, for example, declaring that a woman's murder or attempted murder was a "simple" crime (motivated by passion or jealousy) rather than a counterrevolutionary crime subject to the death penalty. As Akhunbabaev put it in 1940, it was not uncommon for procurators and judges "to classify these crimes in a patently incorrect way, slurring over the political essence of the cases and coming to a softer sentence, which leads not to the reduction of [such] crimes but to their increase."[154] Such readings (or intentional misreadings) of the Soviet penal code reduced the impact of Soviet byt law.

All these problems, too, continued throughout the 1930s and into the 1940s. An internal evaluation of the court system in Namangan province in 1941 was fairly typical. It harshly criticized judicial personnel for failing to classify byt crimes properly and to apply the maximum penalties, for dismissing cases without cause, and for obtaining "illegal" verdicts of not guilty in what was deemed a clear contravention of the facts.[155] In the angry words of an Uzbek Central Committee bureau resolution from late 1939, "The organs of the procuracy and courts, which are obliged to lead a decisive struggle against violations of women's rights, [have instead], through the taciturn and indifferent attitude of some party organizations, in most cases not attached the necessary political meaning to the fact of brutal violence against activist women, [rather] regarding it as byt trifles [bytovye melochi] and in some cases indulging in a mocking attitude toward women."[156]

But by 1939 there could by definition be no such thing as "byt trifles": that was the central point of criminalizing patterns of intimate and social behavior in the hujum. Such patterns were no longer the concern only of women's activists. The investment of huge amounts of political capital in the liberation of Muslim women made such continuing transgressions a matter of grave concern for all true Bolsheviks in Central Asia. Any indulgence of improper gender and family behaviors among Uzbek officials represented a grave danger to the Soviet project—and to Soviet authority as a whole.

Languages of Power: Uzbeks Outside the Party

If Uzbek members of the Soviet judicial and police apparatus found ways to slow or even reverse the campaign to define certain patterns of family life as

---

152. Ibid., ll. 381–83. See also op. 10, d. 1091, l. 6.

153. ÖzRMDA, f. 6, op. 2, d. 462, l. 29.

154. ÖzRMDA, f. 2454, op. 1, d. 412, ll. 147–48.

155. This report is at ÖzRMDA, f. 904, op. 10, d. 91, ll. 47–55. Similar reports from 1941 describing the provinces of Samarqand and Bukhoro are at ll. 58–69 and 72–97, respectively. All such regional courts came under severe scrutiny in a resolution of the Uzbek Commissariat of Justice Collegium, ll. 70–71ob.

156. PDA, op. 15, d. 81, ll. 10–11.

criminal, Uzbek men and women outside the Soviet system also entered the
fray. A fierce battle, both discursive and physical, ensued. When Soviet activists mobilized a mix of Marxism, medicine, and morality to make the case
that so-called traditional ways of life were oppressive, unhealthy, and evil,
their Uzbek opponents subverted Soviet legal and moral spaces to challenge all
of these claims. From their point of view, polygyny, qalin, and underage marriage could just as easily be markers of piety and propriety as crimes. By drawing on their own, supposedly timeless conceptions of Uzbek social customs
and Muslim religious norms, they could threaten to punish anyone who transgressed these non-Soviet codes of proper behavior, such as a woman who unveiled or a Soviet official who threw men in jail for paying qalin.[157] When a
Bolshevik women's activist ventured into a village outside Tashkent in 1929,
to take one extreme example, her body was returned the next day to the city
center in a cart, cut into pieces, with a note attached that read, "Here is your
women's freedom!"[158] Notions of justice, punishment, and retribution—not to
mention the dramatic use of public space—were not solely the property of Soviet prosecutors, judges, and activists.

Uzbeks, Tajiks, Turkmen, and others who for many reasons opposed the
formulation of these new byt crimes also found it comparatively easy to resist
the new rules by manipulating the Soviet judicial system. Since from a Muslim
perspective ultimate judgments about truth and falsity did not fall within the
jurisdiction of a Soviet court, witnesses could impede a trial by corroborating
false alibis, disparaging the victims of byt attacks, or discrediting Soviet officials. In 1929, for example, when the activist Pulatchi Afataboi Tagirova was
murdered by her husband and other male relatives, they were said to have
dragged her corpse to the edge of the village and concocted a story to explain
her death. When Soviet investigators nevertheless found sufficient evidence to
convene a trial, many witnesses appeared to attest to the family's story—although happily for the courts (and the only reason the case later appeared in
published accounts), in the end the truth had been "unmasked."[159] But such
cases appear only on the margins of official records, coming to light only if
and when these schemes to mislead the court failed. Many other invented stories or planted witnesses must have avoided detection.

Angry Uzbek parents likewise launched petition drives to demand the return
of paranjis confiscated from their school-age daughters at Soviet demonstrations.[160] Besieged local officials told their superiors in 1929 that Muslim clerics directed parishioners to continue sending letters of protest about abusive
and coercive tactics to higher authorities long after such tactics had been aban-

157. See the letter to Soviet officials threatening such retribution at RGASPI, d. 1694, l. 50.
158. Strong, *Red Star in Samarkand*, 256.
159. Inoiatov, "Sudy," 26–27.
160. RGASPI, d. 1214, l. 72.

doned.[161] Such allegations, if true, show Uzbeks learning to play the game—using the party's mechanisms of feedback and surveillance to keep Soviet leaders guessing about the behavior and loyalty of their subordinates, thereby undercutting party policy at the grassroots level. One frustrated party report from 1929 alleged that some cases of reported coercion were setups meant to blacken the party's image. Some reputedly involved Uzbek men in drag:

> There have been cases in which men dressed themselves in women's clothes [pretending to be Zhenotdel workers] and tore off women's paranjis with the goal of compromising [our] activist women. There have been cases in which the wives of mullahs have dressed themselves in white clothes, but tore off only new [i.e., valuable] paranjis, saying loudly all the while that they are a commission sent by the Zhenotdel.[162]

In other cases, Soviet courts and procedures were manipulated to work against Soviet goals. We have already seen how Soviet courts unwittingly helped police the boundaries of "proper" qalin payments. Such subversions also undercut party personnel. Some anti-Soviet Uzbeks, showing a sense of ironic humor, went so far as to accuse Bolshevik allies of having transgressed—of all things—Soviet byt laws. In one episode, local clerics succeeded in having several Communists arrested by alleging that they had used force to unveil women.[163] In another case a group of Uzbek men brought charges in Soviet court in 1928 against members of their local mahalla commission. Having mobilized or coached supporting witnesses, they accused the commission of running women's liberation meetings while drunk and of forcing women to attend—in short, of violating the code of conduct expected of Soviet officials. The Soviet court ultimately decided that these accusations were manufactured and convicted the accusers of perjury. The prominent coverage, though, reveals Soviet authorities' deep concern about the dangers of this provocative technique, which threatened to subvert the entire state system of justice.[164]

The very terms of authority in Soviet laws were contested and unstable. Once it became clear that the party treated scientific and public health arguments as "objective" elements beyond debate, indigenous opponents of the new byt laws appropriated this medical and scientific language. Consider the argument in the late 1920s over raising the marriage age for girls. In 1928 a meeting of ninety-five union workers in Surkhondaryo—supposedly one of the most backward regions of Uzbekistan—argued that the minimum marriage age for Uzbek girls should be *reduced,* from 16 to 15. Their argument was

161. RGASPI, d. 2057, l. 61.
162. RGASPI, d. 2056, l. 55.
163. RGASPI, d. 1690, l. 12.
164. N., "Druz'ia chachvana i ichkari," *PV,* 7 May 1928.

clever: "Considering the slower physiological development of Europeans," the resolution declared, "[we] consider it desirable to raise the marriage age for European women to 17 and for men to 19."[165] If Europeans wanted higher marriage ages, that is, Uzbeks had no objection—as long as European rules applied only to Europeans. The problem in Central Asian eyes arose when colonial political structures and Western medical science imposed externally derived norms on a culture and society that felt no need or desire of them. Uzbek unionists here announced their willingness to attack the Bolshevik reification of cultural norms into legal distinctions by subverting their core rationale: the justification of biomedical arguments through each culture's allegedly unique, racially differentiated rate of child development. Unfortunately, party leaders' response to this resolution is not recorded, but they could not have welcomed attempts to appropriate their own banner of objectivity and scientific certainty.

Finally, Uzbek women themselves occupied a unique position in this struggle over law. Both as agents and as the ostensible beneficiaries of Soviet byt liberation, they had far greater latitude than Uzbek men and the potential—if they chose to use it—to point out with comparative freedom the colonialist assumptions and internal contradictions of the new Soviet laws.[166] Women had many more possibilities than men for voicing their fears, anxieties, and even opposition. Given the party's analysis of Central Asian society as fundamentally patriarchal, in Soviet eyes any Uzbek woman who opposed the liberation campaign could not be criminal in the same way as her husband, brother, or father. A young girl by definition could not give her consent to a marriage for qalin, for instance; that was why only the payer and recipient of bride-price were subject to penalties under Soviet law.[167] Bolshevik activists likewise assumed that any local women who voiced opposition to these new laws were only demonstrating their ignorance (which could be rectified through education) or the manipulation and control exercised by their male relatives (which would be overcome through the hujum). In either case, it was virtually inconceivable that such women should be subject to criminal sanctions. Even when

165. ÖzRMDA, f. 904, op. 1, d. 203, l. 106.
166. This argument parallels that of Lynne Viola, who has shown how Russian and Ukrainian women used preconceptions of female weakness and customary roles to lead protests against collectivization. Soviet authorities likewise perceived them as manipulated, not free actors, insofar as they opposed Soviet efforts. See Viola, "*Bab'i Bunty* and Peasant Women's Protest during Collectivization," *Russian Review* 45 (1986): 23–42. David Tyson has argued similarly that in Turkmenistan, women carried out important rituals, such as pilgrimages, that preserved Islamic faith and identity after the official (male) religious establishment had been destroyed. But because women were not seen as culpable and female religiosity was judged ignorant superstition, not a political threat, they were not generally targets of state action. See Tyson, "The Role of Turkmen Women as Custodians of Islam in the Soviet and Post-Soviet Periods," paper presented at Middle East Studies Association of North America, 22–24 Nov. 1996, Providence, R.I.
167. ÖzRMDA, f. 86, op. 1, d. 2772, l. 148, and d. 3933, ll. 88–89.

women led openly defiant protest marches, arrests were made only in exceptional cases.[168]

This view of women's latent sympathy for the Soviet program created spaces for women that did not exist for men. But women, like men, had been socialized into local norms of propriety and decorum, and some took advantage of the resulting opportunities. Mothers as well as fathers arranged marriages for their 13-, 14-, and 15-year-old daughters, and while seeking a good match they also worked to negotiate an advantageous qalin. By the early 1930s, some party activists complained confidentially to their superiors that indigenous women were helping to hide evidence of byt crimes and thus represented a noteworthy part of the problem.[169]

Yet in 1928, female criminals in Central Asia were amnestied en masse, as part of the festivities to mark the Zhenotdel's tenth anniversary. How it would help women's liberation to release criminals may not have been carefully thought through, but all female inmates with less than a year remaining on their sentences were to be freed forthwith (those with more time remaining had their sentences cut in half). Exceptions were made only for groups that should, according to Soviet precepts, not have existed: women convicted of counterrevolutionary crimes, of matchmaking, or of forcing other women into prostitution.[170] The number of women freed by this amnesty appears to have been small, but the implications were plain: women en bloc merited judicial leniency, special treatment, and official favor as revolutionary allies. This approach was rife with obvious contradictions and it had unwanted consequences. Most plainly, the release of female byt offenders hampered efforts to enforce the new laws and weakened the deterrent effect of Soviet justice. A raft of female recidivists finally forced a modification and partial curtailment of the amnesty.[171]

To be sure, most Uzbek women did not declare open opposition to the new byt laws. A small minority of indigenous women actively welcomed the Soviet attack on indigenous forms of patriarchy and worked very hard, at great personal risk, to eradicate female seclusion and subordination. Other local women took advantage of Soviet courts when it was in their interest to do so. Most simply ignored them. But female opposition, where it existed, represented a much deeper threat in principle than is shown by the relatively small number of women willing to stand up and speak out. Zhenotdel and party activists, meanwhile, remained hamstrung by the ideological necessity of treating

168. Such women were usually described as the wives of bois or Muslim clerics; a few ringleaders might be arrested for a short time. See ÖzRMDA, f. 86, op. 2, d. 27, l. 41; and RGASPI, d. 1419, l. 40b; d. 1689, l. 55; and d. 2064, l. 480b.

169. ÖzRMDA, f. 9, op. 1, d. 3385, l. 54.

170. ÖzRMDA, f. 86, op. 1, d. 5885, ll. 476 and 489–92.

171. ÖzRMDA, f. 9, op. 1, d. 3397, l. 950b; f. 86, op. 1, d. 5386, l. 1; and f. 837, op. 6, d. 427, ll. 1–4.

all indigenous women as potential revolutionary allies and by their consequent inability to take action against these recalcitrant women.

The threat these women presented and the symbolic power they wielded are plain in what may have been the most extreme and troubling form of female protest: suicide by self-immolation. While not common, this grisly and profoundly sad phenomenon did occur in early Soviet Central Asia, and in at least some cases appears to have been an act of protest against the hujum.[172] One top-secret local party protocol recounts the story of two young Turkmen schoolgirls in the village of Ak-Sofi who died of their injuries within ninety minutes of dousing themselves with kerosene and setting themselves on fire. They took this step on 7 March 1930, the eve of International Women's Day: lest anyone miss the significance of the timing, they killed themselves in the middle of the town square immediately after a women's liberation meeting. As the local party committee noted, it was a "powerful political event"; within two hours the news reportedly had traveled throughout the surrounding area.[173]

As with other sensitive matters, Soviet lawmakers and officials did their best to hush up the story and discussed it only in private. This tragic episode, though, shows more of the contradictions and ambiguities created by the Soviet approach to women's issues. First, the girls chose a time and a place that explicitly challenged Soviet authority. The hujum itself depended on theatrical demonstrations of unveilings and dramatic piles of paranjis aflame, but here the theatrics of opposition were just as accomplished and even more dramatic: setting women afire rather than their veils. As representatives of youth and as pupils in Soviet schools, moreover, these girls should have stood at the core of indigenous female support for the hujum, not leading the charge against it. The party panic that ensued thus makes sense: local officials immediately dispatched an investigative brigade to explore the girls' connections with the Komsomol and other organizations. Its classified report concluded that the girls had not wanted to participate in Women's Day festivities, but had been forced to do so by the local Komsomol secretary. This coercion apparently provoked their decision to take their own lives, and to do so in a very public way.

As in Chust, however, the local party could not readily make sense of such acts of protest by its ostensible allies. Instead, Bolshevik activists assimilated the story into their preexisting categories of analysis. Women and girls who killed themselves by definition could not be criminals in the eyes of Soviet law. But such a horrific event cried out for someone to be punished—Soviet ju-

172. Women's self-immolation was much discussed in Uzbekistan in the 1980s as a symbol of glasnost, but as an idiom of female protest it has deep historical roots. My study of this phenomenon is in preparation.
173. This protocol, from which information in the next two paragraphs is drawn, is at RGASPI, d. 2432, l. 35.

risprudence could not simply ignore the suicides. Upon further consideration, therefore, the crime took new shape. By the time the local party committee sent its initial report to Tashkent (three days later, on 10 March 1930), the voices of these girls had already been lost. The protocol speaks sadly of them as highly accomplished and motivated pupils, deeply devoted to their studies. Why had they died? Their immolation was not an act of free will, it contended, but rather was the fault of their relatives, who were said to have driven them to suicide and then to have spread "false rumors," first to discredit the local Komsomol and then to depict the self-immolation as an act of political protest. None of this was true, the report concluded—none of it *could* be true—so the girls' families were now to be punished through an exemplary show trial.

Criminality thus took shape in the eye of the beholder. Even so, Central Asian women and girls clearly had the ability to challenge and subvert the Soviet message of liberation at its most vulnerable point, by declaring—whether dramatically or quietly—that they had no need of it. Their actions in doing so, along with those of their male counterparts who faced much more stringent Soviet oversight, suggests something of the scope for resistance remaining in— indeed, partly created by—the strictures of the Stalinist state. Clearly that state held enormous power, in many obvious and crucially important ways. Nevertheless, the complex and creative patterns of popular response and subaltern resistance to Soviet laws show how Uzbek women and men simultaneously found ways to shape the world in which they lived. The final outcome—as measured in the character of Uzbek daily life in the intimate and social spaces of families, neighborhoods, and towns—resulted from an ongoing interplay between these two interwoven and mutually shaping sides, not dictation from one to the other. Even under Stalin, Soviet state power, acting through law and the courts, confronted serious limits in its efforts to govern, much less transform, its colonial Central Asian periphery.

CHAPTER 8

The Limits of Law

The paranji is a dark mark of customary law [odat] on our prosperous, cultured, and happy life. This mark must be rubbed out.

—A letter from eleven female students at the Stalin Communist Agricultural School to *Pravda Vostoka,* 1936

We should like, of course, to send the paranji and chachvon to
hell, but we cannot always get everything we want by issuing
decrees.

—Nadezhda Krupskaia, speaking at the All-Union Conference of Workers among Eastern Women, 1928

In its struggle with the veil the Soviet state flirted with, debated, but ultimately decided *not* to rely on the law as a lever for social change. The hujum
focused on the act of unveiling, after all, so it is potentially illuminating to consider how and why certain strategies—and not others—came to be employed
against the veil. What techniques were deemed appropriate for Soviet power in
the colonial periphery? Which ones, if any, went too far? The question of banning the paranji and chachvon by decree was raised almost immediately after
the hujum was launched in 1927, and it became the focus of intense delibera-
tion on at least three occasions over the next fifteen years. The first wave of debate arose in response to the hujum's difficulties in the late 1920s; the second
appeared during discussions of the Stalin Constitution in 1936; and the third
gripped party members and filled newspapers in 1940, shortly before the USSR
was pulled into World War II. While on each occasion the topic arose for a
different reason, and while the broader context obviously varied widely, one
finds throughout this period a continuing dispute: would a true Bolshevik
want to ban the veil or not?

This debate was vigorous and sometimes sharp, exposing real tensions
within the party; yet one also finds a striking degree of continuity in the argu-

ments employed in 1927, 1936, and 1940. At its root, the dispute revolved around the tension between two countervailing concerns: the perceived efficacy of physical force and legal coercion in bringing about unveiling, on the one hand, and the need in principle for unveiling to be a voluntary, self-conscious act of liberation by women as autonomous actors and historical agents, on the other. The party did seriously and repeatedly consider adding the veil to its canonical list of crimes of daily life. But—curiously perhaps for a regime that showed during the Stalin Revolution little reluctance to confront powerful social groups or to rely on physical force—party officials each time shied away from what appeared the logical culmination of Soviet women's liberation policy. The veil remained legal, albeit strongly discouraged, until the Soviet empire's final collapse. Ultimately the veil *was* legally abolished, but only in 1997–98, at the hands of a post-Soviet, postcolonial government of independent Uzbekistan.[1]

Soviet reluctance to ban the veil represents more than an interesting policy quirk. It is deeply significant, showing the contradictions inherent in the party's simultaneous decisions to use gender liberation as a proxy for socialist revolution and to use law to pursue social and cultural change. It again illuminates the paradoxes of an avowedly anticolonial, liberationist state trying to administer a colonial empire in the name of "civilization," and it further illustrates the relative weakness of Soviet power in Central Asia—according to a core measure of its own choosing—decades after 1917. Finally, it reveals a remarkably disputatious party. Some party activists and leaders felt strongly that the veil should be banned outright, by decree, in order most quickly to bring the benefits of progress, culture, justice, and modernity to Central Asia. Others argued with equal passion that the very idea of such a law was misguided and a betrayal of the party's deepest principles, smacking of the paternalism of tsarist or bourgeois-capitalist European colonial empires. Lacking any blueprint for how to proceed in the Muslim periphery, Soviet policy in Central Asia—even under Stalin—remained an object of continued negotiation, with few answers predetermined and little guidance available from above.

A Cry for Help: The First Wave, 1927–1929

The initial debate on whether to ban the veil arose in 1927, in response to the violence and widespread resistance that quickly greeted the hujum. The idea was not without historical antecedents in the tsarist empire. Before 1917, ja-

---

1. In the late 1990s the Uzbek government launched a broad attack on Islamic "ritual dress," which included a prohibition on female veiling as well as a ban on male beards and other religious attire. Motivated by governmental fear of political Islam and Muslim fundamentalism, this law was enforced mostly in institutions of higher education, and it attracted negative attention from Western human rights organizations (see www.hrw.org/reports/1999/uzbekistan).

didist reformers had discussed the idea of eliminating the paranji at once by issuing a decree, but the notion never gained much steam.[2] During the hujum, both proponents and opponents of the idea said that it had been tried elsewhere, claiming (wrongly) that Atatürk had abolished Turkish women's veils by decree, and that Amanullah Khan had done so in Afghanistan.[3] In the Central Asian context of the hujum, however, when the party started a protracted and very public debate about a possible antiveiling decree, the proposal soon became inextricably identified with Soviet power.

The Soviet Uzbek government portrayed itself as open-minded on the question, as not foreclosing or prejudging any option. No answers were predetermined. As an official report put it in 1927, a decision to outlaw the veil was "possible," and should be discussed "by the broad laboring masses."[4] Party leaders solicited public opinion, sending local activists to canvass the mahallas and saying that they would abide by the popular will.[5] The overall tone was remarkably flexible. In this sense it differed from other colonial contexts and other imperial debates over law, such as the decisions by British authorities in 1829 to outlaw sati in India, or the steps they took a century later to restrict or ban clitoridectomy in parts of East Africa.[6] This Soviet pledge to shape policy in accordance with popular demand also appears at first glance jarringly out of place during the hujum, which was nothing if not confrontational. As Akhunbabaev put it in 1929, "If upon the conclusion of the election campaign the masses themselves finally demand a decree about the chadra, we must meet and satisfy this demand."[7]

2. Mirsaid Sultan-Galiev, "Metody antireligioznoi propagandy sredi musul'man," *Zhizn' natsional'nostei*, no. 29 (127) (1921), 2–3, and no. 30 (128) (1921), 3.

3. On the (alleged) Turkish example, see RGASPI, d. 1694, l. 43, and d. 1696, ll. 6–10 and 23. On Afghanistan, see ÖzRMDA, f. 9, op. 1, d. 3437, l. 16. Atatürk strongly discouraged the veil but never outlawed it: Lois Beck and Nikki Keddie, *Women in the Muslim World* (Cambridge, Mass., 1978), 8–9.

4. ÖzRMDA, f. 736, op. 1, d. 419, l. 40.

5. PDA, op. 5, d. 72, ll. 70–71; RGASPI, d. 1681, ll. 93–950b; d. 1692, l. 64; and d. 2057, ll. 77–78; ÖzRMDA, f. 86, op. 1, d. 6414, l. 14; and A. Nukhrat, "Provedenie kampanii po raskreposhcheniiu zhenshchin Vostoka," *Izvestiia TsK VKP(b)*, no. 2–3 (261–62) (1929), 6.

6. On sati, see Mani, *Contentious Traditions*. The protection of indigenous women from infibulation or "female circumcision" became a cause célèbre in colonial circles during the last decades of British rule in Africa. In 1926 British political and religious authorities in Kenya tried to restrict the practice, requiring that no woman undergo more than a simple clitoridectomy (which was seen as more humane than the complete removal of the external genitalia). Clitoridectomy itself was banned in 1956, during the anticolonial Mau Mau rebellion. The practice had been banned earlier (1946) in Sudan. But in each of these cases local populations usually ignored the laws and restrictions. See Rose Oldfield Hayes, "Female Genital Mutilation, Fertility Control, Women's Roles and the Patrilineage in Modern Sudan," *American Ethnologist* 2 (1975): 617–63; Pedersen, "National Bodies, Unspeakable Acts"; and Thomas, "Ngaitana."

7. "Mestnye rabotniki—ob izdanii dekreta," *Kommunistka*, no. 1 (1929), 32. Liubimova expressed a similar view: "Of course we can say that a decree must be issued—but before this the question needs to be discussed in the localities, and the opinion of the population about this heard" (*Trud i byt zhenshchiny Vostoka*, 110–11).

Such declarations opened a window for genuine debate. Calls for "mass discussion" on such an important issue showed befuddlement within Soviet ranks and a lack of consensus on how to proceed with the party's ostensible showpiece, its women's liberation campaign. The fact that similar issues were under debate elsewhere in the Soviet colonial periphery only underscores the lack of any central blueprint. After intense discussion, authorities in Azerbaijan declined to ban the chadra worn by Azeri women—but simultaneously the Kalmyk Autonomous Republic decided to abolish the *kamzol,* an outer garment designed to constrict female breast development.[8] This uncertainty presented a golden opportunity for lower-level activists to influence policy in Central Asia. Confusion was obvious outside the party as well, where wild rumors circulated about the supposed aim of Soviet officials in outlawing the veil—to turn all Uzbek women into prostitutes.[9]

The lack of direction from above—indeed, party leaders' insistence that wide-ranging public discussion was needed—made it possible for lower-level activists to mobilize or manipulate public opinion. During this period one finds many reports of grassroots demands for a ban on the veil. Such demands—in petitions, letters, speeches, and local resolutions—remained a lasting theme throughout the 1930s.[10] What do they reveal? How strong were these demands, and who was making them? To be sure, much of the impetus for an antiveil decree does appear to have come from below and to have represented a cry for help from the people doing the heavy lifting of the hujum. At least three groups were involved. First and most obviously, the relatively small group of unveiled women had a powerful incentive to support a law that would, they hoped, instantly transform them from members of an embattled minority into pioneers of a heroic majority.[11] As one local Zhenotdel worker from Sirdaryo put it in 1928, many unveiled Uzbek women were saying that

---

8. On the kamzol, see Mariam Tsyn, "Kamzol gubit zdorov'e kalmychki," *Kommunistka,* no. 13 (1929), 45–46; *Trud i byt zhenshchiny Vostoka,* 110–11; Otd. RiD RKP(b), *Docheri revoliutsii* (Moscow, 1923), 144; and Halle, *Women in the Soviet East,* 177. On the Azeri discussions, see RGASPI, d. 1696, especially ll. 6–10, 23, and 35–36; ÖzRMDA, f. 86, op. 1, d. 5885, l. 760; and "Nuzhno li izdat' dekret, zapreshchaiushchii noshenie chadry (Iz stenogramma Zakavkazskogo soveshchaniia rabotnikov sredi zhenshchin 16.VI.1928)," *Kommunistka,* no. 8 (1928), 79–81. The Azeri and Uzbek debates were similar in many ways, and the two discussions influenced each other. The initial discussion in Baku of issuing a decree, for instance, spurred interest in Moscow, and the central Zhenotdel asked its representatives in Central Asia to look into the question (ÖzRMDA, f. 9, op. 1, d. 3368, l. 40). The details of such interactions, however, are complex and lie outside the scope of this book.

9. RGASPI, d. 2064, l. 19. By mid-April 1927 the Central Executive Committee in Old Samarqand was dealing with up to 100 people a day seeking information on whether such a decree had been issued and what it meant. On the rumors and confusion, see d. 1211, l. 207; d. 1214, l. 14; d. 1239, l. 4; and d. 2064, l. 490b.

10. For example, PDA, op. 3, d. 1598, l. 7–70b; ÖzRMDA, f. 86, op. 1, d. 5719, ll. 15–18, and d. 5885, ll. 608 and 686–98; or "Demonstratsiia zhenshchin-uzbechek" and " 'Pust' budet zakon,' " both in *PV,* 28 Apr. 1929.

11. RGASPI, d. 2065, l. 28.

we do not want to hear any more discussions of how the paranji is harmful, of how it hides the sunshine and so on and so forth. We are against
the paranji. But we are still [victims of] spite and vengeance, [directed
against] those of us who have thrown off the paranji, on the part of the
male population, from mullahs, bois, and others. We do not want to take
all the blows on our own spines, we do not want abuse and insults. Tell
us that Soviet Power is against the paranji, that it is taking the paranji
from us, that it is issuing such a law and that all will need to conform to
this law. Everyone will then fulfill the laws of Soviet Power, none of the
men will dare come out against Soviet Power, and the mullahs and bois
will stop tormenting us.[12]

Some Uzbek men in positions of Soviet authority also declared their support,
since such a law would likewise ease their burden in explaining to neighbors
why they did not object if their wives, sisters, daughters, and mothers unveiled.[13]

Many of the "popular demands," though, seem at least in part the products
of orchestration or wishful thinking by local Zhenotdel workers. Many believed that such a law would at last persuade Uzbek women to unveil. These
staff workers may have been too quick to assume the support of most Uzbek
women, and certainly they refused to see any antihujum opinions as represen-
tative of Uzbek society. They preferred to focus on women like the one who reportedly said, "If a law were to be issued [requiring us] to cast off the paranji,
we would cast it off. We would welcome it if such a law were published." The
Zhenotdel said that such demands were heard "more and more often" with
every passing day.[14] Yet when one local women's meeting in 1927 asked those
in attendance their opinions on a wide variety of issues, only one of the 107
women present agreed with the proposition that a decree was needed to ban
the veil—and she was one of the 15 Russian women in attendance.[15] At another congress two years later one speaker announced that she recently had
read a magazine article about the "thousands of women" demanding a decree
against the veil. She went looking for them, but although she visited many
women's meetings, she declared, they were nowhere to be found.[16]

While cracks in the facade of massive popular support for a decree were not
always so visible, they do suggest that disagreement over banning the paranji
was, to a significant extent, a dispute between upper and lower levels of the
Soviet hierarchy. Demands for a decree were real, but they could be traced almost exclusively to the small, beleaguered minority that served as foot soldiers

12. RGASPI, d. 1692, l. 64.
13. ÖzRMDA, f. 86, op. 1, d. 5885, l. 693.
14. RGASPI, d. 1217, l. 55; and ÖzRMDA, f. 736, op. 1, d. 419, l. 40, and f. 837, op. 3, d.
150, ll. 137–38.
15. RGASPI, d. 1204, l. 34.
16. RGASPI, d. 2066, l. 20.

of the women's liberation campaign. Unveiled women and lower-level Zhenot-del activists were the moving forces behind such calls, a fact noted by party leaders who were uncomfortable with the idea of a decree (and perhaps also with the pressure from below).[17] These lower-level personnel, speaking as and for the "masses," hoped public petitions would sway their superiors, since these superiors had promised to be responsive to popular sentiment as mea-sured and reported by rank-and-file activists. "When will there be a decree, why don't you agree to the masses' demand for a decree?" asked a report sent in 1929 by local workers in Osh province to the Central Asian Bureau in Tashkent.[18] The general picture that emerges in the late 1920s is of a strong, albeit not always coordinated, lobbying effort to persuade high party leaders in Tashkent to ban the veil, and of many of these leaders resisting such pres-sure. There were exceptions—some high-ranking Bolsheviks expressed sympa-thy for a decree, but they never carried the day.

The various groups involved in the women's liberation campaign thus had different perspectives on whether to ban the veil. These perspectives tended to vary with individuals' work experiences and proximity to the struggle, and they were expressed through different kinds of arguments. The disputes also highlighted a central tension in the hujum itself. By focusing on the act of un-veiling, the party was requiring a visible act of individual will to show a change in a woman's personal level and political loyalties. But could such an internal shift in consciousness be coerced, forced, or brought about by fiat? Nearly all Soviet women's workers agreed that unveiled women should be pro-tected and that harassment and attacks had to be punished. But beyond that, consensus was difficult to achieve, and bitter disagreements erupted. By map-ping the main lines of argument one can see the frictions within the Soviet hi-erarchy, the conflicts among levels of the party and state apparatus, and the genuine uncertainty about how to proceed.

Arguments in favor of a decree were made on grounds of both principle and practicality. On the practical side, banning the veil could be seen as both ap-propriate and proper given the situation in which activists found themselves. Unveiled women certainly needed protection from violent attacks and street harassment, and many lower-level activists thought outright abolition of the paranji could only help. Such a legal step, they argued, would both increase the number of unveiled women—thus diminishing the opprobrium felt by any in-dividual woman—and give each woman a firm basis on which to announce to her husband and family her decision to unveil.[19] Uzbek women did not want to wear the veil, they said, but were forced to do so by male relatives. These

17. Anna Aksentovich, deputy director of the Central Asia Bureau's Zhenotdel, went so far as to deny that the leadership had proposed the idea, insisting in 1929 that the initiative had come from these other groups (RGASPI, d. 2056, l. 99).

18. Ibid., l. 129.

19. RGASPI, d. 1214, l. 28; d. 1226, l. 63; d. 1717, ll. 4–5; and d. 2057, ll. 7–8; and ÖzR-MDA, f. 86, op. 1, d. 5885, ll. 635–36.

women thus sought the "cover" of such a law—and so did Uzbek men who sympathized with Soviet power and wished their wives to unveil.[20] Such a law would represent a "powerful aid" (*mogushchii lech'*) to women's liberation work by enabling Uzbeks to declare their pro-Soviet feelings without fear of reprisal.[21]

A less optimistic argument was also made on grounds of practicality. It recognized that the Soviet position—despite the confidence the party asserted in the masses' latent sympathy—was in many ways still tenuous. Critics of the hujum pointed to the fact that there was no law requiring women to unveil, and taunted Soviet workers over their impotence to force the issue.[22] One provincial Soviet congress in 1929 declared:

> Without a governmental law banning the wearing of the paranji we will not be able to struggle any longer with those elements of the country for whom the only valid word is a government decree. A law will aid the struggle with the enemies of liberation. It will also ease the situation of many women who walk about unveiled, but who are hindered by their husbands. About this all the delegates who addressed the Congress spoke with one voice.[23]

Activists feared, moreover, that the few places where the hujum had made headway in unveiling Uzbek women—such as the showcase city of Bukhoro—were liable to relapse at any moment. A ban on the paranji would, they hoped, secure the hujum's existing achievements by guarding against backsliding. It would, as the prominent Zhenotdel activist Serafima Liubimova pointed out, both create an atmosphere of support for already unveiled women and make it possible to unmask those enemies who still opposed unveiling.[24]

The case for banning the veil also rested on arguments deeply rooted in Bolshevik principles and the ethos of the hujum. Those in favor of a decree argued that given current conditions in Uzbekistan, the veil was the proper place to focus party efforts, since no other work to liberate women could proceed while the paranji remained. Even when Uzbek women could be persuaded to attend Soviet schools, they learned little when they came to class smothered in their veils. (See Figure 23.) Uzbek women would remain illiterate, unemployed, and ignorant as long as they stayed veiled.[25] Further, there was no reason not to begin immediately, since from a Marxist perspective, the veil was not merely a

20. The Azeri leader Agamaly-Ogly, quoted at K. Ishkova, "Nuzhen li dekret, zapreshchaiushchii noshenie chadry," *Kommunistka*, no. 11 (1928), 60.

21. PDA, op. 5, d. 72, ll. 99–100, also at RGASPI, d. 2057, ll. 34–35.

22. RGASPI, d. 1681, l. 1220b, and d. 2082, l. 1140b. An example of the taunts is at d. 1681, l. 112.

23. "'Pust' budet zakon.'"

24. Serafima Liubimova, "Dekret o chadre i obshchestvo 'Doloi kalym i mnogozhenstvo,'" *Kommunistka*, no. 8 (1928), 74–75.

25. RGASPI, d. 1681, ll. 110 and 1220b.

Figure 23. Uzbek women in a Soviet school, Tashkent, 1929. (Max Penson, courtesy Dina Khojaeva, collection Anahita Gallery, Santa Fe, N.M.)

religious phenomenon. It was by definition linked with a particular stage of socioeconomic relations (the feudal-patriarchal stage), an era that was withering away in the face of Soviet socialism. Whole regions had already cast off the veil, and it was now only proper to administer the paranji a coup de grâce.[26] It was silly and even counterproductive to wait, said a Russian visitor to Central Asia in the early 1930s:

> Much time . . . is being lost. Before giving the former colonies their freedom, they should have been dealt with all the more firmly because of their very subjection. All the mosques and all the Koran schools should have been closed. All the beys, all the mullahs, all the old functionaries should have been arrested and deported. The wearing of the veil should have been prohibited and every infringement punished without mercy. The soil should have been parceled out immediately and the planting of cotton made obligatory. Every case of bribery should have been punished with death, and the children, girls and boys alike, should have been

26. ÖzRMDA, f. 86, op. 1, d. 5885, l. 768.

driven to school by the police. Ten years of such a regime, and the country would have been so modernized that one could have said to its native sons: "There you are! Now carry on for yourselves."[27]

It would be difficult to imagine a clearer (or more patronizing) statement of colonial paternalism. Yet while this comment was made by a nonresident outsider, it matches the thinking of some party members.

The party certainly had not shown reluctance to use decrees elsewhere, whether to bring about change in everyday culture or to introduce new alphabets. No protests had been made in those cases about unwarranted "administrative interference in the more intimate sphere of byt," Liubimova pointed out, and quite rightly so; such objections, she said, would not have blocked such new laws anyway because the laws were, simply, right.[28] Party policy, moreover, was now inconsistent or "ambiguous" (dvusmyslenno) in insisting that party members' families be unveiled while ignoring noncommunists.[29] Yet most of all, issuing a decree to ban the veil fitted perfectly into the logic of the hujum—the word itself meant "attack"—and the time was right, given recent high-level calls for the "intensification" of the women's liberation campaign.[30] To issue such a law would thus be to take action, not merely talk about how to remake Central Asian society. Such a decree was confidently expected to "break the last chains" of women's oppression. As Mariia Muratova, head of the Central Asian Zhenotdel, declared passionately, it would be "a crime" to let such a moment pass by.[31]

Under the combined weight of these arguments the Uzbek government flirted seriously with the idea of banning the veil. As Liubimova put it in 1928,

> There is a pressing need to issue this decree—in order to help still more the real mass movement for unveiling, in order to disarm still further the enemies of Eastern women's liberation, in order to strengthen still further in the consciousness of every Eastern woman [the knowledge that] she is not alone in the struggle with survivals of the slave past, and that behind her stands all the strength and might of Soviet power.[32]

By 1929 a special commission was examining the question. The Uzbek Congress of Soviets drafted a resolution calling for such a law, depicting it in glowing terms as a victory not only for Soviet Central Asia but for the entire colo-

---

27. Quoted by Carlisle, "Modernization," 249.

28. Liubimova declared that even if the women involved in qalin had protested against these laws, their voices would not have dissuaded Soviet authorities ("Dekret o chadre," 75).

29. RGASPI, d. 1681, l. 112.

30. PDA, op. 3, d. 1598, ll. 37–38; and RGASPI, d. 1201, l. 111, and d. 1681, l. 110.

31. Muratova's declaration is at RGASPI, d. 1681, ll. 111–12. The broken chains are cited at Ishkova, "Nuzhen li dekret," 61.

32. Liubimova, "Dekret o chadre," 75.

nized East.[33] Given the force of the arguments and the power of "mass demands" welling up from below, those lobbying for a decree held out great hope that their goal would soon be achieved.

The case against a decree, however, was made just as forcefully by a different set of party leaders and Zhenotdel workers. They, too, used arguments of practicality and principle in opposing such a law, and contended further that it represented a diversion from the party's true priorities. The practical considerations started with a plea for caution among Communists, given the party's insecure position. N. F. Gikalo, a prominent member of the party's Central Asian Bureau and one of the most vehement opponents of a decree, argued that Bolsheviks in Central Asia were surrounded by enemies and thus had to "think and think again" before leaping to conclusions. They must, he said, be "extraordinarily cautious . . . because our enemies can use every word we say. . . . [Our] policy is that the matter is difficult, demanding knowledge, a skillful and cautious approach to the question."[34] Strictly speaking, others pointed out, no law should be necessary, since women in Bukhoro and elsewhere had unveiled without being required to do so.[35]

Using the law to coerce unveiling, further, would probably only backfire. One male Soviet employee in Tashkent told his superiors that "the population is extraordinarily unhappy" about the idea of a decree, "and this unhappiness may in due course take on the character of a mass wave." Another, calling the idea a "serious mistake," warned that the Uzbek population would flee rather than comply.[36] A district-level police official, Abrarkhoja Abrarkhojaev, went even further in 1929:

> The party's decision to consider a decree on unveiling essential greatly surprises me. Such important tasks as the liberation of women and the closing of mosques must be well grounded in the wishes of the people. It is not a secret to any of us what happened to Amanullah Khan, who carried out a series of reforms [in Afghanistan] without considering the byt conditions of the population. The people rose up and overthrew him. We, too, need to remember this.[37]

The ominous message to Soviet authorities could not be missed.

33. RGASPI, d. 2057, l. 134. Calls for such a law are at ÖzRMDA, f. 95, op. 1, d. 1927, l. 227–270b; PDA, op. 5, d. 72, ll. 70–71; and RGASPI, d. 2057, ll. 132 and 134. In 1928 a resolution of the Uzbek Republic's Central Executive Committee considered such a step (ÖzRMDA, f. 86, op. 1, d. 6414, ll. 13–14). Work plans and records of the Commission for the Issuance of a Law on Unveiling, also known as Commission for Struggle with the Paranji, are at RGASPI, d. 2057, ll. 11–13.

34. RGASPI, d. 2065, l. 34. Gikalo's directive to "think and think again" [podumat' i podumat'] is at l. 30. The argument could be reversed: Nukhrat wrote that the mere discussion of a decree could be a powerful factor in persuading women to unveil ("Na bor'bu s perezhitkami rodovogo byta," Sudebnaia praktika RSFSR, no. 3 [1929], 58).

35. This point was made by Zhukova at "Mestnye rabotniki—ob izdanii dekreta," 34.

36. RGASPI, d. 2064, l. 49–49ob.

37. Ibid., l. 49.

From a practical point of view, too, this group contended that legal abolition of the veil simply would not work. The veil was deeply rooted in local culture and economic life, and so could not be abolished at once. Uzbek women were not yet sufficiently organized, and the time was not right. The hujum's existing achievements would be endangered if the veil were outlawed, as women would leave Soviet schools, refuse to attend Soviet meetings, and stop visiting Soviet institutions.[38] Furthermore, the veiled women in the families of many Communists would undercut the credibility of any decree.[39] The indifferent success of other Soviet laws—such as those prohibiting qalin—further proved that the mere existence of rules did not necessarily mean very much. As Akhunbabaev put it, Uzbekistan had enough laws; lax enforcement of those already on the books was the problem, and it cast a pall over the entire effort.[40]

Most crucially, the decree's opponents contended, no such law could work without popular support. In the Soviet Union, according to Antonina Nukhrat, a leader of the central Zhenotdel in Moscow, it was impossible to "pass a law against the will of the overwhelming majority of the laboring population," particularly if it touched on perceived vital interests and identities. Such a law, she declared, would remain nothing more than "empty sounds" (*pustye zvuki*), having no impact on society.[41] In Afghanistan, one government report asserted (incorrectly), Amanullah Khan had outlawed the veil, but his efforts failed without support from the laboring masses: "from [these] brilliant fireworks only smoke remains."[42] In the view of Nukhrat and her allies, notwithstanding the frequent reports of grassroots demands to ban the paranji, the groundwork for such a law had not yet been laid. "Have you really forgotten," asked Gikalo, "how many decrees were issued by Soviet power during the first years of the Revolution? Have all of these laws really been carried out? No. Every decree of the Soviet government demands a mass mobilization, demands a struggle for [its fulfillment]."[43] Party efforts had to concentrate, he and others concluded, on the less glamorous but ultimately more meaningful educational and cultural work that would ensure the hujum's long-term success.[44]

Objections to the proposed decree were also expressed in terms of deeply held principles. Some party leaders felt that calls for a law showed weakness among rank-and-file workers, an overeagerness to find an easy way out of a difficult situation. Banning the paranji, they contended, might mask but could

38. ÖzRMDA, f. 86, op. 1, d. 5885, l. 768; and RGASPI, d. 1226, l. 63, and d. 1717, l. 77.
39. "Mestnye rabotniki—ob izdanii dekreta," 34.
40. "Ne dekret, a glubokaia ekonomicheskaia i politicheskaia rabota nuzhna dlia raskreposhcheniia zhenshchiny," *PV*, 10 May 1929.
41. Nukhrat, "Na bor'bu s perezhitkami rodovogo byta," 58.
42. ÖzRMDA, f. 9, op. 1, d. 3437, l. 16.
43. RGASPI, d. 2065, l. 29.
44. RGASPI, d. 1681, ll. 101–2, and d. 1696, ll. 6–10, 23, and 35–36.

not solve the hujum's problems. By forcing unveiling all at once and without discussion, a decree would enable lower-level workers to skip the hard work of cultural change, education, and leadership by personal example.[45] Speaking in 1929 at the All-Union Conference of Workers among Eastern Women, S. Zhukova, director of the Uzbek Zhenotdel, expressed this view plainly:

> We have [studied] which [social] strata are raising the question of a de-
> cree, [and have] proved that the issue of a decree is being raised by the
> petty bourgeois stratum, and after them the intelligentsia. The erratic
> and unstable among party members are also insisting on a decree. Now,
> for village Communists the unveiling of a wife or relative is certainly a
> revolutionary act. One must have the courage of a revolutionary to go
> against the elements, and such [inconstant] Communists, hoping to hide
> themselves [behind] a decree, are demanding [that one be] issued.[46]

How lower-ranking activists, who faced harassment and attacks every day, felt about being called "erratic and unstable" can only be guessed, but Zhukova's analysis suggests something about relations between levels of the party hierarchy.

An even more fundamental objection to the idea of banning the veil was ideological. Such a decree, this group argued, would violate the party's over-riding need to ensure that unveiling remain an act of free will. If this act was to retain any meaning, it had to come about through education, persuasion, and ultimately individual choice, not through force or threats.[47] Since Uzbek women showed little interest in a decree—Gikalo told a Zhenotdel meeting that the only people who applauded the idea were Zhenotdel workers—it re-mained inappropriate.[48] When one provincial party official, Ashurov, was asked in 1927 what measures should be taken against family members who forbade women to unveil, he declared roundly that such people should be pun-ished with the full force of the law. But when asked what to do about *women* who refused to unveil, Ashurov appeared at a loss. He noted that no law forced a woman to throw off paranji and chachvon, even though it was in her interest to do so. Even Soviet officials could be disciplined only if they forced a female relative to veil or reveil. No such official could be forced to unveil his wife, because that would violate the free choice of the woman involved.[49]

The conclusion that an antiveil decree would harm the hujum and conflict with basic Soviet principles led Gikalo, Nukhrat, Zhukova, and others to argue for a reorientation of party priorities. Debates over banning the veil, they declared, were a distraction from more important work, and represented

---

45. Gikalo made this argument at RGASPI, d. 2065, l. 29.
46. "Mestnye rabotniki—ob izdanii dekreta," 35.
47. PDA, op. 3, d. 1549, ll. 10–100b and 12.
48. RGASPI, d. 2065, l. 24.
49. ÖzRMDA, f. 837, op. 3, d. 150, ll. 176–77.

a "huge mistake."[50] This group argued that, contrary to the assertions of Muratova and Liubimova, the veil itself was not the highest priority of Soviet power, nor should it be the only place for women's liberation work to begin. In their view the paranji was not an end in itself but a symptom of deeper problems. Once practical, everyday work to raise women's educational, economic, and cultural level had been completed, the veil would disappear of its own accord. Passing a law to ban the paranji and chachvon should thus be contemplated only later, once this wider work had run its course—and, in a curious turn of the dialectic, only when such a law was no longer needed. As Breslau explained to a party congress in 1928, "I personally am against issuing a decree at the present time. I think that we must, at present, carry out work on unveiling among our social organizations. We must [do so] among party, Soviet, and social organizations . . . in order to achieve the result of 100 percent unveiling. When all are unveiled, then we can talk about issuing this decree, but now we must work as before."[51] For now, then, the focus of party work had to stay on building the long-range foundation for lasting liberation and on increasing the aktivnost' of the masses, not the empty decrees, parades, or dramatic demonstrations allegedly wanted by lower-level activists. As Gikalo put it, the party needed fewer fine slogans and shouts of "Hurrah!" ("*Yashasin!*") and more hard work.[52]

Opponents of a decree argued that no such law had ever been likely, having been presented only as a question "for discussion" (*v diskussionom poriadke*). They thus denied the clear evidence of high-level sympathy for a ban on the veil, arguing that proponents had exaggerated their support among top party leaders in Tashkent and Moscow.[53] Yet the vigor and depth of debate belie this contention. Sharp exchanges continued throughout 1929 as both sides tried to gain the upper hand. Muratova declared that she could not "in any way" agree with the objections that had been posed, protesting that she and others who favored banning the veil knew full well that such a law would not on its own bring about women's liberation. But after two and a half years of little progress despite all-out effort, she argued, *something* had to be done to make the paranji's abolition possible.[54] Zhukova agreed, apparently changing her mind on the issue, and contradicted her earlier statements by ridiculing the arguments made against a decree and calling such "liberal" attitudes inexplicable. She further noted that no one had expected qalin or underage marriage to disappear overnight when they were forbidden, merely that such laws would

50. RGASPI, d. 1681, ll. 93–95ob, and "Ne dekret, a glubokaia ekonomicheskaia i politicheskaia rabota."
51. RGASPI, d. 1681, l. 106.
52. RGASPI, d. 2065, l. 31. See also d. 1681, ll. 93–95ob.
53. RGASPI, d. 2065, l. 26. Gikalo argued that at a recent conference in Moscow only Azeri women had favored the idea, contending that the chadra (in Azerbaijan) and the paranji (in Central Asia) presented different problems.
54. RGASPI, d. 1681, l. 109.

help in the effort. Likewise, banning the veil would not lead to its immediate disappearance—she was not so naive as that—but it would indubitably be of assistance. Arguments that a law would do more harm than good would have been deemed loopy if made about qalin or underage marriage, she said—only a crank or weirdo (*chudak*) could have said such a thing—and she insisted that they were now just as crazy about the veil. Almost twelve years after the Revolution, she concluded, "we must finish with this question [of the veil] once and for all."[55]

To be sure, a few attempts were made to bridge the gap between these warring sides, and some interesting compromise proposals can be found amid the testy exchanges. Since Communists, Komsomol members, and Soviet workers were already required to unveil their families, one argument ran, perhaps the veil could be banned gradually, step by step, working outward in concentric rings into the wider society. In Azerbaijan, for example, a proposal was made to require all schoolteachers and those pupils who had attended Soviet schools for at least two years—but no others—to cast off their veils.[56] An Uzbek women's activist, Ikramova, mused that perhaps the manufacture and sale—but not necessarily the wearing—of the paranji and chachvon could be banned.[57] Another compromise called for proceeding along generational lines, allowing older Uzbek women (who were thought particularly reluctant to unveil) to retain their paranjis but mandating unveiling for all females under 40.[58] Still another approach drew local distinctions. A decree might be possible in the industrialized Azeri republic, for example, but premature in the laggard, peasant societies of southern Central Asia.[59] Nukhrat suggested that various republic-, province-, and district-level ordinances could eventually serve as the basis for an all-Union law.[60]

Yet as the heated exchanges make plain, such fine distinctions held little promise of achieving consensus or a long-term solution. Both sides felt confident in their views and believed that their opponents not only threatened the women's liberation effort but contradicted the core principles of a true Bolshevik. How, then, could the matter be settled? In mid-1929 an answer came from Moscow. After three years, central authorities had finally made a decision. Aleksandra Artiukhina, deputy chair of the central Zhenotdel in Moscow and thus superior in rank to both Muratova and Zhukova, announced in July 1929 that the Central Committee in Moscow had decided not to ban the veil. Soviet policy in the hujum would henceforth stress economic and cultural work—bringing women into factories, cooperatives, and schools—as the primary means of struggle against the paranji. Such measures

55. Ibid., l. 122–220b.
56. RGASPI, d. 1696, especially ll. 6–10, 23, and 35–36.
57. ÖzRMDA, f. 86, op. 1, d. 5594, l. 235.
58. RGASPI, d. 2057, ll. 7–8.
59. ÖzRMDA, f. 86, op. 1, d. 5885, ll. 768–69.
60. Nukhrat, "Na bor'bu s perezhitkami rodovogo byta," 58.

would be based on a "conscious relationship" with the Eastern woman rather than administrative methods, and would thereby ensure the campaign's future success. Furthermore, she said, "We do not need a law banning the chadra, [nor] do we need discussions about a law; we do not need administrative pressure, but we do want work for women's liberation to continue."[61] According to the Central Committee, then, even the idea of such a law was no longer to be mentioned.

Until this point central authorities had welcomed vigorous debate over whether to ban the veil and paid careful attention to the arguments raised by both sides—indeed, they had held parallel discussions in Moscow. The government's Commission for the Improvement of Women's Labor and Daily Life (KUTB) studied the possibility of banning the veil in Central Asia and Transcaucasia, of forbidding foot-binding among Chinese families, and of outlawing other "harmful customs" that were oppressive to women.[62] All-Union meetings of women's workers in Moscow debated banning the paranji, and many of the same opinions were aired. Iaroslavskii, for instance, expressed sympathy for the idea in late 1928, while women representing the central Commissariat of Justice expressed reservations.[63] As late as May 1929—only two months before Artiukhina announced the new party line—the central KUTB had declared the need to mobilize resources for an all-out campaign in favor of a decree.[64] Even at the highest reaches of power, then, there was little clear vision of what the party should do—and policies could be influenced from below.

Once the decision was finally made, though, lower levels were expected to fall into line. One of the party's most prominent figures—Nadezhda Krupskaia, Lenin's widow—explained that party leaders had determined that such a decree was inappropriate:

> We have introduced revolutionary laws on [women's] equality, which have not yet been fully implemented in daily life, but which have had a stimulating effect. Through our decrees we have forced into place laws that aid liberation in all sorts of ways. And, of course, a law on the paranji could also help liberation. But here it is necessary to know the byt conditions.
>
> It is a complex question. We should like, of course, to send the paranji

---

61. Artiukhina, "Ocherednye zadachi partii po rabote sredi rabotnits i krest'ianok," *Izvestiia TsK VKP(b),* no. 19 (278) (1929), 3.

62. ÖzRMDA, f. 86, op. 1, d. 6570, l. 19. See also f. 9, op. 1, d. 3368, l. 40; f. 86, op. 1, d. 4437, ll. 114 and 265; and d. 5885, ll. 747 and 760. Similar work was under way in parts of the RSFSR: RGASPI, d. 2057, l. 14.

63. "Vsesoiuznyi s"ezd vostochnits," *PV,* 10 Dec. 1928.

64. ÖzRMDA, f. 86, op. 1, d. 5881, l. 63.

and chachvon to hell, but we cannot always get everything we want by issuing decrees.[65]

Krupskaia then struck a careful, temperate note. She urged party members to remember the principles of military strategy: they should remain open to tactical retreats as well as frontal assaults in the effort to unveil and liberate Central Asian women.

But the decision not to ban the veil, however prominent the spokespeople and however well presented their arguments, came as a great surprise and a bitter blow to the lower-level activists and unveiled women who had hoped for legal protection. At the same time, after all, the party was calling for heroic efforts to collectivize the countryside, by force if need be. These women felt crushing disappointment; one prominent Uzbek women's activist, Shadieva, said she cried for two nights straight after she heard the news.[66] These women received little consolation from their superiors, though, hearing only lectures on their proper place in the Soviet system and on the need to adhere to the new party line. One senses a reassertion of power and privilege by leaders uncomfortable with the buffets of lobbying pressure from below, and an attempt to establish or reestablish clear lines of authority and command.

The most visible eruption of jostling between the ranks occurred at a meeting on 11 May 1929, where the decision not to ban the veil was presented and explained to lower-level Zhenotdel activists. Gikalo, who stood among the most stalwart opponents of the proposed decree, was asked to deliver the main report, and he included none of the give-and-take or encouragement of debate that had characterized earlier meetings. His speech offered only a buck-up-and-take-it message for rank-and-file party workers who might not like the decision, but nevertheless had to live with it. While Gikalo noted that their disappointment and frustration were understandable after local activists had worked so hard to prepare the masses for a decree, the question now simply was no longer up for discussion.[67]

Gikalo assured his audience that he had not come to criticize, that he knew they were not guilty of any really serious political errors.[68] At the same time, he told the listening Zhenotdel workers, they must realize that intemperate demands for a ban on the veil did betray a certain Left deviation. And such calls,

65. This speech was reprinted several times. Most of the version quoted here is at L. A. Tul'tseva, "Iz istorii bor'by za sotsial'noe i dukhovnoe raskreposhchenie zhenshchin Srednei Azii (Prazdnovanie 8 Marta, 1920–1927 gg.)," *Sovetskaia etnografiia*, no. 1 (1986), 20, citing N. K. Krupskaia, *Zhenshchina Strany Sovetov—ravnopravnyi grazhdanin* (Moscow, 1938), 56; the final sentence is from N. K. Krupskaia, "Puti raskreposhcheniia zhenshchiny Vostoka (rech' N. K. Krupskoi na Vsesoiuznom soveshchanii rabotnits sredi zhenshchin Vostoka 10.XII.1928)," *Kommunistka*, no. 12 (1928), 12.

66. RGASPI, d. 2065, l. 34.

67. Ibid., l. 2. Gikalo's full report is at ll. 1–36.

68. He reassured these women that he had not come to "beat up on" the *Zhenotdelki*, and that he knew they were "not syndicalists, not individualists": ibid., ll. 26 and 28.

he said, came more from staff workers than from Uzbek women. He compared the situation to the hostile reaction eight years earlier among rank-and-file Communists toward the ending of the militarized system of war communism and the introduction of a more conciliatory, go-slow policy in the NEP. At that time, he said, Lenin had overruled roughly 80 percent of the party's members by pushing ahead with NEP, and time had proved him right. "Of course it is the very simplest thing," Gikalo said, more than a little patronizingly, "to work and not to think. But in such a matter as this, in order to achieve such a great political goal as liberation, it is necessary to think and think again, even if it means you do nothing [right away]."[69] It would be un-Marxist, he implied, for the Zhenotdel to resist the party's decision. Such a call for practical work, after all, held no shame.[70]

Some of his judgments on Zhenotdel work and workers were far from complimentary, and they provoked strong protests and resentment. Gikalo told these women that they had misunderstood basic party doctrines—the importance of economic independence, for example, had been bent by Zhenotdel delegates into such dangerous ideas as Uzbekistan's economic independence from the USSR, women's economic independence from the Soviet Union, or women's total economic independence from men, this latter idea meaning isolation rather than true liberation.[71] He further accused the group of Zhenotdelki of acting as "hysterical women" (isterichki) who failed to create a good moral atmosphere around unveiled women.[72] He accused them, finally, of having an inflated sense of their own importance, with their talk about the party and other Soviet groups as "allies." This language, he pointed out, suggested that their primary loyalty lay to themselves and to women, not to the party or Soviet power as a whole. This sounded like feminist tendencies that undercut Communist loyalties, and such attitudes could not be tolerated. "It appears," he said,

> that you consider yourselves to be popes of the earthly realm, arguing that you have allies: the party, trade unions, Soviet power, and you want these allies to move closer to you, [that is] what you need. And who are you? You are Communists, you are an integral part of the party; you need to talk about how you can move closer to the party, not about how the party can move to you, how the party can work for you.[73]

Angry shouts repeatedly interrupted his speech. "You have not understood [our words] properly, and not expressed [them] precisely," yelled one delegate in disgust. "You can tell me about this after [I finish]," replied Gikalo testily.

69. Ibid., ll. 24 and 30. The quotation is from l. 30.
70. Ibid., ll. 17 and 34.
71. Ibid., l. 27.
72. Ibid., ll. 31 and 33.
73. This quotation and the subsequent exchange are ibid., l. 27.

"But if you don't agree with me, if you object to this, then please read through your own proposals. There you yourselves wrote [these things]. . . . You say that I am misrepresenting everything, but I took this from your proposal." The heckling shows these women refusing to sit passively and listen to criticism from party leaders—people with comfortable jobs who did not, they felt, understand the practical side of women's work. These rank-and-file activists saw their role differently, believing their work to be crucial to Soviet power and thinking that after three years of open debate (in which their participation had, after all, been invited) they had a right to help shape party policy. These tensions did not disappear when Artiukhina and Gikalo drew this wave of debate to a close in mid-1929.

Disagreement in the Socialist Paradise: The Second Wave, 1936–1937

A handful of scattered references aside, the notion of outlawing the veil disappeared from discussion in the early 1930s.[74] Yet contrary to Massell's assertion that the idea of banning the veil was put to rest definitively in 1929, a second wave of debate occurred several years later.[75] The issue resurfaced in 1936–37, as part of the broader process of defining a new "Stalin Constitution." While the wider context had changed and such sharp exchanges could no longer appear in print, one still finds many of the same intraparty tensions on display. The women's liberation effort remained an important arena to legitimize and justify Soviet power in Central Asia, yet the party's policy was still surprisingly open to contention and negotiation, its final shape as yet unknown.

The basic differences between 1927 and 1936 in the wider political context are too obvious to require elaboration. The environment in which party and Soviet officials worked, suffice it to say, changed substantially after Stalin's rise to unquestioned authority in Moscow and the massive upheavals of the first two five-year plans. The idea of banning the veil was revived amid this turmoil, arising in 1936 as part of a broader discussion of Soviet law during the drafting of a new constitution. The decision made by the shah of Iran in 1936 to outlaw the Persian chador does not appear to have been mentioned during this debate, but it may have encouraged Soviet authorities to consider the issue anew.[76] They may have been willing to do so, too, because in crucial ways the wider context had changed surprisingly little since 1927. More than a decade after launching the hujum and well into the Second Five-Year Plan, the initial

---

74. Most references tersely confirmed the party's decision not to ban the veil. The idea of such a decree, according to Evgenii Beliaev, "seems to us of dubious expedience and advisability" (untitled book review in *Antireligioznik*, no. 12 [1930], 102–4). A government resolution of 1930 called the decision "perfectly right" (ÖzRMDA, f. 9, op. 1, d. 3395, l. 77). In 1933 Nukhrat called the discussions in the late 1920s "mistaken" ("Usilit' klassovuiu bditel'nost' i proizvodstvennuiu aktivnost'," *Revoliutsiia i natsional'nosti*, no. 3 [36] [1933], 47).

75. Massell, *Surrogate Proletariat*, 348–53.

76. Guity Nashat, ed., *Women and Revolution in Iran* (Boulder, 1983), 26–29.

fanfare and high hopes had long since given way to quiet despair. The vast numbers of paranjis that continued to dot the streets of virtually every Uzbek city, town, and village represented a continuing affront to Soviet claims of liberation. Some party activists seized the opportunity presented by the discussion of a new constitution to revive the notion of wiping out the paranji in one fell swoop.

The language they used to make their case had changed with the times. "Debate" over banning the veil did not mean the freewheeling exchanges of the late 1920s. The tone of public discussions had shifted unmistakably, and the renewed conversation about a decree followed new scripts. In 1936 each participant had to herald the inevitable success of Soviet policy, while proclaiming stalwart support for the party and humble obeisance to Stalin. "On 13 June we read through the draft of the Stalinist Constitution," began one letter to the editor of *Pravda Vostoka* written by two Uzbek women, Badam Irnazarova and Ugal' Hashimova. "But in order to study [adequately] this great document written by our beloved Stalin, we reread it every day at home after work. We long pondered each article, we discussed [it with each other], remembering our unhappy past [before 1917] and comparing it with our currently happy life." Open criticism of the party hierarchy was no longer permissible; Irnazarova and Hashimova had to voice such ritual adulation before making their main point, a request to abolish the veil: "We think that the new constitution must [include] a point banning the paranji. The paranji—a symbol of oppression and the lack of rights enjoyed by women of the East—must be annihilated. It seems to us that we express the will and desire of all Uzbek women."[77]

In other ways the techniques and arguments resembled those employed earlier. Public opinion, in particular, was invoked and mobilized to pressure lawmakers and party leaders to include a ban on the veil in the new constitution. Throughout June and July 1936, *Pravda Vostoka* published a series of articles, letters, and group petitions under the recurring heading of "The Soviet People Discuss the Draft of a New Soviet Constitution."[78] Most articles described a succession of speakers at provincial conferences denouncing the paranji ("the evil enemy of Uzbek women") and then calling "with one voice" for a ban on the veil. Such meetings then expressed confidence that the people's voice would be heard and that a ban on the veil would find its way into the new constitution.[79] The amount of true discussion here is, of course, debatable. Certainly in

77. Badam Irnazarova and Ugal' Khashimova, "My predlagaem zapretit' parandzhu," *PV,* 30 June 1936.

78. In addition to Irnazarova and Hashimova, see Muradov et al., "Zapretit' noshenie parandzhi," *PV,* 5 July 1936; M. Iarkov, "Kolkhozniki podderzhivaiut predlozhenie o zapreshchenii parandzhi," *PV,* 14 July 1936; and V. Adamovich, "My protiv parandzhi," *PV,* 24 July 1936.

79. The phrase "evil enemy of Uzbek women" is from Muradov et al., "Zapretit' noshenie parandzhi."

1936 such repeated calls for a decree could not have appeared without the sanction or sympathy of top officials. The articles and letters plainly adhered to a script; they meant to give the impression of a massive, grassroots upsurge to abolish the paranji. Irnazarova and Hashimova's initial letter on 30 June, for example, was quickly followed by several reports of local meetings and resolutions echoing their request for a decree.

Yet this debate was at the same time more real than it initially appears. Alongside the required praise for Stalin's genius there was a more biting side to the letters. They carried implicit criticism of the rampant shortcomings and failures in party policy, and repeated arguments from the late 1920s. A decade of the hujum had not rid Uzbekistan of the paranji, first of all; far too many Muslim women still wore this mark of oppression. More had to be done, and the time for action was now. Uzbek women were said to be eager to cast off their veils, being kept in subjection only by the coercion of backward male relatives.[80] Underneath the surface calm and professions of loyalty one thus finds powerful currents of disquiet. The lobbying effort for a decree was more than window dressing: it aimed to put real pressure on decision makers during the brief window of opportunity for shaping the new constitution.

Despite the apparent unanimity of calls to abolish the veil, one finds greater complexity when one reads between the lines. The recurring tensions within Soviet ranks, for example, sometimes surfaced in the public record; in places one can see the muted (or occasionally not so muted) disagreements. Another letter to the editor of *Pravda Vostoka* in July 1936, for example, came from eleven female students at the Stalin Communist Agricultural School who declared their "passionate" support for Irnazarova and Hashimova's proposal to ban the veil. These women, too, observed the Stalinist conventions—offering paeans to liberation through stories of successful unveilings, and opening and closing with strong professions of support for the party. "The paranji is a dark mark of odat on our prosperous, cultured, and happy life," they declared. "This mark must be rubbed out."[81] But most of their letter served just the opposite purpose, pointing out the many reasons a decree was ill advised. Describing one kolkhoz where a majority of women still wore the paranji and chachvon, these students noted how hard it would be to enforce a decree without more and better educational work among rural women. Too often, they continued, unveiling efforts led only to more reveilings, as women were not taught why their actions mattered or how to resist strong harassment. These letter writers promised to visit the countryside themselves to investigate personally what peasant women really wanted—by implication, possibly something other than a decree. Such expressions of "support" hardly show a unanimous public outcry for the immediate abolition of the veil.

This public discussion drew to a close when the Uzbek SSR's new constitu-

80. Iarkov, "Kolkhozniki podderzhivaiut," and Adamovich, "My protiv parandzhi."
81. Saadat Muminova et al., "Parandzha dolzhna byt' zapreshchena," *PV,* 10 July 1936.

tion was completed in late 1936. It outlawed opposition to women's liberation but curiously—despite the weight of "popular demands"—did not abolish the veil.[82] Once again the idea of a decree had been rebuffed, despite a strong and this time organized lobbying campaign. This official decision, once made, was again defended vigorously against disgruntled lower- and mid-level activists. As in 1929, party leaders quashed further discussion and impugned the motives of those who supported a decree. One delegate, A. Kazakova, told the Seventh Uzbek Party Congress in 1937 that the push for a decree had come from comrades who were either unable or unwilling to carry out more useful sorts of educational work among women. Their agitation, furthermore, had only given ammunition to class enemies and clerics.[83] Kazakova heaped scorn on those

> comrades who . . . chatter away about the necessity of issuing a decree and want to resolve this question with administrative methods. This is absolutely incorrect; we have had enormous successes in cotton, in industry, in culture—and we have attained these not by means of decrees or administrative methods, but through mass political work among the population. In this case it is impossible to solve the question of women, of the development of mass political work among them, of the final [success] of women's liberation, by administrative means. This formulation of the question [must] be considered unbefitting a member of the Communist Party [*nepartiinyi*].[84]

After painting such a damning picture of ideological deviation in supporting a decree (such words as "nepartiinyi" carried powerfully negative connotations and even ominous implications in 1936), Kazakova leveled practical criticism at these Communists. They were better at talking than working, she said, and their efforts had done more harm than good.

Yet despite such attempts to shut down discussion, archival records show disagreement continuing to simmer. One local official, Zakharov, declared in mid-1937 that the party could not force a woman to unveil, but should instead concentrate on educational work: "You see, comrades, we cannot tear off the paranji by force, because this would be a political violation of our laws. Women themselves have not yet realized the harm of the paranji, and therefore [still] wear it."[85] Such an analysis appeared to be ideologically sound, given the official view that female unveiling had to be the product of free and conscious individual choice. Even so, Zakharov attracted fire from a visiting party investigator, M. Samokhvalova, who complained that Zakharov used arguments

---

82. Article 121 is quoted by Iuldash Saidov, "V Surkhan-Dar'e oslablena rabota sredi zhenshchin," *PV*, 5 Sept. 1939.

83. See her words in the description of the congress at *PV*, 14 June 1937.

84. PDA, op. 13, d. 3, ll. 220–21.

85. The quotation and Samokhvalova's response are at ÖzRMDA, f. 86, op. 10, d. 772, l. 6.

and quotations from the recent Congress of Soviets merely to shirk his duty and avoid prosecuting cases in which parents had veiled their children. The issue of parent-child relationships raised another set of problems, but Samokhvalova avoided those complexities. She focused on Zakharov's misuse, as she saw it, of the congress's refusal to ban the paranji. His attitude, she argued, was "completely unhealthy" and far too common. Samokhvalova clearly wanted the congress's decision to be reversed and the veil to be banned. Real arguments thus continued to simmer over women's liberation in 1936 and 1937—during the Great Purges, a time when even a whiff of perceived disobedience could trigger the severest sanctions.

Scripts of Power and Reluctance: The Third Wave, 1940–1941

A third and final wave of public discussion of banning the veil began in 1940, only three years after Kazakova had denounced the very idea as "nepartiinyi." In the late 1930s Soviet officials in Central Asia had again shown increasing interest in women's issues: the periodical press devoted significant coverage to such stories, and by 1940 a major campaign to jump-start the hujum seemed to be in the works. After nearly fifteen years of ostensibly all-out effort to eliminate the paranji and chachvon through education and persuasion, Soviet authorities still confronted veils all across Uzbekistan. From the perspective of party leaders, more had to be done—and so the idea of a decree was considered once more. This third wave of discussion was, at least in public, even more heavily scripted. Party activists who favored legal action sensed that at last their time had come. A decree seemed to be at hand: disagreement was not permitted amid the well-orchestrated calls for banning the veil. Yet despite this impressive coordination, no such decree became law. This curious outcome again underscores the party's difficulties in reconciling the use of coercion to bring about liberation, and it illustrates the continuing existence of limits—despite all appearances to the contrary—on Soviet authority in Central Asia.

Mastura Avezova, a Tajik deputy to the USSR Supreme Soviet, reopened the debate in January 1940. Writing in *Pravda,* the Communist Party's flagship newspaper in Moscow, she declared that in Central Asia the paranji had to be wiped out once and for all, and that this could best be done by a law. She proposed that such a law forbid women to wear the paranji or chachvon, and that it punish men who harassed women for casting their veils aside.[86] With the unmistakable imprimatur of high-level approval—Avezova's article appeared very prominently—supporters of a decree seized the opportunity to make their case. This article in *Pravda* launched a tightly controlled script: within days, dozens of "spontaneous" meetings declared (in nearly identical words) their support for a decree, reams of newspaper articles chronicled a huge upsurge of grassroots demands for the veil's eradication, and booklets and pamphlets

86. Mastura Avezova, "Okonchatel'no unichtozhit' parandzhu!" *Pravda,* 15 Jan. 1940.

flooded the region to prove that the paranji and chachvon harmed women and deserved to be abolished.[87]

Whether they meant to test the waters to gauge popular response or they felt genuine sympathy for the notion of banning the veil, top party leaders lent the idea strong support. Avezova's article was reprinted widely throughout Central Asia. Within ten days it appeared on the front page of *Pravda Vostoka*, and her call for a decree was praised in two front-page editorials as right, "a thousand times right."[88] *Pravda* itself continued to report on the campaign throughout the early months of 1940. Thousands of Eastern women had joined in calling for a decree, one article said sympathetically, in a movement that "coincides with the interests of the Soviet woman, the interests of the new socialist society and the new socialist morality. It [should receive] the support of party organizations, and it is receiving such support."[89] This sympathetic evaluation in the Moscow press was quickly republished in *Pravda Vostoka*— lest Soviet officials in Central Asia miss the message.

The official script permitted little room for dissent. Most of the published record shows just one voice: unanimous, repeated calls for a ban on the veil. After the bitter debates of 1927–29 and to a lesser degree those of 1936–37, a decree at last appeared imminent. The "discussion" in 1940 included petitions for abolition, in both the Russian and Uzbek-language press, signed by hundreds of men and women from all across Uzbekistan, from Samarqand to Termiz (Termez).[90] "It is long since time to finish with the paranji," declared one meeting in Qöqon.[91] Eight women wrote that Avezova had "read our minds" in calling for such a decree.[92] In Andijon a member of the city soviet read Avezova's article aloud to a meeting of 2,000 women at a public theater; the meeting then "unanimously" called for a ban on the veil.[93] The main Uzbek-language daily newspaper, *Qizil Özbekiston*, likewise published full-page spreads giving virtually identical opinions from a cross section of Uzbek

87. See the support Avezova received at a meeting in Yangi-Qorghon at PDA, op. 15, d. 383, ll. 47–48. The speakers at a meeting of 230 women in Farghona declared their unanimous support at "Iskorenit' parandzhu!" *PV*, 3 Feb. 1940. See also "Obrashchenie zhenshchin stolitsy Uzbekistana," *PV*, 5 Feb. 1940, and M. Islamova, "Doloi parandzhu!" *PV*, 15 Feb. 1940.

88. The quotation is from "Unichtozhit' parandzhu!" *PV*, 29 Jan. 1940. Her proposal was mentioned sympathetically in the lead editorial on International Women's Day, 8 March 1940. The article was reprinted at *PV*, 25 Jan. 1940.

89. Reprinted as "Proch' parandzhu!" *PV*, 3 Feb. 1940, inaccurately citing the original publication date in *Pravda* as 1 Feb. 1940.

90. One petition with 320 signatories (almost two dozen are named individually) is at Sharipova et al., "Protiv temnoty i nevezhestva," *PV*, 30 Jan. 1940. For Samarqand, see "Obsuzhdeniia stat'i Mastury Avezovoi," *PV*, 3 Feb. 1940, and N. Sharipova, "Zhenshchiny Samarkanda goriacho podderzhivaiut predlozhenie tov. Avezovoi," *PV*, 4 Feb. 1940. A report from "backward" Termiz is "Sobranie zhenshchin goroda Termez," *PV*, 15 Feb. 1940. In the Uzbek press, see, for example, the letter from five peasants at "Bitsin paranchi!" *Jarqin hajat*, no. 1 (42) (1940), 23.

91. "Edinodushnaia podderzhka i odobrenie," *PV*, 6 Feb. 1940.

92. A. Iusupova et al., "Mastura Avezova prochla nashi mysli," *PV*, 4 Feb. 1940.

93. "Edinoglasno odobrili predlozhenie Mastury Avezovoi," *PV*, 6 Feb. 1940.

women: a medical student, a student at the transport institute, a Stakhanovite factory worker, and a People's Artist and All-Soviet deputy, Halima Nasirova.[94] It is difficult to find any ambivalence or ambiguity, so thoroughly was this public record vetted and controlled. Those permitted to speak, virtually without exception, told personal stories of liberation through unveiling and then declared their "passionate," "heartfelt" support for the paranji's abolition. Only rare, indirect signs of editorial autonomy exist. A press review of February 1940 noted approvingly the positive coverage garnered by the anti-veil campaign, but criticized the "apathetic attitude" of a handful of Uzbek- and Tajik-language publications (*Uchkun, Stalin yöli, Bol'shevik, Bol'shevik yöli*). They had reprinted Avezova's article but had failed to report on its subsequent reception among local women.[95] Such demanding criticism shows both the tight restrictions on local editors and the degree to which the public discussion had been scripted.

Stalinist formulas were also observed meticulously in public meetings. Thousands of women gathered in Tashkent on 30 January 1940 for one such festive gathering (complete with dancers and music) to discuss Avezova's proposal to ban the veil. Several top leaders attended, including Usman Yusupov, the first secretary of the Uzbek Communist Party, and coverage was splashed prominently across the pages of local and regional newspapers. The only odd note was struck by the opening speech, delivered not by a heroic young activist but by a voice from the past, 102-year-old Pulat-Oi Abidova—but her words fitted the occasion. To rousing applause, Abidova called on Uzbek women to follow her example and unveil. Only state action, she went on to say, could eradicate the paranji, so a decree was badly needed. The main speaker, Fatima Yoldashbaeva, echoed this call for a decree, as did several others. The speeches recited the usual arguments: they pointed out the bitter pre-Soviet history of Uzbek women, the health risks of wearing a veil, and the transformation brought about in a woman's life by the act of unveiling. The meeting then culminated in a theatrical public unveiling. Those in attendance issued an exhortation to all Uzbek women to join them and then sent a telegram to Comrade Stalin, which—after the requisite praises for his genius—asked him to support this call for a decree. Women still in veils, the telegram pointed out, could not be of full use to the state in its efforts to achieve its glorious goals.[96]

A wide range of arguments thus was mobilized in support of a decree, much of it familiar from earlier debates. The Stalin Constitution of 1936 already protected women's equality and rights in "golden letters" (*altin harflar*), sup-

94. "Pajtaxt xatin-qizlari paranchini taqiqlajdigan dekret," *QÖ*, 2 Feb. 1940. See also the meetings of 500 in Namangan and 400 in Marghilon, at "Paranchini batamam joq qilajlik," *QÖ*, 4 Feb. 1940, and "Ozbekstan pajtaxti xatin-qizlarining ordenli respublikaning barca mihnatkash xatin-qizlariga murachaati," *QÖ*, 5 Feb. 1940.

95. "Protiv parandzhi!" *PV*, 17 Feb. 1940.

96. "Obshchegorodskoe sobranie zhenshchin," *PV*, 1 Feb. 1940, and "Sobranie zhenshchin gor. Tashkenta," *PV*, 2 Feb. 1940.

porters noted carefully, yet Soviet law could do more to help women who still wore the paranji.[97] Banning the veil would help by providing them clear grounds on which to oppose fanatic husbands and male relatives who insisted that they wear this "macabre, medieval cloth."[98] It would help overcome the religious prejudices and superstition that led parents to veil and marry off their 12- and 13-year-old daughters.[99] Far too many women of all ages remained veiled, these activists said, and by 1940 a decree appeared to be the only option that could make a difference.[100] Further, Uzbek women were said to detest the veil because it prevented them from participating in Soviet society and especially because it prevented them from meeting their newly raised production quotas. However implausible this last argument may sound, it was used to underscore the view that such a decree would enable rather than impair Uzbek women's ability to make a truly free choice of how to live.[101]

Soviet scholars did their part to bolster these arguments. Liutsan Klimovich, a well-known specialist on Islam, contended that veiling was not required by Islamic religious doctrine. He further noted that revolutionary law had not shied away from abolishing such dangerous customs as the Kalmyk kamzol or the practice of *shakhsei-vakhsei* (a Shi'a mourning rite, said to require self-mutilation to commemorate the death of Husain, the martyred son of Ali, in 671) in Turkmenistan, Azerbaijan, and Georgia. Then he pointed out the veil's many supposed health risks, including skin and eye diseases along with problems in pregnancy and postnatal care. Since the paranji was physically harmful as well as personally exploitative, he concluded, it too should be abolished.[102]

Once the machinery of state and press had cranked up in early 1940 to argue so strongly for banning the veil, the outcome appeared inevitable. Few cracks marred this public wall of unanimity. Yet even at this stage one finds tensions submerged in the unpublished archival record. One official argued at a closed-door meeting that to debate a decree was to miss the central point. It is "not difficult to issue a decree," he said, but Soviet personnel "need to struggle with those elements that make possible the wearing of paranjis. Our women want to cast off the paranji, but hooligan mullahs prevent them, with

---

97. *Paranchi va cacvan azadlik dushmani* (Tashkent, 1940), 18.

98. The phrase is from "Obrashchenie zhenshchin stolitsy Uzbekistana," *PV*, 5 Feb. 1940. For the argument that a decree would help women stand up for themselves, see "Obsuzhdeniia stat'i Mastury Avezovoi," *PV*, 3 Feb. 1940.

99. "Islam—xatin-qizlarni qul qilish qurali," *QÖ*, 23 Jan. 1940, 18.

100. One article offered a grim depiction of rural veiling to argue that the paranji had to be banned. See Kumrikhon Khaidarova, "Nanesti reshitel'nyi udar feodal'no-baiskim perezhitkam!" *PV*, 8 Feb. 1940.

101. Sanabar Mavlianova et al., "Zhenshchine-kolkhoznitse nenavistna parandzha," *PV*, 14 Feb. 1940.

102. L. I. Klimovich, *Doloi parandzhu!* (Moscow, 1940), especially 53–63. On health, also see Rafail Samoilovich Gershenovich, *Paranji—khotinlar soghligining ashaddiy dushmani* (Tashkent, 1950); and G. Vainshtein, "Chachvan i parandzha—simvol rabstva," *PV*, 30 Jan. 1940. On Shakhsei-Vakhsei, see Keller, *To Moscow, Not Mecca*, 70, 166, and 173.

all their vile tricks they delay this matter. We need to struggle with these elements, and in every possible way struggle for the promotion of women into leadership roles in party and Soviet work. This is where our help is needed."[103]

Other top leaders agreed. Khursan Mahmudova, deputy chair of the Uzbek Supreme Soviet, decried the "shame" (*ujat*) of calls for a decree, arguing that the very idea was fundamentally misguided. It betrayed, she said, a basic mistrust of the party, "a lack of confidence [*ishanmaslik*] in the might of the Communist Party, in the strength of the Soviet people."[104] Communists, she said, should have the strength of their convictions and not doubt that women would in time see the rightness of Soviet emancipation. She pointed to a huge meeting in the October district of Tashkent in June 1940, at which tens of thousands of women had gathered to discuss women's liberation. They declared that the only way to rid Uzbekistan of the paranji was by instilling a "communist spirit" (*kommunistik ruhda*) in the masses, inspiring them with the ideal of service to the collective, and pulling them into Soviet educational programs and social work—not by issuing decrees. Even though such work had so far made little headway, keeping it as the main priority would avoid the ideological difficulties of forcing a woman to unveil and thereby of trying to coerce a leap to revolutionary consciousness.

Archival sources thus offer hints of continuing debate as late as 1940, suggesting that the Stalinist public script does not capture the full story. Official policy on women's liberation—and so perhaps on other matters too—was never merely dictated from above. Consider the final outcome. By March 1940 the idea of banning the veil appeared unstoppable. High-level support from Moscow was plain, and it seemed to augur an outcome different from that of 1929 and 1936. In the late winter and early spring of 1940, the Soviet Uzbek government danced up to the very brink of such a decree. But it backed away, and the periodical press fell silent on the topic for several months, including only the briefest of mentions in *Qizil Özbekiston* on 8 March.[105] By midsummer, when the paranji reappeared as a matter for discussion, a distinct change had occurred. Despite the massive public relations campaign of the previous winter, party leaders clearly had opted once more to retreat. Instead of banning the veil, they chose to support yet more campaigns of exhortation and persuasion—precisely the sorts of effort that had failed to work for the last fifteen years.

Given the prominence and unanimity of the foregoing public campaign, however, not to mention its association with Stalin and Yusupov, among others, party leaders could not simply declare once again that support for a decree was "antiparty." This time, denial was the basic strategy: no policy reversal

103. ÖzRMDA, f. 837, op. 32, d. 2066, l. 60.
104. ÖzRMDA, f. 2454, op. 1, d. 413, l. 43. This "shame" is disparaged at l. 44.
105. "Xalq-ara kommunistik xatin-qizlar kuni," *QÖ*, 8 Mar. 1940, and in the same issue, N. Abdusalamova, "Stalin zamanining xatin-qizlari."

was proclaimed or admitted. No official ever declared that a new course had been chosen, and there was no coordinated attempt to marshal arguments, as Gikalo and Artiukhina had done in 1929 and Kazakova did in 1937, to show that banning the veil was wrong and that the idea should be dropped. The notion simply disappeared, step by step, from public discussions. One *Pravda Vostoka* article in May 1940 mentioned Avezova's call for a decree and told of the impassioned meetings that had followed—fully 4,000 women were said to have unveiled in response to such discussions.[106] Yet it treated Avezova's piece as significant chiefly for sparking a new wave of (voluntary) unveilings. Her call for a decree banning the veil was mentioned, but it was no longer the central theme, nor did it receive editorial support. Another feature story, published a month later, mentioned Avezova's article as the cause of even more unveilings—6,000 in Tashkent alone—but it said nothing at all about the specific contents of her essay, much less expressed support for her ideas.[107] *Qizil Özbekiston* noted in June that "Bolshevik agitation" was succeeding in persuading "thousands" of women to unveil, and that more agitation—not a decree—was needed.[108]

Editors and party leaders appeared content to retreat silently, letting Avezova's "debate" simply peter out. By July 1940 articles about the veil either failed to mention Avezova or did not note that she was interested in legal reforms.[109] The farthest any article would then go was to say that the mere idea of a decree might have salutary effects, even if no such law were ever issued. Of the more than 10,000 women who had discussed Avezova's original essay, for example, more than 3,000 were said to have chosen to unveil.[110] These numbers were small when set against the number of Uzbek women still veiled, but by seeing it this way party activists could persuade themselves that these few heroic women were acting of their own free will, as autonomous agents in the revolutionary cause. Perhaps merely talking about a decree would persuade women to do the right thing and unveil; certainly it avoided the problems and inevitable messiness of an actual decree.

Thus for the third time since Stalin's rise to power the party proved unexpectedly reluctant to confront Uzbek society head-on. The idea of banning the veil once more faded from view, never again to be raised so seriously. Hints do exist that a last-ditch attempt to revive the issue may have been in the works in

106. "Bol'she vnimaniia rabote sredi zhenshchin!" *PV*, 26 May 1940.

107. "Aktivizirovat' rabotu sredi zhenshchin," *PV*, 18 June 1940.

108. See the collection of articles that avoid mentioning a decree at "Paranchiga qarshi bol-shevistik agitatsijani kucajtiramiz," *QÖ*, 17 June 1940; and T. Ibrahimov, "Xatin-qizlar ortasida ishlashga janada i'tibar," *QÖ*, 27 June 1940.

109. Neither Avezova nor a decree is mentioned in "Pokonchit' s parandzhoi—naslediem prokliatogo proshlogo!" *PV*, 2 July 1940. While her name appears in "Ko vsem zhenshchinam or-denonosnogo Uzbekistana," *PV*, 2 July 1940, no specifics are included, merely that she was interested in "the final liquidation of the paranji."

110. "Ko vsem zhenshchinam ordenonosnogo Uzbekistana," *PV*, 2 July 1940.

mid-1941. Writing in *Pravda Vostoka* in late May of that year, Nafisa Hairova called for a renewed campaign against common byt problems afflicting women, such as underage marriage. She focused particular venom on the paranji. Illustrating the continuing depth of everyday patriarchal oppression by pointing again to the veils all too common even in Communists' families, she declared that they must be attacked:

> [Our] successes in the matter of women's liberation cannot be doubted. Yet we cannot rest on our laurels, to give ourselves over to rest. Much more still needs to be done. We cannot forget that we have not yet finally eliminated feudal-serf attitudes toward women. We still have today part of the female population wearing the paranji, that despicable attribute of past slavery and oppression.[111]

This clarion call may have marked the start of a fourth—and perhaps conclusive—wave of legal action against the paranji. But the timing could not have been worse. Within a fortnight German armies had overrun the Soviet western border, and party policy, of necessity, was reoriented completely toward the needs of military defense. Women's liberation, like nearly every other issue, was suddenly harnessed to this end. The resulting political, social, economic, and cultural changes mark a watershed in Soviet history, and bring an end to this story.

Freedom by Force? The Soviet Dilemma

To decree or not to decree? The ongoing and protracted debates show many of the contradictions, tensions, and ambiguities inherent in the party's decision to substitute gender for class in designing a social and cultural revolution for Central Asia. With no road map to point the way, disagreements about precisely what course to take and which tactics to use were perhaps inevitable. But when the hujum adopted an individual act—the casting off of paranji and chachvon—as its proof of cultural modernity, social transformation, and political consciousness, the success of Soviet policy in Uzbekistan came to depend crucially on an act of free will by many individual women. Some of the resulting tensions were expressed in sustained arguments over whether such an act could be brought about by physical force or legal coercion. Men and women in the party continued to disagree, and Soviet policy in Central Asia ultimately was produced by an ongoing process of debate and negotiation, both within the party and in response to outside events.

Party activists had encountered serious difficulties in trying to attack the veil with education and persuasion alone. Such problems fed into a cycle of despair, and many Communists and Soviet government officials came to see the

111. Nafisa Khairova, "Usilit' bor'bu protiv feodal'no-baiskikh perezhitkov," *PV*, 29 May 1941.

idea of banning the paranji as a panacea. Yet three times the Soviet state decided not to proceed with such a decree, showing itself reluctant to push beyond the point at which widespread resistance would be both undeniable and
difficult to suppress.[112] Real discussion, even debate, persisted within the party
on this issue, at unexpected times and to a surprising degree. Even during the
party purges and terror of the late 1930s, one finds Communists fighting to define women's liberation policy through surprisingly frank articulations and
vigorous defenses of their own views. Although the character of public discussion clearly had shifted by the late 1930s, the disagreement and the uncertainty over the outcome never ceased.

Were decisions to leave the veil alone related to decisions elsewhere in the
USSR to strengthen the family and "traditional" values? Most discussions of
Soviet women's and family issues in the 1930s are framed by the idea of a
"great retreat": the view that the Stalinist state shifted away from revolutionary radicalism and toward more socially conservative policies, especially
for urban women; the 1936 decision to outlaw abortion is usually a prime
example.[113] In Uzbekistan the party's unwillingness to ban the veil could
conceivably be seen as fitting into this shift in Soviet policy by representing a
retreat from radical goals. Yet decisions about the veil do not appear to have
been linked to the antiabortion decree, except in the vaguest of ways, or to
most other all-Soviet policies specific to women. Certainly the state's unwillingness to ban the veil did not connote a desire to bolster the traditional
Uzbek family. Rather, it shows the continuing uniqueness and special status
of the Soviet East, where party policy remained flexible and gender issues lay
at the heart of a reconceived Soviet revolution. Whereas women's issues fell
from political prominence in Russia after the Zhenotdel was dissolved in
1930, in Central Asia issues such as the paranji retained their pivotal political and symbolic role. The party debated how best to pursue these issues,
and ultimately—repeatedly—abjured a decree. It did so not to beat a retreat
but to reconceptualize and reshape Bolshevism, the better to transform and
rebuild a new kind of Soviet empire. These complicated local debates and
shifts in party discourse during the 1930s thus say more about Bolshevik attempts to come to grips with a different idiom of Soviet power in the colonial

112. Fannina Halle argued in 1938 that the Soviet state never banned the veil because doing
so would have provoked a "large proportion" of the local population to "embittered resistance"
(*Women in the Soviet East*, 176).

113. Trotsky expressed this view of a Stalinist retreat after his exile. The classic expression is
Nicholas S. Timasheff, *The Great Retreat: The Growth and Decline of Communism in Russia*
(New York, 1946). On women's issues, see Wendy Goldman, *Women, the State, and Revolution:
Soviet Family Policy and Social Life, 1917–1936* (Cambridge, 1993). Scholars have questioned the
degree to which the 1930s should be seen as conservative—full as they were of heroic campaigns
to build a new kind of civilization—and whether such family changes reached the vast number of
Slavic peasant women in the countryside. See Kotkin, *Magnetic Mountain*; and Roberta T. Man-
ning, "Women in the Soviet Countryside on the Eve of World War II, 1935–1940," in *Russian
Peasant Women*, ed. Beatrice Farnsworth and Lynne Viola (New York, 1992), 206–35.

periphery than they do about attitudes toward women in, say, Moscow or Leningrad.

But finally, and perhaps especially remarkable, even the carefully scripted campaign of 1940–41, when to all appearances an antiparanji decree was inevitable, failed to yield such a result. Perhaps the war intervened. Perhaps a sufficient number of party members and Soviet officials realized that such a law would be doomed to fail, or that it would provoke massive resistance. Perhaps too many activists and legislators genuinely believed that women had to be free agents for the social act of unveiling to mean anything. Most likely all these factors and perhaps others played their roles, differing in importance depending on the social actor in question. Certainly, though, the final outcome remains striking. The paranji, that black mark of misery and oppression that was said to mar the future promise and present reality of Soviet socialism, remained always legal under Stalin. Such comparative timidity—an apparent reluctance to act against a recalcitrant populace in one of the most "backward" parts of the USSR—does not fit the usual vision of Soviet life during this period. It shows clearly the limits on state power and the effectiveness of subaltern resistance even during the late 1930s and early 1940s. The party's inability to persuade women to unveil and its grudging decision not to force them to do so show yet another unexpected consequence of the hujum. In launching this campaign the Soviet state had essentially asked what had to be done to make Central Asia Soviet, and it chose an ambitious answer: nothing less than the total fabric of everyday life. But by measuring the success or failure of Soviet power in Uzbekistan by such a sweeping criterion, and by insisting further that the transformation had to happen voluntarily, even Stalin's powerful government had set itself a task at which it was all but bound to fail.

CHAPTER 9

Stalin's Central Asia?

Comrades! One of the clearest victories of the socialist system in Uzbekistan is the liberation of the Uzbek woman and her integration into active social life.

In the past a doomed slave, shut up in the stifling walls of the ichkari, hidden under the paranji, deprived of elementary human rights, the Uzbek woman has now become a fully equal participant in socialist construction.

—Uzbek Party First Secretary Usman Yusupov, addressing the Eighth Uzbek Party Congress, July 1938

All that these Uzbeks and Tajiks know about Karl Marx is that streets are named for him; all they know about Lenin is his statue.

—A Russian visitor to Central Asia, 1932

Soviet power does not matter, it is like smoke. We will be its wind. We will destroy it.

—A Tajik rebel, 1930

The fabric of Central Asian social life in the 1930s has to date been virtually terra incognita. Gregory Massell's pioneering book, like Marianne Kamp's more recent study, ends its coverage in 1929, arguing that bitter resistance thereafter forced Soviet authorities to retreat from the hujum's confrontational tactics. Massell posits that after 1929 the Stalinist state backed away, coming to rely on "systematic social engineering," a slower, more carefully modulated approach to women's liberation.[1] Although this argument sits

1. Massell, *Surrogate Proletariat*, 188.

314

oddly against standard periodizations of Soviet history—1929 is usually seen as a beginning, not the end, of forced social change in the USSR—it has gone largely unquestioned. So has the implication that with this change in tactics, Soviet efforts to transform Uzbek cultural traditions were better positioned for success in the 1930s. Is either judgment accurate? Almost no one has tried to say, although a few writers have asserted that the veil did disappear rapidly after 1929.[2] Given the many traumas weathered by Soviet citizens in the 1930s, from industrialization and collectivization to large-scale party purges and the Terror, such an outcome would not be surprising: the veil and other so-called traditional practices might simply have lost importance amid the broader turmoil and upheaval of the Stalin Revolution.

Yet an investigation of how far Soviet authorities succeeded in transforming Uzbek society in the 1930s turns up several surprises. One is that, Stalin Revolution or no, startlingly little changed after 1929 in the sphere of Uzbek gender relations. One side of this continuity has already been suggested: assertions of retreat notwithstanding, Soviet priorities in Central Asia during the 1930s continued to concentrate on women's liberation, and especially on the veil. By 1930 the veil had been invested on all sides with deep meaning, as a core mark of cultural and ideological affiliation; its donning or doffing served as prima facie evidence of resistance or transformation. As a key trope of Soviet liberation, unveiling remained a centerpiece of public demonstrations, even during the cotton and collectivization campaigns of the 1930s. Celebratory bonfires were still constructed, into which Muslim women dramatically cast their veils. Such theatrics were covered by Soviet newspapers, lauded in state proclamations, and recounted in speeches on International Women's Day. Soviet authorities trumpeted the victory of Stalinist liberation for Muslim women by issuing precisely enumerated statistical claims of success, and proclaimed the culmination of the unveiling campaign by displaying the sort of wide-open, smiling female faces shown in Figure 24.[3] This rhetoric of women's liberation, indeed, remained a central myth of Soviet power and a major component of state legitimacy in Central Asia until 1991—and beyond.

Yet the contemporary evidence, both archival and published, also shows something else altogether: deep despair among Bolshevik authorities in the face of their continuing failure to have much of an impact—at least not the kind of impact they sought—on patterns of Uzbek family life. Some of this despair pokes through the official press, and it even turns up in Soviet propaganda. Despite the heroic oratory and the impressive coercive resources at the

2. William K. Medlin, William M. Cave, and Finley Carpenter, *Education and Development in Central Asia: A Case Study on Social Change in Uzbekistan* (Leiden, 1971), 73; or Shams-ud-din, *Secularisation in the USSR: A Study of Soviet Cultural Policy in Uzbekistan* (New Delhi, 1982), 132.

3. See most Soviet Central Asian newspapers on 8 March in the 1930s. Optimism is less common in the archival record. For a rare upbeat report from 1930, see PDA, op. 5, d. 866, ll. 113–17.

Figure 24. Heroic iconography of unveiling, 1936. (Courtesy RGAKFD.)

disposal of the Stalinist state, the party's continuing efforts during the 1930s to emancipate Uzbek women often had the opposite result: they only strengthened local practices of female veiling and seclusion. Veils actually came to be worn more widely and tenaciously in many parts of Uzbekistan—such as rural villages and the countryside, where veiling had never been universal—and in most circles of indigenous society, including those closest to the party. Given the centrality of the unveiled woman as a defining image of and justification for Soviet power, and the resulting high priority accorded to issues of women's status, this conclusion carries clear implications about the extent of state control over daily life in Soviet Central Asia, and about the lived character of Stalinism in the Soviet empire.

Cultural Power and Hegemony in the 1930s

The Soviet failure to eradicate Uzbek cultural practices of female seclusion stemmed, at root, from the broad inability of party propagandists to subvert the cultural hegemony of the "traditional" values they had in part created. In Gramscian terms, Uzbek women, like men, had from birth imbibed the gender-specific values, beliefs, and behaviors of Muslim society. The customs so abhorred by Bolshevik activists—female seclusion, the veil, polygyny—were supported by a complex web of social, religious, economic, and cultural forces. The Bolshevik Party, by contrast, remained fundamentally alien: Russian (or European), urban, and non-Muslim. Despite the party's efforts to portray local elders and Muslim clerics as class enemies and exploiters of the poor, their positions of status and respect enabled them to shape and disseminate discourses of cultural resistance. And even when Soviet action prevented them from opposing party policies openly, other Muslims did so. To many Uzbeks, the paranji and chachvon had (partly thanks to the Bolsheviks' attack on them) become part of the proper natural order, self-evidently right for upstanding Muslim women—not the horrendous, filthy, disease-ridden means of women's subjugation seen by Bolsheviks. The depth and new strength of such gendered norms of dress and behavior made them nearly impossible to eradicate.[4]

What shapes did this discourse of resistance take? In many ways it continued to develop themes from the late 1920s. Uncompromising denunciations of the infidel (kofir) authorities persisted throughout the 1930s. Combining religious doctrine with new ethno-cultural identities, these freshly established groups of "traditionalists" resisted all efforts to unveil Uzbek women, associating the very idea with prostitution, dishonor, corruption, even loss of nationality. They saw it as particularly important to protect the "inner" domain of women, family, home, and spirituality, where the roots of cultural identity were thought to reside.[5] Muslim clerics made clear the seriousness of this issue, seeing it as part of the sweeping threat posed by other Soviet policies such as collectivization. Sometimes they refused to bury women who opted to unveil, and harassed the nonreligious Soviet funerals that sought to replace them. When in 1930 an unveiled woman died in rural Zerafshon province, for example, popular uproar disrupted her Soviet funeral. According to an internal party report, a crowd gathered during the service, throwing stones and shouting, "A dog's death to a dog! Muslim women who unveil must die!"[6] As late as 1940, party officials complained that mosques that had been officially shut down continued in fact to be active, that many mullahs were preaching against unveiling, and that religious influences were still pervasive. Women heard that God would bar them from heaven if they threw off the paranji, and clergy wives reputedly agitated to prevent them from making such a dire mistake. Uzbek men listened to sermons railing against those husbands—denounced as infidels or unbelievers—who permitted the dishonor of their wives' unveiling.[7] On occasion they too were urged to preserve their nationality and religion, by not shaving their beards.[8]

But such attention to nationalized masculinity remained at best weakly enunciated, always subordinated to the fight over female status, dress, and roles. Muslim traditionalists mobilized an impressive array of techniques to dissuade Muslim women from unveiling, ranging from preaching to street ha-

4. On the power of this hegemony as noted by foreign observers, see Kunitz, *Dawn over Samarkand*, 298–300, or Halle, *Women in the Soviet East*, 175.

5. Chatterjee, *Nation and Its Fragments*, 6 and 121.

6. PDA, op. 5, d. 866, ll. 115–16. This story is dated as 1929 at RGASPI, d. 2066, l. 22.

7. ÖzRMDA, f. 2454, op. 1, d. 412, ll. 129 and 136; and H. Ragajif, "Din ham xatin-qizlar azadlighi," *Jangi jol*, no. 2 (1933), 35.

8. A. Almatinskaia, *Minuvshee: Vospominaniia* (Tashkent, 1971), 140.

rassment to violent attacks. From the Bolshevik perspective, opposition to unveiling in the 1930s was a many-headed hydra. It appeared everywhere, even
among supposed class allies; frustrated activists reported in 1938 that factory
workers in Tashkent still forced their new wives to veil and stay home.[9] Yet
such opposition could be pinned down nowhere in particular—efforts to target
ringleaders seemed to make little difference, or backfired by creating more opposition. Rumors about the ulterior motives behind and alleged dangers of unveiling and women's liberation continued to spread like wildfire. As earlier,
some cast moral aspersions on the characters of individual women who chose
to unveil.[10] Others alleged a variety of unsavory motives for the unveiling campaign, such as permitting Communists to select wives from the ranks of the
unveiled; one kolkhoz outside Tashkent in 1935 refused to send young women
to Soviet meetings without chaperons.[11] Still other rumors held that the ultimate aim of Bolshevik policy, seen in the combination of unveiling and collectivization, was to have all women held in common. In the kolkhoz, peasants
were warned, men and women slept together under one giant blanket, and
wives became common property.[12]

   This everywhere-yet-nowhere resistance annoyed party activists. But religious customs and national-cultural observances continued to structure Uzbek
life, as local men and women were still quite capable of imagining non-Soviet
alternatives and hence of resisting state pressure. Women's liberation was not
the only issue that made such responses possible. Anti-Soviet bands of armed
rebels, the qörboshi, reappeared during the collectivization campaign, for example, and attacked collective farms and Soviet officials in Tajikistan and
Turkmenistan as late as 1933.[13] Even after these groups were brutally suppressed, non-Soviet values appeared to glum party activists all but impossible
to dislodge from the hearts and minds of many Uzbeks. In 1937 a party report
described crowds of up to two thousand women gathering in Tashkent's
mosques, saying that during religious services "they sway their heads all the
time, to the point of exhaustion."[14] Women as well as men continued to par-

9. L. K. (probably Liutsan Klimovich), "Parandzha i chachvan," *Antireligioznik,* no. 2 (1939),
35.
   10. PDA, op. 12, d. 172, ll. 134–37.
   11. ÖzRMDA, f. 86, op. 10, d. 634, l. 250. In 1932 some rural women refused to serve as Soviet delegates, fearing that doing so would indicate a willingness to be abducted by local Communists. This "extraordinary *dikost'* [shyness, savagery, or absurdity] and mistrust of the women," a
party investigator wrote, led the women to return their mandate cards, refusing to have anything
further to do with Soviet efforts (PDA, op. 8, d. 776, l. 24).
   12. These rumors were reported in 1938 and 1933, respectively. See Halle, *Women in the Soviet East,* 195, and Ragajif, "Din ham xatin-qizlar azadlighi," 35. Russian peasants had similar
fears: see Viola, *Peasant Rebels,* 58–59.
   13. On opposition to collectivization in 1930, see the materials from Surkhondaryo at
RGASPI, d. 2343, ll. 7–12, 27–28, 41–43, 55–57, and 71–72. On qörboshi, see also Simon, *Nationalism and Policy,* 106, and Rywkin, *Moscow's Muslim Challenge,* 42.
   14. PDA, op. 13, d. 3, ll. 221–22.

Figure 25. Women conferring with mullah, 1931. (Courtesy RGAKFD.)

ticipate in Muslim social systems, for instance by seeking religious advice from clerics, as shown in Figure 25. Even party members observed such customs, seeking religious burials, carrying out circumcision rituals, and secluding and veiling "their" women.[15] Confidential reports pointed out a clear popular readiness to challenge Soviet policies. One Tashkent resident, Shakirkhoja Tagirkhojaev, declared in February 1937 at an official mahalla meeting that unveiled women had violated shariat and, if married, they could no longer be considered lawful wives.[16] He was quickly arrested, but his willingness to speak out shows the widespread, continuing opposition that characterized "the social opinion of the mahalla."[17]

As before, men were not alone in defying Soviet attempts to unveil Uzbek women. While party officials understandably continued to emphasize the small group of Muslim women who joined the party, frequented women's clubs, and signed up for literacy courses and training programs, other women kept proselytizing for traditional codes of moral behavior, including female veiling.[18] These codes may be called "Uzbek" or "Muslim"; for many indigenous Central Asians, sharp distinctions between such terms were meaningless.

15. See a report from 1939 at PDA, op. 15, d. 1388, ll. 15–21.
16. ÖzRMDA, f. 837, op. 32, d. 346, l. 2.
17. The phrase is from an earlier confidential report: RGASPI, d. 1203, l. 15.
18. For a case from 1937, see PDA, op. 13, d. 3, l. 221.

Together they described the system of cultural practices and beliefs that structured worldviews and daily life, and their staying power was notable among virtually all groups in southern Central Asian society. In extreme cases women again led the violent opposition to their own liberation and to other Soviet policies. One official report in 1930 described an attack in Sartyan, a village near Khorazm, in which 300 "backward women" were so angry about collectivization that they "attacked and fell upon the plenipotentiary for collectivization and the president of the village soviet, aiming to strangle them." Only the timely arrival of the police had saved the lives of these officials. Similar episodes were said to be happening all across Uzbekistan.[19]

The Veiled Empire: Female Seclusion as Social and Political Practice

The preponderance of archival evidence suggests that Uzbek social life had changed far less by 1941 than Bolshevik activists wanted to admit. The cultural hegemony of Uzbek Muslim values still expressed itself in an array of social practices and subaltern responses, ranging from rumors, passivity, and avoidance to subterfuge, sabotage, and violence. Perhaps the clearest behavioral response, however, was the continued—even expanding—practice of female veiling. Veils were probably the most visible aspect of this web of gendered norms and social practices through which Uzbek culture sought to fend off Bolshevik liberation. In a series of confidential fact-gathering missions and investigative reports, party workers throughout the 1930s reported that Uzbeks—both male and female—were defending the paranji with great vigor and tenacity. Sometimes these reports tried to accentuate the positive: in a progress report to superiors in Moscow, for example, antireligious activists in Tashkent wrote in 1936 that only 15–20 percent of Uzbek women remained veiled.[20] After almost ten years of all-out effort, even that figure fell well short of the original high hopes for the veil's total eradication. Yet it still probably overstates Soviet success and ignores the prevalence of veiling as a form of resistance, a way to express a distinctively Muslim, Uzbek, non-Soviet identity. Shortly before his ouster as Uzbek party leader in 1937, Akmal Ikramov conceded that "many" Uzbek women still wore the veil, and the internal material supports this view.[21] Wherever Bolshevik activists and informants gathered data—in urban areas, rural villages, or various social strata—female seclusion appeared to be pervasive, or at least very common, on the eve of war in 1941. One suspects that where party information gathering fell short—especially the remote countryside, but also some towns and Old Cities—the picture was at least as striking.

19. ÖzRMDA, f. 86, op. 1, d. 6574, l. 38. The other specific episodes named were at "Agalyq village in Samarqand province, Vohim village in Andijon, Chust-Pop in Farghona, [and] Bukhoro."
20. PDA(K), op. 12, d. 615, l. 232.
21. PDA, op. 13, d. 3, ll. 220–22.

Bolshevik workers appeared to be in a much stronger position in Uzbek-istan's cities than in the countryside. They had easier access to urban popula-tions and more dependable information. Political control in a large adminis-trative center such as Tashkent could if necessary quickly be backed up by military force. The Russified New Cities, too, provided visible examples of a different way for women and families to live, and offered physical spaces for unveiled women to walk freely. Finally, the government's limited financial re-sources could be concentrated more effectively in cities and large towns to build a support network of women's clubs, schools, and stores. And indeed, the unveiling campaign did succeed to a greater degree in cities. Bukhoro in particular was touted as an exemplary success story, where all women had quickly cast off the veil. Party investigators reported finding few paranjis on the streets of Bukhoro in the 1930s.[22]

But archival reports from most other Uzbek cities suggest that customs of female seclusion and veiling changed little, if at all, during the 1930s. Particu-larly in the mahallas of the virtually all-Muslim Old Cities, such practices ap-peared preeminent. (See Figure 26.) In 1930 one investigator reported that five-eighths of the women living in the Old City of Katta Qorghon, near Samarqand, wore the veil.[23] Years later, in 1936, an antireligious activist com-plained that 90 percent of the women in Old Andijon still wore the paranji and chachvon.[24] Archival photographs from throughout the decade depict veiling as typical among urban Uzbeks; some depict paranjis even in the "success story" of Bukhoro.[25] But party investigators in the 1930s found it easiest to study the urban situation closest to home—meaning, above all, Tashkent, which became the subject of the most detailed and extensive reports. Before 1917, Tashkent had been the tsarist government's main hub in Turkestan; in the early Soviet period it was home to the party's regional leadership (the Sredazbiuro); and in 1930 it replaced Samarqand as the capital city of the Uzbek SSR and thus became the undisputed center of Bolshevik power in Cen-tral Asia. Yet despite—or perhaps because of—this long history of Russian presence, the picture turned up by inspectors in Tashkent was particularly grim.

A series of confidential mahalla investigations in the city highlighted the widespread practice and stubborn persistence of female veiling and seclusion.

22. PDA, op. 10, d. 662, ll. 98–100.

23. ÖzRMDA, f. 86, op. 1, d. 6585, l. 195.

24. PDA(K), op. 12, d. 615, l. 90. For a slightly less bleak view from 1937 of a mahalla in Naryn, a town in Andijon province, see ÖzRMDA, f. 86, op. 10, d. 772, l. 95.

25. Because of their political implications, few such images were published; this fact suggests that they are more likely reflective of everyday practices than the staged Orientalist postcards of the pre-1917 tsarist empire. For veils in Bukhoro, see RGAKFD 09972 and 418095. Other photo-graphs showing urban veils in Uzbekistan between 1930 and 1937 are 281936, 0277939, and 0311344, and ÖzRKFFHMDA 0-84877. Another striking image, at RGAKFD 262640, shows masses of paranjis at the bazaar in Frunze (Kyrgyzstan), illustrating female seclusion among Uzbek communities outside the Uzbek SSR.

Figure 26. Urban market. (Max Penson, courtesy Dina Khojaeva, collection Anahita Gallery, Santa Fe, N.M.)

By all accounts the new Uzbek capital was rife with veiled women. Some were not ethnically Uzbek; in 1936, according to one report, local Jewish women continued to wear the paranji and chachvon.[26] But alarmed party investigators focused on the thousands of Uzbek women who refused to unveil. One report of 1937 bemoaned "the altogether still too great presence of veiled women" as a "fundamental" problem facing the Tashkent party organization. Local Communists kept their wives subjugated, and mahalla censuses showed that at best a third of the local women had unveiled.[27] Another confidential Tashkent investigation of the same year focused on the not-so-aptly-named Red Partisan mahalla and reached a similar conclusion. Local officials came under fire for failing to take an accurate count of the mahalla's unveiled women and for not leading the way by personal example—more than a third of the small group of Communists and Komsomol members kept their wives veiled. Mullahs were free to lead prayers and preach as they wished; they even had the effrontery to cite the Stalin Constitution's promise of religious freedom to do so. Repeated efforts to unveil Uzbek women had culminated in another push just before

    26. ÖzRMDA, f. 86, op. 10, d. 1091, l. 2.
    27. ÖzRMDA, f. 86, op. 10, d. 772, l. 60. A similar report filed in 1931 by the October district women's club reported an 85 percent majority still veiled in some places. It went on to catalogue a litany of other un-Soviet behaviors, such as pulling young girls out of schools, visiting tabibs rather than Soviet doctors, and refusing to teach women to read (op. 1, d. 7287, l. 5).

party investigators arrived, but its success was limited, as shown by the scores of paranjis and chachvons visible on the street.[28]

Bolshevik activists expected some difficulty ending female seclusion in the Old Cities, but the staying power of the veil in other urban locales was a surprise. While most Uzbek women remained oblivious of party messages, even the small group of Uzbek women who could be persuaded or enticed to take paid employment tended to be reluctant to unveil. Some women factory workers in 1930, for example, refused to walk to work without their veils; they removed their paranjis only after arriving at the job.[29] Sometimes even then they refused to unveil. By 1934 Uzbek women accounted for three-quarters of the labor force of a silk-spinning facility in Marghilon, but "a great percentage"— even some members of the Communist Party—insisted on remaining covered, apparently while working.[30] A women's cooperative in Qöqon reported a 60 percent veiled membership in 1932.[31] And many of the women who agreed to work in artels did so only from their homes, thus never experiencing what the Bolsheviks saw as the salubrious psychological effects of participating in a collective workplace. The Zarbdar artel in Marghilon had 250 women workers in 1939, but fully 95 percent were veiled, and 369 of the 553 women working for the Jangi Turmush artel in the now infamous town of Chust reportedly remained veiled and secluded in 1940.[32]

Given the party's enormous ideological investment, it is striking to find non-Soviet ideals of gender roles and women's status maintained so vociferously even in the few real factories that did exist. One local women's worker, Anan'eva, reported confidentially in late 1936 or early 1937 that workers at the Marghilon silk-spinning plant—even those who had worked there for years—showed few signs of raised consciousness or the expected sort of cultural transformation. She named a series of skilled female workers, some with as much as five years' experience, who insisted on staying veiled. Further, she said, nothing had been done "to expose the specific culprits who are hindering women's liberation." Many were men who worked at the factory; some allowed their wives to work there, but only while veiled.[33] Even the classically proletarian experience of industrial labor, then—an experience shared by only a comparative handful of Uzbeks—was not having the expected effects. Marxist class consciousness remained scarce on the ground, among both men

28. This investigation's materials and reports are at ÖzRMDA, f. 837, op. 32, d. 346; here I cite ll. 1, 9, 33–35, and 37.

29. PDA, op. 6, d. 743, ll. 45–47.

30. PDA, op. 9. This reference, from a typescript copy, does not list *delo* or *list*. However, another report from a year later, apparently about the same facility in Marghilon, admitted that 50 percent of female Uzbek staff retained their veils in 1935 (op. 11, d. 1020, ll. 1–2). In 1939 another report bemoaned the fact that seventy of these Marghilon silk-spinners still refused to unveil (op. 15, d. 81, ll. 10–11).

31. ÖzRMDA, f. 86, op. 1, d. 7996, l. 59.

32. PDA, op. 15, d. 81, ll. 10–11; and ÖzRMDA, f. 2454, op. 1, d. 413, l. 57.

33. PDA, op. 13, d. 1169, ll. 1–3.

and women, even in those places where the party most confidently expected to find it.

Bolshevik activists also expected to use the growing, mostly urban network of women's clubs as a built-in support network for liberated women. The provision of a safe space for Muslim women to visit, socialize, and absorb Soviet views on such subjects as women's rights, hygiene, and education was counted upon to lead more or less inexorably to the unveiling of club members. Such successes did occur, but they fell well short of expectations. Party materials on club work among Central Asian women from the early 1930s tended to stress the positive, as most women's clubs claimed a fully or largely unveiled membership.[34] Under closer scrutiny, however, this portrayal unravels. One club in Tashkent claimed a completely unveiled membership, but noted as an aside that most of its women wore veils at home in their mahallas.[35] Another club in Andijon reported in 1930 that 90 percent of its members had unveiled, explaining that only the most recent arrivals had not yet done so—thereby implying something about the thousands of women who had not yet contemplated joining the club.[36] A few reports did not share the optimistic tone: one Tashkent club admitted in 1931 that it had managed to unveil only a quarter of its active members.[37] Another club saw its membership plummet in 1931 from a nominal 510 to only 32 when its rolls were "verified"—that is, when it struck the names of women who no longer visited the club—and of these 32, only 5 were unveiled.[38] Uzbek women remained veiled while participating in Soviet demonstrations, meetings, and elections.[39] A report submitted in February 1930 by a government investigator, Qosimova, after a visit to the Krupskaia women's club in Old Andijon, explains such low success rates:

> The club has very many veiled members. I myself witnessed a meeting, called to discuss the next two weeks' silkworm breeding, to which about 60–70 people came, all dressed in paranjis and chachvons. They sat unveiled at the meeting, but at its conclusion they once again covered themselves and went home. I tried to ascertain the reasons for this phenomenon, and it was explained to me, by the women themselves as well as by the club workers, that earlier all the club's members had been unveiled. Recently, however, after the murders of female activists in Andijon province, many have covered themselves again, some have quit entirely, and the aktivnost' of the women has dropped.[40]

34. See the detailed investigations at ÖzRMDA, f. 86, op. 1, d. 6556, ll. 56–72.
35. ÖzRMDA, f. 9, op. 1, d. 3392, l. 159.
36. ÖzRMDA, f. 86, op. 1, d. 6582, l. 65.
37. Ibid., d. 7287, l. 13.
38. Ibid., d. 7288, l. 5.
39. RGAKFD 416322 and 415398; and ÖzRKFFHMDA 1-46335.
40. ÖzRMDA, f. 86, op. 1, d. 6556, l. 68.

If party activists had such trouble inducing Uzbek women in cities and large towns to unveil, how could they expect to fare in the countryside? The intense collectivization campaigns of the early 1930s had ensured that Soviet authority was felt, sometimes for the first time, in the thousands of rural villages where most Uzbeks lived. Such a brutal introduction did not endear the Bolshevik Party or its ideas to the rural population, and the central government in Tashkent had at best a vague influence on daily life in the many remote areas with little party presence. It therefore comes as no surprise that in those comparatively few rural areas where party investigators could gather detailed information, primarily on collective farms, the data on social attitudes and practices were, from the Bolshevik point of view, disheartening. While scholars have debated the historical extent of rural female seclusion in pre-Soviet Central Asia, by the time of the hujum or shortly thereafter female veiling had evolved into a common practice among rural families that could afford it. Certainly during the 1930s, when the authorities sought desperately to trumpet any success in unveiling, urban or rural, internal party and government materials show that the paranji and chachvon refused to disappear from the countryside. In the early 1930s one kolkhoz reported that its women members flatly refused to work in the fields with men unless they could do so while veiled.[41] Investigators sent in 1932 to scrutinize three rural kolkhozy reported that the majority of women on all three farms wore the veil; at one kolkhoz, Zarbdar, not a single woman was unveiled.[42] Figure 27 shows a typical scene in 1934.

Adherence to female veiling and seclusion appears to have become, if anything, stronger in the countryside during the 1930s, suggesting an important shift in the indigenous practice and meanings of veiling. During the pre-Soviet period, the paranji and chachvon had been worn mainly, albeit not exclusively, by upper-class urban women. By the 1930s, however, they had spread more widely among poor and rural women, and by 1941 had come to be accepted—even by those who did not wear them—as a basic component of Uzbek Muslim identity. As in the 1870s and 1880s, when the paranji had emerged to displace the mursak, the specific features of colonial rule brought about changes in the physical form and cultural connotations of female veiling and seclusion. Given the evidence from collective farms, too, it seems reasonable to suggest that such beliefs and practices may have been even stronger and more prevalent in the many nooks and crannies of rural Uzbekistan that escaped the gaze of Soviet officials.

The passage of time, even in the mid-1930s with Stalin at the height of his powers, seemed not appreciably to help the Bolshevik cause. Later investigations yielded a similar picture, finding widespread veiling and seclusion. In 1936 all the women on Bauman kolkhoz were still veiled, including the wives of local Communists and Komsomol members.[43] Around the same time an-

---

41. PDA, op. 8, d. 775, ll. 11–14.
42. Ibid., d. 776, l. 122.
43. PDA(K), op. 12, d. 638, l. 93.

Figure 27. Rural scene, Andijon province, 1934. (Courtesy ÖzRKFFHMDA.)

other kolkhoz reported a "huge majority" of women wearing paranjis and the few unveiled women too frightened to venture far from home.[44] Even at the end of the decade, Soviet efforts in the countryside made little headway. One official report noted forlornly in late 1938 that three-quarters of the women at one kolkhoz outside Tashkent wore veils every day to the fields, and in the rural district of Aikuran, outside Namangan, fully 90 percent of local women, including some party and Komsomol wives, wore paranjis in 1940.[45]

These findings were confirmed by another detailed investigation of the Namangan area in March 1940. After lambasting local party leaders for ignoring women's issues, and particularly for not devoting any attention to the veil, investigators appended a long list of Communists and Komsomol members with veiled wives. Local collective farms had managed to enlist female members, they conceded, but a glance at the bleak veiling statistics showed how far rural Uzbekistan had yet to go. One kolkhoz had 96 female members, of whom 10 had unveiled; another had 230 female members, but only 40 did not wear paranji and chachvon.[46] The Bolsheviks' failure to remake Uzbek culture—indeed, the unexpected and unwelcome rural momentum in the opposite di-

44. Ibid., l. 53. See also PDA, op. 12, d. 880, ll. 1–11.
45. PDA, op. 15, d. 112, ll. 76–79, and d. 1383, ll. 44–45.
46. Ibid., d. 1383, ll. 49–53.

rection—is well illustrated by the findings of M. Samokhvalova, an Uzbek Komsomol investigator sent to Oltiariq, a district center in Farghona province, in June 1937. Aghast at what she found, she wrote her superiors that "in this district a great number of women are found in paranjis." She explained her findings, giving specific examples:

> Among the women standing in a line for grain I came upon four young girls wearing the paranji. They were 9 or 10 years old, and I tried to strike up a conversation with them, but they stubbornly remained silent. To [my] questions—which kolkhoz are you from, do you go to school or not, what is your name—no answer came.
>
> After this I went to the district executive committee on several matters:
> . . . On the matter of the veil, [I asked] Comrade Salakhutdinov, "Why do you all, here in the district center, have so many women wearing the paranji, both in general [i.e., among adult women] and even down to the little girls, who [also] wear paranjis?"
>
> Comrade Salakhutdinov, the assistant director of the district soviet, together with Comrade Zakharov, principal secretary of the district soviet, said in reply, "Why are you so surprised that you saw five or six girls wearing paranjis, standing in line? You should go out to the villages. There, starting with the elderly women, those who are 90 years old, and ending with the little girls, only 7 years old—they all wear the veil."[47]

In this atmosphere, even party successes could not be taken at face value. The yawning gap between triumphal rhetoric and visibly contrary social reality grew ever more obvious, risking a corrosive impact on Soviet authority and credibility. Anecdotal accounts and statistics continued to proclaim the many women unveiling at festive demonstrations in the 1930s, but there were problems with these claims. First, as in the 1920s, the counting itself was often suspect. Local officials exaggerated successes and minimized failures; sometimes a few unveiled women moved from one demonstration to another, theatrically hurling off a paranji at each place. In other cases, particularly in remote areas, figures were simply invented by local leaders. No data at all were received from still other regions.[48] Second, most women who unveiled did so only briefly. For many reasons—intimidation, fear, discomfort, reluctance, or sim-

---

47. ÖzRMDA, f. 86, op. 10, d. 772, l. 5.

48. A few examples of statistical fudging will suffice. Numbers were withheld from Moscow in a 1931 report at PDA, op. 6, d. 735, ll. 36–50. For a case in 1932 in which Tashkent received only partial information from localities, see op. 9, d. 975, ll. 41–45. For an example of exaggerated figures coming to light in 1939 during a verification, see op. 15, d. 836, ll. 102–6. In my view, figures provided by local and lower-level officials that support official policies or demonstrate success in attaining party goals are more likely suspect than those showing failure or ineptitude. The latter too, of course, could serve personal or institutional agendas, and could be produced (or massaged) by officials—such as, especially, the secret police, and to a lesser extent the control commissions. But as noted above, these secret police reports are not readily accessible after 1929, and so do not affect this analysis.

ply seeing the unveiling effort as a short-term campaign—they soon reveiled once the hubbub of officially sanctioned demonstrations died away. Most of the 500 women who unveiled in Marghilon for the 8 March celebration in 1936, for instance, reveiled within a few months; a similar phenomenon occurred nearly everywhere, even in Bukhoro.[49]

Finally, even the small group of "permanently unveiled" women did not always look the way party activists imagined. A substantial fraction threw off paranji and chachvon, as called for by omnipresent party slogans ("Down with the paranji!"), but devised imaginative, idiosyncratic solutions to the problem of what to wear in their place. Rather than proudly don a red Soviet *kosynka* (triangular kerchief), connoting full European-style liberation and a Soviet affiliation, many women kept their faces fully or partially covered with shawls, scarves, kerchiefs, even tablecloths or a traditional Uzbek *chopon,* the heavy outer robe usually worn by men.[50] Such responses frustrated Soviet activists, but they amounted to a creative reworking of party policy: they offered ways to cast off the paranji and thus claim to be good liberated Soviet women, yet simultaneously to stay upstanding Muslims. "The paranjis and chachvons have been taken off, but the shawls remain, with which the women of the kolkhoz conceal their faces," wrote a labor inspector from a collective farm outside Bukhoro in 1932. "From this we may conclude that in general, the work is very weak on the struggle against byt survivals, and [it] has disappeared on the kolkhozy."[51] Turning away from men they encountered on the street, refusing to show their faces in public, and resisting what the party saw as gainful employment: such unveiled women were not, to put it mildly, what Bolshevik activists had had in mind.

Even where Bolshevik control should have been strongest—in the Soviet elite and party organization itself—adherence to Bolshevik-defined ideals remained more an exception than the rule. Indigenous Communists and Komsomol members were frequently accused by name of keeping their wives secluded and veiled, or not permitting them to leave the home, let alone to take a paying job. Hectoring, intimidation, fines, expulsion, jail time, or even worse had only a limited effect on such behavior.[52] The most rigid forms of female seclusion, after all—such as keeping women home at all times, not merely veiled

49. See a report from 1930 at ÖzRMDA, f. 9, op. 1, d. 3391, l. 4. On Marghilon, see PDA, op. 13, d. 1169, ll. 1–3.

50. PDA, op. 7, d. 879, ll. 199–200, and op. 12, d. 880, ll. 1–11. For an image of unveiled women at an 8 March demonstration who try to hide their faces from the camera, see ÖzRKFFH-MDA 2-607.

51. PDA, op. 9, d. 958, ll. 66–67.

52. Some male Komsomol members in Tashkent still forced their wives to wear the paranji in 1938, according to PDA, op. 14, d. 1092, ll. 1–2. A similar report from Naryn, in Andijon province, in 1936 is at ÖzRMDA, f. 86, op. 10, d. 772, l. 92. A general report from 1940 is at f. 837, op. 32, d. 2066, l. 60.

while in public—had in pre-Soviet times marked elite social status. At least some of the new Soviet elite continued to associate such customs with the possession of power. Adoption of these practices opened them to criticism by political superiors in both Tashkent and Moscow, but Muslim Communist men continued to pay bride-price, marry underage girls, and take multiple wives when they could manage it. Meanwhile their wives, daughters, sisters, and mothers, in overwhelming numbers, remained veiled and often stayed home when they could. Even a few women activists slipped; one, a former village soviet president, reportedly reveiled in 1935.[53]

Top leaders in Tashkent admitted—usually only privately—the extent of the problem. Khursan Mahmudova, deputy president of the Uzbek Supreme Soviet, noted in 1940 that local reports from Farghona and elsewhere made it plain that "we have a situation in which thousands of schoolgirls, under the influence of obscurantists and religious parents and relatives, abandon their studies, marry while still underage, and even wear the paranji."[54] In a separate piece also written in 1940 she gave an overall verdict on Soviet women's liberation efforts. Starting with the required formulas of praise for the leadership of the Communist Party, Soviet government, and the "great Russian people," she asserted that thanks to the great Stalin and his constitution, women in the Soviet Union enjoyed more freedom and possibilities than in any capitalist country. After this formulaic opening, however, Mahmudova's tone sharpened:

> But notwithstanding these successes of ours, in finishing women's true liberation we face serious shortcomings [*kamciliklar*]. In some places the work continues: on feudal-boi relations with regard to women; on disparaging, belittling, and insulting them; on the giving of underage girls into marriage and their sale for qalin; on women's abandonment of work in agriculture and industry; and on the decline of our efforts to pull them into government work, into social and political life, and into education. Among women a great percentage [*anca protsentni*] are illiterate. In consequence of all this, we have not liberated all laboring women from the paranji. As for this [persistence of the veil], it shows the weakness of our mass-political and educational work among women.[55]

As of 1940, then, party leaders were painfully aware that women's liberation in Uzbekistan still had a long way to go.

---

53. PDA(K), op. 12, d. 638, l. 18.
54. ÖzRMDA, f. 2454, op. 1, d. 412, l. 138.
55. Ibid., d. 413, l. 41. She listed a litany of other problems, lingering on byt crimes against women: murder, forced veilings, polygyny, underage marriage, seclusion, attacks, and rape. See d. 412, ll. 127–51, and d. 413, ll. 41–46 and 55–57.

Self-Criticism and Unintended Candor:
Reading Public Sources on Social Practice

These archival materials suggest the continuing existence of limits on Stalinist state authority and Soviet colonial power during the 1930s. Certainly Moscow had proved unable mechanically to work its will on Uzbek society and culture, throwing doubt on any picture of authoritarian, let alone totalitarian, control throughout the USSR. Yet one can also find a similar picture of Uzbek cultural resilience and anti-Bolshevik backlash in published sources. Sometimes one needs to read between the lines of what is said and consider what is left unsaid, but even the visibly sanitized press of the 1930s, with its heroic, optimistic rhetoric, offers hints of how badly the Soviet program of women's liberation through unveiling was faring. The dissonance between what party writers had to say publicly and what their readers could see all around them—all too easily, day after day, at home and on the street—could not be hidden. In some cases the result was double-think or double-speak: the language of public discussion was not necessarily expected to correspond to actual social practice. In others fissures and cracks appeared in the wall of revolutionary rhetoric—gaps through which one can glimpse surprisingly candid views of the persistent problems encountered on the road to liberation.

Many foreign visitors to Soviet Central Asia published their impressions after returning home. The Soviet government tightly controlled the issuance of visas to foreigners, so most Western travelers who reached Central Asia fell into one of two categories: business, industrial, and scientific contacts, or persons thought to be politically sympathetic. Most publications emerged from the second group, and the resulting books and pamphlets tended to parrot (or at least support) the party line. They generally stressed the great leap forward being taken in Central Asia—in women's rights as well as other areas—under the progressive leadership of Stalin and the Bolshevik Party. In 1934, after a brief trip to Central Asia, the prominent black American writer and intellectual Langston Hughes published a pamphlet under Soviet auspices relating his impressions of the area. He stressed what he saw as a lack of racial oppression in the USSR, and used Uzbek women's improved status as a visible demonstration of the emancipation offered by Soviet power.[56] Other socialist-leaning foreign observers published similarly sympathetic portraits of Soviet Central Asia, among them the Americans Anna Louise Strong in 1929 and Joshua Kunitz in 1935, the Frenchman Paul Vaillant-Couturier in 1932, the Austrian Egon Kisch in 1935, and the German Fannina Halle in 1938.[57]

Despite their tendency to stress the bright side of Soviet life—as encouraged

56. Langston Hughes, *A Negro Looks at Soviet Central Asia* (Moscow and Leningrad, 1934), 21–22 and 40–48.

57. Strong, *Red Star in Samarkand*; Kunitz, *Dawn over Samarkand*; Paul Vaillant-Couturier, *Free Soviet Tadjikistan* (Moscow and Leningrad, 1932); Egon Erwin Kisch, *Changing Asia* (New York, 1935); and Halle, *Women in the Soviet East*.

both by their political views and by the filtering and selection by Soviet interpreters and guides of what they saw—these writers nevertheless scattered references throughout their books that show the continuing power of non-Soviet family practices and gender roles. Vaillant-Couturier noted that in 1931 many urban as well as rural women still wore paranjis and chachvons.[58] Three years later, Kunitz observed that "the emotional ramparts built around [the veil] by vested economic interest and religion are well-nigh insurmountable. Despite Bolshevik onslaughts, they have held out in the more inaccessible regions and even in such cities as Tashkent and Samarkand."[59] Still later, in 1938, Halle offered an optimistic account of Soviet women's liberation, stressing in particular that every single woman in Bukhoro had thrown off the veil. Yet she conceded that paranjis were still visible on the streets of all other Uzbek cities, worn by women going about their business or even while taking in a show at the theater. Halle cited an experienced local female doctor's opinion that it would take much longer to change deeply held cultural beliefs and persuade Uzbek women to unveil. Even by Halle's sympathetic accounting, moreover, no more than 5 percent of the women who had cast aside their veils since 1927 remained unveiled—all others had covered themselves again.[60]

Soviet authorities exerted more direct control over Soviet writers than over foreign nationals. The Soviet press, therefore, might be expected to deviate less from official views, and evidence of Bolshevik difficulties should be concomitantly harder to find. To some extent this is so. Most of the Soviet Central Asian periodical and trade press of the 1930s, especially the early 1930s, was mind-numbingly orthodox, reprinting endless portraits of Stalin, citing his speeches at every turn, and exhorting readers to work heroically at fulfilling the Five-Year Plan or boosting the annual cotton harvest. Yet even here an attentive reader finds regular small admissions of the nagging obstacles that hindered women's liberation.

Women's veiled or unveiled status remained a potent symbolic and political issue, serving to show how far Stalinist Central Asia had come, so admissions of trouble might appear disloyal, even treasonous. Yet in Stalinist discourse, obstacles also served a purpose, acting as a foil for the party's heroism. Evidence of opposition ("class struggle") served to justify a further redoubling of efforts and, paradoxically, underscored the correctness of the Bolshevik cause. (As is well known, the huge party purges of the late 1930s were partly justified by Stalin's doctrine that class enemies fought more savagely when on the brink of annihilation.) To some extent, then, opposition was *necessary,* and so it had to be found. This necessity was handy when cases of polygyny, underage marriage, or Communists who kept their wives veiled and secluded came to

58. Cited by Serge Zeyons, *La Révolution des femmes au cœur de l'Asie soviétique* (Paris, 1971), 33.
59. Kunitz, *Dawn over Samarkand,* 275.
60. Halle, *Women in the Soviet East,* 171–75 and 298.

light.[61] Held up as examples of how not to behave, such cautionary tales could by contrast define enlightened Soviet conduct. While such stories seem not to have inflamed as many hearts with outrage as women's activists hoped, they do provide later historians a glimpse of Uzbek family and gender codes.

Articles in the periodical press regularly discussed violations of the various Soviet laws to regulate Uzbek daily life. These byt crimes, ranging from pulling schoolgirls out of school and forcing them to veil all the way up to murder, persisted despite all efforts to quash them. Some of the most egregious cases received prominent coverage, particularly in Uzbek-language women's journals.[62] Russian-language publications also paid attention. An article of 1938 in *Antireligioznik,* for example, illustrated its denunciation of retrograde byt practices by telling several hair-raising stories, including one of a woman attacked the previous December by her "religious fanatic" husband. Angered by her decision to unveil and seek paid employment, he had stabbed her twenty-four times.[63] Such tales persisted into the 1950s and beyond, as the Soviet press regularly showcased continuing examples of byt crime.[64]

The periodical press likewise paid attention to the continuing prevalence of female veiling and seclusion among Uzbek women in other parts of Soviet Central Asia, such as southern Kazakhstan, western Kyrgyzstan, and northeastern Turkmenistan.[65] And within Uzbekistan, according to several published accounts, the paranji and chachvon remained common throughout the 1930s and in some places much longer.[66] For political reasons, of course, Soviet writers could not admit in print that female veiling and seclusion seemed to be increasing in much of Uzbekistan. Nearly all Soviet newspapers and

61. See the example of a ZAGS official who married a 13-year-old girl at "Xatin-qizlar arasida ishlash unutilgan," *QÖ,* 4 Feb. 1936.

62. See the open letter to Uzbekistan's procurator complaining about the persistence of underage marriage and qalin at T. A., "Aciq xat: Qizlarni machburii satghanlar tezdan chavabgarlikga," *Jangi jol,* no. 8–9 (1932), 54–55. A later denunciation of persistent byt crimes is N. Abdusalamova, "Stalin davrining azad xatin-qizlari," *Jarqin haët,* no. 10–11 (28) (1938), 12–13.

63. F. Popov, "O rabote sredi zhenshchin v Uzbekistane," *Antireligioznik,* no. 12 (1938), 14.

64. For Uzbek-language articles and pamphlets bemoaning the veil's persistence, see O. Qosimova, *Özbek khotin-qizlari haqida nimalarni öqish kerak* (Tashkent, 1957), 9–10; in Russian, see G. P. Snesarev, "O nekotorykh prichinakh sokhraneniia religiozno-bytovykh perezhitkov u uzbekov Khorezma," *Sovetskaia etnografiia,* no. 2 (1957), 60–72; or A. A. Abdullaeva and N. P. Sokolov, "Protiv vrednykh obychaev i traditsii," *Trudy Andizhanskogo gosudarstvennogo pedagogicheskogo instituta* 8 (1961): 92–97.

65. S. Shakirdzianov, " 'Bibi-Seshanbe'—religioznyi obriad uzbekskikh zhenshchin," *Vestnik Tsentral'nogo muzeia Kazakhstana,* no. 1 (1930), 91–94. For a later assertion that "it is still not at all uncommon to meet women in paranjis, chachvons, and so forth" on the city streets of southern Kazakhstan, see V. Butler, "O preodolenii religioznykh perezhitkov," *Bol'shevik Kazakhstana,* no. 5 (1940), 50.

66. See P. Kashirin, "O religioznykh perezhitkakh," *Antireligioznik,* no. 5 (1939), 17; L. Klimovich, "Konets, parandzhe!" *Ogonëk,* no. 6 (1940), 4; and M. Sheraliev, "Sudy Uzbekistana v bor'be s perezhitkami feodal'no-baiskogo otnosheniia k zhenshchine," *Sotsialisticheskaia zakonnost',* no. 8 (1955), 23.

journals were based in cities or large towns, too, so their reporting tended to focus on the urban rather than rural scene. Yet amid the required Stalinist hagiographies they did include at least intermittently frank discussion of the issue, and candor actually grew over time. One forlorn newspaper report of 1931 bemoaned the fact that Old Tashkent, unlike Bukhoro, remained virtually completely veiled.[67] Investigative reporters subjected Tashkent, as the Uzbek capital and home to many of Central Asia's most stalwart Bolsheviks, to particular scrutiny. As in the private documents, their verdicts were usually harsh. When asked in 1933 by party officials to judge a "socialist competition" on women's emancipation between Uzbekistan and Turkmenistan, a reporter for the Uzbek-language women's journal *Jangi jol* concluded that fewer than a third of the women in Tashkent's Stalin district had unveiled; she gave the eerily precise tally of 2,895 out of 10,316.[68] By 1940, *Pravda Vostoka* was publishing letters and reports that took veiling in rural Uzbekistan for granted.[69]

If reporters censured cities that lagged in women's unveiling, they had even greater latitude to condemn personal laggards in the middle and lower ranks of the party and government and in Soviet institutions and enterprises. Some newly married factory workers came under fire for pressuring their brides to veil and to quit their jobs in the late 1930s, for example. Usually kulaks, Muslim clerics, or bois were accused of lurking behind the scenes, but the men publicly accused often came from party or Komsomol ranks.[70] One article published by *Jangi jol* in 1934 chronicled relentlessly, mahalla by mahalla, a litany of misconduct by the ethnic Uzbek elite of Tashkent. It focused especially on the city's October district, finding in it widespread byt crimes ranging from polygyny to forced veiling and seclusion. Communists and Komsomol members were seen as fundamental parts of the problem, and in many areas few, if any, women were found to have unveiled. In one mahalla, only two of eleven Komsomol members had unveiled their wives; in another, only five of nineteen Communists had done so. Some refused even to start work on the unveiling

67. "And in Tashkent with every step in the Old City one meets with paranjis and chachvons" ("Istoriia odnogo dogovora," *PV*, 24 Feb. 1931).

68. Nijazxan Hamraqizi, "Stalin rajon miljonlar shartnamasi ustida," *Jangi jol*, no. 2 (1933), 39. See also Mukerrem Shamansuriva, "Paranci azadliq va saghliqni ashaddi dushmanidir: Xatin-qizlar azadlighi ucun ghamxorliq kucajtirilisin," *Jangi jol*, no. 2 (1934), 36.

69. Kumrikhon Khaidarova, "Nanesti reshitel'nyi udar feodal'no-baiskim perezhitkam!" *PV*, 8 Feb. 1940; and F. Iuldashbaeva, "Eshche shire razvernut' rabotu sredi zhenshchin," *PV*, 11 Dec. 1940.

70. Factory workers were blamed at L. K., "Parandzha i chachvan," 35, citing *PV*, 27 Nov. 1938. More typical were the eighteen Komsomol members in Sredne-Chirchik criticized for having veiled younger sisters at V. Bashalov, "Rabota sreda zhenskoi molodezhi—zabytyi uchastok (Uzbekistan, Chechnia, Dagestan)," *Izvestiia TsK VLKSM*, no. 19 (1935), 7–8, and the Communists in Qashqadaryo denounced for having veiled wives at "Xatin-qizlar arasida ishlash unutilgan."

campaign, playing for time by endlessly "preparing." Others, listed by name, forced their wives to veil and stay home, not to work or attend school.[71]

Candor can be glimpsed even in officially sanctioned political discourse. Central Asian party and government conferences, congresses, and high-profile public meetings aired these issues during the 1930s, showing again the tenacity of non-Soviet practices of everyday life. Sometimes, to be sure, these references to "old ways of life" served other agendas. At the Eighth Congress of the Uzbek Communist Party, for instance, held in July 1938, Usman Yusupov, Ikramov's successor as party leader, blamed several terrorist attacks against women on his recently disgraced predecessor. Six women had been murdered in the past two months, he asserted, by "bandits from the Ikramov-Khojaev gang"—hardly a fair accusation against two of the men who inaugurated and led the hujum.[72] More frequently, open discussions of women's liberation were intended to elicit candid information and to steel loyalists' resolve. They used evidence of continuing veiling, seclusion, and polygyny as signs of class struggle, and exhorted Bolshevik true believers to work harder for the Soviet cause. Among the most obvious examples were the two highly visible Congresses of Laboring Female Youth of Uzbekistan, held in Tashkent in October 1935 and November 1938—part of a plan by central Komsomol leaders in Moscow, who convened a nearly simultaneous set of such congresses in several Eastern republics.[73] The two gatherings in Uzbekistan received substantial public attention and prominent newspaper coverage. Both discussed similar issues.[74]

As might be expected on such a public occasion, speakers at the congress in 1935 did not omit the customary formulaic praises of Stalin, nor did they forget to praise the salutary impact of Soviet power on everyday life in Central Asia. The congress's main reports struck a generally upbeat tone, listing all the heroic achievements of women's liberation. Reams of statistics, for instance, showed the new presence, even prominence, of women in various professions. Resistance to Soviet liberation, the continuing presence of byt crime, even the many cases of misconduct by party members: all were subsumed under the general rubric of "class struggle." This explanatory framework implied, reas-

71. "Azadliq dushmanlarigha qarshi!" *Jangi jol*, no. 3 (1934), 3–5.

72. Usman Iusupov, *Otchetnyi doklad VIII S"ezdu Kommunisticheskoi partii (bol'shevikov) Uzbekistana o rabote TsK KP(b)Uz: 2 iiulia 1938 goda* (Tashkent, 1938), 75.

73. "Almost twenty" such congresses were held in non-Russian regions between September and November 1935 ("Zamechatel'nye s"ezdy zhenskoi molodezhi," *Bezbozhnik*, no. 2 [1936], 2).

74. I focus here on the First Congress, the full records of which are at ÖzRMDA, f. 86, op. 10, dd. 632–34. Extensive excerpts were published at *PSTZhMUz*. On press coverage, see *Pravda Vostoka*, 2–21 Oct. 1935. For the similar tone of the Second Congress in 1938, see "OzK(b)P Markazij Komitetining sekretari ortaq Usman Jusupov nutqi: 1938 jil 28 nojabrda Ozbekstan qiz-chuvanlar II sjezdida sozlangan," *Jarqin haët*, no. 10–11 (28) (1938), 4–8; or "Ozbekstan qiz-chuvanlar II sjezdining murachaati: Ozbekstanning hamma jgitlariga va qizlariga, komsomollariga va hamma mihnatkash jashlariga," *Jarqin haët*, no. 10–11 (28) (1938), 9–10.

suringly, that victory over such manifestations of backwardness was ultimately inevitable.[75] Yet social reality outside the congress hall shimmered into view amid the heroic rhetoric, revealing the widespread popular hostility to the Soviet project in general and women's liberation in particular. One young delegate from a kolkhoz said that her husband had threatened to kill her for coming to Tashkent. He announced that her participation in the congress meant disgrace, and that he would no longer live with her.[76] Another delegate, Yoldasheva, told of the continuing power of Muslim clerics, as shown by the ability of mullahs in Farghona to gather crowds of hundreds of women, not only to hear prayers and "counterrevolutionary agitation" but to contribute financially. Yoldasheva further reported that on the collective farms, Komsomol boys and girls could not work together or befriend one another; if they did, she said, rumors quickly spread that they had slept together, and the girl was considered a fallen woman.[77]

As in the periodical press, then, currents of candor ran through the congress debates. The ideological acceptability of discussing a continuing class struggle made it possible to speak about such things. From the perspective of top leaders, too, one reason to convene such meetings across the USSR was to gain just such a fuller and more accurate view of local social dynamics. Moscow had tried for years to elicit such information, mostly unsuccessfully because local party organizations had not proved reliable conduits of information. Komsomol and party leaders in Moscow may have reasoned that they could bypass local elites by bringing in ordinary women as delegates from the localities.

If candid information gathering was a motivation for the First Congress in 1935, it succeeded. The higher leadership—and anyone else who happened to be listening—heard an earful. After passing along their "fiery greetings" to Comrade Stalin and the party, these women typically expressed a wide range of concerns, which as a whole showed their lives as markedly less rosy than the misty-eyed view of Bolshevik propaganda. Byt crimes received a good deal of attention; delegates from all over Uzbekistan decried the continuing practice of polygyny, underage marriage, and the buying and selling of women, all of which remained common, they said, after almost twenty years of Soviet power.[78] Still more egregious was the ongoing violence against unveiled women. While some attacks could be blamed on such class enemies as Muslim clerics and bois, several delegates insisted that the problem went deeper. They pointed to women who were attacked on collective farms by poor peasants, or even by the very Communists and Komsomol members who were supposedly

75. ÖzRMDA, f. 86, op. 10, d. 632, l. 6, and d. 634, ll. 182–84, 232–56, and 267; or PSTZhMUz, 11, 55–57, and 75.

76. ÖzRMDA, f. 86, op. 10, d. 634, l. 282; also PSTZhMUz, 88.

77. ÖzRMDA, f. 86, op. 10, d. 634, ll. 270–71; also PSTZhMUz, 77.

78. See ÖzRMDA, f. 86, op. 10, d. 632, l. 209, and d. 634, ll. 225, 248, 278–81, 291–92, and 311–12; also PSTZhMUz, 24, 50, 63–66, 84, 87, and 89.

defending women's rights.[79] These women begged for more effective protection in a very hostile and dangerous milieu.[80]

The delegates also devoted substantial attention to female seclusion, and their conclusions were bleak. Several noted Bukhoro's comparative success in unveiling its women—speakers from Bukhoro, in fact, expressed shame at the failure of their colleagues from Tashkent and Farghona to measure up.[81] Delegates traded barbs about the relative superiority of their home regions. Although Khorazm usually ranked near the bottom of most Soviet lists as a particularly backward province, one Khorazmi delegate, Babajanova, used the women's liberation campaign to assert her province's progress:

> Everyone knows that there is no railroad in Khorazm. Here, therefore, you can see how we lag behind the other provinces in culture. This notwithstanding, over the past four to five years the province's party and Komsomol organizations have carried out a great deal of work in the area of women's liberation and education. The result of this is as follows: for the past four to five years you have not seen a single woman in a paranji. If you go to Andijon, or to Samarqand, you will see lots of women under the veil. Tashkent is Uzbekistan's single biggest city and its capital, and we, coming from Khorazm, were intoxicated by it. However, wherever you go, everywhere there are women in paranjis. This is why I say, Samarqand, Qöqon, Farghona, and Tashkent—compare yourselves with Khorazm, and you will fear how well Khorazm is doing on women's liberation.[82]

Yet the bragging and sniping could not obscure the generally dismal picture in regard to the veil. Sharp regional distinctions existed, but even in Bukhoro unveiled women were subject to attack, and traditionalist parents and husbands continued to pull girls out of school.[83] Although localized reports make it difficult to generalize about aggregate percentages or the total number of veils remaining, clearly it struck the delegates that among the most obvious measures of Soviet success (or lack thereof) was the huge number of women still veiled in the mahallas of virtually every Uzbek town. Easily a majority of the women in Tashkent's October district remained hidden by paranjis, one report to the congress said, showing the "colossal" amount of work still to be done.[84] In the countryside, too, collective farms were seeing little work on women's issues.

---

79. ÖzRMDA, f. 86, op. 10, d. 632, ll. 224, 271, and 292; also *PSTZhMUz*, 49, 65–66, 84, 94.

80. *PSTZhMUz*, 24 and 82.

81. ÖzRMDA, f. 86, op. 10, d. 634, l. 279. The claim for total success in Bukhoro is at l. 277.

82. Ibid., l. 311; also *PSTZhMUz*, 101. For stark differences in regional economic development, see the statistical comparisons of provincial electrification levels, numbers of public baths, trams, etc., at f. 86, op. 1, d. 8130, l. 71.

83. ÖzRMDA, f. 86, op. 10, d. 634, l. 278.

84. Ibid., l. 263; also *PSTZhMUz*, 73.

Even Komsomol women like the delegates at this very congress, they finally admitted, usually reveiled and stayed secluded as soon as they returned home.[85]

According to delegates' testimony, indeed, the Uzbek Communist and Komsomol elite were little different from other Muslim Uzbeks when it came to female seclusion. Even among the small group of female Komsomol members, veils could be found—one delegate told proudly of her unveiling in 1934, three years *after* joining the Young Communist League, and another implied that some delegates had not unveiled at all before arriving at this very congress.[86] One delegate had been forced by her husband to veil; he also burned her Komsomol membership card when it arrived in the mail.[87] Men like him, the delegates asserted, were fairly typical in Soviet Uzbekistan. According to Rasuleva, from rural Uychin district, a majority of her local leadership—kolkhoz presidents, directors of enterprises, Komsomol cell secretaries—kept their wives veiled, and cases of underage marriage were rife.[88] Sarcasm fairly dripped from Komsomol Secretary Artykov's voice as he described one such Uzbek man from a by now well-known place:

> In Chust district the "Young Communist" Karimov, a worker in the district education office, married according to the old customs, with qalin, eshons, and all the other attributes [of a religious service]. After a few months passed following the wedding, he forced his wife to wear the paranji. When she refused to do so, this "Young Communist," Karimov, in the spirit of the "highest" manner of instruction, started to beat her unmercifully.[89]

Some delegates blamed the reveiling problem on the older generation: one criticized Uzbek parents for forcing their daughters to reveil. Sometimes widespread rumors of imminent attacks frightened unveiled women into donning the veil again. Sometimes the party itself was to blame: one delegate criticized a lack of steady attention to women's work as the main cause for the rapid reveilings after each year's 8 March celebration.[90] Regardless of the explanation, nearly all delegates to the congress agreed that reveilings were epidemic, and that without more effective tactics, no unveiling effort had any hope of success. During 1931–32, according to the delegate Umarova, one group of

85. ÖzRMDA, f. 86, op. 10, d. 634, ll. 269–70. See also f. 837, op. 13, d. 307, l. 6, as cited by N. A. Akopian, "Pervyi s"ezd zhenskoi trudiashcheisia molodezhi Uzbekistana (oktiabr' 1935)," *Nauchnye trudy Tashkentskogo gosudarstvennogo universiteta*, no. 212 (1962), 112.

86. ÖzRMDA, f. 86, op. 10, d. 634, ll. 245 and 269; and *PSTZhMUz*, 64 and 76.

87. ÖzRMDA, f. 86, op. 10, d. 634, l. 297.

88. *PSTZhMUz*, 81–82.

89. ÖzRMDA, f. 86, op. 10, d. 634, l. 249; and *PSTZhMUz*, 66.

90. ÖzRMDA, f. 86, op. 10, d. 632, l. 221, and d. 634, ll. 259 and 270; also *PSTZhMUz*, 71 and 77.

seventy women had unveiled in Qashqadaryo, but by 1935 every single one had again donned the paranji.[91]

All of these proceedings and discussions at the First Congress of Female Youth received prominent press coverage. High-ranking officials took part: Ikramov delivered a major address as first secretary of the Uzbek party. Fervent praise of Stalin remained de rigueur, but the lively congress debate was not censored, as one might have expected. Many of the most critical speeches did find their way into print.[92] They did not openly criticize Stalin, of course—to the contrary, on the surface they attacked anti-Stalinist class enemies—but still, they described candidly what to a Bolshevik eye was the dark underbelly of Uzbek social practices: attacks on women, attempted murders, byt crimes, forced veilings, massive reveilings. The very prominence of this congress's coverage shows that at least some party leaders supported the open airing of such issues, even as Soviet propagandists were proclaiming the full, glorious completion of women's liberation in the USSR. Such tension—or at least dissonance and indecision—within the party further challenges any lingering notions of a tightly controlled, carefully monitored Uzbek state system during the 1930s.

In all of these genres of published sources, therefore, amid the predominant tone of heroism and Stalinist bravura, direct (if selective) admissions of problems could be aired. The degree of openness is less than that in archival materials, but steady low-level candor is undeniably present, especially starting in the mid-1930s. Even some official propaganda about the veil yields indirect evidence. This writing aimed first to associate traditional customs ("the old ways of life," "survivals of the past") with bad and new Soviet alternatives with good. It then sought to demonstrate the inevitability of the triumph of good over evil. Indeed, Soviet publicists implied that the lion's share of this success had already been won, arguing that Uzbek women were already enjoying the fruits of liberation as equal partners in the building of socialism.

In some ways, however, the message of this propaganda was internally inconsistent, even contradictory. To show the primitivism of a pre-Soviet Uzbek past, these writers relied on stylized interpretations of ancient Muslim and Central Asian history. But to make the case more compelling and relevant— to make the reader feel their horror—they also used contemporary evidence, showing the character and meaning of these ostensibly timeless practices through current photographs and anecdotes. They found it easy to locate such material: they had only to look around them. Yet what did such mate-

91. *PSTZhMUz*, 92. For other reveilings, also see ÖzRMDA, f. 86, op. 10, d. 634, ll. 3–5 and 192.

92. In addition to the foregoing references to *PV* and *PSTZhMUz*, see A. Nukhrat, "Usilim antireligioznuiu propagandu sredi natsionalok," *Antireligioznik*, no. 1 (1936), 25–26; and "Zamechatel'nye s"ezdy zhenskoi molodezhi," *Bezbozhnik*, no. 2 (1936), 2–3. The congress's salutary effects—bringing unpleasant facts to light and inspiring redoubled efforts—were acknowledged by V. Tadevosian, "Usilit' bor'bu s prestupleniiami protiv raskreposhcheniia zhenshchin-natsionalok," *Sotsialisticheskaia zakonnost'*, no. 11 (1938), 36.

rials show? They found women in 1940 wearing veils on the trams of Tashkent, on the street, at the bazaar, even while visiting a Soviet antireligious museum.[93] They told of byt crimes and murders in 1939, and related the complaints of still-veiled women all across Uzbekistan. They found women factory laborers keeping paranjis over their faces while working on the assembly line for years on end.[94] They documented, in short, the continuing depth and power of female seclusion. Such materials thus unintentionally confirmed that Soviet liberation had not yet been achieved, and indeed that it had a long way to go. Such propaganda made the Bolshevik triumph seem not so inevitable after all.

The very existence, not to mention timing, of this propaganda onslaught against the veil is another indirect form of evidence about Uzbek female seclusion around 1940. If the assertions of Soviet propaganda were correct and Uzbek women had been completely or at least largely liberated from their centuries-old oppression, one might think a massive, well-coordinated campaign of attacks on the paranji not to be necessary. Yet an upsurge of public discussion did take place in the late 1930s and early 1940s, showing remarkable official interest in an issue that had nominally been put to rest. Newspapers published dozens of articles about the paranji, focusing on its backwardness and alleged health risks, denouncing it as oppressive and evil, and exhorting all Uzbek women who had not yet done so to cast it off.[95] Inspirational drawings of women throwing aside their veils under the glowering eyes of Muslim notables adorned the front covers of journals, as shown in Figure 28. Similar arguments against the veil appeared in mass-market books, booklets, and pamphlets: printed cheaply by the tens of thousands of copies, these publications appeared in increasing numbers around 1939 and continued into the 1950s.[96]

93. See the photographs by Liutsan Klimovich at "Islam—orudie ugneteniia zhenshchiny," *Bezbozhnik*, no. 2–3 (1940), 14–16; and G. Snesareva, "Perezhitki islama i bor'ba s nimi," *Bezbozhnik*, no. 9–10 (1940), 3–5. The veiled women at an antireligious museum in Samarqand are shown in the latter source, above the optimistic caption, "But the day is near when they will come again, with unveiled faces."

94. Liutsan Klimovich, *Doloi parandzhu!* (Moscow, 1940), 44–46 and 59–61.

95. This wave of discussion was sparked by the widely translated and discussed article in *Pravda* by Mastura Avezova, a Tajik member of the USSR Supreme Soviet, in early 1940 (see above, Chapter 8). Among other roughly contemporaneous writings were R. S. Gershenovich, "Chem vredny parandzha i chachvan," *Bezbozhnik*, no. 12 (1938), 7; L. K., "Parandzha i chachvan," 34–35; A. Ozerskii, "Protiv parandzha," *Krest'ianka*, no. 9 (1940), 20–21; L. Klimovich, "Konets, parandzhe!" *Ogonëk*, no. 6 (1940), 4–5; "Bitsin paranchi!" *Jarqin haët*, no. 1 (42) (1940), 23; and "Ozbekistan pajtaxti xatin-qizlarining ordenli respublikaning barca mihnatkash xatin-qizlariga murachaati," *Jarqin haët*, no. 2 (43) (1940), 4–6.

96. Twenty thousand copies of Liutsan Klimovich's brochure about the veil were published in 1940. But his stories of thousands of women unveiling in 1939 in Tashkent and Marghilon suggest that large numbers of women were still available to cast off their veils, and that Soviet efforts had far to go (Klimovich, *Doloi parandzhu!* [Moscow, 1940], 52–53). A similar booklet in Uzbek was published in 1953 in an edition of 30,000 copies, offering nearly unchanged arguments about the veil's health risks and antimodern character. Its retail price of 20 kopecks aimed squarely at a popular audience. See M. Aliev, *Paranji ötmishning sarqiti* (Tashkent, 1953), 23–26.

Figure 28. "From the medieval darkness . . .": unveiling in the face
of class enemies, as seen by a Soviet antireligious journal, 1941.
(*Bezbozhnik,* no. 2 [February 1941], front cover.)

Great effort went into reaching the widest possible audience: articles from the
Russian-language press were translated into Uzbek, for instance, and reprinted
as local primers on women's liberation.[97] Special meetings and demonstrations
were held to discuss the evils of the veil. Some were small, intimate meetings of
a few women with a Soviet activist; others were festive mass affairs held in sta-
diums, attracting thousands of people to listen to speeches and be energized by
banners, dancing, and music. (See Figure 29.) Government observers and re-

---

97. See the pastiche published as *Paranchi va cacvan azadlik dushmani* (Tashkent, 1940),
which included translated newspaper articles on the veil, inspirational exhortations to women, articles by prominent women such as Mahmudova, testimonials from women who had unveiled during the 1930s, and petitions for a decree outlawing the veil. Also translated into Uzbek was V.
Lebedev-Kumach, "Yŏqolsin paranji!" *Ërqin haët,* no. 1 (54) (1941), 10.

Figure 29. Mass rally against the veil, Pushkin Stadium, Tashkent, 1935. (Courtesy ÖzRKFFHMDA.)

porters recorded such demonstrations in photographs and on film, and such "news" imagery was disseminated widely.[98]

Especially when combined with other forms of evidence, this wave of Uzbek- and Russian-language antiparanji propaganda implies strongly that the problem of the veil had not yet been solved. But direct evidence of the veil's survival can also be found even in such thoroughly polemical sources. In 1940, after optimistically asserting that 70–80 percent of Uzbek women were now "[politically] conscious, educated, unveiled, and spending their days in [economically] independent labor," Fatima Yoldashbaeva bemoaned the fact that many women in large cities such as Tashkent, Farghona, Marghilon, and Namangan still wore the veil.[99] Even later, another Soviet propagandist, M. Aliev, discussed how the party had transformed indigenous codes of family practice,

98. Newsreels of meetings in Tashkent in February and March 1940 are at ÖzRKFFHMDA, no. 89 and 93. Another meeting in January 1940, held at Tashkent's Sverdlov Theater, is shown at "Ozbekstan pajtaxti xatin-qizlarining ordenli respublikaning barca mihnatkash xatin-qizlariga murachaati," *Jarqin haët,* no. 2 (43) (1940), 5, and "Tashkent shahar xatin-qizlarining jighilishi," *QÖ,* 1 Feb. 1940.

99. *Paranchi va cacvan azadlik dushmani,* 47. Similar admissions are in the articles by Halima Nasirova, pp. 52–53, and Xadica Karimova, p. 59.

and in particular had liberated Uzbek women from the veil. Writing in 1953, the year of Stalin's death, and after more than thirty-five years of Soviet power, Aliev put his best spin on this story of Bolshevik progress. But even he had to admit the immense work that remained:

> No matter how great our successes in this sphere [of women's libera-tion], we cannot remain satisfied with them, since we will not be able to carry out our work among women without having taken account of the great and serious shortcomings [*katta va jiddiy kamchiliklar*] that [still] exist.
>
> In several districts and provinces of our republic it is still possible to meet women veiled with the paranji and chachvon. Among the women going about daily life while covered by the paranji, there is a sort who want to free their hearts and souls from the paranji and chachvon. They are forced to go about in daily life veiled with paranji and chachvon, however, fearing their husbands and parents, who are under the influ-ence of religious customs and traditions.
>
> In the October, Stalin, and Kirov districts of Tashkent, as well as in the cities of Samarqand and Farghona, it is possible to meet many [women] in a veiled state, wearing paranjis. In the rural districts and cities of Surkhondaryo, Qashqadaryo, Namangan, Bukhoro, and Andi-jon provinces there remains a general tendency for [women] to walk about while veiled with all sorts of outer cloaks, using things like a *das-turkhon*, a *yakhtak*, a *jelak*, or a *chopon* in place of a paranji.[100]

Despite decades of state and party effort, then, the veil was still commonly worn in 1953. Optimists could claim some success, perhaps, in altering its form: instead of a paranji, Aliev noted that some women in the 1950s used a *chopon* (a long outer robe often worn by men), a *jelak* (a kind of short paranji), a *yakhtak* (or *yaktak*, a woman's short unlined summer robe), even a *dasturkhon* (tablecloth). But such incremental adjustments were far less than the ambitious program of 1927 had hoped. Local practices of female seclu-sion, only strengthened by being targeted for all-out attack, had managed to withstand for decades the blandishments and coercion at the disposal of the Soviet metropole and Stalinist state.

Power and Resistance in Stalin's Empire

Soviet authorities devoted continuing attention to the issue of female seclusion in the 1930s and beyond for a very good reason: the tenacious persistence— even expansion—of so-called traditional gender roles and codes of behavior. These practices were seen as inimical to a modern populace and a threat to So-viet values, yet nothing party activists did seemed able to stamp them out. Such

100. Aliev, *Paranji ötmishning sarqiti*, 23.

Bolshevik efforts, in fact, only added to the political resonance of these acts, investing them with a newly antistate component. As in other imperial settings, personal behaviors seen by a metropolitan power as distasteful and uncivilized were—partly on that basis alone—given new local political meanings. The examples of clitoridectomy in British East Africa, peyote ceremonies among Native Americans, and prostitution in India are cases in point: such behaviors could become expressive of antistate sentiments and anticolonial resistance.[101]

Some Muslim women did unveil during the hujum of 1927; a few, mostly in the larger cities, remained unveiled afterward, took up paid work outside the home, and hewed to the Soviet model of women as liberated, fully equal citizens. Moreover, the success of Bolshevik efforts varied by region, generation, and social position, among other variables. Nonetheless, the basic picture of Uzbek family relations and gender roles on the eve of war appeared much like that which impelled the hujum in 1927—except that the paranji had become *more* common in many places. The most obvious change by 1941 was the simple Soviet insistence on declaring, at least in public, that a change had in fact taken place. Such vague, general proclamations of victory in the mostly sanitized, tightly controlled press—in the teeth of abundant everyday evidence to the contrary—may have been the best that Moscow's representatives could do.

Even with all the resources and sanctions of the Stalinist state being brought to bear, decades of all-out effort had failed to transform Uzbek culture the way the Bolsheviks had intended. Most Uzbeks simply refused to live as Bolsheviks, despite the party's unrelenting campaign to persuade them of the merits of a complete cultural overhaul. Ironically, these men and women succeeded in resisting such a transformation partly by using the very categories of ethnonational identity and understandings of nationally emblematic, gendered "traditions" that had been in large part created and universalized by that same party. Many of the specific contents of Uzbek everyday culture were themselves products of this ongoing colonial encounter. Cultural practices of gender and family life had shifted and taken unexpected shape during the years after 1927. But they survived tenaciously, functioning as a basic component of identity, a repository of new political meanings, and an anchor against the state, even during the darkest hours of Stalin's Terror.

101. Pedersen, "National Bodies, Unspeakable Acts"; Thomas, "Ngaitana"; Adams, *Education for Extinction*, 233–34; and Veena Talwar Oldenberg, "Lifestyle as Resistance: The Case of the Courtesans of Lucknow, India," *Feminist Studies* 16 (1990): 259–87.

Conclusion

Where there is power, there is resistance.

—Michel Foucault

On the seventh of March I tore off my veil
But before I reached home
I bought three new paranjis
To veil myself more darkly.

—Satirical song heard among Uzbek women, 1929

Soviet officials and party activists sent to postrevolutionary Central Asia confronted a world very different from the one most had left behind. Each of these men and women faced a difficult process of personal adjustment. Immediately upon arrival at the Tashkent train station in the early 1920s, for example, two prominent Bolshevik women's activists were told as much—"This isn't your Moscow!" (Eto Vam ne Moskva!)[1] Both of these women successfully adapted to what they found in the new Soviet East and ultimately spent years working in Central Asia. Many others, though, fled at the first opportunity to more familiar parts of the USSR. The party as a whole, too, had to adjust to its new empire and rethink what it meant by a "Soviet" policy in the colonial, non-Russian periphery. What would a Soviet society look like in Muslim areas such as southern Central Asia? Party members could only learn by doing what it meant to be Bolshevik in the colonial world, in places that lacked most of the features that classic Marxist theory posited as necessary for socialist revolution. A process of negotiation followed, one that ultimately defined Soviet power in very different terms than in Bolshevik Russia. In the local encounter between Soviet power and Central Asia, both sides emerged transformed.

1. Quoted in Liubimova, *Dnevnik zhenotdelki,* 8.

344

Soviet policy in Central Asia came to focus especially on gender relations as a substitute for class, in the hope that this approach would bring about wholesale revolutionary change. In March 1927 party workers launched a hujum, or assault, against those aspects of daily life, or byt, deemed most oppressive of women—in particular, against customs of female inequality and seclusion. Once such a strategic choice had been made, party activists devised a variety of arguments—political, economic, cultural, hygienic—to encourage men and women in the colonial East to live according to the party's European ideals of women's liberation and gender equality. These activists especially denounced the cotton-and-horsehair veils, known as the paranji and chachvon, that were worn by Uzbek women, and organized massive public demonstrations at which these veils were cast off by the hundreds, hurled to the ground, and with a theatrical flourish set afire.

As we have seen, however, the story of emancipation was rarely so straightforward. Certainly the hujum did not reach the hoped-for culmination and conclusion by October 1927, in time to mark the tenth anniversary of the Bolshevik Revolution. The ongoing encounter between Russians and Central Asians continued long afterward, acted out in a variety of arenas and in the context of continuing Stalinist and colonial rule. Some tsarist colonial policies scarcely changed after 1917—while some became even more obvious and exploitative, such as the rapid expansion of a cotton economy. But under Soviet power, conflict over local cultural issues, and especially over gender politics, ultimately reshaped Uzbek society in ways that the tsarist colonial state never attempted or even contemplated. Party leaders likewise had to rethink the meaning of such basic concepts as Soviet power and Bolshevik policy when they decided to make gender rather than class their highest priority in this part of the non-Russian periphery. Soviet prestige and legitimacy were heavily invested in the effort to bring political consciousness and European notions of progress, modernity, and civilization to these supposedly retrograde colonial backwaters of the tsarist empire. The success or failure of the Soviet state in doing so—and ultimately in overcoming the visible marks of colonial difference and assimilating all Soviet citizens into a unitary socialist society—represented an important part of its claim to leadership in the colonial world, and perhaps even the correctness of its Marxist revolutionary doctrine. To put Central Asia on the ideologically required path to modernity, Bolshevik policy played a key role in forming an "Uzbek" national identity (as it likewise helped shape "Kazakhs," "Turkmen," and others). Even while they helped create powerful and distinct indigenous national identities, though, party workers simultaneously fought over and tried to remake local gender practices, thereby staking a fundamental claim to their own European status and identity.

Many deep issues—of culture, politics, history, religion, gender, health, international relations, and economics, to name just a few—were simultaneously in play in the contest over the veil, in the struggle over this very symbolic, even overdetermined piece of women's clothing. The female body was the chosen terrain for this struggle. Read as a text, this body was taken by all sides to reveal identities, loyalties, and political affiliations, not only of an individual woman but also of her family and entire social network. The conflict over female unveiling launched a dialogue of sorts between European party activists and Muslim traditionalists over the future of Central Asia. This debate emerged from particular contingent choices made in the 1920s. Based largely on mutual misperceptions, it nonetheless had real and often unexpected consequences. In the end this encounter helped to define each side and created the shared mutual perception that the other represented a polar opposite. It thus made both groups more coherent (internally) and more hostile (to each other), while at the same time making life very complicated for the Uzbek women and indigenous socialists who were caught in the middle.

This dichotomous outcome was not inevitable. The precursors of both sides had been complex and multivocal, and even in 1927, views and practices on female veiling and seclusion were fluid, not stable. Many party members thought the issue of veiling a red herring and denounced it as a distraction. Many rural and poor Muslim women, too, had never veiled or been secluded, and there were strong voices of indigenous support (especially among the jadids) for unveiling as a properly Muslim act that would enable renewal and reform. As an unintended consequence of the hujum—of its tactics and its ideological and cultural framework—such competing voices came to be written out of each side and the ambiguities and dissonances muted. "Reform," meaning unveiling, became a Soviet, not jadid, ideal. The voice of indigenous Muslim reformism lost its cultural authority as the party adopted or stole its ideas. "Tradition" came to mean veiling and seclusion—and of *all* Uzbek women, not just those in wealthy urban families. A panoply of associated "traditional" practices (bride-price and polygyny, circumcision ceremonies, religious funerals, pilgrimages, and a host of others) were reimagined as universal; together they became stabilized, and in the end they were nationalized as emblems of the Uzbek people. These practices thus became expressive of an un-Soviet, even *anti*-Soviet identity—a richly ironic outcome, since the Uzbek national identity was itself largely a Soviet creation. The party's own actions, therefore, played an important albeit inadvertent role in spreading the practice of veiling, especially in rural areas, by equating it with Uzbek religio-cultural and now national traditions, and thereby giving it new depth and political meaning.

The particular dynamics of this encounter drove each side to become more univocal, as many of the alternatives that had existed before 1927 came to be seen as unacceptable by all concerned. At the same time, though, both sides of this emerging opposition also came to agree that gender relations were a—or even *the*—proper arena for struggle over the direction of Central Asian politics, culture, and society. This unspoken agreement between Soviet activists and their Muslim opponents may have been the hujum's most fateful consequence. The resultant shifts in the language of cultural identity and the arena of political struggle makes basic elements of Soviet history, such as the purges of the 1930s, appear in a very different light.

By looking from the perspective of the Muslim periphery, one gains new insight into the Stalinist state, seeing more clearly the character and extent of its power and its ongoing negotiations with society. This peripheral perspective iluminates that state's limits, its very real weaknesses in its efforts to extend cultural hegemony to other cultures and its willingness in the end to compromise on even apparently fundamental ideals. Indeed, some Soviet attempts to transform Uzbek society produced results that were the exact opposite of what was intended. Moreover, a good deal of decision making went on at low levels in the party and state hierarchy and at a great distance from Moscow. This approach also enables a glimpse of the complex social and subaltern strategies pursued by individual Uzbek women and men in dealing with an alien state. These strategies ranged from apparent support to active oposition, from studied obliviousness to passive resistance to the spreading of gossip and rumors. They also included varieties of creative subterfuge around questions of law and everyday life.

Lastly, the centrality of the unveiling campaign to the Bolshevik effort and the fierceness of the conflict that ensued over it show how intricately gender relations were interwoven with relations of social and political power in Central Asia, and how women became central to and emblematic of this emerging Uzbek national identity. Both sides were transformed by the contest, and in the Soviet empire gender became a fundamental language of identity, power, and revolution. To many Bolsheviks, the veiled woman was self-evidently an oppressed creature, symbolizing all that was most backward and primitive in the tsarist (capitalist) empire. She showed, they thought, the undeniable need for immediate Soviet uplift and emancipation. To the party's opponents, though, the unveiled woman, equally obviously, meant something else altogether: foreign, colonial control, along with sexual license, poor character, uncertainty over children's patrimony, the explicit denial of God and his law, and ultimately nothing less than the end of the world. Women themselves were the ground for this struggle, and women's own agency thus remained a troublesome and difficult issue. Women's status as conscious actors, as people continually making decisions and individual choices to respond to the world around them, greatly complicated these countervailing narratives of liberation and resistance.

War, Social Change, and the Sovietization of Everyday Life

What happened after 1941? How far did Bolshevik power ultimately change Uzbekistan? History did not end; patterns of gender and family life in Central Asia continued to change and develop in unexpected ways. Clearly the party's efforts failed—at least in their own terms—to transform Central Asian family relations by the time Hitler invaded the USSR. Yet by the early 1960s the situation had changed dramatically. Uzbekistan appeared to many observers re-

Figure 30. Discussing the chachvon and its dangers, Tashkent. (Courtesy RGAKFD.)

markably Sovietized.[2] Most Uzbeks, especially in cities, spoke Russian at work—even at home. They took the occasional bite of pork sausage or the (less occasional) drink of vodka, and faced diminished opprobrium for indulging in such Russian practices. In Uzbek homes, female seclusion decreased and veils at last became an exception, not the rule—the "museum piece" party activists had long sought. (See Figure 30.) Many women worked outside the home, becoming less exotic and Eastern as they mingled with men; their complaints of a "double burden" increasingly resembled those of Russian women. After a major earthquake in 1966, indeed, the rebuilt Tashkent even looked like a Russian Soviet city.[3]

In one sense the seeds of these changes in Soviet Uzbek identity were already present in the 1930s. The continual repetition and inscription of Soviet categories and language—all those heroic congresses, public demonstrations, and newspapers posted in town squares—did, over time, have an impact. Soviet power helped nationalize the Uzbek people and reify their traditions; it created

2. Uzbek colleagues as well as Western scholars such as Terence Emmons and Ronald Suny, who visited Tashkent in the 1960s and 1970s, have shared this impression with me. The Russian sociologist Viktoriia Koroteeva, who studies the contemporary Uzbek mahalla and its change over time, concurs in dating this shift to the early 1960s. Others, such as Michael Rywkin, who lived in and near Samarqand between 1942 and 1946, say that such changes were evident even then (personal communications).

3. A theme developed in detail in my study, now in progress, on earthquakes and empire in the Soviet Union.

all kinds of new vocabularies, public spaces, and social experiences. One might, for that matter, trace the genealogy of this shift even earlier, to the 1920s, 1910s, even the late nineteenth century, back to the indigenous leftists, Communists, and Islamic reformers of prerevolutionary Turkestan. But such seeds are not the same as a wider social or cultural shift, and the trend after 1927 and throughout the 1930s was in the opposite direction. As the historian Adeeb Khalid has shown very effectively, jadid reformism was an important force during the late nineteenth and early twentieth centuries.[4] Yet by the 1930s the jadids as a group had been popularly discredited because of both their personal affiliations and associations with Bolshevism and the Bolsheviks' adoption of many of their programs.

In perhaps the ultimate irony of the women's liberation campaign, in the end it was only a redirection of energies and priorities away from the veil that finally led to the paranji's decline and near-demise. More than anything else, it was the direct and indirect consequences of later historical experiences—especially those of a hugely traumatic world war and slow, painful recovery—that ultimately led to the veil's gradual disappearance over the next two decades. How did this happen? I will suggest several possibilities, the details of which await further research. First, the war years of the 1940s brought a massive influx of non-Muslims to Uzbekistan. The millions of new inhabitants included evacuees and orphans, both Soviet and foreign (especially Poles), in flight from the Nazis, as well as several ostensibly "traitorous" nationalities forcibly deported en masse to Central Asia.[5] This migration brought about a shift in Central Asia's demographic balance far more dramatic than any other in the eighty years of Russian colonial control. The numerical predominance of Uzbeks declined and intercultural contacts increased proportionately, even (especially) in the rural countryside. Evacuated Russian orphans were placed with Uzbek families, for instance.

Wartime factory evacuations from the western borderlands and Russia also brought a huge amount of capital equipment to an area long seen as primitive. Far more industrial complexes arose than were built during the first three five-year plans. This shift changed the area's economic profile not only during the war but afterward as well, as many evacuated plants were left in place after 1945.[6] In the context of a centrally planned economy, further industrial development became at least somewhat self-sustaining, as these enterprises directed

4. Khalid, *Politics of Muslim Cultural Reform.*

5. See Robert Argenbright, "Space of Survival: The Soviet Evacuation of Industry and Population in 1941," in *Beyond the Limits: The Concept of Space in Russian History and Culture,* ed. Jeremy Smith, *Studia Historica* 62 (1999): 207–39; Katherine R. Jolluck, *Exile and Identity: Polish Women in the Soviet Union during World War II* (Pittsburgh, 2002); and Aleksandr M. Nekrich, *The Punished Peoples: The Deportation and Fate of Soviet Minorities at the End of the Second World War* (New York, 1978).

6. Douglas Northrop, "Unplanned War, Planned Economy: Economic Change and Development in Soviet Central Asia, 1928–1945" (unpublished paper, 1992).

higher investment flows to Central Asia. They also created demand for an educated Central Asian workforce, a shift with its own cultural consequences.

Finally, although perhaps harder to demonstrate, the war itself changed people. By 1945 the newly multiethnic population of Uzbekistan had worked together with a clear, single aim—to defeat Nazi Germany and thus to survive. For the first time, Central Asian men had been conscripted successfully into an army directed from Moscow.[7] Sharing in the fight against Hitler and in the almost unimaginably massive casualty counts (roughly 27 million Soviet citizens and soldiers are thought to have perished in the war) may at last have cemented a meaningful Uzbek Soviet identity, and a Soviet loyalty, in a way that was scarcely imaginable before 1941. The experience of Red Army service thousands of miles from home, too, could only have produced profound changes among those soldiers who survived. Today Victory Day is as much a holiday in independent Uzbekistan as in post-Soviet Russia; doorways in traditional Uzbek mahallas proudly boast of the veterans who live inside. The Great Patriotic War lives on in the Uzbek collective memory, helping to create an identity with Soviet as well as Uzbek roots. Thus the war represents a true watershed in Central Asian as well as Soviet history.

A last element of the subtle shifts in Uzbek identity and cultural practices seems to have emerged during the early postwar years. Put most simply, a new generation came of age, one born under Soviet power, to parents who had themselves worked in collective farms or factories rather than in the old villages. The presence of traditionalists, who had emerged to spearhead earlier opposition, diminished with time: already older, they died in large numbers both naturally, of old age, and during the wider traumas of collectivization and war. A younger generation, educated in Soviet schools (see Figure 31), drawing upon the shared experiences and myths of great suffering and ultimate triumph in war, socialized through Red Army service, and less personally familiar with older models of opposition, became Soviet in a way that would have been unimaginable to their grandparents. At this point—at long last—the Soviet government could legitimately claim the allegiance in at least some contexts of more than a small fringe of the population.

Uzbeks did not abandon every ritual seen by the Soviet and European elites as backward: male circumcision rituals remained almost universally practiced, for instance, and the Persian tradition of Navröz, which marks the vernal equinox as a New Year celebration, continued to be observed every March. Uzbek home lives still differed substantially from Russian ones, and intermarriage (especially of Uzbek girls) and interethnic socializing were still fairly unusual. Yet a Soviet identity had joined the Uzbek one, coexisted with it, and henceforth helped to determine loyalties and allegiances. Uzbeks as a group no longer automatically opposed Soviet efforts to modernize and bring progress

7. A tsarist attempt to draft Central Asian men as behind-the-lines labor brigades during the First World War had provoked riots in 1916, and ultimately the idea was dropped.

Figure 31. Stalin in an Uzbek school. (Max Penson, courtesy Dina Khojaeva, collection Anahita Gallery, Santa Fe, N.M.)

to Central Asia. Although a smattering of women continued to live in varying degrees of seclusion, by the late 1960s virtually no one defended the veil publicly, and nearly everyone welcomed the construction of hospitals, schools, and universities—even a metro in Tashkent. The Russians' self-styled European mission appeared, at long last, to have achieved hegemony among Central Asians themselves; this shift marks the true transformation of the region.

This success, fifty years and much pain in the making, is important for many reasons. It helps explain, for example, why Central Asia remained so stable in the late Soviet period. After such bitter, even violent resistance in the 1920s and 1930s, one might reasonably have expected that when state controls finally did loosen, opposition would sprout in Central Asia at the first opportunity. Yet Central Asia remained comparatively quiet during the Thaw of the 1960s, when nationally minded groups in other non-Russian regions began openly to express distinctive ethno-national identities and to stake political claims based on them. Later, during the Gorbachev years, separatist movements emerged across the Soviet Union—most powerfully and visibly in the Baltic republics of Estonia, Latvia, and Lithuania—but they remained weak in Central Asia. With a few exceptions, such as the Alma-Ata riot of December 1986, the region played little role in the interlocking crises that ultimately brought down the USSR. Central Asian governments also showed less leadership turnover or political change in the turmoil that followed the Soviet collapse in 1991. Why?

The war and its aftermath provide an answer. Ironically, Uzbek traditionalists of the 1920s and 1930s had held out war as their great hope, encouraging rumors of an allegedly imminent attack by the USSR's European enemies to smash Soviet power. Such an attack would, not coincidentally, restore the power of devout, self-consciously traditional authorities such as themselves in Central Asia. When war with a European power did come, however, it only served as the glue that held the many parts of the Soviet Union together.

Yet despite this later legacy of Sovietization during the 1940s, 1950s, and 1960s, the paradoxes of the hujum remained. They persist today. While completing research for this book, I lived for almost two years with a wonderful Uzbek family in an older mahalla in Tashkent. They and their neighbors were very pleased that a historian had arrived from America to tell their story to the outside world, and they did everything possible to make my stay pleasant and productive. Their deep pride in country and heritage was shared by the local media: I, along with the handful of other American scholars resident in Uzbekistan, found myself invited regularly to speak at schools, on public occasions, and with interviewers on radio and television. Usually the motive for such invitations was twofold: to demonstrate that outsiders could learn the Uzbek language (despite—or rather because of—the reluctance of most local Russians to do so) and to validate Uzbek greatness by asking for opinions on Uzbekistan's independence (the correct opinion was obvious, at least to those who wished their stay to proceed smoothly).

Most of the people I met in Tashkent and elsewhere assumed that my interest in the "woman question," or *khotin-qizlar masalasi* (in Russian, *zhenskii vopros*) lay in producing the kind of narrative that Soviet newspapers and history books had long subsumed under the general rubric of "women's liberation" (*khotin-qizlar ozodligi* or *raskreposhchenie zhenshchin*). Indeed, in the mid-1990s International Women's Day was still a major holiday in our mahalla. The apparent curiosity, at least to my eyes, of a European socialist holiday, created in Denmark, refracted through Moscow and made emblematic of Bolshevik colonial rule, now being a popular state holiday in the newly independent, postcolonial, and largely Muslim state of Uzbekistan did not seem at all odd to the Uzbeks I knew.[8] These mostly urban and highly educated men and women saw the hujum's legacy of liberation through unveiling as among the most positive outcomes of the Soviet period. They agreed, for the most part, that Uzbekistan still had to cast off legacies of the Russian colonial past and to find its own way, overcoming problems bequeathed by Bolshevik and tsarist rule—problems such as the overproduction of cotton, responsible for the ecological catastrophe of the desiccation of the Aral Sea, and the continuing social costs of Stalin's purges and Terror. At the same time, however, they almost universally spoke warmly of the

8. On the early history of International Women's Day, see Choi Chatterjee, *Celebrating Women: Gender, Festival Culture, and Bolshevik Ideology, 1910–1939* (Pittsburgh, 2002), 18–36.

hujum, pointing to it as a positive mark of Uzbek progress.[9] The fact that today the overwhelming majority of women on the streets of central Tashkent are unveiled is not at all antithetical to their strong Uzbek identity.

This sentiment is shared by the post-Soviet Uzbek government, which has made one of its highest priorities the building of an independent, secular Uzbek nation-state, one based largely on a new and nonreligious image of the modern Uzbek man and woman. It further sees women's liberation as an important political and cultural bulwark against the looming dangers of what it defines as Islamic fundamentalism across the Tajik and Afghan borders. The Uzbek government has thus continued the Soviet custom of publishing panegyrics on 8 March to the activists of the hujum and it supports and protects the monuments that glorify the image of an unveiled woman.[10] It even finally banned the veil, along with male beards and other religious attire—a singularly dramatic step that Stalin never dared to take. Considered as a whole, these efforts to create an emphatically secular national identity are in some ways oddly reminiscent of Bolshevik campaigns of the 1920s and 1930s. The main difference is that now the patriotic urging and the crackdowns on mosques and organized religion emanate from an Uzbek nationalist state, not a foreign colonial power. Whether that distinction makes it easier to impose secularism and social change by fiat (as in, say, Atatürk's Turkey) only time will tell.

Not all the early signs are encouraging. On some issues the postcolonial Uzbek state seems not to have learned from the Soviet experience. In the immediate aftermath of the Soviet collapse, Central Asia showed little sign of organized, politically oriented Islamic activity, for example, and fears of an Iranian-style Muslim revolution seemed vastly overstated in the early 1990s. But in an eerie echo of the 1920s, a subsequent state crackdown on religious practices and personnel helped produce a backlash seen in the formation and growth of Islamist organizations in and around Uzbekistan. Some of these groups use violent tactics: the shadowy Islamic Movement of Uzbekistan (IMU), in particular, has been blamed for a well-coordinated bomb attack in central Tashkent in 1999 that aimed to assassinate the Uzbek president and his cabinet. It failed, and in response the government launched an even harsher crackdown on perceived and potential political opponents. The IMU, meanwhile, according to state allegations, continued to launch regular cross-border raids from bases in northern Afghanistan. Like the Bolsheviks with their hujum, then, the postcolonial Uzbek state has arguably helped to create ex-

---

9. For an example of Western coverage sympathetic to this point of view, see Tom Hundley, "Women Fear Veil of Religious Rebirth," *Houston Chronicle*, 8 Mar. 1992. Hundley quotes women who feel that veiling, particularly when forced, is a brand of "male totalitarianism."

10. On the hujum's anniversaries one finds newspaper articles, interviews with activists, and published memoirs drawing attention to the hujum as a centerpiece of progress. The most obvious physical monument to the hujum is a huge statue of an unveiled woman erected in 1987 to mark its sixtieth anniversary. It now looms over a public square in the Old City of Tashkent.

actly what it wanted most to avoid. By opting to impose a secular vision for
Uzbek national identity and attacking religious institutions to boot, it gave a
gift to the tiny, nascent opposition: the ability to fuse religious and political
messages in a unified antistate language of identity, affiliation, and action.

More recently, after the terrorist attacks of 11 September 2001, the international array of forces shifted radically, in ways that would have been inconceivable in 1927 (or even 1997). By forming a vaguely defined alliance
with the United States to fight a "war against terrorism" from its suddenly
strategic geopolitical location directly north of Afghanistan, the Uzbek government garnered substantial support from Western states newly concerned
about threats from Islamic groups in Central Asia. Its support for gender
equality helped prove its secular bona fides, and also overshadowed or allevi-
ated Western human rights concerns. Western feminist groups, too, shared
some of these priorities and concerns: the treatment of Central Asian and
other Muslim women has continued to be used as a ready gauge of Muslim
society as a whole. Such issues are often taken to show both a level of (or lack
of) enlightenment and progress, and—as in the cartoon shown in Figure 32—
a proclivity for fundamentalist terror. After the attacks of 11 September
2001, for example, Afghan women's burqas served as indisputable proof of
the Taliban regime's medieval character, an apparently irrefutable demonstration of barbarity and oppression that justified war and brooked little disagreement. Western writers and news magazines took it as self-evident that all
Muslim women would yearn for emancipation from the yoke of such fundamentalist tyranny.[11] Western definitions of "liberation" continue to be used,
in other words, usually without question or reflection—and have been invoked by Americans of all political stripes, from radical feminists to Christian
conservatives, just as everyone from missionaries to Stalinists used them
decades ago.[12]

Yet as we know, such assumptions are not always borne out in practice.
Shortly after celebrating International Women's Day in 1995, I walked as
usual the two miles to work at the Uzbek Central State Archive, located in the
Chilonzor district of Tashkent. Near the middle of my commute I passed a
woman dressed in the paranji and chachvon whose supposed eradication
decades earlier I was on my way to study at the archive. The juxtaposition
struck me as remarkable, but it did not seem to trouble her, nor did others on

11. For mainstream media examples, see the cover story in *Time:* Richard Laczyo, "Lifting the
Veil," 3 Dec. 2001, 34–49; and Moni Basu, "Taliban Regime Has Returned Afghan Women to
Dark Ages," *Atlanta Journal-Constitution,* 21 Oct. 2001.

12. For a Christian conservative perspective, see *World* magazine: Marvin Olasky, "Brutality
and Dictatorship," 27 Oct. 2001; or Gene Edward Veith, "Intellectual Burqas," 22 Dec. 2001.
Feminist groups circulated petitions on behalf of Afghan women among American academics in
late 2001 and early 2002; Afghan women were named among *Ms.* magazine's Women of the Year,
2001, "for pursuing everyday acts of resistance in the face of brutal, gender-based oppression"
(*Ms.,* December 2001/January 2002, 52–54).

Figure 32. The veil and Islamic terror, as seen in France in the mid-1990s. (*Le Monde*, 1 Feb. 1995.)

this small, out-of-the-way street even appear to notice her garb. In the mid-1990s, veils could easily be found on the streets of Tashkent—especially in the residential mahallas and throughout the Old City—and they were more common in Namangan and towns in the Farghona Valley. They had been still more widespread a few years earlier, having quickly reappeared soon after Uzbekistan declared its independence.[13] Although they declined in popularity fairly quickly, at least in most areas, this book helps to explain their reappearance sixty-four years after the hujum.

Thanks to the hujum, when Uzbekistan appeared as an independent state in 1991 and Uzbek men and women were able to express their newfound independence in the social arena, they had a deeply gendered vocabulary of national identity on which to draw. Even though paranjis and chachvons had basically disappeared from everyday use by the late 1960s, they remained in the collective cultural memory for decades afterward, possessing clear resonance

13. Shodier Mutahharkhonughlu, "Chodradagi aellar," *Movarounakhr musulmonlari*, no. 1 (1992), 9–13. This development was also noted by Western observers: see Carol J. Williams, "Taking an Eager Step Back to Islam," *Los Angeles Times,* 3 June 1995.

as a defining feature of the Uzbek people. In the early post-Soviet period, therefore, wearing a veil could easily become—and did, at least for some people—an emblem simultaneously expressive of national autonomy and religious freedom.

To be sure, most veils on the streets of Tashkent in the 1990s were not the same paranjis and chachvons that had been worn in the 1920s, 1930s, and 1940s. Fashions had changed and the skills needed to produce horsehair chachvons had become quite rare. Bazaars in the mid-1990s sold newly made paranjis—a fact remarkable in itself—but it was far more difficult to find a chachvon for sale. If one could be located (it took me months), it was usually decades old and bore such a high price that none but the wealthiest of Uzbek families could afford it. In the post-Soviet era, therefore, most Uzbek women who chose to veil did so by borrowing forms of body and facial coverings from other parts of the Muslim world, such as the much less expensive cotton *hijab* (head covering) and *burqu* (face veil) worn by Egyptian women, a kind of veil that leaves the eyes uncovered. Reveiling in the 1990s, then, was less a return to some primordial past than another layer of the modern reworking of perceived cultural patterns and traditions into a new postcolonial political context. Even as it was used explicitly to express an allegedly timeless piety and national identity, the custom of veiling in Central Asia continued to change and adapt to historical circumstances, as it has done elsewhere in the Islamic world.[14]

Although most Western specialists on Central Asia have stressed the impact of either Soviet or traditional influences in shaping contemporary Uzbekistan, it is better to see this area as a hybrid. The labels "Soviet" and "traditional" may seem self-evident, straightforward, stable, fixed, transparent, or mutually opposed, but they are none of these things. Both, rather, are historically produced, fluid, mutually constructing, and continually shifting categories. Central Asian "tradition," in particular, is best seen as a deeply modern product, an ever-changing construct that draws upon cultural practices and religious precepts and refracts them through the challenges of colonial rule and now postcolonial life. How far, then, did Soviet rule change Uzbekistan? In the end, Uzbek traditions and folkways were variously defended, abandoned, and adjusted to changing times; Uzbeks continually reworked and creatively reimagined their customary practices, investing them with an ever-changing variety of political and moral values and associating them with shifting, even contrary individual and collective identities.

The complex and sometimes contradictory mosaic of social life on display today in what the Uzbek president, Islam Karimov, has dubbed the "great state of the future" (*kelajagi buyuk davlat*) thus can be understood only as the

14. Arlene Elowe Macleod, *Accommodating Protest: Working Women, the New Veiling, and Change in Cairo* (New York, 1991); Sherifa Zuhur, *Revealing Reveiling: Islamist Gender Ideology in Contemporary Egypt* (Albany, 1992); and Nilüfer Göle, *The Forbidden Modern: Civilization and Veiling* (Ann Arbor, 1996).

result of the interwoven and overlaid influences of many historical forces and periods. The annual celebration of 8 March, for example, and the continuing valorization of Uzbek women as chemists, historians, dancers, factory workers, and administrators can be explained only by reference to the hard-won successes of the decades-long effort at women's liberation, the effort that was catalyzed and defined by the Bolsheviks' hujum of 1927. Yet the reappearance in 1991 of veils on Uzbek streets as an expression of allegedly traditional but actually newly reconceived national and religio-cultural identities makes sense only as a more unexpected legacy of the hujum. Above all, the modern use of veils as a resurrected national talisman reflects the profound linkage between deep social and cultural identities, on the one hand, and patterns of gendered behavior, on the other, a linkage that the Communist Party's actions in the 1920s and 1930s helped to establish. The resulting complexities have helped to produce the rich matrix of possibilities from which Uzbek men and women today draw their conceptual and cultural vocabularies. Their practical options continue to be shaped by these contradictory historical legacies—legacies that will both constrain and enable developments in Uzbekistan for years to come.

REPORT ON THE WOMEN'S MOVEMENT IN UZBEKISTAN
(20 June 1928)
Based on district-level OGPU materials. Top secret.

State of the [Campaign] Work

After some successes in the women's liberation effort, as shown in the results of the 8 March campaign, this work has notably weakened in recent weeks, and in some locales has stopped completely. This [trend], which has strengthened in connection with the counteragitation of anti-Soviet elements, has come to such a pass that the achievements of the women's liberation campaign in the localities have been reduced to nil.

About the state of work among women in the localities (to put it more accurately, about the absence of such work) [consider] the following materials received from the districts.

In New Chirchik region (Tashkent district) no work at all among women is under way. Both the director of the Zhenotdel and its workers in the party regional committee are equally negligent in this matter. No family circles have been created. In the village of Yangi-Kel'dy a girls' Komsomol cell was organized, but it existed only briefly due to the lack of attention it received from the local organization; the cell met only twice and then disbanded. This situation is seen not only in the villages with an Uzbek population but also in the Russian villages; consider the fact that in Soldat village, the female activist Okuchnikova tried to create a women's circle, but no one helped her and she was forced to abandon women's work.

Struggle against qalin and polygyny is completely absent.

In Shahrisabz region (Qashqadaryo province), not more than 20 of 200 unveiled women attend women's meetings; the others in recent days do not even show themselves on the street. Efforts to draw them to meetings, to reading rooms and clubs are lacking. Zhenotdel workers are not developed politically and have no experience.

In the localities work among women is as absent as it formerly was. Women's circles are not organized. Women's artels (in Zerafshon province) are organized, but poorly.

One month ago in the village soviet no. 10 of Vaganzin district (in the Bogouetdin region of Bukhoro province) almost all women were unveiled. In recent days, however, due to the absence of educational work approximately 80 percent of the women have again veiled themselves. If educational work among women is not carried out, there are grounds to suppose that the process of reveiling among women will accelerate.

Counteragitation by Anti-Soviet Groups in the Village

These facts are characteristic of almost all districts. From the materials at hand it is obvious that almost all work among women has come to nothing. Making use of this, anti-Soviet groups (clergy, bois, merchants, and others) raised their heads and are beginning to carry out their "work," the result of which is, as a rule, the reveiling of women.

The main motives given by these groups in their agitation against the unveiling of women have been:

- The liberation of women concerns only party members and Soviet workers—"let them unveil their own wives."
- To unveil women is to go over to the Russian belief [Orthodoxy]. It is nowhere stated in the Muslim holy books that we are to unveil our wives, and [therefore] if you unveil your wives, God will punish you (Andijon and other districts).
- The state will make them (i.e., unveiled women) into prostitutes, and will do with them as it pleases.
- The goal of unveiling is to make a woman abandon her husband. Unveiled women throw off their husbands and thanks to this many peasant men are left without wives, while the women become prostitutes.
- Women should not be permitted to attend meetings, because there they become Russified and lose their conscience and honor. Besides this, some unveiled women have been mobilized into the army (Qashqadaryo province).

It is characteristic that in some localities (Andijon, Qashqadaryo provinces) the bois and clergy, in their agitation against state measures taken to liberate women, characterize them as measures designed to destroy the Uzbek nationality. "Unveiled women lose their nationality along with the paranji, and cease to be Uzbek women (Andijon province)." "The Uzbek nation, by comparison with others, is very small, and under the existing [state] order Uzbeks, like other nationalities, will not [any longer] be visible in the country (Qashqadaryo province)."

Spreading Provocative Rumors and Intimidation

In order more strongly to intimidate the population, with the aim of distracting it from the liberation of women, the clergy and bois are agitating about the ostensibly rapid fall of Soviet power and about the coming of the English and the Afghans. Thus, one of the merchants of Paishanba village (Zerafshon province), Khoji Rozikov, agitates: "Bosmachi are now being organized, soon the English and the Afghan emir will come; Soviet power will be badly off, because it forces the paranji from our wives, [an act] which God will punish according to the law."

An inhabitant of the Old City of Andijon, Nigmetulla Khoji-Akhunov, judged the measures taken by the state to liberate women by saying, "It is bad that Soviet power is unveiling women and forcing them to violate [illegible]. But never mind—England is already concentrating its forces on the borders and soon will attack Soviet power."

Insulting and Attacking Unveiled Women

Not stopping at intimidation and simple agitation against women's liberation, bois and the clergy have already used methods of insults and attacks against already unveiled women, with the goal of forcing these women once again to don the paranji. This is done through the men who are under their influence, as if spontaneously, in meetings on the street, at official gatherings, etc., where unveiled women are subjected to insults and [illegible] from these elements in the presence of the population at large. Thus, in the Old City of Katta-Qorghon (Zerafshon province), the unveiled activist women's worker Nasretdinova was walking on the street, gathering women together for a meeting. She met the clergyman Khalim Abdul Sufi Zalilov on the street, and in the presence of the people he cursed her with an uncensored tongue and declared: "Whatever you do at home affects only the women busy with you in the household. [But] if you come again into our neighborhood, then you will be expelled."

And Rozyq Hamidov, an inhabitant of the Old City of Katta-Qorghon, beat his wife, Iram-Oi, unmercifully because she had attended a meeting, and warned her that if she repeated her action, she would be killed. In the same manner Tagai Ishbaev, from Raikulya village (Narpai region, Zerafshon province), beat his sister severely because she, against his wishes, had unveiled.

In the village of Faizabad (Qashqadaryo province), the boi Ruzi-Murad Boi Muradov beat his relative Nar-Bibi-Oi Bekbulatova harshly because she wanted to throw off the paranji. Threatening her with murder, he forced her to swear an oath renouncing her decision. The victim complained about him to the village soviet, but the latter did nothing about the boi.

Sadykboi Yusupbaev, Rakhman Mirasulev, and Usman Kazashbaev, inhabitants of Fazyl'man village (Qorghon Tepe region, Andijon province) and opponents of women's liberation, while drunk grabbed the unveiled woman Pashahon Azizova on the street and began in all possible ways to mock her, calling her a prostitute, etc.

Sultan Murad Iskanderov, an inhabitant of Guldrau village, Namangan region, Andijon province, bursting into the home of the peasant woman Tursun-Bibi Urunbaeva (an unveiled woman and member of the village soviet), tried to rape her. Hearing Urunbaeva's shouts, a 50-year-old man ran in, grabbed hold of Iskanderov, and hauled him off to the village soviet. The president of the village soviet, Bekmanbaev, together with the teacher Kholmirzaev, took a bribe from Iskanderov and freed him. Moreover, at Iskanderov's behest they threatened Urunbaeva with arrest and forced her to sign a statement saying that she would have no [further] complaints against him.

These facts show in detail how lower-level Soviet workers have acted in the campaign for women's liberation. Those who are obligated to struggle relentlessly against all manifestations of hostility toward unveiled women are, on the contrary, very often hiding the opponents of women's liberation. These circumstances are enormously important in emboldening [our opponents]; they are in some cases moving from methods of agitation, insults, and assault into full-fledged terror toward those women who dared to transgress the "law" by throwing off the paranji.

Murder of Unveiled Women

In a comparatively short period of time (the past two to three months), Khorazm province alone has seen twelve cases of women being murdered. In Tashkent province there were eight such cases, in Zerafshon province there were two, etc. It is characteristic that in many cases where women are murdered, the actual murderer (the husband, the brother) gives purely familial reasons as the motive for the murder (jealousy, family squabbles, etc.), repudiating political reasons for the murder. But the circumstances in which these murders were carried out (in most cases the victim is either an unveiled woman or a woman who intended to unveil) give grounds to assert that not merely family relations were behind them. These murders were without a doubt, objectively, the "work" of groups hostile to us, groups against the liberation of women—which can be seen from the immediate results of this "work."

On 8 June the unveiled woman Abdan-Bibi was murdered by her husband in Zengi-Ota village, Yangi-Yol region, Tashkent province. She had been an activist, and the Communist cell called her to work in a women's shop. Her husband, Nur-Ali Hasanov, demanded that she not wear a European dress, but she did not agree. They separated. Nur-Ali made a few attempts to force his wife to return to him, but when he saw that his attempts would not succeed, he stabbed her to death. He declared to investigators that he had killed his wife for reasons of jealousy, having caught her with lovers. Another case was in Samarqand province: on 5 June in the village of Sarak-Tepe, Urgut region, the unveiled woman Chuchuk-Oi Djurabaeva was killed. Her husband's brother, Majit Baratov (12 years old), killed her under the influence of a local boi named Umar (the uncle of the deceased). The reason was her removal of the paranji. In Zerafshon province, a peasant named Mardan, living in the village of Uzum, Narpai region, strangled his wife and her mother. The reason: unveiling and the desire to divorce him. In Khorazm province a peasant, Sultan Artykov (Eski-Bagat village, Bagat region), killed his wife, according to his own testimony because she had wanted to leave him. In the same region a peasant in the village of Tadji, Madamin Matchanov, killed his wife with an ax because she quarreled with him and left to return to her father. In the same region of Bagat, another peasant in the village of Alys, Egamberdi Baldirakhmanov, killed his wife and her mother. The reason: she had demanded a divorce (according to him).

Party Members' Attitude [toward the Campaign]

It is not at all uncommon for party members not merely to cover for opponents of women's liberation (this was discussed above), but for themselves to struggle directly against liberation. This is supported by many facts, the most characteristic of which are given below:

- In the city of Nur-Ata (Zerafshon province) a family evening was held at which, in accordance with a resolution of the local party cell, all party members were obliged to attend together with their wives. Some of the party members reacted negatively to this arrangement, did not appear there and did not permit their wives [to attend]. Among these party members were: EPO shop director Tura Khojaev, the policemen Saragul Saibov, Tura Rajabov, and others.
- In Chirak region (Qashqadaryo province), the party members Yoldash Tyuchi, Haidar Yoldashev, Said Nazarov, Khol-Murad Makhamadiev, Shadman Berdiev, and others forced their wives, who had unveiled earlier, once again to wear the paranji.
- The president of the Sultanobod village credit society (Andijon province), Mirabdullaev, through various threats forced his wife, Maksud-Hon, once again to wear the paranji and forbade her to attend school. Other unveiled women followed Maksud-Hon's [example] and again put on the paranji: the wife of the EPO store director, Tash-Tamirov, and others. The party cell did nothing in reaction to this event.
- In a drunken state the police chief Mirzaev (Aim region, Andijon province) broke into the home of Ishan-Hon Sarymsakova, a peasant of Aim village, with the aim of raping her; she had recently unveiled and was an active women's worker and candidate member of the party.
- It was suggested to the union member Abu-Bakir Kholmatov (an inhabitant of the Old City of Andijon) that he unveil his wife in order to serve as an example

to others. Kholmatov responded that his wife would never unveil, since all unveiled women became prostitutes. After this Kholmatov agitated among the population against women's liberation, for the reasons already listed.

- A female inhabitant of the Old City of Andijon, Mastur-hon, expressed a desire
to unveil and to enter the Komsomol. The president of the mahalla commission, the Komsomol member Usmanov, found out about this and protested
against her unveiling, declaring that he, Usmanov, was an opponent of
women's liberation and would fight against it. The result was that Mastur-hon
herself and another woman whom she had persuaded to unveil remained under
the paranji.

- The party member Tash-Temir Qosimov (an inhabitant of Zarkent village,
Yangi-Qorghon region, Andijon province) went with his wife on a pilgrimage to
the Safi-Bulan tomb during the Qurbon holiday [the Muslim Festival of the Sac-
rifice]. He covered her [during this trip]. Other unveiled women, seeing this,
again started to wear the paranji, saying, "Why are the wives of party members
veiling themselves? We can all [therefore] wear the paranji."

Bungling and Distortions of the [Party] Line

Together with the absence of any work in the sphere of women's liberation, in some localities as usual there are cases of bungling by workers, showing an absolute lack of understanding of this question. Thus, in Narpai region (Zerafshon province), the *vakil*
[representative] of Tugai Rabat village, Kholmat Tukhtaev, and the secretary of the village soviet, Klich Muminov, gathered women at a meeting, threatening them with hunting rifles if they did not attend. Women testified [to this] in a statement to the district
executive committee.

The Komsomol member Faizy Yoldashev (an inhabitant of Khoja-Qorghon village,
Khatir region, Zerafshon province) declared at one of the meetings in his village: "If the
good women are going to be unveiled, then we can have a [bazaar] with them."

The president of the Buston village soviet (Bogouetdin region, Bukhoro province)
called several inhabitants of Kasri Ashurak village to see him—the old qörbosh Gha-
furov Qurbon, Turdiev, and others—and announced to them that if they did not unveil
their wives, then he would write an official document about them and send it to the
GPU.

Women's Attitude toward Liberation

The mass of women may be divided into three parts according to their attitude toward
the question of liberation. One part (in truth few, consisting principally of the wives of
clerical figures)[1] have a negative attitude toward liberation and deliberately work
against it. For illustration of this situation consider the following fact: "An inhabitant
of Kara-Palvan village (Yangi-Qorghon region, Andijon province), Muriya-Bibi Akhunbaeva, was invited to read holy books at the funerals of women from that village. Making use of [the fact that] more than 100 women gathered at funerals, Muriya-Bibi
started to agitate among them against the removal of the paranji. Hearing of this, the
president of the village soviet wrote her a letter directing her to cease this agitation.

---

1. All types of sorcerers [and] fortune-tellers, who base their material position on women's ignorance and lack of culture. [Footnote in original.]

Muriya-Bibi read this note, threw her chachvon off and began to shriek hysterically, with the goal of exciting a religious mood in the mass and of attracting [them] all the more to her side."

A different group of women, somewhat greater in number, see liberation through the eyes of their husbands. In this [we see] the centuries-old social, economic, and religious structure of village life (a woman as a thing, the property of her husband). Therefore, to speak of strict, definite opinions on the question of liberation in this group is impossible.

And the third group (female farm laborers, wives of poor peasants, wives of farm laborers) have a positive attitude toward the question of liberation and, in the majority of cases, form the women's aktiv, which provide the bedrock of support for women's work in the village. As an example of this evident aktivnost' by women in the village, [consider the following]. The female peasants of Kasri-Ashuk village (Bogouetdin region, Bukhoro province)—Yadgarova, Ghafurova, Artykova, Kurieva, and other (unveiled) women—appeared before the village soviet and declared their dissatisfaction with the fact that the wives of many Soviet workers remained veiled on the street. On the strength of this [poor example] many peasants did not want to unveil their own wives, and besides this, unveiled women felt unsteady in the [face of] continued counteragitation by the bois and clergy.

Sale of Women

The sale and purchase of women in the village continues to flourish as usual. In Zerafshon province alone seven cases of women being sold have been noted during the past two weeks. In Nurat region, an inhabitant of Oqtosh village, Kasam-Mulla Qodyrov, sold a seven-year-old orphan girl, Samam-Oi, to his fellow villager Altyboi Azimov. He received for her three *tanaps* of dry-farming land and an ox. This situation shows how local organs have fought against this problem with insufficient energy.

[signed]
ASTROV   POPOV
(Chair, Uzbek SSR OGPU)   *(Chief, Military Organization)*

SOURCE: PDA, f. 58, op. 4, d. 1235, ll. 83–92.

GLOSSARY

aktiv (Rus.) wide group of people sympathetic to the party's efforts; includes those who are not Communist Party members

aktivnost' (Rus.) energetic work, devotion to the cause

boi (Uzb.) wealthy person or landlord

bosmachi (Uzb.) bandits; used by urban and Soviet observers to describe qörboshi

byt (Rus.) life, everyday life, daily existence

chachvon (Uzb.) face veil, a mesh of woven horsehair to cover face and hair; worn with paranji

chadra (Azer., from Persian *chador*) garment that covers the body; worn by women in Iran and Azerbaijan, among other places; sometimes used by Russians as a general term for "veil" although it does not cover the face

eshon (Uzb.) Sufi master, shaykh

hujum (Uzb.) assault, attack; also name of campaign against female seclusion and veiling

ichkari (Uzb.) women's or inner quarter of house, not accessible to men not closely related to family

ispolkom (ispolnitel'nyi komitet) (Rus.) executive committee, part of Soviet government

jadid (Uzb.) new; Muslim reform movement in nineteenth- and early twentieth-century tsarist empire

khalat (Uzb.) ceremonial robe

kofir (Uzb.) infidel, unbeliever

Komsomol (Rus.) Young Communist League

korenizatsiia (Rus.) rooting, indigenization, nativization; Bolshevik nationalities policy in 1920s, intended to give Soviet power an indigenous face, particularly by training non-Russians for positions of state and party authority

mahalla (Uzb.) urban neighborhood, especially in Muslim Old Cities

murid (Uzb.) Sufi adept; disciple of a Sufi shaykh

mursak (Uzb.) female veil that predated paranji and chachvon in southern Central Asia

odat (Uzb.) customary law

OGPU (Ob"edinennoe gosudarstvennoe politicheskoe upravlenie) (Rus.) Soviet secret police, 1922–34; later known as NKVD

otin (Uzb.) female Muslim teacher

paranji (Uzb.) body covering or veil, a long cotton robe with false sleeves; drapes over head and holds chachvon in place

proverka (Rus.) verification; carried out by a committee (*proverkom*) that checked and winnowed party membership rolls

qadimists (Uzb.) from *qadimchi,* proponent of old ways, old-fashioned, traditional; conservative Muslim scholars of the ulamo; opposed to reformist jadids

qalin (Uzb.) bride-price; a payment from the groom's family to that of the bride, also expressive of moral and familial bonds

qörboshi (Uzb.) title of prerevolutionary military and police officers in Turkestan and Bukhoro; self-ascription of anti-Soviet bosmachi rebels

qozi (Uzb.) Islamic religious judge

raikom (Rus.) district committee; lower-level party organization

Ramazon (Uzb.) Muslim holy month of Ramadan; concludes with feast (Hayit Ramazon)

shariat (Uzb.) Islamic law

sovchi (Uzb.) matchmaker

Sredazbiuro (Rus.) the party's Central Asian Bureau, based in Tashkent; its chief regional supervisory body

ulamo (Uzb.) ulama; the group of Muslim theologians and scholars responsible for preserving, protecting, and transmitting religious knowledge

yashmak (Turkm.) head covering worn by Turkmen women over hair and mouth

ZAGS (Zapis' aktov grazhdanskogo sostoianiia) (Rus.) Soviet civil registry office

Zhenotdel (Rus.) the party's Women's Department; founded 1919, replaced in 1930 by Zhensektor, or Women's Section

NOTE ON SOURCES

Uzbek women and men responded to the hujum in an enormous range of ways, expressing themselves in overlapping, clashing keys of vociferous support as well as bitter resistance. Decoding these responses requires careful attention to immediate context and particular audience, as well as—where such information is available—the personal histories and sympathies, political and cultural affiliations, and familial, social, and class positions of the people involved. As historians and linguistic anthropologists have shown, it also requires attention to the source frame in which such utterances have been preserved.[1]

This book draws on a broad range of archival and published sources, written from a wide variety of institutional, personal, and political perspectives. Most of these documents are in either Uzbek or Russian, and originated inside the USSR during the 1920s, 1930s, and 1940s; a much smaller quantity, in Turkish and other European languages, comes from outside the USSR. While I use the Uzbek- and Russian-language press (especially *Pravda Vostoka,* the party's newspaper of record in Central Asia), draw on contemporary books and pamphlets, and have gathered a limited number of personal testimonies and oral reminiscences, this book relies above all on almost two years of work in the rich archival collections of Tashkent and Moscow. These collections yield many internal, classified reports prepared by and for party organizations and government bodies at the local, provincial, republican, and regional levels; hundreds of unpublished photographs, newsreels, and feature films; and tens of thousands of pages of judicial records, administrative materials, policy debates, scientific reports, propaganda efforts, and letters and petitions from Soviet citizens. Many are used here for the first time.

Taken together and read with care, these archival materials reveal a rich and nuanced portrait of the complex, ongoing interplay between Soviet power and Uzbek society. But readers should note that this source base has weaknesses as well as strengths; these materials are neither perfect nor transparent, and to some degree they shape the kind of story I am able to tell. For example, although I have tried to hear and incorporate the voices of Uzbek men and women whenever possible, the Soviet provenance of most of my sources makes it more difficult to see the world through Uzbek eyes. The challenges of using the Stalinist periodical press of the 1930s are obvious and well known, but issues of authorship, audience, perspective, selection, and purpose also cloud the most highly classified archival materials, just as they complicate the deceptively straightforward photographic records of everyday life. (Such images were often created for specific purposes, and sometimes they reproduce stereotypes more accu-

---

1. Judith T. Irvine, "Shadow Conversations: The Indeterminacy of Participant Roles," in *Natural Histories of Discourse,* ed. Michael Silverstein and Greg Urban (Chicago, 1996), 131–59, especially 135.

rately than they reflect daily life.)² Statistical data, too, are fraught with special difficulties, owing both to the conscious manipulations or fabrications of their compilers and the shortcomings of Soviet intelligence gathering. Finally, for institutional reasons Soviet secret police summaries, such as the OGPU *svodki* I use extensively, may exaggerate popular anti-Soviet attitudes to show the need for a well-staffed and -funded police force.³

These source issues make it especially difficult to isolate the unfiltered voices of what was a largely rural, illiterate Uzbek society. (The census of 1926 found an aggregate literacy level among Uzbek men of 6.5 percent, for example, and among Uzbek women a level of only 1.0 percent.)⁴ This issue bedevils all historians who study groups with no or few written records: early Native Americans, for instance, or many peasants, some ancient or medieval societies, or children. In the case of modern non-Western societies, postcolonial scholars have further pointed out that when imperial archives exist, they of course preserve imperial records, so the documents they house must be seen as expressions of the institutional interests, social audiences, conceptual languages, and political perspectives of the metropolitan state and its personnel. The result, for some theorists, is a "pregnant silence" of the archive, in Gayatri Spivak's trenchant phrase, in which these documents represent a wall beyond which it is difficult or impossible to go. Indigenous women's voices, in particular, can be seen as being multiply overdetermined, by patriarchy as well as imperialism, and thus now virtually impossible to retrieve.⁵ Yet other scholars of modern empires have found ways to read between the lines of imperial documents, using them in creative and sophisticated ways to extract fresh information and yield new insights. In this regard I take particular inspiration from the remarkable studies of South Asia that have been carried out by the Subaltern Studies Collective, led by Ranajit Guha.⁶ Even Spivak sometimes appears to agree, noting that these official sources show what she calls a "subaltern subject-effect": the view that underneath the sentiments, language, and categories of colonial authorities and

2. Until at least the 1930s, most photographers in Central Asia were non-Muslim outsiders who selected or posed certain images to the exclusion of others. I use some photographs that have a clear propaganda function (such as the image of heroic unveiling); others betray a continuing Orientalist fascination with the East. Sometimes the two motivations merge. Most of the images I use, though, were never published, not least because they contradicted official views, as by showing persistent veiling. While this officially unwelcome content does not make them transparent glimpses of everyday life, it does indicate that in some respects they were less staged to serve state interests. See Graham-Brown, *Images of Women;* Erika Billeter, *Usbekistan: Dokumentarfotografie 1925–1945 von Max Penson* (Bern, 1996); or Ergun Çagatay, *Bir Zamanlar Orta Asya* (Istanbul, 1996).

3. See Sarah Davies, *Popular Opinion in Stalin's Russia: Terror, Propaganda and Dissent, 1934–1941* (Cambridge, 1997); and R. C. Cobb, *The Police and the People: French Popular Protest, 1789–1820* (Oxford, 1970), 3–48. See also the special issues of *Cahiers du monde russe* 40, no. 1–2 (1999); *Kritika* 1, no. 1 (2000); and *Russian Review* 61, no. 1 (2002).

4. These figures are more expressive than exact. But rural literacy was even lower, being officially reported at 3.2 percent and 0.3 percent for Uzbek men and women, respectively. By comparison, 76 percent of Russian men living in Uzbekistan and almost 58 percent of Russian women in the republic were categorized as "literate" (ÖzRMDA, f. 86, op. 1, d. 5884, l. 45).

5. Spivak makes this case most fully in "Can the Subaltern Speak?" especially on pp. 299–304.

6. See the annual *Subaltern Studies.* Another good example—and a model for this study—is Mani, *Contentious Traditions.*

elites, these documents also record and are partly shaped by the actions and will of colonized subjects.[7]

Such a perspective is well suited to Uzbekistan. The newly open archives present an enormous treasure-trove: many millions of documents are now available for perusal. Many of those I use here—such as confidential reports by the secret police and party investigators, an example of which is provided in the appendix—were obviously expressed in and shaped by the pervasive frames of Soviet language and ideology. They therefore can be read both straightforwardly and, as I try to read them, against the grain of their intended use. This approach includes reading as much for what they do not say as for what they wish to express. Reading Soviet reports in this manner can reveal much about their authors, but it also sheds an oblique light on their stated subject: Uzbek society. Yet a startling number turn out not to require such legerdemain, having been written with surprising candor about Bolshevik failings and self-doubts. They make a real effort to engage with, listen to, and transcribe Uzbek voices, even as they categorize, summarize, and classify them according to the party's priorities. Further, as several chapters of this book show, a wide range of other, often unappreciated materials confirm important elements of the stories they tell.

Finally, few if any other sources can do better. Certainly none offers unvarnished, unmediated access to the words—much less the thoughts—of ordinary Uzbeks. Where else might one look? The two most obvious and accessible alternatives are the Uzbek-language press and the views of top Uzbek leaders. While most Soviet publications, especially before the mid-1930s, appeared in Russian, I also use the Uzbek-language press: an array of books, pamphlets, and magazines, as well as key newspapers such as *Qizil Özbekiston*. Especially valuable are the women's journals published by the Uzbek party—*Jangi jol* (1924–34), *Jarqin turmush* (1936–37), *Jarqin hajat* or *Erqin haët* (1938–41), and the later *Özbekiston khotin-qizlari* (1950–66), renamed *Saodat* (1966–). Some Uzbeks, too—men such as Akmal Ikramov and Usman Yusupov, first secretaries of the Uzbek party, and Faizulla Khojaev and Yoldosh Akhunbabaev, presidents of the Uzbek SSR, and women such as the Zhenotdel leader Tojikhon Shadieva—served in highly visible positions of Soviet authority, while many more were lower-level activists. Other Uzbeks also vocally supported the Bolshevik cause, such as the writer Hamza Hakimzoda Niyoziy, who married a Russian woman and received prominent coverage in the Soviet media until (and after) his violent death in 1929. Who were these people? What did they want? Why did they support, or at least appear to support, the Bolshevik cause? They helped shape the hujum and other Soviet policies, and thus played a vital role in defining Soviet power in Central Asia. Fortunately many of their speeches and articles, both published and unpublished, have survived. Local profiles, membership applications, and internal investigations, too, offer much information on rank-and-file Uzbek Communists.

The Uzbek press and Uzbek Communists are both important, and I use these sources accordingly. Yet they are limited, and it would be misleading to see either as a window into Uzbek society as a whole. The Uzbek-language Soviet press was, after all, Soviet. It certainly was not identical to the Russian-language press, but it was produced under similar circumstances by many of the same small minority of political activists and for that reason needs to be read with the same cautions. Indeed, Uzbek-language

7. See her "Subaltern Studies: Deconstructing Historiography," in *Selected Subaltern Studies*, ed. Guha and Spivak (New York, 1988), 13.

Soviet publications, because of their public character and didactic function, are in many ways less revealing than archival sources. And the actively pro-Bolshevik forces in Central Asia were a tiny, almost invisible minority during this period: total party membership in Uzbekistan amounted to much less than 1 percent of the republic's population in 1928, and even that figure includes local Russians, not just indigenous groups.[8] Before privileging Uzbek Communists as the voice of Muslim society, therefore, one needs to keep this social position in perspective.

Other feasible ways to find an Uzbek voice would be to locate an alternate body of sources, to carry out oral histories, or to detect such voices within the Soviet materials. Some émigré publications are available, but they generally were published in the West as polemical attacks on the USSR and are strongly colored by a Turkestani nationalist agenda.[9] Oral history is possible, albeit difficult: seventy years of Soviet mythology regarding the hujum has left its mark. In my experience, many elderly Uzbek men and women now frame their reminiscences by the official story of liberation or unconsciously repeat it. As they do so, some of the complications and nuances that are evident in the contemporary archival and published sources disappear. Oral interviews can be and have been used, most effectively by the historian Marianne Kamp in conversations with former activists and other Uzbek women who played active roles in generating the Soviet narrative of liberation. But although valuable, their stories most effectively illuminate the views of only a small group of Soviet sympathizers, not the vast majority of Uzbek men and women.[10] That leaves the third alternative, reading between the lines of Soviet sources in an attempt to isolate Uzbek perspectives alongside or underneath Soviet interpretations of them. It is an admittedly imperfect method, but still one, as I hope the book shows, that is useful in seeking to understand Central Asian society.

8. The Uzbek party had 34,028 members in July 1928 (ÖzRMDA, f. 86, op. 2, d. 27, l. 34). As we have seen, moreover, many of these Communists did not act in support of party policies on women's liberation.

9. For example, see the work of Baymirza Hayit, including "Turkestan as an Example of Soviet Colonialism," *Studies on the Soviet Union* 1, no. 2 (1961): 78–95; or *Sowjetrussischer Kolonialismus und Imperialismus in Turkestan* (Oosterhout, Netherlands, 1965).

10. Marianne Kamp, "Three Lives of Saodat: Communist, Uzbek, Survivor," *Oral History Review* 28, no. 2 (2001), 21–58. Here and in her other work Kamp tries as far as possible to rely on Uzbek women's voices. She does so by drawing heavily on the Bolshevik Uzbek-language periodical press and on oral historical interviews conducted in the 1990s. But this approach, as Kamp herself admits, best captures the views of only a small number of Uzbek women, those with pro-Bolshevik sympathies, generally higher levels of literacy, and frequently careers as political activists (Kamp, "Unveiling Uzbek Women," 18).

SELECTED BIBLIOGRAPHY

Archival Sources

TASHKENT

Özbekiston respublikasi kinofotofonohujjatlar markaziy davlat arkhivi (ÖzRKFFHMDA)
   Still photographs and documentary films

Özbekiston respublikasi markaziy davlat arkhivi (ÖzRMDA)
   f. 6, op. 2 Upravlenie upolnomochennogo NK RKI SSSR v Srednei Azii
   f. 9, op. 1 Sredne-aziatskii ekonomicheskii sovet
   f. 86, op. 1, 2, 10 TsIK UzSSR
   f. 94, op. 1, 5 Narkompros UzSSR
   f. 95, op. 1 NK RKI UzSSR
   f. 245, op. 1 TsK soiuza "Koshchi" UzSSR
   f. 736, op. 1, 3 Sredneaziatskoe biuro VTsSPS
   f. 737, op. 1 Sovet professional'nykh soiuzov UzSSR
   f. 837, op. 2, 3, 6, 8–10, 13–16, 23, 32 Sovet narodnykh komissarov UzSSR
   f. 904, op. 1, 8, 10, 12, 13, 18 Narkomiust UzSSR
   f. 1714, op. 5, 6, 8 Verkhovnyi sud UzSSR
   f. 2454, op. 1 Prezidium verkhovnogo soveta UzSSR

Prezident devoni arkhivi (PDA)[1]
   f. 58, op. 1–18 TsK KP(b)Uz
   f. 60, op. 1

MOSCOW

Gosudarstvennyi arkhiv Rossiisskoi Federatsii (GARF)
   f. 1235, op. 120, 122, 123, 130 Otdel natsional'nostei VTsIK
   f. 3316, op. 50 TsIK SSSR: Vsesoiuznoe soveshchanie komissii po uluchsheniiu truda i byta zhenshchin Vostoka
   f. 6983, op. 1 Komitet po uluchsheniiu truda i byta zhenshchin rabotnits i krestianok pri prezidium VTsIK RSFSR
   f. 8131, op. 37 Prokuratora SSSR

Rossiisskii gosudarstvennyi arkhiv kinofotodokumentov (RGAKFD)
   Still photographs and documentary films

---

1. PDA is currently closed. As noted in the text, I am grateful to several colleagues for providing archival typescripts and notes.

Rossiisskii gosudarstvennyi arkhiv sotsial'no-politicheskoi istorii (RGASPI)
   f. 62, op. 1–4 Sredneaziatskoe biuro TsK VKP(b)
   f. 81, op. 3 Kaganovich, L. M. (lichnyi fond)
   f. 507, op. 1, 2 Mezhdunarodnyi zhenskii sekretariat Kominterna
   f. M-1, op. 2 TsK VLKSM

UNITED STATES

Anahita Gallery (Santa Fe, N.M.)
   Still photographs

Published Primary Sources

SELECTED CONTEMPORARY PERIODICALS

Uzbek-language periodicals
   Jangi jol
   Jarqin hajat (*Erqin haët*)
   Jarqin turmush (*Erqin turmush*)
   Özbekiston khotin-qizlari (later *Saodat*)
   Qizil Özbekiston
Russian-language periodicals
   Antireligioznik
   Bezbozhnik
   Biulleten' otdela rabotnits i dekhkanok Sredazbiuro TsK RKP(b)
   Bol'shevik Kazakhstana
   Izvestiia TsK RKP(b)
   Izvestiia TsK VKP(b)
   Izvestiia TsK VLKSM
   Kommunistka
   Krest'ianka
   Meditsinskaia mysl' Uzbekistana
   Novyi Vostok
   Ogonëk
   Pravda
   Pravda Vostoka
   Rabotnitsa
   Revoliutsiia i kul'tura
   Revoliutsiia i natsional'nosti
   Sem' dnei
   *Sobranie uzakonenii i rasporiazhenii rabochego i dekhkanskogo pravitel'stva
      UzSSR*
   Sotsialisticheskaia zakonnost'
   Sovetskoe gosudarstvo i pravo
   Sovetskoe pravo
   Sudebnaia praktika RSFSR
   Vestnik iustitsii Uzbekistana
   Vestnik Tsentral'nogo muzeia Kazakhstana

Vlast' Sovetov
Za partiiu
Zhizn' natsional'nostei

CONTEMPORARY BOOKS AND PAMPHLETS

Aliev, M. *Parandji ötmishning sarqiti.* Tashkent, 1953.

Arslanova, Loliakhan. *Uzbechki.* Moscow and Leningrad, 1926.

Chernysheva, A. *Chto dala zhenshchine Vostoka Oktiabr'skaia revoliutsiia.* Tashkent, 1926.

Dobrosmyslov, A. I. *Tashkent v proshlom i nastoiashchem: Istoricheskii ocherk.* Tashkent, 1912.

Docheri revoliutsii. Moscow, 1923.

Gershenovich, Rafail Samoilovich. *Paranji—khotinlar soghligining ashaddiy dushmani.* Tashkent, 1950.

——. *Perezhitki starogo byta i ikh vred dlia zdorov'ia.* Tashkent, 1940.

Halle, Fannina W. *Women in the Soviet East.* London, 1938.

Hughes, Langston. *A Negro Looks at Soviet Central Asia.* Moscow and Leningrad, 1934.

Iusupov, Usman. *Otchetnyi doklad VIII S"ezdu Kommunisticheskoi partii (bol'shevikov) Uzbekistana o rabote TsK KP(b)Uz: 2 iiulia 1938 goda.* Tashkent, 1938.

Kasparova, V. R. *Zhenshchina Vostoka.* Leningrad, 1925.

Kisch, Egon Erwin. *Changing Asia.* New York, 1935.

Klimovich, Liutsan Ippolitovich. *Doloi parandzhu!* Moscow, 1940.

——. *Islam i zhenshchina.* Moscow, 1958.

Kunitz, Joshua. *Dawn over Samarkand: The Rebirth of Central Asia.* New York, 1935.

Larin, Iu. *Evrei i antisemitizm v SSSR.* Moscow and Leningrad, 1929.

Liubimova, Serafima Timofeevna. *Dnevnik zhenotdelki.* Tashkent, 1926.

——. *Kommunist! Esli ty ne khochesh', chtoby narod vymiral, esli ty deistvitel'no zabotish'sia o razvitii narodnogo khoziaistva i kul'tury, esli ty ne bai, ne mulla i ne podderzhivaesh' mull i baev—ty dolzhen rabotat' po raskreposhcheniiu zhenshchin.* Tashkent, 1925.

——. *Sdvigi.* Tashkent, 1925.

Maillart, Ella K. *Turkestan Solo: One Woman's Expedition from the Tien Shan to the Kizil Kum.* London, 1938.

Materialy k otchetu Tsentral'nogo Komiteta KP (bol.) Uzbekistana V-mu Partiinomu kurultaiu. Samarqand, 1930.

Moskalev, V. *Uzbechka.* Moscow, 1928.

Mukhitdinova, Emine. *Revoliutsionnaia zakonnost' i bytovye prestupleniia na Vostoke.* Moscow and Leningrad, 1929.

Niurina, Fanni Efimovna. *Parandzha.* Moscow and Leningrad, 1928.

Nukhrat, Antonina Ivanovna. *Oktiabr' i zhenshchina Vostoka.* Moscow and Leningrad, 1927.

Paranchi va cacvan azadlik dushmani. Tashkent, 1940.

Pervyi s"ezd trudiashcheisia zhenskoi molodezhi Uzbekistana. Tashkent, 1936.

Rezoliutsii III partiinogo kurultaia. Samarqand, 1927.

Rezoliutsii Uzbekskogo Soveshchaniia rabotnikov sredi rabotnits i dekhkanok. Tashkent, 1929.

Smirnov, Nikolai Aleksandrovich. *Chadra (Proiskhozhdenie pokryvala musul'man-skoi zhenshchiny i bor'ba s nim)*. Moscow, 1929.
Sredneaziatskoe 6-e kraevoe soveshchanie rabotnikov sredi zhenshchin. Tashkent, 1928.
Sredniaia Aziia v tsifrakh. Tashkent, 1931.
Stalin, Iosif. *Sochineniia*. 13 vols. Moscow, 1946–53.
Strong, Anna Louise. *Red Star in Samarkand*. New York, 1929.
Trud i byt zhenshchiny Vostoka: Materialy Vsesoiuznogo soveshchaniia komissii po uluchsheniiu byta zhenshchin Vostoka. Moscow, 1928.
Vaillant-Couturier, Paul. *Free Soviet Tadjikistan*. Moscow and Leningrad, 1932.
Vámbéry, Arminius. *Sketches of Central Asia*. London, 1868.
——. *Travels in Central Asia: Being the Account of a Journey from Teheran across the Turkoman Desert on the Eastern Shore of the Caspian to Khiva, Bokhara, and Samarcand Performed in the Year 1863*. New York, 1865.
Vasilevskii, Kazimir. *Islam na sluzhbe kontr-revoliutsii*. Moscow, 1930.
Vsesouiznaia perepis' naseleniia 17 dekabria 1926 g. 59 vols. Moscow, 1927–29.
Vsesoiuznoe soveshchanie otvetstvennykh sekretarei komissii po uluchsheniiu truda i byta zhenshchin. Moscow, 1930.
Za piat' let. Moscow, 1925.
Zelenskii, I. A. *Za raskreposhchenie zhenshchiny*. Tashkent, 1926.

MODERN EDITIONS

Abdurazakova, Sh., et al., comps. *Kommunisticheskaia partiia Uzbekistana i rabota sredi zhenshchin respubliki (1938–1958 gg.): Sbornik dokumentov i materialov*. Tashkent, 1982.
Almatinskaia, A. *Minuvshee: Vospominaniia*. Tashkent, 1971.
Aminova, Rakhima Khadievna, et al., eds. *Kompartiia Uzbekistana v bor'be za reshenie zhenskogo voprosa v period stroitel'stva sotsializma (1917–1937 gg.): Sbornik dokumentov i materialov*. Tashkent, 1977.
Astapovich, Z. A., et al., eds. *Velikii Oktiabr' i raskreposhchenie zhenshchin Srednei Azii i Kazakhstana (1917–1936 gg.)*. Moscow, 1971.
Danilov, V. P., R. T. Manning, and L. Viola, eds. *Tragediia sovetskoi derevni: Kollektivizatsiia i raskulachivanie. Dokumenty i materialy, 1927–1939*. 5 vols. Moscow, 1998–2004.
Engels, Frederick. *Origin of the Family, Private Property, and the State*. New York, 1972.
Finkel'shtein, I. M., ed. *Probuzhdennye Velikim Oktiabrem: Sbornik ocherkov i vospominanii*. Tashkent, 1961.
Lansdell, Henry. *Through Central Asia*. Nendeln, Liechtenstein, 1978.
Murav'yov, Nikolay. *Journey to Khiva through the Turkoman Country*. London, 1977.
Riddell, John, ed. *To See the Dawn: Baku, 1920—First Congress of the Peoples of the East*. New York, 1993.
Tucker, Robert C., ed. *The Lenin Anthology*. New York, 1975.
Tursunov, Kh. T., et al., eds. *Khudzhum—znachit nastuplenie*. Tashkent, 1987.

Secondary Literature

Abdullaev, T. A., and S. A. Khasanova. *Odezhda uzbekov (XIX–nachala XX v.)*. Tashkent, 1978.

Abdullaeva, A. A., and N. P. Sokolov. "Protiv vrednykh obychaev i traditsii." *Trudy Andizhanskogo gosudarstvennogo pedagogicheskogo instituta* 8 (1961): 92–97.

Abdurakhimova, Nadira A. "The Colonial System of Power in Turkistan." *International Journal of Middle East Studies* 34 (2002): 239–62.

Adams, David Wallace. *Education for Extinction: American Indians and the Boarding School Experience, 1875–1928.* Lawrence, Kans., 1995.

Adas, Michael. *Prophets of Rebellion: Millenarian Protest Movements against the European Colonial Order.* Chapel Hill, 1979.

Ahmed, Leila. *Women and Gender in Islam: Historical Roots of a Modern Debate.* New Haven, 1992.

Akiner, Shirin, ed. *Cultural Change and Continuity in Central Asia.* London, 1991.

Akopian, N. A. "Pervyi s"ezd zhenskoi trudiashcheisia molodezhi Uzbekistana (oktiabr' 1935)." *Nauchnye trudy Tashkentskogo gosudarstvennogo universiteta,* no. 212 (1962), 106–15.

Alimova, Dilorom Agzamovna. *Zhenskii vopros v Srednei Azii: Istoriia izucheniia i sovremennye problemy.* Tashkent, 1991.

Allport, Gordon W., and Leo Postman. *The Psychology of Rumor.* New York, 1965.

Allworth, Edward A. *The Modern Uzbeks: From the Fourteenth Century to the Present: A Cultural History.* Stanford, 1990.

Aminova, Rakhima Khadievna. *Oktiabr' i reshenie zhenskogo voprosa v Uzbekistane.* Tashkent, 1975. Abridged and published in English as *The October Revolution and Women's Liberation in Uzbekistan.* Trans. B. M. Meerovich. Moscow, 1977.

Anderson, Michael R. "Islamic Law and the Colonial Encounter in British India." In *Institutions and Ideologies,* ed. David Arnold and Peter Robb, 165–85. Richmond upon Thames, 1993.

Argenbright, Robert. "Space of Survival: The Soviet Evacuation of Industry and Population in 1941." In *Beyond the Limits: The Concept of Space in Russian History and Culture,* ed. Jeremy Smith, *Studia Historica* 62 (1999): 207–39.

Baberowski, Jörg. "Stalinismus als imperiales Phänomen: Die islamischen Regionen der Sowjetunion, 1920–1941." In *Stalinismus: Neue Forschungen und Konzepte,* ed. Stefan Plaggenborg, 113–50. Berlin, 1998.

———. "Stalinismus an der Peripherie: Das Beispiel Azerbaijan, 1920–1941." In *Stalinismus vor dem zweiten Weltkrieg: Neue Wege der Forschung,* ed. Manfred Hildermeier with Elisabeth Müller-Luckner, 307–35. Munich, 1998.

Bacon, Elizabeth E. *Central Asians under Russian Rule.* Ithaca, 1966.

Bakhtin, Mikhail. *The Dialogic Imagination.* Austin, 1981.

Barkey, Karen, and Mark von Hagen, eds. *After Empire: Multiethnic Societies and Nation-Building.* Boulder, 1997.

Barkun, Michael. *Disaster and the Millennium.* New Haven, 1974.

Baron, Beth. "Unveiling in Early Twentieth-Century Egypt: Practical and Symbolic Considerations." *Middle Eastern Studies* 25 (1989): 370–86.

Baxi, Upendra. " 'The State's Emissary': The Place of Law in Subaltern Studies." *Subaltern Studies* 7 (1992): 247–64.

Beck, Lois, and Nikki Keddie. *Women in the Muslim World.* Cambridge, Mass., 1978.

Becker, Seymour. "Russia between East and West: The Intelligentsia, Russian National Identity, and the Asian Borderlands." *Central Asian Survey* 10, no. 4 (1991): 47–64.

——. *Russia's Protectorates in Central Asia: Bukhara and Khiva, 1865–1924.* Cambridge, Mass., 1968.

Benton, Lauren. *Law and Colonial Cultures: Legal Regimes in World History, 1400–1900.* Cambridge, 2002.

Bhabha, Homi K. *The Location of Culture.* London, 1994.

Bikzhanova, M. A. "Mursak—starinnaia verkhniaia odezhda uzbechek g. Tashkenta." *Trudy AN Tadzhikskoi SSR,* no. 120 (1960), 47–53.

Billeter, Erika. *Usbekistan: Dokumentarfotographie, 1925–1945, von Max Penson.* Bern, 1996.

Bourdieu, Pierre. *Language and Symbolic Power.* Ed. John B. Thompson. Cambridge, Mass., 1991.

——. *The Logic of Practice.* Trans. Richard Nice. Stanford, 1992.

Bowen, John R. *Muslims through Discourse: Religion and Ritual in Gayo Society.* Princeton, 1993.

Buttino, Marco. "Ethnicité et politique dans la guerre civile: À propos du bas-macestvo au Fergana." *Cahiers du monde russe* 38 (1997): 195–222.

——. "Study of the Economic Crisis and Depopulation in Turkestan, 1917–1920." *Central Asian Survey* 9, no. 4 (1990): 59–74.

——, ed. *In a Collapsing Empire: Underdevelopment, Ethnic Conflicts, and Nationalisms in the Soviet Union.* Milan, 1993.

Çagatay, Ergun. *Bir Zamanlar Orta Asya.* Istanbul, 1996.

Carlisle, Donald S. "Modernization, Generations, and the Uzbek Soviet Intelligentsia." In *The Dynamics of Soviet Politics,* ed. Paul Cocks et al., 239–64. Cambridge, Mass., 1976.

Cassiday, Julie. *The Enemy On Trial: Early Soviet Courts on Stage and Screen.* De Kalb, Ill., 2000.

Cavanaugh, Cassandra. "Backwardness and Biology: Medicine and Power in Russian and Soviet Central Asia, 1868–1934." Ph.D. diss., Columbia University, 2001.

Chatterjee, Choi. *Celebrating Women: Gender, Festival Culture, and Bolshevik Ideology, 1910–1939.* Pittsburgh, 2002.

Chatterjee, Partha. *The Nation and Its Fragments: Colonial and Postcolonial Histories.* Princeton, 1993.

Chirkov, Petr Matveevich. *Reshenie zhenskogo voprosa v SSSR (1917–1937gg.).* Moscow, 1978.

Cobb, R. C. *The Police and the People: French Popular Protest, 1789–1820.* Oxford, 1970.

Cohn, Bernard. *An Anthropologist among the Historians.* Delhi, 1987.

Comaroff, John L., and Jean Comaroff. *Of Revelation and Revolution: The Dialectics of Modernity on a South African Frontier.* Chicago, 1997.

Cracraft, James, ed. *Major Problems in the History of Imperial Russia.* Lexington, Mass., 1994.

Crane, Diana. *Fashion and Its Social Agendas: Class, Gender, and Identity in Clothing.* Chicago, 2000.

Critchlow, James. *Nationalism in Uzbekistan: A Soviet Republic's Road to Sovereignty.* Boulder, 1991.

Davies, Sarah. *Popular Opinion in Stalin's Russia: Terror, Propaganda, and Dissent, 1934–1941.* Cambridge, 1997.

Dirks, Nicholas B., ed. *Colonialism and Culture*. Ann Arbor, 1992.

Edgar, Adrienne. "The Creation of Soviet Turkmenistan, 1924–1938." Ph.D. diss., University of California, Berkeley, 1999.

Fanon, Frantz. *Black Skin, White Masks*. New York, 1967.

———. *Studies in a Dying Colonialism*. New York, 1965.

Fathi, Habiba. "*Otines:* The Unknown Women Clerics of Central Asian Islam." *Central Asian Survey* 16, no. 1 (1997): 27–43.

Fierman, William, ed. *Soviet Central Asia: The Failed Transformation*. Boulder, 1991.

Firth, Raymond. "Rumor in a Primitive Society." *Journal of Abnormal and Social Psychology* 53 (1956): 122–32.

Fitzpatrick, Sheila. *Stalin's Peasants: Resistance and Survival in the Russian Village after Collectivization*. New York, 1994.

Frierson, Cathy A. *Peasant Icons: Representations of Rural People in Late Nineteenth-Century Russia*. New York, 1993.

Gerth, Karl. "Nationalizing Consumption, Consuming Nationalism: The National Products Movement in China, 1905–1937." Ph.D. diss., Harvard University, 2000.

Getty, J. Arch. *Origins of the Great Purges: The Soviet Communist Party Reconsidered, 1933–1938*. Cambridge, 1985.

Goldman, Wendy Z. *Women, the State, and Revolution: Soviet Family Policy and Social Life, 1917–1936*. Cambridge, 1993.

Göle, Nilüfer. *The Forbidden Modern: Civilization and Veiling*. Ann Arbor, 1996.

Gordon, David C. *Women of Algeria: An Essay on Change*. Cambridge, Mass., 1968.

Gouldner, Alvin. "Stalinism: A Study in Internal Colonialism." *Telos* 34 (1977): 5–48.

Graham-Brown, Sarah. *Images of Women: The Portrayal of Women in Photography of the Middle East, 1860–1950*. New York, 1988.

Gramsci, Antonio. *Selections from the Prison Notebooks of Antonio Gramsci*. Trans. and ed. Quintin Hoare and Geoffrey Nowell Smith. New York, 1973.

Gross, Jo-Ann, ed. *Muslims in Central Asia: Expressions of Identity and Change*. Durham, 1992.

Guha, Ranajit, and Gayatri Chakravorty Spivak, eds. *Selected Subaltern Studies*. New York, 1988.

Hall, Catherine. *Civilising Subjects: Colony and Metropole in the English Imagination, 1830–1867*. Chicago, 2002.

Harker, Richard, et al., eds. *An Introduction to the Work of Pierre Bourdieu: The Practice of Theory*. New York, 1990.

Harris, Colette. "Women of the Sedentary Population of Russian Turkestan through the Eyes of Western Travelers." *Central Asian Survey* 15, no. 1 (1996): 75–95.

Hayden, Carol Eubanks. "Feminism and Bolshevism: The *Zhenotdel* and the Politics of Women's Emancipation in Russia, 1917–1930." Ph.D. diss., University of California, Berkeley, 1979.

Hayes, Rose Oldfield. "Female Genital Mutilation, Fertility Control, Women's Roles, and the Patrilineage in Modern Sudan." *American Ethnologist* 2 (1975): 617–63.

Hayit, Baymirza. *Sowjetrussischer Kolonialismus und Imperialismus in Turkestan*. Oosterhout, Netherlands, 1965.

——. "Turkestan as an Example of Soviet Colonialism." *Studies on the Soviet Union* 1, no. 2 (1961): 78–95.

Hellbeck, Jochen. "Fashioning the Stalinist Soul: The Diary of Stepan Podlubnyi (1931–1939)." *Jahrbücher für Geschichte Osteuropas* 44 (1996): 344–73.

——. "Speaking Out: Languages of Affirmation and Dissent in Stalinist Russia." *Kritika* 1 (2000): 71–96.

Hirsch, Francine. "Empire of Nations: Colonial Technologies and the Making of the Soviet Union, 1917–1939." Ph.D. diss., Princeton University, 1998.

——. "Toward an Empire of Nations: Border-Making and the Formation of Soviet National Identities." *Russian Review* 59 (2000): 201–26.

Ho, Virgil Kit-yiu. "The Limits of Hatred: Popular Attitudes towards the West in Republican Canton." *East Asian History* 2 (1991): 87–104.

Hopkirk, Kathleen. *A Traveller's Companion to Central Asia.* London, 1993.

Hoxie, Frederick E. *A Final Promise: The Campaign to Assimilate the Indians, 1880–1920.* Lincoln, Neb., 2001.

Humphrey, Caroline. *Karl Marx Collective: Economy, Society, and Religion in a Siberian Collective Farm.* Cambridge, 1983.

Husband, William B. *"Godless Communists": Atheism and Society in Soviet Russia, 1917–1932.* De Kalb, Ill., 2000.

——. "Soviet Atheism and Russian Orthodox Strategies of Resistance, 1917–1932." *Journal of Modern History* 70 (1998): 74–107.

Ibragimova, N., and F. Salimova. "Opyt raskreposhcheniia zhenshchin respublik Srednei Azii i Kazakhstana i ego burzhuaznykh falsifikatory." *Kommunist Uzbekistana,* no. 8 (1985), 83–89.

Inoiatov, T. T. "Sudy sovetskogo Uzbekistana v bor'be s feodal'no-baiskimi perezhitkami." *Trudy SAGU* (n.s., Juridical Sciences) 4, no. 124 (1958): 3–42.

Irvine, Judith T. "Shadow Conversations: The Indeterminacy of Participant Roles." In *Natural Histories of Discourse,* ed. Michael Silverstein and Greg Urban, 131–59. Chicago, 1996.

Ismoilov, H. An"anaviy özbek kiyimlari. Tashkent, 1978.

Jolluck, Katherine R. *Exile and Identity: Polish Women in the Soviet Union during World War II.* Pittsburgh, 2002.

Jordanova, Ludmilla. *Sexual Visions: Images of Gender in Science and Medicine between the Eighteenth and Twentieth Centuries.* Madison, 1989.

Kahf, Mohja. *Western Representations of the Muslim Woman: From Termagant to Odalisque.* Austin, 1992.

Kamp, Marianne Ruth. "Pilgrimage and Performance: Uzbek Women and the Imagining of Uzbekistan in the 1920s." *International Journal of Middle East Studies* 34 (2002): 263–78.

——. "Three Lives of Saodat: Communist, Uzbek, Survivor." *Oral History Review* 28, no. 2 (2001): 21–58.

——. "Unveiling Uzbek Women: Liberation, Representation, and Discourse, 1906–1929." Ph.D. diss., University of Chicago, 1998.

Kandiyoti, Deniz. "Women, Islam, and the State: A Comparative Approach." In *Comparing Muslim Societies: Knowledge and the State in a World Civilization,* ed. Juan R. I. Cole, 237–60. Ann Arbor, 1992.

Kaplan, Martha, and John Kelly. "Rethinking Resistance: Dialogics of 'Disaffection' in Colonial Fiji." *American Ethnologist* 17 (1983): 3–22.

Kappeler, Andreas. *Rußland als Vielvölkerreich: Entstehung—Geschichte—Zerfall.* Munich, 1992.

Keller, Shoshana. *To Moscow, Not Mecca: The Soviet Campaign against Islam in Central Asia, 1917–1941*. Westport, Conn., 2001.

——. "Trapped between State and Society: Women's Liberation and Islam in Soviet Uzbekistan, 1926–1941." *Journal of Women's History* 10, no. 1 (1998): 20–44.

Khalid, Adeeb. *The Politics of Muslim Cultural Reform: Jadidism in Central Asia*. Berkeley, 1998.

——. "Society and Politics in Bukhara, 1868–1920." *Central Asian Survey* 19 (2000): 367–96.

——. "Tashkent, 1917: Muslim Politics in Revolutionary Turkestan." *Slavic Review* 55 (1996): 270–96.

Ko, Dorothy. "Bondage in Time: Footbinding and Fashion Theory." *Fashion Theory* 1, no. 1 (1997): 3–27.

——. *Every Step a Lotus: Shoes for Bound Feet*. Berkeley, 2001.

Kocaoglu, Timur, ed. *Türkistan'da Yenilik Hareketleri ve Ihtilaller: 1900–1924*. Haarlem, Netherlands, 2001.

Kotkin, Stephen. *Magnetic Mountain: Stalinism as a Civilization*. Berkeley, 1995.

Landau, Jacob M. *Atatürk and the Modernization of Turkey*. Boulder, 1984.

Laqueur, Thomas. *Making Sex: Body and Gender from the Greeks to Freud*. Cambridge, Mass., 1990.

Lewin, Moshe. *Lenin's Last Struggle*. New York, 1970.

Lewis, Robert A., et al. *Nationality and Population Change in Russia and the USSR: An Evaluation of Census Data, 1897–1970*. New York, 1976.

Lieven, Dominic. *Empire: The Russian Empire and Its Rivals*. New Haven, 2000.

Lobacheva, N. P. *Formirovanie novoi obriadnosti uzbekov*. Moscow, 1975.

Lorimer, Frank. *The Population of the Soviet Union: History and Prospects*. Geneva, 1946.

Macfie, A. L. *Atatürk*. London, 1994.

Macleod, Arlene Elowe. *Accommodating Protest: Working Women, the New Veiling, and Change in Cairo*. New York, 1991.

Mani, Lata. *Contentious Traditions: The Debate on Sati in Colonial India*. Berkeley, 1998.

Manning, Roberta T. "Women in the Soviet Countryside on the Eve of World War II, 1935–1940." In *Russian Peasant Women*, ed. Beatrice Farnsworth and Lynne Viola, 206–35. New York, 1992.

Manz, Beatrice Forbes. "Central Asian Uprisings in the Nineteenth Century: Ferghana under the Russians." *Russian Review* 46 (1987): 267–81.

Martin, Terry. *The Affirmative Action Empire: Nations and Nationalism in the Soviet Union, 1923–1939*. Ithaca, 2001.

Massad, Joseph. *Colonial Effects: The Making of National Identity in Jordan*. New York, 2001.

Massell, Gregory J. *The Surrogate Proletariat: Moslem Women and Revolutionary Strategies in Soviet Central Asia, 1919–1929*. Princeton, 1974.

Medlin, William K., William M. Cave, and Finley Carpenter. *Education and Development in Central Asia: A Case Study on Social Change in Uzbekistan*. Leiden, 1971.

Memmi, Albert. *The Colonizer and the Colonized*. Trans. Howard Greenfeld. Boston, 1965.

Merry, Sally Engle. *Colonizing Hawai'i: The Cultural Power of Law*. Princeton, 2000.

Mitchell, Timothy. *Colonising Egypt.* Cambridge, 1988.

Mubashira, T. *Sovet Sharqi khotin-qizlarini ozod qilish tarikhidan.* Tashkent, 1978.

Mutahharkhonughlu, Shodier. "Chodradagi aellar." *Movarounakhr musulmonlari,* no. 1 (1992), 9–13.

Nashat, Guity, ed. *Women and Revolution in Iran.* Boulder, 1983.

Nekrich, Aleksandr M. *The Punished Peoples: The Deportation and Fate of Soviet Minorities at the End of the Second World War.* New York, 1978.

Normatov, S. *Tadzhikhon.* Tashkent, 1966.

Northrop, Douglas. "Unplanned War, Planned Economy: Economic Change and Development in Soviet Central Asia, 1928–1945." Unpublished paper, 1992.

Oldenberg, Veena Talwar. "Lifestyle as Resistance: The Case of the Courtesans of Lucknow, India." *Feminist Studies* 16 (1990): 259–87.

Ortner, Sherry. "Resistance and the Problem of Ethnographic Refusal." *Comparative Studies in Society and History* 37 (1995): 173–93.

Oshanin, L. V., and V. Ia. Zezenkova, eds. *Voprosy etnogeza narodov Srednei Azii v svete dannykh antropologii.* Tashkent, 1953.

Özbekistonning yangi tarikhi. 3 vols. Tashkent, 2000.

Pal'vanova, Bibi Pal'vanova. *Docheri Sovetskogo Vostoka.* Moscow, 1961.

——. *Emansipatsiia musul'manki: Opyt raskreposhchenie zhenshchiny Sovetskogo Vostoka.* Moscow, 1982.

Park, Alexander. *Bolshevism in Turkestan, 1917–1927.* New York, 1957.

Pedersen, Susan. "National Bodies, Unspeakable Acts: The Sexual Politics of Colonial Policy-Making." *Journal of Modern History* 63 (1991): 647–80.

Peris, Daniel. *Storming the Heavens: The Soviet League of the Militant Godless.* Ithaca, 1998.

Pierce, Richard A. *Russian Central Asia, 1867–1917: A Study in Colonial Rule.* Berkeley, 1960.

Pipes, Richard. *The Formation of the Soviet Union: Communism and Nationalism, 1917–1923.* Cambridge, Mass., 1964.

Poullada, Leon B. *Reform and Rebellion in Afghanistan, 1919–1929.* Ithaca, 1973.

Pratt, Mary Louise. *Imperial Eyes: Travel Writing and Transculturation.* London, 1992.

Pugachenkova, G. A. "K istorii 'parandzhi,' " *Sovetskaia etnografiia,* no. 3 (1952), 191–95.

Qosimova, O. *Özbek khotin-qizlari haqida nimalarni öqish kerak.* Tashkent, 1957.

Raleigh, Donald, ed. *Provincial Landscapes: Local Dimensions of Soviet Power, 1917–1953.* Pittsburgh, 2001.

Roberts, Mary Louise. *Civilization without Sexes: Reconstructing Gender in Postwar France, 1917–1927.* Chicago, 1994.

Ro'i, Yaacov. *Islam in the Soviet Union: From the Second World War to Gorbachev.* New York, 2000.

Rywkin, Michael. *Moscow's Muslim Challenge: Soviet Central Asia.* Armonk, N.Y., 1990.

Said, Edward W. *Orientalism.* New York, 1978.

Sanaqulov, Kh. *Chust: Ommabop tarikhiy-etnografik ocherk.* Tashkent, 1991.

Sanchez, George J. " 'Go After the Women': Americanization and the Mexican Immigrant Woman, 1915–1929." In *Unequal Sisters: A Multicultural Reader in U.S. Women's History,* ed. Ellen Carol DuBois and Vicki L. Ruiz, 250–63. New York, 1990.

Schwartz, Lee. "The Political Geography of Soviet Central Asia: Integrating the Central Asian Frontier." In *Geographic Perspectives on Soviet Central Asia,* ed. Robert A. Lewis, 37–73. London, 1992.

Scott, James C. *Domination and the Arts of Resistance: Hidden Transcripts.* New Haven, 1990.

———. *Seeing Like a State: How Certain Schemes to Improve the Human Condition Have Failed.* New Haven, 1998.

———. *Weapons of the Weak: Everyday Forms of Peasant Resistance.* New Haven, 1985.

Scott, Joan Wallach. *Gender and the Politics of History.* New York, 1988.

Sewell, William H., Jr. "Ideologies and Social Revolutions: Reflections on the French Case." *Journal of Modern History* 57 (1985): 57–85.

Shahrani, M. Nazif. "Central Asia and the Challenge of the Soviet Legacy." *Central Asian Survey* 12, no. 2 (1993): 123–35.

Shams-ud-din. *Secularisation in the USSR: A Study of Soviet Cultural Policy in Uzbekistan.* New Delhi, 1982.

Shirokova, Z. A. *Traditsionnaia i sovremennaia odezhda zhenshchin gornogo Tadzhikistana.* Dushanbe, 1976.

Shukurova, Khudzhuma Samatovna. *Sotsializm i zhenshchina Uzbekistana.* Tashkent, 1970.

Simon, Gerhard. *Nationalism and Policy toward the Nationalities in the Soviet Union: From Totalitarian Dictatorship to Post-Stalinist Society.* Trans. Karen Forster and Oswald Forster. Boulder, 1991.

Slezkine, Yuri. *Arctic Mirrors: Russia and the Small Peoples of the North.* Ithaca, 1994.

———. "From Savages to Citizens: The Cultural Revolution in the Soviet Far North, 1928–1938." *Slavic Review* 51 (1992): 52–76.

———. "Imperialism as the Highest Stage of Socialism." *Russian Review* 59 (2000): 227–34.

———. "The USSR as a Communal Apartment, or How a Socialist State Promoted Ethnic Particularism." *Slavic Review* 53 (1994): 414–53.

Snesarev, G. P. "O nekotorykh prichinakh sokhraneniia religiozno-bytovykh perezhitkov u uzbekov Khorezma." *Sovetskaia etnografiia,* no. 2 (1957), 60–72.

Spivak, Gayatri Chakravorty. "Can the Subaltern Speak?" In *Marxism and the Interpretation of Culture,* ed. Cary Nelson and Lawrence Grossberg, 271–313. Urbana, 1988.

———. "The Rani of Sirmur." In *Europe and Its Others,* ed. Francis Barker et al., 1:128–51. Colchester, 1985.

Starobinski, Jean. *Jean-Jacques Rousseau: Transparency and Obstruction.* Chicago, 1988.

Stoler, Ann Laura. "Carnal Knowledge and Imperial Power: Gender, Race, and Morality in Colonial Asia." In *Gender at the Crossroads of Knowledge: Feminist Anthropology in the Postmodern Era,* ed. Micaela di Leonardo, 51–101. Berkeley, 1991.

———. *Race and the Education of Desire: Foucault's History of Sexuality and the Colonial Order of Things.* Durham, 1995.

———. "Sexual Affronts and Racial Frontiers: European Identities and the Cultural Politics of Exclusion in Colonial Southeast Asia." *Comparative Studies in Society and History* 34 (1992): 514–51.

Sukhareva, O. A., ed. *Kostium narodov Srednei Azii*. Moscow, 1979.

Suny, Ronald Grigor. "Ambiguous Categories: States, Empires, and Nations." *Post-Soviet Affairs* 11 (1995): 185–96.

——. *The Revenge of the Past: Nationalism, Revolution, and the Collapse of the Soviet Union*. Stanford, 1993.

Tett, Gillian. " 'Guardians of the Faith?': Gender and Religion in an (ex) Soviet Tajik Village." In *Muslim Women's Choices: Religious Belief and Social Reality*, ed. Camillia Fawzi El-Solh and Judy Mabro, 128–51. Oxford, 1994.

Thomas, Lynn M. " 'Ngaitana (I Will Circumcise Myself).' " In *Gendered Colonialisms in African History*, ed. Nancy Rose Hunt et al., 16–41. Oxford, 1997.

Thrupp, Silvia L., ed. *Millennial Dreams in Action: Studies in Revolutionary Religious Movements*. New York, 1970.

Timasheff, Nicholas S. *The Great Retreat: The Growth and Decline of Communism in Russia*. New York, 1946.

Tohidi, Nayereh. "Soviet in Public, Azeri in Private: Gender, Islam, Nationalism in Soviet and Post-Soviet Azerbaijan." Paper presented at the Middle East Studies Association of North America, Washington, D.C., 6–10 Dec. 1995.

Tul'tseva, L. A. "Iz istorii bor'by za sotsial'noe i dukhovnoe raskreposhchenie zhenshchin Srednei Azii (Prazdnovanie 8 marta, 1920–1927 gg.)." *Sovetskaia etnografiia*, no. 1 (1986), 12–22.

Tyson, David. "The Role of Turkmen Women as Custodians of Islam in the Soviet and Post-Soviet Periods." Paper presented at the annual conference of the Middle East Studies Association of North America, Providence, 22–24 Nov. 1996.

van der Veer, Peter. *Imperial Encounters: Religion and Modernity in India and Britain*. Princeton, 2001.

Viola, Lynne. "*Bab'i Bunty* and Peasant Women's Protest during Collectivization." *Russian Review* 45 (1986): 23–42.

——. *Peasant Rebels under Stalin: Collectivization and the Culture of Peasant Resistance*. New York, 1996.

——, ed. *Contending with Stalinism: Soviet Power and Popular Resistance in the 1930s*. Ithaca, 2002.

Wagner, William G. *Marriage, Property, and Law in Late Imperial Russia*. Oxford, 1994.

Wang, Ping. *Aching for Beauty: Footbinding in China*. Minneapolis, 2000.

Weber, Eugen. *Peasants into Frenchmen: The Modernization of Rural France, 1870–1914*. Stanford, 1976.

Weiner, Amir. *Making Sense of War: The Second World War and the Fate of the Bolshevik Revolution*. Princeton, 2001.

White, Luise. *Speaking with Vampires: Rumor and History in Colonial Africa*. Berkeley, 2000.

Wood, Elizabeth A. *The Baba and the Comrade: Gender and Politics in Revolutionary Russia*. Bloomington, 1997.

——. *Performing Justice: Agitation Trials in Revolutionary Russia, 1920–1933*. Ithaca, forthcoming.

Woodhull, Winifred. "Unveiling Algeria." *Genders* 10 (1991): 112–31.

Yang, Anand. "Whose Sati? Widow Burning in Early Nineteenth-Century India." *Journal of Women's History* 1, no. 2 (1989): 8–33.

Yegenoglu, Meyda. *Colonial Fantasies: Towards a Feminist Reading of Orientalism*. Cambridge, 1998.

Young, Glennys. *Power and the Sacred in Revolutionary Russia: Religious Activists in the Village*. University Park, Pa., 1997.

Zeyons, Serge. *La Révolution des femmes au cœur de l'Asie soviétique*. Paris, 1971.

Zuhur, Sherifa. *Revealing Reveiling: Islamist Gender Ideology in Contemporary Egypt*. Albany, 1992.